This is the first study of Scottish price history to be published, and a major contibution to the economic and social history of early modern and pre-industrial Britain. Using the remarkable series of 'fiars' prices for grains and other contemporary sources, Alex Gibson and Christopher Smout focus, in particular, on the prices of grain, meal and animal products, and assess how Scots artisans and labourers could survive in an economy that could pay only very low money wages. The authors show how the Scottish people experienced fluctuations in welfare both in the longer term from generation to generation, and within a given life-cycle. They assess the overall standard of living, and examine the nature and adequacy of a diet in which oatmeal was of central importance: their conclusion is that the Scots were poor, but not ill-nourished. The real wage is explored in terms of family survival, and the necessity demonstrated of women and children making substantial cyclical contributions to household income. The Scottish records on prices and wages are a unique historical resource, to which Dr Gibson and Professor Smout have applied both traditional and quantitative historical techniques. In so doing they have produced a path-breaking contribution to the perennial debate on the standard of living of ordinary people prior to the onset of industrialisation.

ALEX GIBSON is a Lecturer in Historical Geography at the University of Exeter.

CHRISTOPHER SMOUT is Historiographer Royal in Scotland, and Director of the Centre for Advanced Historical Studies at the University of St Andrews. Professor Smout is perhaps best known for two seminal works on the social and economic history of the Scottish people, *A History of the Scottish People* (1969) and *A Century of the Scottish People* (1986), in addition to numerous other books and articles.

PRICES, FOOD AND WAGES
IN SCOTLAND 1550–1780

PRICES, FOOD AND WAGES IN SCOTLAND 1550–1780

A.J.S. GIBSON
University of Exeter

and

T.C. SMOUT
University of St Andrews

CAMBRIDGE
UNIVERSITY PRESS

Published by the Press Syndicate of the University of Cambridge
The Pitt Building, Trumpington Street, Cambridge CB2 1RP
40 West 20th Street, New York, NY 10011-4211, USA
10 Stamford Road, Oakleigh, Melbourne 3166, Australia

First Published 1995

Printed in Great Britain at the University Press, Cambridge

A catalogue record for this book is available from the British Library

Library of Congress cataloguing-in-publication data

Gibson, A. J. S. (Alex J. S.)
Prices, food and wages in Scotland, 1550–1780/A. J. S. Gibson and
T. C. Smout
    p. cm.
ISBN 0 521 34656 8 (hc)
1. Prices – Scotland – History.   2. Wages – Scotland – History.
3. Cost and standard of living – Scotland – History.   I. Smout, T. C.
(T. Christopher)   II. Title.
HB235.S4G53   1994
338.4'3664'009411 – dc20   93-41395   CIP
ISBN 0 521 346568 hardback

Contents

Figures

Tables

Acknowledgements

This work commenced with a grant from the Economic and Social Research Council following the initiative taken by the Economic Affairs Committee to encourage work on the history of prices and wages: the study of food was added when it became apparent to us how large a proportion of the wage in Scotland was either paid in food or spent on food. The ESRC was helpfully sympathetic to the additional research costs involved.

Our research could not have succeeded without help from many different scholars. In particular we would like to thank our colleagues at the University of St Andrews, Dr Jane Dawson, Dr R.A. Houston, Dr C.A. Whatley; Dr Lorna Weatherill (now at the University of Newcastle); Mr Robert Smart, the keeper of the muniments of St Andrews University; Dr Michael Moss, his equivalent at the University of Glasgow; Miss Mary Innes, who expertly transcribed data from the St Andrews diet books; Dr Robert Tyson of the University of Aberdeen; Professors Rosalind Mitchison and Alexander Fenton and Dr Julian Goodare and Winifred Coutts of the University of Ediburgh; Dr Nicholas Mayhew of the Ashmolean Museum, Oxford; Dr Maxine Berg of the University of Warwick; Dr Margaret Crawford of Queen's University of Belfast and Dr Robert Thomson of the University of Glasgow. We also wish to express our thanks for the unstinting help of the archivists and librarians of the Scottish Record Office, the National Library of Scotland, Edinburgh Town Council Archives, Aberdeen Town Council Archives and Edinburgh University Library. Edinburgh University Geography Department generously provided access to their facilities for five years, and Terry Bacon of Exeter University Geography Department drew the maps.

Above all, we would like to record our particular indebtedness to Mrs Margaret Richards, who typed and retyped our chapters with an expertise on the word processor and a patience with the authors that was, in each case, truly amazing.

Abbreviations

Publications

APS *Acts of the Parliaments of Scotland, 1124–1707*, twelve volumes (Edinburgh, 1814–75)

EBR *Extracts from the records of the burgh of Edinburgh, 1404–1718*, edited by J.D. Marwick, M. Wood, R.K. Hannay and H. Armet, thirteen volumes (Edinburgh, 1869–1967)

GBR *Extracts from the records of the burgh of Glasgow, 1573–1759*, edited for the Scottish Burgh Society, six volumes (Glasgow, 1876–1911)

OSA [Old] *Statistical account of Scotland, 1791–1799*, edited by Sir John Sinclair: new edition by I.R. Grant and D.J. Withrington, twenty volumes (E.P., Wakefield, 1972–83)

Archives and libraries

NLS National Library of Scotland
SRO Scottish Record Office

A Note on Scottish and English Money

Throughout this book, prices and wage rates are given in pounds, shillings and pence Scots, and the symbol £ is used to denote the pound Scots.

The exchange rate between the English and Scottish pound fluctuated before the Union of Crowns, determined primarily by the bullion content of the two currencies. After 1603, however, the pound Scots was fixed at one-twelfth of the pound sterling. This ratio remained unchanged until in 1707 the pound sterling became the only pound recognised in Great Britain and arrangements were made for calling in Scottish and English coins and reminting them as the coinage of the United Kingdom. Nevertheless, the pound Scots continued to be used as a unit of account in Scotland, particularly in rural areas, for some decades thereafter.

We have rendered all prices and wage rates into pounds Scots, even those from the eighteenth century that were originally quoted in the source as pounds sterling (as in the *Statistical account*), in order to facilitate comparison over time.

In order to compare with English prices and wages of the seventeenth and eighteenth centuries, therefore, it is necessary to divide the Scottish figure by twelve to arrive at the sterling price.

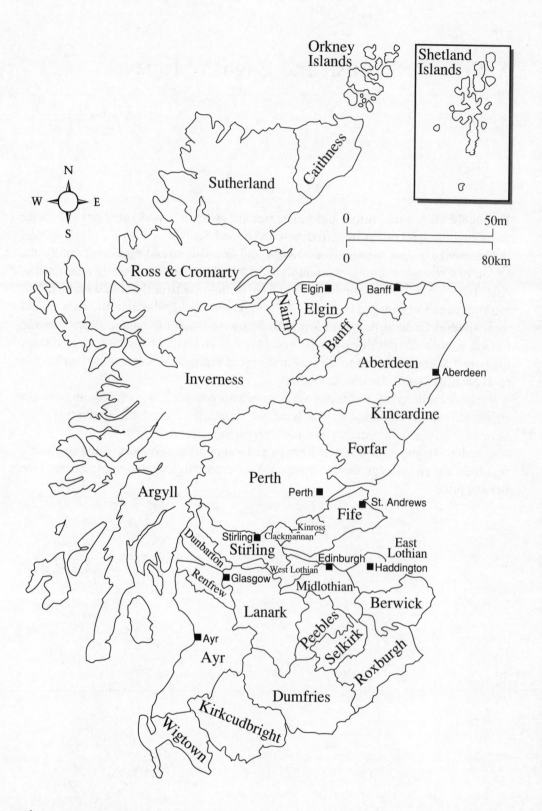

Orkney
Islands

Shetland
Islands

N
W   E
S

Caithness

Sutherland

0   50m

0   80km

Ross & Cromarty

Elgin ■   Banff ■

Nairn

Elgin

Banff

Inverness

Aberdeen

Aberdeen ■

Kincardine

Forfar

Perth

Argyll

Perth ■

Fife   St. Andrews ■

Kinross

Stirling ■   Clackmannan

Dunbarton

Stirling

Edinburgh ■

East
Lothian

Renfrew

West Lothian   Haddington ■

Glasgow ■

Midlothian

Lanark

Berwick

Peebles

Selkirk

Ayr ■

Roxburgh

Ayr

Dumfries

Kirkcudbright

Wigtown

1 ❖ Introduction

In Scotland, the history of prices and wages has until very recently been very much neglected. For the middle ages and the period up to the Union of the Crowns in 1603, the main nineteenth-century work is R.W. Cochran-Patrick's great volumes, *Records of the coinage of Scotland*, which have provided ever since a mine of information on debasement.[1] The record societies, and the Scottish Record Office itself, printed a series of sources from which price quotations can be culled, of which the most useful beyond doubt are the *Exchequer rolls of Scotland*.[2] From these the twentieth-century historians of mediaeval Scotland, whose concerns like those of their predecessors have been almost exclusively political, have made a number of observations on price trends incidental to their main purpose.[3] Recent, more detailed work on the Scottish currency has been undertaken for the middle ages by Stewart, Metcalf, Scott and others[4] and for the price revolution of the sixteenth century by Challis.[5] Nevertheless, the course of commodity prices and wages even in the very critical sixteenth century lacked systematic investigation: there is no volume on the economic or political history of Scotland in that period which contains as much as a single table or graph relative to price history, and scarcely any that contain more than a paragraph or two of generalised comment.[6] Scotland has thus lacked a Thorold Rogers, a William Beveridge or a Phelps Brown and Shiela Hopkins, a Peter Bowden, or a Steve Rappaport, all of whom confined their research to

---

[1] R.W. Cochran-Patrick, *Records of the coinage of Scotland from the earliest period to the Union* (Edinburgh, 1876).

[2] *The Exchequer rolls of Scotland*, 23 volumes (Edinburgh, 1878–1908). Dr. Julian Goodare is analysing both published and unpublished data (1600–34), as part of his study of royal finances.

[3] A.A.M. Duncan, *Scotland: the making of the kingdom* (Edinburgh, 1975); R.Nicholson, *Scotland: the later middle ages* (Edinburgh, 1974); G.W.S. Barrow, *Kingship and unity: Scotland 1000–1306* (London, 1981); A. Grant, *Independence and nationhood: Scotland 1306–1469* (London, 1984). The last named has the fullest treatment and two useful tables. See also work with useful statistical appendices on prices, 1453–1513, Craig Madden, 'The Scottish Exchequer: the finances of the Scottish crown in the later Middle Ages', unpublished University of Glasgow Ph.D. thesis, 1975.

[4] I.H. Stewart, *The Scottish coinage* (revised edition, London, 1967); D.M. Metcalf, *Coinage in medieval Scotland 1100–1600* (British Archaeological Reports, British Series, 45, 1977); W.W.Scott, 'Sterling and the usual money of Scotland, 1370–1415', *Scottish Economic and Social History*, vol. 5 (1985), pp. 4–22.

[5] C.E. Challis, 'Debasement: the Scottish experience in the fifteenth and sixteenth centuries', in Metcalf, *Coinage*, pp. 171–96.

[6] S.G.E. Lythe, *The economy of Scotland in its European setting, 1550–1625* (Edinburgh, 1960); T.C. Smout, *A history of the Scottish people, 1560–1830* (Edinburgh, 1969); G. Donaldson, *Scotland: James V–James VIII* (Edinburgh, 1965); R. Mitchison, *A history of Scotland* (London, 1970); S.G.E. Lythe and J. Butt, *An economic history of Scotland 1100–1939* (Glasgow, 1975); R.A. Dodgshon, *Land and society in early Scotland* (Oxford, 1981), pp. 134–6; J. Wormald, *Court, kirk and community, Scotland 1470–1623* (London, 1981); M. Lynch, *Scotland 1470–1623* (London, 1981). The most ambitious use of price data has been by W. Makey, *The church of the covenant, 1637–1651* (Edinburgh, 1979), especially pp. 3–6, 166–75, 181.

an English (generally to a southern English) scene.[7] Hitherto, indeed, by the standard of most other European countries the Scottish record of scholarship in mediaeval and early modern price history has been extremely meagre. To a substantial degree, however, the gap is now being filled by the labours of Elizabeth Gemmill and Nicholas Mayhew, whose book, *Changing values in medieval Scotland* is due to be published shortly by CUP.

Our own project covers the two centuries from about 1550, and takes up the story where Gemmill and Mayhew will leave it. In terms of previous research this period is scarcely better served than the middle ages. That remarkable series of assessed grain prices compiled on a county basis and known as the 'fiars', which is the subject of chapter 3 of this book, attracted early attention, and in 1963 was the object of Rosalind Mitchison's important and pioneering article on the grain market in seventeenth- and eighteenth-century Scotland.[8] The authors of *Scottish population history* gathered as many fiars as they could find and used them to test the relationship between years of high grain prices and short-term mortality crises.[9] The publication of burgh records provided scattered data on the price of bread and a few other commodities,[10] and more recently, the printing of the Masters of Works' accounts has done the same for building wages.[11] The Scottish History Society also published various account books[12] and J.S. Moore undertook a survey for the SSRC of possible sources for Scottish price history, though this was unfortunately never published.[13] As we go to press, Dr James Kirk is editing for the British Academy records of ecclesiastical patrimony in the reign of Mary Queen of Scots, which will contain much information on prices.[14]

Scholarly discussion of price data has, however, remained exiguous. Walter Makey developed an interesting thesis on the causes of the crisis in Charles I's reign, based on the impact of inflation on rents, but his total discussion amounts to a dozen pages in a monograph on ecclesiastical history. Even for the eighteenth century analysis has been

---

[7] J.E. Thorold Rogers, *A history of agriculture and prices in England, 1259–1793* (6 vols., Oxford, 1866–1902); W. Beveridge *et al.*, *Prices and wages in England from the twelfth to the nineteenth century* (New York, 1939); H. Phelps Brown and S.V. Hopkins, *A perspective of wages and prices* (London, 1981); P. Bowden, 'Agricultural prices, farm profits and rents', and 'Statistical appendix' in J. Thirsk (ed.), *The agrarian history of England and Wales*, vol. IV (Cambridge, 1967); S. Rappaport, *Worlds within worlds: structures of life in sixteenth-century London* (Cambridge, 1989).

[8] R. Mitchison, 'The movements of Scottish corn prices in the seventeenth and eighteenth centuries', *Economic History Review*, 2nd series, vol. 18 (1965), pp. 278–91.

[9] M.W. Flinn (ed.), *Scottish population history from the seventeenth century to the 1930s* (Cambridge, 1977).

[10] See the many volumes published by the Scottish Burgh Record Society between 1868 and 1916 and *Extracts from the records of the burgh of Edinburgh* (ed. J.D. Marwick, M. Wood, R.K. Hannay and H. Armet, thirteen volumes covering the years 1403–1718, Edinburgh, 1869–1967). Some of the data were tabulated in A. Fenton and T.C. Smout, 'Scottish farming before the improvers: an exploration', 1967, *Agricultural History Review*, vol. 13 (1965).

[11] H.M. Paton, *Accounts of the Masters of Works*, vol. I, *1529–1615* (Edinburgh, 1957); J. Imrie and J.G. Dunbar, *Accounts of the Master of Works, 1616–1649* (Edinburgh, 1982).

[12] Among the most useful are *Diary and account book of William Cunningham of Craigends, 1673–1680* (ed. J. Dodds, 1st series, vol. 2, 1887); *Account book of Sir John Foulis of Ravelston, 1671–1707* (ed. A.W.C. Hallen, 1st series, vol. 16, 1894); *The records of a Scottish Cloth Manufactory at New Mills, Haddingtonshire, 1681–1703* (ed. W.R. Scott, 1st series, vol. 46, 1905); *The house book of accompts, Ochtertyre, 1739–9* (ed. J. Colville, 1st series, vol. 55, 1907); *The household book of Lady Grisell Baillie, 1692–1733* (ed. R. Scott–Moncrieff, 2nd series, vol. 1, 1911); *The minutes of the Justices of the Peace for Lanarkshire, 1707–1723* (ed. C.A. Malcolm, 3rd series, vol. 17, 1931); *Ayr burgh accounts, 1534–1624* (ed. G.S. Pryde, 3rd series, vol. 28, 1937).

[13] J.S. Moore, 'Prices and wages in Scotland, 1450–1860', unpublished SSRC report HR 400/1, 1970.

[14] J. Kirk (ed.), *The Books of Assumption: the Scottish ecclesiastical rentals at the Reformation* (British Academy Records of Social and Economic History, forthcoming).

confined, apart from Mitchison's work on the fiars, largely to part of a chapter in Henry Hamilton's *Economic history in the eighteenth century* and to a single article by Valerie Morgan on farm labourers' wages: both these depended heavily on the retrospective observations in Sir John Sinclair's *Statistical account of Scotland* published in the 1790s.[15]

The picture brightens, however, from the time of the first *Statistical account*, itself a mine of information on wages and prices at the onset of the industrial and agricultural revolutions. Bowley and Wood incorporated much Scottish material in their classic studies of farm labourers' wages and, from 1870, of industrial wages.[16] Gourvish gave the debate on the standard of living in the industrial revolution a Scottish dimension with an article on Glasgow and the subject has been taken up again for the same city by Cage.[17] A detailed study was undertaken by Levitt and Smout of Scottish wages and prices in all their regional diversity as illustrated by the poor-law commissioners' investigation of 1843.[18] Hunt included Scotland in his study of British regional wages and Campbell, Roger and Price have each analysed data for the half century or so before the First World War to explore problems of labour costs and welfare.[19] The dark age of Scottish price and wage history does not include the years after around 1780; but it certainly includes everything before.

Our study was chosen to investigate the period between the labours of Gemmill and Mayhew and the start of more intensive research around the close of the eighteenth century. It is intended both as a source book for economic and social historians of the period and as a preliminary attempt to analyse some of the main features of the price and wage history of these two centuries. We have been very aware of the problems consequent upon exploring almost completely unknown territory with restricted resources. Compared to the mediaeval period, the data are more abundant and in certain limited directions more homogeneous. Town-council assessments are most plentiful in the late sixteenth and seventeenth centuries, fiars prices (with a few early exceptions) for 1630–1780 and especially for the eighteenth century. Wherever possible we have concentrated upon long-term or geographically wide series and ignored isolated

---

[15] W. Makey, *The church of the covenant, 1637–1651* (Edinburgh, 1979); H. Hamilton, *An Economic history of Scotland in the eighteenth century* (Oxford, 1963); V. Morgan, 'Agricultural wage rates in late eighteenth-century Scotland', *Economic History Review*, 2nd series, vol. 24 (1971), pp. 181–201; see also T.C. Smout, 'Where had the Scottish economy got to in the third quarter of the eighteenth century?', in I. Hont and M. Ignatieff, *Wealth and virtue: the shaping of political economy in the Scottish Enlightenment* (Cambridge, 1983), pp. 45–72. The most accessible edition of Sinclair's *Statistical account of Scotland* is that published by E.P. of Wakefield under the general editorship of I. Grant and D.J. Withrington, 1973–83.

[16] A.L. Bowley, 'The statistics of wages in the United Kingdom during the last hundred years: part II, agricultural wages, Scotland', *Journal of the Royal Statistical Society*, vol. 62 (1899); A.L. Bowley, *Wages and income in the United Kingdom since 1860* (London, 1937); R. Molland and G. Evans, 'Scottish farm wages from 1870 to 1900', *Journal of the Royal Statistical Society*, series A (general), vol. 113 (1950).

[17] T.R. Gourvish, 'The cost of living in Glasgow in the early nineteenth century', *Economic History Review*, 2nd series, vol. 25 (1972), pp. 65–80; R.A. Cage, 'The standard of living debate: Glasgow, 1800–1850', *Journal of Economic History*, vol. 43 (1983), pp. 175–82.

[18] I. Levitt and T.C. Smout, *The state of the Scottish working class in 1843* (Edinburgh, 1979).

[19] E.H. Hunt, *Regional wage variations in Britain, 1850–1914* (Oxford, 1973); R.H. Campbell, *The rise and fall of Scottish industry, 1707–1939* (Edinburgh, 1980); R.G. Rodger, 'The invisible hand: market forces, housing and the urban form in Victorian cities', in D. Fraser and A. Sutcliffe (eds.), *The pursuit of urban history* (London, 1980), pp. 190–211; S.F. Price, 'Riveters' earnings in Clyde shipbuilding, 1889–1913', *Scottish Economic and Social History*, vol. I (1981), pp. 42–65.

quotations, so we have utilised institutional and estate accounts where they provide data stretching over several decades and the poll tax when it covers a large area of Scotland at a single point in time at the end of the seventeenth century.

In practice, this approach led to a concentration of attention on the prices of basic grain and grain-based foodstuffs (chapters 2–5), on certain animal products (chapter 6) and on the wages in particular of building workers, general labourers and agricultural servants (chapter 8). We largely disregarded other commodity prices, most importantly industrial prices and prices of imported goods, because of the constraints of time and because the scattered nature of the information made valid comparison difficult (though we have included a table of wine prices). Further research would undoubtedly be possible in this area, however: the valuations in the Scottish post-Restoration customs import and export books, for example, appear to be broadly realistic, and when that record series resurfaces under British administration after 1744 more prices are available. Landed archives could similarly yield details of some imported and other commodity prices at the retail level. Coal mining records are of relatively high quality in Scotland and provide quite long runs of data, in particular on miners' wages: because of the constraints of time and a wish not to duplicate the labours of others we largely left their analysis to Dr John Hatcher of Corpus Christi College, Cambridge, who is simultaneously engaged on writing the first volume of the history of the British coal industry. Probate records were a potential source for price history that we failed to exploit: substantial and careful investigation might well yield data over a run of years, at least for certain localities.[20] They are not, however, as consistently full or as useful as English probate records, and their potential has yet to be tested.

In one respect, though, our explorations have gone beyond the conventional limits of a study in prices and wages; chapter 7 is devoted to the examination of food history. We were drawn into this initially by the realisation of how much of the total wage of an agricultural servant (and also of many urban workers) was paid in kind, either as fixed allowances of oatmeal or grain (as with the Lothian hind) or as free meals in the farm kitchen. We felt we should know what was involved in basic Scottish subsistence if we were to make any overall judgements about welfare and the standard of living. This in turn led in chapter 9 to a consideration of Scottish real wages in terms of how much meal the wage could buy and of what remained when subsistence needs, variously defined, had been provided.

The main purpose of this volume is to act as a source book for other scholars and the tables that accompany each chapter contain all the main runs of data. The text of the chapters (as well as the various notes and appendices) explain the pitfalls to be avoided and describe the techniques used in their presentation. The exigencies of space, however, made it impracticable to publish everything we had collected: fortunately, it proved possible to make arrangements to hold the complete data set on computer at the ESRC

---

[20] Some of the possibilities, as well as the shortcomings, of this source are shown in W.K. Coutts, 'Social and economic history of the Commissariot of Dumfries from 1600 to 1665, as disclosed by the registers of testaments', unpublished University of Edinburgh M.Litt thesis, 1982. We have used data from this in chapter 6.

social sciences data archive at the University of Essex (see appendix II), with print-outs deposited in the Scottish Record Office and in St Andrews University Library archives.

One of the disadvantages of formally commencing our study around 1550 is that, although it coincides with an improvement in the volume of available sources, it has limited meaning otherwise as a benchmark in Scottish price history. Scotland, along with other European nations, experienced an inflationary price revolution that occupied the bulk of the sixteenth century and had not completely run its course before the middle of the seventeenth century, though much of its force was exhausted by 1600. It is sensible, therefore, to consider what we can discern about the Scottish price revolution as a whole before we outline the features of the more stable period that followed.

The first point to note is that during the century there was heavy debasement of the Scottish pound in terms of its silver content and, secondly, that this was even heavier for the Scottish pound than for the English pound sterling. There was, though, nothing new in either of these features. Back in the halcyon days of the late thirteenth century, before the outbreak of the Wars of Independence, the pound unit in both countries contained 5,400 grains of silver coin. As late as 1367 they still exchanged at parity. By 1451, the Scottish pound contained 1,178 grains and the English 3,600, with an exchange rate between the two countries of 3:1 – neither country had been able to resist the pressures for devaluation in a Europe increasingly short of silver, but the Scots had been able to resist them less.[21] Nevertheless, as Ranald Nicholson has observed, Scottish experience in the late middle ages was hardly out of line with the general European experience. On the basis of pure silver content, the English pound between 1250 and 1500 depreciated by about 47 per cent, and the Scottish by 82 per cent; but the French *livre tournois* depreciated by about 72 per cent and the *lire* of Milan, Venice and Florence by 87 per cent, 70 per cent and 83 per cent respectively. Plainly medieval Scottish devaluations were not due to the unique greed or incompetence of the Scottish crown, or, since they were 'much the same as that of Florence', to some particular economic backwardness in the region.[22]

The plunge in the bullion content and relative value of the Scottish pound in the course of the sixteenth century, however, was more rapid and extensive than that over any comparable period in the middle ages, and more severe than anywhere else in Europe. Experiments with 'black money' brought the silver in the pound down to about 726 grains (38.59 grams) in the late fifteenth century, but from the mid 1480s to the mid 1520s a period of four decades, monetary stability was maintained in terms of the bullion content of the coinage, and an exchange around 3:1 or 4:1 with sterling remained normal until the 1560s.[23] The 'price revolution' followed. Between the early 1520s and 1603 the silver content of the Scottish pound fell to 144 grains (7.65 grams) and exchange with the

---

[21] Grant, *Independence and nationhood*, p. 240.
[22] R. Nicholson, 'Scottish monetary problems in the fourteenth and fifteenth centuries', in Metcalf, *Coinage*, pp. 105–6.
[23] J.M. Gilbert, 'The usual money of Scotland and exchange rates against foreign coin', in Metcalf, *Coinage*, p. 141.

English pound ultimately rose to 12:1 (figure 1.1). The difference between the two countries was solely due to crown policy. The English had one catastrophic flirtation with debasement in the 1540s (more extreme than anything that ever happened in Scotland) and then rehabilitated sterling so that for most of the second half of the century it retained a silver content about half of what it had been in 1450. The Scots continued to debase their coinage until in 1603 it had fallen 87 per cent below the level of the 1450s. As Challis has demonstrated, it was after about 1540 that the profits of manipulating the mint by debasements gradually became an important way by which the Scottish crown endeavoured to raise money: 'the rot set in during the reign of Mary, but it was in that of her son, James VI, that most damage was done'.[24] It is easy for an Englishman to be shocked, however; the French kings appeared to have followed a policy of raiding their mints similar in its persistence though not in its scale to that of the Scots, whom, indeed, they probably inspired. Again, the European profile of devaluation – including that of Italian and German cities – seems closer to the Scottish experience than to the English. But the extent and seriousness of the inflationary tendencies to which this gave rise to are not to be doubted, nor should the exceptional degree of devaluation in sixteenth-century Scotland in contrast to the rest of Europe be overlooked. At least in terms of the relationship between silver and the money of account, Walter Makey was correct when he observed, 'it would not be impossible to find parallels in other parts of Europe: inflation like money knows no frontiers. But the price rise was much greater in Scotland than it was anywhere else.'[25]

With the data presently available it is difficult to discern what happened to the prices of food in the first half of the sixteenth century (not least because of problems over weights and measures discussed further in chapter 5 below); but the evidence for grain and ale suggests at first only a very gentle upward trend, a doubling in the second quarter, then acceleration amounting to a six-fold increase in grain prices between 1550 and 1600 (illustrated by figures 1.2–1.3, but also see chapter 5), about five-fold for cattle and less for sheep (illustrated by figure 1.4, but also see chapter 6). The last two decades of the century saw by far the steepest inflation for most commodities. Town wages, as far as one can detect their pattern from the limited data of Edinburgh and Aberdeen, lagged in a way that was particularly serious in the 1590s and during some years on either side (see chapters 8 and 9). We should not forget, however, that few Scots were urban wage earners anyway. Nor should we cast stones at the past for allowing inflation to get out of control: between 1970 and 1992 the index of British consumer prices rose six-and-a-half-fold – more than the rise in the price of food in Scotland in the second half of the sixteenth century, and in less than half the time.

The profile of price inflation and of coinage devaluation are strikingly similar, though far from mirror images: by 1580 the silver content of the pound Scots was only a quarter of what it had been in 1500, and by 1601 only one fifth. But inflation was not only, or always, in terms of money of account, or caused solely by a greedy crown. The data are thin, but in terms of pure silver, a gram would have bought about 6 lbs. of Edinburgh

[24] Challis, 'Debasement', in Metcalf, *Coinage*, p. 190.
[25] E.E. Rich and C.H. Wilson (eds.), *Cambridge economic history of Europe*, vol. IV (Cambridge, 1967), p. 458.

wheat bread in the 1530s but only 2 around 1600, with quite a steep fall in terms of silver between the 1580s and the end of the century (see figure 5.4). Other Edinburgh commodity prices (beer, tallow) moved less steeply upwards, perhaps by 15–20 per cent in terms of silver in the last two decades. This pattern is generally in line with the European experience, though Scottish inflation in terms of silver prices was perhaps below the average.[26] This long-term inflation of bread prices in terms of silver points towards an important additional element in the price revolution in Scotland. As in other countries, population pressure was bidding up food prices in the market, following recovery from the late mediaeval demographic crisis, and this was particularly important in the second half of the century. A third possible cause, that inflation was caused by an influx of American silver into northern Europe *via* the Spanish mint, is most improbable in the Scottish case, given the limited extent of Scottish trade with southern Europe and the chronic balance of payments problem in a country with a paucity of acceptable exports and a considerable thirst for imports.

To what extent did the end of the price revolution coincide with the final debasement of the coinage by the Scottish crown in 1601? Following the Union of Crowns in 1603 the pound Scots came to be fixed to the pound sterling at a ratio of 12:1. For one reason or another much of the pressure seemed to be off prices in the first half of the seventeenth century and this, too, is reflected in the wider European experience, whatever the monetary policies of various governments. On the other hand, by 1650 most Scottish prices were higher by at least one quarter, and ale and tallow had doubled in some towns. Wage rates achieved some stability by the 1620s (though they rose again briefly at mid century); but the rise was distinctly less after 1600 than previously: the shifting up represents the last phase of a process by which labour made good some of the earlier lag behind food prices.

For the centry and a half from around 1620 to the end of our study around 1780, however, the outstanding characteristic in the prices of food and labour was the relative stability in the long-term trend of both. True, as illustrated by figures 1.2 and 1.3, the price of meal and grain tended to sag after 1630 compared to the earlier part of the seventeenth century and it rose again on trend after 1680 or 1700. Similarly, returns to labour both on the estate and on the building site seem to have reached a peak in the 1650s, after which they sank back until they enjoyed a further revival after the 1750s. These shifts within the system were not unimportant, as we shall see, but they were slight compared to the ructions caused by the inflation of the sixteenth century and by the inflation of the period that followed 1780 or 1790, with the onset of more intense industrialisation and then war at the close of the eighteenth century. Much of this book is therefore concerned with a long period of relative price stability sandwiched between two of rapid price rises.

It is worth considering for a moment the economic consequences of periods of inflation compared to those of long-term stability. Most obviously, periods of sustained increases in prices hit those whose incomes were inflexible and which were received in money, but benefited those whose incomes from rents or sales rose more quickly than

[26] *Ibid.*, p. 470.

their outgoings: if the inflation was particularly of food prices, the producer who was well placed to enter the market gained at the expense of the consumer who had no small-holding sufficient to meet his food requirements.

At the apex of society, inflation was a problem for the sixteenth-century crown, even though its own actions in raiding the mint for short-term advantage substantially contributed towards it. Many government sources of revenue – for example, the Great Customs – were inflexible. The customs yielded about £3,000 to the crown in late fifteenth century, still only £4,000 in the 1580s, though the silver content of the pound was then less than a third of what it had been at the first date.[27] In the same decade, the mint was yielding a net profit of over £12,000 a year from currency manipulation and between 1585 and 1603 Queen Elizabeth was subsidising the Scottish exchequer to the tune of roughly £35,000 a year. Inflation helped to make Scotland a client state of England.[28]

The crown, though to a much smaller extent than the church, had tried to raise funds by disposing of lands by feu charter in perpetuity to willing buyers in the century before 1550: the fixed annual payments, intended to be a realistic rent at the turn of the century, seemed derisory a hundred years later when they had sunk to a sixth or an eighth of their original burden in real terms and the crown lost accordingly.

The incomes of the larger landowners must have varied according to the way they were able to manage their estates. If they had purchased land on feu charter from church or crown, as a small number did, they would reap a substantial reward. On the other hand, they might suffer from having allowed their own tenants long leases at fixed money rents: the 'kindly tenant' of the late middle ages (so called because he was treated as though he were kin of the landlord), had by custom a long lease that might stretch out a lifetime and become heritable. It would be greatly to the landowners' advantage, in a time of rising prices and rising population, to alter this policy to one of short leases, or even to oblige the tenants to hold at will from year to year; in this way they could take advantage both of constantly altering prices and of sharper competition for holdings. Very possibly they did follow this policy. Sanderson has noted that a high proportion of tenants early in the sixteenth century (and even in the middle of that century) enjoyed long leases and Whyte had described the long lease in the later seventeenth century as a spreading innovation. Perhaps the period between was an interlude in which landowners were tempted to follow, for their own advantage, an untypical short-lease policy.[29] The mid eighteenth-century improvers were to regard the use of short leases, or of no leases, as an example of age-long, dyed-in-the-wool, barbaric bad practice, but the practice was probably not as traditional or, in the price revolution, as irrational, as all that.

[27] Isabel Guy, 'The Scottish export trade, 1460–1599, from the Exchequer Rolls', University of St Andrews M.Phil thesis, 1984, fig. 7.1. By 1597–9 the yield, following reorganisation, had risen to about £9,000: but silver content in the lib. Scots had fallen by a further 20 per cent, since 1582.

[28] Challis, 'Debasement', pp. 184–9. Between 1597 and 1604 the 'total fiscal yield of the coinage' was approximately £293,000. For the English subsidy, see K.M. Brown, 'The price of friendship', in R.A. Mason (ed.), *Scotland and England 1286–1815* (Edinburgh, 1987).

[29] M.H.B. Sanderson, *Scottish rural society in the sixteenth century* (Edinburgh, 1982); I. Whyte, *Agriculture and society in seventeenth century Scotland* (Edinburgh, 1979); K.M. Brown, 'Aristocratic finances and the origins of the Scottish revolution', *English Historical Review*, vol. 104 (1989), pp. 46–87; Dodgshon, *Land and society*, pp. 136–7.

Very many Scottish tenants in arable areas paid most of their rent in kind in the sixteenth and seventeenth centuries, a custom that was to persist to some degree until well into the second half of the eighteenth century. This was certainly mediaeval (or older) in origin. On the other hand, money rent was traditionally more important in upland areas producing cattle or sheep, especially south of the Highland line. Lowland arable rents paid (or at least reckoned) in so many chalders or bolls of oats, bear or wheat were almost invariably the rule in grain-producing areas in 1600. Here, if there was money involved at all, it was a very minor component in the total rental. In these circumstances in fertile arable areas it would not have mattered too much to the laird if his tenants held a life lease or a year-by-year lease. Providing the same quantities of grain were paid over annually, and put on the market rather than consumed in the household, the landowner would get the benefit of any increase in price, though not the benefit of any increase in productivity. One can certainly see the logic of maintaining a tradition of payment of rents in kind in the late sixteenth century as a hedge against inflation. Presumably it was not done again in the similar inflationary period in the late eighteenth and early nineteenth centuries because by then advances in agricultural productivity were so rapid and substantial, the market so efficient and rents so flexible that it would merely have been cumbersome to attempt it.

It has recently been demonstrated that many landowners all over Lowland Scotland became, in the first century after 1550, heavily and increasingly indebted; as early as around 1580 English reports 'paint a fairly startling picture of aristocratic ruin', and debts to Edinburgh merchants grew steeply in the period 1600–30. It is not very clear why. It may be that landowners' expenses were jacked up all round by the example of a nobility abroad and the feeling that they had to maintain a lifestyle closer to that of the French or English nobles they met at court or abroad. It may be that Scottish landowners were by instinct a debtor class whose ambitions were bigger than their pockets, and for the first time they found merchants affluent enough, in the post-Union burghal prosperity, to accommodate them. But it is likely that there were many landowners who were victims of inflation. Possibly some had earlier failed to adjust rental policies in time (e.g., those who had long-lease tenants or 'rentallers' paying fixed money rents in upland areas) and had been living on capital before the merchants came to their rescue. Possibly many were so used to grain prices constantly being adjusted upwards for their rents in kind that they could not curb their ambitions of expenditure in time to cope with the end of inflation, or realise that the days of constantly rising money income had come to an end. Makey has identified an upward jerk in money rents from the second or third decades of the seventeenth century, and Keith Brown has suggested that this might be related to the falling in of long leases that tenants had secured in the disturbed middle decades of the sixteenth century, when manpower had been at a premium for military purposes.[30] He cites the case of the Macleods of Dunvegan, whose rents over the period 1498–1595 rose by 400 per cent (much below inflation), but which

---

[30] Makey, *Church of the covenant*, p. 6; K.M. Brown, 'Aristocratic finances', esp. pp. 56–8; J.J. Brown, 'The social, political and economic influences of the Edinburgh merchant elite' (unpublished University of Edinburgh Ph.D. thesis, 1986).

rose by 600 per cent in the next fifteen years and by a further 700 per cent between 1610 and 1640 when inflation was minimal. The laird recouped his losses when feuding and military spending came to an end. More research on landowners' finances will certainly be needed before any firm conclusion can be drawn.

One class that plainly gained from the price revolution were tenants who at the break up of monastic or other church estates had secured a feu charter and then proceeded to work their own land for what was increasingly a peppercorn rent while selling its produce on a steadily rising market. They became, in effect, small owner-occupiers, 'bonnet lairds' in Scottish phraseology. Dr Sanderson has demonstrated that they were quite a numerous body in aggregate: over half of known feu charters were originally given to the sitting tenants, often those termed the 'kindly tenants'.[31] On the other hand, since they tended to be granted no more than their existing modest holdings, and since many other charters were given for substantial blocks of land to landowners other than existing tenants, it is reasonable to assume that only a small minority of sitting tenants – it would probably work out at about a quarter or a third – actually secured a charter to feu their own farms.[32] The remainder perforce exchanged an ecclesiastical landlord for a lay one, who might, under the pressure of inflation, and especially in the improved political circumstances of the early seventeenth century, become less accommodating. In the later seventeenth and early eighteenth centuries, outside the pastoral south-west, a great many of the bonnet lairds sold up to a larger neighbouring landowner: possibly the gentle but persistent fall in grain prices after 1650 brought pressures which the small independent producer found hard to resist. Something similar happened in England in the first half of the eighteenth century.[33]

At lower social levels than this the long-term effects of the sixteenth-century price inflation might be much less obvious and important than the impact of short-term fluctuations. Tenant farmers unable to obtain a feu charter for their holdings, or to hold on to a long-term lease, would be unable to make many gains from the rising price of food and it is likely enough that, due to land hunger in a situation of rising population rather than due to the price revolution as such, their overall lot would deteriorate. On the other hand, many small tenants were producing basically for their own households and had probably never entered the market on a large scale anyway: as long as harvests were reasonable they would not suffer a much greater degree of poverty than was usually their lot. Farm servants, working for those farmers who did not cultivate the land solely with their own and their families' labour, were generally either subtenants or the children of small tenants and subtenants: they had the advantage in a time of inflation that almost all of their wage was in kind, and as long as the farmer had food to eat, they did.

Craftsmen in the countryside and small burghs – weavers, shoemakers, wrights, smiths and so on – also frequently had small-holdings on which they raised much of their food and enjoyed the right to graze a cow. St Andrews and Anstruther, and possibly other places, had inhabitants known as 'lawburrers' or 'labourers', who had a holding on

---

[31] Sanderson, *Scottish rural society*, p. 81.
[32] T.C. Smout, 'Improvements before the improvers', *Times Literary Supplement*, 1982, p. 389.
[33] G.E. Mingay, *English landed society in the eighteenth century* (London, 1963), esp. chs. 2–4.

the burgh crofts and who probably supplied unskilled heavy work to employers on the side.[34] Only the biggest towns – Edinburgh especially, but also Aberdeen, Dundee, Glasgow and Perth – would have had many who were entirely dependent on what they could earn from their skills at a craft or their muscle power as a labourer. As is more clearly demonstrated in chapter 8 and chapter 9, there was a substantial drop in the purchasing power of such labourers and craftsmen over the period of the price revolution. On the other hand, there were very few long-term gains to be made by wage labour in the long period of price stability that followed, at least until the second half of the eighteenth century. This, at least, contrasts markedly with the English experience, where there were distinct gains for wage earners in the second part of the seventeenth century.

Looking across the curves of data for the entire period 1550–1780, however, what immediately strikes the eye is the small level in short-term variation of day labourers' money wage rates compared to the often extreme amplitude of variation in grain and meal prices. Once the price revolution had run its course, labourers' wages seemed to settle at a traditional price – often 6s. Scots a day – where they might remain for decades. Grain and meal prices, however, had no such stability. To take Fife oatmeal (figure 1.2), for instance, there were five surges in prices in the thirty-year period, 1557–87, on a steeply rising trend, each one of which doubled the figure of three years earlier – though on each occasion there were rapid falls within a year or two thereafter. There is a gap in this series until 1623 (a period covering several dearths), but in the ensuing seventy-seven-year period to 1700, generally on a downward trend after 1650, there were seven surges which brought prices to approximately twice what they had been three years earlier and another two which increased them by more than 50 per cent. In the remaining years, 1700–80, there were only two such instances of doubling, though four of rises in excess of 50 per cent – so this part of the eighteenth century was a good deal less volatile than the sixteenth and seventeenth, but still much more volatile for oatmeal than for the course of wages. And it can be seen from this histogram and also from the Edinburgh wheat data (figure 1.3) how, during the 1790s, volatility returned.

These swings had an obvious effect on wage labour: in one year a man might be able to buy subsistence for himself and dependants with little trouble, but two years later be struggling to feed more than one mouth. These problems are discussed in more detail in chapter 9. They also had a severe effect on small tenants and on farm servants working for payment in kind, in ways that are more difficult to investigate statistically. Surges in food prices came with bad harvests when many small grain farmers who in a good year would sell a surplus found themselves consuming all they had and perhaps even entering the market as potential buyers: so demand was driven up just when supplies for consumption and sale were driven down. The worst sufferers were often, in the end, producers of animals or of animal produce in upland areas, who expected to be able to sell their protein and fats for a larger quantity of calories in the form of Lowland oatmeal, and when they were unable to make the accustomed exchange discovered that their own produce simply contained too few calories to sustain them. In a similar way,

[34] St Andrews University Library: Poll tax records for St Andrews and Anstruther Wester.

high grain prices could drive down the demand for simple textile goods, and cottage producers of woollens were faced with a slump which deprived them of the means to buy grain. To use the terminology associated with Professor Sen's description of famine, they starved because of their lack of 'entitlement' to buy in the market. The exceptionally bad conditions in the north of Scotland in the 1690s must be seen in this context.[35]

Such surges in price were often also associated with heavy emigration – to Poland, Scandinavia and the mercenary armies of Europe in the late sixteenth and early seventeenth centuries, to Ireland in the seventeenth century and to America at certain points in the eighteenth century. Contemporaries more frequently related such movements to the push factors of bad harvests, overpopulation and the failure of subsistence, than to the pull factors of empty lands and good opportunities abroad.[36]

The worst of these surges were often associated with famines, when an increase in prices was accompanied by a sharp increase in mortality. There was nothing novel about famine in Scotland – fifteenth-century chroniclers speak of times when 'thar was ane gret hungyr and deid in Scotland, for the boll of meill was for four punds'.[37] S.G.E. Lythe identified five periods of price increase in the second half of the sixteenth century affecting sixteen years when there were complaints of serious dearth or famine.[38] The authors of *Scottish population history*, attempting to use an objective definition of famine as an increase in mortality 30–50 per cent above the level of the surrounding twenty-five years, found two periods of 'national' famine, covering a total of eight years in the seventeenth century, when death and dislocation were widespread and four periods of 'local' famine, covering a total of seven years, affecting only limited regions. In the eighteenth century they found no 'national' famines, though there were local ones in the periods 1740–2 and 1782–3, especially in the Highlands.[39] It seems safe to conclude, firstly, that the period of the sharpest inflation in the sixteenth century was also the period of most famines, with climatic accident adding to currency debasement and population pressure to compound national troubles; secondly, that relief from general famine was probably the major gain in welfare in Scotland in the eighteenth century. On the other hand, the link between high prices and famine was neither automatic nor general: many increases in prices in the seventeenth and eighteenth centuries came and went without abnormal mortality, no doubt depending on whether the 'entitlement' of the poor could be maintained by opportunities for wage earning on export markets or by efficient distribution of poor relief. Since in times of dearth more would die from disease than from outright hunger, one of the important consequences of maintaining the poor in their own parishes was that they would not then wander around to beg and thus spread epidemics from one part of the country to another.

The end of outright famine was not, in any case, the end of alternating periods of short-term plenty and short-term hardship: these remained, to the end of our period and

[35] A. Sen, *Poverty and famines: an essay on entitlement and deprivation* (Oxford, 1981).

[36] Flinn (ed.), *Scottish population history*, pp. 7–8.

[37] Quoted in Nicholson, 'Scottish monetary problems', p. 111.

[38] Lythe, *The economy of Scotland in its European setting*, pp. 15–23.

[39] Flinn (ed.), *Scottish population history*; T.C. Smout, 'Famine and famine relief in Scotland', in L.M. Cullen and T.C. Smout (eds.), *Comparative aspects of Scottish and Irish economic and social history* (Edinburgh, 1976), pp. 21–31.

beyond, the main source of variation in the standard of living and a feature of personal experience, the memory of which could be handed down for generations. To illustrate this, we conclude our introduction on a less abstract note with two recollections written in the nineteenth century (neither incidentally previously published) of what it was like to live through such a short-term surge in prices. The first concerned the experiences in the spring of 1740 of the narrator's grandfather and great uncle when they were aged eleven and fifteen and pedlar boys round Forfar. The season was one of the worst in the eighteenth century, a time 'of people wandering from Dundee through the country in search of food, and bodies being found in dens and moors with wild herbs in their mouths'. The children found they could neither sell their wares nor beg their bread, but they were befriended by a farm servant girl who let them sleep in the barn unknown to her employer:

In the morning the lass arose before any of the family were astir, awoke them and set them on their way, giving them all she had in her power, viz. half a pease bannock between them; which would make but a poor breakfast for them who had had no supper; yet it seems they had to trudge ten miles before they could procure anything else to eat. At Powrie they went in on a ploughman who was making his brose and solicited a share. He told them he would give them *one* large sup each for a pair of scissors to 'cure' his beard. The terms were certainly hard, but they were forced to comply, and they had no more food until they reached their mother's house at Denhead.[40]

The narrator added the observation that 'we have no cause to regret that our lot was not cast in those "good old times"'. He himself was writing in 1843, itself in one of the bleaker decades of the nineteenth century.

The second illustration is from the son of a Glasgow handloom weaver, writing in 1859 to his own son. He described how his father, unable to get wages owing to him from his employer in the dearth of 1799–1800, found himself completely penniless one Saturday night.

There was nothing in the house to eat, and they had little coals except what was on the fire. They went to bed supperless, and as they had nothing to eat, they thought it better to remain in bed instead of rising on Sunday morning as it was warmer than sitting in a house with neither food nor fire. A rap came to the door on the Sunday morning, and your grandmother rose to see who it was; it turned out to be an acquaintance who was a maid servant in a gentleman's family, and who wanted a letter written to an acquaintance who had enlisted sometime before ... [she] brought with her a few pounds weight of good oatmeal, and some other odds and ends of provisions; she had not money to get paper or pay the postage of the letter, and she brought these articles of provisions instead; she gave your grandmother an idea of what she wanted written, and left her to pile up the letter according to her own taste. Thus the provisions brought so unexpectedly by this woman kept them in a sufficiency of food, till the manufacturer obtained money.[41]

Just as in the previous passage, the occasion is saved by a strange barter transaction which we would be unlikely to find, or to be able to capture, in our tables of statistics or models of possible strategies. This narrator, too, added his moral: 'when I heard these things related, and thought of what has been the state of things since then, I have thought

---

[40] Unpublished memoir, 'Records of the families of Maxwell and Chalmers ... by Alexander Maxwell and his son George' (private possession).

[41] Unpublished diary of John Mackinnon (private possession).

that we ought to be thankful that our lot has been cast in more favourable times'. For the common people who lived through such events, it was always the short-term price fluctuations that mattered more than the long-term trend, for the long-term brought little benefit in a single lifetime before the nineteenth century.

It is important, in the mass of statistical data that follows in this book, to recollect that prices and wages were real things that people paid and received, and on which the quality of their existence, and occasionally indeed their very lives, depended. The inner meaning and interpretation of the data may be subtle and difficult, but they are not merely numerical artifacts gathered to amuse and perplex historians.

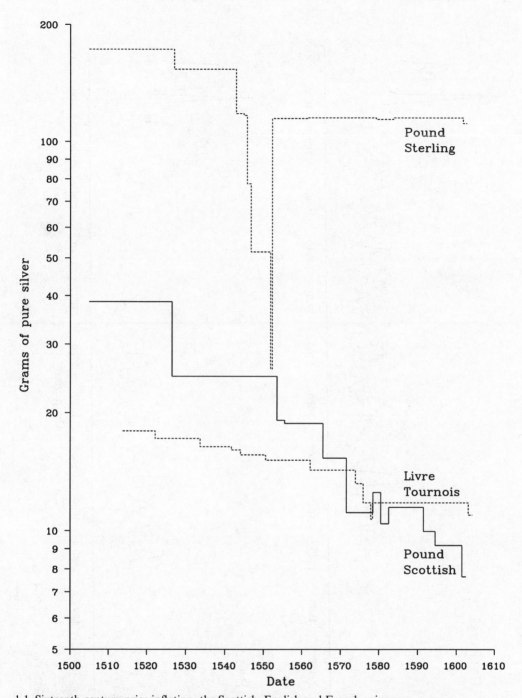

1.1 Sixteenth-century price inflation: the Scottish, English and French coinages

Sources: The value of the Scottish silver coinage has been calculated from I.H. Stewart, *The Scottish Coinage* (London, 1965), which provides details on the fineness and weight of coins, and J.D. Robertson, *A handbook to the coinage of Scotland* (London, 1878), which provides the date of issue of those coins. Clarification of the system of weight is provided by R.W. Cochran-Patrick, *Records of the coinage of Scotland from the earliest period to the Union* (2 vols., Edinburgh, 1876). The value of the English silver coinage is taken from C.E. Challis, *The Tudor coinage* (Manchester, 1978), and that of the French silver coinage (livre tournois) from a table provided in Micheline Baulaut and Jean Meuvret, *Prix des cereales extraits de la Mercuriale de Paris (1520–1698)*, vol. I, 1520–1620 (Paris, 1960), p. 249.

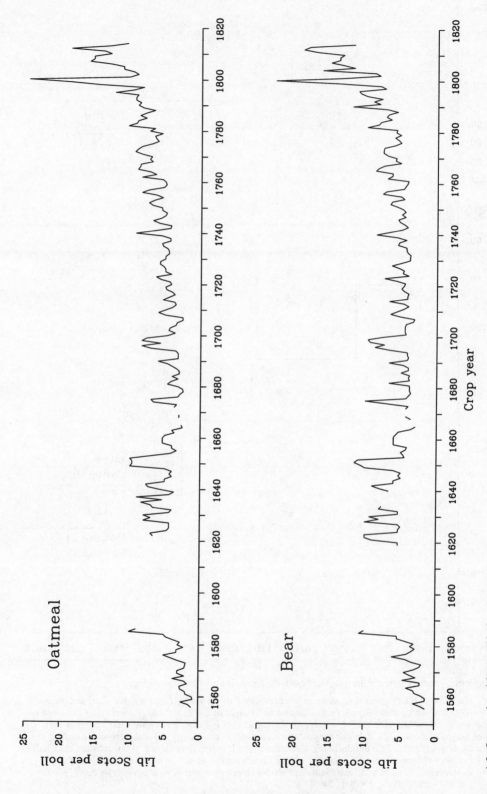

1.2 Oatmeal and bear: Fife fiars, 1556–1814

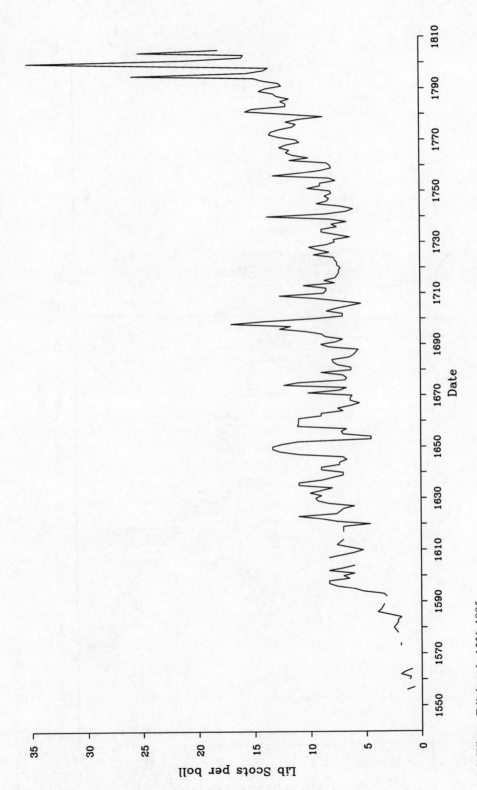

1.3 Wheat: Edinburgh, 1556–1805

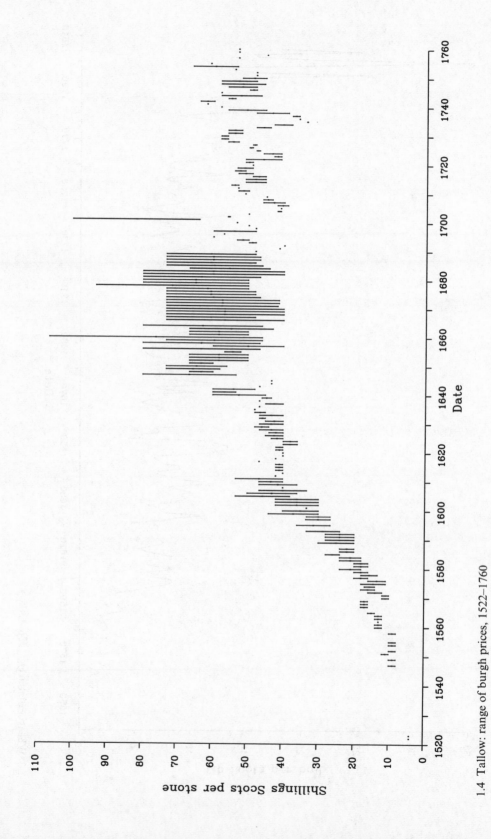

1.4 Tallow: range of burgh prices, 1522–1760

2 ✦ The system of burgh price regulation

1 The burghs and market regulation

The extensive records produced by the town councils constitute one of the richest sources available for the history of prices in early modern Scotland. They contain some of the longest price series available, in many cases pre-dating fiars prices by more than a century. Although posing considerable interpretative difficulties, they provide a detailed record of price trends and fluctuations in a period otherwise largely devoid of reliable price data. The grain and grain-product prices, along with wine prices, derived from the town councils form the tables attached to this chapter, which is intended as a guide to their interpretation.

The majority of the prices to be found in burgh records refer to the products of the principal crafts. Wheatbread, ale, tallow and candle prices appear almost annually in some burgh records, but other commodities such as oatbread, ryebread, wine and various kinds of meat appear at least periodically. Even the price of whisky was occasionally set. The burghs also assessed the price of labour, as we shall see in chapter 8. It is, however, important to acknowledge at the outset that most of these prices do not purport to record current market prices, but rather the price at which such goods were to be sold in the future.

The fact that these were 'statute' prices – statements regarding the price at which certain goods should be sold – raises immediate problems. In the first place, to what extent were these prices actually enforced? This problem hinges on the power of the town authorities to impose their will upon the markets and their ability to uphold their commercial monopolies. In the second place, to what extent were statute prices indicative of more general price movements? Were they, in other words, simple regulatory measures trying to bring order to the market and reflecting current market trends, or was there an element of price manipulation on the part of the burgh authorities? The value of the price statutes to the historian depends on the purpose, justification and success of the price-fixing policies of the burghs. It is thus necessary first to have regard to the structure and organisation of the burghs and their town councils, and therefore to consider their mediaeval origins.

The mediaeval burghs of Scotland were, in essence, communities organised round a market.[1] The first twelfth-century burghs were privileged communities granted exten-

---

[1] For an introduction to the burgh, see A.A.M. Duncan, *Scotland, the making of the kingdom* (Edinburgh, 1975); W.M. Mackenzie, *The Scottish burghs* (Edinburgh, 1949); W.C. Dickinson, *Scotland from the earliest times to 1603* (Edinburgh, 1961); M. Lynch, M. Spearman and G. Stell (eds.), *The Scottish medieval town* (Edinburgh, 1988); M. Lynch (ed.), *The early modern town in Scotland* (London, 1987).

sive rights by the crown to enable them to develop internal and external trade. Very early in their history, each burgh (including those of baronial and ecclesiastical foundation) became self governing, and from this arose the idea of the burgh as a corporate entity, a *communitas*, a notion strengthened in the fourteenth century when each burgh acquired 'feu-ferme' tenure. Instead of being the individual tenants of the king, the burgesses became jointly responsible for a fixed annual sum (the 'ferme') which was to be paid for the 'feu' (a perpetual lease) of their burgh. The burgesses made their own arrangements for raising the annual ferme through land rents, burgh-court fines and petty customs, as well as through the management of the lands, mills and fishings which they held in common.

This financial and administrative autonomy, along with the special economic and trading privileges enjoyed by the burghs, fostered a sense of distinctiveness further emphasised by their possession of special burgh courts. These originally had jurisdiction over all crimes that arose within the burgh boundaries except murder, robbery, rape and arson, but by far the greater part of their time was taken up with issues of nuisance and good neighbourhood – boundary disputes, failures to use the proper weights and measures or to comply with the market regulations, and various similar offences. Under the guidance of the 'Court of the Four Burghs', which concerned itself with general aspects of burgh trade and the welfare of the merchants and was the origin of the subsequent Convention of Royal Burghs, the Scottish burghs became a distinctive entity within the kingdom.

Central to the administration of each burgh was the town council, though it was not until the fourteenth and fifteenth centuries that a standing council seems to have emerged in most burghs. It devolved upon the council to manage the income from the various possessions and rights which the crown had granted to the burgh, notably the common lands, the burgh-court fines, and the petty customs. When this income exceeded the feu-ferme demanded of the burghs the surplus known as the 'Common Good' was devoted to the burgh's common works and common affairs. Thus the town council became responsible for all the expenditure undertaken on the burgh's behalf, and in respect of this financial interest it exercised considerable powers over every facet of burgh life.

This interference was never restricted purely to economic matters, and was reinforced after the Reformation by 'godlie magistrates' with a comprehensive concern for the morals of the population. Many town councils, contributing to clerical stipends, strove to have their own nominees appointed, and burgh control over chaplains and ministers could extend to deprivation of office for absence without cause or prosecution for non-performance of the customary duties. The choice of schoolmasters was theirs, as was the curriculum to be followed in the burgh schools. In Edinburgh the council regulated holidays, determined which books were to be read in each class in the High School and, on one occasion, even concerned itself with the costumes and stage to be used by the pupils.[2] The rules that were laid down regarding the behaviour of the students mirrors a more general concern with the behaviour of the populace.[3] They sought to enforce a

[2] *EBR, 1589–1603*, pp. xvi, 2, 223–4, 233, 364.   [3] *EBR, 1626–41*, p. xxxviii and appendix 6.

rigid observance of Sunday and assumed an inquisitorial supervision over the morals of the burgesses. Acts innumerable were passed against flyting, backbiting, slandering, oaths and opprobrious words. Billiards were condemned, but fencing and dancing (sometimes) encouraged.[4] Much was done in the interests of public morality, such as Edinburgh town council's campaign to stop women wearing plaids over their heads;[5] but much was also done for more practical reasons of the public good. Their act, of 20 August 1673, regulating coaches was in some respects curiously modern, decreeing that they should be numbered, fares limited, and galloping in the streets forbidden.[6] All in all, the degree to which the town councils legislated on almost every aspect of burgh life seems positively meddlesome to modern eyes. As I.F. Grant describes their records, 'pages might be filled with examples of "village pump legislation"'.[7]

The power of the councils, albeit within a strictly local context, cannot be overemphasised. It remained unimpaired into the seventeenth century and many features continued into the eighteenth. The magistrates of the Scottish burghs were people of consequence who expected to be treated with great respect. In Edinburgh the magistrates were attended by halberdiers when holding their courts, and were required to wear 'comlie and decent apparell' so that they might be 'discerned from other common burgesses and be mair reverenced by the people subject to their charge'.[8] Although the necessity for repeated strictures regarding issues of good behaviour and good neighbourhood might hint at a certain ineptness at enforcing their own regulations, it cannot be doubted that in them was vested an almost absolute authority over the day-to-day activities of the burgh. This authority, although wielded with enthusiasm in many spheres, was never exercised more fully than in protecting and controlling the economy of the burgh and its market.

The burghs operated on the basis of their trading privileges and a large part of the political effort of individual burghs and the Convention of Royal Burghs was directed towards defending them. Such developments as the granting of privileges to unfree burghs, or of particular trading monopolies to individuals, and all other threats to the livelihood of existing burghs were vigorously opposed – and not without reason. It was tacitly understood or definitely stated in all acts granting or confirming the Royal Burghs' privileges that in return they must shoulder a definite proportion of the taxes that were required by the crown. From 1554 this amounted to a sixth of the national burden. As they often argued, though not always successfully, anything which threatened their monopolistic control of trade also threatened their ability to pay their share of taxation.

This concern led to much 'protective legislation'. It was upon the burgesses that this burden of taxation fell and naturally their privileges, as craftsmen or merchants, had to be protected. Town council records are full of the necessary discriminatory legislation directed against 'unfreemen' (i.e., those who were not burgesses) both within and without the burgh. In Dumbarton, to give one characteristic example, no beef or tallow

---

[4] *EBR, 1655–65*, pp. lxvii, 131.   [5] *EBR, 1626–41*, p. li.
[6] *EBR, 1665–80*, p. lviii. With the exception of the prohibition of galloping, modern 'Hackney carriages' work under very similar council by-laws.
[7] I.F. Grant, *The social and economic development of Scotland before 1603* (Edinburgh, 1930), p. 397.
[8] *EBR, 1589–1603*, pp. 39, 44, 47, 378.

was to be sold to unfreemen before 2 p.m., and even thereafter 'the freemen to be preferit'.[9] Elsewhere shops belonging to unfreemen were forcibly closed, apothecaries were specifically forbidden to sell spices, and the merchants' sole right to undertake foreign trade was rigorously upheld. The Convention of the Royal Burghs played an important role in all this, and individual burghs were often required to report on the extent to which they were observing the regulations.[10]

The legislation did not stop at general enactments or special actions against individual defaulters. Edinburgh was particularly active in its campaign to subordinate the neighbouring port of Leith to its own jurisdiction and market. A town council act of 1609 illustrates the vindictive character of such restrictions in decreeing that no candlemaker was to send his candles to the port, but rather that the people of Leith had to come to Edinburgh to buy them.[11] Edinburgh was equally rigorous against the suburban towns outwith the burgh walls, notably Potterrow and Canongate. In 1574 the town council went to the length of drawing up a rota of persons who, month by month, were to represent the burgh's case against Canongate before the Lords of Session.[12] Central to the burghs' trading privileges was the possession of a market, and defending this was a particularly important aspect of 'protective legislation'. Indeed, so successful were the burghs that until 1517 not a single legal market was held outside a Royal Burgh, and thereafter the situation changed only slowly before the seventeenth century.[13]

Such was the importance of burgh markets that the authorities laid down detailed regulations as to their operation, for instance in respect of the weight, price and quality of bread or the quality and price of meat, fish and ale. Moreover, the baxters, brewers and butchers were all obliged to offer for sale to any burgess whatever merchandise they might have in stock. Such legislation occurs throughout the history of the burghs down to the seventeenth century and sometimes beyond.

Protecting the burgesses against the activities of unfreemen was one reason for regulating the market. The protection of the consumer was another, achieved, for example, through the prohibition of 'regrating' – the buying up of more goods than were required for immediate consumption in order to sell again at a profit.[14] Throughout the mediaeval period and later regrating was considered a most heinous crime against the community, for with limited markets and deficient transport came the real danger that the market might be cornered. Occasionally the regulations were more relaxed. In mid fifteenth-century Aberdeen, butter, cheese and eggs were not to be bought and resold before 1 p.m.; presumably permitting these activities to take place during the rest of the day.[15]

Determining trading standards also protected the consumer: this rested to a large

[9] J. Irving, *Dumbarton burgh records, 1627–1746* (Dumbarton, 1860), p. 35.
[10] T. Pagan, *Convention of the Royal Burghs* (Glasgow, 1926), p. 129.   [11] *EBR, 1604–26*, pp. xx, 55.
[12] J.D. Marwick, *Edinburgh guilds and crafts* (Scottish Burgh Records Society, Edinburgh, 1909), pp. 53, 81, 106, 109.
[13] A. Ballard, 'The theory of the Scottish burgh', *Scottish Historical Review*, 12 (1916), pp. 22, 28.
[14] Regrating was defined in 1592 (*APS*, vol. 3, p. 576) as buying up goods at a market only to sell them in the same market or within a radius of four miles.
[15] John Stuart, *Extracts from the council register of the burgh of Aberdeen*, vol. I, *1398–1570* (Spalding Club, Aberdeen, 1844), p. 16 (9 June 1448).

degree on ensuring that the proper weights and measures were used, at first those proper to each individual burgh, but later, through the activities of the Convention of the Royal Burghs and the Scottish Parliament, those deemed standard for the whole country. It also involved such regulations as ensuring that the baxters stamped their initials on every loaf of bread sold so that breaches of the statutes regarding the weight and price of bread might be more readily pursued, outlawing the sale of fly-blown meat, and even prohibiting the adulteration of sweets. In most cases the purpose of such regulations is self evident, but the reasoning behind some of the earlier rules, such as that 'no shoemaker ought to tan hides but such as have horns and ears of equal length', is less obvious.[16]

The other major concern of the burgh authorities was to ensure that there was an open market. There was to be no secret selling in lofts or cellars and all goods for sale had to be displayed openly. This concern lies juxtaposed with the economic foundation of the burgh – the monopoly. The two apparently dissonant ideas were brought together by the concept of the community. The burgh was a restricted trading community founded upon a monopolistic control of trade, but its privileges were to be enjoyed in common by all those who had a right to them. Thus if an unexpected ship arrived in harbour all burgesses admitted to trading rights must have an equal opportunity to buy. Similarly, if in mediaeval times the burgh decided on some 'wild adventure' (the term given for sending a ship forth with export goods), then the freighting was to be done publicly so that all might have an equal chance of participating. This equality was maintained in the market place; the forestaller, buying goods before they reached the market stalls, was, like the regrater, considered an enemy of the community and punished accordingly.

The control of prices also falls within this area of consumer protection, though there is a sense in which the price statutes were also designed to protect the craftsman from undue competition. As discussed below, it seems to have been the case that the products of the principal food-processing crafts were priced (in theory at least) according to the cost of the necessary raw materials, plus an allowance due to the craftsman for his labour and profit. To take the example of wheatbread, in the sixteenth and seventeenth centuries it was generally understood that 140 lbs. of bread should be sold at a price equal to the cost of a boll of wheat plus the allowance given to the baxter for baking it into bread. By setting the price in this way the consumer might be protected from unreasonably high bread prices, but the craftsman was also guaranteed a suitable return for his labour (as long as the allowance was sufficient and the council honest in its appraisal of wheat prices).

Though serving both purposes, it was the protection of the consumer which seems to have been paramount. The burghs were often urged to action by central government, as in the period 1530–60 when 'repeated exhortations were made to burgh magistrates . . . to control or reduce food prices'.[17] It was often expressly stated that prices were being set because the craftsmen were placing too exorbitant a value on their labour. However, not only craftsmen were affected. By setting the price of craftwork, the town councils

---

[16] *EBR, 1528–1557*, pp. 154, 157, 161, 166; *EBR, 1665–80*, p. lvii; C. Innes and R. Renwick (eds.), *Ancient laws and customs of the burghs of Scotland*, vol. I, p. 75, Statuta gilda, c.24.   [17] Lynch, *Early modern towns*, p. 74.

effectively also set a ceiling on the prices that craftsmen could pay for their raw materials. This is expressed most openly by a proclamation from Edinburgh town council dated 11 October 1595 warning baxters and brewers to buy no dearer wheat, malt or barley than would allow them to sell a 16 oz. loaf for 12d. or a pint of ale for 12d.[18] If, as seems likely, baxters and brewers were the main purchasers of these materials within the burgh, the council would have been able to influence the prices of both the final product and the raw materials. It could certainly ensure that there was no undue profiteering at any stage in the process from the storehouse to the food on the citizen's table.

This bias towards the consumer is reflected by the attitude of the town councils towards the unfree craftsmen. Although their activities were contrary to the craftsmens' legal monopoly in the burghs, unfreemen were permitted to engage in some trading activities. In Edinburgh, according to M. Wood, 'it is impossible not to conclude that the council connived at the breach of the statutes regarding unfreemen for the sake of the fines involved and that unfree trades pursued their business at the risk of prosecution when the council was free to turn attention to them'.[19] Moreover, the town councils of Aberdeen and Edinburgh went so far in the recognition of the unfreemen's trading role as to set prices for the produce of both free and unfree craftsmen; in Aberdeen for ale, and in Edinburgh for wheatbread. In both burghs the produce of the unfreemen was to be cheaper than that of the freemen; the reasoning being that the unfreemen required a smaller allowance for raw materials, labour costs and profit than the freemen.[20] The unfree craftsmen were, of course, subject to other restrictions; otherwise, by selling cheaper produce, they would soon have cornered the market.

In Culross, and perhaps other towns, there was a special 'land market' where country fleshers could come to sell their meat separately from the town fleshers: this gave rise to trouble in 1655 when the town fleshers set their dogs on the country fleshers, and by 'their girning, tanting and mocking of them', drove them away: the town council intervened to protect the 'outland fleshers', as their activities provided a way of keeping meat prices within bounds. They had no time for the town fleshers 'seiking suche heighe pryces for their flesh as they do'. It was not as though their meat was always of good quality: a few years later the council confiscated a carcase from one of the town fleshers and presented it to the unfortunate inmates of the Town Hospital because it was 'blawin' – fly blown.[21]

This concern with the consumer rather than the producer or seller of food may reflect the balance of power within the town councils of the Scottish burghs. Town government was generally dominated by a guild most of whose members were merchants and their interests led them from time to time into conflict with various craft incorporations. Furthermore, even within the circle of craftsmen, the baxters, fleshers and candlemakers

[18] *EBR, 1589–1603*, p. 140.   [19] *EBR, 1604–1626*, p. xiv.

[20] In March of 1658 the baxters of Edinburgh were granted an allowance of 40s. Scots per boll of wheat. This was for the production of 140 lbs. of wheatbread. The 'utland' baxters, however, were to produce a quarter more bread for this 40s. allowance 'be reasone of their easie burthens in the country and unequallitie of the fynes of the bread conforme to the fynes of Edinburgh bread' (*EBR, 1655–1665*, p. 89). This condemnation of the fineness of the bread implies that the 'utland' baxters were baking more bread per boll than the 140 lbs. required of the town's baxters. The 'easie burthens' reflects the fact that the unfreemen were not subject to the taxation that was levied on the craftsmen in the burgh and thus their 40s. allowance was provided for the baking of more bread than was required of the town's baxters.

[21] D. Beveridge, *Culross and Tulliallan* (Edinburgh, 1885), vol. I, pp. 131, 279; vol. II, p. 49.

were not among the most prestigious trades. In Edinburgh from 1583, for example, eight out of twenty-four of the seats on the council were reserved for craftsmen, but the baxters' deacons were only allowed to attend on specified occasions while others (such as the hammermen) were granted permanent representation. In addition, the craftsmen were, of course, consumers as well as producers and all had an interest in holding down the price of those goods they themselves did not provide. The political pressure must always have been to keep prices as low as possible.

Occasionally it indeed appears as if the burgh authorities were too enthusiastic in their attempts to act on behalf of the consumer. The town council in Dundee seems to have succumbed to such temptation in 1561, when the baxters of the town successfully complained to the Court of Session that the magistrates were setting the price of wheatbread regardless of fluctuations in the cost of wheat.[22] That the baxters found it necessary to pursue such an action in a higher court emphasises how little power they wielded within the burgh itself. Moreover, as such an appeal was a slow, cumbersome and expensive process, the baxters must have been sorely pressed to have embarked on such a course. Notwithstanding this political weakness, however, no burgh could sanction the ruin of the crafts which ministered to the immediate needs of its citizens. Pricing policies must ultimately have reflected this factor.

Something of this emerged on those occasions when a higher authority, in the shape of Parliament or Privy Council, tried to intervene directly in price fixing. An attempt was made in 1535 to establish a commission of 'certane lordis and utheris', sitting with the Provost of Edinburgh, which would 'mak sik statutis and ordinancis as they sall think maist expedient for the commoun wele to cause all craftsmen within the toun of Edinburgh and utheris of the realme to make gude and sufficent stuff and sell the samin of ane competent price'.[23] From the wording of the preamble to this act it would seem that it was principally a response to the high prices being charged by craftsmen. This legislation does not appear to have had any immediate effect, but it may have laid the foundation for the two acts of price intervention attempted by the Privy Council in the 1550s. In December 1551 it pronounced on the price at which malt, ale and wheatbread was to be sold in Edinburgh, Leith, Musselburgh, Tranent, Seton, Newbattle, Dalkeith, Canongate, Duddingston, Lasswade, 'and uthiris townys nixt adjacent to this burgh [of Edinburgh]'. This enactment seems, however, to have been completely ignored, at least by the town council of Edinburgh: during 1552 burgh statute prices followed courses quite independent of Privy Council, and were considerably more sympathetic to the food producers. Whereas the Privy Council had commanded the four-penny loaf to weigh 22 ounces, malt to be no dearer than £3 for nine firlots, and ale not to exceed 3d. a pint,[24] the Edinburgh statute prices in 1552 were as follows as shown in table 2A.

Only a little more successful was an act of the Privy Council of 11 January 1556, which decreed that the freemen baxters of the burghs should sell 14 ounces of wheatbread for four pennies. This price was duly noted by the Convention of the Royal Burghs and adopted by Edinburgh town council on the same day, but next month Edinburgh was

[22] A. Warden, *Burgh laws of Dundee* (London, 1872), p. 337. [23] *APS*, vol. 2, p. 351.
[24] R.K. Hannay, *Acts of the Lords of Council in public affairs, 1501–1554* (Edinburgh, 1932), pp. 611–14.

Table 2A *Regulation of wheatbread, malt and ale by Edinburgh town council, 1552*

	Weight of 4d. wheat loaf		Price of malt	Price of ale
	Town	Outland	(9 firlots)	(pint)
10 Feb.	—	—	£3.8.0	4d.
8 April	16 oz.	20 oz.	—	—
27 May	13 oz.	17 oz.	—	—
26 July	16 oz.	20 oz.	—	—
9 Aug.	15 oz.	24 oz.	—	—
7 Oct.	26 oz.	30 oz.	—	4d.

Note, incidentally, how outland baxters were expected to provide more bread for 4d. than the town baxters.

again setting prices on its own account. In 1581 Parliament reaffirmed that 'setting the ordour and price on all stuff' within each burgh was the responsibility of the provost and baillies.[25] This act, which was expressly aimed at 'the stancheing of dearth of victuallis', also called upon 'everie erle, lord, barone, alsweill within regalitie as ryeltie' to determine and enforce such prices within their own jurisdictions.

This extension of the principle of price control to the landward parts of the kingdom had first been made by Parliament in 1494 and was confirmed in 1535. However, though this act still had the force of law in the seventeenth century,[26] there is little evidence of price regulation outside the burghs. Very few price statutes are to be found in the extracts of the barony and regality court records which have been printed[27] and, at least until the Justices of the Peace attempted to determine wages and occasional prices related to wages (such as shoe leather) in the seventeenth century, there is no sign of a controlled economy in the countryside comparable to that of the burghs.

2 The system of assize

The main legal guarantee that prices fixed by town councils would not become hopelessly out of line with the price of raw materials originated in the mediaeval system of assize, which also needs to be explained if we are to see how the system worked in subsequent centuries. The imposition by the crown of these carefully defined rules determining how prices should be set appears very early in the history of the burghs. The idea which lay behind them has already been mentioned; that any product of craftwork should be priced according to the cost of the necessary raw materials, plus an allowance to cover the costs and profits that were due to the craftsmen. Following this principle,

[25] J.D. Marwick (ed.), *Records of the Convention of the Royal Burghs of Scotland, 1295–1714* (Edinburgh, 1870), vol. 1, p. 556; *EBR, 1528–1557*, p. 230; *APS*, vol. 3, p. 225.

[26] *APS*, vol. 2, pp. 238, 346; J.A. Clyde, *Hope's Major Practicks, 1608–1633* (Stair Society, Edinburgh, vol. 3, 1937 and vol. 4, 1938).

[27] Of the various barony and regality records printed by the Scottish History Society, etc. only those for the Barony of Carnwath mention local price statutes: W.C. Dickinson (ed.), *The court book of the barony of Carnwath, 1523–1542* (Scottish History Society, 3rd series, vol. 29, 1937), pp. lxv–lxvi, 25, 59.

any competent authority could construct a table giving the price of craftwork according to the total cost of the raw materials plus labour. This is just what David I did in the early twelfth century to produce the earliest known Scottish assize for bread.[28] Using 2d. intervals between 10d. and 24d. per boll of wheat, this assize determined the proper weight of three sorts of half-penny loaves; a 'lefe wele bakyn and dry', a 'lefe wele bakyn and new', and one which was 'wastel qwhyte and well bultyd'. From this assize it would seem that for the cost of a boll of wheat there was to be sold either 1,008 oz. of 'wastel qwhyte' bread, 960 oz. of 'wele bakyn and new' bread, or 912 oz. of 'wele bakyn and dry' bread.[29] Two other early assizes, the 'Assize panis denarii'[30] and the 'Assize panis oboli',[31] are internally inconsistent, although the latter (which dates from between 1306 and 1329) appears to have been based on that of David I, with 1,008 oz. of 'Pastus panis' or 912 oz. of 'Panis coctus et ficcatus' to be sold for the cost of a boll of wheat.

It must be emphasised that in these, as in most other assizes, what was described as the 'cost' of a boll of wheat actually included a fixed allowance granted to the baxters for baking it into bread. This is demonstrated by the fact that the tables of assize establish a linear relationship between the so-called 'cost' of wheat and the price at which bread made from that wheat was to be sold. If the 'cost' of wheat meant simply the price of the raw material, to which the baxters' allowance was additional, then such a relationship could only have obtained if, firstly, the amount of bread baked per boll decreased as the price of wheat rose, or, secondly, if the allowance granted to the baxters increased as the price rose. The former is unlikely, and contrary to all common sense, but the latter would at least have incorporated into the assize an elegant mechanism of 'index-linking' the baxters' earnings to the price of wheat. There is, however, plenty of evidence to show that this was not the case, although admittedly none from as early as the reign of David I. Most telling is a statement made by Edinburgh town council in 1680 that 'the pais of wheat[bread] to be according to the rait of wheat at eleven pound per boll; the ordinarie allowance to the baxters being included in the said pryce', and a petition of 1657 made by the baxters to Edinburgh town council which maintained that their allowance of 20s. per boll had not been increased since 1555.[32] It seems certain that the baxters' allowance did not vary with the cost of wheat and therefore that the 'cost' of wheat referred to in the tables of assize actually included that allowance.

The same idea underpinned two early Scottish assizes relating ale to malt,[33] the later of which is said to have been made by King William (1165–1214). The first gives the price of a gallon of ale according to the cost of a chalder of malt at 3s.4d. intervals between 6s.8d. and £1.6s.8d., and the second gives the price of a gallon of ale according to the cost

[28] *APS*, vol. 1, p. 675 (in repaged form); 'The assize of the breade after the price of the qwhete throw the auld assize of King David.'
[29] The boll and ounce are not the measures used in later centuries. It seems impossible to relate these to the measures used later in the mediaeval period.
[30] *APS*, vol. 1, p. 679 (in repaged form); 'Assisa panis denarii', date and provenance uncertain.
[31] *APS*, vol. 1, p. 50 (in repaged form); 'Assisa panis oboli', taken from the Ayr Mss. which dates from the reign of Robert I (1306–1329).
[32] *EBR, 1655–1665*, p. 89; *EBR, 1665–1680*, p. 393.
[33] *APS*, vol. 1, p. 675; 'Of the assize of ail eftir the malt' and 'The assize of aill made by King William' (and thus 1165–1214).

of a chalder of malt at 5s. intervals between 10s. and £2. Although both are internally consistent, the first is based on 160 gallons of ale being sold for the cost of a chalder of malt whereas the second is founded on 240 gallons of ale per chalder of malt. This second assize thus determines that 120 pints of ale should be sold for the cost of a boll of malt.[34] It is significant that as late as the mid seventeenth century this was the ratio most commonly used to determine the price of ale in both Aberdeen and Stirling, even though no intervening statutes or assizes have been found to confirm that of King William.[35]

Once again, just as the 'cost' of the wheat in the bread assizes included the baxters' allowance, so the 'cost' of the malt in the ale assizes included the brewers' allowance, along with all the other incidental costs incurred in brewing a boll of malt into ale. With 120 pints of ale to be sold at this price, it must follow that this was the actual quantity of ale to be brewed from each boll of malt. These assizes were therefore regulating the quality as much as the price of ale. It is interesting to note that the former seems to have remained unchanged between the twelfth and seventeenth centuries. If these assizes were used to determine prices in the burghs, it would have limited the degree to which the merchants, or anyone else, could abuse their control of the town council – the statute price of wheatbread or ale was to be calculated from the current price of wheat or malt plus the allowance given to the baxters or brewers.

It was absolutely central to the assizes that the price of a commodity should be determined with direct reference to the price of the raw materials from which it was made. This was so fundamental that a town council could effectively set the price of craftsmen's produce without having to mention the actual price of that produce. For instance, the authorities in Edinburgh believed the relationship between the price of wheat and wheatbread to be so well known that sometimes they found it unnecessary to record the statute price of bread.[36] Thus on 12 April 1492 it was reported that; 'It is fundin and delyuerit be an assyse that the pais suld be given of the penny laiff to the baxteris after the raitt of quheit to 10s.6d. the boll.' The same was true of the relationship between malt and ale. Thus on 17 January 1492, 'The best quheitt in the mercat was fundin be assyse for 12s. [the boll]; item, the laid of malt for 20s.' With well-known tables of assize relating wheat prices to bread prices, and malt to ale prices, such statements were clearly sufficient warning to the baxters and brewers of the price at which bread and ale should be sold.

For general conclusions about the reliability and usefulness of prices derived from this system of town council statute and assize, the reader should turn now to the final section of this chapter. The intervening sections here probe particular problems relating to different commodities that were the subject of burgh price regulation, and which appear in the tables appended to this chapter.

---

[34] This presumes the gallon to contain 8 pints and the chalder 16 bolls. Neither assumption is certain, though the fact that the ratio is that found in later centuries does support such an interpretation.

[35] A short table is to be found in the minutes of the town council of Aberdeen for 7 October 1586. This gives the price of a pint of ale according to the price of malt at one pound intervals between two and four pounds per boll. It is based on the assumption that 120 pints of ale should be sold for the cost of a boll of malt.

[36] *EBR, 1403–1528*, pp. 61–2.

3 The link between wheat and wheatbread prices in Edinburgh (table 2.3)

In the case of Edinburgh, it is possible both to illustrate in elaborate detail how the system worked, and (for this burgh alone) to derive a series of wheat prices from the known quotations of bread prices (see tables 2.1 and 2.3). Although explicit details are not always available, recording the price of both the wheat and the bread that was to be made from it was a sufficiently common practice to allow us to chart the relationship between the two from 1495 to 1681. Care must be taken, however, as the terminology used does change, and the situation was highly complex.

The earliest reference to the statute price of wheatbread in Edinburgh, of 24 February 1495, makes it quite clear that it was based on the price of wheat in the market: 'The assys fand the quheit in the market the last market day at 11s. [the boll] and ordains thame [the baxters] to furneis the pais according thairto, quhilk is 13 unces 3 quarteris for the penny laif.'[37]

In fact, as table 2B shows, the price of bread in Edinburgh was set according to the 'market price' of wheat in both 1495 and 1528. This terminology presumably referred to the cost of the wheat without the allowance for the baxters; hence the lower ratio between the cost of wheat and wheatbread. In contrast, from 1548 to 1573 the documents refer to the price at which wheat was 'commonly sold', and from 1653 to 1681 bread was priced 'according to the rate of wheat'.

A distinct change occurred after about the middle of the sixteenth century. Thereafter 2,240 oz. (140 lbs.) of bread was to be sold for the cost of a boll of wheat as given in the council statutes. This suggests that from that date the price of wheat as it was 'commonly sold' and the 'rate of the wheat' both refer to the total cost of baking a boll of wheat into bread. They both, in other words, include the baxters' allowance.

It follows from this that Edinburgh town council reckoned that 2,240 oz. (140 lbs.) of fine bread should be baked from each and every boll of wheat. This is confirmed by an act of the Privy Council of 11 January 1555 which decreed 'if any man delivers wheat to a Baxter to be baked for hire, that he receive seven score pound weight of baked bread good and sufficient stuff',[38] and by Alexander Hunter who stated in 1624 that 'there should be made 140 lbs. weight of bread of very fine wheat bread out of every boll of wheat'.[39] In governing the relationship between wheat prices and bread prices, the assize therefore also determined the extraction rate of flour from wheat, and thus the quality of the bread to be produced by the baxters (see discussion in appendix I).

The town council in Edinburgh permitted the sale, and set the price, of coarser varieties of bread. In 1624 it published a table of assize giving the proper weight of 12d. and 6d. loaves of 'first' or 'finest bread', 'second' or 'four' bread, and 'masloche' bread (with a rye content) according to the price of wheat at one pound intervals between £3 and £16 the boll.[40] Once again, the 'price of wheat' must have included the baxters'

---

[37] *EBR, 1403–1528*, p. 69.
[38] J.D. Marwick (ed.), *Recs. Conv. Royal Burghs, 1295–1714*, vol. 1, p. 556.
[39] Alexander Hunter, *A treatise of weights, mets and measures of Scotland* (Edinburgh, 1624; reprinted, Amsterdam, 1974, p. 2).   [40] *EBR, 1604–1626*, pp. 249, 409.

Table 2B *Regulation of wheatbread by Edinburgh town council, 1495–1681*

Date	Weight of loaf	Cost of loaf		Price of wheat (per boll)	Weight of bread sold for price of one boll
24 Feb. 1495	13¾ oz.	1d.	'market price'	132d.	1,815 oz.
1 Feb. 1528	11½ oz.	1d.	'market price'	144d.	1,656 oz.
7 Dec. 1548	20 oz.	4d.	'commonly sold for'	432d.	2,160 oz.
11 Sep. 1550	20 oz.	4d.	'commonly sold for'	432d.	2,160 oz.
11 Jan. 1556	14 oz.	4d.	'commonly sold for'	640d.	2,240 oz.
24 Feb. 1556	17 oz.	4d.	'commonly sold for'	520d.	2,210 oz.
20 Apr. 1556	16 oz.	4d.	'commonly sold for'	560d.	2,240 oz.
17 Oct. 1573	13 oz.	4d.	'commonly sold for'	720d.	2,340 oz.
21 Dec. 1653	14 oz.	12d.	'according to rate of'	1,920d.	2,240 oz.
30 Jun. 1654	7⁷⁄₁₆ oz.	6d.	'according to rate of'	1,800d.	2,231 oz.
26 Oct. 1655	7 oz.	6d.	'according to rate of'	1,920d.	2,240 oz.
10 Dec. 1656	5⅝ oz.	6d.	'according to rate of'	2,400d.	2,250 oz.
23 Dec. 1657	5⅞ oz.	6d.	'according to rate of'	2,286d.	2,238 oz.
27 Jan. 1664	10³⁄₁₆ oz.	12d.	'according to rate of'	2,640d.	2,241 oz.
13 Jul. 1664	12⅜ oz.	12d.	'according to rate of'	2,160d.	2,228 oz.
9 Feb. 1670	14 oz.	12d.	'according to rate of'	1,920d.	2,240 oz.
8 Nov. 1676	14 oz.	12d.	'according to rate of'	1,920d.	2,240 oz.
13 Mar. 1678	14 oz.	12d.	'according to rate of'	1,920d.	2,240 oz.
Aug. 1681	11³⁄₁₆ oz.	12d.	'according to rate of'	2,400d.	2,238 oz.

allowance and, once again, the price of the 'finest' bread was determined on the basis that 140 lbs. (2,240 oz.) of bread was to be baked from each boll of wheat. The price of the 'four' bread shows that about 2,980 oz. of this bread was to be baked from each boll of wheat, whilst the price of the 'masloche' bread shows that about 3,730 oz. of this clearly inferior bread was to be baked from each boll. The cheaper, coarser breads were a consequence of higher extraction rates being used in the grinding and bolting of the flour used, though in the case of the 'masloche' bread there presumably was, as its name implies, some mixing of the wheat flour with rye, and perhaps pease or bearmeal.

These three different types of bread only appear in the price statutes from November 1636 to April 1668. The ratio between them was always 3:4:5. After 1668 the price statutes revert to reporting only the price of the 'finest' bread, but, with the price relationship between the three sorts now well established, the price of the two coarser varieties was effectively set by the inevitable phrase – 'and the rest of the bread to be confrome thereto'. A similar terminology is sometimes found prior to 1624, and there is some evidence to suggest that more than one type of bread was also permitted during the late sixteenth and early seventeenth centuries. There was certainly a very high quality bread known as 'mayne' bread. This came to the attention of the burgh authorities in years of scarcity because it required a low, and thus wasteful, extraction rate of flour. As the town council explained in 1595:

in consideratioun of the present dearth . . . bayking and using of mayne floure and mayne breid is mair superfluous, serving the appetyte of delicate persouns and ane destruction of vivers rather than necessar to ane commoun weill . . . na baxters of this burgh baik, haif or sell any mayne floure or mayne breid.[41]

Unhappily for the commonweal, a marginal note records that this 'Tuik na effect'. The periodic outlawing of such bread, in 1600, 1601, 1612 and 1650,[42] as well as in 1595, records the frequent concern of the town council with scarcity. The two instances in which the rules were relaxed and mayne bread expressly permitted, in 1603 and 1615,[43] record years of plenty. Unfortunately, in only two instances is there any evidence of the quality of this bread. In 1610 a 12d. loaf of mayne bread was to weigh 9 oz. whilst a 12d. loaf of the 'finest' wheat bread was to weigh 17 oz. If the latter bread was baked at a rate of 140 lbs. per boll, then the mayne bread must have been baked at a rate of 74 lbs. 2 oz. per boll. In 1615, on the other hand, when a 12d. loaf of 'finest' wheatbread weighed 14 oz., the mayne bread was still to be sold at 12d. for 9 ounces. This implies that 90 lbs. of mayne bread was to be baked from a boll of wheat. It is possible, of course, that the baxters were permitted a higher allowance for making mayne bread and that the amount to be baked from each boll of wheat would therefore be somewhat less than these figures suggest. Whatever the precise arrangement, it was clearly a very fine and expensive bread.

With regard to the three principal types of bread sold in the seventeenth century the assizes were quite explicit. A carefully defined weight of each sort was to be baked from each boll. This was then to be sold at a price equal to the cost of that wheat plus the baxters' allowance for baking it into bread. It follows, therefore, that through the imposition of these rules the only means by which the merchant-dominated town council of Edinburgh (and also of Glasgow)[44] could influence the price of bread, was either by misrepresenting the price of wheat or by keeping the allowance given to the baxters as low as possible.

Consider first the allowance which was granted to the baxters to cover their various costs and to provide for their livelihood. On 9 November 1657 a committee was set up by Edinburgh town council to consider a petition by the baxters regarding this allowance. It was argued by the baxters that 'considering the great chairges and burtherns the baxters of this burgh now are subject into mair nor fomerlie' their allowance of 20s. per boll established in 1555, and affirmed in 1597 and 1626, was now too low and should be increased. The committee concurred and recommended that henceforth the allowance should be increased to 40s. Scots per boll for the freemen baxters. The report was approved by the town council and took force on 17 March 1658.[45]

This was a remarkable decision. A doubling of the allowance was a huge increase, even allowing for the fact that in the 1650s there appears to have been some upward pressure

---

[41] *EBR, 1589–1603*, pp. 142–3.
[42] *EBR, 1589–1603*, pp. 268, 279–80; *EBR, 1604–1629*, p. 94; *EBR, 1642–1655*, p. 230.
[43] *EBR, 1584–1603*, p. 321; *EBR, 1604–1629*, p. 129.
[44] Glasgow town council recorded the cost of wheat alongside their bread statutes on some forty-five occasions between 1661 and 1737. There is no doubt that, as in Edinburgh, this 'cost' included the baxter's allowance and that 140 lbs. of bread should be baked from each boll of wheat (*GBR*, passim).
[45] *EBR, 1655–1665*, p. 89.

on wages in several sectors. However, according to the baxters, the allowance had remained unchanged since 1555. If so, the baxters must have suffered severely in the intervening century, when the cost of wheat and ale in Edinburgh rose roughly eight-fold and six-fold respectively and even labourers and masons obtained at least four-fold wage increases over this period. In fact, even the doubling of the allowance in 1658 would have been insufficient to recover the ground lost by the baxters over the preceding century, though there seems to have been little or no further increase in the allowance until well into the eighteenth century. In Glasgow the allowance was reported to be 48s. per boll in 1739 and 1740, whilst in Dundee it was still only 40s. per boll in 1741.[46]

There may, nevertheless, be good grounds for believing the baxters' statement that the allowance had remained unchanged since 1555. Restricting the allowance was one way in which the town council could influence the price of bread, and doubtless the baxters had to make do with whatever allowance they were granted, mitigating its effects by evading the price statutes whenever they could.[47]

In calculating the table of wheat prices in Edinburgh (table 2.3) we have accepted the baxters' statement that their allowance remained at 20s. per boll between 1555 and 1657.[48] Being doubled, it also seems reasonable to presume that the allowance then remained at the new level until at least 1702, the last year in which the town council set the price of bread under its old authority. In knowing the baxters' allowance throughout this period it thus becomes possible to determine, at least in theory, the actual market price of wheat upon which the statute price for wheatbread was based.

If the town council was honest in its examination of the price of wheat in the market, then this series provides an unparalleled insight into the movement of wheat prices from 1556 to 1702, and allows the series provided by the fiars to be pushed back by some seven decades. But there may be a suspicion that, as the pressure was on the town council to keep bread prices as low as possible, they may not have been entirely honest in their appraisal of market prices. Whether or not this was the case can only be tested through a comparison with other wheat price series. In the early years it is only against the prices recorded in the Exchequer Rolls that any comparison can be made. Occasionally the

[46] *GBR, 1739–59*, pp. 27, 78; W. Hay, *Charters, writs and public documents of the Royal Burgh of Dundee, 1292–1880* (Dundee, 1880), p. 158.

[47] This still leaves the implication that the allowance granted to the baxters in 1555 may have been exceptionally favourable. One possible explanation for this may lie with the fact that for a brief period in the mid sixteenth century the craftsmen, and with them possibly the baxters, found themselves powerful enough greatly to enhance their economic and political standing within the burghs. The craftsmen forged an alliance with Mary of Guise, the Queen Regent, who was in dispute with the merchants over three ordinances she had recently passed, including one which transferred the power to set prices from the burgh authorities to the Privy Council. The craftsmen may have been able to take advantage of this conflict by negotiating directly with the Queen Regent – offering her their support in return for the repeal of the 1555 Act and certain other privileges (Grant, *Social and economic development*, pp. 431–2). It seems quite plausible that, at a time when the craftsmen's alliance with Mary resulted in a favourable interpretation of their political and economic status, they also managed to negotiate an exceptionally profitable allowance for their labour. It is probably not coincidental that this was also a period in which the Privy Council, and not the burgh authorities, had the power to set prices. Its role may have been short lived, but the Privy Council seems to have established the principle that 140 lbs. of bread was to be baked from each boll of wheat. The rule that the baxters should receive 20s. for baking that 140 lbs. of bread may also have originated with this intervention.

[48] It should be noted that the allowance granted to the malt makers, although it did increase between 1552 and 1677, only did so by some 67 per cent; the allowance being proportional to 4s. on every boll of malt produced in 1552 and 6s.8d. on every boll by 1667.

prices calculated from the Edinburgh wheatbread series appear somewhat low, but, in general, the comparison gives no reason to doubt the validity of this calculated series of Edinburgh wheat prices.

This comparison is, however, far from ideal, but when after 1626 the series can be compared with the Midlothian fiars, the correspondence is generally quite close. Only in 1653 and 1654 was the price difference greater than 25 per cent, and this particular dislocation was perhaps because the town authorities were unwilling to accept that the preceding six years of exceptionally high prices were really over. Alternatively, a more subtle factor may have been at work in these two years. During the preceding period of scarcity the burgh authorities had been setting the price of bread on the basis of unrealistically low wheat prices; the fiars were reporting prices that were, on average, more than 10 per cent above those the burgh authorities were willing to accept. Because of this, presuming that the baxters had to buy their wheat at a price somewhat closer to the fiars, they must have either accepted a lower allowance or been baking bread that was coarser than usual. Perhaps the relatively high price of bread in 1653 and 1654 – with the hidden extra allowance it would have given the baxters – was some sort of *quid pro quo* for lower profits over the preceding few years.

Leaving aside the anomalous situation of 1653 and 1654, the relationship between the fiars' prices and those used by the town council to set the price of bread was a close one, though there are a few years in which the baxters were apparently having to sell the bread for less than the cost of the wheat from which it was baked.[49] A total of forty-three price comparisons between 1626 and 1702 returns a correlation coefficient (PMCC) of 0.86. The town council prices were lower than the fiars, but the difference was negligible, on average less than 3 per cent, and swallowed up by the much greater annual variation between the two prices. More problematic is the fact, as discussed in chapter 3, that the fiars themselves tended to underestimate actual market prices. In view of this it would seem that the town councils' prices also tended to underestimate market prices by about 10 per cent even though it was often stated that the council based their calculations on the 'maximum' price of wheat. In part this may have reflected the fact that the bread price for any year was usually set relative to the price of wheat in November when grain prices were at their lowest, but then this timing may itself have reflected the magistrates' anxiety to keep bread prices as low as possible. However, if taken too far the baxters were likely to respond in kind by baking bread that was marginally coarser and by stretching the wheat, and their allowance, that little bit further.

In 1681 the main Edinburgh series ends abruptly, although the town council records do contain one further reference to the price of wheatbread – in 1702. Three decades later, in March 1733, such prices begin to be recorded again, this time in the *Caledonian Mercury* and the *Scots Magazine*. By now, of course, the prices were set under the authority of the British statutes. A number of Acts of Parliament from 1709 to 1773

---

[49] In 1628, for instance, wheat, according to the fiars, cost £8.6s.8d. per boll. The baxters were required to sell their bread at 8d. for 10 oz. This would have given a return of only £7.9s.4d. for every 140 lbs. of bread sold – the amount that was meant to be baked from each boll. This is a most unlikely situation; the baxters must have been able to obtain wheat at a cheaper price than indicated by the fiars, or to evade the statutes by baking a very much coarser bread than usual.

Table 2C *Regulation of wheatbread by local and national statutes, 1624–1773*
Quantity of bread (oz. avoirdupois) to be baked from one Winchester bushel of wheat

		First quality	Second quality	Third quality
Edinburgh statute,	1624	608 oz.	810 oz.	1,013 oz.
English statute,	1707	556 oz.	834 oz.	1,111 oz.
British statute,	1709	555 oz.	790 oz.	1,113 oz.
British statute,	1757	543 oz.	723 oz.	982 oz.
British statute,	1762	543 oz.	723 oz.	965 oz.
British statute,	1773	728 oz.	832 oz.	971 oz.

Note: In the Edinburgh statute first quality was described as 'finest', second quality as 'four', third quality as 'masloche'. In the English and British statutes the terminology is respectively 'white', 'wheaten' and 'household'. The equivalents may well not be exact.

determined the quality of the three types of bread that were to be subject to price regulation: white, wheaten and household bread.[50] As the price of 'white' bread was only periodically given from 1733, from that date the figures in table 2.1 refer to the cost of 'wheaten' bread. The implications of this in terms of comparisons with earlier Edinburgh prices and with Glasgow prices are discussed in a footnote to that table.

The eighteenth-century statutes applied the same principle as the twelfth-century assize of David I in Scotland and the thirteenth-century assize of Henry III in England;[51] that a certain weight of bread was to be sold at a price equal to the cost of the wheat plus the labour that was required to produce it. From these acts the quality of the three sorts of bread can be compared with the three varieties sold in seventeenth-century Edinburgh (see table 2C).[52]

Although these acts define the relationship between the price of bread and the total cost of the wheat plus labour required to produce it, there is no eighteenth-century evidence regarding the allowance given to the baxters. Without this it is impossible to determine the actual price of wheat upon which the price statutes for bread were based, but alternative series for wheat are of course by then available from the fiars.

4 Bread prices in other burghs (tables 2.1, 2.2)

Unfortunately, similar considerations bedevil any comparable attempt to establish the wheat prices which lay behind the series of sixteenth- and seventeenth-century statute prices for bread that are available for other Scottish burghs (see tables 2.1 and 2.2).

In Glasgow, as in Edinburgh, the town council set the price of bread on the fixed

[50] 8 Anne, c.18, 1709. 31 Geo. II, c.29, 1757. 3 Geo. III, c.11, 1762. 13 Geo. III, c.62, 1773.
[51] 51 Hen. III, c.1, 1266.
[52] To make the 1623 Scottish figure comparable to English and British statutes, the boll has been taken to be equivalent to 4 Winchester bushels, and the size of the Scottish troy ounce to be 1.086 times the Imperial avoirdupois ounce. 51 Hen III c.1 still regulated English assize in 1707. There is some evidence that the British assize of 1709 was not in fact adopted in Scotland.

Table 2D *Regulation of oatbread by Stirling town council, 1638*

When a boll of oatmeal sold for	12d. baps should weigh	10d. baps should weigh	8d. baps should weigh	6d. baps should weigh
£ 5.0.0	16 oz.	14 oz.	11½ oz.	10 oz.
£ 6.0.0	14 oz.	12 oz.	10 oz.	9¼ oz.
£ 7.0.0	11½ oz.	9¼ oz.	8 oz.	7½ oz.
£ 8.0.0	9½ oz.	7 oz.	7½ oz.	6 oz.
£ 9.0.0	8¼ oz.	6 oz.	6½ oz.	5¼ oz.
£10.0.0	7½ oz.	5½ oz.	5¼ oz.	4¾ oz.

understanding that 140 lbs. Scottish Troy of finest wheat bread was to be baked from each boll of wheat. Unfortunately, it is only for 1739 that we know the baxter's allowance (48s. per boll) and thus no estimates can be made on the basis of bread prices regarding the likely market price of wheat in Glasgow. Neither do we know the baxter's allowance in either Aberdeen or Stirling, but in any case in these two burghs there was a variable relationship between the statute price of bread and the cost of wheat as noted by their town councils. In Aberdeen we can compare the statute price of wheatbread with the reported cost of wheat for a total of twenty-three years between 1581 and 1630. Unlike Edinburgh and Glasgow, no common relationship emerges, though there is undoubtedly some logic behind these statutes. For instance, wheat was reported to have cost £8 on nine separate occasions; on five of those the price of bread was set as if 120 lbs. had to be sold for the price of a boll of wheat, on one occasion as if 140 lbs. had to be thus sold, and on three further occasions as if 160 lbs. had to be sold. This was no random variation, but the logic of the price statutes seems impossible to determine now, particularly without the benefit of a complete table of assize. Perhaps in Aberdeen the 'cost' of a boll of wheat did not include the baxters' allowance or, if it did, perhaps the allowance varied from one year to the next. Alternatively, the quality of the bread may have changed from one year to another, responding, perhaps, to the scarcity or otherwise of wheat.

A similar situation prevailed in Stirling. On forty-four occasions between 1601 and 1664 the town council recorded the statute price of wheatbread along with the price of wheat upon which it was based. Once again an irregular relationship emerges, but one which appears neither random nor illogical. Here the price of wheat stood at £8 the boll on eight occasions. On two of those the price of bread was set on the basis that 160 lbs. had to be sold for the cost of a boll; on a further two occasions 150 lbs., and on four other occasions 140 lbs. It impossible to discern what lay behind this variation, but the same factors noted at Aberdeen probably played their part.

Wheat was not the only grain involved in such calculations. Stirling town council produced a table (table 2D) of assize in 1638 for calculating the price of oatbread with respect to that of oatmeal.[53]

[53] R. Renwick, *Extracts from the records of the royal burgh of Stirling, 1519–1666* (Glasgow, 1887), p. 180.

It is clear that the relationship that this table of assize forges between the price of oatmeal and the price of oatbread is far from straightforward. When oatmeal was sold at £5 per boll the 12d. baps were to weigh 16 oz., but the 6d. baps (which we might expect to have weighed 8 oz.) were to provide a full 10 oz. of bread. This difference is maintained whatever the price of oatmeal; thus when it was £10 the boll and the 12d. baps weighed 7 oz., the 6d. baps weighed 4¾ oz. and not the 3½ oz. that might have been expected. A similar discrepancy emerges when comparing the amount of bread received at different oatmeal prices; thus the 16 oz. for 12d. received when oatmeal was £5 the boll compares favourably with the 7½ oz. for 12d. received when meal was twice as expensive.

In Edinburgh and Glasgow the 'cost' of wheat in equivalent assizes included the cost of the labour required to bake it into bread and there was thus a linear relationship between the 'cost' of wheat and the price of wheatbread, but such does not seem to have been the case here. There is certainly no linear relationship between the price of oatmeal and that of oatbread and, in any case, the table specifically refers to the price at which the oatmeal was sold. It would seem, therefore, that the baxters' allowance was additional to the given price of oatmeal. How this allowance was to be applied is, however, hard to determine. Had there been a fixed allowance per boll then the oatbread would have become relatively cheaper the more expensive the meal. Similarly, a fixed allowance per bap would have resulted in oatbread that was relatively cheaper the bigger the bap. Yet the opposite was true in both cases. The changing relationship between the price of oatmeal and oatbread must have been a consequence of either changing allowances or a changing amount of bread being baked from each boll of oatmeal, or perhaps of a combination of both. There is no explicit evidence on the way the allowance or quality of bread may have varied, but the only logical supposition is that the baxters' allowance increased with the price of meal (perhaps designed as an equitable response to the higher cost of living that such would entail), or that the amount of bread to be baked from a boll of meal increased as the size of the baps became smaller. This would mean that the cheaper baps were also the coarsest.[54]

---

[54] The sort of equation that lay behind this table might have run along the following lines:

Cost of baking oatbread from a boll of oatmeal			Weight of 6d. and 12d. baps with the amount of bread baked from each boll of meal			
			-- 12d. bap --		-- 6d. bap --	
Oatmeal	+ Allowance	= Total	Wt./bap (oz.)	Total (oz.)	Wt./bap (oz.)	Total (oz.)
£5.0.0	£1.0.0	£6.0.0	16	1,920	10	2,400
£8.0.0	£2.0.0	£10.0.0	9½	1,900	6	2,400
£10.0.0	£2.16.0	£12.16.0	7½	1,920	4¾	2,432

Although this does greatly simplify the 'Table of Ait Breid', the fact that these equations are consistent (give or take a few ounces) does suggest that the principle behind them is correct. The value of the allowance and the amount of the bread baked into the 12d. and 6d. baps is, however, purely notional and runs from an initial assumption that the allowance was £1.0s.0d. per boll when oatmeal stood at £5.0s.0d. Whatever their actual values, the ratios between them must have been as given in the table. That is to say, when the price of oatmeal increased the baxters' allowance actually kept slightly ahead of the increase. Also, whatever the actual amount of bread baked from each boll of meal, it had to have been 25 per cent greater when baked into 6d. baps than when into 12d. baps. The seventeenth-century housewife choosing her oatbread in Stirling did so knowing that the 6d. loaf was both the cheapest and the coarsest, and that the 12d. loaf was both the most expensive and the finest.

This assize of oatbread seems to have been both more equitable and more flexible than that which determined wheatbread prices in Edinburgh and Glasgow. The contemporary baxter may have been grateful, but it does confuse the relationship between the price of oatbread and oatmeal. If similar considerations lay behind the price statutes for wheatbread made in burghs other than Edinburgh and Glasgow, then it is small wonder that it is now impossible to establish how wheatbread prices were calculated in those burghs.

Why Edinburgh and Glasgow should stand so distinct from the other burghs is unclear, but it does not seem that such was the intention. On 10 January 1604 Aberdeen town council noted that in Edinburgh 16 oz. of wheat bread was being baked for 12d., but in their own town only 14 oz., 'notwithstanding that this town should be conforme to them'.[55] Similarly, the Convention of Royal Burghs determined in 1655 that 'the pais of wheat bread of all sorts to be conform to the pais of Edinburgh'.[56] It is unclear whether it was the actual price of bread or the manner in which it was to be determined that was to be thus standardised throughout the country, but neither actually occurred, and in Aberdeen and Stirling, the price of bread seems to have reflected more than just the price of wheat. In these burghs a changing baxters' allowance or quality of bread may have been as important a cause of fluctuations in the price of bread as variations in the cost of grain.

Such factors could only ever have had limited effects, however. On the one hand, the baxters must always have been able to make a living, and, on the other, the bread was unlikely to have become either exceptionally fine or excessively coarse. The bread price statutes undoubtedly provide a general guide to the major long-term trends, and are particularly valuable in charting the course of the sixteenth-century 'price revolution'.

5 Malt and ale (tables 2.7, 2.8)

Malt and ale were also products regularly subject to price control, appearing in the documentary record even more frequently than wheatbread (see tables 2.7 and 2.8). The principle that lay behind price statutes for ale was precisely the same as that which lay behind those for wheatbread – a certain quantity of ale was to be brewed from each boll of malt (or ground malt)[57] and this was to be made available at a price equal to the cost of that malt plus the cost of the labour and materials required to brew it into ale. The cost of malt was the main variable and that, in turn, depended on the quality of the grain harvest; periodically, usually in October or November of each year, it was necessary for each town council to determine the price at which ale was to be sold in the future. Particularly rapid fluctuations in the price of malt called for action at other times of the year, as on 30 May 1635 when the town council of Dumbarton decided that, because of price rises in the raw materials 'a visitation to be maid in the eftirnoon of aill and beir, to test and, if worthie, to increase the price'.[58]

---

[55] Aberdeen town council register, vol. 41, p. 495.
[56] *Recs. Conv. Royal Burghs*, vol. III, p. 402.
[57] In Edinburgh it was expressly stated on four occasions between 1566 and 1600 that the price of ale was being set with regard to the price of ground malt. On all other occasions the town council referred merely to malt, but it is possible that such also referred to ground malt.   [58] Irving, *Dumbarton records*, p. 47.

From the late twelfth century until the mid seventeenth century the common rule seems to have been that 120 pints of ale should be brewed from each boll of malt. This underpinned King William's table of assize (1165–1214) and occured as late as 1644 in an act of the Scottish Parliament which decreed that; 'the excise of aill shall be uplifted allowing to everie boll of broune Malt conteyning four firlottes of prickmet within the Kingdome 15 gallons of aill'.[59]

In Aberdeen and Stirling, this remained the usual ratio between the cost of malt and the price of ale, though there was some variation.[60] In these two burghs, although the 'cost' of the malt must have included the brewers' allowance, nowhere is it stated what that allowance may have been. These statutes, even when they refer to the so-called 'cost' of malt, thus only provide a general guide to movements in the price of that article.

The price of malt reported in other burgh records did not always include an allowance for the brewers. In Edinburgh the relationship between the price of ale and malt varied considerably, although of the twenty-four occasions between 1505 and 1600 when the price of both ale and malt was given, on six occasions exactly 240 pints of ale were to be sold at a price equal to the reported cost of a 'laid' (of nine firlots) of malt. This works out at $106\frac{2}{3}$ pints per boll: this lower ratio, as well as its greater variation, reflects the fact that here the given price of malt does not seem to have included an allowance for the brewers. In fact, in Edinburgh the reported price of malt was itself a 'statute' price. Thus on the 24 February 1556 the provost, baillies and council declared that, since the price of bear (the usual grain from which malt was made) was 36s., 'the nyne furlettis grundin malt of the auld mesour to be sauld for 4 lib. and the pynt aill 4d.'.[61]

Malt was, of course, as much a product of craftwork as ale and its price was regulated in exactly the same way – an allowance being set for the manufacture of each boll of malt. In seventeenth-century Aberdeen the allowance was in kind (a proportion of raw material given in lieu of cash) but in Edinburgh it was in money.[62]

Parliament itself first defined the malt makers' allowance in kind – in 1503 it was to be no more than one boll of bear on every chalder of malt produced, but by 1536 it was defined in terms of cash – the 'difference' between the price of the boll of bear and malt being set at 2s.[63] Although no further acts can be found, the records of Edinburgh town council and the Privy Council show the allowance to have increased to 4s. by 1552, to 6s.8d. by 1677, and to 10s. in 1679.[64] The difficulty here is that although the 'difference' is known (at least in these years) this was not necessarily the allowance given to the malt makers; a boll of bear need not have produced exactly a boll of malt. A St Andrews diet account of 1597[65] states that the manufacture of each boll of malt required 18 pecks of

[59] *APS*, vol. 6(1), p. 240.
[60] The price of malt and ale is given in Aberdeen on twenty-three occasions between 1581 and 1635. On thirteen occasions 120 pints of ale could be bought for the given price of malt and never did the ratio fall below 100 pints or rise above $133\frac{1}{3}$ pints. In Stirling there was more variation, but of the fifty-six occasions when both malt and ale prices were given the ratio was 120 pints per boll sixteen times and within plus or minus 10 pints of that no less than forty times. In Aberdeen the variation seems to reflect the price (and thus the scarcity) of the malt – the higher the price of the malt the more ale that was brewed from each boll.
[61] *EBR, 1528–1557*, p. 238.   [62] Aberdeen town council register, vol. 27; *EBR, 1528–1557*, pp. 162–3.
[63] *APS*, vol. 2, pp. 245, 351.
[64] *Register of the Privy Council* (3rd series), vol. 5, pp. 97–9; *ibid.*, vol. 6, pp. 365–9.
[65] NLS, Crawford and Balcarres Mss: untitled St Andrews University diet account, 1597.

bear. A 'Barley and Malt Book' of 1773–83,[66] on the other hand, shows that only 8 bolls of barley were required to manufacture every 10 bolls of malt. These very different ratios may reflect the use of different measures, the production of different qualities of malt, or even the relative productivity of bear and barley, but without knowing the ratio that Parliament and the Privy Council had in mind when determining the price 'difference' between bear and malt it is clearly impossible to establish the allowance they were granting to the malt makers.

Without this information on the process of malting bear in the sixteenth and seventeenth centuries, and without any knowledge of the allowance granted to the brewers for producing their ale, it is impossible to establish the relationship between the 'market' price of malt and the price given in the burgh records – be it a 'statute' price (as in Edinburgh) or one which included an allowance for the brewers (as in Aberdeen and Stirling). This difficulty is exacerbated by the fact that, from 1644, Parliament imposed an excise duty on ale and beer of 4d. per pint.[67] This excise is recorded in the Kirkcudbright statutes from October of 1644, but elsewhere it goes unnoted. It may, however, be the cause of a sudden discrepancy which emerged in the ratio between ale and malt prices in Stirling in 1663 and 1664. The situation was even more complicated in Edinburgh. Although the national excise duty was reduced to only 2d. per pint in 1647, six years later Edinburgh was granted a special imposition on top of the excise for the express purpose of repaying the council's debts.[68] Originally 4d. per pint, this imposition reached as much as 12d. per pint in December 1658.[69] By 1666 it had dropped to 2d. per pint,[70] a level at which it remained well into the eighteenth century.[71]

During the 1650s and 1660s most of the burghs stopped recording the price of ale in their council records. In part this may have reflected the growing role of the Privy Council in determining ale prices. As early as 1598 and 1620 the Privy Council attempted to set the price of ale (with only limited success in both instances),[72] but its main function was to define how the price was to be established in each burgh and 'landwart paroche'. Although not actually empowered to do so until an Act of the Scottish Parliament of 1669, in 1666 the Privy Council established a table (table 2E) relating ale prices to the price of the bear.[73]

This table of assize was renewed (and slightly modified) in 1676 and 1697[74] but it was left to the 'shireffes, justices of peace and magistratts of burghs to putt this act in due execution within their respective bounds'.

---

66 SRO, GD 44/52/100(12), 'Gordon Castle barley and malt book, 1773–1783'. In the early nineteenth century it was generally recognised that a given quantity of barley would produce a greater quantity of malt (William Cobbet, *Cottage economy*, 1926 edition, London, p. 13).   67 *APS*, vol. 6(1), p. 76a.

68 *APS*, vol. 6(1), p. 727; vol. 6(2), pp. 753, 780.   69 *EBR, 1655–1665*, pp. xxxv–xxxvii.

70 *Register of the Privy Council* (3rd series), vol. 2 , pp. 130–2.

71 *APS*, vol. 8, p. 49; vol. 8, p. 182; vol. 9, p. 206 and app. 169; vol. 9, p. 310.

72 In both 1598 *Register of the Privy Council* (1st series), vol. 5, p. 507 and 1620, *ibid.*, vol. 12, p. 157, the council set the price of ale at 1s. per pint. The 1598 ordinance took effect in Aberdeen and Edinburgh, but in Kirkcudbright ale was to be sold at 8d. per pint. In 1620 Aberdeen and Edinburgh again set the price at 1s. per pint, but this time both Kirkcudbright and Glasgow erred – setting prices at 8d. and 9d. respectively.

73 *APS*, vol. 7, p. 574; *Register of the Privy Council* (3rd series), vol. 2, pp. 130–2. It was proclaimed on 18 January: by 7 February the magistrates of Culross had taken cognisance of it. Beveridge, *Culross*, vol. I, p. 332.

74 *Register of the Privy Council* (3rd series), vol. 5, pp. 69–72; vol. 6, pp. 365–9.

Table 2E *Regulation of ale by Privy Council, 1666*

When a boll of best rough bear is bought for	The pint of best ale and beer shall be sold for	Pints of ale per boll rough bear
£ 6.0.0	12d.	120
£ 8.0.0	20d.	96
£10.0.0	24d.	100

Table 2F *Regulation of ale by Privy Council, 1680*

When the weigh barley costs	and the weigh of rough bear costs	then the pint of ale shall be sold at	Pints of ale per weigh of rough bear
7 merks	6 merks	14d.	80
8 merks	7 merks	16d.	80
9 merks	8 merks	18d.	80
10 merks	9 merks	24d.	65.4
11 merks	10 merks	26d.	66.6
12 merks	11 merks	28d.	67.7
13 merks	12 merks	30d.	68.6

As the table 2E shows, there was a variable relationship between the price of bear and the price of ale. Possibly because of this the Privy Council's table of assize was soon found to be unsatisfactory. In 1680 it was deemed necessary to establish a new table (table 2F).[75]

The 'weigh' was the boll defined by weight rather than, as before, by measure. First introduced in December 1679,[76] the 'weigh' was originally intended to vary with the season, being of 15 stone 'troas' from the harvest until the following 15 April, but of only 14 stone 'troas' thereafter.[77] In 1680, this complication was abandoned and the 'weigh' was redefined as 15 stone throughout the year. Although the price of ale given in the table was said to have included the excise, at this time at 2d. per pint, the table does seem somewhat contradictory; when bear stood at 6, 7 or 8 merks per boll the price of ale (excluding the excise) was clearly determined from the fact that 80 pints were brewed from each boll. When it cost 9 merks or more per boll the ratio was variable – the ale always, in fact, being 4d. more than it would have been if exactly 80 pints were brewed from each boll. Perhaps there was a logic in this that is now lost, but whatever the case the Privy Council's new table was to have no more lasting impact on the method by which ale prices were determined than its predecessor.

[75] *Register of the Privy Council* (3rd series), vol. 6, pp. 530–33.
[76] *Register of the Privy Council* (3rd series), vol. 6, pp. 365–9. This act of the Privy Council also first established the boll of oatmeal as of 8 stone 'troas', a weight confirmed by an Act of Parliament of 1696 (*APS*, vol. 10, p. 34).
[77] This would allow for the drying of the grain whilst in storage.

In Aberdeen the price of ale continued to be set by the town council until 1680. The price had, however, stabilised at 2s. per pint in 1644 and was still at that level in 1680 when the town council last set the price of ale. This seems to reflect a change in attitude towards the pricing of ale which was to occur throughout Scotland. By the eighteenth century the price of the different qualities of ale had become so well established that they came to be known as 2s. or 3s. ale. Thus we read that at Kelly in Fife in 1713[78] a barrel of 2s. ale and half a barrel of 3s. ale were brought from Dundee. After the Union and the imposition of English currency, these in due course became known as 'two-penny' and 'three-penny' ale. With this the very idea that a certain quantity of ale should be brewed from a boll of malt or bear and sold at a cost equal to that malt or bear plus the labour required to brew it into ale was finally abandoned. Gradually the 'fixed' prices of ale became merely names for different qualities. Today in most Scottish public houses seventy-shilling and eighty-shilling beers are available, but of course their price per pint has long varied with market forces and the Chancellor's decisions on duty.

6 Oatbread, ryebread, horse corn, wine, etc. (tables 2.4, 2.5, 2.6, 2.9)

The use of tables of assize, or at least the idea that the price of any product of craftwork should be related to the cost of the necessary raw materials plus the cost of the labour required to make it, was not restricted to wheatbread and ale. Table 2.4 is concerned with oatbread. The 1638 regulations relating the price of oatbread in Stirling to the price of oatmeal have already been discussed, and a similar table must have been used in Aberdeen between 1612 and 1643 where, in years of scarcity, the baxters were permitted to bake oatbread and to sell it at a price set relative to the price of oatmeal.[79] The same was probably true in Kirkcudbright, Old Aberdeen and Banff where oatbread was also occasionally subject to price regulation, although it is only with respect to the former that a reasonably lengthy price series is available. Of course, oatmeal itself was also a product of craftwork and should, therefore, also have been subject to some form of price control. In fact, only in Dunfermline on 11 October 1575 is the price of oatmeal known to have been determined by a town council:

The Quhilk Day the assyse all in ane voce statutis and ordanis that malt be sauld for 56s. the boll, aill for 6d. the pynt, maill for 30d. the peck, and gif the maill makeris willfullie mixis thair maill with dust or seeds the samyn to be escheatit and thay dischargit of thair freedom for zeir and a day.[80]

Given its importance to the majority of the inhabitants of the Scottish burghs, it is notable that oatmeal does not generally seem to have been subject to price regulation. Presumably it was brought to the burgh already ground by millers in the countryside, and its price was deemed to be beyond burgh control.

Ryebread was another product that came to the attention of the burgh authorities, but

[78] SRO, GD45/18/1249, 'The spending at Kelly in 1713'.
[79] The ratio between the price of oatmeal and oatbread was, however, variable. The was a maximum of 2,700 oz. and a minimum of 2,240 oz. oatbread sold at a price equal to the given cost of the oatmeal.
[80] A. Shearer, *Extracts from the burgh records of Dunfermline in the sixteenth and seventeenth centuries* (Dunfermline, 1951), p. 12.

Table 2G *Regulation of ryebread by Aberdeen town council, 1603–15*

	When a boll of rye is sold for	Price of bread per lb.	Ryebread shall be made per boll
June 1603	£6.0.0	4.6d.	2,400 oz.
Oct. 1603	£6.0.0	8.7d.	2,462 oz.
Oct. 1606	£5.0.0	8.0d.	2,400 oz.
May 1615	£8.0.0	12.8d.	2,400 oz.
Oct. 1615	£8.0.0	12.8d.	2,400 oz.

only rarely. On five occasions between 1603 and 1615 Aberdeen town council set the price of ryebread, always linking it explicitly to the price of rye (table 2G).

On four of those occasions 2,400 oz. of ryebread were to be sold at a price equal to the given cost of a boll of rye – the implication of this uniformity being, once again, that the reported price of rye included an allowance for the baxters. In Edinburgh, the price of 'ryebread' was purportedly determined by the town council eight times between 1636 and 1643, but in this case it seems almost certain that the term was generally used to describe what was commonly known as 'masloche' bread, essentially a poor quality wheat loaf mixed with rye. Only once, in 1606, was it explicitly linked to the current cost of a boll of rye, and then in a way that implied that 3,840 oz. of bread was to be made from each boll of rye, a figure very different from that found in Aberdeen.[81] Perhaps the size of the boll was different, the quality of the ryebread was inferior, or the allowance to the baxters much higher. It is impossible now to tell.

The other grain product that was commonly subject to burgh price regulation was 'oats'. This was not, however, in the context of town council prices, an article for human consumption: the statutes often described it as 'Horse Corn', and its price was given alongside that for hay and the twenty-four hours' stable fee as part of the mechanism to regulate the activities and earnings of the 'stabilleris'. A limited series is available for Elgin, with more extensive series relating to Aberdeen, Edinburgh and Stirling (tables 2.5 and 2.6). It is difficult to determine to what extent these prices included an allowance for the stablers and whether they therefore overstate the price at which oats could have been bought in the open market.

Other products subject to price control included wine and whisky. How the price of the latter was established is unclear, but it is, in any case, only known to have been subject to price regulation in Dumbarton, and then only occasionally. Wine, for which excellent series of 'statute' prices are available from Edinburgh (table 2.9), was, at least during the last quarter of the sixteenth century, priced according to its original cost, the current exchange rate, and the cost of bringing it to Scotland – with an allowance for leakage and the merchant's profit included in the calculation.[82] This Edinburgh price

---

[81] *EBR, 1604–1626*, p. 25.

[82] *EBR, 1573–1589*, pp. 93–4, 129; *EBR, 1589–1603*, p. 31; J. Irving (ed.), *Dumbarton burgh records, 1627–1746* (Dumbarton, 1860).

may in fact have been of significance throughout Lowland Scotland: Stirling town council in 1623 ordered all wine to be sold for 'only' 12d. a pint more than it is in Edinburgh.[83] Presumably the justification for regulating wine prices lay in the fact that with only limited trade, individual merchants importing wine from the continent would have had, even if only for short periods, a monopolistic control of the supply to the burgh. Without some form of control they would have found it tempting to abuse that monopoly.

This was a consideration which might apply equally to imported grains in time of dearth. Thus in 1596 the town council in Edinburgh regulated the price, and quantity that could be sold to each buyer, of a cargo of victual from London, and did much the same again in 1600.[84]

On one occasion, famine prompted a general proclamation regarding the price at which various grains should be sold. On orders from Privy Council, Edinburgh town council, on 29 April 1699, fixed the price of wheat, bear and oats at £17, £13 and £12 per boll and the price of oatmeal, peasemeal and bearmeal at £13.12s.0d., £10.0s.0d. and £8.8s.0d. respectively.[85] These appear, however to have been the only occasions when any town council attempted to limit grain prices in this way.

These regulations relative to wine and grain represent something of a departure from those already considered. Their objective was not to define a price and quality of a product and thereby control craftsmens' earnings, but was rather to achieve the more immediate and straightforward goal of keeping prices in the market as low as possible, the intention being to limit profiteering. This more general concern with prices in the market – as opposed to the specific control of craftsmens' earnings and the price of their products – was expressed by many intermittent statutes regarding various other products. Butter, cheese, eggs and milk were occasionally subject to price control – always as a response to unusually high prices being charged in the market. Other items which appear in the burgh records include such diverse subjects 'wyld mete and tame foulis', fish, fruit, figs and raisins, and even sweets.[86] Whether the rarity of these statutes belies a more widespread concern with such items is difficult to determine, but the available price quotations are certainly too few and far between to allow for any meaningful analysis. Prices which related the fleshers' and candlemakers' crafts were also regulated by burgh statutes in the same way as bread or ale, but they are considered separately in chapter 6.

7 Non-statute prices (tables 2.10, 2.11, 2.12)

Burgh records also sometimes include a few prices other than those associated with statutes. They occasionally include, for instance, references to the 'liquidated' price of various grains – prices which represented a legal judgement on the price of various grains

[83] R. Renwick, *Extracts from the records of the burgh of Stirling* (Glasgow, 1887), p. 158.
[84] *EBR, 1589–1603*, pp. 156, 265.   [85] *EBR, 1689–1701*, p. 245.
[86] *EBR, 1665–1680*, pp. 94, 285, 292; John Stuart, *Extracts from the council register of the burgh of Aberdeen*, vol. I, *1398–1570* (Aberdeen, 1844), p. 75; Cosmo Innes, *Extracts from the council register of the burgh of Aberdeen*, vol. II, *1570–1625* (Spalding Club, Aberdeen, 1898), p. 31.

through which debts and contracts could be settled.[87] Another quite different class of price data refers to grain bought or sold on behalf of the council. For instance, in Edinburgh in 1699, 100 bolls of oatmeal were purchased by the council for the 'use of the poor' at a cost of £13.6s.8d. per boll.[88] Other burghs also found it necessary to purchase grain and the price was occasionally noted.[89] A policy restricted to years of dearth, these prices are both intermittent and exceptional.

Of slightly more value are the series of prices relating to the sale or valuation of grain received by various town councils as rent from their common lands or in connection with payments of duty on imports. Such series are not as widespread as might be wished, as most burghs feued or set in tack for long periods their common lands and other possessions. Even when such were let by the council the records are not always complete. Edinburgh, for instance, had its 'Boroughmuir fermes', but only occasionally was the price of the grain received from the tenants noted in the council records.[90] In Ayr, however, the sale of the 'mill-ferme' of malt and oatmeal and of the 'Alloway-ferme' of bear was regularly noted and provides a valuable series of grain prices for the period 1583–1623 (table 2.10). In Perth, on the other hand, rents in kind appear to have been commuted into money payments early on, and from 1615 to 1685 the tenants of the Blackfriars and Charterhouse Crofts were required to pay rent on the basis of the value of bear as noted in the council records (table 2.11). A comparable series of prices is also available for Aberdeen between 1631 and 1670 (table 2.12). Here a levy was exacted on imported grain which could be paid in kind or in cash. Known as the 'Syseboll' when levied on non-freeman, and the 'St Nicholas Mett' when levied on burgesses, the council records note the price received through the sale of the wheat, bear, oatmeal, malt, rye and peas collected in kind.

A final category of price data to be found in the burgh records concerns reports made to, or by, various town councils regarding the price at which grain was bought, sold, valued or assessed by bodies other than the town council. It is in the Perth burgh records, for instance, that the county fiars for bear and meal for 1703–57 are to be found. In the same burgh, from 1665 through to 1685, the town council met with the kirk session of Perth to fix the price of the teind victual (bear and meal) for the parish and these prices are also recorded in the burgh records (table 2.11). Unfortunately, such price data are usually very restricted in scope, and too sparse to allow for meaningful analysis.

8 The effectiveness of burgh price regulation

The annual statutes undoubtedly provide a most important price series; the question remains as to how effective the system was in regulating the sale price of items such as bread and ale. To test this we need to know actual market prices. Sometimes the council records themselves provide this information, as at Edinburgh where on 15 December

---

[87] Shearer, *Dunfermline*, pp. 2, 116.   [88] *EBR, 1689–1701*, p. 244.
[89] For instance, W. Cramond, *The annals of Banff*, New Spalding Club (1891 and 1893), 1751, 1766, 1773 and 1775.
[90] *EBR, 1589–1603*, pp. 33, 210, and Edinburgh City Chambers MSS. Treasurers' accounts, vol. II, 1581–96 for a short series of malt and wheat prices, 1585–8 (pp. 185, 195, 255, 259, 265, 285, 320 and 435).

1529 the town council set the price of a gallon of ale at 1s.4d. while admitting that the common price before the enactment was from 1s.8d. to 2s. a gallon.[91] Intermittent references to known sale prices can be found from other sources, but these are only of limited value. Aberdeen University, for instance, was paying 6d. per pint for ale in September 1579 and 2s. per pint in May 1650,[92] precisely the prices laid down by the town council for those years. In Edinburgh, on the other hand, the Duke of Lennox, whilst Commissioner to the Scottish Parliament in 1607, paid just over 16d. per pint for the 95 gallons of ale purchased for his household.[93] This was 4d. per pint more than the statutes for that year permitted – but then perhaps the Duke was being supplied with ale of a particularly high quality. Considerations of this sort bedevil any attempt to assess the effectiveness of the statutes from the few comparisons that can be made.

The problem must, therefore, be approached from a different angle; what powers did the burgh authorities have to enforce their price legislation and to what extent were they willing to call upon them? The earliest references to the powers available to the burgh authorities show them to have been very severe indeed. In 1532 the baxters in Edinburgh were ordered to keep the statutes regarding the price and weight of bread 'under payne of tynsall of thair fredome and escheiting of thair bread'.[94] In a similar vein, an assize of 1573 in Dunfermline declared that: 'the first browster that can be apprehendit to sell 7d. aill hir fatt [vat] to be brokin and tyn [lose] her freedom for ane zeir and pay 40s. of unlaw'.[95]

The statute price at this time was 6d. per pint. The 'maill makeris' were also threatened with such a penalty two years later.[96] If a baxter, brewer or any craftsman, were to be deprived of their freedom they would no longer have been able to ply their trade – a most effective deterrent if the burgh authorities were willing to carry it out. It was, however, such a severe punishment that it could only ever have been used as a last resort,[97] and it is unlikely that many burghs would have taken such a step lightly.

By the end of the sixteenth century fines had become the principal deterrent. In 1589 Edinburgh town council declared that the baxters were to conform to the statutes 'under payne of 40s. and escheitting of the breid swa oft as thai failyie'.[98] These fines the burgh authorities were quite willing to impose; in Old Aberdeen six brewers were fined 26s.8d. each for selling 16 and 20 penny ale and 16 and 18 penny beer when the statute prices were 12d. and 14d. respectively. Four baxters were also fined 13s.8d. each for selling bread of the wrong weight.[99] Often the fines were set according to the value of the goods in question. In October 1609 the town council of Dunfermline fined Robert Phillane and Archibald Douglas, both of whom were malt makers, for:

[91] *EBR, 1528–1557*, p. 17.
[92] Liber rationum Collegii Aberdonensis, 1 September 1579 and 10 May 1650; transcribed and printed in Cosmo Innes, *Fasti Aberdonenses* (Spalding Club, Aberdeen, 1859).
[93] Household account of Ludovick, Duke of Lennox, when Commissioner to the Parliament of Scotland, 1607, pp. 160–91 in *Miscellany of the Maitland Club*, vol. I, Maitland Club, vol. 25 (Edinburgh, 1834).
[94] *EBR, 1403–1528*, p. 217, 30 July 1523.   [95] Shearer, *Dunfermline*, p. 3, 30 October 1573.
[96] *Ibid.*, p. 12, 11 October 1575.
[97] By an act of Parliament of 13 June 1496, the forfeiture of a craftsman's freedom was the prescribed punishment for a third offence (*APS*, vol. 2, p. 238).   [98] *EBR, 1589–1603*, p. 380.
[99] Minute book of the court of Old Aberdeen, vol. I, 18 April 1608.

contravention of the lait actis maid at the last Head Court in selling thair malt dearer nor aucht merks 6s. 8d. the boll and in refusing to sell the samin to the nytbours under ten merks the boll and uttering of distanefull and contemptuous language to sundry nytbours desyring malt.[100]

Often we hear no more than that certain individuals were declared in 'unlaw' of the court – a phrase which usually implies a fine, but may occasionally amount to no more than a warning. In Dunfermline on 18 May 1620 'unlaw' was imposed on George Smeiton for selling 'Dutch' beer (probably German in fact) for 18d. the pint, when the statutory price was only 12d.[101] In Dumbarton, in 1638, the council records note that the baxter was fined 54s. 'for selling light bread'. This was, perhaps, as severe a punishment as the town council dared impose, as there was only one baxter in the burgh. He had been enticed from Stirling only two years previously by the council's promise 'to pay the first year's maill on his baikhous, and to be maid burgess also gratis'.[102] Here, as in many of the smaller burghs, the town council was probably unwilling to exercise their full powers. In Dunfermline, for instance, George Pearson was convicted of forestalling, the statutory penalty being £40, which the Council 'relentit to 40s'.[103]

The burgh authorities undoubtedly had the power to enforce their price legislation, but without a detailed study of the court books it is impossible to establish how expedient they found it to use that power. It seems probable that the policy of the authorities would have varied from one burgh to the next, and would have evolved with changing economic circumstances – but these are issues we have not been able to pursue. Craftsmen were undoubtedly convicted and fined for breaking the price statutes, but the available evidence suggests that this occurred only infrequently. Whether this obscures a more widespread, or even endemic, contravention of the statutes is difficult to assess, but it appears most unlikely. Many of the burghs were regularly setting the price of the principal craft products for over a century and a half, and may have been doing so long before their records begin to speak of such; it seems improbable that they would have continued to do this if the statutes were without relation to the economic life of the burghs.

An even more important factor restricting the extent to which the statutes would have been ignored lay with the fact that they established the maximum price at which goods could be sold. An individual craftsman was unlikely to get much custom if he alone charged more than was permitted – the housewife would always favour those who sold their goods at the designated price. In fact, a craftsman could only successfully flout the price statutes if all his competitors were doing likewise, hence the disfavour with which craft combinations were viewed. There is occasional evidence that such wholesale contravention of the statutes did occur,[104] but there is absolutely nothing to suggest that this was a permanent feature of burgh life. Neither should we expect it to have been; the 'brewers, bakers and candlestick makers' would have been expert enough in their respective trades to have known more subtle methods of protecting their profits than

---

[100] Shearer, *Dunfermline*, p. 68.   [101] *Ibid.*, p. 120.
[102] Irving, *Dumbarton records*, p. 54; *ibid.*, p. 49.   [103] Shearer, *Dunfermline*, p. 120.
[104] In January 1499 it was reported by the town council in Edinburgh that 'The haill browsters wer in use to callit in and convict for breking the statutes, as at 8 January 1498 thair is callit and convict at anes to the nummer of fyftie wyffes. The 11 of January the said yeir the nummer of sixty wyffes' (*EBR, 1403–1528*, p. 104). This is the only time such a widespread prosecution of craftsmen or women is known to have occurred.

simple price manipulation. The adulteration of bread and ale must have been a fact of life long before it came into prominence during the course of the nineteenth century. It would probably have been the quality rather than the price of goods which varied when the price statutes failed to reflect actual market conditions. It appears, therefore, that while it would have been quite impossible for councils to have insulated themselves from long-term price trends in the market, or even to have proceeded regardless of short-term fluctuations, town council statute prices were especially designed to hold the prices of baxters', brewers' and other craftsmen's product at a relatively steady rate, or at least one steadier than that of the raw materials. With this qualification in mind, they can be used with some confidence.

INTRODUCTION TO TABLES 2.1–2.12

The records of the Scottish burghs provide three types of price information, all of which appear in the tables which follow. The most common are the 'statute' prices which were meant to determine the maximum price at which products of craftwork such as wheatbread (table 2.1), oatbread (table 2.4), horse oats or corn (tables 2.5 and 2.6) and ale (table 2.8) were to be sold within the burgh. The price of imported wine in Edinburgh (table 2.9) was also established through a statute price mechanism, although in this case to prevent profiteering by merchants rather than craftsmen.

The second type of price information arises because these prices were often set on the basis of the current price of the raw materials from which the products of craftwork were to be made, plus an allowance due to the craftsmen for their costs and reasonable profit. As discussed in the text, the 'reported' price of wheat (table 2.2) and malt (table 2.7) usually, though not invariably, included that allowance. These tables must therefore be used with caution as the reported price must exceed the actual market price upon which they were based. Only in Edinburgh is the amount allowed to any group of craftsmen known; some evidence exists (as discussed in the text) to chart the allowance due to Edinburgh baxters between 1556 and 1681 and this has enabled us to deduce the contemporary price of wheat on the basis of the statute price for wheatbread (table 2.3).

As a rule the town council statutes were promulgated each November and, unless particularly severe short-term price movements demanded more immediate intervention, were intended to remain in force until the following November. As we have endeavoured to provide only one price for each calender year, tables 2.1–2.9 record prices set in November or, if no statutes were laid down in that month, those set in December or, failing that, any set (or reported) earlier in the calender year. These we presume still to have been current in November.

As 'statute' prices were meant to apply from the November of the year in which they were set until the following November, and the 'reported' prices were those current in November of the year in question, both effectively describe the price environment of the crop year which commenced during the calendar year referred to. As such, these prices may be compared directly with the fiars prices which are the subject of chapter 3.

The third type of price information contained within these tables refers to the sale of grain grown or collected by the town council. Much miscellaneous information of this nature is to be found, but precious few series. Tables 2.10–2.12 ostensibly refer to the price obtained by various town councils for victual sold by them, although in fact they are clearly summary 'accounting prices'. In Ayr (table 2.10) the sale appears to have been of bear, malt and oatmeal received by way of rent from the Town Mill and the Alloway lands. In Perth (2.11) the sale was of the bear grown on the Blackfriars and Charterhouse Crofts, as well as of the bear and oatmeal received by way of teind from the parish as a whole. In Aberdeen (2.12) the sale was of a series of grains received by way of the two petty customs known as the sysboll (levied on non-freemen) and the St Nicholas Mett (levied on burgesses of the town). In all three tables the dates to which prices refer are crop years and are thus directly comparable to the other town council price series.

A consideration which underlies all of the series we offer concerns the weights and measures to which particular prices refer. Wheatbread and oatbread prices seem straightforward in that, with the exception of those figures which have been footnoted, all prices were almost certainly per pound Scottish Troy. As discussed in appendix I, however, this system of weight may have changed significantly following an Act of Parliament of 19 February 1618. The size of the bolls of wheat, oats, malt, bear, rye and peas used in the different burghs is even more problematic. There is some debate concerning the evolution of the national standards (see appendix I), but in any case until the very end of our period the use of various local measures is much more likely. Appendix I reviews the available evidence concerning the size of these local measures of grain capacity although, as this evidence is primarily drawn from eighteenth-century sources, its applicability for earlier periods is uncertain.

Similar problems beset comparisons between the price of ale as recorded in different burghs in that either the national standard or the local measures discussed in appendix I may have been used. The situation with regard to ale is further confused by the excise which was imposed on ale. This was first exacted nationally following a 1644 Act of Parliament (*APS*, vol. 6, part 1, pp. 76a, 238a) although only for Kirkcudbright records, as footnoted in table 2.8, do the records explicitly refer to this excise. In Kirkcudbright, as elsewhere, when no specific mention is made of the excise it is impossible to tell whether or not it was included in the given price. All known references to the excise have been footnoted in the tables.

Sources

Aberdeen: John Stuart (ed.), *Extracts from the council register of the burgh of Aberdeen, vol. I, 1398–1570* (Spalding Club, Aberdeen, 1844); Cosmo Innes, *Extracts from the council register of the burgh of Aberdeen, vol. II, 1570–1625* (Spalding Club, Aberdeen, 1898); Gordon DesBrisay, 'Authority and discipline in Aberdeen, 1650–1700', unpublished University of Aberdeen Ph.D. thesis, 1989; L.B. Taylor, *Aberdeen shorework accounts, 1596–1670* (Aberdeen, 1972); Aberdeen town council register, vols. 17–58, 1541–1701 (containing proceedings of the council, and the baillie, guild and head courts),held at the Town House, Aberdeen.

Ayr: George S. Pryde, *Ayr burgh accounts, 1534–1624* (Scottish History Society, 3rd series, vol. 28, Edinburgh, 1937).

Banff: William Crammond, *The annals of Banff* (New Spalding Club, 2 vols., Aberdeen, 1891 and 1893).

Dumbarton: Joseph Irving, *Dumbarton burgh records, 1627–1746* (Dumbarton, 1860).

Dunfermline: Andrew Shearer, *Extracts from the burgh records of Dunfermline in the sixteenth and seventeenth centuries* (Carnegie Dunfermline Trust, 1951); Erskine Beveridge, *Burgh records of Dunfermline, 1488–1589* (Edinburgh, 1917); David Masson, *Register of the Privy Council of Scotland, vol. 3, 1578–1585* (Edinburgh, 1880), p. 751.

Edinburgh: J.D. Marwick, M. Wood, R.K. Hannay and H. Armet, *Extracts from the records of the burgh of Edinburgh, 1403–1701* (13 vols., Edinburgh, 1869–1967); Robert K. Hannay, *Acts of the Lords of Council in Public Affairs, 1501–1554; selections from the Acta Dominorum Concilii* (Edinburgh, 1932). Eighteenth-century wheatbread prices from the *Scots Magazine* and the *Caledonian Mercury*.

Elgin: William Crammond, *The records of Elgin, 1234–1800* (New Spalding Club, 2 vols., Aberdeen, 1903 and 1908).

Glasgow: J.D. Marwick and R. Renwick, *Extracts from the records of the burgh of Glasgow, 1573–1759* (Scottish Burgh Records Society, vols. 11–12, 16, 19, 22 and 29, Glasgow, 1876–1911).

Haddington: SRO, B30/13/3–4, 'Burgh council minutes, 1605–1624'.

Kirkcudbright: C.H. Armet, *Kirkcudbright town council records, 1576–1658* (2 vols., privately printed, Edinburgh, 1939 and 1958); SRO, T.644, 'Kirkcudbright town council minutes, 1578–1658'.

Perth: Perth Museum and Art Gallery, no. 270, James Scott, 'Prices of victual at Perth, 1525–1685'; SRO, B59/16, 'Register of Acts of Council', SRO, B59/17, 'Index to Perth register of acts of council'; SRO, PE1/1/100, 'Index to Perth council minutes'.

Stirling: Robert Renwick, *Extracts from the records of the royal burgh of Stirling, AD 1519–1666* (Glasgow, 1887).

Table 2.1 *Wheatbread (per lb.): town council statutes, 1495–1782*

Date	Aberdeen d.	Edinburgh d.	Glasgow d.	Stirling d.	Miscellaneous d.
1495		1.16			
1503		1.00			
1523		3.20			
1526				1.60	
1527					
1528		1.39			
1529		1.77			
1535		1.88			
1536		1.23			
1539		1.88			
1540					
1541	1.77				Elgin 1.33
1542	1.45				
1543	1.77				
1544	2.28				
1545	2.91			2.90	
1546	2.67				
1547	1.60	3.20			
1548		3.20		2.00	Banff 1.77
1549	2.28				Elgin 2.0; Banff 1.77
1550	2.46	3.20			Elgin 2.28
1551	2.67	3.20			Elgin 2.28; Banff 2.46
1552	2.28	2.46			
1553	1.60	1.77			
1554	1.60				
1555	2.00				
1556		4.00			Elgin 2.91
1557	2.28	2.85			
1558	1.77				
1559	2.00				
1560	2.67	3.56			
1561	3.20	3.39			
1562	5.32	4.92			
1563	3.55	4.27			
1564	3.20	3.20			
1565					
1566	2.67				Jedburgh 4.0
1567	3.20				
1568	3.20				
1569	3.20	3.20			
1570	3.20				Elgin 2.66
1571	3.20				Elgin 4.0
1572	4.00				Elgin 3.2
1573	4.57	4.92			
1574	4.57	4.92	4.57		
1575	4.57		4.00		Elgin 3.2; Dunfermline 5.33
1576	3.55		4.57		
1577	3.55		5.33		
1578	3.55	5.33	5.33		
1579	4.57		5.33		
1580	4.57	6.00	5.33		Elgin 4.0

Table 2.1 *(cont.)*

Date	Aberdeen d.	Edinburgh d.	Glasgow d.	Stirling d.	Miscellaneous d.
1581	4.92		5.33		Elgin 5.33
1582	4.92	5.33	5.33		Elgin 3.55
1583	5.32	5.65	5.81		
1584	5.32	4.80			
1585	6.86		5.81		Dunfermline 6.85
1586	8.00	8.53			
1587	8.00	9.14			
1588	6.86				
1589	6.86	7.53	8.00		
1590	7.10				
1591					
1592	7.10	7.11			
1593	8.00	7.53			
1594	10.67	10.66			
1595	12.00	12.00			
1596		14.77			
1597	16.00	16.00			
1598	12.00	16.00			
1599	16.00	12.80	11.63		
1600		12.00	11.63		
1601		12.00		12.80	Perth 12.0
1602		16.00		14.77	
1603	14.76	12.00		12.00	
1604	13.71	12.00			Perth 10.66
1605	13.71		10.66	12.80	
1606	13.71	12.00	16.00		Haddington 13.71
1607	13.71	16.00	13.33	12.80	Perth 10.66
1608	13.71			14.77	Haddington 13.71
1609	12.00	12.00		12.00	
1610	10.67	10.67	13.33	12.00	
1611	12.00		12.00	13.71	
1612	9.84	14.77	12.00		
1613	16.00			12.00	Dunf. 13.71; Hadd. 16.0
1614		13.71		12.80	
1615	17.45			14.77	
1616	17.45			15.36	Haddington 16.0
1617	13.71	13.71		13.71	Haddington 16.0
1618	16.00	13.71		14.77	Haddington 16.0
1619	16.00	13.71		14.77	Haddington 13.71
1620	16.00	9.60		12.00	Haddington 10.67
1621	16.00	14.77		14.77	
1622	19.20	17.16		16.00	
1623	24.00	20.62	16.00	19.20	
1624	19.20	14.77	16.00	16.00	Haddington 12.0
1625	16.00	14.22	10.66	13.71	
1626	16.00	12.00	10.66	12.80	
1627	16.00	12.00	10.66		
1628	16.00	12.80	16.00	14.77	Banff 12.0
1629	24.00	13.71	16.00	16.00	
1630	21.32	18.85	16.00	17.45	Banff 12.0
1631	16.00	15.52	10.66	16.00	Banff 12.0
1632	21.32	17.16		17.16	
1633		16.00	10.66	16.00	
1634	17.16	14.63	13.33	15.36	
1635	24.00		19.20		
1636	24.00	21.33	16.00	21.33	
1637	19.20	16.34	19.20	18.28	
1638	17.45	13.71	17.45	14.62	
1639	13.71	13.71		13.71	
1640	16.00	13.71	12.30	12.00	
1641		17.16		16.00	

Table 2.1 *(cont.)*

Date	Aberdeen d.	Edinburgh d.	Glasgow d.	Stirling d.
1642		17.16		20.21
1643	15.44	14.63		16.34
1644				15.67
1645				
1646		13.71		
1647		19.20	17.77	17.16
1648	24.00	24.00	24.00	
1649	25.60	23.27	24.00	23.27
1650	25.60	19.20	32.00	
1651	13.71		31.03	
1652	25.60	19.95		
1653	25.60	15.12	16.00	24.00
1654	13.71	10.31		
1655		13.71		
1656	13.71	17.07		
1657	14.76	16.34		
1658	17.45	20.76	17.06	
1659	19.20	24.00	17.06	
1660	19.20	20.62		
1661	17.45	22.42	17.13	
1662			17.16	
1663			18.84	15.51
1664	17.45	15.52	12.00	13.71
1665	16.00		18.84	
1666	13.71	15.52	12.00	
1667	13.71	13.71	13.71	
1668	13.71	12.91	11.17	
1669	13.71		13.71	
1670	13.71	13.71	14.77	
1671	13.71		18.28	
1672	16.00		14.55	
1673	16.00	13.71	13.71	
1674	12.80		23.09	
1675	15.36		22.58	
1676	21.32	13.71	13.71	
1677	14.76		13.71	
1678	14.76	13.71	14.62	
1679	14.76		16.34	
1680	14.76	16.97	15.43	
1681	13.71	17.16	16.34	
1682	12.00		14.77	
1683	12.00		16.25	
1684	12.00		17.13	
1685	13.71		15.36	
1686	13.71		14.62	
1687	13.71		14.55	
1688	13.71		13.71	
1689	13.71		15.43	
1690			15.42	
1691			15.42	
1692			15.42	
1693			15.43	
1694			21.33	
1695			20.56	
1696			24.00	
1697	16.00		22.42	
1698			27.42	
1699			24.00	
1700			17.45	
1701	16.00		17.16	

Table 2.1 *(cont.)*

Date	Glasgow d.	Edinburgh[1] d.	Edinburgh[2] (Scot. standard) d.	Date	Edinburgh[1] d.	Edinburgh[2] (Scot. standard) d.
1702	17.16	14.77	14.77	1743	10.28[3]	15.30
1703	17.16			1744	12.02[3]	17.89
1704	18.07			1745	11.29[3]	16.80
1705	18.07			1746	16.50	22.61
1706	12.96			1747	15.00	20.56
1707	13.71			1748	18.00	24.67
1708	17.16			1749	15.75	21.59
1709	24.00			1750	15.75	21.59
1710	22.42			1751	18.00	24.67
1711	18.07			1752	17.25	23.64
1712	18.07			1753	18.00	24.67
1713	18.07			1754	16.50	22.61
1714	18.07			1755	16.50	22.61
1715	18.84			1756		
1716	18.84			1757	15.76[3]	23.46
1717	18.84					
1718	18.84					
1719	17.16			1766	19.88[3]	25.69
1720	17.16			1767	20.83[3]	26.92
1721	18.07			1768	21.56	25.66
1722	18.84			1769	20.63	24.55
1723	19.81					
1724	18.10					
1725	20.61			1772	24.00	28.56
1726	20.62					
1727	18.84					
1728	22.42			1777	22.50[3]	29.27
1729	21.48			1778	20.63[3]	26.84
1730	17.16			1779	19.88	23.81
1731						
1732	15.51					
1733	18.07	10.97[3]	16.33	1782	24.75[3]	32.19
1734	19.81					
1735	19.82					
1736						
1737	17.16					
1738						
1739	16.52	12.37[3]	18.41			

1 From 1733 all Edinburgh prices have been drawn from press reports rather than Town Council records. They were, nevertheless, set by the Town Council, albeit now under the authority of British statutes regarding the assize of bread. Of the three sorts of bread alluded to in these statutes, only the price of wheatbread was invariably given and it is to this that the table refers. To compare with prices in Edinburgh up to and including 1702, and with the Glasgow price series which continued to follow the pre-Union Scottish assize right through until 1739, allowance must be made for the fact that the amount of bread to be produced from a fixed quantity of wheat (and thus the quality of that bread) varied over time.

The Scottish assize determined that 2,240 oz. Scottish Troy of finest bread should be baked from each boll of wheat. According to the English assize which took force in Scotland on 1 May 1707, 833.5 oz. avoirdupois of wheatbread was to be baked from each bushel of wheat. This assize, in Edinburgh at least, appears not to have been superceded by that of Anne, 1709, but rather remained in force until that of George II, 1757, took effect on 29 September 1758. According to this, 723.75 oz. avoirdupois of wheatbread was to be produced from each bushel of wheat. This in turn was superseded by the assize of George III, 1773, which took effect on 29 September, 1773, and required that 728.4375 oz. avoirdupois of wheatbread be produced from each bushel of wheat. This remained in force until the Edinburgh series ends in 1782.

2 The equivalent cost of a pound Scottish Troy of 'finest' bread produced at a rate of 2,240 oz. Scottish Troy per boll wheat. Although a derived price series which assumes that the assizes operated as discussed above, that there were exactly 4 bushels to the boll, and that 1.086 oz. avoirdupois equalled 1 oz. Scottish Troy, this should nevertheless aid comparison with both the contemporary Glasgow series and all earlier series.

3 These prices are per pound Imperial avoirdupois and should be multiplied by 1.086 to calculate equivalent price per pound Scottish Troy. All other eighteenth-century Edinburgh prices, having been derived from the cost of a peck loaf said to weigh 16lbs. Scottish Troy (or 17lb. 6oz. Imperial avoirdupois), are given per pound Scottish Troy.

Table 2.2 *Wheat and wheatbread: Aberdeen and Stirling statutes, 1526–1664*

	Aberdeen				Stirling		
Date	Wheat (per boll) L. s. d.		Wheatbread (per lb.) d.	oz. bread per boll	Wheat (per boll) L. s. d.		Wheatbread (per lb.) d.	oz. bread per boll
1526					0 16 0		1.60	1,920
1545					1 18 0		2.91	2,508
1548					1 6 0		2.00	2,496
1581	3 6 8		4.92	2,597				
1588	4 0 0		6.86	2,238				
1593	4 6 8		8.00	2,080				
1594	6 13 4		10.67	2,399				
1595	8 0 0		12.00	2,560				
1598	9 0 0		12.00	2,880				
1599	8 0 0		16.00	1,920				
1600								
1601					7 0 0		12.80	2,100
1602					9 6 8		14.77	2,427
1603	10 0 0		14.76	2,600	8 0 0		12.00	2,560
1604								
1605					8 13 4		12.80	2,600
1606	10 0 0		13.71	2,800				
1607					8 0 0		12.80	2,400
1608					10 0 0		14.77	2,600
1609	8 0 0		12.00	2,560	7 0 0		12.00	2,240
1610					7 0 0		12.00	2,240
1611	8 0 0		12.00	2,560	8 13 4		13.71	2,427
1612	6 13 4		9.84	2,602				
1613	8 0 0		16.00	1,920	8 0 0		12.00	2,560
1614					8 0 0		12.80	2,400
1615	10 13 4		17.45	2,346	9 6 8		14.77	2,427
1616	10 13 4		17.45	2,346	9 6 8		15.36	2,333
1617	8 0 0		13.71	2,240	8 0 0		13.71	2,240
1618	12 0 0		16.00	2,880	8 10 0		14.77	2,210
1619	8 0 0		16.00	1,920	8 6 8		14.77	2,167
1620	8 0 0		16.00	1,920	6 0 0		12.00	1,920
1621	8 0 0		16.00	1,920	9 0 0		14.77	2,340
1622	10 0 0		19.20	2,000	10 0 0		16.00	2,400
1623					12 0 0		19.20	2,400
1624					11 0 0		16.00	2,640
1625					8 0 0		13.71	2,240
1626	9 0 0		16.00	2,160	7 0 0		12.80	2,100
1627								
1628					8 10 0		14.77	2,210
1629					10 0 0		16.00	2,400
1630	12 13 4		21.32	2,281	10 13 4		17.45	2,347
1631					9 6 8		16.00	2,240
1632					10 0 0		17.16	2,238
1633					9 6 8		16.00	2,240
1634					8 13 4		15.36	2,167
1635								
1636					12 0 0		21.33	2,160
1637					10 13 4		18.29	2,239
1638					8 13 4		14.63	2,275
1639					8 0 0		13.71	2,241
1640					7 0 0		12.00	2,240
1641					9 6 8		16.00	2,240
1642					12 0 0		20.21	2,280
1643					9 6 0		16.34	2,193
1644					8 13 4		15.67	2,124
1647					10 0 0		17.17	2,238
1649					13 6 8		23.27	2,200
1653					14 0 0		24.00	2,240
1663					9 0 0		15.52	2,227
1664					8 0 0		13.71	2,241

Table 2.3 *Wheat and wheatbread: Edinburgh statutes, 1556–1681*

Date	Wheatbread (per lb.) d.	Implied wheat price (per boll) s. d.	Date	Wheatbread (per lb.) d.	Implied wheat price (per boll) s. d.
1/1556	4.57	33 4	10/1617	13.71	140 0
2/1556	3.77	23 11	11/1618	13.71	140 0
4/1556	4.00	26 8	11/1619	13.71	140 0
9/1557	2.85	13 2	10/1620	9.60	92 0
1/1560	2.91	13 11	11/1621	14.77	152 4
7/1560	4.27	29 9	5/1622	17.07	179 1
10/1560	3.56	20 8	10/1622	17.16	180 3
11/1561	3.39	19 7	11/1623	20.62	220 6
12/1562	4.92	37 5	10/1624	14.77	152 4
8/1563	4.27	29 9	10/1625	14.22	145 11
6/1564	3.41	19 10	11/1626	12.00	120 0
7/1564	3.20	17 4	11/1627	12.00	120 0
10/1564	3.20	17 4	11/1628	12.80	129 4
10/1569	3.20	17 4	10/1629	13.71	140 0
11/1573	4.92	37 5	12/1630	18.85	200 0
12/1573	5.65	45 10	10/1631	15.52	161 0
9/1574	4.92	37 5	11/1632	17.16	180 3
9/1578	5.33	42 3	11/1633	16.00	166 8
10/1578	5.33	42 3	11/1634	14.63	150 8
10/1580	6.00	50 0	11/1636	21.33	228 11
12/1580	7.68	69 7	11/1637	16.34	170 8
6/1582	5.33	42 3	10/1638	13.71	140 0
8/1583	6.00	50 0	11/1639	13.71	140 0
10/1583	5.65	45 10	11/1640	13.71	140 0
11/1583	5.33	42 3	12/1641	17.16	180 3
10/1584	4.80	37 8	11/1642	17.16	180 3
7/1586	8.53	79 7	10/1643	14.63	150 8
9/1587	6.74	58 7	5/1646	13.71	140 0
10/1587	9.14	86 8	11/1647	19.20	204 0
12/1587	8.53	79 6	11/1648	24.00	260 0
10/1589	7.53	67 10	11/1649	23.27	251 6
6/1592	6.40	54 8	2/1650	19.20	204 0
11/1592	7.11	62 11	10/1652	19.95	212 9
10/1593	7.53	67 10	10/1653	15.12	161 0
6/1594	10.67	104 5	12/1653	13.71	140 0
10/1595	12.00	120 0	6/1654	12.91	130 7
10/1596	14.77	152 4	11/1654	10.31	100 3
4/1597	17.45	183 8	10/1655	13.71	140 0
9/1597	16.00	166 8	12/1656	17.07	179 1
6/1598	16.00	166 8	12/1657	16.34	170 8
8/1599	14.77	152 4	11/1658	20.76	202 2
11/1599	12.80	129 4	11/1659	24.00	240 0
3/1600	12.80	129 4	12/1660	20.62	200 6
5/1600	14.22	145 11	1/1661	22.42	221 7
10/1600	13.71	140 0	1/1664	18.85	179 11
1/1601	12.00	120 0	7/1664	15.52	141 0
11/1602	16.00	166 8	2/1666	15.52	141 0
12/1602	18.29	193 4	2/1667	13.71	120 0
10/1603	13.71	140 0	4/1668	12.91	110 7
12/1604	12.00	120 0	2/1670	13.71	120 0
10/1607	16.00	166 8	1/1673	13.36	115 10
11/1609	12.00	120 0	6/1673	13.71	120 0
6/1610	11.29	111 9	11/1676	13.71	120 0
10/1610	10.67	104 5	3/1678	13.71	120 0
11/1612	14.77	149 0	1/1680	16.97	158 0
6/1614	13.71	140 0	8/1681	17.16	160 3
10/1614	13.71	140 0			

Table 2.4 *Oatbread (per lb.): town council statutes, 1575–1701*

Date	Aberdeen	Elgin	Kirkcud-bright		Date	Aberdeen	Kirkcud-bright
	d.	d.	d.			d.	d.
1575		2.28			1642	12.48	13.71
					1643		
					1644		13.71
1580		2.66			1645		
1581		4.00			1646		13.71
1582		2.66			1647		13.71
					1648	12.19	13.71
					1649		
1596			9.14		1650		13.71
1597			9.14		1651		13.71
					1652	12.80	13.71
					1653	12.80	13.71
1600			9.14		1654	7.10	
1601			9.14		1655		
1602			9.14		1656	7.10	13.71
1603			9.14		1657	7.10	13.71
					1658	8.53	
					1659	9.84	
1606			9.14		1660	9.14	
					1661	8.26	
					1662		
1609			9.14		1663		
1610			9.14		1664	8.25	
1611			9.14		1665	7.54	
1612	9.85				1666	7.10	
1613			9.14		1667		
1614	8.52		9.14		1668	8.00	
1615			9.14		1669	8.00	
1616	9.13		9.14		1670	7.54	
1617			9.14		1671	7.10	
1618			9.14		1672	8.00	
1619					1673	7.10	
1620			9.14		1674	7.10	
1621			9.14		1675	8.00	
1622			13.71		1676	10.67	
1623			9.14		1677	6.40	
1624			9.14		1678	6.40	
1625					1679	5.84	
1626			9.14		1680	5.84	
1627			9.14		1681	5.57	
1628			9.14		1682	6.40	
1629			9.14		1683	6.40	
1630	12.21		13.71		1684	6.40	
1631	7.32		9.14		1685	6.40	
1632					1686	6.40	
1633			9.14		1687	6.40	
1634			13.71		1688	6.40	
1635	11.90		13.71		1689	6.40	
1636	11.90						
1637			9.14				
1638	9.84		13.71		1697	9.14	
1639			13.71				
1640			13.71		1701	9.14	

Table 2.5 *Horse oats (per boll): Aberdeen, Edinburgh and Elgin statutes, 1508–1613*

Date	Aberdeen	Edinburgh			Elgin
	Great oats s. d.	Best corn s. d.	Second corn s. d.	Corn (unspecified) s. d.	Horse corn s. d.
1508		5 4	4 0		
1529		8 0	6 8		
1541					5 4
1546		14 8	10 8		
1547					
1548				10 8	
1549					9 4
1550					10 8
1551		13 4	10 8		9 4
1552	10 8				
1553					
1554		13 4	10 8		
1555		13 4	10 8		
1556					
1557		16 0	13 4		
1560		16 0	13 4		
1561					
1562		21 4	18 8		
1570					10 8
1571					13 4
1572					13 4
1580		32 0	26 8		
1581					16 0
1582					20 0
1583					
1584	24 0				
1585	24 0				
1586					
1587				40 0	
1588					
1589		40 0	39 4		
1590	42 8				
1591	42 8			56 0	
1592	42 8			48 0	
1593	53 4				
1600				80 0	
1606	80 0				
1610	64 0				
1611				96 0	
1613	106 8				

Table 2.6 *Horse oats (per boll): Stirling statutes, 1525–1664*

Date	Fine wheat oats L. s. d.	Carse oats L. s. d.	Dryfield oats L. s. d.
1525		0 6 8	
1545		0 10 8	0 8 0
1554		0 6 8	0 5 4
1555		0 9 4	0 6 8
1556		0 10 8	0 8 0
1562		0 16 0	0 12 0
1566		0 16 0	0 10 8
1599		3 4 0	2 2 8
1600		2 13 4	1 12 8
1601		2 8 0	1 12 0
1602	5 6 8	3 4 0	2 0 0
1603	4 0 0	2 8 0	1 12 0
1604	4 0 0		2 0 0
1605		4 0 0	2 8 0
1606			
1607	4 0 0	3 4 0	2 2 8
1608	4 8 0	3 4 0	2 8 0
1609	4 0 0	2 13 4	2 0 0
1610	4 0 0	2 13 4	2 0 0
1611	4 0 0	2 13 4	2 0 0
1612			
1613	4 16 0	3 12 0	2 13 4
1614	4 16 0	3 12 0	2 0 0
1615	5 6 8	3 4 0	2 13 4
1616	4 16 0	3 12 0	2 8 0
1617	4 16 0	4 0 0	2 13 4
1618	4 16 0	4 0 0	2 13 4
1619	4 0 0	3 4 0	1 12 0

Date	Fine wheat oats L. s. d.	Carse oats L. s. d.	Dryfield oats L. s. d.
1620	3 4 0	2 2 8	1 12 0
1621	4 16 0	3 4 0	2 2 8
1622	5 6 8	4 16 0	2 8 0
1623	6 8 0	4 0 0	2 13 4
1624	4 16 0	3 4 0	2 0 0
1625	4 0 0	2 13 4	2 0 0
1626	3 6 8	2 13 4	1 12 0
1627			
1628	4 0 0	2 13 4	1 12 0
1629	5 6 8	4 0 0	2 0 0
1630	6 8 0	4 16 0	2 8 0
1631	4 16 0	3 4 0	2 2 8
1632	4 16 0	3 4 0	2 2 8
1633	5 6 8	3 6 8	2 2 8
1634	5 6 8	4 0 0	2 13 4
1635			
1636	8 0 0	6 8 0	2 2 8
1637	5 6 8	4 0 0	3 4 0
1638	4 16 0	4 0 0	2 13 4
1639	4 5 4	3 4 0	2 2 8
1640	4 0 0	3 4 0	2 2 8
1641	6 8 0	4 16 0	2 13 4
1642	5 6 8	4 0 0	2 13 4
1643	5 6 8	4 0 0	2 13 4
1644	5 6 8	4 0 0	2 13 4
1645			
1646			
1647	6 0 0	5 0 0	3 4 0
1648			
1649	8 0 0	6 13 4	5 6 8
1653	8 0 0	6 13 4	5 6 8
1663	3 13 4	2 8 0	1 8 0
1664	3 6 8	2 13 4	1 8 0

Table 2.7 *Malt (per boll): town council statutes, 1505–1635*

Date	Aberdeen s. d.	Edinburgh s. d.	Stirling s. d.	Date	Aberdeen s. d.	Stirling s. d.
1505		11 0		1601		123 4
				1602		153 4
				1603	120 0	133 4
1520			13 4	1604	100 0	
1521			12 0	1605		126 8
1522			12 0	1606		
				1607	120 0	106 8
				1608		106 8
1525			16 0	1609	120 0	113 4
1526			16 0	1610		126 8
1527			16 0	1611	120 0	116 8
1528				1612	160 0	
1529			14 4	1613		140 0
				1614		120 0
				1615	160 0	140 0
1545			30 0	1616	160 0	
1546		32 0	30 0	1617	120 0	
1547		30 4		1618		
1548		22 3	24 0	1619	120 0	
1549				1620	106 8	
1550		33 9	44 0[1]	1621	160 0	
1551		23 1		1622	160 0	
1552		23 1		1623		
1553		16 0		1624	120 0	
1554		23 1	16 0	1625		
1555		23 1	28 8	1626	100 0	
1556		35 7	36 0	1627	133 4	
1557		26 8[3]				
1558						
1559		31 1		1635	213 4	
1560		31 1				
1561						
1562			40 0[1]			
1563		39 9				
1566		38 3[4]	33 0[1]			
1567			37 0[2]			
1578		84 5[4]				
1581	66 8					
1582	50 0	59 3[3]				
1583		48 11				
1587		80 0				
1589		65 2[5]				
1592		56 11				
1593	86 8					
1594	133 4					
1598	133 4					
1599	133 4		146 8			
1600		106 8[5]	120 0			

1 Price set in January 2 Price set in April
3 Price per boll of 'old measure' 4 Price per boll of ground malt
5 Price per boll of ground malt 'with the charitie'

Table 2.8 *Ale (per pint): town council statutes, 1504–1680*

Date	Aberdeen[1] d.	Banff d.	Edinburgh d.	Stirling d.	Miscellaneous d.
1504			2.0		
1505			1.5		
1506			1.0		
1507	1.0		1.5		
1516			1.5		
1520			2.5	2.0	
1521					
1522				1.5	
1523				2.0	
1524					
1525				1.5	
1526					
1527				2.5	
1528				1.5	
1529			2.0		
1530			2.0		
1531			2.5		
1536			2.0		
1541					Elgin 1.5
1542					
1543	2.0				
1544	2.0				
1545	2.0		2.0	3.0	
1546			4.0		
1547	2.0		4.0		
1548		1.5	4.0	3.0	
1549	2.5	2.5			Elgin 2.5
1550	2.5	3.0	4.0		Elgin 2.5
1551	2.5	2.5			Elgin 2.5
1552	2.0		4.0		
1553	1.5	1.5			
1554	2.0			2.0	
1555	2.0		4.0	3.0	
1556			4.0	4.0	Elgin 4.0
1557			3.0		
1558	2.0				
1559	2.0		3.5		
1560	3.0		4.0		
1561	3.0				
1562	4.0[2]		5.0	4.0	
1563	4.0		4.0		
1564	2.0		3.0		
1565					
1566	2.5		5.0		Jedburgh 5.0
1567	3.0				
1568	3.0				
1569	3.0		4.0		

1 The Aberdeen town council often set the price of ale produced and sold by both freemen's and unfreemen's (sometimes craftsmen's) wives. The former's ale (which is recorded here) always cost more, whilst the latter, in some years, were actually prohibited from selling ale within the burgh.
2 The price of beer sold by freemen's wives was also set this year; to cost 6d. per pint.

Table 2.8 *(cont.)*

Date	Aberdeen d.	Edinburgh d.	Glasgow d.	Kirkcud-bright d.	Stirling d.	Miscellaneous d.
1570	3.0[1]					Elgin 3.0
1571	3.0					Elgin 3.0
1572	3.0					
1573	4.0					Dunfermline 6.0
1574	4.0	6.0	6.0			Dunfermline 6.0
1575	4.0		7.0			Dunferm. 6.0; Elgin 4.0
1576	4.0	5.0	6.0			
1577	5.0		7.0			
1578	5.0	6.0	6.0	4.0		
1579	6.0		6.0			
1580	6.0	6.0	7.0	6.0		Elgin 4.0
1581	6.0	9.0	7.0	8.0		Elgin 6.0
1582	5.0	6.0	8.0			Elgin 4.0
1583	4.0	6.0	8.0			
1584	6.0	6.0[2]	8.0	6.0		
1585	8.5		10.0			Dunfermline 8.0
1586				8.0		
1587		8.0		6.0		
1588	6.0			6.0		
1589	6.0	7.0	10.0	6.0		
1590	8.0			8.0		
1591		8.0		6.0		
1592	8.0	8.0		6.0		
1593	8.0	8.0		8.0		
1594	12.0	10.0	10.0	8.0		
1595		12.0	16.0	12.0		
1596		12.0		12.0		
1597	12.0	12.0		12.0		
1598	12.0	12.0		8.0		
1599	12.0	14.0	16.0	8.0	14.0	
1600		12.0	16.0	8.0	12.0	
1601		12.0		12.0	12.0	Perth 10.0
1602	14.0	16.0		12.0	14.0	
1603	12.0	12.0		8.0	12.0	
1604	10.0	12.0				Perth 10.0
1605	12.0		12.0		12.0	Haddington 14.0
1606	12.0	12.0	16.0[3]			Dunf. 16.0;[4] Hadd. 14.0
1607	12.0	12.0	16.0		12.0	Perth 10.0
1608	20.0				12.0	Perth 10.0
1609	12.0	12.0		12.0	12.0	Perth 12.0
1610	12.0	13.0	16.0	12.0	12.0	Perth 12.0; Hadd. 12.0
1611	14.0		16.0	12.0	12.0	
1612	16.0	16.0	20.0	16.0		Perth 12.0
1613	16.0	16.0		12.0	14.0	Dunfermline 16.0[4]
1614		16.0		12.0	12.0	
1615	16.0	16.0		12.0	14.0	
1616	16.0	14.0		12.0	12.0	Perth 12.0: Hadd. 16.0
1617	12.0	14.0		12.0	12.0	Perth 16.0; Hadd. 14.0
1618	16.0	16.0[5]		12.0	14.0	Haddington 14.0
1619	14.0	12.0			12.0	Haddington 13.0
1620	12.0	12.0		8.0	9.0	Haddington 12.0
1621	16.0	14.0		12.0	16.0	
1622	16.0	16.0		16.0	16.0	
1623		20.0	24.0	16.0	24.0	
1624	16.0	14.0	16.0	12.0[3]	12.0	Haddington 14.0

1 From this date Aberdeen town council set the price of beer sold by freemen's wives; in 1570 it cost ½d. more per pint than ale, from 1571 to 1593 it cost 1d. more per pint with the exception of 1578 when it cost 1½d. more. From 1597 to 1635 it cost 2d. more, and from 1636 to 1642 it cost 4d. more per pint.

2 Outlands ale to be sold at 5d. per pint. 3 Beer to be sold at 4d. per pint more than ale.

4 Price for 'thrice the standard pint'. (This standard pint may have been the English pint.)

5 From this date Edinburgh town council began to set the price of double (or strong) and single (or small) ale; the former was invariably set (and it is to this which the table refers). When single ale was referred to it was always half the cost of double ale.

Table 2.8 *(cont.)*

Date	Aberdeen	Banff	Edinburgh	Glasgow	Kirkcud- bright	Stirling	Miscellaneous
	d.	d.	d.	d.	d.	d.	d.
1625	16.0	12.0[1]	12.0	16.0[2]	12.0	12.0	
1626	12.0		12.0	12.0	12.0	12.0	
1627	16.0		14.0	16.0	12.0		Dumbarton 16.0[6]
1628	16.0	12.0	16.0	20.0	12.0	14.0	Dumbarton 16.0
1629	16.0		14.0	20.0	12.0	16.0	Dumbarton 16.0
1630	20.0	14.0	16.0	20.0	12.0	16.0	
1631	12.0	12.0	14.0	16.0	12.0	12.0	
1632	16.0	16.0	16.0[3]			14.0	
1633			16.0	16.0	12.0	14.0	Dumbarton 16.0
1634	20.0		16.0	16.0	12.0	16.0	
1635	24.0	16.0		20.0	12.0		
1636	20.0	16.0	18.0	20.0	16.0	18.0	
1637	16.0	12.0	16.0	16.0	12.0	16.0	
1638	16.0		12.0	16.0	12.0	12.0	
1639	14.0		12.0	16.0	12.0	12.0	
1640	16.0	12.0	14.0	16.0	12.0	12.0	
1641	16.0		16.0			16.0	Dunfermline 14.0
1642	20.0	16.0	20.0		16.0	20.0	
1643	16.0		14.0			14.0	
1644	24.0		14.0	20.0	12.0[4]	12.0	
1645				24.0	12.0		
1646			14.0		12.0[4]		
1647			16.0	24.0	16.0[5]	16.0	
1648	24.0		18.0	24.0	16.0		
1649	24.0		20.0	24.0	16.0[5]	20.0	Elgin 20.0[7]
1650	24.0			28.0	20.0		
1651	24.0			32.0	24.0		
1652	24.0		20.0	32.0	20.0		
1653	24.0		16.0	24.0	16.0	24.0	
1654			24.0	20.0	16.0		
1655				24.0			
1656	24.0			24.0	20.0[5]		
1657	24.0				20.0[5]		
1658	24.0		16.0				
1659	24.0		28.0				
1660	24.0		24.0				
1661	24.0						
1662							
1663			24.0			16.0	
1664	24.0		24.0			12.0	
1665	24.0		20.0				
1666	24.0						
1667	24.0		20.0				
1668	24.0		20.0				
1669	24.0						
1670	24.0						
1671	24.0						
1672	24.0						
1673	24.0						
1674	24.0						
1675	24.0						
1676	24.0						
1677	24.0						
1678		12.0					
1679	24.0						
1680	24.0						

1 Banff town council also set the price of beer; from 1625 to 1635 at 2d. per pint more than ale, from 1636 to 1642 at 4d. per pint more than ale, but at the same price in 1678.

2 Glasgow town council also set the price of beer, always at 4d. per pint more than ale.

3 From this date Edinburgh town council began to regularly set the price of beer; from 1632 to 1647 at 4d. per pint more than ale with the exception of 1636 when it was 2d. per pint more expensive. In 1648 beer was again 2d. more expensive, but from 1652 to 1665 beer and ale were to be sold at the same price.

4 Excluding 'ane plak at the pint' (4d.) for the excise.   5 Including the excise.

6 In Dumbarton beer was always to cost 4d. per pint more than ale.   7 Beer at the same price as ale.

Table 2.9 *Wine (per pint): Edinburgh statutes, 1517–1699*

Date	Bordeaux s. d.	Claret s. d.	White s. d.	Undefined s. d.	Miscellaneous s. d.
9/1517		0 8			
6/1520		0 6	0 6		
10/1520				1 0	
2/1544			1 4		2 0 (Romany)
1/1546		1 6	1 6		
10/1546					1 0 (Romany)
12/1546	1 0	1 0			1 4 (Romany)
					1 8 (Rens)
5/1547	0 10				
3/1548				1 2	
5/1548				1 0	
12/1548	1 0	1 1	1 1	1 0	0 10 (Rochell)
1/1550				1 2	
5/1550				1 0	
9/1557				1 4	
10/1560	1 2				1 0 (Sherand)
11/1560	1 4				1 4 (Sherand)
4/1562				1 0	
1/1563	0 8				0 6 (Rochell)
11/1564	1 4				
6/1565				1 2	
12/1565				1 2	
10/1566				1 0	
1/1575					6 6 (Seck)
3/1576	2 6				2 2 (Rochell)
					2 2 (Sherand)
12/1576				3 0	
12/1577				3 4	
4/1578				3 4	
11/1578					1 8 (Rochell)
12/1579				2 8	
8/1580	3 0				
9/1580				3 0	
12/1583				2 8	
2/1587	6 0			5 8	
12/1587	5 4				
1/1590	6 0				
12/1590	6 4				
10/1594	6 8				8 0 (Seck)
12/1596	8 0			8 0	

Date	Claret s. d.	French s. d.	Seck s. d.	Spanish s. d.	Miscellaneous s. d.
7/1661			36 0		
3/1664		16 0	36 0	36 0	36 0 (Canarie)
					12 0 (White)
5/1667	18 0		40 0		36 0 (Ranish)
					12 0 (White)
4/1668	16 0	16 0	30 0		
3/1670			36 0	36 0	
12/1675		28 0			
11/1676		20 0			
1/1680				32 0	
12/1682		22 0			
4/1688		18 0			
12/1697	32 0		44 0		36 0 (Canarie)
1/1699			40 0		

Table 2.10 *Bear, malt and oatmeal (per boll): Mill and Alloway fermes, Ayr, 1583–1623*

Crop Year	Alloway Ferme beir L. s. d.	Mill Ferme malt L. s. d.	Mill Ferme oatmeal L. s. d.	Crop Year	Alloway Ferme beir L. s. d.	Mill Ferme malt L. s. d.	Mill Ferme oatmeal L. s. d.
1583		2 16 8		1605	5 0 0	5 16 8	4 0 0
1584				1606	5 0 0		
1585		3 6 8		1607			
1586		5 0 0		1608	5 6 8	5 6 8	4 0 0
1587		3 3 4		1609	5 13 4	5 3 4	4 0 0
1588		3 6 8		1610	5 6 8	5 10 0	3 13 4
				1611	6 0 0	6 0 0	5 0 0
1592		4 0 0		1612	6 13 4	6 13 4	5 6 8
1593		6 0 0		1613	6 13 4		
1594		5 6 8		1614	6 13 4		
1595		6 13 4		1615	6 13 4		
1596		16 0 0		1616	7 6 8		
1597	6 0 0	9 0 0		1617	7 0 0		
1598	5 0 0			1618	6 0 0		
1599	5 0 0	8 1 4		1619	4 0 0		
1600	5 0 0	5 13 4		1620	3 0 0		
1601	5 6 8			1621	6 13 4		
1602	6 0 0	9 0 0	6 0 0	1622	9 0 0	10 0 0	8 0 0
1603	5 0 0	5 10 0	4 0 0	1623	8 0 0	13 6 8	8 0 0
1604	5 0 0						

Table 2.11 *Bear and oatmeal (per boll): Perth council and session, 1615–1685*

Crop Year	Farm bear L. s. d.	Crop Date	Farm bear L. s. d.	Teind bear L. s. d.	Teind meal L. s. d.
1615	5 0 0	1665	4 0 0		3 6 8
1616	6 0 0	1666	4 13 4		4 0 0
1617	5 13 4	1667	5 0 0		4 0 0
1618		1668	4 13 4		3 13 4
1619	5 0 0	1669	5 0 0	4 13 4	3 13 4
1620		1670			
1621	6 13 4	1671	6 0 0	5 6 8	5 6 8
1622	7 0 0	1672	5 6 8	4 13 4	4 0 0
1623	9 0 0	1673	4 13 4	4 0 0	5 0 0
		1674	8 0 0	7 6 8	6 0 0
		1675	11 0 0	10 6 8	7 6 8
1631	5 6 8	1676	4 13 4	4 6 8[1]	3 6 8
1632	5 13 4	1677	4 13 4	4 13 4	3 0 0
1633	7 0 0	1678	4 6 8	4 3 4	2 13 4
1634	7 6 8	1679[2]	4 6 8	4 3 4	3 6 8
1635	9 0 0	1680	4 3 4	4 0 0	3 6 8
1636	8 6 8	1681	5 0 0	4 16 8	4 16 8
1637	7 0 0	1682	7 13 4	7 13 4	5 0 0
1638	5 0 0	1683	5 0 0	5 0 0	3 6 8
1639		1684	4 10 0	4 10 0	4 0 0
1640	5 0 0	1685	4 13 4	4 13 4	3 13 4
1641	8 0 0				

1 This is the price attached to the bear from the north part of the parish, from the south part the bear was only £4.3.4
2 If the money was not payed within a fortnight tenants were to pay an extra merk (13s. 4d.) per boll.

Table 2.12 *Grain prices (per boll): St. Nicholas Metts, Aberdeen, 1630–1669*

Crop Year	Wheat L. s. d.			Beir L. s. d.			Oatmeal L. s. d.			Malt L. s. d.			Rye L. s. d.			Peas L. s. d.		
1630	10	0	0	8	0	0	6	13	4	8	0	0						
1633	10	0	0	8	13	4	8	0	0	9	6	8	8	0	0			
1634	10	0	0	8	13	4	8	0	0	9	6	8						
1635	12	0	0	8	0	0				9	6	8	8	6	8	10	13	4
1636	12	0	0	8	0	0	6	0	0	8	6	8						
1637	9	0	0	5	0	0												
1638	8	0	0	5	6	8	4	0	0									
1639	6	0	0	4	0	0	3	6	8	4	0	0						
1640	8	0	0	6	0	0	4	0	0									
1641	10	0	0	8	0	0				9	0	0				9	0	0
1642	11	0	0	9	0	0	6	13	4	9	0	0				9	0	0
1643	8	0	0	6	0	0	5	0	0	8	0	0						
1644	9	0	0	5	8	0	5	6	8									
1645	6	13	4	5	6	8												
1646																		
1647				7	6	8												
1648	15	0	0	12	0	0	12	0	0	12	8	0	9	6	8	16	0	0
1649	11	6	8	10	6	8	10	0	0	13	6	8	6	13	4	13	6	8
1650	12	0	0	8	0	0				8	0	0				12	0	0
1651				8	0	0	6	13	4	9	0	0						
1652	12	0	0	6	13	4	6	0	0	4	5	0						
1653	9	0	0	4	0	0												
1654	6	0	0	4	0	0	4	13	4									
1655	5	0	0	4	13	4	4	0	0	4	13	4						
1656	6	0	0	4	0	0				5	6	8						
1657	7	6	8	5	0	0	4	16	0	5	0	0						
1658				5	13	4	5	6	8	6	0	0						
1659				6	13	4												
1660				6	0	0												
1661				6	0	0				6	13	4						
1662				5	6	8												
1663				4	0	0	4	0	0									
1664				4	0	0												
1665				4	0	0												
1666				4	13	4				4	0	0						
1667	5	0	0	5	0	0	5	6	8									
1668				4	0	0												
1669	5	16	0	4	0	0	4	0	0									

3 ✣ The system of county fiars

The practice, common throughout much of the seventeenth century and the whole of the eighteenth, whereby sheriffs held annual courts to determine the prevailing price of the commonest sorts of grain in their counties, has long been appreciated by scholars attempting to chart the movement of prices in early modern Scotland.[1] Termed 'fiars', many of these price series survive, and some provide an almost unbroken record of grain prices from the mid seventeenth to the twentieth centuries. The fiars were not finally abolished until the Local Government (Scotland) Act of 1973. However, although apparently providing what is beyond doubt the most comprehensive and uniform source on Scottish grain prices available (tables 3.1–3.19), they also pose interpretative difficulties. A detailed appraisal of their purpose, method of calculation and value as a guide to actual market prices is clearly necessary.

The derivation and meaning of the word 'fiars' and the origin of the practice of 'striking' such prices are both obscure. The word itself seems to mean 'market price'. Identical in meaning to Middle English 'feor' and Old French 'feur', it is derived from the Latin 'forum' in the sense of a market, and hence market price.[2] However, it is clear that sheriffs did not hold courts to strike the county fiars prices just as an academic exercise. In one sense, they were, in the words of a not disinterested critic, 'conventional prices struck for a particular purpose'.[3] After the Teinds Act of 1808 that purpose was primarily to provide a valuation of grain upon which stipends could be converted from payment in grain to payment in money, but even as late as the end of the nineteenth century fiars prices were still used for many other ancient purposes.

In some few counties ... old feu-duties exist that depend on the fiars. Crown-duties, thirlage, multures, are also mentioned in parts. The chief interest, apart from that of the ministers, is found in the valuations of crop which are made between outgoing and incoming tenants on farms. These in many parts of Scotland seem to be based on the fiars.[4]

---

[1] For instance, R.C. Mossman, 'On the price of wheat at Haddington from 1627–1897', *The Accountants' Magazine*, vol. 4 (1900), pp. 94–110; R. Mitchison, 'The movements of Scottish corn prices in the seventeenth and eighteenth centuries', *Economic History Review*, 2nd series, vol. 18 (1965), pp. 278–91; M.W. Flinn *et al.*, *Scottish population history from the seventeenth century to the 1930s* (Cambridge, 1977), appendix B.

[2] D. Littlejohn, 'Aberdeenshire fiars', *Miscellany of the New Spalding Club*, vol. 2 (Aberdeen, 1906), p. 3; Scottish Office and the Board of Agriculture and Fisheries, Committee on Fiars Prices in Scotland, *Fiars prices in Scotland* (HMSO, London, 1911), p. 4 (henceforth *1911 report*).

[3] D. Hunter, *Report of the committee on fiars prices to the General Assembly of the Church of Scotland* (Edinburgh, 1895), p. 22 (henceforth *1895 report*).　　[4] *Ibid.*, p. 24.

In fact, it seems that the fiars constituted a most important yardstick in the economic life of the country.

The value of the gross amount of property, in rents, stipends, feu-duties, out-going crops, and bargains in victual, made with reference to the fiars, which is determined in our fiar courts in one day, far exceeds that determined in all the other courts of the kingdom in the course of a year.[5]

Such was the position when it was made explicit in the nineteenth century. The uses to which the fiars were put in earlier centuries were presumably similar, although there is little explicit evidence upon which to base such an assumption. Certainly the calculation of money equivalents for rents and multures still reckoned in kind must then have been of the first importance. In the Act of Sedurunt of the Lords of Council and Session of 1723 the purpose of the fiars was simply stated; 'to liquidate the price of victual in divers processes that come before them [the Sheriffs], and subordinate juricatories'.[6]

When the fiars were first stuck is as uncertain as their original purpose. Fiars courts were referred to as an existing institution by an Act of the Scottish Parliament of 1584,[7] and the earliest known series dates from 1556. This provides an unbroken series of bear and oatmeal prices for Fife until 1586, although the record is then blank until 1619.[8] There is also some evidence that Commissary Courts were striking fiars from the mid sixteenth century.[9] Whatever their origin, surviving series are rare before the 1630s, and it is not until the eighteenth century that annual fiars prices are to be found for the majority of Scottish counties.

The fiars price series tabulated below have been extracted from many sources. Several lengthy runs have been published (mainly in the eighteenth and nineteenth centuries); notably those for the counties of Aberdeen, Midlothian (Edinburgh), East Lothian (Haddington), West Lothian (Linlithgow) and Fife,[10] as well as for most other counties for the period 1756–76.[11] These series are complemented and extended here by a number drawn from various manuscript sources; some from Sheriff Court records, some from estate records deposited at the Scottish Record Office and some from a miscellany of less obvious sources.[12]

With these county series we must mention those recorded by the Lord Treasurer's Remembrancer's Office and known as the 'Exchequer' fiars,[13] which are available for

[5] *Report of the General Assembly's committee on the fiars; presented to the Assembly in 1831*, Parliamentary papers, 1834, vol. 49, p. 5 (henceforth *1831 report*).
[6] Court of Session, *Acts of Sedurunt of the Lords of Council and Session* (Edinburgh, 1811), p. 278.
[7] *APS*, vol. 3, p. 304.
[8] It is uncertain whether this gap is due to the temporary abandonment of striking annual fiars or a loss of the relevant documentary record.   [9] Littlejohn, 'Aberdeenshire', p. 3; *1911 report*, p. 4.
[10] Littlejohn, 'Aberdeenshire', pp. 2–43; A. Bald, *The farmer and corn dealer's assistant* (Edinburgh, 1780), pp. 394–427; G. Barclay, 'Account of the parish of Haddington', *Transactions of the Society of Antiquaries of Scotland*, vol. I (Edinburgh, 1792); R.C. Mossman, 'On the price of wheat'; J. Trotter, *General view of the agriculture of the county of West Lothian* (London, 1811), appendix 5; J. Sinclair, 'A table of the fiars of the county of Berwickshire, 1689 to 1792 inclusive', *OSA*, vol. 3, p. 208; R. Kerr, *General view of the agriculture of the county of Berwick* (London, 1813); Flinn *et al.*, *Scottish population history*, appendix B, pp. 489–98.
[11] Bald, *Assistant*, pp. 393–419.
[12] The introduction to the tables contains a full list of the manuscript and other sources from which we have extracted fiars prices. Although we undertook an extensive search for such data, with these prices being recorded by many individuals for many purposes, it seems likely that further series may yet be unearthed in the Scottish Record Office and other public or private collections.   [13] SRO, E. 5/5, 'Exchequer fiars, 1708–1786'.

most counties from 1708 and which were calculated directly from the county fiars. A return was made from each county to the Exchequer where a small deduction known as the 'King's (or Queen's) Ease' was made. These Exchequer fiars then formed the standard for the conversion to money of dues payable to the crown in kind. Analysis of the Exchequer fiars for the period 1760–9 show that, almost invariably, the difference between them and the county fiars amounted to exactly 12s. Scots per boll. This was the case for 297 of the 310 price comparisons which could be made. Where the difference was other than of 12s. per boll there is every indication that this was the result of simple arithmetic error. With over 95 per cent of the Exchequer fiars being precisely 12s. per boll less than their respective county fiars the former may provide a useful, if imperfect, guide to the fiars prices in those counties in years for which no other evidence survives. Great care, however, must be taken for it is known, for example, that in those many years when the local sheriff court in Ross-shire did not meet, the fiars for the county were fixed in Exchequer simply by taking two-thirds of the Fife fiars. Indeed, Mitchison judges that 'no reliable series survive for the eighteenth or seventeenth centuries anywhere north of the Great Glen'.[14] It is at present an open question whether or not using the Exchequer fiars can realistically augment the patchy coverage of northern and western counties in the eighteenth century, and we have not, partly for considerations of space, tabulated them here.

Objections raised against the fiars in the nineteenth and early twentieth centuries, mainly by clerical critics who felt they were being deprived of the true value of their teinds, throw some light on how the fiars were traditionally determined. Perhaps most significantly, these show that the methods used varied considerably from county to county and were rarely above criticism. For instance, the Committee of the General Assembly of the Church of Scotland in 1831 declared that:

It is manifest that in the mode of conducting the business of our fiars courts, there is anything but uniformity; that not one of the various methods followed is free from objection; that, in short, they are all in a greater or less degree defective.[15]

These remarks were echoed in 1852 by G. Paterson, who declared that the methods of striking the fiars in the various counties were 'different, inconsistent and contradictory', and the manner of conducting the process 'loose, inefficient and incorrect'. He concludes that no one can be surprised 'that the result should be unsatisfactory'.[16] In fact it was an Act of the Court of Session in 1723, itself a response to the great increase in the use made of the fiars in the early eighteenth century, which provided the first condemnation of the way in which fiars prices were then arrived at:

the said fiars are struck, and given out by the Sheriffs, without due care and enquiry into the current and just price; and that when some Sheriffs proceed in striking the fiars by way of inquest, yet they get not sufficient evidence to the jury; and that other Sheriffs proceed arbitrarily and without an inquest; and that some of them entirely neglect to strike fiars, which creates great uncertainty, and much delay and expense in the administration of justice.[17]

[14] Mitchison, 'Corn prices', p. 279.   [15] *1831 report*, p. 4.
[16] G. Paterson, *An historical account of the fiars in Scotland* (Edinburgh, 1852), p. 4.
[17] *Acts of sederunt of the Lords of Council*, p. 278.

The Act's own provisions were, however, less than comprehensive; it reads as if it was directed as much against the total neglect of the fiars as against the arbitrary methods used to strike them. Much was still left to the discretion of the sheriffs – they were not asked to name a true average price (although the Court of Session had in 1685 explicitly ordained that the fiars be based on 'the current prices for which victual in the county was in use to be sold yearly'), nor were they told which grains should be quoted or which measures used. At least the Act appointed certain other conditions which must have helped to introduce more regular procedures. It determined, firstly, that fiars should be struck in all counties, secondly, that they should be struck between the 4 and 20 February, and published on or before the 1 March, thirdly, that they should be based on the price at which the various grains common in each county had been bought and sold, 'especially since the 1st November immediately preceding', and lastly that all this should be done with the aid of a jury of fifteen men of knowledge and skill, of whom no fewer than eight should be heritors.

The reports of the nineteenth century show that even these provisions, which the Court of Session itself chose not to enforce on a number of occasions,[18] had only limited impact. As late as 1900 a departmental committee appointed by the Board of Agriculture concluded that 'the way in which the fiars prices are at present arrived at is eminently unsatisfactory',[19] and in 1911 the report of the Parliamentary Committee on Fiars Prices in Scotland maintained that 'there is great diversity in the procedure', leading to 'a difference in results, between counties adjoining and similar in circumstances'.[20]

Such criticism appears damning at first sight, but it does not necessarily invalidate the usefulness of the fiars to the historian. Mitchison in her analysis of the Scottish grain market of the seventeenth and eighteenth centuries came to optimistic conclusions regarding their utility as a guide to prices:

They may not be an exact mirror of average prices, but if we are to doubt their general reliability as a local record in the eighteenth century we have to accept that the landowners of Scotland, who were often merchants too, who had the main share in fixing them and who both paid and received large sums on their basis, did not know what they were doing. It is these considerations that make the fiars prices of Scotland an adequate tool for the historian, while the coverage they give to the country is better than that of any other price series so far advanced for England.[21]

The accuracy of this assessment, and the extent to which fiars prices may be used as a guide to actual market prices, and to their trends and variations, are our next concerns.

There are several related questions which must be addressed. First, to what extent do the fiars provide a useful measure of price movements through time? This does not demand that they should represent actual grain prices in the market, only that short- and long-term movements in market prices are sufficiently mirrored by movements in the fiars. Second, do they provide a measure of price variation between counties in the same year? Is it justifiable, in other words, to use the fiars to describe regional price differences? Finally, to what extent do they represent the actual price at which individuals would have been able to purchase grain? In chapter 9 we consider the purchasing power of

[18] *1895 report*, p. 6.   [19] *1911 report*, p. 3.   [20] *1911 report*, p. 5.
[21] R. Mitchison, 'Corn prices', p. 280.

labour in early modern Scotland – do the fiars provide a realistic measure of the cost of oatmeal in the market against which we may contrast the earnings of craftsmen and labourers?

The Report of the Committee on Fiars Prices of the General Assembly in 1895 does not at first inspire confidence in the use of the fiars for our second purpose, as a completely reliable guide to regional price variation. Drawing attention to the variety of ways in which the fiars continued to be struck in different counties, the committee observed that:

Much must depend on the mode of striking, when the value of a chalder for 1893 could in Lanark be £14.9s.2d., while in Renfrew it was only £13.9s.3½d.; or again in Dumfries, £13.1s.6d., while in Wigtown, £12.3s.3½d.; or again in Clackmannan, £13.17s.0½d., while in Kinross, £13.10s.9½d.; or, as surprising as any, in Argyll, £14.6s.7d., while in Ayr, £13.6s.6d. In these days of quick communication, when prices tend, like water, towards a common level, it is difficult to understand how counties practically adjacent can show such discrepancy in their fiars.[22]

There was up to a 7 per cent difference between the higher and lower citations in adjacent counties in the illustrations given here, presumably the most telling the committee could find.

Nor, it would seem, do unadjusted fiars provide an accurate measure of retail prices. Observing that the wholesale transactions of middlemen were used to establish the fiars, the same committee further commented:

Hence, perhaps, the constant and very wide difference between the fiars for oatmeal for instance, and the lowest price at which oatmeal can be bought retail. When a minister receives his meal stipend at a rate of 15s. per boll, and cannot buy his meal for domestic purposes at less than 18s.4d., he has some ground for dissatisfaction.[23]

But this, and other reports of the nineteenth century, should not be read uncritically. All were careful to emphasise that their objective was 'not to raise or lower the fiars, but to get them struck on correct principles',[24] but each was also undoubtedly arguing the case of the clergy; a case which rested upon discrediting the fiars (so the clergy's income could be established by a more equitable and less volatile arrangement) or, at the very least, upon proving the fiars to be unjustifiably low in relation to actual market prices. It is hardly coincidental that the two principal reports of the nineteenth century, of 1831 and 1895, both emerged after a period of falling grain prices and thus falling clerical incomes.

Yet the case put forward on behalf of the clergy was a strong one. The reports of 1831 and 1895 produce much evidence, surely pertinent to earlier centuries, on the wide variety of methods by which fiars prices were struck in different counties. Consider first the evidence that was admitted in the various fiar courts. A crucial point is over what part of the year evidence was taken on the price of grain, since, as discussed in chapter 4, prices varied greatly during the course of a year. If the county fiars were determined with respect to different portions of the year their levels were bound to be different – even if

---

[22] *1895 report*, p. 35.   [23] *Ibid.*, p. 20.   [24] *1831 Report*, p. 5.

each county experienced precisely the same monthly price trends. The earliest date from which evidence on transactions was admitted for the Candlemas fiars[25] was usually 1 November (as laid down by the Act of Sederunt of 1723 and observed in fourteen counties), but in some courts evidence was admitted from as early as 1 October. In Haddington, as we know from other evidence over the period 1721–95,[26] there was, on average, a 4.2, 5.7, 6.9 and 4.3 per cent drop in the price of wheat, oats, barley and pease respectively between the last week in September and the last week of October. Similarly, in Edinburgh over the period 1741–95, the retail price of oatmeal fell, on average, by exactly 2 per cent over the same four-week period. More significantly, in some years this drop in both Haddington and Edinburgh could exceed 20 per cent: the inclusion of price evidence from October transactions would have had a marked effect on the overall average in such years. Similarly, the majority of counties did not accept evidence of transactions made after the last week in February or first week in March. But in five (Clackmannan, Dunbarton, Elgin, Ross and Cromarty) the period extended no further than 20 February and in Berwickshire no further than Candlemas itself (2 February).

Restricting the period for which evidence may be used also had the more general effect of lowering the fiars relative to the overall annual average price. Once again, both Haddington and Edinburgh provide some relevant evidence. Comparing the average monthly wholesale price of grain in Haddington between November and February inclusive (the usual period from which evidence was taken) against the average monthly price over the twelve-month period November to October shows that the former was often appreciably lower. Between 1721 and 1795, while the price between November and February was very close to the fiars, the twelve-month average was 4 per cent higher for wheat, 6 per cent higher for oats, 3.3 per cent higher for barley and 7.7 per cent higher for pease. In some years the difference could be very much more dramatic; thus whilst the November–February average for wheat reported in the press in 1794–5 was 13 per cent higher than the fiars price for the 1794 crop, the corresponding November to October average was no less than 44.8 per higher than the fiars price.

Calculations of the reported price of oatmeal in Edinburgh 1741–89 tell a similar story. Thus, while the average monthly retail price between November and February was 5.6 per cent higher than the (wholesale) fiars, the average monthly price over the whole year was 7.3 per cent higher than the fiars. Once again, the difference was sometimes much greater, as in 1768–9 when the November–February average was 11.1 per cent greater than the fiars for the 1768 crop, but the full November to October average was 22.2 per cent above the fiars price.[27]

The timing of the fiars was thus clearly an important consideration, and there is no doubt that in this respect the clergy had some very real grounds for complaint. The report of 1831 explains the increase in prices after the striking of the fiars thus:

---

[25] The majority of surviving fiars prices were the so-called 'Candlemas fiars'. These were nominally struck at Candlemas, 2 February. However, a few 'Lammas fiars' (1 August) have survived, for Lanarkshire until 1704, Berwickshire until 1722, Aberdeenshire until 1723, and Roxburghshire into the nineteenth century.

[26] These figures are taken from the monthly market prices for wheat, bear, oats and pease in Haddington recorded in the *Scots Magazine*. See chapter 4 below.   [27] See chapter 4 below.

In the first or earliest part of the season, there is an influx into the markets of raw, ill-preserved, inferior grain; and during the subsequent, but particularly latter part of it, they are over supplied, in consequence of the farmers pushing the sales of their produce, in order to be prepared for the payment of their Candlemas rents. By the time, however, the fiars are fixed, the markets are relieved from these distressing causes; and in the ordinary run of years, prices, finding their natural level, rise.[28]

This was further exacerbated, the report maintained, in the south-western counties of Wigtown and Kirkcudbright because they received large quantities of Irish grain early in the season – keeping the price of locally grown grain lower than it would otherwise have been, and much lower than it would become later in the season. The recommendation of the 1831 report was therefore that:

The period embraced by the averages, which is little more than some months, is clearly too short. It should be extended from the beginning of March to the first week of May, and from November retrospectively, so as to include all transactions in the crop of that year. On this point all intelligent farmers and corn-dealers are agreed.[29]

A further point of concern emphasised in the reports was that the evidence tended to come from merchants and other middlemen. This had two consequences; first, that the evidence related to wholesale and not retail prices, and, second, that it generally referred only to large transactions. In fact, in seven counties small sales were specifically excluded. This touches upon how an average was then deduced. In twenty-six counties quantities were taken into account when calculating average prices, i.e., a weighted average was being sought. But in the counties of Aberdeen, Banff, Edinburgh, Lanark, Renfrew and Roxburgh, and sometimes in Clackmannan, Fife, Kinross and Kirkcudbright, quantities were not considered. The difference this could make to the calculated average is obvious and, as smaller quantities tend to be sold more often and at higher prices, the fiars price would be relatively higher where a weighted average was not employed.

Such differences in the evidence accepted by the courts were probably less important than the variety of methods employed in actually striking the fiars. The Act of Sederunt of 1723 merely directed the Sheriff to appoint a jury of fifteen men, of whom at least eight were to be heritors, who should 'pass upon inquest, and return their verdict on the evidence underwritten, or their own proper knowledge concerning the fiars for the preceding crop, of every kind of victual of the product of the sheriffdom'.[30]

There was no guidance on how that verdict should be determined, and each court tended to follow its own method. The use of a jury's 'own proper knowledge' was a much criticised power and, although not always exercised, in some counties it could have a marked effect on the fiars:

In Aberdeenshire the majority of the jury is composed not only of heritors, but almost always of the same heritors, unless death render a change necessary; and some of them are said to have been every year on the jury for the last 40 years. The verdict of the jury rarely corresponds with the average calculated according to the quantities of which evidence has been given.[31]

---

[28] *1831 report*, p. 3.   [29] *Ibid.*, p. 4.   [30] *Acts of Sederunt of the Lords of Council*, p. 278.
[31] *1831 report*, p. 2. It was noted in this report that over the previous 20 years the fiars of Aberdeen were about 7 per cent lower than in the neighbouring counties of Banff, Kincardine, Forfar and Elgin.

The report of 1911 further maintained that in Aberdeen, until 1812, the jury acted 'on their own proper knowledge . . . without any evidence at all'.[32] The reports were careful not to question the honesty of the jurors in exercising this power but, as it was put in 1895, 'as the interests of those who serve on the jury are always in the direction of lower fiars, the power, if it exists at all, is one which honourable men would be scrupulous in exercising'.[33]

This was a criticism both of the use of the jury's 'own proper knowledge' in the determination of the fiars and of the jury itself. In fact, in the report of 1831, observing the success of the Haddington fiars (which had always been struck without a jury), it was recommended that the jury be dispensed with entirely, 'what can be more anomalous in principle, or more unfair in its practical tendency, than the rule which requires that a majority of the jurymen shall be persons interested in the verdict which they have to pronounce?'.[34]

Such a bias might, however, have been more evident in the nineteenth century than earlier. At the time of these complaints little except the minister's stipend was calculated from the fiars and it was in the heritor's interest to maintain a low money equivalent, but when heritors had received rents and multures calculated in kind but paid in money the opposite interest prevailed. Thus the earliest relevant evidence as to setting the level of the fiars, the case of Mundie *contra* Craigie of Craigie heard before the Court of Session in December 1685, declares them to be 'not only far above true prices, but penal'; the court ordered that fiars should be struck according to 'the current prices for which victual in the country was in use to be sold yearly', and 'appointed the same to be proved by such witnesses as were heritors and merchants, who were in use to trade victual there'.[35]

The use, and potential abuse, of the jury's 'own proper knowledge' was not the only way in which the striking of fiars varied from one county to the next. Consider how the various courts dealt with the problem of insufficient evidence for a specific grain. According to the 1895 report, in most cases no return was made, but in some counties an average of the previous three years was taken, whilst in others the price was taken from a neighbouring county, and in yet others witnesses offered their own opinion.[36] This was a problem which related primarily to bear, a grain which was gradually replaced by barley in the course of the eighteenth and nineteenth centuries. The conservatism of the fiars courts was such that prices for bear continued to be struck long after the grain had all but disappeared. In the 1890s bear fiars were struck in some counties by making a deduction from the fiars for barley; of 2s. Sterling per quarter in Inverness and Dunbarton, and of 3s.6d. sterling per quarter in Ayr. Fortunately, this is a problem which was unlikely to have been serious until after 1780.

Of more general significance, however, was the variable manner in which fiars prices

[32] *1911 report*, p. 4.   [33] *1895 report*, pp. 18–19.   [34] *1831 report*, p. 4.

[35] Henry Home (Lord Kames), *The decisions of the Court of Session from first institution to the present time* (Edinburgh, 1791), vol. I, pp. 311–12.

[36] *1895 report*, p. 21. The report lists these various practices without ascribing them to particular counties. SRO, SC 9/67/1/1, 'Minutes anent the fiars of the Shire of Sutherland for the years 1738–1742' explicitly states that the fiars for these five years were all struck on 9 September 1743.

for various qualities of grain were set. This was a practice given explicit approval by the 1723 Act of Sedurunt, but striking different rates according to quality, 'which experience has shown to be good and profitable', was never enforced and many courts continued to strike but one rate. Those which did strike multiple rates followed quite different methods, although everywhere the aim was to distinguish between grains of different qualities. In some counties it was recognised that different areas produced grains of different quality and thus a distinction was made along geographical lines. Hence the Lammermuir and Merse rates for Berwickshire, the Carse, Dryfield and Muirland rates for Stirlingshire, and the Deall-land and Muirland rates for Linlithgowshire. In Perthshire, two rates were struck for both oats and beare; called merely 'first' and 'second' these, at least in the nineteenth century, actually seem to have referred to grain from the carselands and highland fringe respectively. Such a practice was approved of in later years because it avoided the problem, discussed in the 1831 report, of striking a rate on the strength of a biased sample of the county's transactions. Thus in Kirkcudbright-shire a sufficient number of witnesses was seldom attracted from its richest grain districts owing to the distance of those districts from the county town. In Kincardineshire, also, too few representations were made about the price of grain from the most fertile area, around Montrose, and too many from the less fertile area, around Stonehaven, so the fiars were too low.[37]

Elsewhere other methods were used; in nineteenth-century Banff and Lanark the first and second fiars were distinguished by weight. The first barley weighed 54 lbs. or more per bushel, the second less than 54 lbs. per bushel. In Kinross a most peculiar method was used. An average price was first calculated, then 1s. per quarter added to make the first fiar, and 1s. per quarter deducted to make the second fiar. But by far the most common method was to distinguish between the different varieties of each grain. Thus in Kincardineshire different rates were struck for White and Brockit oats and in Ayrshire for White and Grey oats. In Stirlingshire, not only was there the distinction already noted between Carse, Dryfield and Muirland oats, but also between Black, Brucked, Grey and Airseed oats. In Aberdeenshire fiars are to be found for Great, Brockit and Small oats; bear and Wair bear; meal and White meal; as well as for Ferme and Mercat bear, malt, wheat, rye and pease.[38] The distinction between the Ferme and Mercat fiars does not appear to have been one of quality, but rather one of destination: 'Ferme bear would be that which was presentable for payment of rent, and which would as a general rule fall to be delivered at the laird's house. Mercat bear would be the same commodity prepared for, transported to and sold in the market'.[39] This distinction was, however, short lived. The last crop for which the Ferme and Mercat fiars' prices for wheat, rye and pease differed was 1630; for malt the crop of 1649; for bear the crop of 1655; and for meal the crop of 1669.

Aberdeenshire was also unique in that the three varieties of oats and two of bear were each given fiars both 'with' and 'without' fodder. The fodder usually added a few shillings to the price, the outstanding exception being the crop of 1696 for which the fiars

[37] *1831 report*, p. 3.   [38] For a full discussion of the Aberdeenshire fiars see Littlejohn, 'Aberdeenshire'.
[39] *Ibid.*, p. 10.

prices for all the grains 'with' and 'without' fodder were the same. Whether this means that there was no straw, or that which there was had no value whatsoever, it illustrates the impracticality of using the difference between the fiars 'with' and 'without' fodder as a guide to the actual price of fodder. In the tables which follow, only the fiars 'without fodder' have been included, although all the series are recorded by Littlejohn and are held on computer.[40]

There remains one final method used to establish different rates which must be considered. The Court of Session in 1771 stated that, 'the method of striking fiars in East Lothian is by much the best' and the Committee on Fiars Prices of 1895 could only add that, 'if fiars prices are to be struck at all, they could not be struck more equitably'.[41] The method was singular, as illustrated by George Barclay's 1792 description of the procedure followed by the Sheriff Depute of Haddington:[42]

In place of calling a jury, he has been in the use of annually, in the end of February or beginning of March, to summon before himself betwixt 60 and 80 buyers and sellers of all the different kinds of grain of the preceding crop, from the several quarters of the county; those he examines upon oath, as to the different prices at which they have been bought and sold, and, from this evidence strikes the Fiars in the following manner: He collects the total quantity proved of each species of grain, and, from this he finds the medium price of one boll; then he collects the total quantity of what is sold above the general medium, and finds the medium of that; he collects, in the next place, all that is sold below the general medium, and finds the medium thereof. To each of these mediums he adds $2\frac{1}{2}$ per cent and the medium of what is sold above the general medium with the forsaid addition, constitutes the first Fiars; the general medium, with the forsaid addition, constitutes the 2nd Fiars; and the medium of what is sold below the general medium, with the like addition, constitutes the 3rd Fiars.[43]

Perhaps it is the rigour of this method which makes the comparison between the average November–February wholesale price in the Haddington market as reported in the press and the fiars such a close one.

The very different methods employed in different counties undermines the value of using the fiars records, in unadjusted form, as a direct guide to actual differences in the price at which grain was traded in different counties. For instance, whereas in Linlithgow witnesses were to be questioned about the highest price they had paid, received, or heard of having been paid or received for each type and quality of grain,[44] in Haddington an arithmetic mean of all transactions was calculated. A straight comparison between two such counties would inevitably be misleading. Moreover, the timing of the fiars, let alone the composition of the jury and the nature of the evidence they considered, meant that fiars everywhere were likely to understate the average price at which grain was sold through the year as a whole, even if – as was certainly the case in Haddington – they were

---

[40] See appendix II.   [41] *1895 report*, p. 29.   [42] George Barclay, 'Parish of Haddington'.

[43] The addition of 2.5 per cent to the average is said to have been originally because above four-fifths of the grain of East Lothian sold by the fiars is sold at six months' credit (2.5 per cent), while the grain taken up for ascertaining the fiars was all sold for ready money: Davidson, *Report on the fiars of East Lothian* (Edinburgh, 1850). After 1808 the addition was defended by ministers as compensation for the long-delayed payment of stipend. The stipend was legally earned on the 29 September, but was not paid until the following March.

[44] SRO, GD 98/vol. 18, p. 382; 'Rules to be observed in making the feirs of the shireffdome of Linlithgow, 13 February 1702'.

very close to the wholesale price at which grain was sold during the months from which evidence on transactions was adduced.

A further difficulty is that each county continued to use its own local measures; often well into the nineteenth century. To a certain extent this can be overcome for the late eighteenth century as much evidence exists on the size of the measures of capacity by which grain was sold at that time. A table of conversion deduced from this evidence is provided in appendix I but weights and measures evolved with time and there is no guarantee that the measures used in the late eighteenth century were the same as those used at the time of the earliest fiars.

But one very important question remains to be answered. Even if the very nature of the fiars impedes any simple comparison between their levels in different counties, and qualifies the extent to which we may use them as a literal measure of market prices, especially retail prices, can they still provide an insight into long-term trends and short-term fluctuations? Here the answer must surely be positive, for although each court followed its own methods there is no reason to suspect that each also chopped and changed between methods. Moreover, it cannot be doubted that juries kept half an eye on the fiars set in previous years whilst they were striking the current one; as the 1723 Act of Sedurunt put it, they would have used 'their own proper knowledge concerning the fiars of the preceding cropt'. It seems most unlikely, therefore, that fiars prices would have moved on a trend that was contrary to market prices, and extremely probable that they would have been a close reflection.

Such a contention is supported by a series of comparisons between fiars prices and the price at which grain is known to have been traded in various counties. This is, of course, no absolute test of the accuracy of the fiars as it is certain that whatever prices we can now uncover constitute but a tiny proportion, and probably a quite biased sample, of the transactions which actually took place in any county. The evidence for Haddington is probably exceptional in this respect as the monthly market prices recorded from 1721 in the *Caledonian Mercury*, the *Edinburgh Courant* and the *Scots Magazine* seem to have been based on as broad, if not broader, sample of transactions as the fiars (see chapter 4). The Haddington fiars were struck in a remarkably careful way and they do tend to follow very closely the general movement in market prices shown in the press, though, as we have already noted, the fiars prices for wheat, oats, barley and pease were, on average, 4.0, 6.0, 3.3 and 7.7 per cent higher over the twelve-month period than over the period during which the fiars were struck. In chapter 4 we also discuss the relationship between the Edinburgh (Midlothian) fiars and the reported retail transaction prices in the Edinburgh meal market. The correspondence is, as at Haddington, reassuringly close (see figure 3.1).

Both the above situations are based on press reports of prices. If we turn to actual account books, the picture is not very different. To take an example from East Lothian, farm-gate sales of oats and bear made by John Nisbet of Dirleton between 1668 and 1702 (table 3.24) were, on average, made at a price 11.5 and 13.5 per cent higher than their respective fiars,[45] but still the fiars prices and the sales moved in the same direction. Such

---

[45] SRO, GD 6/1504 and 1542; Contracts between William Nisbet of Dirleton (in East Lothian) and various merchants. Carriage, usually between North Berwick and Leith, seems to have been paid by the purchaser.

differences may have been largely a consequence of the timing of the fiars, but elsewhere the wholesale–retail factor seems to play its part. Two miles outside Cupar in Fife, between 1769 and 1784, Lady Balgarvie was purchasing oats and oatmeal at a price 17.5 and 10 per cent higher, on average, than their respective fiars (table 3.20).[46] Other price series from Fife confirm this quite substantial difference between the fiars and the price at which grain was actually bought and sold. Bear and oatmeal prices recorded in Craighall estate rentals between 1663 and 1679 (table 3.21) were, on average, 13.7 and 12.3 per cent higher than contemporary fiars.[47] Similarly, the bear and oatmeal sold by the masters of the Pittenweem Sea Box between 1658 and 1755 (table 3.22) fetched, on average, 5.8 and 18.1 per cent more than their respective fiars would have led us to expect the grain to have been worth.[48] Finally, between 1722 and 1777 the 'accounting' price used on the Buchannan estate in Stirlingshire to deduct from servants' fees the cost of the oatmeal with which they were supplied was, on average, just over 10 per cent higher than the current fiars price for oatmeal (table 3.23).[49] This was despite the fact that the Stirlingshire fiars may have been more reliable than most, as it is known that a book recording transactions in the market was kept to help the jury with its decisions.[50] In all these cases, however, as figures 3.1–3.4 show, there was generally an admirable correlation between the trends or fluctuations shown by the fiars and by known market transactions from manuscript accounts.

Clearly the fiars must be used with some caution, but as a general guide to the movement of grain prices in early modern Scotland they are, to use Mitchison's words, 'an adequate tool for the historian', and are undoubtedly without parallel with respect to their coverage of the country.

As for the use which may be made of the oatmeal fiars in determining the level of real wages (a goal pursued in chapter 9), clearly certain allowances must be made for the time of year at which the fiars were struck and for the fact that they were determined largely on the evidence of wholesale transactions. An increase of 10 per cent on the fiars would seem to provide a useful guide to the approximate price at which oatmeal could have been bought in the market over the year as a whole. It is possible that this differential would have been smaller in the earlier part of the period for which fiars are available, when the pressure was on heritors to keep them high and methods of assessment less often subject to an organised jury. The figure of 10 per cent is, however, also amply borne out by the evidence of oatmeal prices in Edinburgh, 1741–89, considered in the next chapter.

[46] St Andrews University Library Mss., Lady Balgarvie's Account Book.
[47] Bear and meal prices from Craighall estate rentals taken from J.A. di Folco, 'Aspects of seventeenth century social life in Central and North Fife' (unpublished M.Phil. thesis, St Andrews, 1975).
[48] St Andrews University Library Mss., Pittenweem sea box book, 1633–1755.
[49] SRO, GD 220/6; Miscellaneous Montrose accounts for the estate of Buchanan, 1722–91. See A. Gibson, 'Proletarianization? The transition to full-time labour on a Scottish estate, 1723–1787', *Continuity and Change*, vol. V (1990), pp. 357–89.   [50] Mitchison, 'Corn prices', p. 279.

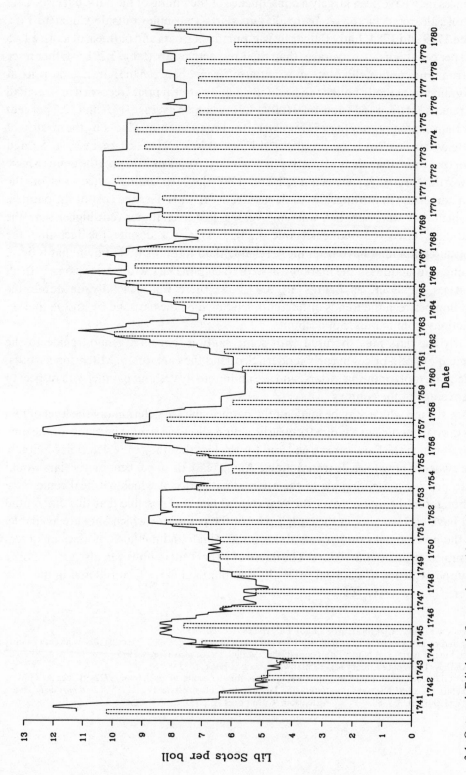

3.1 Oatmeal: Edinburgh fiars and monthly meal market, crops 1740–1780

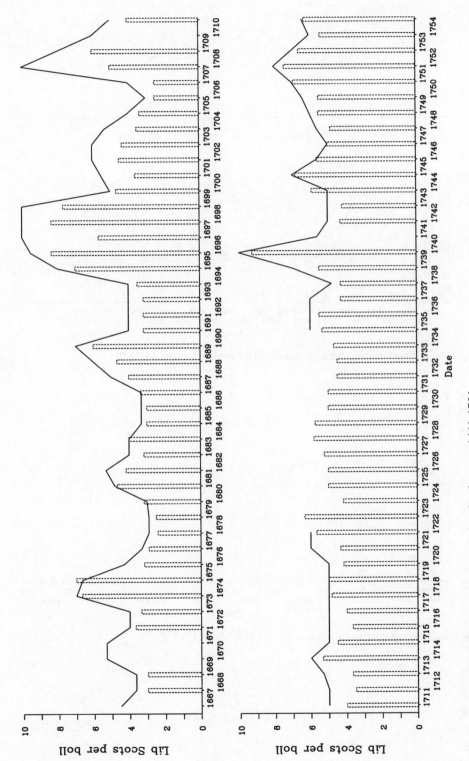

3.2 Oatmeal: Fife fiars and Pittenweem sea box book, crops 1666–1754

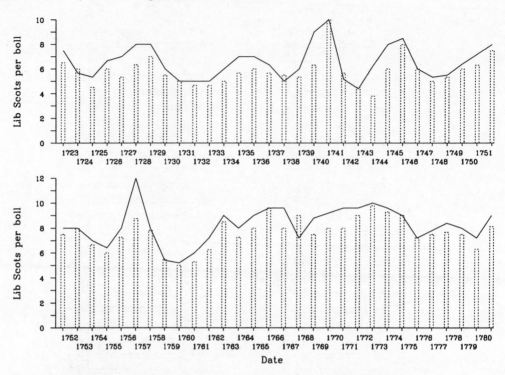

3.3 Oatmeal: Stirlingshire fiars and Buchanan estate accounts, crops 1722–80

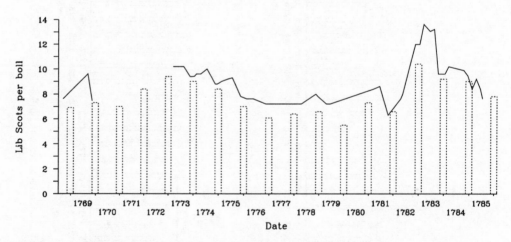

3.4 Oatmeal: Fife fiars and Lady Balgarvie's accounts, crops 1768–85

INTRODUCTION TO TABLES 3.1–3.24

Although determined, or 'struck', for similar purposes throughout Scotland, the fiars price series which follow can be compared one to another only with caution. First, as discussed in the text, there were important technical differences in the way in which the fiars were actually arrived at in different counties. The consequence of this in terms of the comparability of the various fiars is impossible to assess in any quantitative manner. Second, there was considerable variation in the size of the grain measures used in different counties. As described in appendix I, virtually every county had its own boll measure. To take but one cautionary example, table 3.10 lists the wheat fiars for the counties of Aberdeen, Ayr, Banff, Berwick, Clackmannan, Dumfries and Edinburgh from 1725 to 1780. As far as can be determined (largely on the basis of comparisons made in the last quarter of the eighteenth century) the capacity of the wheat bolls used in these counties were 10,754, 8,602, 9,265, 12,902, 9,513, 26,557 and 8,944 cubic inches respectively. One may thus contrast (a) the given fiars prices for crop 1756 (which would probably have been struck with respect to local measures) against (b) their equivalent prices per Linlithgow boll (the supposed Scottish standard) of 8,789 cubic inches capacity.

Aberdeen	Ayr	Banff	Berwick	Clackmannan	Dumfries	Edinburgh
a) £12.12.0	£14. 8.0	£12.12.0	£10.14.0	£12. 0.0	£33.12.0	£13. 4.0
b) £10. 6.0	£14. 4.3	£11.19.1	£ 7. 5.9	£11. 1.9	£11. 2.5	£12.19.5

Clearly a very different comparison is made once the size of the boll used in the different counties is taken into account; although the unexpectedly low value for Berwickshire does cast doubt on whether the local measure referred to by our late eighteenth-century witnesses was actually used with respect to the fiars. Such difficulties in establishing for certain what measures were used at what dates have persuaded us that we should not here attempt to adjust the fiars data in any way.

Fiars prices always refer to crop years; that is to say that the price given was ascribed to the crop harvested in the year stated even though the price was actually set in the early part of the subsequent year. Thus prices which refer to wheat harvested in 1756, would have been 'struck' in, or shortly after, February 1757, and would, at least in theory, have reflected the level of prices in the wholesale markets between November 1756 and February 1757.

In addition to the fiars, and largely as a control against which their veracity may be judged, we provide in tables 3.20–3.24 a series of miscellaneous prices extracted from various estate records. The fullest detail is provided by Lady Balgarvie's accounts regarding her purchases of oats and oatmeal near Cupar in Fife (table 3.20). Here both the year in which the grain was harvested and the actual transaction date is recorded. At Dirleton, East Lothian (table 3.24), only the contract date is recorded, although it is probably safe to assume that sales taking place up to and including August were of grain from the preceding year's crop, whilst those from September onwards were from the crop of the year in which the sale took place. The tables for Craighall in Fife (table 3.21) and Buchanan in Stirlingshire (table 3.22), on the other hand, refer to 'accounting' prices which the respective estate managements used for their own purposes. How closely these mirrored local market prices is difficult to assess, though it seems unlikely that they could have diverged significantly from them.

Sources

The following list comprises all the sources we have consulted. Not all have been used in compiling tables 3.1–3.19, for these represent but a selection from our full database, available as described in appendix II. A. Bald, *The farmer and corn dealer's assistant* (Edinburgh, 1780) provides tables of fiars prices for most of the Scottish counties for the period 1756–76 and M.W. Flinn (ed.), *Scottish population history* (Cambridge, 1977) includes an appendix of selected series (principally oatmeal) for the period 1619–1826. These have only been noted below if they provide fiars data which are otherwise unavailable. All known manuscript sources have been noted, even if they duplicate other material. Finally, although we have not utilised them for reasons discussed in the text, the Exchequer fiars, 1708–86 (SRO, E.5/5) constitutes a potentially fruitful additional source.

Aberdeenshire	1619–20 and 1628–1850 from D. Littlejohn, 'Aberdeenshire fiars', *Miscellany of the New Spalding Club*, vol. 2 (Aberdeen, 1906), pp. 2–43.
Ayrshire	1658–1821 from SRO, SC 6/85/20.
	1667–71, 1697 and 1740–80 from SRO, GD 25/9/Box 1.
	1691–6 from SRO, GD 109/3943.
	1704–1833 from SRO, SC 6/78/1.
Banffshire	1756–76 from Bald, *Assistant*, p. 395.
Berwickshire	1689–1792 from J. Sinclair, 'A table of the fiars of the county of Berwick', *OSA*, vol. 3, p. 208. 1756–67 from SRO, GD 1/651/16.
Buteshire	1756–76 from Bald, *Assistant*, p. 397.
Clackmannanshire	1756–76 from Bald, *Assistant*, p. 398.
Dumfriesshire	1624 from SRO, GD 6/1056.
	1756–76 from Bald, *Assistant*, p. 400.
Dunbartonshire	1756–76 from Bald, *Assistant*, p. 399.
Edinburgh	1626–1779 from SRO, GD 69/282 (also in Bald, *Assistant*, pp. 423–7).
	1640–1931 from SRO, GD 224/1066 (also as SRO, RH2/4/109, pp. 112–20).
Elginshire	1756–76 from Bald, *Assistant*, p. 402.
Fife	1556–86 from SRO, GD 26/12/1.
	1619–34 (bear) and 1619–1826 (oatmeal) from M.W. Flinn, *Scottish population*, appendix B.
	1640–1814 from SRO, GD 26/12/11 (and duplicate GD 26/12/34).

Forfarshire (Angus)	1611–18 from SRO, GD 30/2191.
	1649–69 from SRO, GD 16/27/217.
	1756–76 from Bald, *Assistant*, p. 404.
	1764 from SRO, GD 45/23/86.
	1779–1833 from SRO, GD 16/27/82.
Glasgow (Commissariot)	1670–1705 (bear and oatmeal) from SRO, GD 22/3/758.
	1664–1776 (oatmeal) from Glasgow University Archives, Mss. 26652 and 26670. 1756–76 (bear and oatmeal) from Bald, *Assistant*, p. 411.
Haddingtonshire	1605–24 from SRO, B 30/13/3.
	1627–1786 from G. Barclay, 'Account of the parish of Haddington', *Transactions of the Society of Antiquaries of Scotland*, vol. 1 (Edinburgh, 1792), appendix 3.
	1627–1897 (wheat) from R.C. Mossman, 'On the price of wheat at Haddington, 1627–1897', *Accountants' magazine*, vol. 4 (1900), pp. 94–110.
	1647–48 from SRO, GD 150/2625.
	1652–87 from SRO, GD 110/683.
Inverness-shire	1756–76 from Bald, *Assistant*, p. 406.
Kincardineshire	1675–86 from SRO, GD 49/378.
	1756–76 from Bald, *Assistant*, p. 407.
Kinross-shire	1763–76 from Bald, *Assistant*, p. 408.
Kirkcudbrightshire	1662–76 from SRO, GD 10/501.
	1756–76 from Bald, *Assistant*, p. 409.
Lanarkshire	1691–1830 from SRO, SC 38/19/1.
Linlithgowshire (West Lothian)	1654–1808 from J. Trotter, *General view of the agriculture of the county of West Lothian* (Edinburgh, 1811), appendix 5.
	1661–71 from SRO, GD 103/2/77. 1714 and 1722 from SRO, GD 30/2191. 1731–45 from SRO, GD 6/1059. 1771–76 from SRO, GD 45/19/259.
Nairnshire	1756–76 from Bald, *Assistant* (Edinburgh, 1780), p. 413.
Perthshire	1630–1710 from SRO, SC 49/22/1.
	1702–56 from Perth Town Council Archives, B 59/17/3. 1630–1785 from Perth Museum and Art Gallery Archive, No. 270.
Renfrewshire	1756–76 from Bald, *Assistant*, p. 415.
Roxburghshire	1669–72 from SRO, GD 6/1057/1 and GD 6/1057/2.
	1756–76 from Bald, *Assistant*, p. 416–17. 1633–1825 (oatmeal) from M.W. Flinn, *Scottish population*, appendix B.
Stirlingshire	1682–1777 from SRO, SC 67/57/19.
	1774–80 from SRO, SC 67/28/2.
Wigtownshire	1756–76 from Bald, *Assistant*, p. 419.

Table 3.1 *Oatmeal and bear: county fiars, 1556–1624*

| Crop year | Fife | | Forfar | | |
	Oatmeal L. s. d.	Bear L. s. d.	Oatmeal L. s. d.	Wheat L. s. d.	Bear L. s. d.
1556	1 0 0	1 6 8			
1557	1 8 0	2 0 0			
1558	2 10 0	3 0 0			
1559	0 16 0	1 7 0			
1560	0 18 0	1 6 8			
1561	1 16 0	1 18 0			
1562	1 18 0	2 16 8			
1563	2 12 0	3 0 0			
1564	2 13 4	4 0 0			
1565	1 12 0	2 2 0			
1566	2 0 0	2 2 0			
1567	3 13 4	4 10 0			
1568	2 0 0	2 13 4			
1569	3 0 0	3 11 8			
1570	3 0 0	4 6 8			
1571	2 0 0	3 0 0			
1572	1 18 0	2 3 4			
1573	1 16 0	1 18 0			
1574	3 0 0	3 6 8			
1575	4 0 0	4 3 4			
1576	5 0 0	6 0 0			
1577	3 3 4	4 0 0			
1578	3 3 4	3 6 8			
1579	2 3 4	2 16 8			
1580	3 0 0	3 10 0			
1581	2 13 4	3 0 0			
1582	3 13 4	4 3 4			
1583	4 13 4	5 6 8			
1584	5 0 0	5 6 8			
1585	10 0 0	10 13 4			
1586	9 0 0	10 0 0			
1611			5 0 0	6 13 4	5 6 8
1612				8 0 0	7 6 8
1613			4 0 0	6 13 4	6 13 4
1614			5 6 8	7 0 0	6 0 0
1615			6 0 0	8 0 0	7 0 0
1616			4 13 4	6 13 4	5 6 8
1617			4 6 8	7 6 8	5 0 0
1618			4 10 0	6 13 4	5 0 0
1619		5 6 8			
1620		5 6 8			
1621		9 0 0			
1622	6 13 4	10 0 0			
1623	7 0 0	10 0 0			
1624	4 13 4	5 6 8			

Table 3.2 *Oats: county fiars, 1628–1674*

Crop year	Aberdeen Great oats[1] L. s. d.	Aberdeen Small oats[1] L. s. d.	Edinburgh L. s. d.	Fife L. s. d.	Haddington[2] L. s. d.	Linlithgow L. s. d.	Perth L. s. d.
1628	6 6 8	2 13 4					
1629	5 0 0	3 0 0					
1630	3 10 0	2 0 0					
1631	3 0 0	1 10 0					
1632	4 10 0	2 10 0					
1635					6 0 0		
1636					5 6 8		
1640				5 13 4	8 0 0		
1641				7 6 8	7 0 0		
1642				7 13 4	6 0 0		
1643				5 0 0	5 0 0		
1644				5 0 0	6 0 0		
1645			4 0 0	4 0 0	3 0 0		
1646			3 13 4		3 10 0		
1647			6 6 8		6 6 8		
1648			9 6 8		8 0 0		
1649	7 0 0	3 6 8	10 0 0	9 13 4	8 0 0		
1650	6 6 8	2 16 8	10 0 0	10 13 4	11 0 0		
1651	6 0 0	2 13 4	10 0 0	9 6 8	10 13 4		
1652	6 13 4	3 6 8	7 10 0	8 0 0	8 10 0		
1653			2 13 4	3 13 4	4 6 8		3 0 0
1654			2 13 4	4 0 0	2 13 4	3 6 8	
1655	4 3 4	1 16 8	3 6 8	3 6 8	3 13 4	3 6 8	4 6 8
1656	3 13 4	1 16 0	4 3 4	4 0 0	4 13 4		4 0 0
1657	3 13 4	1 16 0	4 0 0	3 13 4	4 13 4	3 13 4	3 6 8
1658				5 6 8	6 13 4	5 3 4	4 13 4
1659			6 10 0	5 6 8	6 16 0		7 6 8
1660			6 10 0	5 6 8	6 0 0	5 13 4	6 13 4
1661			6 6 8	5 0 0	5 13 4	6 0 0	5 6 8
1662			4 13 4	3 13 4	4 15 0	4 6 8	4 13 4
1663			4 13 4	4 0 0	4 6 8	4 0 0	4 0 0
1664			3 6 4	2 10 0	3 0 0	2 13 4	3 0 0
1665	3 13 4	1 13 4	3 6 4	2 13 4	3 13 4	3 6 8	3 6 8
1666	4 0 0	2 0 0	4 0 0		4 0 0	3 13 4	3 6 8
1667	5 0 0	2 0 0	3 16 0		3 8 0	3 6 8	3 13 4
1668	3 6 8	1 16 0	4 0 0	3 0 0	3 0 0	3 6 8	3 6 8
1669	3 13 4	1 13 4	3 6 8	3 0 0	3 13 4	3 3 4	3 13 4
1670	4 6 8	2 0 0	5 0 0		4 6 8	4 6 8	5 0 0
1671			6 0 0		5 14 0	5 0 0	4 6 8
1672			4 13 4	3 13 4	4 0 0	4 0 0	3 6 8
1673			4 13 4	3 6 8	4 8 0	4 6 8	3 13 4
1674			8 6 8	6 13 4	8 12 0	6 13 4	6 13 4

1 Aberdeen prices are for great and small oats without fodder. Prices for these grains with the fodder are invariably slightly higher. Figures in italics are for fiars which were struck between July and November rather than, as was usual, in or around February. Great oats were occasionally refered to as 'whyt' oats.

2 Haddington prices are for first oats. Prices for second oats are published in Flinn, *Scottish Population History*, 1977.

Table 3.3 *Oats: county fiars, 1675–1724*

Crop year	Aberdeen		Ayr		Berwick		Edinburgh
	Great oats[1]	Small oats[1]	White oats[2]	Grey oats[2]	Merse oats	Lammer-muir oats	
	L. s. d.	L. s. d.	L. s. d.	L. s. d.	L. s. d.	L. s. d.	L. s. d.
1675							7 16 0
1676	*3 13 4*	*1 13 4*					3 10 0
1677	*3 10 0*	*1 10 0*					3 13 4
1678	*3 0 0*	*1 6 8*					3 10 0
1679	*3 6 8*	*1 6 8*					4 0 0
1680	*3 0 0*	*1 6 8*					4 0 0
1681	*3 13 4*	*1 16 0*					5 0 0
1682	*4 0 0*	*1 13 4*					5 8 0
1683							4 13 4
1684							4 6 8
1685							4 2 0
1686							4 0 0
1687							4 2 0
1688							4 13 4
1689					4 10 0	4 4 0	5 14 0
1690	6 0 0	3 0 0			4 16 0	4 10 0	6 15 0
1691	4 0 0	2 0 0			2 16 0	2 12 0	4 6 8
1692	4 0 0	2 0 0			3 4 0	3 0 0	4 0 0
1693	4 0 0	2 0 0			3 12 0	3 6 0	4 8 0
1694	4 6 8	2 0 0			3 16 0	3 12 0	4 16 0
1695	6 0 0	2 13 4			5 6 0	5 4 0	7 6 8
1696	8 0 0	3 0 0			6 13 4	5 0 0	10 0 0
1697	7 0 0	2 13 4			4 16 0	4 0 0	6 13 4
1698	10 0 0	4 0 0			8 0 0	5 0 0	12 0 0
1699	8 0 0	3 0 0			7 13 4	6 6 8	9 0 0
1700	6 10 0	2 13 4			4 0 0	3 0 0	6 0 0
1701	5 0 0	2 0 0			3 10 0	3 0 0	4 3 4
1702	4 6 8	2 0 0			3 8 0	3 0 0	6 0 0
1703	4 0 0	2 0 0			3 12 0	3 4 0	5 10 0
1704	4 13 4	2 0 0			3 6 8	3 0 0	5 6 8
1705	4 3 4	1 13 4			3 14 0	3 6 8	4 13 4
1706	4 0 0	1 6 8			2 0 0	1 12 0	3 6 8
1707	4 6 8	2 0 0			2 18 0	2 12 0	3 18 0
1708	5 6 8	2 13 4			4 6 0	3 18 0	6 10 0
1709	5 6 8	2 0 0			5 12 0	4 18 0	7 10 0
1710	5 6 8	2 13 4			4 16 0	4 4 0	6 3 4
1711	4 6 8	1 16 0			4 4 0	3 18 0	4 19 4
1712	3 13 4	2 0 0			3 4 0	2 16 0	4 14 0
1713	5 0 0	2 13 4	4 10 0	3 16 0	3 12 0	3 0 0	5 0 0
1714	5 0 0	2 10 0	6 0 0		4 4 0	3 12 0	5 6 8
1715	4 13 4	2 13 4	5 0 0	3 0 0	3 14 0	3 2 0	5 6 8
1716	4 6 8	2 0 0	5 6 8	4 0 0	3 10 0	3 4 0	4 13 4
1717	5 0 0	3 0 0	4 13 4	3 6 8	3 16 0	3 8 0	5 10 0
1718	4 13 4	2 0 0	5 6 8	3 6 8	4 0 0	3 14 0	5 4 0
1719	5 0 0	2 0 0	5 0 0	4 0 0	5 8 0	5 4 0	5 18 0
1720	4 0 0	1 16 8	4 16 8	3 6 8	3 16 0	3 12 0	5 10 0
1721	4 6 8	2 0 0	4 16 8	2 10 0	3 12 0	3 7 0	5 3 4
1722	5 6 8	2 13 4	6 0 0	4 0 0	4 10 0	4 4 0	5 18 0
1723	6 0 0	2 13 4	5 6 8	4 0 0	5 8 0	4 16 0	6 8 0
1724	4 3 4	1 13 4	4 10 0	3 0 0	4 4 0	4 0 0	5 3 4

1 Figures in italics are for fiars which were struck between July and November rather than, as was usual, in or around February.
2 The boll of oats was stated to be of 8 Winchester bushels.

Table 3.3 *(cont.)*

Crop year	Fife L. s. d.	Haddington L. s. d.	Kincardine White oats L. s. d.	Kincardine Brockit oats L. s. d.	Lanark L. s. d.	Linlithgow Oats L. s. d.	Linlithgow Great oats L. s. d.
1675	7 0 0	7 13 4	6 0 0	4 3 4		6 13 4	
1676	3 3 4	3 6 8	4 3 4	3 0 0		2 16 0	
1677	2 18 0	3 10 0	4 0 0	2 10 0		3 0 0	
1678	2 8 0	3 0 0	3 0 0	2 6 8		2 13 4	
1679	2 10 0	3 13 4	4 0 0	2 10 0		4 0 0	
1680	3 0 0	4 0 0	4 0 0	2 13 4		4 0 0	
1681	4 13 4	5 0 0	4 0 0	3 0 0		5 8 0	
1682	4 3 4	5 16 0	4 13 4	3 13 4		4 10 0	
1683	3 3 4	3 16 0	4 0 0	2 13 4		3 13 4	
1684	4 0 0	4 6 8	4 0 0	2 13 4		3 13 4	
1685	3 0 0	3 13 4	3 13 4	2 13 4		3 6 8	
1686	3 0 0	3 13 4	3 13 4	2 13 4		4 0 0	
1687	3 0 0	3 14 0				3 13 4	
1688	4 0 0	4 10 0				4 10 0	
1689	4 13 4	5 6 8				5 0 0	
1690	6 0 0	6 4 0				5 13 4	
1691	3 3 4	3 16 0			3 6 8	3 10 0	
1692	3 0 0	4 0 0			3 6 8	3 10 0	
1693	3 3 4	4 10 0			4 6 8	4 0 0	
1694	3 10 0	4 16 0			4 10 0	4 13 4	
1695	6 10 0	7 0 0			6 6 8	6 6 8	
1696	7 0 0	9 0 0			6 13 4	8 0 0	
1697	5 3 4	6 6 8				5 0 0	
1698	7 13 4	10 10 0				10 0 0	
1699	7 13 4	9 10 0				6 13 4	
1700	4 13 4	6 0 0			5 0 0	4 13 4	
1701	3 10 0	4 6 8			3 6 8		4 0 0
1702	4 10 0	4 13 4			4 0 0		5 6 8
1703	4 6 8	5 0 0			4 13 4		5 0 0
1704	3 10 0	5 0 0					4 16 8
1705	3 3 4	4 10 0					4 0 0
1706	2 6 8	2 16 0					2 13 4
1707	2 6 8	4 0 0					3 0 0
1708	4 16 8	5 8 0					5 0 0
1709	5 10 0	7 6 8					6 15 0
1710		6 0 0					6 5 0
1711	4 0 0	5 0 0			3 13 4		4 6 8
1712	3 10 0	4 12 0					4 6 8
1713	3 10 0	5 0 0			4 0 0		4 6 8
1714	4 16 8	5 6 8			5 6 8		5 0 0
1715	4 5 0	5 6 0			4 0 0		5 10 0
1716	3 10 0	4 10 0			3 13 4		4 5 0
1717	3 16 8	5 6 0			4 10 0		4 16 0
1718	4 10 0	5 2 0					4 15 0
1719	4 16 8	6 2 0			5 0 0		5 3 4
1720	4 0 0	5 10 0			4 0 0		5 0 0
1721	4 3 4	4 18 0			4 0 0		4 10 0
1722	5 10 0	5 13 4			5 6 8		6 0 0
1723	5 16 8	6 5 0			6 0 0[1]		5 16 0
1724	4 0 0	5 2 0			3 16 0		4 0 0

1 From this date, documents explicitly state that 'seed excepted'.

Table 3.3 *(cont.)*

Crop year	Linlithgow Small oats	Perth	Stirling White carse oats	White dryfield oats	Brucked oats	Grey oats
	L. s. d.	L. s. d.	L. s. d.	L. s. d.	L. s. d.	L. s. d.
1675		6 0 0				
1676		3 6 8				
1677		3 0 0				
1678		3 0 0				
1679		3 0 0				
1680		3 6 8				
1681		5 0 0				
1682		4 10 0	5 6 8	5 6 8	4 6 8	2 13 4
1683		3 13 4	4 10 0	4 10 0	3 10 0	2 5 0
1684		3 13 4	3 16 8	3 16 8	3 3 0	1 16 8
1685		3 6 8	4 0 0	4 0 0	3 3 4	1 16 8
1686		3 13 4	4 16 8	3 13 8	3 6 8	2 10 0
1687		3 13 4	4 13 4	4 5 0	3 6 8	2 3 4
1688		4 0 0	4 16 8	4 13 4	3 16 8	2 10 0
1689		5 6 8	5 13 4	5 0 0	4 6 8	2 10 0
1690		6 13 4				
1691		3 13 4	4 6 8	3 0 0	2 3 4	2 3 4
1692		3 0 0				
1693		3 6 8	4 6 8	3 6 8	3 6 8	2 3 4
1694		4 0 0	5 6 8	4 0 0	4 3 4	2 13 4
1695		5 6 8	7 0 0		5 10 0	3 10 0
1696		7 0 0	7 0 0	5 6 8	5 0 0	3 10 0
1697		5 0 0	5 10 0	5 0 0	4 6 8	3 0 0
1698		7 10 0	9 6 8	8 0 0	7 3 4	4 3 4
1699		8 0 0	8 6 8	8 0 0	6 3 4	4 16 8
1700		4 13 4	5 3 4	4 13 4	3 10 0	2 13 4
1701	3 6 8	3 13 4	4 13 4	4 3 4	3 6 8	2 3 4
1702	5 0 0	5 0 0	5 6 8	5 6 8	4 6 8	2 16 8
1703	4 0 0	4 6 8	5 6 8	5 3 4	4 13 4	3 0 0
1704	4 3 4	3 13 4	4 16 8	4 10 0	3 10 0	2 10 0
1705	3 6 8	3 10 0	4 13 4	4 6 8	3 3 4	2 3 4
1706	2 4 0	2 10 0	3 10 0	3 3 4	2 16 8	1 13 4
1707	4 5 0	3 0 0	4 5 0	4 0 0	3 4 0	2 2 6
1708	6 13 4	5 0 0	5 6 8	5 0 0	4 0 0	2 10 0
1709	6 0 0	6 0 0	7 0 0	6 16 8	5 0 0	3 6 8
1710	5 6 8	5 6 8	6 0 0	5 13 4	5 3 4	3 3 4
1711	3 18 4	3 13 4	4 0 0	3 16 8	3 0 0	2 3 4
1712	3 10 0	3 13 4	4 3 4	4 0 0	3 6 8	2 0 0
1713	3 16 8	4 0 0	4 13 4	4 13 4	3 6 8	2 6 8
1714	4 10 0	5 6 8	6 6 8	5 16 8	5 3 4	3 4 0
1715	4 10 0	4 0 0	5 6 8	5 0 0	4 6 8	2 13 4
1716	3 13 4	4 3 4	4 6 8	4 0 0	3 6 8	2 0 0
1717	4 0 0	4 0 0	5 0 0	4 13 4	3 16 8	2 10 0
1718	4 6 8	4 10 0	5 0 0	4 13 4	4 0 0	2 13 4
1719	4 13 4	5 0 0	5 6 8	5 0 0	4 0 0	2 13 4
1720	4 10 0	4 0 0	4 0 0	4 10 0	3 10 0	2 6 8
1721	4 0 0	4 0 0	4 10 0	4 0 0	2 13 4	2 6 8
1722	5 10 0	6 6 8	6 3 4	6 0 0	4 3 4	3 0 0
1723	5 6 8	7 0 0	5 13 4	5 10 0	4 13 4	2 16 8
1724	3 13 4	4 6 8	4 0 0	3 13 4	3 0 0	2 0 0

Table 3.4 *Oats: county fiars, 1725–1780*

Crop year	Aberdeen Great oats L. s. d.	Aberdeen Small oats L. s. d.	Ayr White oats[1] L. s. d.	Ayr Grey oats[1] L. s. d.	Banff L. s. d.	Berwick Merse oats L. s. d.	Berwick Lammer-muir oats L. s. d.
1725	4 0 0	2 0 0	6 0 0	5 0 0		4 12 0	4 6 0
1726	4 6 8	2 0 0	6 6 8	3 3 0		4 0 0	3 16 0
1727	4 13 4	2 6 8	6 0 0	5 0 0		4 4 0	4 0 0
1728	5 13 4	2 13 4	6 17 0	5 0 0		5 8 0	5 2 0
1729	5 0 0	2 0 0	6 0 0	4 0 0		4 10 0	4 0 0
1730	4 6 8	1 13 4	4 16 0	3 0 0		3 14 0	3 11 0
1731	5 0 0	1 16 8	5 0 0	4 0 0		4 0 0	3 12 0
1732	4 13 4	1 13 4	4 10 0	3 10 0		3 4 0	2 16 0
1733	4 13 4	2 0 0	4 10 0	2 10 0		4 0 0	3 16 0
1734	5 0 0	2 0 0	4 0 0	2 5 0		3 16 0	3 10 0
1735	5 3 4	1 16 8	4 16 0	3 12 0		4 16 0	4 12 0
1736	5 0 0	1 16 8	4 16 0	3 12 0		5 2 0	4 14 0
1737	4 13 4	2 0 0	4 7 0	2 8 0		4 12 0	4 4 0
1738	4 0 0	1 6 8	6 8 0	4 0 0		3 6 0	3 0 0
1739	5 6 8	2 13 4	7 0 0	4 16 0		4 4 0	3 12 0
1740	7 0 0	3 0 0	9 12 0	6 8 0		7 10 0	6 10 0
1741	6 0 0	2 6 8	6 8 0	5 0 0		4 6 0	4 0 0
1742	5 0 0	2 0 0	4 16 0	3 4 0		4 0 0	3 14 0
1743	3 12 0	1 4 0	4 0 0	2 16 0		3 0 0	2 14 0
1744	6 13 4	2 13 4	6 8 0	4 0 0		4 4 0	3 0 0
1745	6 0 0	3 0 0	9 12 0	6 0 0		6 0 0	5 14 0
1746	5 6 8	1 16 0	6 13 4	5 6 8		4 7 0	3 16 0
1747	4 13 4	1 10 0	5 4 0	4 0 0		3 10 0	3 7 0
1748	5 0 0	2 0 0	5 6 8	4 0 0		4 14 0	4 10 0
1749	4 10 0	2 0 0	6 0 0	4 0 0		4 12 0	4 8 0
1750	5 0 0	2 0 0	6 13 4	4 0 0		4 8 0	4 6 0
1751	6 6 8	3 0 0	7 12 0	4 16 0		6 6 0	5 14 0
1752	6 10 0	3 10 0	7 4 0	4 16 0		6 0 0	5 14 0
1753	6 0 0	4 0 0	7 4 0	4 16 0		5 16 0	5 8 0
1754	4 13 4	2 0 0	6 8 0	4 5 4		4 8 0	4 0 0
1755	6 10 0	3 15 0	8 0 0	6 0 0		5 14 0	5 0 0
1756	8 0 0	4 0 0	9 12 0	7 4 0	8 10 0	7 4 0	6 6 0
1757	6 10 0	4 0 0	9 12 0	7 4 0	8 0 0	6 17 0	6 5 0
1758	5 6 8	2 13 4	5 12 0	4 0 0	5 6 6	4 0 0	3 16 0
1759	3 16 0	1 16 0	5 4 0	4 0 0	4 2 0	3 12 0	3 6 0
1760	4 4 0	1 16 0	6 8 0	4 0 0	4 0 0	4 4 0	3 18 0[2]
1761	4 10 0	2 10 0	7 10 0	5 4 0	4 16 0	3 16 0	3 6 0
1762	8 0 0	4 0 0	10 0 0	6 8 0	7 16 0	8 0 0	7 4 0
1763	6 4 0	2 8 0	7 12 0	5 4 0	5 14 0	4 12 0	4 4 0
1764	7 0 0	3 0 0	7 12 0	5 4 0	6 10 0	5 6 0[2]	4 16 0
1765	8 0 0	4 0 0	11 8 0	7 12 0	7 10 0	6 18 0	6 6 0
1766	8 0 0	4 0 0	10 16 0	7 4 0	7 10 0	7 10 0	6 10 0
1767	7 0 0	3 10 0	10 10 0	6 8 0	7 4 0	6 6 0	5 14 0
1768	5 16 0	3 0 0	8 0 0	4 0 0	5 2 0	4 14 0	4 4 0
1769	6 0 0	3 0 0	9 12 0	4 16 0	6 6 0	5 11 0	4 16 0
1770	7 4 0	4 0 0	9 12 0	4 16 0	7 10 0	6 3 0	5 8 0
1771	8 8 0	4 0 0	9 6 0	6 0 0	8 0 0	7 4 0	6 0 0
1772	8 14 0	4 4 0	8 16 0	5 8 0	8 8 0	7 1 0	6 0 0
1773	9 0 0	5 0 0	9 16 0	5 8 0	8 0 0	6 15 0	6 0 0
1774	9 0 0	4 0 0	9 12 0	6 0 0	8 0 0	6 9 0	6 8 0
1775	7 10 0	4 10 0	8 0 0	4 16 0	6 12 0	4 16 0	4 12 0
1776	6 0 0	3 4 0	8 8 0	5 8 0	5 8 0	4 12 8	3 13 0
1777	6 12 0	4 4 0	8 8 0	4 16 0		5 11 0	5 2 0
1778	6 6 0	3 12 0	9 4 0	6 0 0		5 14 0	5 0 0
1779	6 0 0	3 0 0	7 4 0	6 0 0		4 7 0	4 4 0
1780	6 6 0	3 12 0	8 0 0	6 0 0		6 3 0	5 16 0

1 The boll of oats was stated to be of 8 Winchester bushels.

2 Different values are given in a note of the fiars for Berwick in the Marchmont Granary Book, 1753-67 (SRO, GD 1/651/66); £3.10.0 for Lammermuir oats in 1760 and £5.0.0 for Merse oats in 1764.

Table 3.4 *(cont.)*

Crop year	Bute L. s. d.			Clackmannan L. s. d.			Dumfries L. s. d.			Edinburgh L. s. d.			Elgin L. s. d.			Fife L. s. d.		
1725										5	13	4				4	0	0
1726										5	6	8				4	10	0
1727										5	10	0				4	13	4
1728										6	16	0				5	6	8
1729										6	0	0				5	0	0
1730										4	12	0				4	10	0
1731										5	2	0				4	10	0
1732										4	9	0				4	0	0
1733										5	0	0				4	0	0
1734										5	0	0				4	3	4
1735										5	16	0				4	13	4
1736										5	12	0				5	0	0
1737										5	6	0				4	8	0
1738										4	2	0				3	6	8
1739										5	12	0				4	13	4
1740										8	14	0				7	13	4
1741										5	12	0						
1742										4	10	0				4	0	0
1743										3	10	0				3	12	0
1744										5	12	0				4	12	0
1745										6	12	0				5	10	0
1746										5	12	0				5	3	4
1747										4	12	0				4	12	0
1748										5	8	0				4	13	4
1749										5	8	0				4	12	0
1750										5	12	0				4	18	0
1751										7	0	0				5	13	4
1752										7	4	0				6	8	0
1753										6	6	0				5	18	0
1754										5	8	0				4	13	4
1755										6	12	0				5	8	0
1756	10	16	0	7	0	0	16	0	0	9	0	0				6	12	0
1757	9	6	0	7	4	0	16	16	0	7	4	0	7	10	0	6	13	4
1758	6	12	0	5	5	0	11	0	0	5	4	0	4	10	0	4	15	0
1759	6	12	0	4	12	0	9	12	0	4	16	0	4	10	0	4	8	0
1760	7	10	0	4	16	0	9	12	0	5	0	0	4	6	8	4	6	0
1761	8	8	0	5	8	0	12	0	0	5	8	0				4	13	4
1762	10	4	0	7	12	0	22	0	0	9	0	0				7	4	0
1763	8	8	0	6	13	4	14	8	0	6	6	0				5	16	8
1764	9	0	0	7	0	0	14	8	0	7	6	0	6	0	0	6	12	0
1765	11	8	0	8	0	0	21	12	0	8	14	0	9	0	0	8	6	8
1766	10	16	0	8	8	0	18	0	0	8	11	0	8	10	0	7	13	4
1767	9	18	0	8	0	0	16	16	0	8	8	0	7	0	0	7	10	0
1768	9	6	0	6	6	0	14	8	0	6	0	0	6	0	0	5	6	8
1769	10	10	0	7	4	0	16	16	0	6	18	0	6	0	0	5	18	0
1770	10	16	0	7	4	0	18	0	0	7	4	0	7	4	0	5	12	0
1771	10	16	0	8	8	0	20	16	0	8	16	0	8	10	0	7	0	0
1772	10	16	0	7	16	0	21	0	0	8	14	0	9	0	0	6	13	4
1773	10	16	0	7	16	0	19	4	0	8	8	0	9	0	0	7	0	0
1774	9	18	0	8	2	0	19	4	0	8	2	0	9	0	0	6	17	0
1775	8	14	0	6	12	0	16	0	0	6	0	0	7	10	0	5	16	0
1776	8	8	0	6	6	0	14	8	0	6	0	0	6	0	0	5	6	0
1777										6	6	0				5	8	0
1778										6	12	0				5	12	0
1779										5	8	0				5	0	0
1780										6	12	0				5	12	0

Table 3.4 *(cont.)*

Crop year	Forfar L. s. d.	Haddington L. s. d.	Inverness L. s. d.	Kincardine L. s. d.	Kinross L. s. d.	Kirkcudbright L. s. d.
1725		5 16 0				
1726		5 8 0				
1727		5 14 0				
1728		7 4 0				
1729		6 10 0				
1730		4 16 0				
1731		4 14 0				
1732		4 4 0				
1733		5 2 0				
1734		5 0 0				
1735		6 0 0				
1736		5 16 0				
1737		5 0 0				
1738		4 0 0				
1739		5 18 0				
1740		9 0 0				
1741		6 0 0				
1742		4 12 0				
1743		4 0 0				
1744		6 8 0				
1745		6 18 0				
1746		5 8 0				
1747		4 16 0				
1748		5 6 0				
1749		5 10 0				
1750		5 10 0				
1751		7 4 0				
1752		7 10 0				
1753		7 2 0				
1754		5 6 0				
1755		6 12 0				
1756	6 18 0	9 0 0	6 6 6	7 10 0		10 0 0
1757	6 10 0	8 2 0	6 19 10	7 0 0		12 0 0
1758	5 8 0	5 2 0	4 13 4	5 10 0		6 12 0
1759	4 18 0	4 15 3	4 13 4	5 6 8		5 12 0
1760	4 10 0	4 16 0	4 13 4	4 0 0		6 0 0
1761	4 14 0	5 3 0	4 13 4	4 16 0		
1762	7 10 0	9 8 9	8 0 0	8 0 0		12 12 0
1763	6 10 0	6 10 0	6 0 0	6 0 0	5 8 0	10 4 0
1764	7 6 0[1]	7 10 9	7 4 0	8 0 0	6 6 0	9 0 0
1765	9 0 0	9 0 3	8 0 0	9 12 0	8 0 0	14 8 0
1766	8 10 0	8 15 6	8 0 0	8 0 0	7 10 0	10 0 0
1767	8 0 0	8 10 0	6 13 4	8 0 0	7 12 0	11 8 0
1768	6 0 0	6 8 3	6 0 0	6 0 0	5 6 8	8 8 0
1769	6 10 0	7 4 0	6 6 0	6 12 0	6 0 0	10 4 0
1770	6 12 0	7 4 3	7 4 0	7 4 0	6 0 0	10 16 0
1771	7 10 0	8 11 6	9 0 0	9 0 0	7 10 0	12 12 0
1772	7 10 0	8 18 3	9 0 0	9 12 0	6 18 0	12 0 0
1773	7 16 0	8 14 9	7 4 0	8 0 0	6 10 0	12 0 0
1774	8 0 0	8 13 0	8 0 0	9 0 0	6 12 0	12 0 0
1775	7 4 0	6 9 3	8 0 0	8 0 0	6 0 0	10 16 0
1776	5 8 0	6 5 9	6 0 0	6 0 0	5 8 0	8 14 0
1777		7 4 9				
1778		7 5 3				
1779	5 14 0	5 16 3				
1780	5 14 0	7 6 0				

1 Explicitly described as white oats in this year by SRO, GD 45/12/86.

Table 3.4 *(cont.)*

Crop year	Lanark L. s. d.	Linlithgow Great oats L. s. d.	Linlithgow Small oats L. s. d.	Nairn L. s. d.	Perth L. s. d.	Renfrew L. s. d.
1725	5 0 0	5 6 8	4 13 4		4 13 4	
1726	4 15 0	5 0 0	4 10 0		4 16 8	
1727	5 10 0	5 3 4	4 15 0		5 0 0	
1728	6 0 0	6 6 8	5 16 8		5 13 4	
1729	5 0 0	5 4 0	4 10 0		5 6 8	
1730	3 13 4	4 10 0	3 18 0		4 6 8	
1731	3 16 0	4 10 0	4 0 0		4 13 4	
1732	3 12 0	3 18 0	3 10 0		4 6 8	
1733	4 0 0	4 10 0	4 0 0		4 10 0	
1734	4 10 0	4 19 0	4 11 0		4 13 4	
1735	5 6 8	5 11 0	5 3 0		4 16 8	
1736	5 6 0	5 6 8	4 14 6		5 3 4	
1737	4 10 0	5 4 0	4 16 0		4 16 8	
1738	3 15 0	4 0 0	3 15 0		4 0 0	
1739	5 6 0	5 4 0	4 16 0		5 10 0	
1740	8 0 0	8 10 0	8 0 0		7 5 0	
1741	5 0 0	5 8 0	4 15 0		4 13 4	
1742	4 0 0	4 0 0	3 10 0		4 10 0	
1743	3 5 0	3 16 6	3 5 8		4 0 0	
1744	4 7 0	4 13 4	4 0 0		5 0 0	
1745	6 13 5	6 16 0	6 0 0		6 0 0	
1746	5 0 0	5 0 0	4 12 0		5 0 0	
1747	4 0 0	4 8 0	4 0 0		4 10 0	
1748	4 16 0	4 14 0	4 4 0		4 13 4	
1749	4 18 0	4 16 0	4 0 0		4 16 0	
1750	5 12 0	5 10 0	4 18 0		5 0 0	
1751	6 10 0	6 10 0	6 0 0		6 0 0	
1752	6 6 0	7 0 0	6 0 0		6 0 0	
1753	6 0 0	6 12 0	6 0 0		5 0 0	
1754	5 0 0	5 6 0	4 18 0		5 0 0	
1755	4 16 0	6 6 0	5 18 0		5 10 0	
1756	7 10 0	8 8 0	7 10 0	8 0 0	7 0 0	8 10 0
1757	7 0 0	7 10 0	6 14 0	8 0 0	6 10 0	8 0 0
1758	4 16 0	5 2 0	4 6 0	5 0 0	5 0 0	5 0 0
1759	4 12 0	4 16 0	4 0 0	4 16 0[1]	4 6 0	5 8 0
1760	4 5 0	4 14 0	4 0 0	4 10 0	4 5 0	5 4 0
1761		5 12 0	4 16 0	5 0 0	5 10 0	6 12 0
1762	8 0 0	8 8 0	7 4 0	8 0 0[1]	7 0 0	8 14 0
1763	6 0 0	6 6 0	5 16 0	6 0 0	5 16 0	6 12 0
1764	7 12 0	7 4 0	6 6 0	6 12 0[1]	7 0 0	6 18 0
1765	8 0 0	8 10 0	8 0 0	8 16 0[1]	8 0 0	9 4 0
1766	8 10 0	9 0 0	8 8 0	8 10 0[1]	7 15 0	8 0 0
1767	9 0 0	8 8 0	7 10 0	8 10 0	7 0 0	8 2 6
1768	6 6 0	6 0 0	5 8 0	5 12 0[1]	6 0 0	6 12 0
1769	7 10 0	7 4 0	6 4 0	6 0 0[1]	6 0 0	8 2 0
1770	7 4 0	7 0 0	6 0 0	7 4 0	6 6 0	8 14 0
1771	8 8 0	8 2 0	7 0 0	9 0 0	7 16 0	8 7 8
1772	7 16 0	8 2 0	7 4 0	9 6 0	7 10 0	8 2 0
1773	8 8 0	8 2 0	7 4 0	8 2 0	8 2 0	8 8 0
1774	8 8 0	7 16 0	6 6 0	8 8 0	7 4 0	7 9 4
1775	6 0 0	6 4 0	5 6 0	7 12 0	6 6 0	6 14 0
1776	6 6 0	6 0 0	5 2 0	6 6 0	5 16 0	7 10 0
1777		6 0 0	5 2 0		6 0 0	
1778		6 10 0	5 2 0		6 0 0	
1779		5 11 0	5 5 0		5 8 0	
1780		6 0 0	5 5 0		6 6 0	

1 According to Bald (*The Farmer and Corn Dealers' Assistant*, Edinburgh, 1780, p. 413) these prices 'are not in the Fiars, but are filled up in the same proportion to other Grains as they bear in those years when mentioned in the Fiars'.

Table 3.4 *(cont.)*

Crop year	Roxburgh	Stirling White carse oats	Stirling White dryfield oats	Stirling Brucked oats	Stirling Grey oats	Wigtown
	L. s. d.	L. s. d.	L. s. d.	L. s. d.	L. s. d.	L. s. d.
1725		5 10 0	5 0 0	3 13 4	2 13 4	
1726		5 0 0	4 0 0	4 0 0	2 10 0	
1727		6 0 0	5 6 8	4 0 0	3 6 8	
1728		6 6 8	6 0 0	5 16 8	3 6 8	
1729		5 0 0	4 13 4	4 0 0	2 10 0	
1730		4 10 0	4 5 0	3 13 4	2 8 0	
1731		4 13 4	4 6 8	3 15 0	2 8 0	
1732		4 10 0	4 6 8	3 10 0	2 4 0	
1733		4 13 4	4 10 0	4 0 0	2 10 0	
1734		5 6 8	5 0 0	4 6 8	2 13 4	
1735		5 13 4	5 6 8	4 10 0	2 13 4	
1736		5 10 0	5 5 0	4 13 4	2 10 0	
1737		5 10 0	5 0 0	4 0 0	2 10 0	
1738		4 10 0	4 5 0	4 0 0	2 8 0	
1739		5 13 4	5 13 4	4 13 4	2 16 8	
1740		8 10 0	8 10 0	7 0 0	4 5 0	
1741		5 6 0	5 0 0	4 10 0	2 10 0	
1742		4 8 0	4 4 0	4 0 0	2 6 0	
1743		3 6 0	3 3 0	3 0 0	1 16 0	
1744		5 6 8	4 13 4	4 6 8	2 13 4	
1745		6 10 0	6 5 0	6 0 0	3 10 0	
1746		5 6 0	5 0 0	4 13 4	3 0 0	
1747		4 15 0	4 10 0	3 15 0	2 8 0	
1748		4 13 8	4 6 8	4 0 0	2 8 0	
1749		5 4 0	4 15 0	4 0 0	2 4 0	
1750		6 0 0	5 10 0	4 12 0	2 14 0	
1751		5 10 0	5 10 0	4 2 6	2 15 0	
1752		7 0 0	6 10 0	6 0 0	4 0 0	
1753		6 0 0	5 15 0	5 0 0	3 0 0	
1754		5 10 0	5 3 4	4 13 4	2 13 4	
1755		6 5 0	6 5 0	5 15 0	3 12 0	
1756	9 0 0	7 12 0	7 12 0	6 12 0	4 0 0	12 0 0
1757	9 6 0	6 16 0	6 16 0	6 0 0	3 10 0	11 0 0
1758	5 2 0	5 13 0	4 12 0	4 0 0	2 12 0	8 0 0
1759	4 16 0	4 10 0	4 10 0	4 0 0	2 5 0	5 10 0
1760	4 10 0	4 14 0	4 14 0	4 0 0	2 0 0	6 0 0
1761	4 16 0	5 10 0	5 5 0	4 10 0	2 8 0	7 0 0
1762	10 16 0	7 5 0	7 0 0	6 0 0	3 0 0	12 0 0
1763	6 0 0	6 5 0	6 0 0	5 0 0	2 10 0	11 10 0
1764	8 0 0	7 0 0	6 16 0	6 0 0	3 0 0	9 0 0
1765	9 12 0	7 16 0	7 16 0	7 0 0	3 10 0	10 0 0
1766	9 12 0	7 10 0	7 0 0	6 0 0	3 0 0	10 0 0
1767	8 8 0	8 0 0	7 14 0	6 14 0	4 10 0	10 16 0
1768	6 0 0	6 6 0	6 0 0	5 8 0	4 0 0	9 12 0
1769	7 4 0	7 10 0	7 4 0	6 12 0	4 0 0	10 16 0
1770	6 12 0	7 4 0	7 0 0	6 10 0	4 0 0	12 0 0
1771	9 0 0	7 16 0	7 4 0	6 12 0	4 4 0	12 0 0
1772	9 12 0	7 10 0	7 4 0	6 18 0	4 16 0	12 12 0
1773	9 0 0	8 8 0	8 0 0	7 0 0	6 0 0	13 4 0
1774	9 0 0	8 0 0[1]	7 10 0	7 0 0	4 16 0	12 0 0
1775	6 12 0	6 0 0	5 14 0	4 10 0	9 10 0	12 0 0
1776	6 0 0	6 6 0[1]	6 0 0	5 8 0	4 10 0	10 4 0
1777		6 12 0[1]	6 6 0	6 0 0	4 10 0	
1778		6 6 0				
1779		5 8 0				
1780		6 0 0				

1 Different values for these years are given in the Book for the Quarterly Fyars for Stirling Shire (SRO, GD 67/28/2). Those struck at the February courts were: crop 1774, £8.8.0; crop 1776, £6.0.0; and crop 1777, £6.0.0.

Table 3.5 *Oatmeal: county fiars, 1625–1674*

Crop year	Aberdeen Mercat oatmeal[1] L. s. d.	White oatmeal[1] L. s. d.	Ayr L. s. d.	Edinburgh L. s. d.	Fife L. s. d.
1625					4 6 8
1626					4 6 8
1627					4 6 8
1628	*6 13 4*	*8 0 0*			8 0 0
1629	*5 6 8*	*6 13 4*			7 0 0
1630	*4 6 8*	*5 6 8*			8 0 0
1631	*3 0 0*	*4 0 0*			4 6 8
1632	*5 0 0*	*6 13 4*			4 0 0
1633					6 13 4
1634					7 0 0
1635				8 6 8	8 6 8
1636				8 6 8	5 6 8
1637				6 13 4	9 0 0
1638					4 6 8
1639				4 5 4	3 13 4
1640				4 5 4	5 13 4
1641					7 6 8
1642				7 0 0	7 13 4
1643				6 13 4	5 0 0
1644				6 13 4	5 0 0
1645				5 6 8	4 0 0
1646				3 6 8	4 6 8
1647				7 6 8	4 0 0
1648				10 0 0	5 0 0
1649	*7 0 0*	*8 0 0*		11 0 0	10 0 0
1650	*6 13 4*	*8 0 0*		11 0 0	9 13 4
1651	*6 0 0*	*8 0 0*		11 0 0	9 13 4
1652	*6 6 8*	*7 0 0*		8 0 0	10 0 0
1653				3 6 8	4 0 0
1654				3 6 8	4 3 4
1655	*4 0 0*	*4 13 4*		7 10 0	3 6 8
1656	*3 0 0*	*4 0 0*		5 0 0	4 0 0
1657	4 13 4	3 6 8		5 0 0	4 0 0
1658			5 6 8		5 6 8
1659			5 6 8	7 0 0	5 6 8
1660			8 0 0	7 0 0	5 6 8
1661			9 0 0	6 6 8	5 0 0
1662			5 6 0		3 13 4
1663			5 1 4	5 0 0	4 0 0
1664			3 6 8	4 0 0	2 10 0
1665	*3 0 0*	*4 0 0*	5 0 0	4 9 0	2 13 4
1666	*4 0 0*	*5 0 0*	4 5 8	4 16 0	
1667	*4 6 8*	*5 6 8*	4 13 4	4 3 4	
1668	*4 0 0*	*4 0 0*	4 0 0	4 0 0	3 0 0
1669	*4 0 0*	*4 3 4*	3 10 0	4 8 0	3 0 0
1670	*4 3 4*	*5 0 0*	5 6 8	5 6 8	
1671			5 16 8	6 13 4	
1672			4 10 0	5 6 8	3 13 4
1673			5 13 4	5 0 0	3 6 8
1674			9 6 8	9 6 8	6 13 4

1 Aberdeen 'ferme oatmeal' was usually, and from 1670 was always, the same price as 'mercat' oatmeal. Figures in italics are for fiars which were struck between July and November rather than, as was usual, in or around February.

Table 3.5 *(cont.)*

Crop year	Forfar L. s. d.			Glasgow Commissary L. s. d.			Linlithgow L. s. d.			Perth L. s. d.			Roxburgh L. s. d.		
1625															
1626															
1627															
1628															
1629															
1630										9	0	0			
1631										4	13	4			
1632										6	13	4			
1633										8	0	0	11	0	0
1634										8	13	4	12	0	0
1635										9	0	0[2]	14	0	0
1636										8	0	0	12	10	0
1637										7	0	0	10	0	0
1638										4	13	4	8	0	0
1639										4	0	0	7	0	0
1640										5	6	8	11	10	0
1641										7	0	0	11	0	0
1642										6	13	4	8	10	0
1643										6	0	0			
1644										5	6	8	7	10	0
1645										6	0	0	7	13	4
1646										6	6	8	9	10	0
1647										7	6	8	12	0	0
1648										13	6	8	18	0	0
1649	8	0	0							9	0	0	15	0	0
1650	8	0	0							10	13	4	18	0	0
1651	10	0	0							10	13	4	13	6	8
1652	7	6	8							10	0	0	10	0	0
1653	3	6	8							3	6	8	5	10	0
1654	2	10	0				2	13	4	3	0	0	4	4	0
1655	2	13	4				4	0	0	4	6	8	2	10	0
1656	*3*	*6*	*8*[1]							4	0	0	8	10	0
1657	3	13	4				4	13	4	4	0	0	8	6	8
1658	4	13	4				6	0	0	4	6	8	10	13	4
1659	6	0	0							7	6	8	11	10	0
1660	5	0	0				6	16	8	6	13	4	10	0	0
1661	5	0	0				6	0	0[2]	5	6	8	10	0	0
1662	4	0	0				5	0	0	4	13	4	6	10	0
1663	3	6	8				4	13	4[2]	4	0	0	7	0	0
1664	2	13	4	3	3	4	3	6	8	3	0	0	6	0	0
1665	2	10	0	5	13	4	4	0	0	3	6	8			
1666	4	0	0	5	0	0	4	0	8[2]	3	13	4			
1667	4	3	4	5	0	0	4	0	0	4	0	0			
1668	3	13	4	4	6	8	4	0	0	4	0	0			
1669	3	13	4	3	6	8	3	13	4	4	0	0[2]			
1670				6	5	0	5	6	8	5	0	0			
1671				6	0	0	5	16	8	5	0	0			
1672				4	10	0	4	10	0	4	0	0			
1673				5	16	8	4	17	0	4	0	0			
1674				9	0	0	8	10	0	6	13	4			

1 In 1656 no Candlemas fiar was struck. That from the Lammas court has been entered.

2 Flinn (*Scottish Population History*, 1977) reports different values for oatmeal in Linlithgow (1661 at £6.13.4, 1663 at £5.13.4, and 1666 at £4.8.0) and in Perth (1635 at £7.0.0 and 1669 at £3.13.4).

Table 3.6 *Oatmeal: county fiars, 1675–1724*

	Aberdeen		Ayr	Berwick	Edinburgh	Fife
Crop year	Mercat oatmeal [1] L. s. d.	White oatmeal [1] L. s. d.	L. s. d.	L. s. d.	L. s. d.	L. s. d.
1675			8 10 0		8 0 0	7 0 0
1676	*3 3 8*	*4 3 8*	3 13 4		4 0 0	3 3 4
1677	*3 0 0*	*3 16 8*	3 6 8		4 0 0	2 18 0
1678	*2 13 4*	*3 10 0*	3 12 0		4 0 0	2 8 0
1679	*2 13 4*	*4 0 0*	6 0 0		4 13 4	2 10 0
1680	2 13 4	3 6 8	5 6 8		4 16 0	3 3 4 [3]
1681	3 10 0	4 3 4	6 0 0		5 6 8	4 13 4
1682	*5 6 8*	*6 6 8*	4 13 0		5 12 0	4 3 4
1683			5 6 8		4 13 4	3 3 4
1684			4 3 4		4 8 0	4 0 0
1685			4 6 8		4 6 8	3 0 0
1686			6 0 0		4 5 0	3 0 0
1687			6 10 0		4 9 0	3 6 8
1688					5 0 0	4 0 0
1689			6 13 4	5 16 0	5 18 0	4 13 4
1690	5 6 8	6 6 8	6 10 0	6 0 0	6 16 0	6 0 0
1691	3 6 8	4 3 4	4 0 0	4 0 0	4 8 0	3 3 4
1692	4 0 0	4 6 8	4 16 8	4 6 0	4 3 4	3 3 4
1693	3 6 8	4 13 4	6 0 0	4 16 0	4 16 0	3 3 4
1694	4 0 0	4 13 4	6 6 8	5 12 0	5 0 0	3 10 0
1695	5 6 8	6 13 4	7 0 0 [3]	7 10 0	7 15 0	7 0 0
1696	6 0 0	8 0 0	9 0 0	10 0 0	11 12 0	8 6 8 [2]
1697	6 13 4	8 0 0	6 0 0 [3]	6 8 0	7 9 8	5 13 4
1698	10 13 4	12 0 0	10 0 0	12 0 0	13 4 0	8 6 8
1699	8 0 0	9 0 0	8 0 0	8 16 0	10 0 0	7 13 4
1700	5 6 8	6 13 4	6 13 4	4 16 0 [3]	6 13 4	4 13 4
1701	3 13 4	4 13 4	4 10 0	3 18 0	4 16 0	3 12 0
1702	4 0 0	4 13 4	5 6 8	4 16 0	7 0 0	4 10 0
1703	3 13 4	4 6 8	4 13 4	4 18 0	6 5 0	4 6 8
1704	4 0 0	4 13 4	4 13 4	4 6 8 [3]	6 0 0	3 10 0
1705	3 10 0	4 6 8	4 13 4	4 0 0	5 6 8	3 6 8
1706	2 13 4	4 0 0	4 13 4	2 10 0	4 0 0	2 10 0
1707	3 6 8	4 3 4	4 6 8	3 12 0 [3]	4 10 0	2 10 0
1708	4 13 4	5 6 8	6 6 8	6 0 0	7 4 0	5 0 0
1709	5 0 0	5 13 4	7 0 0	7 12 0	8 10 2	6 0 0
1710	5 0 0	5 13 4	6 0 0	5 17 0 [3]	7 4 0	
1711	3 6 8	4 0 0	4 13 4	5 0 0	6 0 0	4 0 0
1712	3 0 0	4 0 0	4 6 8	4 4 0	5 6 8	3 10 0
1713	4 0 0	4 13 4	4 10 0	4 12 0	6 0 0	3 13 4 [3]
1714	4 6 8	5 0 0	6 6 8	5 8 0	6 0 0	5 6 8
1715	3 6 8	4 13 4	5 3 4	4 12 0	6 0 0	4 10 0
1716	3 6 8	4 6 8	5 0 0	4 10 0	5 0 0	3 13 4
1717	4 3 4	5 0 0	5 0 0	5 0 0	6 0 0	4 0 0
1718	4 3 4	4 13 4	5 6 8	5 0 0	6 0 0	4 16 8
1719	4 6 8	5 0 0	5 3 4	5 8 0	6 8 0	5 0 0
1720	3 10 0	4 6 8	5 0 0	4 8 0	6 0 0	4 3 4
1721	3 10 0	4 10 0	4 16 8	4 10 0 [3]	6 0 0	4 6 8
1722	5 0 0	5 13 4	6 0 0	5 8 0	6 8 0	5 13 4
1723	5 10 0	6 0 0	5 6 8	5 10 0	6 18 0	6 6 8
1724	3 6 8	4 10 0	4 10 0	4 16 0	5 6 8	4 3 4

1 Figures in italics are for fiars which were struck between July and November rather than, as was usual, in or around February.

2 From this date the fiars refer to the price of oatmeal by both weight and measure. This series continues to refer to the price according to the boll by measure.

3 Flinn (*Scottish Population History*, 1977) reports different values for oatmeal in Ayr (1695 at £7.3.4 and 1697 at £6.3.4), Berwick (1700 at £4.4.0, 1704 at £4.6.0, 1707 at £4.4.0, 1710 at £5.8.0 and 1721 at £6.0.0) and in Fife (1680 at £3.0.0 and 1713 at £3.13.4).

Table 3.6 *(cont.)*

Crop year	Glasgow Commissary L. s. d.	Kincardine L. s. d.	Lanark [1] L. s. d.	Linlithgow L. s. d.	Perth L. s. d.	Roxburgh L. s. d.	Stirling L. s. d.
1675	7 16 8	5 0 0		7 6 8	6 13 4		
1676	3 16 8	3 13 4		3 6 8	3 6 8		
1677	3 13 4	3 0 0		3 6 8	3 0 0		
1678	3 13 4	3 0 0		3 0 0	3 0 0		
1679	5 14 8	3 6 8		4 16 8	3 6 8		
1680	5 0 0	4 0 0		4 10 0	3 13 4		
1681	6 6 8	4 3 4		5 6 8	5 6 8		
1682	5 13 4	4 13 4		5 6 8	4 13 4	8 13 4	5 13 4
1683	5 16 8	4 0 0		4 0 0	4 0 0	6 13 4	4 13 4
1684	4 6 8	4 0 0		4 10 0	3 13 4	8 8 0	4 3 4
1685	4 8 0	3 13 4		4 6 8	3 6 8	7 0 0	4 6 8
1686	5 3 4	3 13 4		4 13 4	3 13 4	7 5 0	5 16 8
1687	5 4 4			5 0 0	4 0 0	7 0 0	5 0 0
1688	5 6 8			5 0 0	4 0 0	8 0 0	5 0 0
1689	6 8 0			5 13 4	5 6 8	10 0 0	6 6 8
1690	7 0 0			6 6 8	6 13 4	12 0 0	
1691	4 18 4		4 0 0	4 0 0	4 0 0	6 8 0	4 10 0
1692	4 10 0		4 6 8	4 0 0	3 6 8	7 0 0	
1693	5 3 4		5 6 8	4 10 0	3 6 8	8 10 0	4 13 4
1694	7 0 0 [2]		5 13 4	5 6 8	4 0 0	10 0 0	5 13 4
1695	8 7 4		8 0 0	8 0 0	5 6 8	14 10 0	8 3 4
1696	9 13 4		10 13 4	9 0 0	7 10 0	16 0 0	8 6 8
1697	6 13 4 [2]			6 0 0	5 6 8	12 0 0	6 6 8
1698	11 0 0			12 0 0	9 0 0	20 0 0	9 13 4
1699	9 6 0			9 0 0	9 0 0	15 0 0	8 13 4
1700	6 2 4		6 0 0	5 12 0	5 0 0	9 0 0	5 13 4
1701	5 0 0		4 10 0	4 16 8	4 0 0	7 10 0	4 16 8
1702	5 15 0		5 6 8	6 13 4	5 6 8	10 0 0	5 13 4
1703	5 12 8		5 10 0	5 12 0	4 6 8 [3]	9 12 0	5 13 4
1704	5 0 0			5 6 8	3 13 4	10 0 0	5 3 4
1705	4 10 0			4 10 0	3 13 4	8 0 0	4 16 8
1706	3 13 4			3 6 8	2 13 4	5 12 0	3 13 4
1707	4 11 4			3 10 0	3 3 4	6 13 4	4 5 0
1708	7 0 0			5 10 0	5 0 0	10 10 0	6 0 0
1709	8 0 0			8 0 0	6 6 8	13 10 0	7 0 0
1710	7 1 4			7 4 0	5 6 8	11 10 0	6 6 8
1711	4 17 8		4 5 0	5 0 0	3 13 4	8 10 0	4 3 4
1712	4 16 0			5 0 0	3 13 4	8 0 0	4 13 4
1713	5 5 0		4 15 0	5 6 8	4 3 4	9 0 0	5 0 0
1714	6 12 8		6 0 0	6 0 0	5 10 0	9 12 0	6 13 4
1715	5 19 8		5 0 0	6 0 0	5 0 0	9 0 0	5 13 4
1716	5 1 4		4 10 0	5 0 0	4 3 4	8 0 0	4 10 0
1717	5 8 4		5 5 0	5 8 0	4 0 0	9 0 0	5 6 8
1718	5 13 4			5 10 0	4 13 4	9 0 0	5 13 4
1719	5 16 5		5 6 8	5 16 0	5 0 0	11 0 0	5 13 4
1720	5 5 9		4 10 0	4 0 0	4 0 0	9 0 0	4 10 0
1721	5 12 0		5 0 0	5 6 8	4 0 0	9 0 0	5 0 0
1722	6 15 8		6 5 0	6 10 0	5 16 8	10 10 0	6 10 0
1723	5 15 4		6 5 0 [4]	6 6 8	6 6 8		6 0 0
1724	4 11 6		4 7 6	4 16 0	4 3 4		4 10 0

1 Lanark prices are for first or best oatmeal. Prices for second oatmeal are published in Flinn, *Scottish Population History*, 1977.

2 Values of £6.13.4 in 1694 and £10.13.4 in 1697 are given in the Accounts of the Ordinary Revenue of the College of Glasgow, 1664-1774 (Glasgow University Archive, 26652 and 26670).

3 From this date the fiars refer to the price of oatmeal by weight.

4 From this date the boll is explicitly stated to be 'according to weight'.

Table 3.7 *Oatmeal: county fiars, 1725–1780*

Crop year	Aberdeen		Ayr	Banff	Berwick	Bute
	Mercat oatmeal L. s. d.	White oatmeal L. s. d.	L. s. d.	L. s. d.	L. s. d.	L. s. d.
1725	4 16 8	5 8 8	6 10 0		5 4 0	
1726	4 6 8	5 6 8	6 10 0		4 12 0	
1727	4 13 4	5 6 8	6 0 0		5 2 0	
1728	5 13 4	6 0 0	7 10 0		5 16 0	
1729	4 13 4	5 13 4	6 0 0		5 12 0	
1730	4 3 4	5 0 0	4 0 0		4 0 0	
1731	4 13 4	5 6 8	5 0 0		4 4 0	
1732	3 6 8	4 10 0	4 10 0		3 10 0	
1733	4 6 8	5 0 0	5 12 0		4 16 0	
1734	4 13 4	5 6 8	5 16 0		4 16 0	
1735	5 6 8	6 0 0	6 13 0		5 4 0	
1736	4 13 4	5 6 8	6 4 0		5 2 0	
1737	4 13 4	5 6 8	5 6 8		5 4 0	
1738	3 13 4	4 3 4	5 6 0		4 0 0	
1739	5 6 8	6 0 0	6 13 0		5 12 0	
1740	7 0 0	8 0 0	10 0 0[2]		9 2 0	
1741	5 6 8	6 0 0[1]	6 0 0		5 0 0	
1742	4 0 0	4 16 8	4 10 0		4 4 0	
1743	3 4 0	3 18 0	3 12 0		3 6 0	
1744	5 10 0	6 6 8	6 13 4[2]		5 12 0[3]	
1745	7 10 0	6 13 4	9 0 0		6 8 0	
1746	4 16 0	5 13 4	6 8 0		5 0 0	
1747	3 16 0	4 16 0	5 8 0		4 0 0	
1748	4 13 4	5 6 8	5 16 8[2]		5 0 0	
1749	4 3 4	5 0 0	6 0 0		4 16 0	
1750	4 13 4	5 6 8	6 6 8[2]		5 0 0	
1751	6 13 4	7 10 0	7 10 0		7 4 0[3]	
1752	6 13 4	7 10 0	7 4 0		6 18 0	
1753	5 10 0	6 6 0	8 0 0		6 0 0	
1754	4 13 4	5 6 8	6 12 0		4 16 0	
1755	6 6 8	7 0 0	7 12 0		6 0 0	
1756	8 0 0	9 0 0	10 8 0	8 6 6	8 8 0	10 16 0
1757	7 4 0	8 4 0	8 8 0	7 13 3	7 4 0[3]	9 6 0
1758	4 6 8	5 0 0	5 4 0[2]	4 16 0	4 8 0	6 12 0
1759	3 16 0	4 8 0	5 4 0	4 0 0	4 0 0	6 12 0
1760	4 0 0	4 13 4	6 3 0[2]	4 0 0	4 14 0	7 10 0
1761	4 10 0	5 6 8	7 4 0	5 0 0	4 16 0	8 8 0
1762	8 0 0	9 4 0	9 12 0	8 0 0	8 16 0	10 4 0
1763	5 10 0	6 8 0	7 4 0	6 0 0	5 16 0	8 8 0
1764	7 0 0	8 0 0	7 12 0	7 0 0	6 4 0	9 0 0
1765	8 8 0	9 10 0	10 16 0	8 14 0	8 0 0	11 8 0
1766	8 0 0	9 2 0	9 12 0	8 4 0	7 16 0[3]	10 16 0
1767	7 0 0	7 16 0	8 16 0	8 0 0	7 6 0[3]	9 18 0
1768	5 16 0	6 15 0	7 4 0	6 0 0	5 14 0	9 6 0
1769	6 0 0	7 0 0	9 0 0	6 12 0	6 3 0[3]	10 10 0
1770	7 10 0	8 12 0	9 4 0	8 0 0	6 18 0	10 16 0
1771	8 8 0[1]	9 12 0	9 12 0	8 8 0	7 16 0	10 16 0
1772	8 14 0	10 0 0	8 16 0[2]	8 14 0	8 0 0	10 16 0
1773	8 0 0	9 6 0	9 4 0	8 2 0	7 10 0	10 16 0
1774	8 14 0	10 0 0	8 8 0	8 14 0	7 8 0	9 18 0
1775	7 4 0	8 8 0	6 16 0	6 12 0	6 0 0	8 14 0
1776	5 6 8	6 4 0	7 4 0[2]	5 8 0	5 3 4	8 8 0
1777	6 16 0	7 16 0	8 0 0		6 0 0	
1778	6 6 0	7 4 0	8 0 0		6 0 0	
1779	5 14 0	6 15 0	6 12 0		4 13 0	
1780	6 12 0	7 10 0	8 0 0		6 9 0	

1 The boll of white meal was stated to weigh 9 stones from 1741; that of mercat meal 8 stones from 1771.

2 Flinn (*Scottish Population History*, 1977) reports different values for these dates but must be considered of doubtful veracity as both SRO, SC 6/85/20 and SRO, GD 109/3943 record the values as given here.

3 Flinn (*Ibid.*) reports these fiars prices as follows; 1744 at £6.2.0, 1751 at £7.0.0, 1757 at £8.8.0, 1766 at £10.8.0, 1767 at £9.15.0 and 1769 at £8.3.0.

Table 3.7 *(cont.)*

Crop year	Clackmannan L. s. d.	Dumfries L. s. d.	Dunbarton L. s. d.	Edinburgh L. s. d.	Elgin L. s. d.	Fife L. s. d.	Forfar L. s. d.
1725				6 13 4		5 0 0	
1726				6 0 0		5 0 0	
1727				6 8 0		5 4 8	
1728				7 8 0		5 16 0	
1729				6 12 0		5 14 8	
1730				5 4 0		5 0 0	
1731				5 14 0		5 0 0	
1732				5 0 0		4 10 0	
1733				6 0 0		4 10 0	
1734				6 0 0		4 14 0	
1735				6 12 0		5 6 8	
1736				6 8 0		5 10 0	
1737				6 6 0		4 6 0 [1]	
1738				4 18 0		4 6 0	
1739				6 12 0		5 10 0	
1740				10 4 0		9 5 0	
1741				6 8 0		5 2 0	
1742				5 0 0		4 6 0	
1743				4 10 0		4 4 0	
1744				7 0 0		5 18 0	
1745				7 12 0		6 16 0	
1746				6 6 0		5 12 0	
1747				5 4 0		5 0 0	
1748				6 0 0		4 16 8	
1749				6 8 0		5 10 0	
1750				6 8 0		5 10 0	
1751				8 4 0		6 18 0	
1752				8 0 0		7 8 0	
1753				7 4 0		6 12 0	
1754				6 0 0		5 8 0	
1755				7 4 0		6 6 0	
1756	8 12 0	19 4 0	10 0 0	10 0 0		8 8 0	
1757	8 0 0	21 12 0	8 16 0	8 4 0		7 8 0	7 4 0
1758	5 15 0	14 8 0	5 15 0	6 0 0		5 4 8	5 12 0
1759	5 8 0	12 16 0	5 12 0	5 4 0		4 18 0	5 2 0
1760	5 10 0	14 8 0	6 0 0	5 14 0		5 0 0	5 0 0
1761	6 0 0	16 0 0	7 0 0	6 6 0		5 8 0	5 6 0
1762	8 10 0	28 16 0	9 4 0	10 0 0		8 8 0	8 0 0
1763	7 10 0	21 12 0	7 7 0	7 0 0		6 8 0	6 12 0
1764	8 0 0	20 16 0	8 8 0	8 0 0	5 6 8	7 4 0	7 12 0
1765	9 12 0	28 16 0		9 12 0	8 0 0	9 0 0	9 18 0
1766	9 12 0	24 0 0	10 2 0	9 6 0	7 2 0	8 14 0 [1]	9 0 0
1767	9 6 0	20 16 0	9 0 0	9 4 0	6 5 0	8 12 0	8 8 0
1768	7 10 0	16 0 0	9 8 0	7 4 0	5 6 8	6 18 0	7 4 0
1769	8 0 0	20 16 0	9 6 0	8 8 0	5 6 8	7 6 0	7 0 0
1770	8 0 0	22 8 0	9 12 0	8 8 0	6 8 0	7 0 0	7 4 0
1771	9 6 0	26 8 0	9 12 0	10 0 0	8 10 0	8 8 0	8 8 0
1772	9 12 0	27 4 0	9 12 0	10 0 0	7 16 0	9 8 0	8 14 0
1773	9 12 0	26 8 0	9 8 0	9 0 0	7 10 0	9 0 0	8 14 0
1774	9 6 0	25 12 0	7 8 0	9 6 0	7 4 0	8 8 0	9 4 0
1775	7 10 0	25 12 0	7 16 0	7 4 0	6 8 0	7 0 0	8 0 0
1776	7 4 0	22 8 0	7 16 0	7 4 0	5 6 8	6 1 6	6 3 0
1777				7 4 0		6 8 0	
1778				7 12 0		6 12 0	
1779				6 0 0		5 10 0	6 0 0
1780				8 0 0		7 6 0	6 18 0

1 Flinn (*Scottish Population History*, 1977) reports the price for 1737 at £5.3.4 and for 1766 at £8.14.8.

Table 3.7 *(cont.)*

Crop year	Glasgow Commissary L. s. d.			Inverness L. s. d.			Kincardine L. s. d.			Kinross L. s. d.			Kirkcudbright L. s. d.			Lanark L. s. d.			Linlithgow L. s. d.		
1725	6	10	4													6	0	0	6	0	0
1726	6	0	0													5	12	0	5	10	0
1727	6	18	8													5	12	0	5	15	0
1728	7	13	2													7	6	8	7	0	0
1729	5	17	4													5	15	0	5	16	0
1730	5	2	8													4	6	8	5	0	0
1731	5	2	2													4	7	6	4	12	0
1732	5	0	0													3	17	6	4	11	0
1733	5	17	4													5	0	0	5	5	0
1734	6	8	0													5	15	0	5	13	0
1735	6	11	6													6	5	0	6	6	8
1736	6	8	0													6	2	0	6	1	0
1737	6	0	0													5	6	8	5	16	0
1738	6	0	0													4	10	0	4	18	0
1739	7	10	8													6	6	8	6	3	0
1740	12	0	0													11	0	0	10	0	0
1741	5	16	0													6	0	0	6	0	0
1742	5	0	0													4	10	0	4	10	0
1743	4	4	0													3	16	0	4	5	0
1744	6	5	0													5	10	0	6	0	0
1745	9	14	8													7	13	4	8	0	0
1746	6	12	0													6	0	0	5	18	0
1747	5	8	0													4	16	0	5	0	0
1748	6	0	0													5	0	0	5	8	0
1749	6	6	8													5	16	0	6	0	0
1750	7	0	0													6	6	0	6	6	0
1751	9	1	6													8	0	0	8	0	0
1752	8	13	4													8	0	0	8	0	0
1753	8	4	0													7	0	0	7	10	0
1754	6	12	0													5	16	0	5	19	0
1755	8	6	8													7	0	0	7	0	0
1756	11	0	0	6	6	6	7	10	0				15	0	0	9	0	0	9	12	0
1757	9	0	0	6	19	10	6	10	0				15	0	0	8	5	0	8	0	0
1758	6	0	0	4	13	4	5	4	0				11	0	0	5	10	0	5	16	0
1759	5	16	0	4	13	4	4	16	0				9	12	0	4	12	0	5	8	0
1760	6	4	0	4	13	4	4	0	0				11	0	0	5	0	0	5	6	0
1761	7	4	0	4	13	4	4	16	0							6	10	0	6	3	0
1762	10	8	0	8	0	0	7	4	0				17	2	0	9	0	0	9	0	0
1763	7	16	0	6	0	0	6	0	0	6	6	0	17	0	0	6	14	0	7	0	0
1764	9	4	0	7	4	0	7	1	0	7	10	0	16	16	0	7	16	0	8	0	0
1765	10	16	0	8	0	0	8	5	6	9	12	0	19	4	0	10	0	0	9	12	0
1766	10	16	0	8	0	0	8	0	0	8	16	0	18	0	0	9	6	0	9	12	0
1767	9	12	0	6	13	4	7	4	0	9	0	0	14	8	0	9	12	0	9	4	0
1768	8	4	0	6	0	0	6	0	0	7	4	0	10	16	0	6	18	0	7	4	0
1769	9	9	4	6	6	0	6	0	0	7	12	0	14	8	0	8	10	0	8	4	0
1770	9	8	0	7	4	0	6	12	0	7	12	0	14	8	0	8	12	0	8	4	0
1771	9	10	0	9	0	0	8	0	0	9	4	0	15	0	0	10	4	0	9	6	0
1772	10	13	4	9	0	0	9	0	0	9	12	0	16	16	0	9	6	0	9	12	0
1773	10	4	0	7	4	0	8	0	0	9	6	0	16	16	0	9	6	0	9	0	0
1774	9	4	0	8	0	0	8	15	6	9	0	0	16	16	0	9	0	0	9	3	0
1775	7	16	0	8	0	0	7	0	0	7	4	0	14	8	0	6	12	0	7	4	0
1776	8	8	0	6	0	0	5	8	0	7	4	0	12	0	0	7	4	0	6	18	0
1777																			7	4	0
1778																			7	10	0
1779																			6	8	0
1780																			8	0	0

Table 3.7 *(cont.)*

Crop year	Nairn L. s. d.	Perth L. s. d.	Renfrew L. s. d.	Roxburgh L. s. d.	Stirling L. s. d.	Wigtown L. s. d.
1725		4 10 0			6 0 0	
1726		4 13 4			5 6 8	
1727		5 0 0			6 6 8	
1728		5 13 4			7 0 0	
1729		5 6 8		11 0 0	5 10 0	
1730		4 10 0		9 10 0	5 0 0	
1731		4 16 8		9 0 0	4 13 4	
1732		4 10 0		7 16 0	4 13 4	
1733		4 13 4		10 0 0	5 0 0	
1734		5 0 0		9 0 0	5 13 4	
1735		5 0 0		11 0 0	6 0 0	
1736		5 0 0		11 10 0	5 13 4	
1737		4 16 8		10 0 0	5 10 0	
1738		4 10 0		8 0 0	5 6 8	
1739		5 10 0		10 0 0	6 6 0	
1740		8 0 0		18 10 0	10 0 0	
1741		5 0 0		9 10 0	5 13 4	
1742		4 13 4		8 0 0	4 10 0	
1743		4 2 0		7 0 0	3 16 0	
1744		5 10 0		10 10 0	6 0 0	
1745		6 0 0		12 12 0	8 0 0	
1746		5 5 0		9 12 0	6 0 0	
1747		4 16 0		8 0 0	5 0 0	
1748		5 0 0		8 10 0	5 6 8	
1749		5 3 4		9 12 0	6 0 0	
1750		5 0 0		9 12 0	6 6 0	
1751		6 10 0		15 0 0	7 10 0	
1752		6 10 0		13 12 0	8 0 0	
1753		5 5 0		10 16 0	6 13 4	
1754		4 16 0		8 16 0	6 0 0	
1755		5 16 0[1]		11 10 0	7 5 0	
1756	8 0 0	7 10 0	11 8 0	14 0 0	8 15 0	13 0 0
1757	8 0 0	7 0 0	9 0 0	13 4 0	7 16 0	12 0 0
1758	5 0 0	5 6 0	5 12 0	8 6 0	5 10 0	8 0 0
1759	4 16 0	4 16 0	5 15 6	7 16 0	5 0 0	7 4 0
1760	4 10 0	5 0 0	6 5 0	7 12 0	5 6 0	8 0 0
1761	5 0 0	5 10 0	7 8 0	9 0 0	6 5 0	9 0 0
1762	8 0 0	7 8 0	10 0 0	16 0 0	8 10 0	12 16 0
1763	6 0 0	6 10 0	7 12 0	10 10 0	7 5 0	12 0 0
1764	6 12 0	7 10 0	8 16 0	12 0 0	8 0 0	10 16 0
1765	8 16 0	8 8 0	11 4 0	16 0 0	9 12 0	12 0 0
1766	8 10 0	8 2 0	11 4 0	15 4 0	8 0 0	12 0 0
1767	8 10 0	7 8 0	10 6 0	13 12 0	9 0 0	12 0 0
1768	5 12 0	7 12 0	8 4 0	10 16 0	7 10 0	12 0 0
1769	6 0 0	6 12 0	9 12 0	12 0 0	8 0 0	12 0 0
1770	7 4 0	6 18 0	9 12 0	12 0 0	8 0 0	12 12 0
1771	9 0 0	9 0 0	10 6 8	14 8 0	9 0 0	14 8 0
1772	9 6 0	8 8 0	10 0 0	16 0 0	9 16 0[1]	16 0 0
1773	8 0 0	9 12 0	9 16 0	15 6 0	9 6 0	16 0 0
1774	7 12 0	9 8 0	9 4 0	14 8 0	9 0 0[2]	16 0 0
1775	7 12 0	7 4 0	7 16 0	11 8 0	7 4 0	14 8 0
1776	6 0 0	7 4 0	7 18 0	10 0 0	7 10 0	12 16 0
1777		7 8 0		11 2 0	7 13 0[2]	
1778		7 4 0		11 8 0	7 10 0	
1779		7 4 0		9 0 0	6 6 0[1]	
1780		8 12 0		12 12 0	8 2 0	

1 Flinn (*Scottish Population History*, 1977) reports the Perth fiar for 1755 at £5.10.0 and the Stirling fiars for 1772 and 1779 at £9.6.0 and £6.12.0 respectively.

2 Different values for these years are given in the Book for the Quarterly Fyars for Stirling Shire (SRO, SC 67/28/2). Those struck at the February courts were: crop 1774, £9.6.0 and crop 1777, £7.10.0.

Table 3.8 *Wheat: county fiars, 1626–1674*

Crop year	Aberdeen[1] L. s. d.			Edinburgh L. s. d.			Fife L. s. d.			Haddington[2] L. s. d.			Linlithgow L. s. d.			Perth L. s. d.		
1626				7	0	0												
1627										10	0	0						
1628	*9*	*0*	*0*	8	6	8				12	0	0						
1629	*8*	*0*	*0*	9	6	8				13	6	8						
1630	*7*	*0*	*0*	9	10	0				14	0	0				13	0	0
1631	*6*	*13*	*4*	9	0	0				15	0	0				9	0	0
1632	*9*	*0*	*0*	10	0	0				11	0	0				10	0	0
1633				9	0	0				9	13	4				9	6	4
1634				8	0	0				7	0	0				10	13	4
1635				11	0	0				15	6	8				12	0	0
1636				11	0	0				14	0	0				13	0	0
1637				9	0	0				11	0	0				9	0	0
1638				8	0	0				7	0	0				6	13	4
1639				7	0	0				9	0	0				5	6	8
1640				7	0	0										8	0	0
1641				9	0	0				10	0	0				9	0	0
1642				9	0	0				9	10	0				9	6	8
1643				7	6	8				8	0	0				8	0	0
1644				7	6	8				8	10	0				7	0	0
1645				6	13	4				7	0	0				8	13	4
1646				7	0	0				7	0	0				7	6	8
1647				11	0	0				11	0	0				10	13	4
1648				12	13	4				15	0	0				13	6	8
1649	*11*	*0*	*0*	13	6	8	12	13	4	11	0	0				12	0	0
1650	*12*	*0*	*0*	13	6	8	13	6	8	14	6	8				13	6	8
1651	*11*	*0*	*0*	12	10	0	14	0	0	13	10	0				13	6	8
1652	*12*	*0*	*0*	11	0	0	12	0	0	11	0	0				11	13	4
1653				4	10	0	6	0	0	7	0	0				6	0	0
1654				4	10	0	6	0	0	5	0	0	4	13	4	5	0	0
1655	*7*	*0*	*0*	7	0	0	6	6	8	6	13	4	5	13	4	6	13	4
1656	*5*	*6*	*8*	7	3	4	6	0	0	8	0	0				6	0	0
1657	*7*	*0*	*0*	6	13	4	6	0	0	7	13	4	6	6	8	6	0	0
1658							9	6	8	12	0	0	11	0	0	8	0	0
1659				11	0	0	7	10	0	12	0	0				9	0	0
1660				11	0	0	8	0	0	10	0	0	10	0	0	9	0	0
1661				11	0	0	8	0	0	11	10	0	10	0	0	10	0	0
1662				9	0	0	8	6	8	9	10	0	9	6	8	8	0	0
1663				9	0	0	8	0	0	8	6	8	8	10	0	7	0	0
1664				7	0	0	6	13	4	6	13	6	6	6	8	6	0	0
1665	*6*	*0*	*0*	7	10	0	6	0	0	7	0	0	7	0	0	6	0	0
1666	*6*	*0*	*0*	6	6	8				5	0	0	5	6	8	4	13	4
1667	*6*	*0*	*0*	5	10	0				5	3	4	5	6	8	5	6	8
1668	*6*	*0*	*0*	6	6	8	4	13	4	6	10	0	5	10	0	5	0	0
1669	*6*	*0*	*0*	6	6	8	5	6	8	6	10	0	6	0	0	5	0	0
1670	*7*	*0*	*0*	6	3	4				6	0	0	6	3	4	6	0	0
1671				10	3	4				11	0	0	9	6	8	8	0	0
1672				7	6	8	5	0	0	6	13	4	6	13	4	5	6	8
1673				6	13	4	5	0	0	6	13	4	6	0	0	5	6	8
1674				12	6	8	9	6	8	12	17	4	11	0	0	10	0	0

1 These prices are for 'mercat' wheat. 'Ferme' wheat was, after 1630, always the same price. Figures in italics are for fiars struck between July and November rather than, as was usual, in or around February.

2 Haddington prices are for 'first' wheat. Prices for 'second' wheat are published in Flinn, *Scottish Population History*, 1977. That series does not commence until 1651.

Table 3.9 *Wheat: county fiars, 1675–1724*

Crop year	Aberdeen[1] L. s. d.			Ayr L. s. d.			Berwick L. s. d.			Edinburgh L. s. d.			Fife L. s. d.			Haddington L. s. d.		
1675										11	0	0	10	0	0	11	10	0
1676	*6*	*0*	*0*							6	16	0	6	13	4	7	6	8
1677	*5*	*6*	*8*							6	13	4	5	0	0	7	3	4
1678	*7*	*0*	*0*							7	0	0	5	0	0	8	0	0
1679	*8*	*0*	*0*							9	0	0	6	0	0	9	13	4
1680	6	13	4							6	5	0	4	13	4	6	12	0
1681	6	13	4							6	5	0	5	13	4	6	6	8
1682	*6*	*0*	*0*							7	10	0	6	0	0	8	0	0
1683										7	18	0	5	0	0	7	0	0
1684										8	0	0	6	13	4	7	6	8
1685										6	8	0	4	16	8	6	6	8
1686										6	0	0	5	0	0	6	6	8
1687										5	16	0	4	13	4	5	10	0
1688										5	12	0	4	16	8	5	6	8
1689							6	0	0	8	6	8	6	0	0	8	6	0
1690	9	6	8				7	5	0	9	0	0	7	6	8	9	6	0
1691	6	13	4				5	12	0	7	12	0	5	6	8	7	14	0
1692	6	13	4				7	10	0	7	0	0	5	6	8	7	0	0
1693	7	0	0				8	0	0	8	12	0	6	13	4	8	16	0
1694	8	13	4				6	10	0	8	18	0	8	0	0	8	12	0
1695	10	13	4				8	0	0	10	6	8	9	6	8	10	0	0
1696	9	6	8				9	12	0	12	13	4	9	0	0	13	0	0
1697	12	0	0				10	0	0	11	13	4	10	6	8	12	0	0
1698	17	0	0				11	0	0	17	0	0	12	0	0	16	0	0
1699	13	6	8				11	13	4	14	0	0	12	0	0	15	0	0
1700	12	0	0				7	0	0	9	13	4	7	0	0	9	13	4
1701	7	6	8				5	10	0	7	0	0	6	0	0	6	13	4
1702	7	10	0				5	0	0	7	0	0	6	0	0	6	6	8
1703	7	10	0				7	0	0	8	10	0	6	13	4	8	14	4
1704	8	0	0				5	16	0	7	14	0	6	6	8	7	13	4
1705	6	0	0				5	9	0	6	10	0	5	0	0	6	4	0
1706	5	0	0				4	0	0	5	6	8	4	10	0	5	0	0
1707	6	0	0				5	16	0	7	6	8	5	6	8	7	0	0
1708	8	0	0				7	13	4	9	10	0	7	13	4	9	0	0
1709	12	0	0				10	10	0	12	13	4	10	10	0	12	13	4
1710	9	0	0				6	10	0	8	15	0				8	4	0
1711	7	0	0				7	13	8	8	10	0	6	13	4	8	0	0
1712	7	0	0				6	10	0	8	10	0	7	0	0	8	0	0
1713	8	0	0	10	0	0	9	10	0	10	10	0	8	10	0	11	0	0
1714	6	0	0	8	0	0	7	0	0	7	14	0	7	0	0	7	10	0
1715	6	13	4	9	0	0	6	0	0	8	13	4	6	5	0	8	12	0
1716	6	0	0	10	0	0	6	0	0	7	13	4	6	10	0	7	10	0
1717	7	0	0	9	0	0	6	10	0	7	10	0	7	0	0	7	14	0
1718	6	0	0	10	0	0	5	6	0	7	6	8	7	10	0	7	6	8
1719	6	13	4	9	0	0	6	0	0	7	6	8	7	0	0	7	12	0
1720	5	6	8	9	0	0	5	0	0	7	4	0	6	0	0	7	13	4
1721	6	0	0	10	0	0	6	0	0	7	10	0	7	6	8	8	0	0
1722	6	13	4	10	0	0	7	0	0	7	10	0	8	10	0	9	0	0
1723	7	0	0	8	0	0	6	15	0	7	14	0	7	16	8	8	0	0
1724	7	0	0	7	0	0	8	0	0	7	16	0	6	13	4	8	13	4

1 Figures in italics are for fiars which were struck between July and November rather than, as was usual, in or around February.

Table 3.9 *(cont.)*

Crop year	Kincardine L. s. d.			Lanark L. s. d.			Linlithgow L. s. d.			Perth L. s. d.			Stirling L. s. d.		
1675	7	0	0				10	0	0	10	0	0			
1676	6	13	4				6	0	0	6	13	4			
1677	6	0	0				6	0	0	6	0	0			
1678							6	6	8	5	6	8			
1679	6	13	4				8	13	4	6	13	4			
1680	6	0	0				6	0	0	5	0	0			
1681	6	0	0				6	0	0	6	0	0			
1682	6	13	4				6	0	0	6	0	0	7	0	0
1683	6	0	0				6	6	8	6	0	0	7	0	0
1684	6	0	0				6	6	8	6	13	4	8	6	8
1685	6	0	0				6	0	0	5	6	8	6	13	4
1686	6	0	0				5	13	4	5	6	8	7	0	0
1687							5	6	8	5	0	0	7	0	0
1688							5	0	0	4	13	4	7	0	0
1689							7	0	0	7	6	8	10	6	8
1690							8	0	0	9	0	0			
1691				8	0	0	6	13	4	5	6	8	8	0	0
1692				8	0	0	6	10	0	5	13	4			
1693				8	13	4	8	0	0	6	13	4	8	6	8
1694				11	0	0	8	0	0	8	0	0	10	6	8
1695				12	0	0	8	10	0	8	0	0	11	0	0
1696				12	0	0	11	10	0	10	0	0	11	0	0
1697							9	0	0	10	0	0	12	13	4
1698							15	0	0	13	6	8	16	6	8
1699							13	6	8	12	13	4	14	0	0
1700				9	0	0	8	16	0	7	0	0	8	13	4
1701							6	6	8	6	0	0	8	10	0
1702				8	0	0	6	13	4	6	0	0	7	0	0
1703				8	10	0	8	0	0	6	0	0	7	13	4
1704							7	2	0	6	0	0	8	3	4
1705							6	0	0	5	0	0	7	0	0
1706							4	6	8	4	0	0	5	0	0
1707							7	0	0	6	0	0	8	10	0
1708							7	13	4	7	6	8	8	13	4
1709							12	0	0	10	0	0	12	0	0
1710							8	15	0	7	6	8	9	0	0
1711							7	3	4	6	10	0	8	0	0
1712							8	1	0	6	13	4	9	0	0
1713							8	15	0	8	0	0	9	0	0
1714							7	0	0	6	13	4	8	3	4
1715							8	10	0	7	0	0	8	6	8
1716							7	10	0	7	0	0	9	0	0
1717							7	0	0	6	13	4	7	10	0
1718							7	5	0	7	0	0	7	0	0
1719							7	6	8	6	13	4	7	0	0
1720							6	13	4	5	6	8	6	13	4
1721							7	8	0	6	13	4	8	0	0
1722							8	6	8	9	0	0	8	13	4
1723				8	13	4	8	0	0	7	13	4	7	10	0
1724				8	0	0	7	5	0	7	0	0	8	0	0

Table 3.10 *Wheat: county fiars, 1725–1780*

Crop year	Aberdeen L. s. d.			Ayr[1] L. s. d.			Banff L. s. d.			Berwick L. s. d.			Clackmannan L. s. d.			Dumfries L. s. d.			Edinburgh L. s. d.		
1725	8	10	0	9	0	0				8	6	0							9	12	0
1726	8	0	0	9	6	8				7	16	0							8	4	0
1727	8	6	8	10	0	0				8	6	0							9	5	0
1728	8	0	0	11	0	0				8	8	0							10	0	0
1729	7	10	0	10	0	0				7	4	0							8	8	0
1730	6	0	0	8	0	0				6	0	0							7	14	0
1731	6	0	0	8	0	0				5	6	0							7	16	0
1732	6	0	0	8	0	0				5	0	0							6	6	0
1733	6	13	4	6	12	0				7	4	0							7	13	4
1734	6	13	4	6	8	0				8	0	0							8	18	0
1735	6	13	4	8	0	0				7	10	0							8	18	0
1736	6	13	4	9	12	0				7	10	0							7	10	0
1737	6	13	4	8	0	0				7	16	0							8	0	0
1738	6	0	0	8	10	0				6	8	0							6	12	0
1739	7	0	0	9	0	0				6	16	0							8	3	0
1740	11	0	0	13	4	0				11	8	0							13	15	0
1741	8	0	0	7	16	0				7	4	0							8	10	0
1742	7	0	0	6	10	0				6	0	0							6	12	0
1743	5	0	0	5	4	0				4	16	0							6	0	0
1744	7	0	0	8	0	0				5	4	0							7	2	0
1745	9	0	0	9	12	0				9	0	0							9	6	0
1746	8	0	0	7	4	0				7	4	0							8	8	0
1747	6	13	4	6	16	0				7	4	0							8	4	0
1748	8	0	0	8	8	0				8	6	0							8	12	0
1749	8	0	0	8	0	0				7	4	0							8	0	0
1750	7	10	0	9	12	0				7	4	0							8	2	0
1751	9	0	0	9	12	0				9	0	0							10	2	0
1752	9	0	0	9	12	0				8	0	0							9	0	0
1753	8	0	0	9	0	0				7	12	0							9	0	0
1754	7	0	0	8	8	0				6	12	0							7	12	0
1755	8	0	0	9	12	0				7	4	0							8	4	0
1756	12	12	0	14	8	0	12	12	0	10	14	0[2]	12	0	0	33	12	0	13	4	0
1757	11	0	0	13	4	0	11	0	0	9	12	0	10	0	0	38	8	0	10	16	0
1758	8	8	0	9	12	0	8	10	0	7	4	0	9	0	0	28	16	0	9	0	0
1759	7	4	0	8	8	0	8	0	0	7	0	0	8	10	0	25	12	0	8	0	0
1760	7	10	0	9	0	0	8	0	0	8	0	0	8	6	0	24	0	0	8	2	0
1761	8	0	0	9	12	0	8	0	0	6	12	0	8	10	0	27	4	0	8	8	0
1762	10	4	0	12	0	0	11	2	0	9	0	0	10	16	0	36	0	0	11	14	0
1763	8	8	0	10	16	0	8	8	0	8	10	0	10	0	0	28	16	0	10	0	0
1764	10	0	0	12	0	0	10	10	0	9	4	0[2]	10	16	0	32	0	0	11	8	0
1765	10	16	0	12	12	0	12	0	0	10	0	0	12	0	0	38	8	0	12	0	0
1766	12	0	0	12	12	0	12	0	0	10	16	0	11	2	0	33	12	0	11	14	0
1767	12	0	0	11	8	0	12	0	0	10	9	0[2]	11	8	0	33	12	0	12	12	0
1768	10	4	0	12	0	0	11	8	0	9	0	0	11	8	0	38	8	0	12	0	0
1769	9	0	0	10	16	0	10	16	0	8	16	0	10	4	0	35	4	0	10	16	0
1770	10	10	0	10	4	0	10	10	0	8	12	0	10	10	0	35	4	0	11	2	0
1771	12	12	0	12	12	0	12	0	0	11	4	0	12	0	0	38	8	0	12	12	0
1772	13	0	0	13	16	0	12	12	0	11	6	0	13	4	0	40	0	0	13	10	0
1773	12	12	0	13	4	0	12	12	0	12	8	0	12	0	0	43	4	0	13	7	0
1774	12	3	0	12	12	0	12	12	0	10	8	0	12	0	0	43	4	0	12	12	0
1775	9	18	0	12	0	0	10	16	0	8	16	0	10	4	0	36	0	0	11	8	0
1776	9	12	0	11	8	0	9	12	0	9	0	8	9	18	0	35	4	0	11	2	0
1777	11	2	0	13	16	0				11	4	0							12	0	0
1778	10	10	0	11	8	0				9	0	0							10	16	0
1779	8	8	0	9	12	0				7	10	0							8	14	0
1780	10	16	0	11	8	0				10	16	0							12	0	0

1 The boll of wheat was stated to be of 4 Winchester bushels.

2 Different values are given in a note of the fiars for Berwick in the Marchmont Granary Book, 1753–67 (SRO, GD 1/651/16); £10.0.0 in 1756, £13.16.0 in 1764 and £10.16.0 in 1767.

Table 3.10 *(cont.)*

Crop year	Elgin L. s. d.	Fife L. s. d.	Forfar L. s. d.	Haddington L. s. d.	Kincardine L. s. d.	Kinross L. s. d.	Kirkcud -bright L. s. d.
1725		8 10 0		10 0 0			
1726		7 16 8		8 12 0			
1727		8 10 0		9 10 0			
1728		8 10 0		10 0 0			
1729		8 0 0		9 0 0			
1730		6 13 4		8 0 0			
1731		6 13 4		7 4 0			
1732		5 6 8		6 0 0			
1733		6 0 0		8 2 0			
1734		7 6 8		9 0 0			
1735		8 3 4		9 0 0			
1736		7 10 0		7 17 0			
1737		7 0 0		8 0 0			
1738		6 0 0		6 12 0			
1739		7 6 8		8 4 0			
1740		13 0 0		13 10 0			
1741				8 8 0			
1742		5 16 8		6 15 0			
1743		5 6 8		5 16 0			
1744		7 13 4		6 18 0			
1745		8 12 0		9 10 0			
1746		8 10 0		8 2 0			
1747		6 13 4		8 4 0			
1748		7 12 0		8 14 0			
1749		7 13 4		8 0 0			
1750		7 3 4		8 2 0			
1751		8 6 8		10 6 0			
1752		8 6 8		9 0 0			
1753		8 0 0		9 0 0			
1754		7 10 0		7 5 0			
1755		7 16 0		8 6 0			
1756		10 0 0	10 10 0	13 10 0	10 0 0		
1757	11 0 0	9 3 4	9 6 0	10 16 0	11 0 0		
1758	8 10 0	7 13 4	8 12 0	9 0 0	8 0 0		
1759	7 0 0	6 10 0	7 10 0	7 17 3	7 10 0		
1760	7 2 0	7 6 8	8 0 0	8 2 0	7 10 0		
1761		8 0 0	8 6 0	8 17 9	8 0 0		
1762		10 13 4	11 0 0	11 12 6	10 0 0		
1763		7 13 4	8 0 0	10 3 6	8 0 0	7 10 0	
1764	9 0 0	9 0 0	9 15 0[1]	11 6 3	9 12 0	9 0 0	
1765	12 0 0	11 6 8	11 14 0	12 4 9	11 8 0	11 0 0	
1766	11 0 0	9 10 0	10 10 0	12 0 3	12 0 0	9 0 0	
1767	12 0 0	10 16 0	12 0 0	12 13 3	12 0 0	12 0 0	
1768	9 0 0	11 8 0	12 0 0	12 8 9	11 0 0	11 8 0	
1769	9 6 0	10 0 0	10 16 0	10 15 9	9 12 0	9 0 0	19 4 0
1770	9 0 0	8 16 0	9 12 0	10 16 0	10 0 0	9 18 0	19 4 0
1771	12 0 0	11 2 0	12 0 0	12 7 9	12 0 0	9 12 0	19 4 0
1772	12 0 0	11 0 0	12 0 0	13 8 6	12 12 0	12 12 0	
1773	12 0 0	11 4 0	12 0 0	13 17 0	12 0 0	12 0 0	21 12 0
1774	12 0 0	10 13 4	12 12 0	12 11 3	12 12 0	12 0 0	21 4 0
1775	9 6 0	9 18 0	10 4 0	11 7 0	9 12 0	9 12 0	19 4 0
1776	8 14 0	8 18 0	10 16 0	11 7 6	9 12 0	10 0 0	16 16 0
1777		10 2 0		12 1 3			
1778		9 0 0		10 13 3			
1779		7 6 0	8 8 0[1]	9 0 6			
1780		10 10 0	11 8 0[1]	12 2 3			

1　These fiars are for white wheat. The fiars for red wheat were as follows; 1764 at £9.6.0 (SRO, GD 45/12/86), 1779 at £7.16.0 and 1780 at £10.16.0 (SRO, GD16/27/82). The remaining fiars in this series refer merely to 'wheat', but may be presumed to refer to white wheat as the fiar for 1764 was reported in SRO, GD 45/12/86 to be £9.15.0.

Table 3.10 *(cont.)*

Crop year	Linlithgow L. s. d.			Perth L. s. d.			Renfrew L. s. d.			Roxburgh L. s. d.			Stirling L. s. d.		
1725	10	0	0	9	0	0							9	10	0
1726	8	5	0	8	0	0							8	10	0
1727	8	13	4	8	10	0							9	0	0
1728	9	0	0	8	10	0							10	0	0
1729	8	4	0	7	10	0							8	13	4
1730	7	10	0	6	13	4							7	10	0
1731	7	10	0	6	13	4							7	10	0
1732	5	18	0	5	13	4							6	10	0
1733	6	16	6	7	10	0							8	0	0
1734	8	16	0	8	0	0							9	0	0
1735	8	11	0	8	0	0							8	10	0
1736	8	5	6	7	6	8							7	15	0
1737	7	15	0	6	13	4							7	0	0
1738	6	2	0	6	0	0							6	10	0
1739	8	0	0	8	0	0							8	10	0
1740	14	0	0	11	0	0							14	10	0
1741	8	0	0	7	6	8[1]							7	10	0
1742	6	8	0	6	0	0							6	12	0
1743	6	0	0	6	0	0							6	0	0
1744	6	10	0	7	0	0							7	10	0
1745	9	0	0	9	0	0							8	10	0
1746	8	8	0	8	12	0							8	10	0
1747	7	12	0	8	0	0							8	10	0
1748	8	16	0	8	0	0							8	12	0
1749	8	0	0	7	10	0							8	0	0
1750	8	4	0	8	0	0							8	13	4
1751	9	7	0	9	10	0							9	6	0
1752	8	16	0	9	0	0							8	10	0
1753	9	0	0	8	0	0							9	0	0
1754	7	18	0	7	10	0							8	0	0
1755	8	4	0	8	0	0							8	8	0
1756	13	4	0	12	0	0				12	0	0	12	0	0
1757	10	10	0	10	0	0				11	8	0	10	16	0
1758	9	0	0	8	0	0				9	0	0	9	0	0
1759	8	0	0	7	4	0				8	8	0	7	16	0
1760	8	0	0	7	10	0				8	10	0	8	2	0
1761	8	14	0	8	0	0				8	14	0	8	2	0
1762	11	12	0	10	0	0				12	12	0	10	4	0
1763	9	14	0	8	14	0				10	4	0	9	0	0
1764	10	15	0	9	12	0				12	0	0	9	12	0
1765	12	0	0	11	8	0				13	4	0	12	0	0
1766	10	16	0	10	10	0				12	12	0	10	16	0
1767	12	0	0	11	0	0				13	4	0	11	8	0
1768	12	0	0	11	8	0				10	16	0	11	8	0
1769	10	0	0	10	4	0				10	16	0	10	4	0
1770	9	16	0	9	12	0	10	4	0	10	16	0	10	4	0
1771	11	8	0	11	8	0	12	1	0	12	0	0	12	0	0
1772	12	6	0	11	10	0	13	8	0	13	16	0	13	10	0
1773	13	4	0	12	12	0	13	10	0	15	0	0	14	0	0
1774	12	0	0	12	6	0	12	4	6	13	4	0	12	0	0[2]
1775	10	16	0	10	16	0	10	10	0	11	8	0	10	10	0[2]
1776	9	18	0	10	10	0				11	8	0	10	10	0[2]
1777	12	0	0	11	2	0							12	0	0[2]
1778	10	10	0	10	0	0							10	10	0
1779	8	14	0	8	8	0							8	14	0
1780	11	14	0	12	0	0							11	14	0

1 From this date the fiars refer to both 'best' and 'second' wheat although this series continues to report the price of best wheat.

2 Different values for these years are given in the Book for the Quarterly Fyars for Stirling Shire (SRO, SC 67/28/2). Those struck at the February courts were: crop 1774, £15.6.9; crop 1775, £10.16.6; crop 1776, £11.8.0; and crop 1777, £11.14.0.

Table 3.11 *Bear and barley: county fiars, 1625–1674* [1]

	Aberdeen			Ayr[3]	Edinburgh
Crop year	Bear[2] L. s. d.	Mercat bear[2] L. s. d.	Wair bear[2] L. s. d.	L. s. d.	L. s. d.
1625					
1626					6 13 4
1627					
1628	*7 13 4*	*7 0 0*			7 6 8
1629	*6 13 4*	*6 0 0*			8 6 8
1630	*5 3 4*	*4 13 4*			9 10 0
1631	*4 0 0*	*4 0 0*			6 0 0
1632	*6 10 0*	*6 10 0*			7 10 0
1633					8 10 0
1634					8 0 0
1635					9 0 0
1636					9 0 0
1637					7 0 0
1638					6 0 0
1639					6 0 0
1640					6 0 0
1641					8 0 0
1642					9 0 0
1643					6 13 4
1644					6 13 4
1645					5 6 8
1646					5 0 0
1647					7 6 8
1648					10 0 0
1649	*8 0 0*	*8 0 0*			11 0 0[4]
1650	*8 0 0*	*7 13 4*			10 13 4
1651	*7 13 4*	*7 13 4*			11 0 0
1652	*7 6 8*	*7 6 8*			10 0 0
1653					4 13 4
1654					4 13 4
1655	*5 0 0*	*5 0 0*	*3 6 8*		6 13 4[4]
1656	*4 0 0*	*4 0 0*	*2 13 4*		6 6 8
1657	*4 6 8*	*4 6 8*	*2 13 4*		6 6 8
1658				6 0 0	
1659				6 0 0	6 6 8
1660				8 0 0	6 6 8
1661				11 0 0	9 0 0
1662				5 6 8	7 10 0
1663				5 6 8	7 0 0
1664				3 13 0	5 13 4
1665	*4 0 0*	*4 0 0*	*3 0 0*	5 0 0	5 13 4[5]
1666	*4 6 8*	*4 6 8*	*3 0 0*	5 13 4	6 0 0
1667	*5 6 8*	*5 6 8*	*3 0 0*	4 5 0	6 10 0
1668	*4 13 4*	*4 0 0*	*2 13 4*	5 0 0	6 0 0
1669	*4 3 4*	*4 3 4*	*3 6 8*	4 10 0	6 0 0
1670	*5 0 0*	*5 0 0*	*3 13 4*	5 0 0	6 0 0
1671				6 0 0	6 6 8
1672				4 6 8	6 13 4
1673				5 6 8	6 6 8
1674				11 6 8	9 13 4

1 Although bear and barley were quite distinct, the documents from which these series have been drawn often fail to record which was being considered. No distinction between the two grains is thus made in the column headings although all reliable evidence concerning the replacement of bear by barley has been noted.

2 Aberdeen prices for bear and wair bear are 'without fodder'. Prices for these grains 'with fodder' were slightly higher. Aberdeen 'ferme bear' was usually, and from 1656 was always, the same price as the 'mercat' bear listed here. Wair bear was bear grown on ground manured with seaweed. Figures in italics are for fiars which were struck between July and November rather than in February.

3 The boll of bear was stated to be of 8 Winchester bushels.

4 Flinn (*Scottish Population History*, 1977) reports the Edinburgh fiar for 1649 as £10.13.6 and that for 1655 as £6.11.6.

5 Rough bear also appears from this date.

Table 3.11 *(cont.)*

Crop year	Fife L. s. d.			Forfar L. s. d.			Glasgow Commissary L. s. d.			Haddington[2] L. s. d.			Linlithgow L. s. d.			Perth L. s. d.		
1625	5	6	8															
1626	5	0	0															
1627	5	6	8							8	13	4						
1628	10	0	0							10	0	0						
1629	8	0	0							12	0	0						
1630	9	6	8							11	0	0				10	0	0
1631	5	6	8							13	0	0				5	13	4
1632	5	6	8							8	6	8				7	13	4
1633	8	0	0							8	6	8				9	0	0
1634	7	13	4							5	0	0				9	6	8
1635										10	0	0				10	0	0
1636										10	0	0				10	0	0
1637										8	0	0				8	0	0
1638										4	13	8				5	6	8
1639										8	0	0				4	6	8
1640	6	13	4							8	8	0				6	13	4
1641	8	0	0							9	0	0				8	0	0
1642	9	0	0							8	0	0				8	0	0
1643	6	0	0							6	13	4				7	0	0
1644	6	0	0							7	0	0				6	0	0
1645	5	0	0							5	0	0				7	6	8
1646	5	6	8							5	6	8				6	6	8
1647	5	0	0							7	10	0				9	0	0
1648	6	0	0							9	3	0				13	6	8
1649	10	0	0	8	0	0				10	0	0				9	6	0
1650	10	13	4	9	6	8				15	0	0				11	0	0
1651	11	10	0	10	13	4				14	0	0				11	0	0
1652	11	0	0	9	0	0				9	13	4				11	6	8
1653	4	10	0	4	0	0				6	0	0				4	13	4
1654	4	13	4	3	0	0				5	0	0	4	0	0	4	13	4
1655	5	0	0	4	0	0				6	0	0	5	16	8	5	6	8
1656	4	6	8	4	6	8[1]				6	13	4				4	13	4
1657	4	3	4	4	6	8				9	10	0	4	13	4	4	13	4
1658	6	0	0	5	6	8				9	0	0	6	13	4	6	0	0
1659	6	0	0	5	6	8				8	0	0				7	6	8
1660	6	0	0	5	6	8				7	0	0	6	3	4	6	13	4
1661	6	0	0	6	0	0				8	13	4	7	13	4	7	0	0
1662	5	13	4	5	6	8				7	0	0	6	13	4	6	0	0
1663	5	6	8	4	13	4				6	6	8	5	3	4	5	6	8
1664	3	13	4	3	6	8				4	10	0	3	13	4	3	13	4
1665	3	0	0	2	13	4				4	6	8	4	0	0	4	0	0
1666				4	10	0				5	0	0	4	6	8	4	6	8
1667				4	13	4				5	10	0	4	13	4	4	13	4
1668	3	13	4	3	6	8				5	10	0	4	13	4	4	13	4
1669	4	6	8	3	6	8				6	13	4	4	13	4	4	13	4
1670							5	0	0	5	13	4	4	16	8	5	0	0
1671							6	6	8	6	4	0	5	6	8	5	13	4
1672	4	6	8				4	3	4	6	0	0	4	13	4	4	13	4
1673	4	0	0				5	0	0	6	4	0	4	13	4	4	13	4
1674	7	0	0				9	0	0	10	9	0	8	10	0[3]	8	0	0

1 In 1656 no Candlemas fiar was struck. That from the Lammas court has been entered.

2 Haddington prices are for first barley. Prices for second barley are published in Flinn, *Scottish Population History*, 1977 although that series does not commence until 1651.

3 This series continues in table 3.12 as 'best bear'.

Table 3.12 *Bear and barley: county fiars, 1675–1724*

Crop year	Aberdeen			Ayr[2]	Berwick	
	Bear[1]	Mercat bear[1]	Wair bear[1]		Merse bear	Lammer-muir bear
	L. s. d.	L. s. d.	L. s. d.	L. s. d.	L. s. d.	L. s. d.
1675				11 0 0		
1676	*4 3 4*	*3 16 8*	*3 0 0*	4 13 4		
1677	*4 0 0*	*3 16 0*	*2 16 0*	4 0 0		
1678	*3 10 0*	*3 10 0*	*2 13 4*	3 13 4		
1679	*3 13 4*	*3 13 4*	*2 13 4*	6 0 0		
1680	3 6 8	3 6 8	2 6 8	5 13 4		
1681	4 0 0	4 0 0	2 13 4	6 0 0		
1682	*5 6 8*	*6 0 0*	*4 10 0*	6 13 4		
1683				6 0 0		
1684				4 13 4		
1685				4 13 4		
1686				6 6 8		
1687				7 6 8		
1688						
1689				7 0 0	4 12 0	4 4 0
1690	6 0 0	6 0 0	4 10 0	7 6 4	6 12 0	6 0 0
1691	4 0 0	4 3 4	3 0 0	4 16 0[3]	3 16 0	3 12 0
1692	4 0 0	4 0 0	3 0 0	4 16 8[3]	4 6 8	4 0 0
1693	4 0 0	4 0 0	3 0 0	5 11 8	5 0 0	4 16 0
1694	4 13 4	4 13 4	3 0 0	6 13 4	4 16 0	4 12 0
1695	6 13 4	6 13 4	5 6 8	7 16 8	5 10 0	5 6 0
1696	8 13 4	8 13 4	7 0 0	12 0 0	9 16 0	7 10 0
1697	9 0 0	9 0 0	6 13 4	7 3 6[4]	7 0 0	6 0 0
1698	11 6 8	11 6 8	9 6 8	12 0 0	10 0 0	7 0 0
1699	9 6 8	9 6 8	6 13 4	10 0 0	9 0 0	7 14 0
1700	6 13 4	6 13 4	4 13 4	9 0 0	6 10 0	5 10 0
1701	4 13 4	4 6 8	3 13 4	5 3 4	4 16 0	4 8 0
1702	4 6 8	4 6 8	3 13 4	5 13 4	4 4 0	3 14 0
1703	4 6 8	4 6 8	3 6 8	5 6 8	5 10 0	4 16 0
1704	4 13 4	4 13 4	3 0 0	5 0 0	4 16 0	4 8 0
1705	4 13 4	4 6 8	3 0 0	5 0 0	5 6 0	4 16 0
1706	4 0 0	4 0 0	2 0 0	5 0 0	3 6 0	2 16 0
1707	4 6 8	4 6 8	3 0 0	4 13 4	3 14 0	3 9 0
1708	5 0 0	5 0 0	3 6 8	6 6 8	5 10 0	5 1 0
1709	6 13 4	6 13 4	4 13 4	8 0 0	7 0 0	6 0 0
1710	6 0 0	5 0 0	4 0 0	7 0 0	6 0 0	5 6 0
1711	4 6 8	4 6 8	2 16 8	5 0 0	5 8 0	5 4 0
1712	4 0 0	4 0 0	2 13 4	5 0 0	4 0 0	3 12 0
1713	5 6 8	5 6 8	4 0 0	6 8 0	5 10 0	5 0 0
1714	5 6 8	5 6 8	3 16 8	8 6 8	6 0 0	5 8 0
1715	4 6 8	4 6 8	3 6 8	6 0 0	4 12 0	4 2 0
1716	4 6 8	4 6 8	3 0 0	5 13 4	4 4 0	3 18 0
1717	5 6 8	5 6 8	3 13 4	5 0 0	4 12 0	4 0 0
1718	5 0 0	5 0 0	4 0 0	5 6 8	5 0 0	4 14 0
1719	5 13 4	5 13 4	4 13 4	5 10 0	6 0 0	5 12 0
1720	4 13 4	4 13 4	4 0 0	5 3 4	5 10 0	5 0 0
1721	5 6 8	5 6 8	4 6 8	4 16 8	4 8 0	4 3 0
1722	6 6 8	6 6 8	5 0 0	6 0 0	5 10 0	5 0 0
1723	6 13 4	6 13 4	5 13 4	7 0 0	6 4 0	5 8 0
1724	4 13 4	4 13 4	3 16 8	5 0 0	5 8 0	5 0 0

1 Figures in italics are for fiars which were struck between July and November rather than, as was usual, in or around February.

2 The boll of bear was stated to be of 8 Winchester bushels.

3 Different values are given in SRO, GD 109/3943; £4.16.8 in 1691 and £5.0.0 in 1692.

4 According to GD 25/9/Box 1, the fiar for crop 1697 was £7.0.0

Table 3.12 *(cont.)*

Crop year	Edinburgh L. s. d.			Fife L. s. d.			Glasgow Commissary L. s. d.			Haddington L. s. d.			Kincardine L. s. d.			Lanark L. s. d.		
1675	12	0	0	10	0	0	9	0	0	11	12	0	6	0	0			
1676	7	0	0	4	6	8	4	13	4	5	6	8	4	3	4			
1677	7	0	0	4	0	0	3	16	8	5	6	8	4	0	0			
1678	5	12	0[1]	3	13	4	3	6	8	5	3	4	4	0	0			
1679	6	13	4	3	16	8	5	6	8	5	10	0	4	0	0			
1680	6	0	0	3	16	8	4	14	0	5	6	8	4	3	4			
1681	6	0	0	3	16	8	5	3	4	5	6	8	4	0	0			
1682	8	13	4	6	13	4	7	6	8	8	10	0	6	0	0			
1683	5	18	0[2]	3	16	8	5	0	0	5	16	0	4	6	8			
1684	5	16	0	4	0	0	4	1	3	5	6	8	4	13	4			
1685	5	14	0	3	16	8	4	6	8	5	9	0	4	3	4			
1686	6	10	0	5	0	0	5	6	8	6	12	0	4	0	0			
1687	5	15	0	4	0	0	5	10	4	5	6	8						
1688	5	14	0	4	0	0	5	0	0	5	6	8						
1689	6	5	0	4	13	4	6	6	8	6	0	0						
1690	8	13	0	6	13	4	7	13	4	8	16	0						
1691	5	18	0	4	3	4	5	9	0	5	3	0				4	6	8
1692	6	0	0	4	0	0	4	10	0	5	14	0				4	0	0
1693	6	5	0	4	3	4	4	13	4	6	7	0				4	16	8
1694	6	6	8	4	3	4	6	6	0	6	5	0				5	10	0
1695	8	5	0	6	13	4	7	4	8	8	0	0				8	0	0
1696	12	0	0	8	13	4	9	11	2	12	0	0				10	13	4
1697	9	10	0	7	6	8	7	0	0	9	6	8						
1698	13	6	8	9	6	8	10	0	0	14	0	0						
1699	12	13	4	9	13	4	10	6	8	12	6	8						
1700	9	10	0	7	10	0	7	5	0	9	6	8				7	0	0
1701	6	6	8	4	6	8	5	0	0	6	0	0				4	6	8
1702	6	13	4	4	10	0	5	10	2	6	6	8				5	6	8
1703	7	3	4	4	10	0	5	14	4	7	10	0				5	0	0
1704	6	15	0	4	10	0	5	0	0	6	6	4						
1705	6	12	0	4	6	8	4	13	4	6	0	0						
1706	5	2	0	3	6	8				4	13	4						
1707	5	6	8	3	3	4				5	0	0						
1708	7	6	8	5	3	4				7	0	0						
1709	8	15	0	6	10	0				8	16	0						
1710	8	10	0							8	0	0						
1711	7	6	8	4	13	4				7	0	0				4	6	8
1712	6	6	8	4	0	0				6	0	0						
1713	6	10	0	4	13	4				7	0	0				4	10	0
1714	7	14	0	6	13	4				7	6	8				6	13	4
1715	6	16	0	4	3	4				6	12	0				5	0	0
1716	6	5	0	4	3	4				5	10	0				4	10	0
1717	5	14	0	4	0	0				5	15	0				4	13	4
1718	6	12	0	4	13	4				6	10	0						
1719	7	0	0	5	0	0				7	10	0				5	0	0
1720	6	15	0	4	13	4				6	15	0				4	10	0
1721	6	3	4	4	10	0				5	18	0				4	0	0
1722	6	18	0	5	13	4				6	18	0				6	10	0
1723	8	5	0	7	6	8				8	4	0				7	0	0
1724	6	5	0	4	0	0				6	13	4				4	15	0

1 Muirland bear appears in this year's fiars (at £4.6.8 per boll).
2 Barley bear (sometimes designated just 'barley'), blauded bear and rough bear are consistently set from this date. This series is for 'barley bear'.

Table 3.12 *(cont.)*

Crop year	Linlithgow				Perth			Stirling					
	Best bear L. s. d.			Muirland bear L. s. d.			Bear L. s. d.		Bear L. s. d.		Carse bear L. s. d.		Dryfield bear L. s. d.
1675	10	0	0				10	0	0					
1676	4	0	0				4	13	4					
1677	4	3	4				4	13	4					
1678	3	15	0				4	3	4					
1679	4	13	4				4	3	4					
1680	4	3	4				4	0	0					
1681	4	13	4				5	0	0					
1682	7	0	0				6	13	4	7	0	0		
1683	4	10	0				4	13	4	4	10	0		
1684	4	6	8				4	6	8	4	3	4		
1685	4	6	8				4	6	8	4	6	8		
1686	5	13	4				5	0	0	5	6	8		
1687	5	0	0				4	6	8	4	13	4		
1688	5	0	0				4	10	0	4	13	4		
1689	5	0	0				5	13	4	5	13	4		
1690	7	6	8				8	0	0					
1691	4	13	4				5	0	0	5	0	0		
1692	4	13	4				4	0	0					
1693	5	0	0				4	6	8	4	13	4		
1694	5	3	4				4	13	4	5	6	8		
1695	7	6	8				6	13	4	8	0	0		
1696	11	0	0				9	10	0	9	6	8		
1697	7	0	0				7	0	0	7	10	0		
1698	10	13	4				10	0	0	11	10	0		
1699	11	0	0				10	10	0	9	13	4		
1700	7	0	0				7	0	0	8	6	8		
1701	5	10	0	4	16	8	5	0	0	5	0	0		
1702	6	0	0	5	0	0	5	0	0	5	13	4		
1703	6	0	0	5	6	8	5	0	0	5	6	8		
1704	6	0	0	5	10	0	4	10	0	4	16	8		
1705	5	6	8	5	0	0	4	10	0	5	6	8		
1706	4	0	0	3	10	0	3	10	0	4	0	0		
1707	4	6	8	4	0	0	3	13	4	4	13	4		
1708	6	10	0	6	3	4	5	13	4	6	0	0		
1709	7	15	0	7	0	0	6	13	4	8	0	0		
1710	7	16	8	7	0	0	6	6	8	7	0	0		
1711	5	15	0	5	3	4	4	13	4	4	10	0		
1712	5	16	0	5	6	0	4	0	0	4	13	4		
1713	5	6	8	5	0	0	5	0	0	5	0	0		
1714	7	10	0[1]	6	13	4	6	6	8	7	16	8		
1715	6	13	4	6	0	0	4	13	4	6	0	0		
1716	5	0	0	4	13	4	4	6	8	4	10	0		
1717	5	0	0	4	10	0	4	5	0				4	16	8	4	10	0
1718	5	13	4	5	5	0	4	18	4				5	6	8	5	0	0
1719	5	16	0	5	6	8	5	6	8				5	6	8	5	0	0
1720	6	0	0	5	13	4	4	6	8				5	0	0	4	13	4
1721	5	15	0	5	3	4	4	13	4				5	0	0	4	13	4
1722	6	10	0	6	0	0	6	3	4[2]				6	13	4	6	0	0
1723	7	10	0	6	12	0	8	0	0				6	10	0	6	3	4
1724	5	8	0	5	0	0	5	3	4				4	13	4	4	10	0

1 Described in SRO, GD 30/2191 as 'deall land bear'.

2 From this date the fiars refer to both 'best' and 'second' bear although this series continues to record the price of best bear.

Table 3.13 *Bear and barley: county fiars, 1725–1780*

Crop year	Aberdeen Bear L. s. d.	Aberdeen Mercat bear L. s. d.	Aberdeen Wair bear L. s. d.	Ayr[1] L. s. d.	Banff L. s. d.	Berwick Merse barley[2] L. s. d.
1725	5 10 0	5 13 4	5 0 0	6 3 4		
1726	5 13 4	5 13 4	4 10 0	6 10 0		
1727	6 0 0	6 0 0	4 13 4	6 1 4		
1728	7 0 0	7 0 0	5 13 4	8 10 0		
1729	6 0 0	6 0 0	4 13 4	6 6 8		
1730	5 0 0	5 0 0	3 6 8	4 13 4		
1731	5 13 4	5 13 4	4 13 4	5 0 0		
1732	4 16 8	4 16 8	3 10 0	4 13 4		
1733	5 6 8	5 6 8	4 10 0	5 0 0		
1734	5 10 0	5 10 0	4 13 4	5 2 0		
1735	5 13 4	5 13 4	4 13 4	5 5 0		
1736	6 0 0	6 0 0	5 0 0	5 5 0		
1737	6 0 0	6 0 0	5 0 0	4 0 0		
1738	4 13 4	4 13 4	3 13 4	6 16 0		
1739	6 6 8	6 10 0	5 6 8	8 10 8		
1740	9 0 0	8 0 0	7 0 0	11 4 0		
1741	7 0 0	7 0 0	5 13 4	7 12 0		
1742	6 0 0	6 0 0	5 0 0	5 12 0		
1743	4 10 0	4 4 0	3 10 0	4 1 4[3]		
1744	7 0 0	7 0 0	5 6 8	7 12 0		
1745	8 0 0	8 0 0	6 10 0	11 4 0[3]		
1746	6 13 4	6 13 4	5 6 8	7 16 0		
1747	5 6 8	5 6 8	4 0 0	6 0 0		
1748	6 13 4	6 13 4	5 0 0	7 16 0		
1749	6 0 0	5 6 8	4 16 8	6 12 0		
1750	5 10 0	5 3 4	4 3 4	7 16 0		
1751	7 0 0	6 13 4	5 6 8	9 12 0		
1752	6 10 0	7 10 0	8 0 0	8 8 0		7 0 0
1753	6 0 0	7 4 0	7 10 0	10 0 0		7 0 0
1754	6 0 0	6 0 0	4 6 8	8 0 0		4 16 0
1755	7 6 8	7 0 0	5 6 8	9 12 0		5 10 0
1756	10 0 0	10 0 0	8 0 0	12 12 0	10 0 0	9 9 0
1757	9 0 0	9 0 0	7 0 0	10 16 0	9 0 0	7 10 0
1758	6 0 0	6 0 0	5 0 0	6 0 0	5 10 0	4 13 0
1759	5 14 0	5 14 0	4 0 0	6 0 0	5 10 0	4 16 0
1760	5 2 0	5 2 0	4 0 0	6 16 0	5 10 0	4 16 0
1761	5 14 0	5 14 0	4 0 0	8 12 0	5 0 0	4 8 0
1762	9 0 0	9 0 0	7 0 0	10 0 0	9 0 0	7 16 0
1763	8 0 0	8 0 0	5 10 0	9 4 0	8 0 0	6 10 0
1764	8 8 0	8 8 0	6 0 0	9 8 0	8 8 0	6 9 0
1765	10 0 0	10 0 0	7 10 0	13 4 0	9 0 0	7 0 0
1766	11 0 0	11 0 0	8 0 0	12 12 0	10 0 0	9 3 0
1767	9 0 0	9 0 0	7 0 0	11 8 0	8 8 0	7 1 0
1768	7 0 0	7 0 0	5 10 0	7 4 0	6 6 0	5 2 0
1769	7 10 0	7 10 0	6 0 0	12 0 0	7 10 0	6 8 0
1770	8 8 0	8 8 0	6 6 0	11 12 0	9 0 0	6 18 0
1771	8 8 0[4]	9 6 0	8 0 0	14 0 0	9 12 0	8 0 0
1772		11 2 0	8 8 0	11 8 0	10 10 0	9 0 0
1773		9 12 0	7 12 0	12 12 0	9 12 0	8 0 0
1774		10 10 0	7 0 0	11 8 0	10 10 0	8 5 0
1775		9 6 0	8 0 0	10 0 0	8 14 0	6 18 0
1776		6 6 0	6 0 0	9 0 0	6 12 0	5 0 0
1777		8 0 0	7 14 0	11 8 0		6 18 0
1778		7 16 0	7 4 0	10 16 0		6 12 0
1779		6 18 0	6 12 0	9 6 0		4 19 0
1780		7 4 0	6 18 0	9 12 0		6 6 0

1 The boll of bear was stated to be of 8 Winchester bushels.

2 Prior to crop 1752 Merse bear and Lammermuir bear were recorded (see next page); from 1752 Merse bear became Merse rough bear and the fiar for Merse barley was struck.

3 Different values are given in SRO, GD 25/9/Box 1; £4.1.8 in 1743 and £10.16.0 in 1745.

4 From crop 1772 only bear 'with fodder' is listed.

Table 3.13 *(cont.)*

| Crop year | Berwick | | Bute | Clackmannan | Dumfries | Dunbarton |
| | Merse bear | Lammermuir bear | | | | |
	L. s. d.	L. s. d.	L. s. d.	L. s. d.	L. s. d.	L. s. d.
1725	6 6 0	5 16 0				
1726	5 12 0	5 0 0				
1727	6 12 0	6 0 0				
1728	7 4 0	6 18 0				
1729	5 12 0	5 0 0				
1730	4 6 0	4 4 0				
1731	4 10 0	4 0 0				
1732	3 14 0	3 4 0				
1733	5 0 0	4 10 0				
1734	4 16 0	4 8 0				
1735	5 2 0	4 10 0				
1736	6 17 0	5 17 0				
1737	6 10 0	5 14 0				
1738	4 16 0	4 4 0				
1739	5 2 0	4 4 0				
1740	8 14 0	7 16 0				
1741	5 16 0	5 4 0				
1742	6 0 0	5 2 0				
1743	3 18 0	3 6 0				
1744	4 10 0	3 6 0				
1745	5 14 0	5 2 0				
1746	5 5 0	4 10 0				
1747	5 6 0	5 0 0				
1748	5 16 0	5 4 0				
1749	4 16 0	4 8 0				
1750	4 12 0	4 4 0				
1751	6 6 0	5 14 0				
1752	6 8 0[1]	5 16 0				
1753	6 6 0	5 14 0				
1754	4 8 0	4 0 0				
1755	5 0 0	4 10 0				
1756	8 17 0	8 0 0	12 6 0	9 12 0	21 0 0	10 0 0
1757	6 18 0	6 0 0	9 10 0	9 0 0	24 0 0	8 16 0
1758	4 1 0	4 0 0	6 12 0	5 16 0	13 0 0	5 15 0
1759	4 10 0	4 1 0	6 12 0	6 0 0	13 0 0	6 0 0
1760	4 4 0	3 18 0	7 10 0	5 12 0	14 0 0	6 0 0
1761	4 0 0	3 15 0	8 8 0	6 0 0	15 0 0	7 10 0
1762	7 4 0	6 12 0	10 4 0	8 12 0	24 0 0	8 10 0
1763	5 18 0	5 10 0	9 6 0	9 0 0	21 0 0	8 17 0
1764	5 10 0	5 6 0	9 18 0	9 0 0	19 10 0	8 18 0
1765	6 14 0	6 6 0	12 18 0	11 14 0	25 16 0	
1766	8 11 0	8 0 0	12 18 0	11 0 0	24 0 0	10 2 0
1767	6 15 0	6 11 0	10 4 0	10 6 0	19 4 0	9 0 0
1768	4 10 0	4 10 0	9 18 0	8 0 0	16 0 0	7 16 0
1769	5 14 0	5 2 0	12 12 0	9 0 0	16 0 0	9 16 0
1770	6 10 0	6 2 0	12 12 0	9 12 0	20 16 0	9 12 0
1771	7 0 0	6 10 0	12 12 0	10 0 0	26 8 0	9 6 0
1772	8 8 0	8 0 0	12 12 0	11 2 0	27 0 0	9 18 0
1773	7 8 0	7 4 0	12 12 0	10 16 0	22 4 0	10 4 0
1774	7 4 0	7 0 0	9 18 0	10 10 0	24 0 0	9 6 0
1775	6 6 0	6 0 0	10 4 0	9 6 0	21 12 0	8 14 0
1776	4 17 6	4 4 0	9 12 0	7 16 0	14 8 0	7 10 0
1777	6 6 0	6 0 0				
1778	6 6 0	6 0 0				
1779	4 13 0	4 10 0				
1780	5 14 0	5 14 0				

1 From crop 1752 Merse bear becomes known as Merse rough bear.

Table 3.13 *(cont.)*

Crop year	Edinburgh L. s. d.	Elgin L. s. d.	Fife L. s. d.	Forfar L. s. d.	Glasgow Commissary L. s. d.	Haddington L. s. d.	Inverness L. s. d.
1725	7 0 0		4 16 8			6 13 4	
1726	6 6 0		4 13 4			6 6 0	
1727	7 9 0		5 6 8			7 16 0	
1728	9 0 0		6 6 8			9 0 0	
1729	6 13 4		5 0 0			6 12 0	
1730	5 13 4		3 16 8			5 12 0	
1731	5 16 0		3 16 8			5 8 0	
1732	5 5 0		3 15 0			4 12 0	
1733	6 5 0		4 3 4			6 2 0	
1734	6 5 0		4 6 8			6 2 0	
1735	6 7 0		4 6 8			6 6 0	
1736	7 2 0		5 10 0			7 4 0	
1737	7 0 0		5 6 8			7 4 0	
1738	5 18 0		4 6 8			5 10 0	
1739	7 4 0		5 12 0			7 4 0	
1740	10 12 0		8 10 0			11 2 0	
1741	6 13 4					6 9 0	
1742	6 13 4		5 0 0			6 18 0	
1743	5 12 0		4 3 4			5 0 0	
1744	6 6 0		4 12 0			6 6 0	
1745	7 0 0		5 5 0			7 4 0	
1746	7 0 0		5 10 0			6 12 0	
1747	6 14 0		4 10 0			6 16 0	
1748	6 16 0		5 0 0			6 16 0	
1749	6 6 0		4 10 0			6 3 0	
1750	6 7 0		4 16 8			6 2 0	
1751	7 4 0		5 13 4			7 4 0	
1752	7 16 0		6 12 0			7 18 0	
1753	8 8 0		6 6 8			8 6 0	
1754	6 5 0		4 13 4			6 3 0	
1755	6 12 0		5 2 0			6 9 0	
1756	10 0 0		7 13 4	8 8 0	9 19 8	10 4 0	6 6 6
1757	8 17 0	7 10 0	7 3 4	8 0 0	8 0 10	9 0 0	6 19 10
1758	6 6 0	4 10 0	4 15 0	6 0 0	4 14 2	6 6 0	4 13 4
1759	6 5 0	4 13 4	4 10 0	5 15 0	5 11 4	6 5 0	4 13 4
1760	6 3 0	4 6 8	4 5 0	5 10 0	5 12 8	5 17 0	4 13 4
1761	6 6 0		4 2 0	5 2 0	6 1 10	5 9 0	4 13 4
1762	8 11 0		7 0 0	7 4 0	8 1 7	9 4 6	8 0 0
1763	8 2 0		6 6 8	7 4 0	7 19 0	8 10 0	6 0 0
1764	8 5 0	6 0 0	6 6 0	7 10 0[1]	7 19 4	8 15 0	7 4 0
1765	9 18 0	9 0 0	8 13 4	9 18 0	9 14 6	10 1 0	8 0 0
1766	10 16 0	8 10 0	8 5 0	9 12 0	10 6 4	11 15 0	8 0 0
1767	8 8 0	7 0 0	7 8 0	8 16 0	8 12 2	9 6 6	6 13 4
1768	7 1 0	6 0 0	5 3 4	6 6 0	7 7 0	7 14 9	6 0 0
1769	8 2 0	6 0 0	5 18 0	6 12 0	8 6 5	8 15 9	6 6 0
1770	8 5 0	7 10 0	5 16 0	7 0 0	8 14 0	8 10 6	7 4 0
1771	9 15 0	8 10 0	7 0 0	8 14 0	9 10 8	9 14 3	9 0 0
1772	10 10 0	9 0 0	7 12 0	9 6 0	9 15 0	11 0 0	9 0 0
1773	10 8 0	9 0 0	7 12 0	9 0 0	9 7 0	11 5 9	7 4 0
1774	9 15 0	9 0 0	7 10 0	9 6 0	9 13 0	11 0 9	8 0 0
1775	8 7 0	8 0 0	6 0 0	8 0 0	8 8 0	8 15 6	8 0 0
1776	7 4 0	6 0 0	5 3 0	6 3 0	6 12 0	7 3 9	7 4 0
1777	8 5 0		5 10 0			8 10 9	
1778	8 8 0		6 0 0			8 11 0	
1779	6 15 0		5 4 0	6 0 0[2]		6 16 9	
1780	8 8 0		5 17 0	6 18 0[2]		8 12 0	

1 Although this series of prices (1756-76) taken from Bald (*The Farmer and Corn Dealers' Assistant*, Edinburgh, 1780) is said to refer to 'bear', SRO, GD 45/12/86 ascribes this 1764 fiars price to 'barley' whilst recording 'Chester bear' at £6.16.0 per boll.

2 These prices, taken from SRO, GD 45/12/86, refer to barley bear. Chester bear was recorded to have been £5.8.0 for crop 1779 and £6.0.0 for crop 1780.

Table 3.13 *(cont.)*

Crop year	Kincardine L. s. d.	Kinross L. s. d.	Kirkcudbright L. s. d.	Lanark L. s. d.	Linlithgow Best bear L. s. d.	Blandart bear L. s. d.	Muirland bear L. s. d.
1725				5 6 8	6 10 0		5 13 4
1726				4 15 0	5 15 0		5 1 8
1727				5 10 0	7 0 0		6 0 0
1728				7 0 0	8 3 4		7 12 0
1729					6 0 0		5 10 0
1730				4 5 0	5 4 0		4 10 0
1731				3 16 0	5 0 0		4 10 0
1732				3 15 0	4 17 0		4 4 0
1733				5 10 0	6 0 0		5 4 0
1734				4 10 0	5 18 0		5 10 0
1735				6 10 0	6 3 0		5 17 0
1736				5 16 0	6 9 0		5 19 0
1737				5 13 4	6 11 0		5 17 0
1738				5 4 0	6 0 0		5 12 0
1739				6 10 0	7 2 0		6 10 0
1740				10 10 0	10 10 0		10 0 0
1741				6 3 4	6 5 0		5 12 0
1742				5 6 0	6 5 0		5 15 0
1743				3 16 0	5 6 8		4 10 0
1744				5 17 0	5 18 0[1]	5 12 0	5 3 0
1745				7 0 0	7 3 0	6 8 0	5 12 0
1746				6 0 0	6 18 0	6 8 0	6 0 0
1747				4 16 0	6 0 0	5 10 0	5 6 0
1748				5 16 0	6 5 0	5 18 0	
1749				5 10 0	6 0 0	5 14 0	5 7 0
1750				6 0 0	6 6 0	5 16 0	5 10 0
1751				7 0 0	7 4 0	6 18 0	6 6 0
1752				7 6 8	7 16 0	7 10 0	6 14 0
1753					8 10 0	7 10 0	7 0 0
1754				5 12 0	6 0 0	5 12 0	5 0 0
1755				5 18 0	6 18 0	6 8 0	5 18 0
1756	8 0 0		12 0 0	9 0 0	9 12 0	9 0 0	8 10 0
1757	7 10 0		12 12 0	9 0 0	8 10 0	7 18 0	7 12 0
1758	5 6 8		8 0 0	5 0 0	6 5 0	5 10 0	5 0 0
1759	5 0 0		7 4 0	4 12 0	6 4 0	5 12 0	5 0 0
1760	4 16 0		7 4 0	4 10 0	5 15 0	5 0 0	4 10 0
1761	4 10 0			5 10 0	6 6 0	5 14 0	5 0 0
1762	7 4 0		13 16 0	7 14 0	8 2 0	7 8 0	6 18 0
1763	6 12 0	6 5 0	13 4 0	6 0 0	8 0 0	7 4 0	6 12 0
1764	7 4 0	6 6 0	12 0 0	8 0 0	8 2 0	7 10 0	6 15 0
1765	9 0 0	9 0 0	16 0 0	9 12 0	10 4 0	9 10 0	8 14 0
1766	10 0 0	8 0 0	13 4 0	9 6 0	10 16 0	10 4 0	9 12 0
1767	8 0 0	8 0 0	16 0 0	9 10 0	8 7 0	8 5 0	7 17 0
1768	7 0 0	5 10 0	10 16 0	6 6 0	6 12 0	6 0 0	5 12 0
1769	6 6 0	6 6 0	11 8 0	8 10 0	8 4 0	7 4 0	6 12 0
1770	7 0 0	6 0 0	12 12 0	7 10 0	8 8 0	7 8 0	6 6 0
1771	8 10 0	7 6 0	15 12 0	9 6 0	9 9 0	8 9 0	7 16 0
1772	10 0 0	9 0 0	15 0 0	8 14 0	9 18 0	9 0 0	8 8 0
1773	8 0 0	8 0 0	15 0 0	9 12 0	10 10 0	9 6 0	8 14 0
1774	9 12 0	8 0 0	14 8 0	8 8 0	9 6 0	8 4 0	7 4 0
1775	7 18 0	6 6 0	13 4 0	6 6 0	8 6 0	7 8 0	6 12 0
1776	5 8 0	5 8 0	8 8 0	6 6 0	7 4 0	6 6 0	5 14 0
1777					8 5 0	7 4 0	6 12 0
1778					8 5 0	7 4 0	6 12 0
1779					7 10 0	6 18 0	6 6 0
1780					8 8 0	7 16 0	7 4 0

1 From this date 'best bear' becomes known as 'barley bear'.

Table 3.13 *(cont.)*

Crop year	Nairn	Perth	Renfrew	Roxburgh	Stirling Carse bear	Dryfield bear	Wigtown
	L. s. d.	L. s. d.	L. s. d.	L. s. d.	L. s. d.	L. s. d.	L. s. d.
1725		5 0 0			5 13 4	5 5 0	
1726		5 0 0			5 5 0	5 0 0	
1727		6 0 0			7 0 0	6 13 4	
1728		6 10 0			7 0 0	6 6 8	
1729		5 6 8			5 6 8	5 3 4	
1730		4 13 4			4 10 0	4 3 4	
1731		4 13 4			4 13 4	4 10 0	
1732		4 10 0			4 13 4	4 10 0	
1733		5 0 0			5 6 8	5 3 4	
1734		5 0 0			5 0 0	4 13 4	
1735		5 0 0			5 13 4	5 10 0	
1736		5 16 8			5 15 0	5 12 0	
1737		5 6 8			5 15 0	5 10 0	
1738		5 0 0			5 10 0	5 0 0	
1739		6 0 0			7 0 0	7 0 0	
1740		8 13 4			10 0 0	10 0 0	
1741		5 6 8			5 12 0	5 6 8	
1742		5 13 4			5 13 4	5 12 0	
1743		5 0 0			4 5 0	4 0 0	
1744		5 6 8			5 13 4	5 6 8	
1745		6 0 0			7 10 0	7 0 0	
1746		5 10 0			7 0 0	6 10 0	
1747		5 6 8			5 10 0	5 5 0	
1748		5 10 0			5 12 0	5 6 8	
1749		5 6 8			5 10 0	5 0 0	
1750		5 6 8			6 10 0	6 0 0	
1751		6 6 0			7 0 0	6 13 4	
1752		7 0 0			8 10 0	8 0 0	
1753		6 6 0			7 15 0	7 15 0	
1754		5 6 8			5 18 0	5 12 0	
1755		6 6 0			7 10 0	7 5 0	
1756	8 0 0	8 10 0	11 0 0	12 0 0	9 10 0	9 10 0	9 0 0
1757	9 0 0	7 10 0	9 0 0	9 12 0	8 0 0	7 15 0	11 0 0
1758	5 0 0	5 6 0	5 10 0	5 8 0	5 13 4	5 10 0	9 0 0
1759	5 8 0	5 8 0	5 10 0	5 14 0	5 10 0	5 8 0	7 10 0
1760	5 2 0	5 0 0	5 18 0	5 8 0	5 10 0	5 5 0	8 0 0
1761	5 0 0	5 0 0	7 6 0	5 8 0	6 0 0	5 15 0	9 0 0
1762	8 0 0	7 0 0	8 14 0	10 16 0	8 6 0	8 0 0	15 0 0
1763	6 0 0	7 10 0	8 10 0	8 14 0	8 0 0	7 14 0	12 10 0
1764	7 4 0	7 10 0	8 16 0	9 0 0	9 0 0	8 14 0	10 10 0
1765	8 16 0	10 0 0	11 17 0	10 4 0	11 8 0	11 8 0	12 12 0
1766	8 10 0	9 0 0	11 8 0	12 0 0	10 16 0	10 4 0	12 12 0
1767	8 10 0	8 0 0	10 18 0	9 0 0	10 4 0	9 14 0	10 16 0
1768	5 14 0	6 0 0	8 0 0	6 18 6	7 16 0	7 12 0	10 0 0
1769	6 6 0	7 0 0	10 7 6	8 8 0	8 10 0	8 6 0	10 0 0
1770	7 4 0	7 0 0	9 9 0	8 8 0	8 14 0	8 8 0	13 4 0
1771	9 0 0	8 8 0	10 11 3	9 18 0	10 4 6	9 6 0	14 8 0
1772	9 6 0	9 0 0	10 10 0	10 16 0	10 10 0	10 0 0	15 0 0
1773	9 0 0	9 0 0	11 2 0	10 16 0	10 10 0	10 0 0	15 0 0
1774	9 6 0	9 0 0	10 4 4	10 16 0	10 0 0[1]	9 12 0[1]	15 0 0
1775	8 0 0	7 10 0	9 0 0	8 8 0	8 8 0	8 0 0[1]	13 16 0
1776	6 12 0	6 6 0	8 8 0	6 6 0	7 16 0	7 0 0	9 18 0
1777		6 12 0			8 8 0	8 2 0	
1778		6 18 0			8 8 0	8 2 0	
1779		6 3 0			7 4 0	6 12 0	
1780		6 18 0			8 5 0	7 16 0	

1 Different values for these years are given in the Book for the Quarterly Fyars for Stirling Shire (SRO, SC 67/28/2). Those struck at the February courts were: crop 1774, Carse bear at £11.14.0 and dryfield bear at £10.16.0, and crop 1775 dryfield bear at £8.8.0. From 1774, SRO, SC 67/57/19 records, in addition to Carse, dryfield and (appearing for the first time) muirland 'bear', both Carse and dryfield 'barley'. This table continues to refer to the price of Carse and dryfield 'bear'.

Table 3.14 *Malt and rye: county fiars, 1628–1674*

Crop year	Aberdeen Malt[1] L. s. d.			Fife Malt L. s. d.			Linlithgow Malt L. s. d.			Aberdeen Rye[1] L. s. d.			Fife Rye L. s. d.			Perth Rye L. s. d.		
1628	*8*	*0*	*0*							*6*	*13*	*4*						
1629	*6*	*13*	*4*							*5*	*6*	*8*						
1630	*6*	*6*	*8*							*4*	*6*	*8*						
1631	*4*	*6*	*8*							*3*	*0*	*0*						
1632	*6*	*13*	*4*							*4*	*0*	*0*						
1649	*8*	*6*	*8*	11	0	0				*6*	*13*	*4*	10	0	0			
1650	*8*	*6*	*8*							*6*	*13*	*4*	10	13	4			
1651	*8*	*6*	*8*							*6*	*0*	*0*	9	6	8			
1652	*8*	*0*	*0*	13	6	8				*6*	*0*	*0*	9	0	0			
1653				6	0	0							4	0	0			
1654				5	0	0	4	13	4				4	0	0			
1655	*5*	*0*	*0*	7	0	0	7	0	0	*4*	*3*	*4*						
1656	4	0	0	5	6	8				3	0	0	4	0	0			
1657	*4*	*13*	*4*	5	6	8	5	6	8	3	6	8	4	0	0			
1658				7	6	8	7	0	0				6	0	0			
1659				6	15	0							6	0	0			
1660				6	15	0	7	0	0				5	6	8			
1661				7	6	0	8	0	0				5	6	8			
1662				7	0	0	6	13	4				4	0	0	4	0	0
1663				6	0	0	5	16	8				4	0	0			
1664				5	0	0	4	0	0				3	6	8			
1665	*4*	*0*	*0*	4	0	0	4	13	4	3	6	8	3	6	8	3	6	8
1666	4	6	8				4	13	4	4	0	0				3	0	0
1667	5	6	8				5	6	8	4	0	0				4	0	0
1668	4	0	0	5	0	0	5	6	8	4	0	0	3	0	0			
1669	4	3	4	5	6	8	5	3	4	3	6	8	3	6	8			
1670	5	0	0				5	6	8	4	3	4				4	13	4
1671							5	16	8									
1672				5	6	8	5	3	4				4	0	0			
1673				5	0	0	5	0	0				3	6	8			
1674				8	0	0	9	0	0				8	0	0			

1 These prices are for 'mercat' malt and rye. 'Ferme' malt and rye were usually, and from 1650 were invariably, the same price as their 'mercat' equivalents. Figures in italics are for fiars struck between July and November rather than, as was usual, in or around February.

Table 3.15 *Malt and rye: county fiars, 1675–1724*[1]

Crop year	Aberdeen Malt[2] L. s. d.	Fife Malt L. s. d.	Linlithgow Malt L. s. d.	Stirling Malt L. s. d.	Aberdeen Rye[2] L. s. d.	Fife Rye L. s. d.	Perth Rye L. s. d.
1675		11 0 0	10 13 4			8 0 0	
1676	*3 16 8*	5 6 8	4 6 8		*3 10 0*	3 13 4	
1677	*3 6 8*	4 10 0			*3 6 8*	2 18 0	
1678	*3 10 0*	4 6 8	4 2 8		*3 0 0*	2 10 0	
1679	*3 13 4*	4 13 4	5 0 0		*3 6 8*	3 0 0	
1680	3 6 8	4 10 0			3 0 0	3 10 0	
1681	4 0 0	4 6 8			3 6 8	5 0 0	
1682	*4 0 0*	7 6 8		7 6 8	*3 6 8*	4 6 8	
1683		4 10 0	5 0 0	4 13 4		3 10 0	
1684		4 10 0		4 10 0		4 0 0	
1685		4 6 8	4 12 0	4 10 0		3 6 8	3 6 8
1686		5 12 0	6 0 0	5 6 8		3 0 0	3 13 4
1687		4 10 0		5 0 0		3 6 8	3 6 8
1688		4 10 0	5 6 8	5 0 0		4 0 0	4 0 0
1689		5 6 8	5 6 8	6 0 0		4 13 4	5 6 8
1690	6 0 0	7 10 0	7 13 4		5 0 0	6 0 0	6 13 4
1691	4 0 0	4 13 4	5 6 8	5 0 0	4 0 0	3 10 0	3 6 8
1692	3 6 8	4 13 4	5 0 0		4 0 0	3 0 0	3 6 8
1693	4 0 0	4 13 4	5 6 8	4 13 4	4 0 0	3 3 4	3 6 8
1694	4 13 4	4 16 4	5 6 8	5 10 0	4 0 0	3 15 0	4 0 0
1695	6 13 4	7 10 0	7 10 0	8 0 0	5 6 8	7 0 0	4 13 4
1696	8 13 4	9 13 4		10 3 4	6 0 0	7 0 0	6 13 4
1697	9 0 0	10 10 0		8 6 8	8 0 0	5 6 8	5 6 8
1698	11 6 8	10 10 0	11 0 0	12 0 0	10 0 0	8 6 8	7 10 0
1699	8 0 0	10 0 0		11 0 0	7 13 4	7 13 4	9 0 0
1700	6 13 4	8 0 0	7 13 4	8 13 4	5 6 8	4 10 0	5 0 0
1701	4 6 8	4 16 8	5 6 8	5 13 4	4 13 4	3 6 8	4 0 0
1702	4 0 0	5 0 0	6 0 0	5 10 0	4 13 4	4 10 0	5 0 0
1703	3 13 4	5 0 0	6 0 0	6 0 0	4 0 0	4 6 8	4 6 8
1704	4 0 0	5 3 4	6 0 0	5 3 4	4 0 0	3 10 0	3 13 4
1705	4 0 0	5 0 0	5 10 0	5 0 0	3 0 0	3 6 8	4 0 0
1706	3 6 8	4 0 0	4 0 0	4 13 4	3 0 0	2 10 0	2 13 4
1707	3 6 8	3 16 8	4 13 4	4 13 4	3 6 8	2 6 8	3 3 4
1708	4 13 4	5 13 4	6 10 0	6 0 0	4 13 4	4 13 4	5 0 0
1709	6 13 4	7 0 0	7 10 0	7 10 0	5 0 0	5 10 0	6 13 4
1710	5 0 0		8 0 0	7 0 0	5 0 0		5 6 8
1711	4 0 0	5 6 8	5 13 4	5 3 4	3 13 4	4 0 0	3 13 4
1712	3 6 8	4 10 0	5 13 4	4 13 4	3 6 8	3 10 0	3 13 4
1713	4 13 4	5 6 8	5 13 4	5 6 8	4 0 0	3 10 0	4 0 0
1714	4 13 4	7 6 8	7 6 8	7 10 0	4 6 8	4 16 8	5 10 0
1715	4 3 4	4 13 4	6 10 0	6 0 0	3 6 8	4 0 0	5 0 0
1716	3 13 4	4 13 4	5 6 8	4 13 4	3 6 8	3 10 0	4 0 0
1717	4 13 4	4 10 0	5 0 0	5 0 0	4 3 4	3 16 8	4 0 0
1718	4 6 8	5 6 8	5 6 8	5 0 0	4 0 0	4 10 0	4 6 8
1719	4 13 4	5 10 0	5 6 8	5 6 8	4 6 8	4 16 8	5 0 0
1720	4 0 0	5 6 8	5 10 0	5 0 0	3 10 0	4 0 0	4 0 0
1721	4 13 4	5 0 0	5 13 4	5 0 0	3 10 0	4 6 8	4 0 0
1722	5 13 4	6 3 4	6 6 8	6 6 8	5 0 0	5 10 0	5 16 8
1723	5 13 4	7 16 8	7 0 0		5 10 0	5 16 8	6 13 4
1724	4 3 4	5 0 0	5 6 8	5 0 0	4 0 0	4 3 4	4 3 4

1 Also available, but excluded due to lack of space, is a series of malt prices for Lanark; crops 1694-96, 1700-3, 1711, 1713, 1715 and 1723-1830.

2 Figures in italics are for fiars struck between July and November rather than, as was usual, in or around February.

Table 3.16 *Malt and rye: county fiars, 1725–1780*

Crop year	Aberdeen Malt L. s. d.			Fife Malt L. s. d.			Linlithgow Malt L. s. d.			Stirling Malt L. s. d.			Aberdeen Rye L. s. d.			Fife Rye L. s. d.			Perth Rye L. s. d.		
1725	5	6	8	6	4	8	6	13	4	6	0	0	4	0	0	4	10	0	4	10	0
1726	5	6	8	6	0	0	6	0	0	6	0	0	4	6	8	4	15	0	4	13	4
1727	6	0	0	6	13	4	7	6	8	7	6	8	4	13	4	5	0	0	4	6	8
1728	6	6	8	7	3	4	8	0	0	8	0	0	5	13	4	4	13	4	5	0	0
1729	6	0	0	6	12	0	6	10	0	6	0	0	5	0	0	4	16	8	5	6	8
1730	4	3	4	5	6	8	6	0	0	5	6	8	4	3	4	4	0	0	4	0	0
1731	5	13	4	5	6	8	5	13	4	5	5	0	4	13	4	3	13	4	4	6	8
1732	4	13	4	5	0	0	5	5	6	5	6	8	3	6	8	3	6	8	4	0	0
1733	5	0	0	5	6	8	6	10	0	6	0	0	4	6	8	3	8	0	4	6	8
1734	4	16	8	5	6	8	6	3	4	5	10	0	4	0	0	4	0	0	4	13	4
1735	5	6	8	5	16	8	6	18	0	5	13	4	4	13	4	3	13	4	4	0	0
1736	5	10	0	6	13	4	7	8	6	6	10	0	4	13	4	4	10	0	5	0	0
1737	5	10	0	6	13	4	7	0	0	6	10	0	4	13	4	4	8	0	5	0	0
1738	4	13	4	5	16	8	7	5	0	6	0	0	4	0	0	3	13	4	4	0	0
1739	6	0	0	6	13	4	7	18	0	7	10	0	5	0	0	3	18	0	5	10	0
1740	8	0	0	9	13	4	11	0	0	10	10	0	8	0	0	7	6	8	8	0	0
1741	7	0	0				7	5	0	6	10	0	5	6	8				5	0	0
1742	6	0	0	6	0	0	5	12	0	6	10	0	5	0	0	4	0	0	4	13	4
1743	4	0	0	5	5	0	5	12	6	5	3	0	3	15	0	3	6	8	4	0	0
1744	6	0	0	6	0	0	6	13	4	6	0	0	5	6	8	4	3	4	4	6	8
1745	7	10	0	6	5	0	8	0	0	7	15	0	6	13	4	4	5	0	5	10	0
1746	6	8	0	6	16	8	7	10	0	8	0	0	4	16	0	4	0	0	5	5	0
1747	6	0	0	6	0	0	6	10	0	6	13	4	4	16	0	4	0	0	3	13	4
1748	6	0	0	6	0	0	7	0	0	6	13	4	4	16	0	3	12	0	4	13	4
1749	5	6	8	6	0	0	6	12	0	6	10	0	4	16	0	3	10	0	5	0	0
1750	5	6	8	6	0	0	7	6	0	7	0	0	4	16	0	4	5	0	4	10	0
1751	6	13	4	6	15	0	8	0	0	7	13	4	6	0	0	4	8	0	7	0	0
1752	7	10	0	8	0	0	8	0	0	8	10	0	6	0	0	5	0	0	6	13	4
1753	7	0	0	7	16	8	9	10	0	9	0	0	5	0	0	5	6	8	5	5	0
1754	6	0	0	6	0	0	7	0	0	6	13	4	4	16	0	3	18	0	3	15	0
1755	6	13	4	6	6	0	7	15	0	8	0	0	5	6	8	4	10	0	4	12	0
1756	9	10	0	9	3	4	10	12	0	10	0	0	6	12	0	6	0	0	6	0	0
1757	9	0	0	8	10	0	10	0	0	9	10	0	6	10	0	5	15	0	5	0	0
1758	6	0	0	6	5	0	7	5	0	6	8	0	4	16	0	4	10	0	4	10	0
1759	6	0	0	6	0	0	7	0	0	6	10	0	4	0	0	3	10	0	3	16	0
1760	5	2	0	6	0	0	7	0	0	7	0	0	4	8	0	3	12	0	5	0	0
1761	6	0	0	6	0	0	8	0	0	7	0	0	4	10	0	4	0	0	4	0	0
1762	8	10	0	8	10	0	9	12	0	9	6	0	8	0	0	5	8	0	5	10	0
1763	8	8	0	8	0	0	10	0	0	9	0	0	5	12	0	5	0	0	5	6	0
1764	8	10	0	8	0	0	9	16	0	10	0	0	7	0	0	5	0	0	5	10	0
1765	10	0	0	10	10	0	12	0	0	11	8	0	8	0	0	6	6	0	6	0	0
1766	10	10	0	10	0	0	12	12	0	12	0	0	8	0	0	6	0	0	6	16	0
1767	8	8	0	9	8	0	11	8	0	10	14	0	6	10	0	4	0	0	6	0	0
1768	7	0	0	7	3	4	8	0	0	9	0	0	6	0	0	5	0	0	4	16	0
1769	7	4	0	7	18	0	10	4	0	8	17	0	6	0	0	4	15	0	5	0	0
1770	8	8	0	7	14	0	10	10	0	9	18	0	7	10	0	4	13	4	5	5	0
1771	8	14	0	9	6	0	11	10	0	11	8	0	8	8	0	6	0	0	6	0	0
1772	9	12	0	10	0	0	12	0	0	10	16	0	8	14	0	5	8	0	6	6	0
1773	9	12	0	10	0	0	12	12	0	11	10	6	8	0	0	6	0	0	6	12	0
1774	10	10	0	9	15	0	12	0	0	11	4	0	8	14	0	5	10	0	6	0	0
1775	8	8	0	8	0	0	10	16	0	9	6	0	7	4	0	5	8	0	5	14	0
1776	6	4	0	7	5	0	9	12	0	9	0	0	5	6	8	4	12	0	6	6	0
1777	8	8	0	7	10	0	10	10	0	9	12	0	6	16	0	6	0	0	6	0	0
1778	8	4	0	8	0	0	10	10	0				6	6	0	5	0	0	6	0	0
1779	8	0	0	7	6	0	9	18	0				5	14	0	4	11	0	4	10	0
1780	8	8	0	9	0	0	11	2	0				6	12	0	4	16	0	6	0	0

Table 3.17 *Pease and beans: county fiars, 1628–1674*

Crop year	Aberdeen Pease[1]			Edinburgh Pease			Fife Pease and beans[2]			Haddington Pease			Linlithgow Pease			Perth Pease		
	L.	s.	d.	L.	s.	d.	L.	s.	d.	L.	s.	d.	L.	s.	d.	L.	s.	d.
1628	*9*	*0*	*0*															
1629	*6*	*0*	*0*															
1630	*5*	*13*	*4*															
1631	*6*	*13*	*4*															
1632	*5*	*6*	*8*															
1640				4	13	4												
1642				7	6	8												
1643				5	0	0												
1644				6	0	0												
1645				4	10	0												
1646				4	0	0												
1647				5	6	8												
1648				9	0	0												
1649	*8*	*0*	*0*	11	0	0	11	0	0	11	0	0						
1650	*7*	*13*	*4*	9	0	0	10	13	4[2]									
1651	*7*	*13*	*4*	9	0	0	11	10	0[2]	11	0	0						
1652	*10*	*13*	*4*	9	0	0	12	0	0	5	0	0						
1653							4	0	0	3	0	0				4	13	4
1654				2	0	0	4	0	0	5	0	0	2	0	0	3	0	0
1655	*5*	*0*	*0*	5	0	0	4	0	0	4	0	0	5	16	8			
1656	4	0	0	3	10	0	4	0	0	4	0	0						
1657	4	3	4	3	13	4	4	0	0	7	0	0	3	6	8	4	13	4
1658							6	0	0	12	0	0	6	0	0			
1659				5	6	8	6	0	0	12	0	0						
1660				5	6	8	5	6	8	5	10	0	6	6	8			
1661				5	13	4	5	6	8	5	13	4	6	0	0	6	13	4
1662				3	10	0	4	0	0	3	10	0	3	13	4	5	0	0
1663				4	0	0	4	0	0	4	0	0	3	6	8	5	6	8
1664				2	13	4	3	6	8	2	15	0	2	10	0	3	6	8
1665	*4*	*0*	*0*	4	6	0	3	6	8	5	0	0	4	6	8	4	0	0
1666	*5*	*6*	*8*	3	13	4				3	14	0	3	16	8	4	0	0
1667	*5*	*6*	*8*	4	0	0				4	5	0	3	13	4	5	0	0
1668	*5*	*0*	*0*				4	0	0	3	0	0	3	0	0	4	13	4
1669	*4*	*13*	*4*	3	3	4	3	6	8	3	4	0	3	0	0	4	0	0
1670	*5*	*0*	*0*	3	10	0				4	0	0	4	0	0	5	0	0
1671				6	0	0							5	16	8	5	6	8
1672				4	6	8	4	13	4	5	10	0	4	10	0	5	6	8
1673				6	0	0	4	0	0	7	10	0	4	13	4	5	0	0
1674				11	0	0	8	0	0	12	12	0	8	10	0	8	0	0

1 These prices are for 'mercat' pease. 'Ferme' pease was usually, and from 1631 was invariably, the same price. Figures in italics are for fiars struck between July and November rather than, as was usual, in or around February.

2 Pease and beans were listed separately, but (with the exception of 1650 and 1651) when both were given they were always returned with the same fiars price. In 1650 pease were £10.13.4 and beans £9.13.4 per boll; in 1651 pease were £11.10.0 and beans £9.13.4 per boll. (No beans prices were struck in 1656-58, 1665-71 or 1674.)

Table 3.18 *Pease and beans: county fiars, 1675–1724*

Crop year	Aberdeen Pease [1]			Berwick Pease			Edinburgh Pease			Fife Pease and beans [2]			Haddington Pease		
	L.	s.	d.	L.	s.	d.	L.	s.	d.	L.	s.	d.	L.	s.	d.
1675							8	10	0	9	10	0	9	8	0
1676	*5*	*0*	*0*				3	6	8	3	13	4	3	0	0
1677	*4*	*10*	*0*				3	0	0	2	18	0	3	2	0
1678	*4*	*0*	*0*				3	0	0	2	10	0	2	16	0
1679	*4*	*0*	*0*				4	6	8	3	10	0	4	0	0
1680	4	0	0				5	16	0	4	0	0	5	4	0
1681	4	6	8				5	10	0	6	0	0	5	13	4
1682	*4*	*6*	*8*				5	0	0	5	0	0	7	0	0
1683							4	0	0	3	10	0	3	13	4
1684							4	0	0	4	0	0	5	12	0
1685							3	12	0	3	6	8	3	13	4
1686							5	16	0	4	13	4	5	16	0
1687							3	12	0	3	6	8	3	15	0
1688							5	0	0	5	0	0	5	0	0
1689				4	4	0	4	10	0	4	13	4	5	0	0
1690	8	0	0	6	10	0	7	18	0	8	0	0	8	8	0
1691	5	0	0	4	0	0	4	0	0	4	3	4	4	12	0
1692	5	6	8	4	0	0	4	0	0	3	10	0	4	6	0
1693	5	6	8	4	0	0	4	6	8	3	13	4	4	6	0
1694	5	6	8	4	0	0	5	3	4	3	15	0	4	12	0
1695	8	0	0	7	0	0	8	6	8	8	0	0	9	0	0
1696	9	0	0	7	10	0	11	14	0	8	0	0	10	0	0
1697	9	0	0	7	0	0	6	13	4	7	0	0	6	12	0
1698	14	0	0	10	10	0	13	0	0	9	10	0	14	0	0
1699	10	0	0	8	10	0	10	3	4	10	0	0	10	6	8
1700	8	0	0	4	0	0	5	0	0	5	0	0	5	13	4
1701	5	6	8	3	0	0	3	3	4	3	10	0	3	0	0
1702	5	0	0	3	12	0	5	0	0	5	0	0	5	0	0
1703	4	13	4	3	16	0	4	10	0	4	3	4	4	13	4
1704	5	0	0	3	12	0	4	10	0	4	0	0	4	13	4
1705	4	13	4	4	8	0	5	0	0	4	13	4	5	10	0
1706	4	0	0	1	18	0	2	16	0	2	13	4	3	0	0
1707	4	0	0	2	10	0	3	0	0	2	13	4	2	14	0
1708	5	6	8	5	0	0	5	6	8	4	13	4	5	3	4
1709	6	13	4	6	10	0	7	0	0	6	0	0	7	3	4
1710	5	13	4	5	14	0	6	13	4				7	3	4
1711	5	0	0	4	0	0	4	0	0	3	10	0	4	0	0
1712	4	0	0	3	0	0	3	16	0	3	10	0	4	0	0
1713	5	0	0	7	10	0	8	0	0	6	13	4	8	10	0
1714	5	6	8	6	10	0	6	0	0	7	6	8	7	10	0
1715	5	6	8	5	0	0	5	13	4	4	10	0	6	6	8
1716	5	0	0	3	6	0	3	6	8	3	0	0	3	16	0
1717	5	6	8	3	12	0	4	0	0	3	10	0	4	6	0
1718	5	6	8	3	10	0	4	0	0	3	16	8	3	18	0
1719	6	0	0	5	16	0	5	0	0	4	13	4	6	12	0
1720	4	6	8	4	0	0	5	0	0	3	13	4	4	12	0
1721	6	0	0	5	0	0	5	0	0	5	0	0	5	15	0
1722	6	13	4	6	0	0	7	0	0	6	0	0	6	13	4
1723	7	0	0	5	10	0	6	12	0	7	16	8	6	13	4
1724	5	0	0	5	0	0				4	13	4	5	2	0

1 Figures in italics are for fiars struck between July and November rather than, as was usual, in or around February.

2 Pease and beans were listed separately, but when both were given they were always returned with the same fiars price. (No beans prices were struck in 1675, 1676, 1681, 1683, 1685–87, 1689–1701, or 1710.)

Table 3.18 *(cont.)*

Crop year	Kincardine Pease			Lanark Pease			Linlithgow Pease			Perth Pease			Stirling Pease and beans		
	L.	s.	d.	L.	s.	d.	L.	s.	d.	L.	s.	d.	L.	s.	d.
1675	6	0	0				8	0	0	10	0	0			
1676	4	3	4				3	3	4	4	13	4			
1677	4	0	0				3	0	0	3	13	4			
1678	4	0	0							3	6	8			
1679	4	0	0				5	0	0	4	0	0			
1680	4	3	4				2	13	4	4	0	0			
1681	4	0	0				5	0	0	6	0	0			
1682	6	0	0				5	13	4	6	0	0	5	13	4
1683	4	6	8				3	13	4	4	0	0	4	3	4
1684	4	13	4				4	0	0	4	0	0	3	13	4
1685	4	3	4				3	0	0	4	0	0	3	10	0
1686	4	0	0				5	12	0	4	6	8	5	0	0
1687							3	3	4	4	6	8	5	0	0
1688							5	6	8	5	0	0	5	0	0
1689							4	10	0	6	0	0	5	13	4
1690							6	13	4	8	0	0			
1691				4	0	0	3	13	4	4	13	4	3	11	4
1692				4	6	8	4	0	0	4	0	0			
1693				4	16	8	4	0	0	4	6	8	3	16	8
1694				5	13	4	5	0	0	4	13	4	5	6	8
1695				8	0	0	7	10	0	7	0	0	7	13	4
1696				10	13	4	8	0	0	9	0	0	6	16	8
1697							5	0	0	7	0	0	6	10	0
1698							10	0	0	10	0	0	10	6	8
1699							9	0	0	11	0	0	10	0	0
1700				4	13	4	4	0	0	6	0	0	5	0	0
1701				4	6	8	3	10	0	4	6	8	4	6	8
1702							5	0	0	6	0	0	5	6	8
1703							4	0	0	4	6	8	5	0	0
1704							4	13	4	4	10	0	4	3	4
1705							4	0	0	5	0	0	4	6	8
1706							2	0	0	3	6	8	3	3	4
1707							3	6	8	3	13	4	4	0	0
1708							5	6	8	5	3	4	5	6	8
1709							7	0	0	6	13	4	7	0	0
1710							6	6	8	7	13	4	6	13	4
1711							3	5	0	3	13	4	3	6	8
1712							3	6	0	4	0	0	3	3	4
1713							6	13	4	6	0	0	5	6	8
1714							6	0	0	7	0	0	7	0	0
1715							5	10	0	5	0	0	5	0	0
1716							3	0	0	4	3	4	3	3	4
1717							3	0	0	4	5	0	3	10	0
1718							4	6	8	4	0	0	4	6	8
1719							5	0	0	5	0	0	4	13	4
1720							6	0	0	4	3	4	3	6	8
1721							4	8	0	4	6	8	4	0	0
1722							7	0	0	6	6	8	7	0	0
1723				7	0	0	6	0	0	7	10	0	6	0	0
1724				4	10	0	3	12	0	4	13	4	3	6	8

Table 3.19 *Pease and beans: county fiars, 1725–1780*

Crop year	Aberdeen Pease L. s. d.			Banff Pease L. s. d.			Berwick Pease L. s. d.			Clackmannan Pease L. s. d.			Dumfries Pease L. s. d.			Edinburgh Pease L. s. d.		
1725	6	0	0				7	10	0							7	10	0
1726	7	0	0				4	4	0							4	12	0
1727	6	13	4				6	4	0							5	10	0
1728	8	0	0				5	12	0							6	12	0
1729	6	6	8				4	0	0							5	10	0
1730	4	3	4				3	6	0							3	4	0
1731	4	6	8				3	10	0							3	6	0
1732	4	13	4				3	12	0							3	12	0
1733	4	13	4				4	0	0							4	4	0
1734	5	6	8				4	0	0							4	10	0
1735	5	13	4				4	16	0							5	4	0
1736	6	0	0				6	6	0							6	0	0
1737	6	0	0				7	0	0							6	6	0
1738	5	0	0				3	6	0							3	18	0
1739	6	0	0				3	16	0							5	10	0
1740	9	12	0				11	0	0							12	0	0
1741	8	10	0				4	16	0							5	12	0
1742	6	0	0				4	10	0							4	10	0
1743	4	4	0				2	16	0							3	12	0
1744	7	0	0				3	6	0							4	16	0
1745	8	0	0				6	12	0							6	6	0
1746	6	6	8				3	12	0							4	10	0
1747	6	0	0				3	18	0							4	10	0
1748	6	0	0				3	16	0							4	0	0
1749	5	0	0				3	9	0							4	4	0
1750	5	0	0				3	18	0							5	15	0
1751	7	10	0				6	0	0							7	10	0
1752	8	0	0				8	0	0							8	0	0
1753	6	0	0				5	4	0							6	6	0
1754	6	0	0				3	16	0							4	16	0
1755	6	13	4				4	16	0							6	6	0
1756	9	0	0	8	6	8	10	14	0	7	10	0	19	4	0	10	0	0
1757	8	10	0	7	4	0	6	8	0	9	6	0	22	8	0	8	0	0
1758	6	0	0	4	16	0	4	4	0	4	10	0	12	16	0	5	16	0
1759	4	8	0	4	0	0	4	16	0	4	0	0	12	16	0	3	12	0
1760	5	0	0	4	0	0	4	10	0	5	6	0	11	4	0	4	16	0
1761	5	0	0	5	0	0	3	6	0	5	4	0	12	16	0	4	16	0
1762	8	0	0	8	0	0	5	16	0	8	0	0	25	12	0	7	10	0
1763	8	0	0	6	0	0	5	14	0	7	10	0	14	8	0	7	4	0
1764	8	0	0	7	0	0	6	18	0	8	0	0	14	8	0	7	4	0
1765	8	0	0	8	14	0	6	3	0	10	0	0	24	0	0	7	16	0
1766	8	10	0	8	4	0	7	10	0	9	0	0	19	4	0	8	14	0
1767	8	0	0	8	0	0	7	8	0	9	0	0	19	4	0	8	14	0
1768	8	0	0	6	0	0	7	16	0	5	14	0	14	8	0	8	2	0
1769	8	0	0	6	12	0	5	8	0	7	4	0	16	0	0	6	12	0
1770	8	0	0	8	0	0	6	8	0	7	10	0	17	12	0	6	18	0
1771	8	8	0	8	8	0	5	12	0	8	0	0	24	0	0	8	8	0
1772	8	14	0	8	14	0	7	8	0	9	0	0	19	4	0	9	0	0
1773	8	14	0	8	2	0	6	0	0	7	10	0	19	4	0	7	10	0
1774	9	12	0	8	14	0	5	16	0	8	8	0	20	16	0	7	10	0
1775	9	0	0	6	12	0	4	16	0	6	18	0	19	4	0	6	6	0
1776	6	0	0	5	8	0	4	10	8	6	6	0	16	0	0	6	0	0
1777	7	16	8				5	10	0							6	0	0
1778	6	12	0				4	10	0							5	14	0
1779	5	14	0				4	0	0							4	16	0
1780	6	12	0				5	0	0							6	0	0

Table 3.19 *(cont.)*

Crop year	Fife Pease and beans[1]	Forfar Pease	Haddington Pease	Kincardine Pease	Kinross Pease	Lanark Pease
	L. s. d.	L. s. d.	L. s. d.	L. s. d.	L. s. d.	L. s. d.
1725	5 10 0		8 6 0			
1726	5 0 0		5 12 0			
1727	5 0 0		5 14 0			
1728	4 18 0		7 0 0			7 10 0
1729	4 6 8		5 4 0			5 0 0
1730	3 0 0		3 4 0			4 0 0
1731	3 3 4		3 8 0			3 16 0
1732	3 8 0		3 16 0			3 13 4
1733	3 6 8		4 12 0			
1734	3 6 8		4 0 0			4 10 0
1735	3 12 0		5 10 0			5 10 0
1736	5 6 8		6 6 0			6 6 0
1737	5 8 0		6 10 0			6 0 0
1738	3 12 0		4 0 0			4 0 0
1739	4 10 0		4 18 0			6 3 4
1740	8 13 4		13 4 0			11 0 0
1741			5 8 0			6 0 0
1742	4 0 0		4 12 0			4 10 0
1743	3 6 8		3 2 0			3 12 0
1744	4 0 0		4 16 0			5 12 0
1745	4 13 4		6 14 0			7 0 0
1746	4 0 0		4 10 0			4 10 0
1747	3 8 0		4 14 0			4 4 0
1748	3 12 0		3 18 0			4 16 0
1749	3 10 0		3 9 0			4 13 4
1750	6 0 0		5 0 0			6 0 0
1751	5 13 0		7 10 0			7 10 0
1752	7 0 0		8 6 0			8 8 0
1753	6 0 0		7 2 0			6 0 0
1754	3 18 0		4 14 0			5 6 0
1755	4 12 0		6 6 0			6 0 0
1756	7 6 8	7 4 0	10 0 0	7 10 0		9 0 0
1757	7 13 4	6 13 4	8 2 0	7 0 0		9 0 0
1758	4 15 0	5 6 0	4 16 0	5 0 0		5 0 0
1759	3 6 0	3 10 0	3 15 3	4 16 0		4 4 0
1760	4 5 0	4 10 0	4 12 0	4 16 0		4 0 0
1761	4 0 0	3 12 0	4 17 3	4 16 0		5 10 0
1762	7 0 0	6 12 0	8 0 0	7 4 0		8 0 0
1763	5 16 8	6 12 0	6 14 0	6 0 0	5 6 8	6 6 0
1764	5 14 0	7 0 0	7 3 9	7 0 0	5 12 0	8 0 0
1765	8 6 8	9 12 0	7 17 3	8 6 0	8 10 0	9 0 0
1766	7 10 0	8 14 0	9 1 6	8 0 0	7 10 0	9 0 0
1767	7 10 0	8 0 0	9 6 9	8 0 0	8 0 0	9 10 0
1768	5 12 0	6 0 0	8 15 9	6 8 0	5 0 0	7 0 0
1769	5 18 0	6 0 0	6 6 6	6 0 0	5 18 0	7 10 0
1770	5 10 0	6 0 0	6 11 9	6 12 0	5 6 0	7 4 0
1771	6 0 0	7 10 0	7 15 6	8 0 0	6 0 0	9 3 0
1772	6 6 0	7 10 0	8 15 6	9 0 0	7 10 0	9 0 0
1773	6 13 4	7 4 0	7 12 0	7 4 0	7 16 0	8 2 0
1774	6 12 0	7 10 0	7 13 3	9 0 0	6 6 0	9 0 0
1775	5 16 0	7 4 0	6 5 6	8 0 0	6 0 0	6 6 0
1776	5 0 0	5 2 0	5 13 0	5 8 0	5 7 0	6 6 0
1777	5 6 0		6 13 6			
1778	4 10 0		5 11 6			
1779	4 2 0	4 4 0	4 17 3			
1780	5 12 0	5 5 0	6 1 9			

1 Pease and beans were listed separately, but were always returned with the same fiars price.

Table 3.19 *(cont.)*

Crop year	Linlithgow Pease L. s. d.	Perth Pease L. s. d.	Renfrew Pease L. s. d.	Roxburgh Pease L. s. d.	Stirling Pease and beans L. s. d.
1725	5 10 0	5 6 8			5 0 0
1726	4 0 0	5 0 0			4 0 0
1727	5 15 0	5 6 8			6 0 0
1728	6 12 0	5 13 4			6 13 4
1729	4 0 0	5 0 0			4 5 0
1730	3 6 8	4 0 0			3 0 0
1731	3 10 0	4 6 8			3 15 0
1732	3 4 0	4 0 0			3 4 0
1733	4 5 6	4 6 8			4 10 0
1734	3 12 0	4 13 4			4 0 0
1735	4 18 0	4 10 0			5 4 0
1736	5 9 0	5 6 8			5 6 8
1737	5 10 0	5 10 0			5 10 0
1738	4 0 0	4 10 0			4 0 0
1739	5 6 0	5 10 0			6 0 0
1740	10 0 0	9 0 0			10 0 0
1741	5 15 0	5 10 0			5 6 8
1742	4 0 0	4 13 4			4 0 0
1743	3 5 4	4 0 0			3 6 0
1744	4 10 0	5 0 0			4 10 0
1745	7 2 0	5 10 0			6 15 0
1746	4 9 0	4 6 8			5 10 0
1747	4 0 0	4 0 0			3 15 0
1748	3 15 0	4 6 8			3 15 0
1749	4 0 0	4 10 0			3 15 0
1750	6 0 0	6 0 0			6 10 0
1751	7 0 0	6 0 0			6 0 0
1752	7 10 0	7 0 0			8 0 0
1753	6 4 0	6 0 0			6 0 0
1754	4 12 0	4 0 0			4 13 4
1755	6 0 0	5 15 0			6 15 0
1756	8 10 0	7 10 0	11 8 0	12 0 0	8 10 0
1757	8 0 0	7 4 0		9 0 0	8 15 0
1758	4 4 0	5 0 0		5 14 0	4 10 6
1759	3 12 0	4 0 0		5 0 0	4 0 0
1760	4 16 0	5 0 0		5 10 0	5 0 0
1761	4 16 0	4 10 0		5 8 0	4 18 0
1762	8 0 0	6 0 0		10 0 0	8 0 0
1763	6 12 0	5 16 0		9 12 0	7 0 0
1764	7 4 0	6 10 0		8 8 0	8 0 0
1765	8 8 0	9 0 0		9 12 0	10 0 0
1766	9 0 0	7 15 0		10 16 0	9 0 0
1767	8 0 0	8 0 0		11 8 0	9 0 0
1768	6 18 0	6 0 0		9 18 0	6 6 0
1769	6 12 0	5 8 0		7 4 0	7 10 0
1770	6 12 0	5 8 0	9 0 0	7 16 0	6 18 0
1771	7 10 0	7 4 0		7 16 0	8 8 6
1772	7 16 0	7 4 0	10 16 0	10 4 0	7 16 0
1773	6 18 0	7 10 0	10 0 0	9 0 0	7 16 0
1774	7 4 0	7 4 0	9 18 0	9 0 0	7 16 0[1]
1775	5 17 0	6 6 0	9 13 0	7 4 0	6 6 0[1]
1776	5 14 0	5 2 0	8 12 0	6 0 0	6 12 0
1777	5 18 0	4 16 0			6 0 0[1]
1778	5 14 0	4 16 0			5 14 0
1779	4 13 0	4 10 0			4 16 0
1780	6 4 0	6 0 0			6 0 0

1 Different values for these years are given in the Book for the Quarterly Fyars for Stirling Shire (SRO, SC 67/28/2). Those struck at the February courts were: crop 1774, £7.10.10; crop 1775, £7.0.0; and crop 1777, £5.14.0.

Table 3.20 *Oats and oatmeal: Lady Balgarvie's accounts, Fife, 1767–1784*

Crop year	Transaction date	Oats L. s. d.			Oatmeal L. s. d.			Crop year	Transaction date	Oats L. s. d.			Oatmeal L. s. d.		
1767	9/1768				7	12	0	1778	11/1778				8	0	0
									12/1778				7	16	0
1768	9/1769				9	12	0		4/1779				7	4	0
									6/1779				7	4	0
1769	11/1769	6	6	0	7	7	0								
								1780	10/1780	6	0	0			
1772	1/1773	10	4	0					11/1780	6	0	0			
	3/1773	8	14	0	10	4	0		12/1780	7	4	0			
	4/1773				10	4	0		3/1781	7	16	0	8	8	0
	5/1773				10	4	0		6/1781	7	16	0	8	12	0
	6/1773	9	0	0	10	4	0	1781	10/1781	6	12	0	6	6	0
	8/1773	9	12	0	10	4	0		11/1781	6	12	0			
1773	11/1773				9	8	0		12/1781	6	12	0			
	12/1773	7	11	2	9	8	0		4/1782	6	15	0	7	12	0
	1/1774				9	8	6		5/1782	7	10	0	8	0	0
	2/1774				9	12	0	1782	11/1782	9	18	0	12	0	0 [1]
	4/1774	8	0	0	9	12	0		12/1782	9	18	0			
	7/1774				10	0	0		1/1783	10	10	0	12	0	0
1774	11/1774				8	16	0		3/1783	11	2	0	13	12	0 [2]
	12/1774	7	0	0	8	16	0		6/1783				13	1	0
	2/1775	7	0	0	9	0	0		8/1783				13	4	0
	5/1775				9	4	0	1783	10/1783	8	8	0 [3]	9	12	0
	6/1775	7	16	0					11/1783				9	12	0 [4]
	7/1775				9	6	0		12/1783	8	14	0			
1775	11/1775				7	16	6		1/1784				9	12	0
	12/1775	6	9	0					2/1784	9	0	0			
	2/1776	6	6	0	7	12	0		3/1784	9	18	0	10	4	0
	4/1776	6	0	0	7	12	0	1784	10/1784				9	18	0
	5/1776	6	0	0	7	12	0		12/1784	8	14	0	9	9	0
1776	11/1776	5	14	0	7	4	0		1/1785	9	0	0			
	2/1777	6	0	0	7	4	0		2/1785				8	8	0
	4/1777	6	0	0	7	4	0		3/1785	9	0	0			
	7/1777	6	6	0	7	4	0		4/1785				9	4	0
1777	11/1777	6	0	0					5/1785	9	12	0			
	1/1778				7	4	0		6/1785				8	8	0
	3/1778				7	4	0		7/1785	7	16	0	7	12	0
	4/1778				7	4	0								
	5/1778	6	12	0											

1 Also at £10.16.0   2 Also at £12.0.0   3 Also at £7.4.0   4 Also at £9.3.0

Table 3.21 *Bear and oatmeal: Craighall estate records, Fife, 1663–1679*

Crop year	Bear L. s. d.			Oatmeal L. s. d.			Crop year	Bear L. s. d.			Oatmeal L. s. d.		
1663	5	10	0	4	10	0	1672	4	10	0	4	0	0
1664	3	13	4	3	0	0	1673	4	6	8	4	0	0
1665	3	6	8	3	6	8	1674	8	0	0	8	0	0
1666	4	0	0	4	0	0	1675	11	0	0	5	0	0
1667	5	6	8	5	0	0	1676	4	13	4	3	13	4
1668	4	13	4	3	10	0	1677	5	6	8	3	0	0
1669	4	13	4	3	13	4	1678	4	10	0	3	0	0
1670	4	13	4	5	0	0	1679	4	10	0	4	10	0
1671	5	6	8	5	0	0							

Table 3.22 *Bear and oatmeal: Pittenweem Sea Box, Fife, 1658–1755* [1]

Crop year	Bear L. s. d.			Oatmeal L. s. d.			Crop year	Bear L. s. d.			Oatmeal L. s. d.		
1658	6	13	4	6	0	0	1702	4	13	4	6	0	0
1659	6	13	4	6	0	0	1703	5	6	8	6	0	0
1660	5	13	4				1704	5	0	0	5	6	8
1661	5	6	8				1705	4	13	4	4	0	0
1662	6	0	0				1706	3	13	4	3	0	0
1663	6	0	0				1707	3	13	4	4	0	0
1664	4	0	0				1708	6	0	0	10	0	0
1665	3	6	8				1709	7	0	0	8	0	0
1666	3	10	0	3	10	0	1710	6	2	0	6	0	0
1667	4	10	0	4	10	0	1711	5	8	4	5	0	0
1668	4	13	4	3	13	4	1712	4	6	0	5	0	0
1669	5	0	0	3	13	4	1713	4	15	0	5	6	8
1670	4	13	4	5	6	8	1714	6	13	4	6	0	0
1671	5	6	8	5	6	8	1715	4	13	4	5	0	0
1672	4	10	0	4	0	0	1716	4	6	8	5	0	0
1673	4	6	8	4	0	0	1717	4	10	0	5	0	0
1674	8	0	0	7	0	0	1718	5	1	0	5	0	0
1675	10	0	0	6	13	4	1719	6	0	0	5	0	0
1676	4	13	4	4	6	8	1720	4	12	0	5	0	0
1677	4	6	8	3	6	8	1721	4	16	0	6	0	0
1678	4	0	0	2	18	0	1722	6	0	0	6	0	0
1679	4	0	0	2	18	0							
1680	4	0	0	3	0	0							
1681	4	0	0	4	16	0	1735	4	10	0	6	0	0
1682	6	13	4	5	6	8	1736	5	15	0	6	0	0
1683	4	0	0	4	0	0	1737	5	10	0	6	0	0
1684	4	0	0	4	0	0	1738	4	7	0	4	16	0
1685	4	0	0	3	6	8	1739	5	15	0	7	0	0
1686	5	3	4	3	6	8	1740	8	8	2	10	0	0
1687	4	6	8	3	6	8 [2]	1741	5	5	0	5	12	0
1688	4	6	8	5	0	0	1742	5	7	0	5	0	0
1689	4	18	4	6	0	0	1743	4	0	0	5	0	0
1690	7	0	0	7	0	0	1744	4	6	8	5	0	0
1691	4	6	8	4	0	0	1745	5	0	0	7	0	0
1692	4	19	0	4	0	0	1746	5	16	0	5	12	0
1693	4	13	4	4	0	0	1747	4	12	0	5	0	0
1694	4	13	4	4	0	0	1748	5	8	0	5	12	0
1695	7	6	8	8	0	0	1749	4	13	4	6	0	0
1696	8	6	8	9	10	0	1750	5	0	0	6	8	0
1697	7	18	0	10	0	0	1751	5	16	8	7	0	0
1698	11	0	0	10	0	0	1752	6	18	0	8	0	0
1699	10	10	0	10	0	0	1753	6	11	8	7	0	0
1700	7	6	8	5	0	0	1754	4	17	4	6	0	0
1701	4	10	0	5	10	0	1755	5	4	0	6	8	0

1　When more than one sale is given in any year, the price quoted refers to the largest quantity sold.

2　From this date the oatmeal is explicitly stated to be 'fine meal'.

Table 3.23 *Oatmeal: Buchanan estate 'accounting' price, Stirlingshire, 1722–1780*

Crop year	Oatmeal L. s. d.			Crop year	Oatmeal L. s. d.			Crop year	Oatmeal L. s. d.		
1722	7	10	0	1742	4	8	0	1762	9	0	0
1723	5	13	4	1743	6	5	0	1763	8	0	0
1724	5	6	8	1744	8	0	0	1764	9	0	0
1725	6	13	4	1745	8	10	0	1765	9	12	0
1726	7	0	0	1746	6	0	0	1766	9	12	0
1727	8	0	0	1747	5	6	8	1767	7	4	0
1728	8	0	0	1748	5	10	0	1768	8	16	0
1729	6	0	0	1749	6	8	0	1769	9	4	0
1730	5	0	0	1750	7	4	0	1770	9	12	0
1731	5	0	0	1751	8	0	0	1771	9	12	0
1732	5	0	0	1752	8	0	0	1772	10	0	0
1733	6	0	0	1753	7	0	0	1773	9	12	0
1734	7	0	0	1754	6	8	0	1774	9	0	0
1735	7	0	0	1755	8	0	0	1775	7	4	0
1736	6	6	8	1756	12	0	0	1776	7	16	0
1737	5	0	0	1757	8	0	0	1777	8	8	0
1738	6	0	0	1758	5	8	0	1778	8	0	0
1739	9	0	0	1759	5	4	0	1779	7	4	0
1740	10	0	0	1760	6	0	0	1780	9	0	0
1741	5	3	4	1761	7	4	0				

Table 3.24 *Bear, wheat, oats: Dirleton victual contracts, East Lothian, 1668–1702*

Date of contract	Bear L. s. d.			Wheat L. s. d.			Oats L. s. d.			Date of contract	Bear L. s. d.		
2/1668	6	0	0							1/1683	8	13	4
2/1669							3	4	0	2/1683	8	6	8[2]
4/1670							3	8	0	2/1683	8	13	4[2]
5/1670							4	0	0	4/1683	8	0	0
6/1670							4	0	0				
1/1671	6	10	0										
7/1671							5	6	8	12/1691	5	7	0
12/1671				10	0	0				8/1692	5	16	0
1/1672	6	6	8										
4/1672	5	0	0							12/1696	12	0	0
10/1675				6	3	4							
										1/1698	9	10	0
										1/1699	13	10	0
1/1677				13	8	4							
8/1677	12	0	0[1]										
8/1677	6	13	4[1]							3/1702	8	10	0
6/1678							3	10	0	5/1702	9	10	0
5/1679	4	4	0	9	0	0							
7/1679							3	8	0				

1 In August 1677, 300 bolls of bear were sold for £12.0.0 and 113 bolls for £6.13.4.

2 In February 1683, 150 bolls of bear were sold for £8.6.8 and 20 bolls for £8.13.4.

4 ❖ Press reports of monthly market prices

The grain price series so far considered all provide a relatively coarse description of price movements; the fiars courts and town councils generally only set prices on an annual basis. Whilst this is of little consequence with regard to the assessment of longer-term movements, short-term price fluctuations, notably those within the year, are effectively obscured. For an insight into these, however, it is possible to turn to the quite remarkable series of monthly market prices recorded in the *Caledonian Mercury* and *Scots Magazine*. These chart the price of wheat, oats, barley and pease in East Lothian markets from 1721, and the price of oatmeal, peasemeal and bearmeal in Edinburgh from 1741. Such is the quality of this evidence that it not only provides a rare opportunity to trace in detail short-term price fluctuations, but also to examine both the relationship between those prices and the annually struck fiars and also the character of the annual cycle of grain price fluctuation. There are, however, a number of interpretative difficulties associated with this data which must be addressed before turning to the actual price series.

The bulk of this price data has been extracted from issues of the *Scots Magazine*. Prices of first, second and third wheat, oats, barley and pease begin to appear regularly in a small table headed simply 'Haddington Prices' from the March issue of 1741. These prices were still being reported well into the nineteenth century although tables 4.1–4.4, which record the prices fetched by 'first' wheat, oats, barley and pease, have been brought to a close in 1785,[1] though in the accompanying figures we have been able to show data to 1795. No information is provided in the original source on how the prices were either collected or calculated, although the date of the market to which the prices refer is almost invariably given. This was usually the first Friday of the month, suggesting that the editor of the *Scots Magazine* used the most recent prices he had to hand at the time of going to press.[2]

For a record of the price of grain in East Lothian prior to March 1741, it is necessary to

---

[1] In addition to those prices recorded here, we have available on computer quotations for first wheat, oats, barley and pease through to 1820 and for third wheat, oats, barley and pease for the period 1741–1781.

[2] It should be noted that the *Scots Magazine* was published sometime after the end of the month to which it was accredited. Thus the August edition, for instance, would have been published around the end of the second week of September. This meant that the *Scots Magazine* could usually report the prices fetched at the first Friday market of the month in which it was published. Sometimes, however, the edition, for whatever reason, was unable to report on the first market of the month and instead recorded the prices fetched on the last Friday market of the preceding month. For the sake of consistency, we have tabulated such prices as if they referred to the following month. This ensures that there is always only one set of prices per month and that they are at approximately four-week intervals.

turn to local newspapers. Prices in the Haddington and Dalkeith markets are recorded in the *Edinburgh Courant* from as early as May 1708, but these are most irregular and it is not until the *Caledonian Mercury* begins to note the price of grain in 1721 that anything like a complete series commences. This paper was usually published three times each week and, from May 1721, reported weekly on the price of wheat, oats, barley and pease at the Haddington market. To conform with the material available in the *Scots Magazine*, prices have been extracted and tabulated at monthly intervals.[3] For a period after March 1741 prices can be found in both the *Scots Magazine* and the *Caledonian Mercury* and are always identical.

From 1721 through to 1734 the *Caledonian Mercury* always reported prices at Haddington. But from August 1734 prices at Gifford were also noted. This was a weekly market held each Tuesday established by the Marquis of Tweeddale.[4] Throughout the rest of 1734 prices were recorded from both Gifford and Haddington, but during 1735 and 1736 the *Caledonian Mercury* began to report almost exclusively on prices at Gifford. The 1737 and 1738 volumes are missing from the National Library of Scotland, but by the time the series recommences in January 1739 the prices fetched in the Haddington market were once again the only ones reported. From then until 1795 all prices refer to Haddington. As Gifford lies but four miles to the south of Haddington and no significant price difference existed during the few months of 1735 when prices from both markets were being recorded, no distinction has been made in tables 4.1–4.4 between prices at the two markets.

There are three interrelated questions raised by these price series. First, were the markets dealing primarily with wholesale or retail transactions? Second, what was meant by the designation of grain prices as being 'first', 'second' or 'third'? And finally, how were the prices reported by the *Caledonian Mercury* and *Scots Magazine* actually determined? There is little hard evidence upon which to answer these questions, but some issues can be clarified.

Haddington was the principal market in one of Scotland's most important grain-growing districts and as such was primarily a wholesale market. That is to say, the majority of transactions which took place in the market would have been between local farmers and merchants, with the bulk of the produce presumably destined for Edinburgh. This conclusion is supported by the remarkably close correspondence between the fiars price for each grain and the average monthly price over the period November to February during which, as discussed in chapter 3, evidence was drawn for the purpose of striking the fiars. Between 1721 and 1795 there are fifty-two years for which prices are available for all four months and in those years the fiars prices for first wheat, oats, barley and pease were, on average, 100.2, 98.5, 103.5 and 98.8 per cent of the average price of those grains over the period November to February. This suggests that the monthly market price quotations were established by more or less the same method as

---

[3] The prices ascribed to any month refer to the first market of the month unless that was held after the 7th of that month. In such cases prices referring to the market held closest to the 1st of the month have been extracted. Thus prices taken from the *Scots Magazine* and *Caledonian Mercury* are directly comparable. Prices ascribed to any month in tables 4.1–4.4 should thus be read as referring to the beginning of that month.

[4] *Caledonian Mercury*, 5 August 1734.

the fiars and that both referred to the same commodity. As it is known that the fiars were determined on the evidence of farmers regarding the prices of the grains they had sold,[5] this would suggest that the monthly market price quotations also referred to the prices obtained by farmers selling their grain wholesale in the market.

Drawing such a parallel with the fiars also throws light on both the meaning of the terms 'first', 'second' and 'third' applied to the various grains and how their prices were determined. As has already been discussed in chapter 3, in East Lothian three fiars prices were ascribed to each grain and they were determined by a most peculiar method. A third of all the farmers in the county were called upon towards the end of February 'to depose as to the quantities, kinds, and prices of grain of the previous crop sold by them'. The Sheriff Clerk then proceeded to work out for each grain a weighted average price for all the transactions. This average was designated as the medium, or 'second', fiar. The Sheriff Clerk then took a weighted average of all the transactions made at a price above that medium and designated it the 'first' fiar. A weighted average of all the transactions made below that price was then calculated and designated as the 'third' fiar.[6]

The use of precisely the same terms in the monthly price statistics reported by the press (as opposed to the more usual 'best', 'worst', etc.), along with the observed correspondence between the fiars and the average price over the period November to February, suggests that very much the same method lay behind the calculation of monthly price statistics as the fiars. This must have demanded very time-consuming attention to detail on the part of the market's officials, but it constitutes the most plausible account of how the monthly quotations were determined.

There is therefore every reason to believe that these figures constitute an accurate and consistent guide to monthly wholesale prices in East Lothian over much of the eighteenth century. In tables 4.1–4.4 we have collected together all available quotations for 'first' wheat, oats, barley and pease, and for a more immediate impression of how prices fluctuated month by month, figures 4.1–4.4 have been compiled. These chart the monthly prices reported in the press alongside the fiars prices struck each year by the Sheriff Clerk.[7]

There are two general points to be drawn from these graphs. The first merely confirms what has already been demonstrated statistically; that fiars prices, set in late February or early March, generally reflect very closely the price at which grain was sold over the preceding four months. Although discrepancies can be found in particular years, the only significant periods during which this correspondence does not hold are for oats over the periods 1721–29 and 1739–41 and for barley throughout most of the 1720s and 30s. So notable are these temporary discordances that one must suspect that, for whatever

---

[5] D. Hunter, *Report of the committee on fiars prices to the General Assembly of the Church of Scotland* (Edinburgh, 1895), p. 28.

[6] To each of these calculated averages the Sheriff Clerk added 2.5 per cent to allow for the fact that whilst the evidence used in striking the fiars referred to transactions made 'in ready money', the bulk of the grain that was to be valued according to the fiars was sold at six months' credit – the cost of which was 2.5 per cent. Such an artificial adjustment would presumably not have been made in preparing the market price statistics reported in the press.

[7] In figures 4.1–4.4 the fiars price is marked by a dashed-line column which extends from November of the crop year in question to the following February. It thus embraces the period for which evidence was admitted in striking the fiars.

reason, the fiars system had broken down or had been somehow perverted. The second concerns the way in which prices moved over the course of the year and how in certain years prices could reach levels scarcely hinted at by the fiars. A particularly notable year in this respect is 1757. For each of the four principal grains sold at Haddington the fiars struck at the beginning of the year, which is to say for the crop of 1756, were at their highest level since the crop of 1740, but from the fiars alone one would never guess how bad the situation really was. In fact, what the monthly prices show is that wheat prices peaked in May of 1757 at a level 20 per cent higher than the preceding fiars, oats in August 33 per cent higher, and barley and pease in March 42 and 44 per cent higher respectively.

Annual movements in fiars prices, which are all that can be charted for most of Scotland for virtually all of the period with which we are concerned, clearly tell only part of the story. In years such as 1729, 1740, 1741, 1757 and 1793, grain prices in Haddington reached levels markedly higher than the fiars would suggest and, at least as importantly, throughout the eighteenth century price movements experienced from month to month were often of a magnitude comparable to those experienced from one year to the next.

Underlying such very short-term price movements was, of course, a strongly seasonal cycle of grain prices – the general character of which can be described by calculating the average monthly price of each grain expressed as a percentage of the average annual price. This takes no account, however, of whether prices were generally falling, rising or holding steady and is thus a dubious guide to the influence of purely seasonal factors on price movements. For that reason, alongside the cycle of average price movements at Haddington for the period 1721 to 1795 we have, in figures 4.5 and 4.6, also plotted the same statistic for just those years in which prices were, on a year-on-year basis, relatively stable.[8] However one looks at annual price movements their extravagantly cyclical nature is evident.

As already mentioned, the monthly figures refer to those prices current during the first week of each month: and all four grains show much the same pattern, especially clearly in those years when the underlying price trend was stable. Each was at its most expensive in early August just prior to the commencement of the harvest; prices then fell off sharply through August, September and October until, towards the end of the harvest in late October, they began to flatten out. In years of stable prices, wheat was lowest in November, pease in December, and oats and barley in January, but all four grains showed similar erratic movements at a low level throughout these months. Only during February and March did prices leap forward once more. Thereafter, although temporarily pegged back over April and May, prices rose steadily to their early August maximum.

The most obvious feature of these seasonal price curves is the sustained drop over the course of the harvest, but other features are less easy to explain. That some prices continued to drop over the course of the winter is a case in point; oats and barley reached their lowest prices so long after the end of the harvest that their delayed release on to the market must have been an important factor. The universal increase in prices in March

---

[8] For the purpose of these calculations, a price rise or fall of less than 10 per cent between August of the year in question and the preceding August is taken to mean that the year was one of relatively stable prices.

and April was explained by the fact that grain, still damp early in the year, was drying out: thus it was observed that 'corn of equal quality, if sold when new threshed in March, will fetch a higher price at that time than if it had been threshed and sold a month sooner in the season'.[9] A further characteristic was the marked drop in prices which occurred during the late spring. Pease prices declined markedly during April, whilst wheat and barley prices fell sharply during May. Even oats prices were pegged back somewhat during these months. As there seems no reason to presume a fall-off in demand at this time of year, one can only suppose that tenant farmers were selling off increased quantities of grain in search of cash to pay their termly rent.

One final observation which can be drawn concerns the relative magnitude of the seasonal price fluctuations experienced by each grain. During those years in which the underlying price trend was stable, wheat, barley, oats and pease showed average seasonal price ranges of 9.6, 10.6, 15.0 and 17.4 per cent respectively. Such differences between grains are difficult to explain, although they may reflect the manner in which farmers released their stocks, the manner in which merchants purchased supplies, or their relative keeping qualities. In the case of wheat, the grain with the least pronounced seasonal price range, it probably also reflects the fact that wheatbread was still something of a luxury in Scotland. There must have been many whose preferred diet was of wheatbread but who, when prices began to rise beyond their means, switched to the less costly meals made from pease, barley and oats. Such substitution would have exacerbated the seasonal price fluctuations of these latter grains, though never to the extent that they became as expensive as wheat.

For those dependent upon purchased supplies of grain, these short-term price movements would have been of great practical consequence. For example, on average, a pound spent on oats in Haddington at the beginning of February would in theory have obtained over 15 per cent more calories than a pound spent on oats at the beginning of August, unless the difference in moisture content cancelled the benefit. But the evidence available from Haddington is limited if we wish to pursue this line of enquiry; the prices quoted in the press refer to wholesale transactions and there are, moreover, no returns for meal – and it was upon oatmeal that the vast majority of Scots depended at this time. For this, however, we can turn to one further set of data recorded in the *Scots Magazine*.

Alongside the table of market prices at Haddington, the *Scots Magazine* printed, under the simple heading 'Edinburgh', the price of oatmeal, bearmeal and peasemeal in pence Scots per peck. Commencing in 1741, these prices were also being reported well into the nineteenth century although tables 4.5–4.7 have been brought to a close at the end of 1795.[10] The fact that prices are given in pence Scots per peck shows that they refer to retail transactions; and presumably to retail transactions made in the Edinburgh meal market. This conclusion is supported by the fact that the Edinburgh fiars for oatmeal (which, as discussed in chapter 3, were likely to have referred to wholesale prices) were, over the forty-nine years between 1741 and 1795 for which comparative data exist,

---

[9] G. Buchan-Hepburn, *General view of the agriculture and rural ecomony of East Lothian* (Edinburgh, 1794), p. 43.
[10] From February 1746 to March 1755 the *Scots Magazine* also reported the price of wheatbread. Occasionally this was the price set by the town council – these reports were used for table 2.1. More often, however, it was the price of wheatbread in the markets; we have not tabulated this short run of prices.

significantly lower (5.3 per cent) than the average monthly price over the period November to February during which evidence was drawn for the purpose of striking the fiars (see figure 3.1).

Unfortunately, unlike the series compiled from the wholesale transactions at Haddington, we have little hint of the mechanisms by which these monthly prices were determined. As discussed in chapter 2, wheatbread prices were almost certainly governed by town council statutes, but the provenance of the meal prices is much less clear. There may have been some formal arrangement whereby transactions made in the market were registered, but given the conditions which obtained in the meal market, this seems most improbable. Much more likely is that opinions were taken, perhaps even on an *ad hoc* basis, on the price at which the three different types of meal had been selling on the day concerned. There is, however, no reason to suppose that the various meal prices reported by the *Scots Magazine* are inconsistent or inaccurate.

As with the Haddington grain price series, the Edinburgh meal price series provide an opportunity to address both the nature of short-term price fluctuations and the seasonal cycle of price movements. As in Haddington, 1757 witnessed a particularly marked discrepancy between the prevailing fiars price (for crop 1756, struck in February or March 1757) and the level to which prices apparently climbed later in the year. Thus whilst the Edinburgh fiar for crop 1756 was set at £10.0s.0d. Scots per boll, oatmeal was fetching the equivalent of £12.8s.0d. Scots per boll throughout the second quarter of the year; a 24 per cent price rise effectively obscured by the fiars which, in fact, actually fell back to £8.4s.0d. Scots per boll by the time they were next struck in February or March 1758.

As illustrated by figure 4.7, such peaks lasting a few months at most interrupted the general run of oatmeal and peasemeal prices in Edinburgh just as they did the general run of grain prices in Haddington. The magnitude of the seasonal element of short-term price fluctuations was, however, very much less marked in Edinburgh than in Haddington. This can be seen clearly by comparing average monthly grain prices in Haddington, 1724–95 (figures 4.5 and 4.6) with average monthly meal prices in Edinburgh, 1741–95 (figures 4.8 and 4.9). Even allowing for the fact that the vertical scale of the latter two figures has been exaggerated (to ensure the relatively small price differentials can be picked out), the difference is clear. It would appear that the Edinburgh housewife buying oatmeal, bearmeal and peasemeal in the retail market was protected from the sharper fluctuations of the wholesale market for oats, barley (bear) and pease.

As basic necessities, the demand for all three types of meal would have been highly inelastic and thus it is towards the supply of these commodities we must turn for an explanation of their relative price stability. Two particular factors are likely to have conspired to minimise very short-term price movements. First, oatmeal, bearmeal and peasemeal were all manufactured commodities; the ultimate cost of which had to cover more than just the price of the raw materials from which they were manufactured. Second, the meal market in Edinburgh would presumably have been both highly competitive and, crucially, supplied by merchants with the facilities and resources to store substantial quantities of grain for considerable periods.

The effect of the manufacturing process on the nature of short-term price fluctuations would have been relatively minor. All meal prices had to cover the cost of labour and fixed costs, which would tend slightly to dampen the impact of fluctuations in the cost of the raw materials. For instance, if, on average, 10 per cent of the final price of oatmeal was to cover labour and other fixed costs, a 50 per cent increase in the price of oats would be transformed into a 45 per cent increase in the price of oatmeal. The greater the proportion of such costs incorporated within the price of oatmeal, the greater the degree to which oatmeal prices would be protected from swings in the price of oats. Unfortunately, without detailed mill accounts it is impossible to directly calculate the costs involved in the manufacture of oatmeal. However, making the assumption that oatmeal on sale in Edinburgh was largely manufactured from oats grown in East Lothian and traded in the Haddington market, one might attempt indirectly to estimate those fixed costs by comparing the price of oatmeal in Edinburgh with that of oats in Haddington. Using Swinton's estimates regarding the amount of oats required to produce a boll of oatmeal,[11] it emerges that, over the period 1741–95 (for which we have 603 months of comparative data),[12] the boll of Edinburgh oatmeal which cost, on average, £8.9s.5d. Scots required £7.17s.2d. Scots worth of Haddington oats; a 'profit' of 12s.3d. per boll of oatmeal. This represented 7.2 per cent of the final price, and would, of course, have had to cover all the costs of transport, labour, fuel and the depreciation of fixed capital.

More significant in reducing fluctuations, however, is the fact that Edinburgh merchants would not buy oats in Haddington in equal quantities throughout the year. They were, after all, petty capitalists with the financial resources and facilities to store grain, and may have attempted to purchase the damper oats when prices were at their lowest (generally January and February) and then attempted to sell the manufactured oatmeal as prices began to rise later in the year, though the cost advantage might have been reduced by a lower yield. Their ability to take advantage of cheap months and avoid dear months would in any case help to iron out price fluctuations for the consumer. An exactly similar effect would arise from their opportunities to buy in cheaper markets than Haddington, since Edinburgh sat at the centre of a well-developed grain market and could readily bring in supplies from as far north as the Moray Firth or Orkney. Merchants could supply the capital with grain drawn from a wide area according to the cheapness and quality of available supplies and would not have been as tied to the

[11] J. Swinton, *Proposal for Uniformity of Weights and Measures* (Edinburgh, 1789) provides a table of the various amounts of oatmeal which could be produced from a series of bolls of oats which weighed from 164 lbs. 7 oz. to 230 lbs. 4 oz. Scottish Troy. Although he states that a boll of oats could weigh considerably less than 164 lbs. 7 oz., he reckoned that such grain was unlikely to have been brought to the market for sale. Taking the upper quartile of those values Swinton tabulates (to allow for the fact that the Haddinton prices are for 'first' oats) it seems reasonable to proceed on his estimate that a boll of oatmeal weighing 128 lbs. Scottish Troy would require 1.03 bolls of oats for its manufacture.

[12] Analysis has been undertaken without taking account of the actual time it would have taken for the oats purchased in Haddington to have been processed and transported to Edinburgh. This, in fact, does not appear to have led to any lag between price movements in Haddington and Edinburgh. Product moment correlation coefficients of 0.95, 0.94, 0.90 and 0.86 have been calculated from a direct comparison of prices, a one-month, two-month and three-month time lag in the oats price series respectively. It would appear that oatmeal prices in Edinburgh tended to reflect the contemporary price of oats in Haddington rather than the price of the oats from which the meal had actually been made.

success or otherwise of the local harvest as might have been the case in provincial towns such as Perth or Aberdeen. The case of Edinburgh may, therefore, have been rather unusual.

Notwithstanding the relative stability of meal prices in Scotland's capital, it would be wrong to suppose that very short-term price movements (many of which followed a broadly cyclical pattern) were of small consequence. Seasonal price fluctuations in years with a stable trend suggest that there was relatively little variation between the first and second halves of the year, though prices were of course always lower in the first half. But, as figure 4.9 demonstrates, monthly price fluctuations were very significant in years when underlying prices were either rising or falling. There would have been few years to match the wild price movements already noted in 1757 (when the same cash outlay could have purchased very nearly 20 per cent more oatmeal in January than in August), but year-on-year price movements in excess of 10 per cent were experienced in very nearly two-thirds of all the years for which we have detailed monthly price data. When that movement was in an upward direction the difference between what could be bought in January as opposed to February was substantial. Perhaps if families could make bulk purchases in January and February to cover their needs for the rest of the year substantial savings could be made, but the fact of the matter was that few families dependent on purchased meal supplies could adopt such a strategy. Oatmeal would have been purchased whenever there was available cash, and what that cash could obtain would vary with the seasons and in line with the success or otherwise of the harvest. For families on tight budgets (and chapter 9 suggests that these would have comprised the majority of the wage-dependent labouring classes) price fluctuations may well have translated directly into fluctuations in the amount of food that was bought. What the monthly press reports on the price of oatmeal, bearmeal and peasemeal tell us is that when a poor harvest was expected, August and September could have been months of very real hardship for a significant proportion of the capital's population.

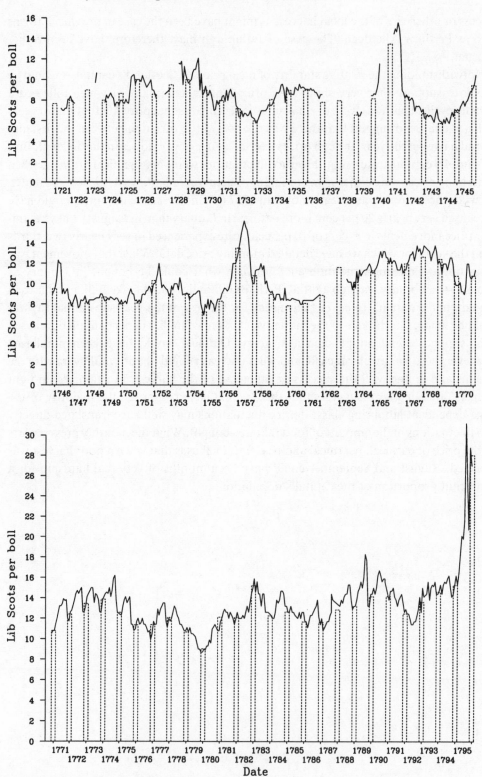

4.1 'First' wheat: Haddington fiars and monthly market prices, crops 1720–95

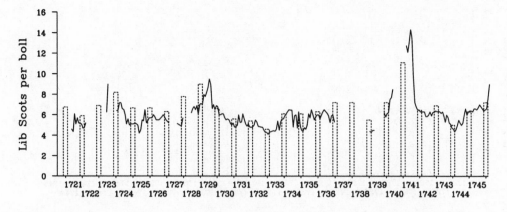

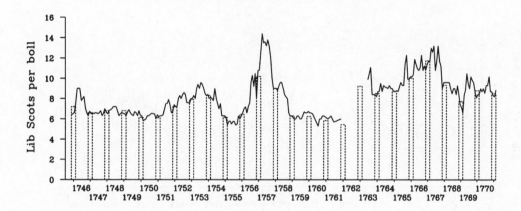

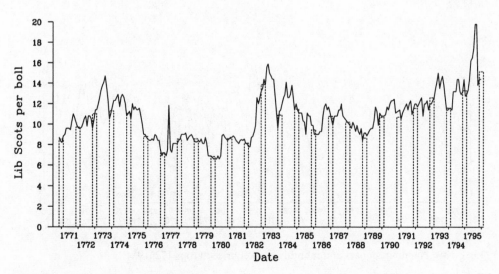

4.2 'First' barley: Haddington fiars and monthly market prices, crops 1720–95

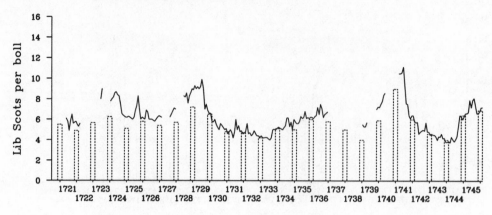

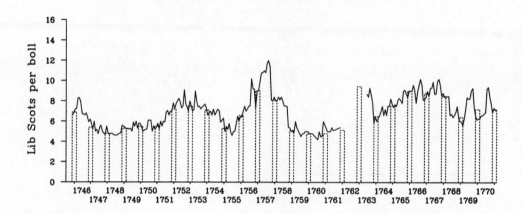

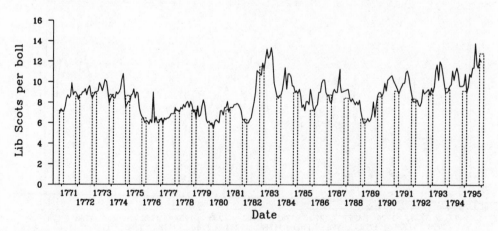

4.3 'First' oats: Haddington fiars and monthly market prices, crops 1720–95

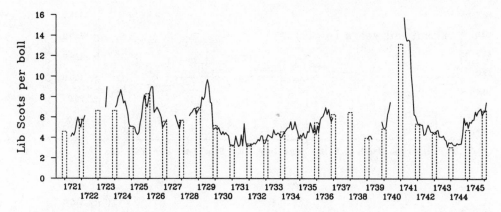

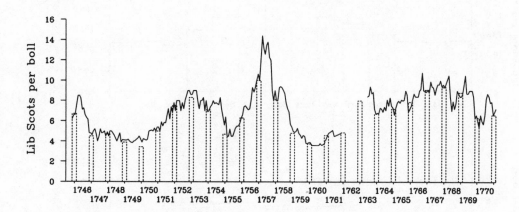

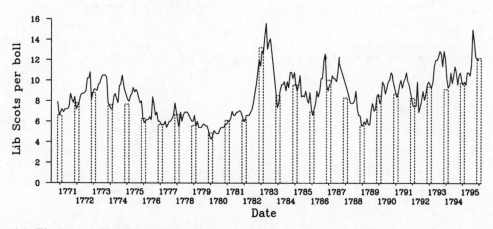

4.4 'First' pease: Haddington fiars and monthly market prices, crops 1720–95

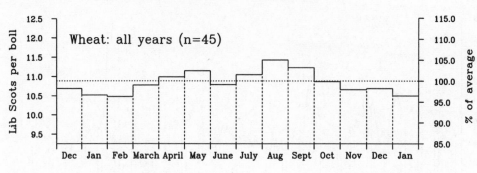

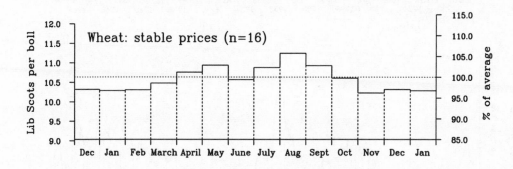

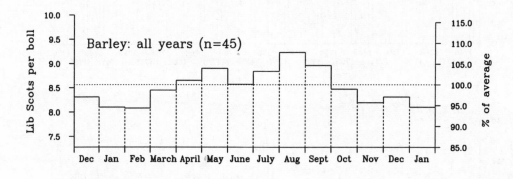

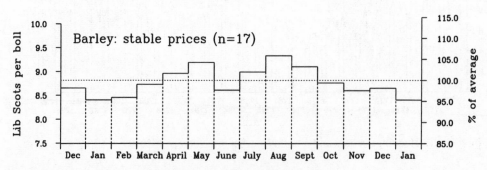

4.5 Average monthly wheat and barley prices: Haddington, 1724–95

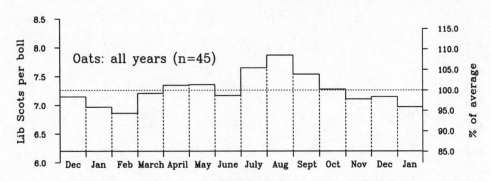

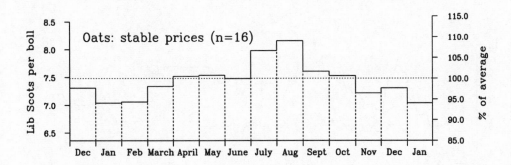

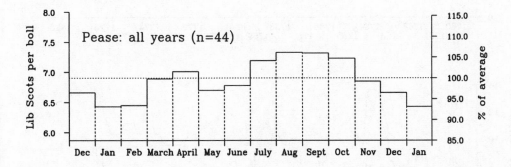

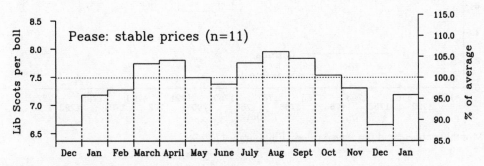

4.6 Average monthly oats and pease prices: Haddington, 1724–95

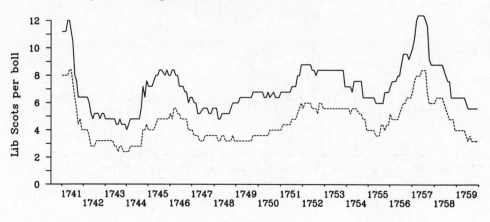

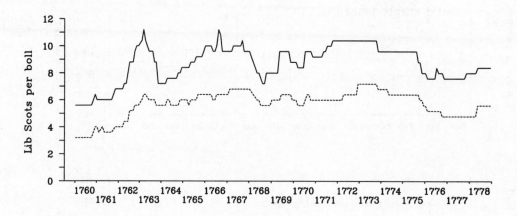

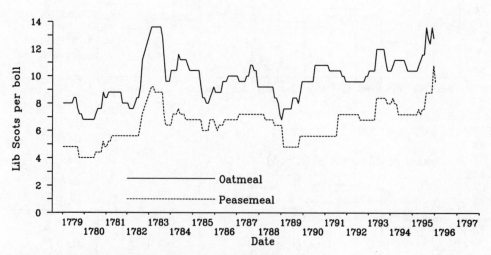

4.7 Monthly oatmeal and peasemeal prices: Edinburgh, 1741–95

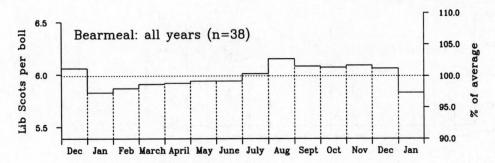

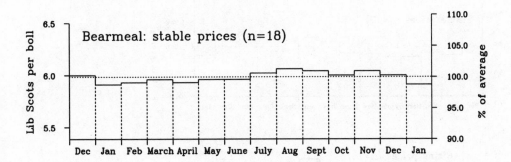

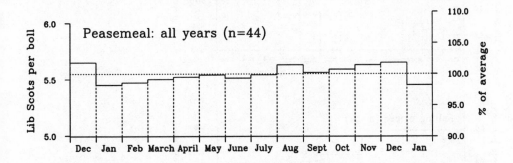

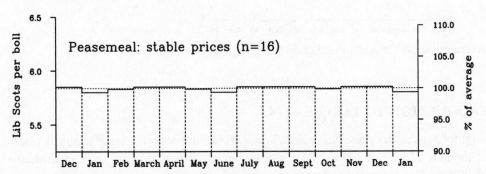

4.8 Average monthly bearmeal and peasemeal prices: Edinburgh, 1741–95

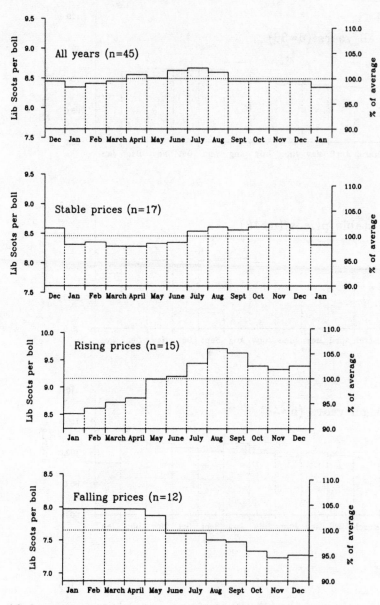

4.9 Average monthly oatmeal prices: Edinburgh, 1741–95

INTRODUCTION TO TABLES 4.1–4.7

The eighteenth-century press has provided us with two important series of monthly price data; the first of wholesale prices for wheat, barley, oats and pease in East Lothian (usually at the Haddington market) and the second of retail prices for oatmeal, bearmeal and peasemeal in Edinburgh. The former commences in May 1721 with data extracted from the *Caledonian Mercury* and, from March 1741, from *The Scots Magazine*, whilst the latter derives entirely from *The Scots Magazine* and commences in January 1741. Both series have been compiled from short tables found towards the rear of each issue of the magazine and, although we have only tabulated prices until 1785 and 1795 respectively, both were reported well into the nineteenth century.

The Scots Magazine was usually published during the second week of each month and appears to have used the most recent price data the editor had to hand. With respect to wholesale prices in Haddington this usually meant from the first Friday market of the month, although sometimes prices were reported to have come from the market held on the last Friday of the preceding month. Edinburgh retail prices were never ascribed a specific date, but we may safely assume that they too usually refer to the first week of the month in which they were published.

The *Caledonian Mercury* was published two or three times a week and wholesale prices in East Lothian were usually reported on a weekly basis. For the sake of comparability with the figures derived from *The Scots Magazine*, we have extracted from the *Caledonian Mercury* those prices which refer to the first market of the month unless this was after the seventh, in which case we have extracted prices from the market closest to the first of the month. This ensures that throughout the period covered by these tables, prices consistently refer to the beginning of the month in question.

Little is known about the manner in which Edinburgh prices were derived and we can only assume that the editor of the *The Scots Magazine* (which was published in Edinburgh) simply observed what prices were being fetched in the meal market at the time of going to press. There is certainly no evidence of a more formal mechanism of assessment.

The provenance and meaning of the East Lothian wholesale prices are clearer. Except for a short period from August 1734 through to the end of 1736, it was the Haddington market from which prices were drawn. However, during the second half of 1734, the *Caledonian Mercury* reports on prices in both Haddington and Gifford. Then, from January 1735 until at least the end of 1736, only prices from Gifford were noted. How long this situation prevailed is uncertain as the 1737 and 1738 issues of the *Caledonian Mercury* are missing from the National Library of Scotland. However, once we are able to pick the series up in January 1739, prices were once more being drawn from the Haddington market. In spite of this, whilst we have taken prices for Haddington whenever possible, as Gifford is only four miles to the south of Haddington no distinction has been drawn between the two markets in tables 4.1–4.4.

Whether they are attributed to either the Haddington or Gifford market, the tables of prices to be found in both the *Caledonian Mercury* and *The Scots Magazine* always refer to first (or best), second and third 'qualities' of grain. As discussed in the main text, this so mirrors the terminology of the fiars that a similar mechanism of assessment was probably being employed. That is to say that the price of the 'second' wheat (or barley, oats or pease) was the weighted average of *all* transaction prices; the 'first' wheat price, meanwhile, was the weighted average of all transaction prices *above* that mean price, whilst the 'third' wheat price was the weighted average of all transaction prices *below* that mean. Tables 4.1–4.4 refer to the price of 'first' wheat, barley, oats and pease.

Table 4.1 *First wheat (per boll): Haddington monthly market prices, 1721–1785*

Date	January L. s. d.	February L. s. d.	March L. s. d.	April L. s. d.	May L. s. d.	June L. s. d.	July L. s. d.
1721	--	--	--	--	7 4 0	7 0 0	7 0 0
1722	7 18 0	7 16 0	7 14 0	--	--	--	--
1723	--	--	--	--	--	9 14 0	10 13 0
1724	7 16 0	8 10 0	8 4 0	8 9 0	8 14 0	8 7 0	8 4 0
1725	8 0 0	7 15 0	7 14 0	8 2 0	7 16 0	7 14 0	9 0 0
1726	--	10 0 0	9 16 0	10 8 0	10 0 0	--	9 5 0
1727	--	8 3 0	--	--	--	--	--
1728	--	--	--	--	--	11 12 0	11 10 0
1729	9 13 0	9 17 0	10 0 0	10 14 0	11 0 0	11 0 0	11 12 0
1730	9 8 0	8 12 0	8 10 0	9 0 0	8 12 0	7 18 0	7 0 0
1731	8 8 0	8 10 0	7 18 0	9 0 0	8 0 0	8 16 0	9 2 0
1732	6 8 0	6 8 0	7 0 0	6 8 0	6 15 0	6 14 0	6 10 0
1733	5 16 0	5 18 0	--	--	7 0 0	7 0 0	7 0 0
1734	7 14 0	--	--	8 16 0	8 14 0	8 18 0	9 10 0
1735	8 12 0	8 13 0	8 12 0	8 12 0	9 6 0	9 2 0	9 0 0
1736	9 2 0	9 2 0	9 0 0	9 4 0	9 0 0	9 1 0	8 16 0
1737	--	--	--	--	--	--	--
1738	--	--	--	--	--	--	--
1739	6 18 0	6 11 0	6 10 0	6 18 0	--	--	--
1740	8 14 0	8 12 0	9 2 0	9 16 0	11 12 0	--	--
1741	--	--	14 10 0	15 0 0	14 14 0	15 12 0	15 0 0
1742	8 8 0	8 0 0	8 3 0	8 6 0	8 0 0	7 0 0	7 10 0
1743	6 6 0	6 6 0	6 13 0	6 9 0	6 12 0	6 10 0	6 4 0
1744	6 0 0	5 14 0	6 4 0	5 16 0	6 7 0	6 0 0	5 16 0
1745	7 4 0	7 0 0	7 9 0	7 14 0	8 0 0	7 10 0	7 18 0
1746	9 14 0	10 10 0	12 6 0	12 0 0	12 0 0	9 0 0	9 10 0
1747	7 16 0	8 2 0	8 10 0	8 18 0	8 9 0	7 12 0	7 16 0
1748	8 0 0	8 8 0	8 8 0	8 8 0	8 8 0	--	8 12 0
1749	8 6 0	8 6 0	8 12 0	8 8 0	8 14 0	8 12 0	8 10 0
1750	8 8 0	8 0 0	--	8 6 0	8 0 0	8 14 0	--
1751	8 3 0	8 8 0	8 2 0	8 18 0	9 0 0	8 18 0	9 6 0
1752	10 0 0	10 6 0	11 0 0	12 0 0	10 18 0	9 12 0	9 18 0
1753	9 16 0	9 8 0	10 0 0	10 0 0	10 0 0	9 8 0	10 12 0
1754	9 0 0	8 10 0	8 14 0	8 16 0	9 0 0	9 0 0	--
1755	8 0 0	7 12 0	8 10 0	7 10 0	8 8 0	8 2 0	8 0 0
1756	9 0 0	9 6 0	9 12 0	9 10 0	9 6 0	9 10 0	10 0 0
1757	13 4 0	--	15 0 0	15 12 0	16 4 0	15 12 0	15 6 0
1758	11 6 0	11 8 0	11 8 0	11 10 0	12 0 0	11 8 0	11 16 0
1759	9 6 0	8 16 0	8 8 0	9 0 0	9 0 0	9 0 0	8 8 0
1760	8 8 0	8 8 0	8 12 0	--	--	--	8 8 0
1761	--	8 8 0	--	8 8 0	8 8 0	8 8 0	--
1762	--	--	--	--	--	--	--
1763	--	--	--	--	10 13 0	10 10 0	10 4 0
1764	11 5 0	10 4 0	11 8 0	10 16 0	11 2 0	11 6 0	11 8 0
1765	11 2 0	11 8 0	11 12 0	12 0 0	12 12 0	13 4 0	12 12 0
1766	12 12 0	12 0 0	12 6 0	12 6 0	12 0 0	11 8 0	11 8 0
1767	12 0 0	12 6 0	12 18 0	12 18 0	13 4 0	12 6 0	12 18 0
1768	13 16 0	--	--	13 7 0	13 4 0	12 6 0	12 18 0
1769	12 0 0	11 2 0	12 0 0	12 0 0	12 0 0	11 8 0	12 0 0
1770	9 18 0	9 18 0	10 4 0	9 6 0	9 6 0	9 0 0	9 14 0
1771	10 16 0	11 8 0	12 0 0	12 12 0	13 4 0	13 4 0	13 8 0
1772	12 12 0	12 15 0	13 6 0	13 16 0	14 8 0	14 14 0	14 8 0
1773	14 2 0	14 8 0	14 14 0	15 0 0	15 0 0	13 10 0	14 8 0
1774	14 2 0	14 8 0	14 11 0	14 8 0	15 0 0	14 2 0	14 14 0
1775	12 7 0	12 6 0	13 4 0	13 16 0	14 2 0	13 10 0	13 16 0
1776	11 14 0	12 0 0	11 8 0	11 11 0	12 0 0	11 8 0	11 8 0
1777	11 14 0	11 8 0	11 8 0	12 18 0	12 6 0	12 18 0	13 4 0
1778	11 14 0	12 0 0	12 12 0	13 4 0	12 18 0	12 6 0	12 0 0
1779	11 2 0	10 13 0	11 2 0	10 10 0	10 10 0	10 7 0	10 4 0
1780	9 0 0	8 18 0	9 6 0	9 6 0	9 18 0	9 12 0	10 19 0
1781	11 14 0	12 0 0	12 12 0	12 18 0	12 12 0	12 12 0	12 0 0
1782	12 12 0	12 0 0	12 0 0	12 0 0	12 6 0	12 0 0	12 12 0
1783	15 18 0	14 11 0	15 12 0	14 8 0	14 8 0	13 4 0	14 8 0
1784	12 6 0	12 0 0	12 0 0	12 12 0	13 16 0	13 10 0	13 16 0
1785	12 12 0	12 12 0	13 4 0	12 12 0	12 12 0	12 6 0	12 3 0

August L. s. d.	September L. s. d.	October L. s. d.	November L. s. d.	December L. s. d.	Average L. s. d.
7 4 0	7 4 0	8 2 0	8 2 0	8 8 0	--
--	--	--	--	--	--
--	--	--	--	--	--
7 8 0	7 16 0	7 16 0	7 10 0	8 0 0	8 1 2
10 5 0	10 8 0	10 10 0	9 11 0	10 0 0	8 17 11
--	9 14 0	10 0 0	9 0 0	9 0 0	9 13 8
8 12 0	--	--	9 0 0	9 4 0	--
11 16 0	9 10 0	11 6 0	10 10 0	10 0 0	--
12 2 0	9 0 0	10 12 0	8 10 0	8 16 0	10 4 8
7 2 0	8 0 0	7 12 0	8 0 0	7 19 0	8 2 9
8 12 0	8 8 0	8 16 0	7 10 0	7 6 0	8 7 2
6 12 0	7 0 0	6 8 0	6 6 0	6 4 0	6 11 1
7 0 0	7 4 0	7 12 0	7 12 0	7 10 0	6 19 2
9 12 0	9 0 0	7 16 0	9 6 0	9 0 0	8 16 7
9 12 0	9 4 0	9 6 0	9 6 0	9 2 0	9 0 7
8 16 0	8 10 0	8 4 0	8 12 0	8 12 0	8 16 7
--	--	--	--	--	--
--	--	--	--	--	--
--	--	--	8 10 0	8 10 0	--
--	--	--	--	--	--
13 10 0	9 0 0	8 16 0	8 6 0	8 12 0	12 6 0
7 9 0	7 10 0	7 6 0	6 18 0	7 4 0	7 12 10
5 18 0	6 14 0	7 4 0	6 6 0	6 0 0	6 8 6
6 7 0	6 18 0	6 9 0	7 4 0	7 0 0	6 6 3
8 1 0	--	8 18 0	9 0 0	9 6 0	8 0 0
9 0 0	9 6 0	9 10 0	8 10 0	8 6 0	9 19 4
8 8 0	8 6 0	8 8 0	8 16 0	8 4 0	8 5 5
--	8 12 0	9 0 0	9 0 0	--	8 10 8
8 8 0	8 12 0	8 11 0	8 6 0	8 0 0	8 8 9
9 10 0	9 0 0	9 0 0	8 6 0	8 8 0	8 11 2
9 7 0	9 15 0	9 10 0	9 0 0	10 0 0	9 0 7
9 14 0	9 10 0	9 8 0	9 0 0	8 14 0	10 0 0
10 0 0	8 18 0	9 0 0	9 0 0	9 2 0	9 12 0
9 6 0	9 6 0	8 0 0	--	6 18 0	8 13 0
7 6 0	8 0 0	8 10 0	8 10 0	8 10 0	8 1 6
10 12 0	12 0 0	12 0 0	12 0 0	12 12 0	10 9 0
14 8 0	12 12 0	10 16 0	10 2 0	10 0 0	13 10 6
10 0 0	10 6 0	9 12 0	9 6 0	9 3 0	10 15 3
8 12 0	8 8 0	9 12 0	8 8 0	8 10 0	8 15 8
8 8 0	8 0 0	8 0 0	8 8 0	--	--
--	--	--	9 0 0	--	--
--	--	--	--	--	--
10 4 0	10 4 0	9 9 0	10 4 0	9 12 0	--
11 8 0	11 14 0	12 0 0	11 14 0	11 2 0	11 5 7
13 4 0	13 4 0	12 12 0	12 12 0	12 0 0	12 6 10
11 8 0	12 0 0	11 2 0	11 8 0	11 8 0	11 15 6
13 16 0	13 4 0	13 10 0	12 18 0	13 4 0	12 18 6
13 4 0	13 16 0	13 4 0	12 0 0	12 6 0	13 0 1
12 12 0	12 12 0	12 0 0	10 10 0	9 18 0	11 13 6
12 0 0	12 0 0	10 16 0	10 10 0	10 16 0	10 5 8
13 18 0	13 14 0	13 16 0	12 0 0	11 14 0	12 12 10
14 14 0	15 0 0	12 12 0	12 12 0	13 4 0	13 13 5
14 5 0	13 16 0	12 12 0	12 12 0	13 16 0	14 0 3
15 18 0	16 4 0	13 16 0	12 12 0	--	14 10 5
14 2 0	11 8 0	11 8 0	10 16 0	10 19 0	12 12 10
11 2 0	10 13 0	10 16 0	9 18 0	10 10 0	11 4 0
13 10 0	13 10 0	11 14 0	11 2 0	12 0 0	12 6 0
11 8 0	11 8 0	11 2 0	10 16 0	10 16 0	11 17 0
9 12 0	9 0 0	9 0 0	8 14 0	8 14 0	9 19 0
11 3 0	11 8 0	11 2 0	10 16 0	10 16 0	10 3 8
12 12 0	12 6 0	12 0 0	11 8 0	12 0 0	12 4 6
13 4 0	12 12 0	--	14 8 0	15 0 0	12 15 9
14 8 0	12 12 0	--	12 12 0	12 9 0	14 0 10
14 14 0	14 14 0	14 8 0	13 4 0	13 4 0	13 7 0
12 0 0	12 12 0	12 0 0	12 12 0	12 12 0	12 9 9

Table 4.2 *First barley (per boll): Haddington monthly market prices, 1721–1785*

Date	January L. s. d.			February L. s. d.			March L. s. d.			April L. s. d.			May L. s. d.			June L. s. d.			July L. s. d.		
1721	--			--			--			--			4	12	0	4	7	0	6	2	0
1722	4	14	0	4	14	0	5	4	0	--			--			--			--		
1723	--			--			--			--			--			6	5	0	9	0	0
1724	6	8	0	6	8	0	7	4	0	7	4	0	6	12	0	6	10	0	6	0	0
1725	5	2	0	5	4	0	5	2	0	5	0	0	4	4	0	4	10	0	5	10	0
1726	--			5	14	0	6	0	0	5	16	0	5	10	0	--			5	10	0
1727	--			5	4	0	--			--			--			--			--		
1728	--			--			--			--			--			6	4	0	6	12	0
1729	7	2	0	7	0	0	8	0	0	7	16	0	8	4	0	8	14	0	9	10	0
1730	6	16	0	6	0	0	6	0	0	6	2	0	6	2	0	5	14	0	5	10	0
1731	4	16	0	4	17	0	5	0	0	6	0	0	5	5	0	5	6	0	6	2	0
1732	4	16	0	4	16	0	5	0	0	5	10	0	5	6	0	4	17	0	4	17	0
1733	4	2	0	4	6	0	--			--			4	9	0	4	8	0	4	12	0
1734	5	18	0	--			--			6	10	0	6	9	0	6	9	0	4	16	0
1735	4	10	0	4	8	0	4	15	0	4	12	0	5	0	0	6	2	0	5	14	0
1736	6	0	0	5	12	0	6	0	0	6	6	0	6	10	0	6	6	0	6	3	0
1737	--			--			--			--			--			--			--		
1738	--			--			--			--			--			--			--		
1739	4	8	0	4	6	0	4	10	0	4	10	0	--			--			--		
1740	6	3	0	6	4	0	7	10	0	7	14	0	8	10	0	--			--		
1741	--			--			12	15	0	12	2	0	13	0	0	14	6	0	13	10	0
1742	6	6	0	6	6	0	6	6	0	6	6	0	5	17	0	5	17	0	6	0	0
1743	6	6	0	6	7	0	6	6	0	6	3	0	6	6	0	5	17	0	5	6	0
1744	4	13	0	4	7	0	4	12	0	5	0	0	5	10	0	5	4	0	5	0	0
1745	6	8	0	6	8	0	6	6	0	6	12	0	6	12	0	6	10	0	6	14	0
1746	6	12	0	7	10	0	9	0	0	9	0	0	9	0	0	7	16	0	8	0	0
1747	6	10	0	6	12	0	6	10	0	6	12	0	6	12	0	6	10	0	6	12	0
1748	6	10	0	6	16	0	6	18	0	7	0	0	7	4	0	--			7	4	0
1749	6	10	0	6	6	0	6	14	0	6	18	0	6	12	0	6	8	0	6	6	0
1750	6	6	0	5	16	0	--			6	0	0	6	6	0	6	6	0	--		
1751	6	4	0	6	6	0	6	6	0	6	8	0	6	18	0	7	10	0	7	10	0
1752	7	4	0	7	4	0	8	0	0	8	6	0	8	0	0	8	8	0	8	12	0
1753	8	0	0	8	6	0	8	0	0	9	0	0	9	8	0	9	0	0	9	12	0
1754	8	0	0	8	2	0	8	0	0	7	16	0	9	0	0	8	0	0	--		
1755	6	4	0	5	8	0	5	15	0	5	16	0	5	10	0	5	15	0	5	15	0
1756	6	12	0	7	0	0	7	4	0	6	12	0	7	4	0	7	12	0	9	12	0
1757	10	16	0	--			14	8	0	13	10	0	13	12	0	13	4	0	13	16	0
1758	9	0	0	8	16	0	9	6	0	9	12	0	9	12	0	9	0	0	8	8	0
1759	6	3	0	6	0	0	6	0	0	6	6	0	6	6	0	6	0	0	6	0	0
1760	6	12	0	6	12	0	6	10	0	--			--			--			5	6	0
1761	--			6	0	0	--			6	6	0	6	0	0	5	14	0	--		
1762	--			--			--			--			--			--			--		
1763	--			--			--			--			9	16	0	9	18	0	10	10	0
1764	8	14	0	8	14	0	9	10	0	8	14	0	9	6	0	9	3	0	9	2	0
1765	8	14	0	8	16	0	8	14	0	9	4	0	9	12	0	9	6	0	9	6	0
1766	10	4	0	10	7	0	11	18	0	11	8	0	11	0	0	10	16	0	11	2	0
1767	11	14	0	11	14	0	13	0	0	12	12	0	13	4	0	10	16	0	11	14	0
1768	9	12	0	--			--			9	12	0	9	0	0	8	10	0	9	0	0
1769	7	4	0	6	12	0	8	8	0	8	17	0	10	10	0	9	9	0	9	0	0
1770	8	8	0	8	8	0	9	0	0	8	14	0	9	0	0	8	11	0	9	6	0
1771	8	4	0	8	17	0	9	0	0	9	12	0	9	12	0	9	12	0	9	9	0
1772	9	12	0	9	12	0	9	14	0	10	1	0	10	10	0	10	16	0	9	16	0
1773	11	8	0	11	8	0	12	0	0	12	12	0	13	6	0	13	16	0	14	2	0
1774	11	14	0	12	6	0	12	6	0	12	12	0	12	18	0	11	14	0	12	12	0
1775	11	5	0	10	10	0	12	0	0	11	8	0	11	14	0	11	8	0	11	8	0
1776	8	14	0	8	10	0	8	8	0	8	8	0	8	11	0	8	8	0	9	0	0
1777	7	4	0	7	4	0	6	18	0	7	10	0	11	17	0	7	10	0	7	5	0
1778	8	11	0	9	0	0	9	0	0	9	0	0	9	3	0	8	8	0	8	14	0
1779	8	5	0	8	8	0	8	5	0	8	11	0	8	2	0	8	2	0	8	14	0
1780	6	12	0	6	12	0	6	12	0	6	18	0	6	12	0	6	18	0	8	17	0
1781	8	14	0	8	14	0	8	17	0	8	14	0	8	8	0	8	5	0	8	2	0
1782	8	2	0	7	16	0	7	16	0	8	14	0	8	16	0	9	6	0	9	18	0
1783	14	8	0	13	16	0	15	12	0	15	18	0	15	0	0	14	14	0	14	8	0
1784	11	8	0	12	0	0	12	12	0	12	18	0	14	2	0	12	12	0	12	12	0
1785	11	8	0	11	2	0	11	2	0	11	2	0	10	7	0	10	4	0	9	0	0

August L. s. d.			September L. s. d.			October L. s. d.			November L. s. d.			December L. s. d.			Average L. s. d.		
5	2	0	5	14	0	5	4	0	5	3	0	5	2	0	--		
--			--			--			--			--			--		
--			--			--			--			--			--		
5	2	0	5	12	0	5	0	0	5	2	0	5	2	0	6	0	4
5	8	0	6	10	0	5	4	0	5	8	0	5	14	0	5	4	8
--			5	16	0	6	0	0	5	16	0	5	10	0	5	14	8
5	3	0	--			--			4	18	0	5	14	0	--		
6	16	0	6	10	0	6	18	0	6	1	0	7	0	0	--		
9	0	0	6	12	0	7	0	0	6	10	0	6	18	0	7	13	10
5	12	0	5	10	0	5	4	0	5	0	0	5	4	0	5	14	6
5	12	0	5	2	0	4	18	0	5	2	0	4	16	0	5	4	8
4	16	0	4	16	0	4	10	0	4	6	0	4	6	0	4	16	4
5	8	0	4	10	0	5	6	0	5	12	0	5	12	0	4	16	6
5	18	0	6	0	0	4	14	0	6	6	0	4	19	0	5	15	10
6	10	0	6	0	0	5	10	0	5	16	0	6	0	0	5	8	1
5	18	0	5	5	0	5	18	0	6	0	0	5	6	0	5	18	8
--			--			--			--			--			--		
--			--			--			--			--			--		
--			--			--			6	4	0	5	16	0	--		
--			--			--			--			--			--		
9	16	0	7	4	0	6	16	0	6	10	0	6	10	0	10	4	10
6	6	0	5	18	0	6	5	0	6	5	0	6	8	0	6	3	4
6	0	0	5	15	0	5	4	0	5	2	0	4	14	0	5	15	6
5	4	0	6	0	0	6	12	0	6	0	0	6	6	0	5	7	4
7	0	0	--			6	12	0	6	8	0	6	10	0	6	10	10
8	4	0	7	0	0	6	12	0	6	6	0	6	15	0	7	12	11
6	16	0	6	6	0	6	11	0	7	0	0	6	13	0	6	12	0
--			6	6	0	6	10	0	6	12	0	--			6	15	6
6	14	0	6	12	0	6	6	0	6	16	0	6	7	0	6	10	9
6	11	0	6	10	0	6	10	0	6	0	0	6	8	0	6	5	3
7	18	0	7	8	0	6	12	0	6	14	0	7	8	0	6	18	6
8	8	0	7	12	0	7	12	0	7	10	0	8	0	0	7	18	0
9	8	0	9	0	0	8	10	0	8	6	0	8	8	0	8	14	10
7	0	0	7	10	0	6	6	0	--			6	6	0	7	12	0
5	8	0	5	10	0	6	6	0	6	0	0	6	6	0	5	16	1
10	6	0	9	4	0	10	10	0	8	0	0	10	16	0	8	7	8
13	4	0	12	0	0	10	0	0	9	0	0	9	0	0	12	0	10
8	4	0	8	0	0	6	12	0	6	6	0	6	6	0	8	5	2
6	6	0	6	14	0	6	12	0	6	12	0	6	15	0	6	6	2
6	0	0	6	0	0	6	6	0	6	6	0	--			--		
--			--			--			6	0	0	--			--		
--			--			--			--			--			--		
11	2	0	8	8	0	8	8	0	8	8	0	8	4	0	--		
9	0	0	9	6	0	9	0	0	9	0	0	8	14	0	9	0	3
11	8	0	12	6	0	9	18	0	9	18	0	10	4	0	9	15	6
12	6	0	10	16	0	11	5	0	10	16	0	11	8	0	11	2	2
13	4	0	11	14	0	11	5	0	9	0	0	9	12	0	11	12	5
9	0	0	8	8	0	9	6	0	8	8	0	7	7	0	8	16	3
10	4	0	9	16	0	9	12	0	8	14	0	8	2	0	8	17	4
9	6	0	10	4	0	8	14	0	8	14	0	8	6	0	8	17	7
10	4	0	11	0	0	10	13	0	10	4	0	9	15	0	9	13	6
10	16	0	10	16	0	10	10	0	9	12	0	10	10	0	10	3	9
14	14	0	13	10	0	12	6	0	10	10	0	11	2	0	12	11	2
12	18	0	12	12	0	12	0	0	10	16	0	--			12	4	4
11	11	0	10	16	0	10	0	0	9	0	0	9	0	0	10	16	8
8	17	0	8	8	0	8	8	0	7	10	0	6	18	0	8	6	8
8	2	0	8	2	0	8	2	0	8	2	0	8	8	0	8	0	4
8	17	0	9	0	0	8	14	0	8	8	0	8	5	0	8	15	0
8	2	0	6	18	0	6	18	0	6	18	0	6	15	0	7	16	6
9	0	0	8	14	0	8	11	0	8	8	0	8	11	0	7	13	9
8	8	0	8	10	0	8	8	0	8	11	0	8	2	0	8	9	5
12	12	0	12	0	0	--			13	4	0	13	10	0	10	3	1
14	8	0	12	12	0	--			9	12	0	11	5	0	13	15	8
12	18	0	13	16	0	12	12	0	11	8	0	12	0	0	12	11	6
11	2	0	10	16	0	10	16	0	9	18	0	9	18	0	10	11	3

Table 4.3 *First oats (per boll): Haddington monthly market prices, 1721–1785*

Date	January L. s. d.			February L. s. d.			March L. s. d.			April L. s. d.			May L. s. d.			June L. s. d.			July L. s. d.		
1721	--			--			--			--			6	2	0	5	16	0	4	18	0
1722	5	10	0	5	6	0	5	12	0	--			--			--			--		
1723	--			--			--			--			--			8	0	0	9	0	0
1724	7	16	0	8	0	0	8	4	0	8	12	0	8	14	0	8	8	0	8	6	0
1725	6	4	0	6	6	0	6	4	0	6	2	0	6	0	0	6	4	0	6	18	0
1726	--			6	0	0	6	18	0	6	14	0	6	0	0	--			6	0	0
1727	--			6	4	0	--			--			--			--			--		
1728	--			--			--			--			--			8	6	0	8	4	0
1729	8	18	0	9	6	0	9	0	0	9	4	0	9	0	0	9	4	0	9	18	0
1730	6	12	0	5	16	0	5	15	0	6	0	0	5	10	0	5	4	0	5	0	0
1731	4	12	0	4	15	0	5	0	0	4	15	0	4	4	0	4	16	0	6	0	0
1732	4	13	0	4	16	0	5	12	0	4	12	0	4	14	0	4	8	0	4	11	0
1733	4	8	0	4	4	0	--			--			4	5	0	4	2	0	4	0	0
1734	5	5	0	--			--			5	0	0	5	4	0	5	8	0	6	3	0
1735	5	16	0	5	12	0	5	12	0	5	16	0	6	6	0	6	2	0	6	4	0
1736	6	4	0	6	2	0	6	6	0	6	8	0	7	4	0	6	10	0	7	10	0
1737	--			--			--			--			--			--			--		
1738	--			--			--			--			--			--			--		
1739	5	10	0	5	6	0	5	6	0	5	14	0	--			--			--		
1740	7	4	0	7	10	0	7	16	0	8	8	0	8	12	0	--			--		
1741	--			--			10	10	0	10	10	0	10	12	0	11	3	0	9	6	0
1742	6	8	0	5	16	0	5	14	0	5	15	0	4	12	0	4	16	0	4	18	0
1743	4	10	0	4	12	0	4	10	0	4	10	0	4	7	0	4	0	0	4	7	0
1744	3	16	0	3	18	0	3	15	0	4	6	0	4	1	0	3	17	0	4	1	0
1745	6	6	0	6	12	0	6	12	0	6	14	0	7	18	0	7	4	0	7	18	0
1746	7	4	0	7	4	0	8	6	0	8	6	0	7	18	0	6	14	0	6	14	0
1747	5	16	0	5	4	0	6	0	0	5	0	0	5	4	0	4	15	0	5	7	0
1748	4	16	0	4	14	0	4	16	0	4	16	0	4	13	0	--			4	12	0
1749	5	8	0	5	4	0	5	6	0	5	4	0	5	6	0	5	0	0	5	18	0
1750	5	10	0	5	0	0	--			5	4	0	5	4	0	6	2	0	--		
1751	5	16	0	5	5	0	6	0	0	5	10	0	6	0	0	5	18	0	6	18	0
1752	7	5	0	7	14	0	8	0	0	8	5	0	7	18	0	7	6	0	7	10	0
1753	7	10	0	7	0	0	7	3	0	9	0	0	8	0	0	7	8	0	7	10	0
1754	6	12	0	6	16	0	7	0	0	6	12	0	7	4	0	6	12	0	--		
1755	5	0	0	5	10	0	5	4	0	5	16	0	5	0	0	4	12	0	5	0	0
1756	6	8	0	7	0	0	7	10	0	7	0	0	7	4	0	7	10	0	7	10	0
1757	9	0	0	--			10	16	0	10	16	0	11	0	0	10	16	0	11	14	0
1758	8	0	0	8	0	0	8	8	0	8	2	0	8	8	0	8	0	0	7	10	0
1759	5	2	0	4	16	0	6	0	0	5	8	0	5	2	0	4	16	0	4	10	0
1760	4	16	0	4	16	0	4	16	0	--			--			--			4	4	0
1761	--			5	0	0	--			5	0	0	5	8	0	5	2	0	--		
1762	--			--			--			--			--			--			--		
1763	--			--			--			--			8	5	0	8	14	0	8	8	0
1764	6	0	0	6	6	0	6	12	0	7	0	0	7	10	0	6	12	0	7	4	0
1765	7	8	0	7	14	0	7	10	0	8	2	0	8	6	0	8	2	0	7	16	0
1766	9	0	0	9	0	0	9	12	0	9	0	0	7	16	0	9	0	0	9	12	0
1767	9	0	0	8	10	0	9	6	0	9	6	0	9	18	0	8	14	0	8	14	0
1768	8	8	0	--			--			8	10	0	6	12	0	6	15	0	6	8	0
1769	6	0	0	5	12	0	6	6	0	7	4	0	8	8	0	8	4	0	8	5	0
1770	6	6	0	6	6	0	6	12	0	6	12	0	6	15	0	6	18	0	9	4	0
1771	7	2	0	7	2	0	7	12	0	8	8	0	8	14	0	8	8	0	8	12	0
1772	8	5	0	8	14	0	8	14	0	9	0	0	9	0	0	9	6	0	8	14	0
1773	9	0	0	9	0	0	9	2	0	9	18	0	9	12	0	9	2	0	9	12	0
1774	8	14	0	8	8	0	8	8	0	9	0	0	8	16	0	9	0	0	9	6	0
1775	8	2	0	8	0	0	8	14	0	8	16	0	9	6	0	8	8	0	9	0	0
1776	6	0	0	6	3	0	6	3	0	5	17	0	6	6	0	6	0	0	9	0	0
1777	6	9	0	5	17	0	6	9	0	6	6	0	6	9	0	6	9	0	6	12	0
1778	7	4	0	7	1	0	7	10	0	7	7	0	7	16	0	7	10	0	7	19	0
1779	7	4	0	6	8	0	7	13	0	6	12	0	6	15	0	7	13	0	8	5	0
1780	6	0	0	5	8	0	6	2	0	6	6	0	6	3	0	6	0	0	7	4	0
1781	7	1	0	7	10	0	7	10	0	7	10	0	7	16	0	7	16	0	7	18	0
1782	6	0	0	6	0	0	6	0	0	6	6	0	6	10	0	7	7	0	8	0	0
1783	11	17	0	11	5	0	12	6	0	13	4	0	12	6	0	12	12	0	13	7	0
1784	8	14	0	8	14	0	9	6	0	10	4	0	11	8	0	9	6	0	10	16	0
1785	9	3	0	8	17	0	9	6	0	8	14	0	7	10	0	7	16	0	7	4	0

August L. s. d.	September L. s. d.	October L. s. d.	November L. s. d.	December L. s. d.	Average L. s. d.
5 16 0	6 10 0	5 12 0	5 14 0	5 16 0	--
--	--	--	--	--	--
--	--	--	--	--	--
7 12 0	6 11 0	6 8 0	6 6 0	6 4 0	7 11 9
7 6 0	8 6 0	7 0 0	6 0 0	6 4 0	6 11 2
--	5 16 0	6 0 0	6 4 0	6 7 0	6 4 4
6 4 8	--	--	7 2 0	7 0 0	--
8 12 0	7 12 0	8 6 0	8 12 0	9 0 0	--
9 1 0	7 0 0	7 10 0	6 18 0	6 12 0	8 9 3
5 12 0	5 8 0	5 4 0	5 0 0	5 2 0	5 10 3
5 0 0	5 8 0	4 16 0	4 18 0	4 12 0	4 18 0
4 18 0	4 12 0	4 8 0	4 8 0	4 5 0	4 13 1
4 4 0	5 0 0	5 1 0	5 0 0	5 2 0	4 10 7
6 3 0	5 6 0	5 15 0	5 0 0	6 0 0	5 10 4
6 16 0	6 2 0	6 4 0	6 2 0	6 5 0	6 1 5
7 2 0	6 4 0	6 10 0	6 12 0	6 15 0	6 12 3
--	--	--	--	--	--
--	--	--	--	--	--
--	--	--	7 0 0	7 5 0	--
--	--	--	--	--	--
7 12 0	7 10 0	6 8 0	6 2 0	6 8 0	8 12 1
5 0 0	4 18 0	5 14 0	4 16 0	4 16 0	5 5 3
4 6 0	4 12 0	4 3 0	4 4 0	3 16 0	4 6 5
4 7 0	5 8 0	6 8 0	6 6 0	6 0 0	4 13 7
8 2 0	--	6 12 0	6 12 0	6 16 0	7 0 6
6 12 0	6 16 0	6 8 0	5 18 0	6 4 0	7 0 4
5 12 0	5 0 0	4 16 0	4 14 0	5 10 0	5 4 10
--	4 16 0	4 16 0	5 12 0	--	4 16 9
5 10 0	6 0 0	5 6 0	5 16 0	5 16 0	5 9 6
6 2 0	5 0 0	5 11 0	5 4 0	5 8 0	5 8 6
7 1 0	6 12 0	7 0 0	7 0 0	7 16 0	6 8 0
9 2 0	7 14 0	7 8 0	7 0 0	8 0 0	7 15 2
7 4 0	7 8 0	7 10 0	7 14 0	7 6 0	7 11 1
7 4 0	7 0 0	5 18 0	--	6 6 0	6 14 4
5 0 0	5 16 0	6 10 0	6 0 0	6 10 0	5 9 10
10 4 0	9 4 0	9 4 0	7 6 0	9 0 0	7 18 4
12 0 0	11 8 0	8 2 0	8 0 0	8 8 0	10 3 7
7 10 0	7 10 0	5 8 0	5 8 0	5 0 0	7 5 4
4 16 0	4 16 0	5 0 0	5 0 0	5 0 0	5 0 6
5 0 0	4 10 0	4 10 0	6 0 0	--	--
--	--	--	5 8 0	--	--
--	--	--	--	--	--
9 6 0	8 12 0	7 16 0	5 17 0	6 10 0	--
6 12 0	7 11 0	7 10 0	8 5 0	7 14 0	7 1 4
9 0 0	9 2 0	8 14 0	8 8 0	9 0 0	8 5 2
10 4 0	9 12 0	8 2 0	8 4 0	8 8 0	8 19 2
9 18 0	10 4 0	9 12 0	8 11 0	8 16 0	9 4 1
6 12 0	6 18 0	7 10 0	6 9 0	6 0 0	7 0 2
9 0 0	9 6 0	7 10 0	6 12 0	6 3 0	7 7 6
9 8 0	8 8 0	7 16 0	6 18 0	7 7 0	7 7 6
9 18 0	8 14 0	9 0 0	9 0 0	8 14 0	8 8 8
9 6 0	9 12 0	8 14 0	8 8 0	8 14 0	8 17 3
10 4 0	10 0 0	9 0 0	7 18 0	8 8 0	9 4 8
10 4 0	10 16 0	9 0 0	7 10 0	--	9 0 2
8 18 0	7 10 0	6 18 0	6 12 0	6 8 0	8 1 0
6 0 0	6 12 0	6 0 0	6 0 0	6 6 0	6 7 3
6 18 0	6 18 0	6 18 0	7 10 0	7 4 0	6 13 3
8 2 0	7 10 0	8 2 0	7 16 0	7 1 0	7 11 6
7 13 0	6 6 0	6 0 0	6 3 0	5 17 0	6 17 5
7 4 0	6 15 0	7 10 0	7 10 0	8 2 0	6 13 8
7 16 0	7 10 0	7 4 0	6 6 0	6 6 0	7 6 11
9 0 0	11 2 0	--	10 16 0	10 13 0	7 19 5
12 9 0	9 18 0	--	8 14 0	8 8 0	11 9 7
10 16 0	10 10 0	9 12 0	9 12 0	9 0 0	9 16 6
8 2 0	8 2 0	7 16 0	9 6 0	8 8 0	8 7 0

Table 4.4 *First pease (per boll): Haddington monthly market prices, 1721–1785*

Date	January L. s. d.	February L. s. d.	March L. s. d.	April L. s. d.	May L. s. d.	June L. s. d.	July L. s. d.
1721	--	--	--	--	4 2 0	4 9 0	4 4 0
1722	5 16 0	5 14 0	6 3 0	--	--	--	--
1723	--	--	--	--	--	7 0 0	9 0 0
1724	7 0 0	7 4 0	8 0 0	8 4 0	8 14 0	8 0 0	7 8 0
1725	5 2 0	5 2 0	5 0 0	4 10 0	4 6 0	4 10 0	5 10 0
1726	--	8 10 0	9 0 0	9 0 0	6 9 0	--	7 0 0
1727	--	5 15 0	--	--	--	--	--
1728	--	--	--	--	--	6 3 0	6 8 0
1729	6 17 0	6 18 0	8 0 0	7 15 0	8 0 0	9 4 0	9 14 0
1730	5 0 0	4 16 0	5 0 0	4 12 0	4 6 0	4 12 0	4 6 0
1731	3 5 0	3 5 0	4 4 0	3 12 0	3 3 0	3 6 0	4 6 0
1732	3 4 0	3 8 0	3 7 0	3 10 0	3 8 0	3 12 0	3 17 0
1733	3 18 0	4 6 0	--	--	4 0 0	4 16 0	4 8 0
1734	4 8 0	--	--	5 0 0	5 0 0	5 12 0	4 16 0
1735	4 6 0	4 2 0	4 10 0	4 0 0	4 0 0	4 13 0	4 11 0
1736	5 4 0	4 12 0	5 16 0	6 0 0	6 2 0	6 10 0	7 0 0
1737	--	--	--	--	--	--	--
1738	--	--	--	--	--	--	--
1739	3 18 0	4 4 0	4 4 0	3 18 0	--	--	--
1740	4 18 0	5 2 0	6 6 0	6 16 0	7 10 0	--	--
1741	--	--	15 16 0	14 0 0	13 10 0	13 12 0	13 10 0
1742	5 6 0	5 8 0	5 6 0	5 6 0	4 6 0	4 8 0	4 18 0
1743	4 8 0	4 14 0	4 16 0	4 3 0	4 3 0	4 2 0	4 5 0
1744	3 12 0	3 8 0	3 6 0	3 6 0	3 10 0	3 8 0	3 9 0
1745	5 0 0	5 12 0	5 10 0	5 16 0	5 16 0	6 12 0	6 4 0
1746	6 12 0	7 10 0	8 10 0	8 10 0	8 5 0	7 2 0	7 5 0
1747	4 12 0	5 0 0	5 4 0	4 14 0	4 0 0	4 10 0	5 4 0
1748	4 10 0	5 0 0	5 0 0	4 16 0	4 12 0	--	4 0 0
1749	4 2 0	4 2 0	4 4 0	4 0 0	3 18 0	3 17 0	4 0 0
1750	3 18 0	4 5 0	--	4 2 0	4 4 0	5 0 0	--
1751	5 8 0	5 0 0	5 18 0	5 10 0	5 17 0	5 16 0	6 11 0
1752	7 0 0	8 0 0	8 0 0	8 0 0	7 0 0	7 16 0	7 4 0
1753	8 12 0	9 0 0	9 0 0	9 0 0	8 0 0	7 4 0	8 0 0
1754	7 0 0	7 8 0	7 12 0	8 0 0	7 14 0	7 16 0	--
1755	6 8 0	4 10 0	4 10 0	5 4 0	4 10 0	4 10 0	4 18 0
1756	6 12 0	7 8 0	7 10 0	7 6 0	7 2 0	7 4 0	8 0 0
1757	10 0 0	--	14 8 0	13 4 0	12 12 0	13 10 0	13 16 0
1758	8 0 0	8 0 0	9 6 0	9 8 0	9 6 0	9 0 0	8 14 0
1759	5 0 0	4 18 0	5 0 0	5 6 0	4 16 0	4 12 0	4 6 0
1760	3 18 0	3 12 0	3 12 0	--	--	--	3 12 0
1761	--	4 16 0	--	5 0 0	5 2 0	4 10 0	--
1762	--	--	--	--	--	--	--
1763	--	--	--	--	7 4 0	8 8 0	8 10 0
1764	6 16 0	6 15 0	7 6 0	7 4 0	6 18 0	7 8 0	7 1 0
1765	6 12 0	7 6 0	7 16 0	8 0 0	7 16 0	8 2 0	8 0 0
1766	7 10 0	8 2 0	8 14 0	8 8 0	8 8 0	8 8 0	9 0 0
1767	9 2 0	8 16 0	9 18 0	9 8 0	9 6 0	8 12 0	9 4 0
1768	9 6 0	--	--	10 10 0	8 8 0	7 0 0	7 19 0
1769	8 8 0	8 14 0	9 12 0	10 10 0	8 14 0	8 14 0	9 0 0
1770	6 0 0	5 8 0	6 12 0	6 0 0	5 14 0	6 12 0	8 4 0
1771	6 18 0	7 4 0	6 18 0	7 4 0	7 4 0	7 4 0	7 10 0
1772	7 10 0	7 16 0	8 10 0	8 14 0	8 14 0	8 16 0	9 0 0
1773	9 3 0	9 2 0	9 0 0	9 12 0	9 14 0	10 4 0	10 10 0
1774	7 4 0	7 4 0	8 8 0	8 14 0	8 5 0	7 16 0	9 9 0
1775	8 2 0	7 19 0	8 10 0	8 14 0	9 6 0	8 17 0	9 2 0
1776	5 17 0	6 0 0	6 4 0	6 3 0	6 9 0	6 3 0	8 8 0
1777	5 14 0	5 14 0	5 13 0	6 0 0	5 8 0	5 14 0	6 0 0
1778	6 0 0	5 8 0	6 18 0	6 0 0	6 12 0	6 18 0	6 18 0
1779	6 12 0	5 10 0	6 0 0	5 8 0	5 8 0	5 8 0	5 14 0
1780	4 5 0	4 12 0	5 2 0	4 18 0	4 16 0	4 16 0	5 2 0
1781	6 0 0	6 0 0	6 6 0	7 0 0	6 12 0	6 12 0	6 18 0
1782	6 0 0	6 12 0	6 12 0	6 12 0	6 18 0	7 4 0	7 16 0
1783	12 18 0	12 12 0	14 8 0	15 12 0	13 1 0	13 16 0	14 2 0
1784	7 16 0	9 0 0	9 12 0	9 12 0	9 18 0	9 0 0	9 18 0
1785	9 12 0	9 0 0	9 12 0	10 10 0	8 8 0	8 11 0	8 8 0

August L. s. d.	September L. s. d.	October L. s. d.	November L. s. d.	December L. s. d.	Average L. s. d.
4 12 0	5 10 0	6 0 0	5 10 0	5 0 0	--
--	--	--	--	--	--
--	--	--	--	--	--
7 12 0	7 0 0	6 8 0	5 6 0	5 2 0	7 3 2
6 0 0	7 8 0	8 4 0	7 8 0	7 0 0	5 16 8
--	6 8 0	6 0 0	5 0 0	5 4 0	6 19 0
6 4 0	--	--	4 17 0	5 14 0	--
6 10 0	6 16 0	6 18 0	6 6 0	6 12 0	--
9 2 0	7 10 0	7 8 0	4 16 0	4 18 0	7 10 2
4 10 0	4 6 0	4 4 0	3 6 0	3 6 0	4 7 0
3 4 0	5 8 0	3 16 0	3 2 0	3 5 0	3 13 0
3 14 0	4 4 0	4 4 0	3 8 0	3 10 0	3 12 2
4 6 0	4 10 0	4 8 0	4 0 0	4 2 0	4 5 4
4 18 0	5 12 0	5 0 0	4 12 0	3 18 0	4 17 7
5 10 0	5 0 0	4 10 0	5 6 0	4 7 0	4 11 3
6 6 0	6 16 0	6 1 0	5 12 0	6 0 0	5 19 11
--	--	--	--	--	--
--	--	--	--	--	--
--	--	--	5 12 0	5 0 0	--
--	--	--	--	--	--
10 6 0	8 12 0	6 6 0	6 4 0	5 14 0	10 15 0
5 6 0	4 18 0	4 12 0	4 12 0	4 9 0	4 17 11
3 18 0	3 15 0	3 3 0	3 12 0	3 10 0	4 0 9
3 9 0	4 8 0	6 0 0	5 6 0	5 12 0	4 1 2
6 12 0	--	6 18 0	6 4 0	6 12 0	6 1 5
6 12 0	6 6 0	6 3 0	4 16 0	4 16 0	6 17 3
4 16 0	4 17 0	5 0 0	4 10 0	4 18 0	4 15 5
--	4 16 0	3 18 0	4 3 0	--	4 10 6
4 1 0	4 4 0	4 6 0	4 10 0	4 4 0	4 2 4
5 2 0	5 0 0	5 6 0	5 0 0	5 8 0	4 14 6
7 4 0	6 4 0	7 8 0	6 16 0	7 16 0	6 5 8
8 0 0	8 10 0	9 0 0	9 0 0	8 12 0	8 0 2
8 0 0	8 6 0	7 0 0	8 0 0	6 18 0	8 1 8
7 12 0	8 6 0	7 4 0	--	5 12 0	7 8 4
5 6 0	5 10 0	5 10 0	5 15 0	6 6 0	5 4 9
9 6 0	8 17 0	9 6 0	10 0 0	10 13 0	8 5 4
12 6 0	12 0 0	9 0 0	8 0 0	9 0 0	11 12 4
7 16 0	7 4 0	6 18 0	5 14 0	5 8 0	7 17 10
4 12 0	4 10 0	3 16 0	3 16 0	3 18 0	4 10 10
3 16 0	3 12 0	3 14 0	3 16 0	--	--
--	--	--	4 16 0	--	--
--	--	--	--	--	--
9 8 0	8 14 0	8 17 0	7 4 0	6 14 0	--
8 2 0	7 10 0	8 6 0	7 10 0	7 6 0	7 6 10
8 2 0	9 0 0	8 12 0	6 18 0	7 4 0	7 15 8
9 3 0	10 16 0	9 0 0	9 0 0	8 17 0	8 15 6
9 12 0	9 12 0	10 0 0	9 8 0	9 12 0	9 7 6
7 4 0	7 16 0	9 0 0	8 14 0	8 8 0	8 8 6
9 0 0	9 0 0	8 8 0	6 6 0	6 12 0	8 11 6
8 14 0	8 8 0	7 16 0	7 18 0	6 12 0	6 19 10
8 14 0	8 2 0	7 16 0	8 8 0	7 4 0	7 10 6
10 4 0	10 4 0	10 16 0	8 2 0	8 16 0	8 18 6
10 10 0	10 10 0	10 4 0	7 16 0	7 10 0	9 9 7
9 12 0	10 10 0	9 12 0	9 0 0	--	8 14 0
8 17 0	8 5 0	7 16 0	8 0 0	6 6 0	8 6 2
7 14 0	6 12 0	6 18 0	6 0 0	6 0 0	6 10 8
6 0 0	6 6 0	6 12 0	7 16 0	6 18 0	6 2 11
6 18 0	6 12 0	6 6 0	6 0 0	6 0 0	6 7 6
5 14 0	5 11 0	5 11 0	5 2 0	4 10 0	5 10 8
5 8 0	5 8 0	5 8 0	5 14 0	5 14 0	5 1 11
6 18 0	7 1 0	7 0 0	6 12 0	6 0 0	6 11 7
8 14 0	9 12 0	--	12 0 0	11 8 0	8 2 6
12 18 0	11 8 0	--	--	7 7 0	12 16 2
9 6 0	10 16 0	10 16 0	10 4 0	10 16 0	9 14 6
9 0 0	8 2 0	7 16 0	8 17 0	7 4 0	8 15 0

Table 4.5 *Oatmeal (per peck): Edinburgh, 1741–1795*

Date	January s. d.		February s. d.		March s. d.		April s. d.		May s. d.		June s. d.		July s. d.	
1741	14	0	14	0	14	0	15	0	15	0	14	0	13	0
1742	8	0	8	0	8	0	7	6	6	6	6	0	6	6
1743	6	0	6	0	6	0	6	0	6	0	6	0	5	6
1744	5	0	5	6	6	0	6	0	6	0	6	0	6	0
1745	9	0	9	0	9	0	9	6	10	0	10	0	10	6
1746	10	0	10	6	10	6	10	0	10	0	9	0	9	0
1747	8	0	7	6	7	6	6	6	6	6	--	--	7	0
1748	7	0	7	0	6	0	6	0	6	6	6	6	6	6
1749	7	6	7	6	8	0	8	0	8	0	8	0	8	0
1750	8	6	8	6	8	6	8	0	8	0	8	6	8	0
1751	8	6	8	6	8	6	8	6	8	6	8	6	9	0
1752	11	0	11	0	11	0	11	0	11	0	10	6	10	6
1753	10	6	10	6	10	6	10	6	10	6	10	6	10	6
1754	9	0	9	0	9	0	8	6	9	6	9	6	--	--
1755	8	0	8	0	8	0	8	0	7	6	7	6	7	6
1756	9	0	9	6	9	6	9	6	10	0	10	0	11	0
1757	12	6	13	6	15	0	15	6	15	6	15	6	15	6
1758	11	0	11	0	11	0	11	0	11	0	10	6	10	0
1759	8	0	8	0	8	0	8	0	8	0	7	6	7	0
1760	7	0	7	0	7	0	7	0	7	0	7	0	7	0
1761	7	6	7	6	--	--	7	6	7	6	7	6	7	6
1762	8	6	8	6	8	6	9	0	9	0	10	0	11	0
1763	--	--	13	0	14	0	13	0	--	--	12	0	12	0
1764	9	0	9	0	9	0	9	6	9	6	9	6	9	6
1765	10	6	10	6	10	6	10	6	11	0	11	0	11	0
1766	12	6	12	6	12	6	12	6	12	0	12	0	12	6
1767	12	0	12	0	12	0	12	6	12	6	12	6	12	6
1768	12	0	--	--	--	--	--	--	10	0	10	0	9	6
1769	10	0	10	0	10	0	10	0	12	0	12	0	12	0
1770	11	0	11	0	10	6	10	6	10	6	10	6	12	0
1771	11	6	11	6	11	6	11	6	12	0	12	0	12	6
1772	13	0	13	0	13	0	13	0	13	0	13	0	13	0
1773	13	0	13	0	13	0	13	0	13	0	13	0	13	0
1774	12	0	12	0	12	0	12	0	12	0	12	0	12	0
1775	12	0	12	0	12	0	12	0	12	0	12	0	12	0
1776	10	0	9	6	9	6	9	6	9	6	9	6	10	6
1777	9	6	9	6	9	6	9	6	9	6	9	6	9	6
1778	10	0	10	0	10	0	10	0	10	6	10	6	10	6
1779	10	0	10	0	10	0	10	0	10	0	10	0	10	6
1780	8	6	8	6	8	6	8	6	8	6	8	6	9	0
1781	10	6	11	0	11	0	11	0	11	0	11	0	11	0
1782	10	0	9	6	9	6	9	6	10	0	10	6	10	6
1783	--	--	17	0	17	0	17	0	17	0	17	0	17	0
1784	13	0	13	0	13	0	13	0	14	6	14	0	14	0
1785	13	0	13	0	13	0	13	0	11	6	10	6	10	6
1786	11	0	11	0	11	0	11	0	12	0	12	0	12	0
1787	12	6	12	0	12	0	12	0	12	0	12	6	12	6
1788	11	6	11	6	11	6	11	6	11	6	11	6	11	6
1789	8	6	9	6	9	6	9	6	9	6	9	6	10	6
1790	12	0	12	0	12	0	12	0	12	0	12	0	13	6
1791	13	6	13	6	13	0	13	0	13	0	13	0	13	0
1792	12	0	12	0	12	0	12	0	12	0	12	0	12	0
1793	13	0	13	0	13	0	13	0	15	0	15	0	15	0
1794	13	0	13	6	14	0	14	0	14	0	14	0	14	0
1795	13	0	13	0	13	0	13	6	14	0	14	6	14	6

August s. d.		September s. d.		October s. d.		November s. d.		December s. d.		Average s. d.	
10	0	9	6	8	0	8	0	8	0	11	10½
6	6	6	6	6	0	6	6	6	6	6	10¼
5	6	6	0	5	6	5	6	5	6	5	9½
6	0	7	0	9	0	8	0	9	6	6	8
10	6	--	--	10	0	10	6	10	0	9	10
9	0	8	6	8	6	7	6	8	0	9	2½
7	0	7	0	6	6	6	6	7	0	7	0
6	6	6	6	7	0	7	6	7	6	6	8½
8	0	8	0	8	6	8	6	8	6	8	0½
--	--	8	6	8	0	8	0	8	0	8	3
9	0	9	0	10	0	10	0	11	0	9	1
10	0	10	6	10	6	10	6	10	6	10	8
10	6	10	6	10	6	10	6	9	0	10	4½
9	6	9	6	8	0	8	0	8	0	8	10½
7	6	7	6	8	6	8	6	8	6	7	11
12	0	12	0	12	0	11	6	12	0	10	8
15	0	14	6	11	6	11	0	11	0	13	10
9	6	9	6	8	0	8	0	8	0	9	10½
7	0	7	0	7	0	7	0	7	0	7	5½
7	0	7	0	7	0	7	6	8	0	7	1½
7	6	7	6	--	--	8	6	--	--	6	10
11	0	11	0	12	0	12	6	12	6	10	3½
12	0	11	0	11	0	9	0	9	0	11	7
9	6	9	6	10	0	10	0	10	6	9	6½
11	6	11	6	11	6	11	6	12	0	11	1
14	0	13	6	12	0	12	0	12	0	12	6
12	6	13	0	12	0	12	0	12	0	12	3½
9	0	9	0	10	0	10	0	10	0	--	--
12	0	12	0	12	0	11	0	11	0	11	2
12	0	12	0	12	0	11	6	11	6	11	3
12	6	12	6	13	0	13	0	13	0	12	2½
13	0	13	0	13	0	13	0	13	0	13	0
13	0	13	0	13	0	12	0	12	0	12	10
12	0	12	0	12	0	12	0	12	0	12	0
12	0	11	0	11	0	10	0	10	0	11	6
10	0	10	0	10	0	9	6	9	6	9	9
9	6	9	6	9	6	10	0	10	0	9	7
10	6	10	6	10	6	10	6	10	6	10	4
10	6	9	6	9	0	9	0	8	6	9	9
9	6	9	6	9	6	11	0	10	6	9	2
11	0	11	0	10	0	10	0	10	0	10	8½
11	6	14	0	--	--	--	--	--	--	--	--
16	0	14	0	12	0	12	0	12	0	15	3
14	0	14	0	13	6	13	0	13	0	13	6
10	0	10	0	10	6	11	0	11	6	11	5½
12	6	12	6	12	6	12	6	12	6	11	10½
13	6	13	6	13	0	13	0	11	6	12	6
11	6	10	6	10	6	10	0	9	0	11	0
10	6	10	6	10	0	11	0	12	0	10	0½
13	6	13	6	13	6	13	6	13	6	12	9
13	0	13	0	12	6	12	6	12	0	12	11
12	0	12	0	12	0	12	6	12	6	12	1
15	0	15	0	14	0	13	0	13	0	13	11
14	0	13	6	13	0	13	0	13	0	13	7
17	0	16	0	15	6	17	0	16	0	14	9

Table 4.6 *Bearmeal (per peck): Edinburgh, 1741–1795*

Date	January s. d.		February s. d.		March s. d.		April s. d.		May s. d.		June s. d.		July s. d.	
1741	--	--	--	--	--	--	9	6	10	0	10	0	--	--
1742	5	0	5	0	5	0	4	0	3	6	3	6	4	0
1743	--	--	--	--	5	0	4	0	4	6	--	--	--	--
1744	--	--	--	--	--	--	3	6	4	0	4	6	4	6
1745	5	0	5	0	5	0	5	0	5	6	5	6	5	6
1746	6	0	6	0	7	0	7	0	7	0	6	6	6	0
1747	5	0	5	0	5	0	4	6	4	6	--	--	--	--
1748	5	0	5	0	--	--	--	--	5	0	5	0	--	--
1749	--	--	--	--	--	--	5	0	5	6	5	6	6	0
1750	5	0	6	0	6	0	6	0	6	0	6	0	6	0
1751	6	0	6	0	6	0	6	0	6	0	6	0	6	0
1752	7	0	7	0	7	0	7	0	7	0	7	0	7	0
1753	7	0	7	0	7	0	7	0	7	0	7	0	7	0
1754	6	6	6	6	6	0	7	0	7	0	7	0	--	--
1755	5	6	5	6	5	6	5	6	5	0	5	0	5	0
1756	6	0	6	0	6	0	6	0	6	0	6	6	7	0
1757	8	6	9	6	10	0	10	0	10	0	10	6	10	6
1758	7	6	7	6	7	6	7	6	7	6	7	6	7	0
1759	5	0	5	0	5	0	5	0	5	0	5	0	4	0
1760	--	--	--	--	5	0	5	0	5	0	5	0	5	0
1761	5	0	5	0	--	--	5	0	5	0	5	0	5	0
1762	5	0	5	0	5	0	5	6	5	6	5	6	6	6
1763	--	--	8	0	8	0	8	0	--	--	8	0	8	0
1764	7	0	7	0	7	0	7	6	7	6	7	6	7	6
1765	7	6	7	6	7	6	7	0	7	6	7	6	7	6
1766	8	0	8	0	8	0	8	0	7	6	7	6	8	0
1767	8	0	8	6	8	6	9	0	9	0	9	0	9	0
1768	8	0	--	--	--	--	--	--	7	6	7	6	7	0
1769	7	0	7	0	7	0	7	0	7	6	7	6	7	6
1770	7	6	7	6	7	0	7	0	7	0	7	0	7	6
1771	7	6	7	6	7	6	7	6	7	6	8	0	8	0
1772	8	0	8	0	8	0	8	0	8	0	8	0	8	0
1773	8	6	8	6	8	6	8	6	8	6	8	6	8	6
1774	8	6	8	6	8	6	8	6	7	6	7	6	7	6
1775	7	6	7	6	7	6	7	6	7	6	7	6	8	0
1776	7	0	6	6	6	6	6	6	6	6	6	6	6	6
1777	6	0	6	0	6	0	6	0	6	0	6	0	6	0
1778	6	0	6	0	6	0	6	0	7	0	7	0	7	0
1779	6	0	6	0	6	0	6	0	6	0	6	0	6	0
1780	5	0	5	0	5	0	5	0	5	0	5	0	5	6
1781	6	6	7	0	7	0	7	0	7	0	7	0	7	0
1782	7	0	7	0	7	0	7	0	7	0	7	0	7	0
1783	--	--	11	0	11	0	11	0	11	0	11	0	11	0
1784	8	0	9	0	9	0	9	0	9	6	9	0	9	0
1785	8	6	8	6	8	6	8	6	8	6	7	6	7	6
1786	8	0	8	0	8	0	8	0	8	0	8	6	8	6
1787	8	6	9	0	9	0	9	0	9	0	9	0	9	0
1788	9	0	9	0	9	0	8	6	8	6	8	6	8	6
1789	8	0	7	0	7	0	7	0	7	0	7	0	7	0
1790	7	0	7	0	7	0	7	0	7	0	7	0	7	0
1791	7	0	7	0	7	0	7	0	7	0	7	0	7	0
1792	10	0	10	0	10	0	10	0	10	0	10	0	10	0
1793	10	0	10	0	10	0	10	0	11	0	11	0	12	0
1794	11	0	12	0	10	6	10	6	10	6	10	6	10	6
1795	10	6	10	6	11	0	12	0	12	0	12	0	12	0

August s. d.		September s. d.		October s. d.		November s. d.		December s. d.		Average s. d.	
7	0	7	0	5	0	5	0	4	6	--	--
4	0	4	0	4	0	4	6	4	6	4	3
--	--	4	6	4	0	--	--	--	--	--	--
4	6	--	--	--	--	5	0	5	0	--	--
6	0	--	--	6	0	6	0	6	0	5	6
6	0	6	0	6	0	5	0	5	0	6	1½
5	0	4	6	4	6	5	0	--	--	--	--
--	--	--	--	4	6	--	--	--	--	--	--
6	0	6	0	6	0	--	--	--	--	--	--
--	--	6	0	6	0	6	0	6	0	5	11
6	0	6	0	6	6	6	6	7	0	6	2
7	0	7	0	7	0	7	0	7	0	7	0
7	0	7	0	7	0	7	0	6	6	6	11½
7	0	7	0	7	0	7	0	5	6	6	8
5	0	5	0	5	0	5	0	5	6	5	2½
7	6	7	6	8	0	8	0	8	6	6	11
11	0	9	6	8	0	8	0	7	6	9	5
6	0	6	0	--	--	5	6	5	0	6	9½
4	0	4	6	4	6	5	0	5	0	4	9
5	0	5	0	5	0	5	0	5	0	5	0
5	0	5	0	--	--	5	0	--	--	--	--
6	6	6	6	7	6	7	6	7	0	6	1
8	0	8	0	7	6	7	0	7	0	7	9
7	6	7	6	7	0	7	6	7	6	7	4
8	0	8	0	8	0	8	0	8	0	7	8
8	0	8	0	8	0	8	0	8	0	7	11
9	0	9	0	9	0	8	0	8	0	8	8
7	0	7	0	7	0	7	0	7	0	--	--
7	3	7	6	7	6	7	6	7	6	7	4
7	6	7	6	7	6	7	6	7	6	7	4
8	0	8	0	8	0	8	0	8	0	7	9½
8	0	8	0	8	0	8	0	8	6	8	0½
8	6	8	6	8	6	8	6	8	6	8	6
7	6	7	6	7	6	7	6	7	6	7	10
8	0	8	0	7	0	7	6	7	0	7	6½
6	6	6	6	6	6	6	0	6	0	6	5½
6	0	6	0	6	0	6	0	6	0	6	0
7	0	7	0	7	0	7	0	7	0	6	8
6	0	6	0	5	6	5	6	5	0	5	10
6	0	6	0	6	0	7	0	6	0	5	6
7	0	7	0	7	0	7	0	7	0	5	2½
8	0	9	0	--	--	--	--	--	--	--	--
11	0	9	0	8	0	8	0	8	0	10	0
9	0	9	0	9	0	8	6	8	6	8	10½
7	6	7	6	8	6	8	6	8	6	8	2
8	6	8	6	8	6	8	6	8	6	8	3½
9	0	9	0	9	0	9	0	9	0	8	11½
8	6	8	0	8	0	8	0	8	0	8	5½
7	0	7	0	7	0	7	0	7	0	7	1
7	0	7	0	7	0	7	0	7	0	7	0
10	0	10	0	10	0	10	0	10	0	8	3
10	0	10	0	10	0	10	0	10	0	10	0
12	0	12	0	11	0	11	0	11	0	10	11
10	6	10	6	10	6	10	6	--	--	10	8
14	0	12	0	13	0	14	0	14	0	12	3

Table 4.7 *Peasemeal (per peck): Edinburgh, 1741–1795*

Date	January s. d.		February s. d.		March s. d.		April s. d.		May s. d.		June s. d.		July s. d.	
1741	10	0	--	--	--	--	10	0	10	6	10	6	--	--
1742	5	0	5	0	5	0	4	6	3	6	3	6	3	6
1743	4	0	4	0	4	0	4	0	4	0	3	6	3	6
1744	3	0	3	0	3	6	3	6	3	6	3	6	3	6
1745	5	0	5	0	5	0	5	0	5	6	6	0	6	0
1746	6	6	6	0	7	0	7	0	6	6	6	6	6	0
1747	5	0	4	6	4	6	4	6	4	0	--	--	4	0
1748	4	6	4	6	4	0	4	0	4	6	4	6	4	0
1749	4	0	4	0	4	0	4	0	4	0	4	0	4	0
1750	4	6	4	6	4	6	4	6	4	6	4	6	5	0
1751	5	0	5	6	5	6	5	6	5	6	5	6	6	0
1752	7	0	7	6	7	6	7	6	7	6	7	0	7	0
1753	7	0	7	0	7	0	7	0	7	0	7	0	7	0
1754	7	0	7	0	6	6	7	0	7	0	7	0	--	--
1755	5	0	5	0	5	0	5	0	4	6	4	6	4	6
1756	6	6	6	0	6	0	6	0	6	0	6	6	7	0
1757	8	6	9	6	10	0	10	0	10	0	10	6	10	6
1758	7	6	8	0	8	0	8	0	8	0	7	6	7	0
1759	5	0	5	0	5	0	5	0	5	0	4	6	4	0
1760	4	0	4	0	4	0	4	0	4	0	4	0	4	0
1761	5	0	4	6	--	--	5	0	4	6	4	6	4	6
1762	5	0	5	0	5	0	5	6	5	6	5	6	6	6
1763	--	--	7	6	8	0	8	0	--	--	7	6	7	6
1764	7	0	7	0	7	0	7	6	7	6	7	0	7	0
1765	7	6	7	6	7	6	7	0	7	6	7	6	7	6
1766	8	0	8	0	8	0	8	0	7	6	7	6	8	0
1767	8	0	8	6	8	6	8	6	8	6	8	6	8	6
1768	8	6	--	--	--	--	--	--	7	6	7	6	7	0
1769	7	6	7	6	7	6	7	6	7	6	8	0	8	0
1770	7	6	7	6	7	0	7	0	7	0	7	0	7	6
1771	7	6	7	6	7	6	7	6	7	6	7	6	7	6
1772	7	6	7	6	7	6	8	0	8	0	8	0	8	0
1773	9	0	9	0	9	0	9	0	9	0	9	0	9	0
1774	8	6	8	6	8	6	8	6	8	0	8	0	8	0
1775	8	0	8	0	8	0	8	0	8	0	8	0	8	0
1776	7	0	6	6	6	6	6	6	6	6	6	6	6	6
1777	6	0	6	0	6	0	6	0	6	0	6	0	6	0
1778	6	0	6	0	6	0	6	0	7	0	7	0	7	0
1779	6	0	6	0	6	0	6	0	6	0	6	0	6	0
1780	5	0	5	0	5	0	5	0	5	0	5	0	5	6
1781	6	0	6	6	6	6	7	0	7	0	7	0	7	0
1782	7	0	7	0	7	0	7	0	7	0	7	0	7	0
1783	--	--	11	6	11	6	11	0	11	0	11	0	11	0
1784	8	0	9	0	9	0	9	0	9	6	9	0	9	0
1785	8	6	8	6	8	6	8	6	8	6	7	6	7	6
1786	8	0	7	6	8	0	8	0	8	0	8	6	8	6
1787	8	6	9	0	9	0	9	0	9	0	9	0	9	0
1788	9	0	9	0	9	0	8	6	8	6	8	6	8	6
1789	8	0	6	0	6	0	6	0	6	0	6	0	6	0
1790	7	0	7	0	7	0	7	0	7	0	7	0	7	0
1791	7	0	7	0	7	0	7	0	7	0	7	0	7	0
1792	9	0	9	0	9	0	9	0	9	0	9	0	9	0
1793	8	6	8	6	8	6	8	6	10	6	10	6	10	6
1794	10	0	10	6	10	0	10	0	9	0	9	0	9	0
1795	9	0	9	0	9	0	9	6	9	0	9	6	9	6

August s. d.		September s. d.		October s. d.		November s. d.		December s. d.		Average s. d.	
8	0	7	0	5	6	6	0	5	0	--	--
4	0	4	0	4	0	4	0	4	0	4	2
3	0	3	6	3	6	3	0	3	0	3	7
3	6	3	6	5	0	5	0	5	6	3	10
6	0	--	--	6	0	6	0	6	0	5	7
6	0	6	0	6	0	5	0	5	0	6	1½
4	6	4	6	4	6	4	6	4	6	4	5½
4	0	4	0	4	0	4	6	4	0	4	2½
4	0	4	0	4	6	4	6	4	6	4	1½
--	--	5	0	5	0	5	0	5	0	4	9
6	0	6	0	6	6	7	0	7	6	5	11½
7	0	6	6	7	6	7	6	7	0	7	2½
7	0	7	0	7	0	7	0	7	0	7	0
6	6	6	6	6	0	6	0	5	0	6	6
5	6	5	6	5	0	5	6	5	6	5	0½
7	6	7	6	8	0	8	0	8	0	6	11
10	6	8	6	7	6	7	6	7	6	9	2½
6	0	6	0	6	0	6	0	5	0	6	11½
4	6	4	0	4	0	4	0	4	0	4	6
4	0	4	0	4	0	4	6	5	0	4	1½
4	6	4	6	--	--	5	0	--	--	--	--
6	6	6	6	7	0	7	0	7	0	6	0
7	6	7	6	7	0	7	0	7	0	7	5½
7	0	7	0	7	0	7	6	7	6	7	2
7	6	8	0	8	0	8	0	8	0	7	7½
8	0	8	0	8	0	8	0	8	0	7	11
8	6	8	6	8	6	8	6	8	6	8	5½
7	0	7	0	7	0	7	0	7	0	--	--
8	0	8	0	8	0	8	0	7	6	7	9
8	0	8	0	7	6	7	6	7	6	7	5
7	6	7	6	7	6	7	6	7	6	7	6
8	0	8	0	8	0	8	0	9	0	7	11½
9	0	9	0	9	0	8	6	8	6	8	11
8	0	8	0	8	0	8	0	8	0	8	2
8	0	8	0	7	6	7	6	7	0	7	10
6	6	6	6	6	0	6	0	6	0	6	5
6	0	6	0	6	0	6	0	6	0	6	0
7	0	7	0	7	0	7	0	7	0	6	8
6	0	6	0	5	0	5	0	5	0	5	9
5	6	5	6	5	6	6	6	6	0	5	4½
7	0	7	0	7	0	7	0	7	0	6	10
8	0	9	0	--	--	--	--	--	--	--	--
11	0	9	0	8	0	8	0	8	0	10	1
9	0	8	6	8	6	8	6	8	6	8	9½
7	6	7	6	8	6	8	6	8	6	8	2
8	6	8	6	8	6	8	6	8	6	8	3
9	0	9	0	9	0	9	0	9	0	8	11½
8	6	8	0	8	0	8	0	8	0	8	5½
6	0	6	0	6	0	7	0	7	0	6	4
7	0	7	0	7	0	7	0	7	0	7	0
9	0	9	0	9	0	9	0	9	0	7	10
8	6	8	6	8	6	8	6	8	6	8	9½
10	6	10	6	10	6	10	0	10	0	9	9
9	0	9	0	9	0	9	0	--	--	9	5
11	0	11	0	11	0	11	0	13	6	10	2

5 ✦ Trends and fluctuations in grain-price movements

1 Long-term trends to ca.1650

In the three preceding chapters we have laid out and explained a series of price tables for grains and grain-based foods, drawn from burghal records, from fiars and from monthly press reports. The purpose of this chapter is to attempt a broad description and interpretation of both long-term and short-term trends, to give our figures a context.

First, however, it is worth explaining again that throughout the foregoing tables and in the course of this chapter, our use of dates refers to 'crop years'. Thus when we state, for example, that '1622 was a dear year', what we are saying is that prices were high following the crop of 1622, which begins to be cut in the early autumn of 1622 and is the basis of burgh assessments set around November 1622 and of the fiars struck in or around February 1623. In either case the price structure determined by that harvest ruled until supply conditions were altered by expectations concerning the following harvest in the late summer or autumn of 1623. This needs to be borne in mind by, for example, demographic historians trying to correlate prices with mortality in the spring of the calendar year 1623 or social historians interested in vagrancy in the summer of the same calendar year. In each case the relevant price statistic is headed in our tables 1622, not 1623. The price statistic headed 1623 refers to a crop that only began to be gathered in the autumn of the calendar year 1623.

For the earliest part of our study, certainly until around 1630, we are heavily dependent for the interpretation of grain price movements on the evidence of assessed prices of the town councils, considered in chapter 2, along with certain data drawn from the Exchequer Rolls after 1600 made available to us from his own researches by Dr Julian Goodare. What they can tell us of the price revolution in Scotland may be swiftly summarised, although, as ever, conclusions are liable to be undermined by the uncertain evolution of Scottish weights and measures at this early date.

For the first half of the sixteenth century, the figures that we have collected are very scattered but certainly show a tendency for prices to lift, right from the first decade, and perhaps to double in the course of the second quarter. In Edinburgh, wheatbread was twice as expensive comparing 1528–36 with 1547–51, and ale, about 1½d. a pint in 1504–16, was 4d. by 1546–52. Malt prices in Stirling also more than doubled between the 1520s and the later 1540s. Wine was about 6d.–8d. a pint at the start of the century, a shilling or more by the 1550s. Such trends are roughly consonant with what was happening elsewhere in Europe; grain prices in England, for example, also approximately doubling between the early 1520s and the early 1550s.[1]

The second half of the century provides more data and evidence of a much steeper and accelerating price rise. It began unevenly. Ale and wine prices were still much the same in Edinburgh in the later 1560s as in the early 1550s, but Edinburgh wheatbread was 30 per cent up, and Aberdeen ale nearly 40 per cent up. The fiars prices in Fife reveal an even stronger underlying upward trend: Fife oatmeal, comparing 1556–9 with 1566–9, was 90 per cent more expensive, and bear was 70 per cent up (figures 5.1–5.3). Thereafter everything bounded ahead, fuelled by an underlying inflation from dearth to dearth. The earliest surviving series of Fife fiars for oatmeal and bear ends with the crop of 1586, but for the last four years of their quotation oatmeal was five times, and bear four times, the average of the first four years beginning with the crop of 1556. The estimated price of wheat in Edinburgh also grew by between three and four times between mid century and the mid 1580s; but it had grown to eight times as high as the late 1550s figure by the late 1590s. Wheatbread in Aberdeen and Edinburgh, 2½d. or 3d. a pound around 1550, was 4d. around 1575 and 9d. by 1586; it doubled again to 16d. by 1597. In good years the price fell, but not to old levels. Ale, 4d. a pint in Edinburgh around 1550, reached 8d. in 1581 and 12d. by 1597 – a more moderate rate of inflation than other grain-derived foodstuffs. Wine, about 1s. in mid century, was 3s. by 1576 and 8s. by 1596 – a faster rise even than for wheat. Animal prices are considered in chapter 6, but it is worth observing here that, just as in England, the rate of inflation was not as great for beasts as for grains in the second half of the century (though it had probably been similar in the first half). We see a five-fold increase in cattle prices (and less for sheep) between about 1550 and about 1600, compared to something over a six-fold rise in grain prices.

All of this, though, was much faster inflation than in England where the average wholesale price of all grains momentarily touched, in 1596–7, a point about three times the level of mid century, and then fell back to one about twice that level, whereas animal prices barely doubled in the same period.[2] The difference need not surprise us, of course, as we have seen in chapter 1 how the Scottish crown pursued a policy of repeated debasement in some ways closer to that of France (though more extreme) than to that of England, where Elizabeth's ministers strove to maintain the bullion content in the coinage. A different perspective on inflation in Scotland appears from figure 5.4, which shows that in terms of the quantity of bread that could be purchased per gram of silver, there was relatively little deterioration before the mid 1580s, but then a rapid fall of purchasing power by about one half between that point and the end of the century. Presumably that was when demographic pressures became paramount. Calculated in terms of silver, English and Scottish inflation rates appear much more comparable.

Scottish prices were driven upwards, therefore, both by state monetary policy and by population pressures that appeared catastrophic in bad harvests. The underlying trend presented an extremely grave situation for those dependent on cash incomes who could not raise them at the same rate. Such would include, for example, the crown, dependent

[1] Joan Thirsk (ed.), *The agrarian history of England and Wales*, vol. IV, *1500–1640* (Cambridge 1967), pp. 817–18.
[2] *Ibid.*, p. 820.

on relatively inflexible rents or feu duties or traditional levels of customs dues, nobles with tenants on long or secure leases with rents paid in cash, urban labourers without access to allowances in kind. It is not surprising that everywhere such losers would try to adjust the bargain – the crown by increased taxation, the lairds by preferring where they could rents in kind and tenants at will, the labourer possibly by requesting more cash and the option of a food wage. Similarly it is likely that, with differential returns from animals and grain, those who could shift land use from pasture to arable would do so and those who could not would suffer even more.

The price revolution had not exhausted itself by the start of the seventeenth century, but it began to change its character when after the Union of the Crowns there was no further monetary debasement, the pound Scots being tied to the pound sterling at a ratio of 12:1. In Scotland, bread and grain prices in the first two decades increased little after 1603, even falling back from the highest levels of the dearth years of the late 1590s and the turn of the century. But it was not everywhere so; examination of the tables shows that there were years of high prices in some localities, especially during the second decade. Thereafter, in the very severe dearth following 1621, in the later 1620s, and in bad years of the 1630s and 1640s, many prices well exceeded those of 1596–7. Wheatbread in Edinburgh and Aberdeen, for instance, rose from 16d. to as high as 24d. per pound, though relapsing when the crises passed to 13d. or less. That was fairly typical of such grain-based prices as we have. The prices that the comptroller received in Exchequer for wheat and oats paid as feu duties, collected by Dr Goodare for the early seventeenth century, probably moved more sluggishly than other prices, as they were only slowly adjusted to the market. Yet, comparing the years 1601–4 to 1631–4, they rose over the three decades by 28 per cent and 81 per cent respectively. This may represent the royal effort to recoup profits foregone in earlier years. No price as much as doubled in the first half of the seventeenth century except ale, which did so in some towns, notably Aberdeen. Here it seems to have risen by less than the average in the sixteenth century, so perhaps this early seventeenth-century surge can be seen as a catching-up process by the brewers, allowed by the magistrates once earlier runs of dearth eased. A cheaper pint was available in Stirling and Kirkcudbright than in Edinburgh, Glasgow or Aberdeen, but who is to say it was the same quality?

Certainly by the late 1650s, the price revolution had come to an end. The only goods that can be followed even with sparse data all the way through from ca.1500 to the middle of the seventeenth century are wheatbread and ale in the Edinburgh assessments: in the former the overall inflation was about eighteen-fold, in the latter about twelve-fold, in a period of 150 years.

2 Long-term trends, ca.1650–1780

The price historian's task is eased from the 1630s by a slowly increasing number of fiars prices for oatmeal and grain, supplementing town council assessments. As the latter begin to be discontinued, mainly at the end of the seventeenth century, the fiars increased more rapidly and give an impressive regional coverage by the mid eighteenth century.

Within the period 1650–1780, the second half of the seventeenth century was, like the first half, marked by great instability of prices between years. These short-term fluctuations can obscure the long-term trend, but, as figures 5.5–5.8 demonstrate in their graphing of eleven-year means of the fiars from 1630 to 1780, there was nevertheless a steady tendency for prices to fall from mid century until the late 1670s. During the 1680s this trend reversed and, leaving aside the distortion caused by the crisis of the late 1690s, there was a tendency clearly evident in the figures for fiars prices to creep upward again. This was more apparent for oatmeal and wheat than for bear and pease, which did not move ahead until around the middle of the eighteenth century. For all grains in all counties, however, the increase was always more pronounced in the 1760s than in earlier decades. Where there is a long enough run of data, the impression of average price levels over the 150-year period 1630–1780 is of an asymmetrical and very flattened U-shaped curve, distorted into a W only by the bulge in average prices caused by the abnormally severe short-term crisis of the late 1690s discussed in the following section.

These long-term trends were universal both between different grains and in the different counties of Scotland. The seventeenth-century data are thinnest, but suggest almost a halving in prices before the later 1670s for oats, oatmeal and perhaps wheat, with a rather smaller drop for bear. The falling trend may indeed begin well before the middle of the century, only to be interrupted by scarcities in the 1640s, which were exacerbated by military problems. It is interesting that in any case this fall must predate the impact of most of the tendencies towards better farming detected by Dodgshon and Whyte in their studies of seventeenth-century agrarian society, as well as any improvement in the climate as charted by Lamb and Parry.[3] Nor is there any hint of improved communications to aid grain movements. This makes alteration on the supply side less likely as an explanation of price trends at this point than a shift in demand, probably brought about by a combination of economic depression and an easing of the demographic pressures that had fuelled inflation since the later sixteenth century. One can postulate some decline of population similar to that detected by Wrigley and Schofield in England after 1650. Perhaps in the Scottish case it was associated with an impact on the birth rate from the heavy emigration (especially of young males) to Poland, Scandinavia, the Low Countries and Ulster, notable in the 1620s and 1630s. In the second half of the seventeenth century, the population of Aberdeen and Dundee dropped, and even Edinburgh probably failed to grow substantially.[4] Export industries were doing badly after ca.1640, and the number of net grain consumers may have fallen more rapidly than the number of net grain producers, especially if those tempted into cottage textile industries in good times began to move back to full time food production.

[3] R.A. Dodgshon, *Land and society in early Scotland* (Oxford, 1981); I. Whyte, *Agriculture and society in seventeenth-century Scotland* (Edinburgh, 1979); H.H. Lamb, *Climate, history and the modern world* (London, 1982); M.L. Parry, 'Secular climatic change and marginal agriculture', *Transactions of the Institute of British Geographers*, no. 64 (1975), pp. 1–13.

[4] E.A. Wrigley and R.S. Schofield, *The population history of England, 1541–1871* (Cambridge, 1981); M.W. Flinn (ed.), *Scottish population history from the seventeenth century to the 1930s* (Cambridge, 1977), especially part 3; M. Perceval-Maxwell, *The Scottish migration to Ulster in the reign of James I* (London, 1973); A. Bieganska, 'A note on the Scots in Poland, 1550–1800', in T.C. Smout (ed.), *Scotland and Europe 1200–1850* (Edinburgh, 1986), pp. 157–66; R. Gillespie, *Colonial Ulster: the settlement of east Ulster 1600–1641* (Cork, 1985).

The sharpest price falls are in the 1650s and 1660s, perhaps related in the short term to the bubonic plague of the late 1640s and the impact of smallpox, noted for the first time as a serious killer in several places in the 1660s.[5] Indications that the price of meal and wheat fell more than bear could be due to differing elasticities for food and ale and would be consistent with some drop in population.

One would expect the heavy mortality of the 'ill years' of the later 1690s to continue to keep prices low after the dearth had passed. Tyson has suggested that population levels may have dropped by about 13 per cent in this crisis and had not been fully restored even by 1755.[6] Certainly the opening years of the new century saw some very low prices, but after about 1705 there are indications that Scotland very slowly started to pull out of the price trough for grain that had ruled in years of reasonable harvest over the previous thirty years. As figures 5.5–5.8 graphically demonstrate, oatmeal and wheat prices were creeping upwards everywhere except Edinburgh, where it was not until the 1730s and 1740s that an upward trend becomes apparent. Bear remained more sluggish until the 1730s when there was a marked upturn – in Ayrshire a dramatic one. Such records as there are for peas and beans show a bouncing, cyclical pattern with little upward shift before 1750. The early part of the 1760s reveals a general rise on every graph, bringing prices on to a higher plateau: the overall gain from 1705 was usually more than 50 per cent, and in some cases close to doubling by the early 1770s, though a slight (and temporary) dip in the last five years before 1780 somewhat obscures the extent of the gain. The vigour of price increases in the 1760s was immediately reflected in the sharp increase in the activities of improving landowners: building new villages, surveying their estates and enclosing commonty as investment in agriculture was encouraged by better returns.[7]

The profile and scale of Scottish grain-price movements in the seventeenth and eighteenth centuries are different in certain respects from those of England. Mingay and John, relying mainly on wheat prices series from Winchester and Exeter in the south, charted a fall in prices beginning after the Restoration and continuing well into the eighteenth century to reach their nadir in the 'agricultural depression' of 1730–50.[8] Bowden, drawing more recently on a much more extensive data set, 1640–1750, for many grains and several regions, emphasised the rather moderate nature of the downward trend; less pronounced than in Scotland in the seventeenth century, but equally continuing through the first half of the eighteenth century without reversal.[9] Differences

[5] Flinn (ed.), *Scottish population*, pp. 133–64.

[6] R.E. Tyson, 'Contrasting régimes: population growth in Ireland and Scotland during the eighteenth century', in R.A. Houston *et al.* (eds.), *Conflict and identity in the social and economic history of Ireland and Scotland* (forthcoming). See also R.E. Tyson, 'Famine in Aberdeenshire, 1695–1699: anatomy of a crisis', in D. Stevenson (ed.), *From lairds to louns: country and burgh life in Aberdeen, 1600–1800* (Aberdeen, 1986), pp. 32–51; R.E. Tyson, 'The population of Aberdeenshire, 1695–1755: a new approach', *Northern Scotland*, vol. 6 (1985), pp. 113–32.

[7] I.H. Adams, 'Economic process and the Scottish land surveyor', *Imago Mundi*, vol. 27 (1975), pp. 13–18.

[8] G.E. Mingay, 'The agricultural depression, 1730–1750', *Economic History Review*, 2nd series, vol. 8 (1955–6); G.E. Mingay, *English landed society in the eighteenth century* (London, 1963), pp. 54–6; A.H. John, 'The course of agricultural change, 1660–1760, in L.S. Presnell (ed.), *Studies in the industrial revolution* (London, 1960); for a dissenting note, see M.W. Flinn, 'Agricultural productivity and economic growth in England, 1700–1760: a comment', *Journal of Economic History*, vol. 26 (1966), pp. 93–8.

[9] P.J. Bowden, 'Agricultural prices, wages, farm profits and rents', in *The agrarian history of England and Wales*, vol.V *1640–1750* (ed. Joan Thirsk) (Cambridge, 1985) part 2, chapter 13 and appendix 3.

between the two countries could be due to the depth of the late seventeenth-century economic depression in Scotland, where there was no comparably large and healthy industrial and urban consumer sector to keep up prices. Equally, the earlier Scottish recovery could reflect a better economic performance after the Union of 1707 than has been suspected. There is no disagreement that in the last three decades of our period, 1750–80, when England and Scotland both enjoyed renewed population growth, both countries also experienced generally buoyant prices for the main grains.

3 Short-term fluctuations before 1700

As we explained in chapter 1, for most people in Scotland, and especially for consumers, the most important feature of grain prices was not the long-term trend but the more dramatic short-term fluctuations, particularly those severe enough to bring hunger or outright famine. For the sixteenth century and until 1630, the town council assessments are again our main source, and we cannot be sure that, in their efforts to control as well as to reflect market prices, local authorities did not try to flatten peaks, fill troughs, delay upward movements for a time and try to either shorten or to prolong a period of high bread and ale prices when wholesale grain prices were also high, depending on whether they were more concerned about the consumer paying too much for manufactured goods or the producer being squeezed of his profits. The series for oatbread for Kirkcudbright (table 2.4) provides a striking instance of the refusal of a local authority to reflect market forces except in a spasmodic and jerky fashion. This may be an explanation for the apparent lack of synchronisation of certain peaks in different places, as shown by burgh assessed prices compared to later fiars prices: it should not, without further confirmation, be taken as evidence that the grain market was working less effectively earlier than it did at the end of the seventeenth century.

Some sixteenth-century and early seventeenth-century crises leap off the page as soon as the statistics are examined: the first is 1523, when wheatbread at Edinburgh was at twice the level of any other quotation between 1495 and 1547. How long this crisis lasted, or whether it stood alone in the first four decades of the sixteenth century, we cannot say as very few price quotations survive. Then the harvests of 1562, 1573–5, 1585–7, 1594–9, 1602, 1621–4, 1628–30 and 1635–8 all attracted high prices in more than one place. But the sources are thin even after 1550, and it is most unlikely that we have been able to pick up every year of crisis in this period. For example, how far was the 1558 crop dear outside Fife? Secondly, there do seem to be occasions when prices moved decisively in different directions in different corners of the country, as though the market was indeed disjointed. 1576–8, for example, appears to have been a period of low steady grain prices in Aberdeen, rising prices in Glasgow and falling prices in Fife. Similarly, how seriously should we take the high prices in Aberdeen for the harvests of 1615–16, when there was little stir in the Forfar fiars?

Without demographic records in these early years we cannot say as much about the impact of famine as we would like. Within our study period we know in general terms that there was famine mortality in the bad years of the 1580s and 1590s and a fuller examination has been made elsewhere, using early parish registers, of the severe mortality associated with high prices and vagrancy in the dearth that commenced with the bad harvest of 1621.[10] The latter does indeed stand out as much the sharpest peak in prices in the first quarter of the sixteenth century (see figures 5.1 and 5.2), following two decades of relatively more benign experience, but we are again reminded that prices in these circumstances are not everything: following the 1623 harvest, Aberdeen's prices for wheatbread exceeded those of all other Scottish burghs, but mortality was not, apparently, very high in the north-east. It is tempting to relate that fact to the prosperity of the local plaiding trade which, in this period, was probably the most successful export-oriented domestic industry in Scotland. With the earnings and savings of that trade, perhaps, the peasantry of the north-east were able to stave off the consequences of a dearth more fatal in the south, in parishes like Dumfries, Melrose, Dunfermline and Burntisland which lacked such a staple to provide the wherewithal to buy when the crops failed.

Once we come to the dear harvests of 1628–30, 1635–8 and the lesser peaks in the early 1640s we begin to have the benefit, rather sketchy at first, of fiars data from Fife, Haddington, Midlothian and Perthshire, with some from Aberdeen and Roxburgh (tables 3.2–3.19: figures 5.9–5.10). There are some interesting features. In 1628–30, and again in several years of the 1630s, the Fife fiars for oatmeal and the comptroller's Exchequer prices for oats and wheat exceeded those of the dearth of 1621–3, though historical demographers can find no evidence that mortality ever hit comparable levels.[11] Perhaps there was less vagrancy to spread infection and no co-incidence with epidemic diseases such as typhus.

The crisis of crops 1647–52 is better covered, though still only by the same range of localities as began to appear in the 1630s. It stands out instantly with the later 1690s as one of two peaks in the entire period 1630–1780 when prices were exceptionally high for an unusually long period (see figures 5.9 and 5.10). Like the early 1620s and the late 1690s, it was associated with famine mortality, though due to the scarcity of the parish burial records in these years of civil and ecclesiastical dislocation, it is difficult to measure its comparative seriousness in terms of either the numbers dying or the extent of the area affected. The impression of demographers, however, is that it was much more limited than the other two great crises, perhaps serious in Argyll and the northern Lowlands, but hardly catastrophic elsewhere.[12]

The same crisis was visible in England, though not necessarily with mortal effects. Bowden calls it a 'final paroxysm' of the price revolution.[13] In Scotland, it appears in some wheatbread series (figure 5.1) as the culmination of a century of inflation. How far it was caused, or exacerbated, by the turmoils associated with war and English invasion cannot be readily assessed. Presumably throughout Great Britain dislocated communications and the demand of armies to be fed in an environment of bad harvests drove prices above what they would have been in peacetime conditions, but invasion itself did not end trade. One contemporary explained: 'when our own corns failed us the English

[10] Flinn (ed.), *Scottish population*, pp. 197–226.   [11] *Ibid.*, pp. 127–8.   [12] *Ibid.*, p. 151.
[13] Bowden, 'Agricultural prices', p. 1.

nation did bring in abundantly wheat, beans, peas and such like and brought down the dearth of our mercats by expectation'.[14]

In this crisis there is a rough, though not precise, uniformity of experience across Scotland and between grains despite the varying circumstances of war. There are fiars data for Fife, Midlothian, Haddington and Forfar in the south-east core, with Aberdeenshire, Perth and Roxburghshire beyond: and it covers (though not in a complete series for each), four grains (oats, bear, wheat, rye), oatmeal and two pulses (peas and beans), supplemented by data from assessed prices in the towns. In most cases where the data cover the beginning and the end, it can be seen that prices started to rise with the crop of 1647 and to subside with the crop of 1652. The precise experience differed from place to place, but everywhere there were three or four bad years which in several cases were the most expensive of the century. The scale and universality of the rise, including that for the less popular rye, peas and beans which like oatmeal itself stood at twice the level of previous and subsequent years, indicate both the inelastic nature of the demand for grain foods and the need which arose to substitute one kind of grain for another. There are however, some signs of wartime dislocation in the fact that years of high prices were not everywhere synchronised even down the east coast.

This crisis was followed by an uneventful quarter of a century, with only locally significant clusters of fairly high prices focused on 1659–60. Wheatbread and oatbread in the burghs, Haddington wheat and peas and Roxburgh oatmeal were all up in these years.

More important was the dearth of 1674–5, again accompanied by the doubling or near-doubling of the great majority of the fiars prices for which we have records – not only in the south-east and Perthshire but also now for meal in Ayr and Glasgow and bear in Glasgow. There is no indication that prices rose higher in the west or in Perthshire than in the east, or that the rate of increase was greater, but contemporaries perceived a danger of famine throughout the western Lowlands, Borders, Argyll and the 'toun of Perth' in 1675 unless grain imports were allowed. The problem of the uplands was not just high grain prices: tenants had been hit by extremely severe weather in the early months of 1674, when storms and the 'thirteen drifty days' of late February had wiped out flocks of sheep and cattle and destroyed the farmers' ability to trade meat for grain – a further reminder that famines are caused not only by high prices for food but also by an absence of the wherewithal to buy that food. Burial levels were significantly higher in these years than in most of those in the surrounding decades, though there were several epidemics about and the exact relationship between price and mortality is, as ever, hard to determine.[15]

The remainder of the 1670s and the 1680s saw a return to low prices, interrupted by a faint upward movement with the crops of 1681 and 1682 and a slightly stronger one with those of 1689 and 1690. The latter had more impact in that it influenced all prices, whereas the former was hardly detectable in some – for example wheat, or Aberdeenshire peas – which is a sure sign that scarcity was not marked enough to lead to widespread

---

[14] R. Law, *Memorialls: or, The memorable things that fell out within this island of Brittain from 1638 to 1684* (Edinburgh, 1818), p. 5.   [15] Flinn (ed.), *Scottish population*, pp. 159–63.

substitution. The run of low prices was, however, dramatically interrupted in the 1690s by the most famous dearth of all, the so-called 'ill years of King William' which occupied most of the period from 1695–1699. There are signs that it began in the extreme north – Orkney and Shetland – as early as the crop of 1693, but we have no fiars data to illustrate it there.[16]

The crisis has elsewhere been described from the point of view of the grain imports brought in as relief and from the point of view of the mortality it caused.[17] In a situation of poor weather across the northern hemisphere, evidently associated with unusual sunspot activity, most of Europe, including England, experienced higher prices than for decades. The general climatic picture was of poor weather in the first part of the decade especially in southern England and in France, leaving Scotland comparatively free, but according to Ian Whyte (*pers. comm.*) in the second part of the decade rain and cold engulfed Scotland and Scandinavia, associated with a shift of the Gulf-Stream south-wards, and an extension of the Arctic icefields that brought several Eskimos to Scotland in their kayaks. Ireland, England and France at this point were less badly affected.

The Scottish fiars prices show little increase before 1695, when the harvest failed. It failed again in 1696 and in 1698; 1697 was a respite in most localities and the high prices then and in 1699 were perhaps caused more by rundown of grain in stock than by the weather. By 1700 a good, plenteous harvest brought the problem to an end, and five years of very low prices followed. The extent of population loss was very variable but obviously more severe than anything since the early 1620s, probably more severe even than that. A few upland parishes in the north may have lost at least a third of their population; it has been estimated that Aberdeenshire as a whole might have lost one fifth; the overall decline for Scotland (caused by emigration and a decline in births as well as by mortality) has been put as high as 13 per cent. There are signs that the peak of mortality differed somewhat from region to region, but 1697 and 1699 were the worst years. Some other countries, for example England, had high prices but no particular peak in mortality; others, like Finland, had even higher famine-related mortality.[18]

The profiles of the fiars prices in these years are very reminiscent of 1647–52, though with more synchronised peaks. It is not clear that prices were generally higher in the later 1690s than around 1650, nor that the leap above the preceding price level was much greater. Why, then, should famine mortality and population loss have been so much more prominent?

The answer may lie partly in the length of the period of dearth. In 1647–52, there were three or four very high years in succession, flanked by rather lower ones. In 1695–9 there were again usually three or four very dear harvests – often in 1695, almost always 1696, 1698 and 1699. The success of the 1697 harvest brought partial relief in the southern half of Scotland for every grain except wheat, but in the one northern county for which there are records, Aberdeenshire, this break did not occur. The price of oats slightly faltered:

---

[16] *Ibid.,* p. 165.

[17] T.C. Smout, *Scottish trade on the eve of Union, 1660–1707* (Edinburgh, 1963), pp. 165–7, 179–82, 202, 246–9. Flinn (ed.), *Scottish population,* pp. 166–85; Tyson, 'Famine in Aberdeenshire'.

[18] Wrigley and Schofield, *Population history of England*; E. Jutikkala, 'The great Finnish famine in 1696–7', *Scandinavian Economic History Review,* vol. 3 (1955), pp. 48–63; Flinn (ed.), *Scottish population,* pp. 164–86.

those of oatmeal, bear, wheat and rye went steadily up, to achieve their peaks the following year. The crop of 1698 was usually the most expensive everywhere. Mortality was abnormally high in Aberdeenshire, especially in the calendar years 1697 and 1699, where there is some evidence that fiars prices failed to reflect, for the reasons discussed in chapter 4, the sharpest peaks of grain prices; it has been suggested that here a boll of oatmeal may have reached £16 Scots, or four times the pre-famine price.[19] In the south-east of Scotland the worst calendar year for deaths was generally 1699.

Tyson has also related the depth of the crisis in the north-east both to the difficulties over poor relief in the disputes between Episcopalian and Presbyterian authorities after 1690 and to the simultaneous decline of the export trades in stockings and plaiding which in earlier decades had provided the small tenants and cottars who were the country knitters and weavers with cash to buy grain. With their income gone, they were doubly helpless against the high prices. No doubt throughout Scotland the problem of dearth was to some degree exacerbated by inefficient poor relief and by the deep commercial crisis of the time; the strain of grain imports affected not only the balance of trade but even the amount of coin circulating in the country.[20]

On the other hand it is not clear that at the close of the 1690s the Scottish economy was more seriously affected than it had been in the midst of the military campaigns against Montrose and Cromwell. There may of course have been a difference in that the economic crisis at the end of the 1640s was the first to hit Scotland after a number of decades in which the commercial sector had evidently prospered, whereas the dearth of the late 1690s hit an economy which had been in a situation of commercial stagnation or decline for some time: thus the funds available for charitable donations and ordinary poor relief may have been much lower than previously. But all of this demands more research.

4 Short-term fluctuations, 1700–80

In contrast to the seventeenth century, and especially to its closing years, the first forty years of the eighteenth century witnessed a long period without famine and without many significant short-term fiars price fluctuations (figures 5.9 and 5.10). The most anxious years probably followed the crops of 1708–10, which saw renewed starvation in Europe and increases in all grain prices everywhere in Scotland, though of varying magnitude and duration. While fiars prices were always well below those of the late 1690s, they were generally at least as high as those of 1689–90 and often comparable with those of the troubled year 1674. For wheat prices especially, the crop of 1709 was a big peak everywhere, even in Aberdeen. For the much more important oat crop and oatmeal, however, the increase was comparatively insignificant in the north, although of somewhat greater magnitude elsewhere. Only a few parishes even in the south, however, complained of distress among the poor and the parish registers reveal no obvious ill effects. No evidence has come to light to support Henry Hamilton's observation that in

---

[19] Tyson, 'Famine in Aberdeenshire'.
[20] Tyson, 'Famine in Aberdeenshire', pp. 35–6; Smout, *Scottish trade*, pp. 124–8.

1709 in Scotland 'famine again brought desolation to the countryside and starvation to countless people'.[21] That is unwarrantably pessimistic.

Although many grain prices crept upwards during the following three decades, there was little drama. Occasionally one grain or another had a moderately dear year in one or two counties – fiars prices for wheat in Haddington and Edinburgh in 1713, oats in Berwickshire in 1719, pease in Haddington, Fife and Berwickshire in 1713–14, malt in Fife in 1714 were all above average, but the disjointed, unsynchronised nature of these movements indicates no very serious disruption. Most fiars prices were up again following the harvests of 1722 and 1723, when imports of victual from Ireland reached a peak,[22] but it is again significant that oats and meal in Edinburgh and Haddington were only slightly raised and that wheat everywhere in the east barely stirred. There were small movements later in the 1720s and 1730s, again mainly unsystematic and insignificant. For labour, the even nature of the seasons must have appeared a merciful contrast with earlier generations.

In the crop years 1739 and 1740 the peace was shattered by another subsistence crisis of the old type, which ran through Europe from Ireland to Prussia and Austria and caused very serious mortality, particularly in Ireland and Norway. In Scotland, the problem was precipitated by a light harvest in 1739, followed by a bitter winter. The fiars prices quite fail to show the extent of the problem, which only became evident after they had been struck in February 1740. Thereafter grain prices began to climb very steeply, though unfortunately the monthly price data for Haddington are too sketchy to show the full extent of the increase. The worst grain riots of the century broke out in Edinburgh in October 1740 following the summer droughts and prospects for an even greater shortfall of supply which the populace believed led the grain merchants to horde their stocks. The fiars prices for the crop 1740 were the highest in the first half of the century. For oatmeal, oats, bear, wheat and rye in the south of Scotland, on both east and west coasts, prices were up by at least 30–60 per cent compared with 1739 and had often doubled compared with 1738. For peas, important as a food crop in the south-east, in Haddington and Berwickshire the 1740 crop was nearly three times as expensive as the 1739 crop.

That there was suffering in Scotland is plain: the outbreak of grain riots in Edinburgh and elsewhere as far north as Cromarty testified to the resentment of the poor that grain exports and distilling were not formally suspended. Some famine-induced mortality occurred. It was quite widely reported among the Highland population, where the severe winter had decimated the cattle and reduced purchasing power; hardship also led to some rise in deaths among the urban and industrial workforce in the Lowlands.[23] On the other hand, there was no great leap in mortality as there was in seventeenth-century crises, or in the contemporary crisis in Ireland, Norway and Austria.

Professor Post has discussed reasons for the differential mortality in thirteen

[21] Flinn (ed.), *Scottish population*, p. 211; H. Hamilton, *An economic history of Scotland in the eighteenth century* (Oxford, 1963), p. 7.
[22] L.E. Cochran, *Scottish trade with Ireland in the eighteenth century* (Edinburgh, 1985), p. 100.
[23] Flinn (ed.), *Scottish population*, p. 219.

European countries in this crisis, reaching the conclusion that the most important variable was the effectiveness of national systems of poor relief, high in England and Prussia, for example, but low in the countries worst affected.[24] It was certainly true in Scotland that much greater efforts were made by local authorities and landowners to import food and distribute it at cost price than had been the case in the 1690s. On the other hand, in Scotland, unlike in many European countries where the crisis was spread over up to four years, the period of very high prices was quite restricted. Under these circumstances even in the seventeenth century a general surge of mortality would not have been expected. Possibly the relief efforts of the authorities in 1740 and 1741, sharpened, no doubt, by the menace of rioters in the streets, helped to check speculation and hoarding, and therefore to make the following season a cheap year. What was the relative contribution of better weather or better charity in Scotland compared to, say, Norway, would be hard to say.

The fiars prices of the next forty years had a different character from the previous period. They were somewhat more unsteady and, more importantly, were from the 1750s set against a more steeply rising trend. The harvests of 1744 and 1745 were followed by high fiars, and complaints were heard of scarcity in Perthshire, upland Dumfriesshire and Tiree, even of famine in Orkney.[25] The prices for oats, oatmeal and bear in Ayrshire and Aberdeenshire were nearly as high or even higher than in 1740. Disruption of markets from the Jacobite rising can perhaps account for the sharp short-term hike in prices on the Haddington market in the first half of 1746 (see figures 4.1–4.4).

Thereafter, in the period down to 1780, there was upward pressure on prices in 1751–2, 1756–7, 1762, 1765–6 and 1770–3. Of these, 1756–7 was probably much more serious than the fiars indicate. As we saw in chapter 4, the fiars prices at Haddington again understate what really occurred, as the main price increase came between March and August 1757, while fiars had been struck in or around February on the basis of prices following the 1756 harvest. For the main grains, the peaks reported in the press in 1757 were between 20 and 42 per cent above the prevailing fiars, and touched or even exceeded the levels of the summer of 1741. John Ramsay of Ochtertyre in Stirlingshire noted this season as one of the first occasions on which the high price of grain had been 'alleviated by the plenty of potatoes, a root which twenty years before had been confined to gentlemen's gardens'.[26] From the fiars for the 1762 crop, it looks as if 1763 would have been nearly as bad, but there were few problems to which contemporaries drew attention.

The crisis of 1771–3, however, created much worse social dislocation, with reports of near famine in the Hebrides and grain riots in Dumfries, Perth and Dundee.[27] In the fiars price tables the levels in the early 1770s do not seem unduly above those of the immediately surrounding years, though they come at the culmination of a decade in which the tendency towards increased prices had been marked. The heart of the problem

---

[24] J.D. Post, *Food Shortage, climatic variability and epidemic disease in preindustrial Europe: the mortality peak in the early 1740s* (Ithaca, 1985).   [25] Flinn (ed.), *Scottish population*, pp. 223–4.
[26] Quoted in R.N. Salaman, *The history and social influence of the potato* (Cambridge, 1949), p. 392.
[27] Flinn (ed.), *Scottish population*, pp. 231–3; S.G.E. Lythe, 'The Tayside meal mobs, 1772–3', *Scottish Historical Review*, vol. 46, pp. 26–36.

lay, however, as much in the reduced purchasing power of vulnerable sectors of the population as in inflation. The bad winter of 1771–2 caused heavy losses among Highland cattle, leading to a shortage of cash to buy grain on the islands: industrial depression exacerbated by the crash of the Ayr Bank in 1772 threw thousands out of work, especially in the linen trade so important to the Tayside towns. There was no general disaster, but one sees here, as so often in the history of short-run grain price movements, that a surge in prices is only one element determining whether or not there will be either an increase in deaths, or a rise in social discontent, or both.

It is not our concern to pursue price history in detail past 1780, but a glance at, for example, figures 1.2–1.3, 4.1–4.4 and 4.7 demonstrate that severe fluctuations were to be a feature of the remainder of the century. The year 1782 was regarded by the reporters to Sir John Sinclair's *Statistical Account* as witnessing the most serious harvest shortfall for decades. Starvation was then narrowly averted in the Lowlands, but not everywhere in the Highlands. Several times in the 1790s the situation became grave indeed. A prolonged period of inflation began in this decade, which was to drive prices up more rapidly than at any time since the sixteenth century. That story, however, lies beyond the confines of this study.

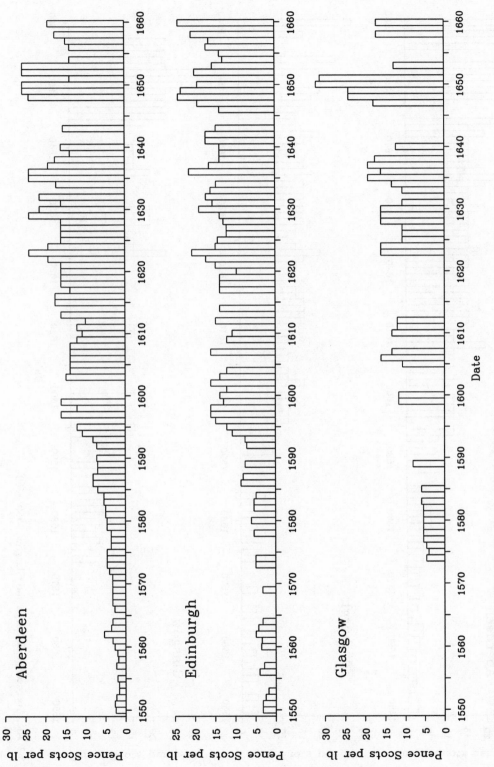

5.1 Wheatbread: Aberdeen, Edinburgh and Glasgow, 1550–1660

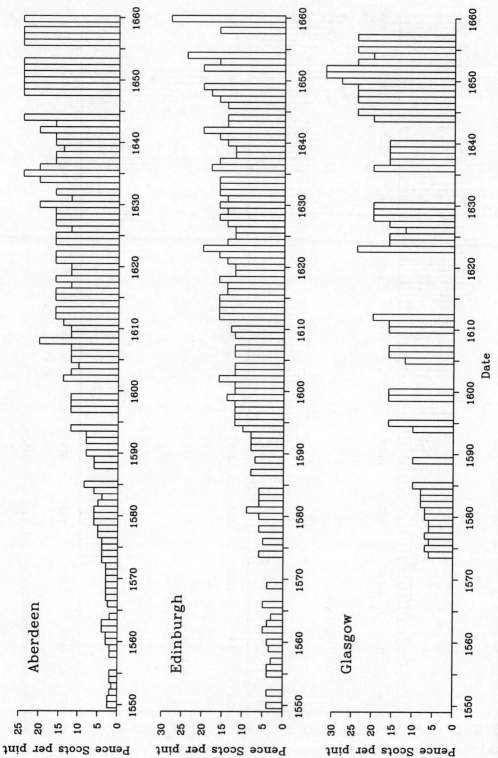

5.2 Ale: Aberdeen, Edinburgh and Glasgow, 1550–1660

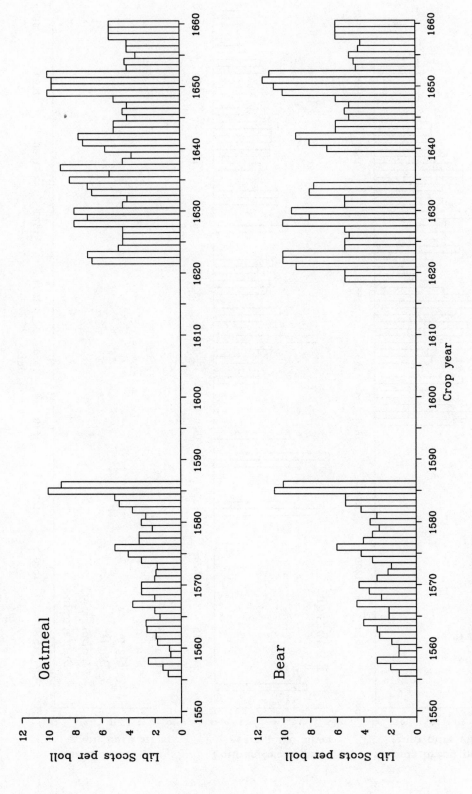

5.3 Oatmeal and bear: Fife, crops 1556–1660

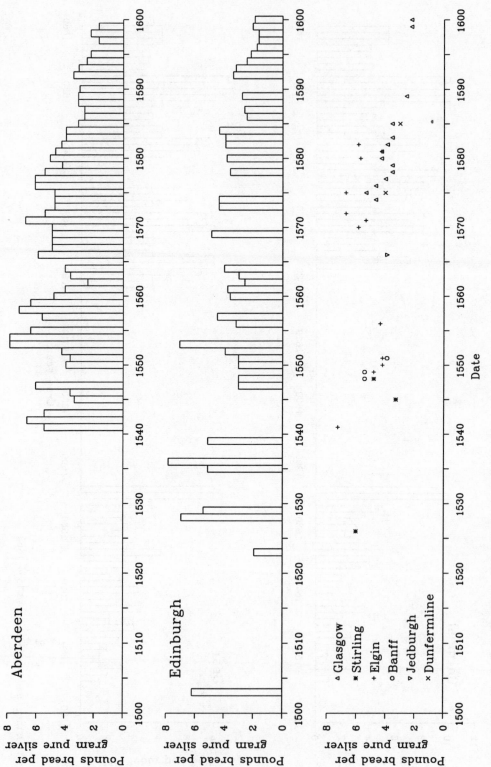

5.4 The purchasing power of silver: wheatbread equivalents, 1506–1600

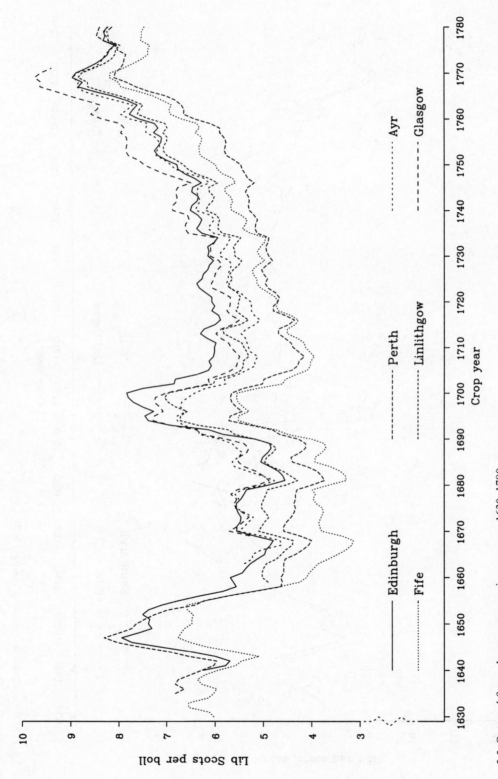

5.5 Oatmeal fiars: eleven-year moving average, 1630–1780

Lib Scots per boll

Crop year

Edinburgh

Fife

Perth

Linlithgow

Ayr

Glasgow

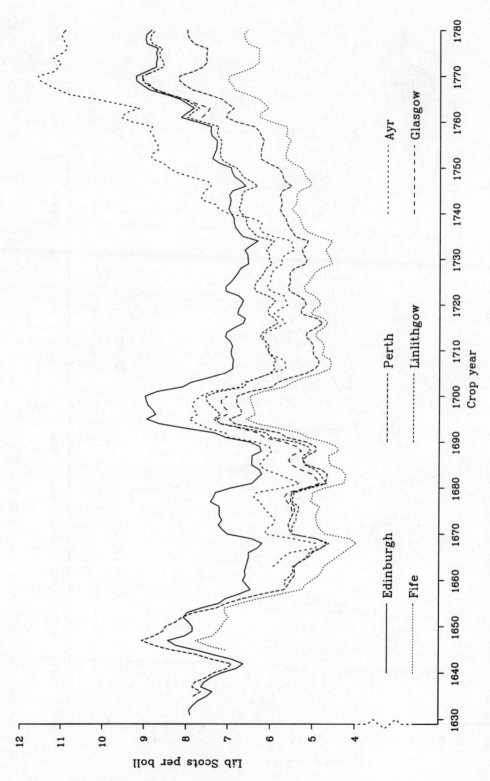

5.6 Bear fiars: eleven-year moving average, 1631–1780

Edinburgh

Fife

Perth

Linlithgow

Ayr

Glasgow

Lib Scots per boll

Crop year

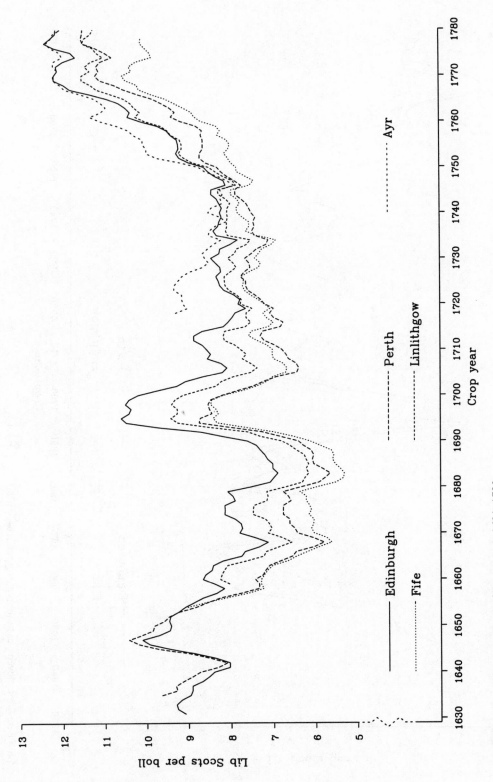

5.7 Wheat fiars: eleven-year moving average, 1631–1780

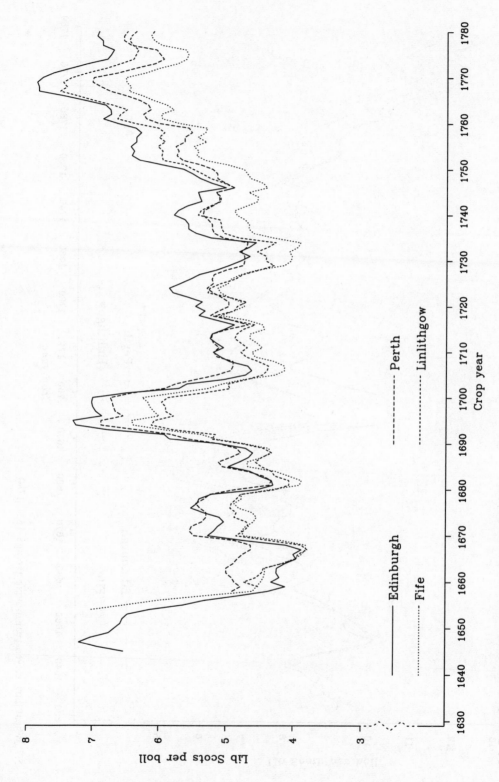

5.8 Pease fiars: eleven-year moving average, 1645–1780

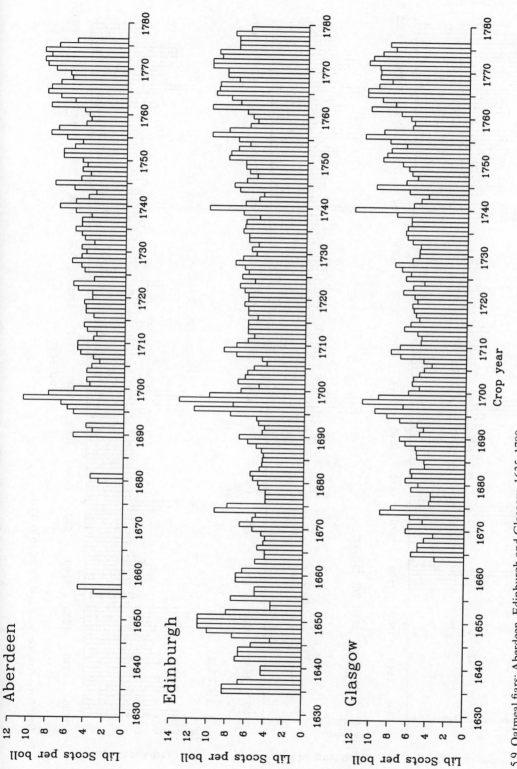

5.9 Oatmeal fiars: Aberdeen, Edinburgh and Glasgow, 1635–1780

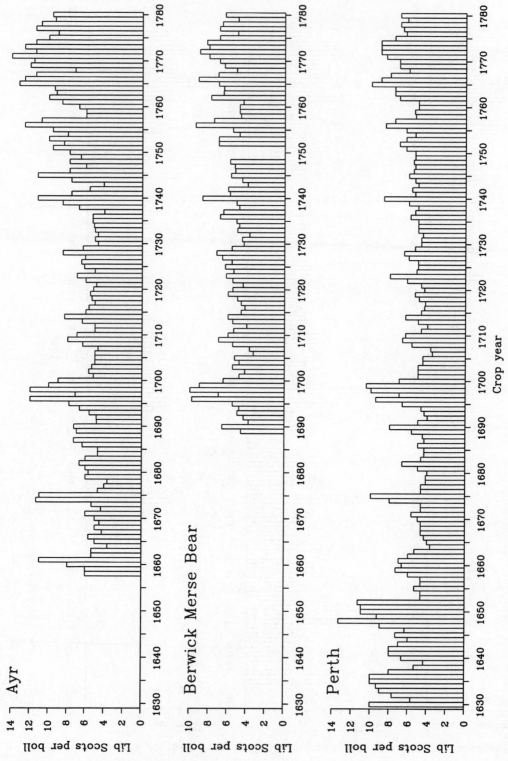

5.10 Bear fiars: Ayr, Berwick and Perth, 1630–1780

6 ✧ The price of animals and animal products

1 Meat and livestock prices: introduction (tables 6.1–6.16)

The tables in this chapter bring together evidence on Scottish meat and livestock prices, together with prices of tallow, candle, butter and eggs from the sixteenth century to around 1780. Price quotations are very sparse before the middle of the sixteenth century, but even thereafter few good series are available. The suite of tables, considered as a whole, provide a fair indication of long-term price trends; for short-term movements, the St Andrews University meat purchase accounts, (tables 6.1–6.3), the various eighteenth-century price series (tables 6.12–6.16) and, of course, the Leven and Melville monthly price series 1690–1702 (table 6.11) are the most useful, though as usual all need to be used with caution. The tallow price series (tables 6.17–6.19) may also be useful in tracing short-term movements in sheep prices, but these have their own particularly complex interpretative problems, discussed in the next section.

The question of typicality is particularly difficult with regard to livestock prices. Precisely when in the year any given quotation refers is often unknown, yet, as the Leven and Melville series demonstrates, prices varied significantly according to the season. Moreover, it is seldom stated exactly how old, and never how big, any of the cattle or sheep referred to in the miscellaneous series may have been when bought or sold. Even apparently straightforward terms contain ambiguities. The term 'cattle' or 'nolt' includes both oxen and cows ('kye'). Oxen, though, may be powerful draught animals used for the plough, worn-out beasts destined for a final feeding up before slaughter, or young animals at four years old ready for the drove (otherwise 'stots', 'marts' or bullocks, though the last term is also used for younger animals). Cows (also used generically to mean cattle) similarly might be young animals ready for the drove, or milk cows sold with or without their calves. Sheep included wedders and ewes as the commonest distinction. Then there were various categories of immature animals. The price difference occasioned by an extra year's fattening is well illustrated by the relative cost and price of the stock bought and sold at Buchanan (table 6.16).

A few points on specific sources and the price quotations used in the various tables should be mentioned. Tables 6.1–6.3, though with significant gaps, are much the longest series for meat from a single source, and drawn from the diet books of the colleges of St Andrews University from the sixteenth century to the eighteenth. The colleges regularly noted the price of carcases bought for the table and, after 1750, of the going price for fresh meat per stone or per pound. For the sake of consistency, we have restricted ourselves to noticing only the price of meat bought in the last quarter of the year. In a similar way, the colleges noted the prices of butter and eggs, and tables 6.20 and 6.21 provide the only long-run series of quotations that we have been able to find for either commodity. Despite being institutional, there is enough variation in the purchases of the St Andrews colleges to provide confidence that these are buyer's prices in a real market.[1]

The Exchequer Rolls, one of the most valuable sources for the sixteenth century, contain a great number of livestock prices, some of which form the backbone of table 6.4.[2] These are mostly to be found in the accounts of the *ballivi ad extra* and those of the comptroller. The former comprise the submissions made by those accountants responsible for the collection of the rents and renders due from the crown's demesne. The accountant *charged* himself with all the money and produce that was due – reporting its collection or explaining why it could not be collected – and *discharged* himself of any responsibility for money or produce that was then paid out – either as his own costs or as gifts, liferents, etc. to third parties. The balance he paid to the comptroller (on paper at least) and these payments are noted in the latter's accounts. Both the charge and discharge sides of the accounts include many valuations, particularly by way of the commutation of rents in kind, but these do not seem to have reflected actual market prices. Set in tack, or established by custom, these often remained constant for many years, even decades, occasionally centuries, showing only sudden movements – always up. These obviously misleading valuations have been disregarded.

A more generally reliable guide is provided by the price of livestock actually sold by the accountant. As he had to discharge himself of the responsibility of delivering the livestock to the comptroller, and had instead to deliver the cash received through its sale, both the number of beasts sold and their price had to be recorded. Unfortunately, a substantial proportion of these sales were to those presenting the livestock in the first place (and were thus probably both on favourable terms and on paper only), or were made under long-term contracts or understandings with the purchaser. The most blatant 'contract' prices have also been ignored, but even when these have been removed there undoubtedly remains a degree of price inertia in the Exchequer data which would not have been reflected in actual market prices.

An average price (the mean unless there was a particularly prominent mode) has been calculated, where appropriate and subject to the exclusions mentioned above, from the Exchequer price quotations for each year. The date given refers to the start of the accounting year which usually ran from July to July. This is to make the Exchequer prices more directly comparable with the town council statutes (generally set in November) and the fiars prices (usually set in February but dated to the previous crop year). The remaining price quotations in both the 'miscellaneous' tables (tables 6.4 and 6.10) are a medley of transaction prices, contemporary estimates and valuations, as indicated in the source column to the tables themselves. Quotations occasionally refer to

[1] We are extremely grateful to Miss Mary M. Innes for extracting the data from the diet books of the colleges of St Leonard's, St Mary's, St Salvator's and United College, held in the archives of the University of St Andrews.
[2] *Exchequer Rolls of Scotland, Rotuli Scaccarii Regum Scotorum*, 1264–1600 vols. 14–23 (Edinburgh, 1893–1908).

cattle and sheep carcases, but as there is no observable difference between such prices and those of their live counterparts this has not been noted in the tables.

Table 6.5 makes use of the price data collected by Winifred Coutts from Dumfries testamentary inventories, covering much of the period between 1600 and 1662.[3] Like Exchequer data, however, the information is likely to have been biased on the low side (as probate prices so often were, in order to keep down the duty payable), and also not to reflect immediately year-by-year variation: they appear, however, at least to indicate trends. A very different kind of valuation was that put on stolen beasts by Privy Council in their attempt to bring a measure of justice to the victims of raids, and these quotations were particularly numerous around 1600 (table 6.6).[4] Just as the Exchequer quotations and inventory data often reflected price inertia and low values and so tended to be understatements in a period of inflation, so these appear to have included a punitive element of exaggerated damages, and tended to be overstatements. It is most unlikely that Privy Council would want to see the guilty party emerge with profit from their thieving, and a high price would also help the pursuer with legal costs. Nevertheless they, too, are interesting in respect to the trends they show. It is unclear whether the price given represents what it was reckoned to be at the time the court was sitting, or retrospective for the time of the actual raid (justice could take up to a decade to catch up with the miscreants). On one occasion, though, the point was made in the record that the value of the sheep in question related to what the price had been ten years earlier when the raid occurred, and it was indeed set at a level substantially below those relating to more contemporary cases.[5]

Privy Council was also involved through the Justices of the Peace in a national investigation into animal prices that took place in 1626 and 1627 (table 6.7). This produced one of the most comprehensive and interesting sets of data that we have located over the entire period, providing a unique opportunity to investigate different price levels between animals of various types and ages across ten Lowland counties.[6] The background was a sudden increase in prices that had taken place in 1626, which led Privy Council to place restrictions on the export of wool, cattle, sheep and hides to England. The increase was blamed on demand from the south – an Aberdeenshire commentator, for example, said that no beasts were available to local people because buyers from the Mearns, Angus, Fife and the counties south of Edinburgh had bought them up for sale to Englishmen, and from Kincardineshire came the warning that 'the puir men laboraris salbe forcit to quyte ther tillage gif remeid be nocht provydit speidalie'. Of particular concern was the high price of plough oxen. The problem may also have been related to the dearth of grain two years previously when many young animals would have been slaughtered to provide cash and food in what had been the most severe famine for

[3] W.K. Coutts, 'Social and economic history of the Commissariot of Dumfries from 1600 to 1665, as disclosed by the registers of testaments', unpublished University of Edinburgh M.Litt. thesis, 1982, vol. 2, appendix IV and V. In calculating the annual means from this data, very eccentric price quotations have been disregarded.

[4] *Register of the Privy Council* (1st series) (Edinburgh 1877–98), esp. vols. 6–7.

[5] *Ibid.*, vol. 6, p. 437.

[6] *Ibid.* (2nd series), vols. 1 and 2 (Edinburgh, 1899–1900). Most of the information is in vol. 1, pp. lxxxv–lxxxvii, 670–8 and vol. 2, pp. 553–6, 618.

decades.[7] In any case the Council's prohibitions on export had only limited effect; from Selkirk came the comment that the regulations had prevented the English from coming into 'geyf ane full pryce to the poore folk that hes grittest neit thairof' while not preventing 'the transportatioun quhilk is maid contenualie be some off the richest sorte', and from Haddington came the warning that between May and August above 2,000 beasts had been transported through the county for sale in England despite the restrictions.

The Privy Council, in an attempt to monitor the situation, asked the Justices of the Peace to report to them the market price of wool, oxen, cattle and sheep between May and August, within their bounds. This was an unprecedented demand on men who, in Scotland, had only been used sparingly as an arm of government since their introduction by James VI. In some counties there was no response at all: Sir John Leslie of Wardes, the man entrusted in Aberdeenshire with convening the justices, wrote to say that he was unaquainted with such public business and that in any case he was not someone whom the justices would respect. In others, the response was inadequate – the justices of Fife simply reported the price of flesh was 'a thrid and above darrer nor they wer within thir few years'. Most of the respondents, however, apparently took their responsibility seriously, though they gathered the prices in different ways. In Roxburghshire the justices gave their own considered opinion from personal experience – 'be our sensour, knawledge and pluralitie of voittis'. In Berwickshire they employed two experts to survey the markets, who reported in 1627 with a tart reminder to the justices 'to get ws ane competent fiall for our pains and viewing of the marcatis thir nyne or ten weikis or ellis ye will get slack service heirefter'. In Angus the justices report was 'found be our owne knowledge, and lykewayes be the informatione of diverse and sindrie inhabitantis of good and honest conversatione', and a similar proceeding was followed in Selkirk.

These differences have to be borne in mind when considering, for example, the sharply varying prices of oxen reported in Selkirk and in Roxburgh. On the other hand, the highest prices for oxen are likely to be found in the most fertile counties where the upper range is represented by heavy draught animals rather than by young beef animals ready for the drove, as would be the case in a county with little tillage, like Selkirk. The report refers to the price of English draught oxen, from Teviotdale, used on large mains farms in East Lothian, and worth a great deal more than ordinary plough beasts. We have listed all the prices as close to the original categories of cattle and sheep as possible, but we have not given any wool prices, partly because of ambiguities in the qualities and measurements used in the returns, and partly because we have found too few surviving wool prices from other periods to construct a series. We would nevertheless draw attention to this data for other scholars interested in wool prices.

Of the remaining tables of livestock prices, the Aberdeen and Edinburgh Statute price series (tables 6.8 and 6.9) stand distinct. Taken from the records of the respective town councils,[8] these represent an attempt to regulate the price of beef and mutton in the two

---

[7] M.W. Flinn (ed.), *Scottish population history from the seventeenth century to the 1930s* (Cambridge, 1977), pp. 117–26.

[8] The Aberdeen prices have been extracted from unpublished volumes of the Town Council Register held at the Town House, Aberdeen. The Edinburgh prices have been taken from J.D. Marwick *et al.* (eds.), *Extracts from the records of the burgh of Edinburgh.*

burghs. How successful, or how responsive to market forces, these statutes were is impossible to determine, but as with similar price assessments for grain, it is inherently unlikely that they could remain unrelated to market prices for long. These prices, it should be remembered, were price *maxima*. That the town councils strove to establish the price of beef and mutton indicates that they had in mind some idea of a standard beast – though it must be noted that as often as not they felt unable to set the price of beef and merely stipulated that it should be sold at a price 'according to its goodness'. Certainly more assessed prices of this kind exist (or have existed) than we have quoted. Privy Council in 1620, for example, surveyed a whole range of meat and other prices set by Edinburgh town council,[9] and in 1669 the Court of Session allowed the magistrates to 'exact the oathes of the poultriemen and innkeepers concerning their contravention of the acts lately made for the price of the fowll drest and undrest'.[10]

The Leven and Melville monthly price series, 1690–1702 (table 6.11) refers to the cost of beef, veal, mutton and lamb purchased for the use of the household.[11] Considerable quantities were purchased, though the amount varied greatly from month to month and year to year. An average figure (once again the mean unless a particularly prominent mode emerged) has been calculated for each month.

The prices of cattle at Carskey[12] and Knockbuy[13] in Argyll (tables 6.12 and 6.13) are related to rent payments: the estate in each case was involved in taking animals from their tenants and disposing of them in the market to drovers and others, crediting the peasants with the proceeds to set against the rent. The Carskey data differentiate between various categories of cattle.

The prices of cattle at Park estate, Wigtownshire (table 6.14), and of cattle and sheep at Melville estate, Fife (table 6.15), have been taken from annual valuations made of the stock on each estate.[14] The former is a much more detailed valuation – often valuing each beast individually – whilst the latter generally ascribes a single value, which we presume to have been an average value, for each type of cattle or sheep. Both appear to reflect market prices; the former often giving a valuation explicitly on the basis of the price that was actually paid for the stock.

The prices of cattle and sheep at Buchanan,[15] as table 6.16 makes clear, refer directly to transaction prices. These accounts, though detailed, do not permit a breakdown by age, though there was usually about a year's age difference between those bought and sold. The farm at Buchanan was apparently fattening stock for the Glasgow market, keeping cattle and sheep for between three months and three years before selling them. The often substantial price difference between those bought and sold reflects this fact.

[9] *Register of the Privy Council* (1st series), vol. 7, p. 181.
[10] Court of Session, *Acts of Sederunt of the Lords of Council and Session, from the 15th of January 1553, to the 11th of July, 1790* (Edinburgh, 1790).
[11] SRO, GD 26/6/132/1–14, Leven and Melville Mss., 'House day books, containing daily accounts of provisions consumed'.
[12] F.F. Mackay (ed.), *Macneill of Carskey: his estate journal 1703–1743* (Edinburgh, 1955).
[13] E.R. Cregeen, 'The tacksmen and their successors: a study of tenurial reorganisation in Mull, Morvern and Tiree in the early 18th century', *Scottish Studies*, vol. 13 (1969), p. 136, together with notes provided to the authors by the late Dr Cregeen.
[14] SRO, GD 26/5/559, Leven and Melville Mss., 'Account book of Melville Estate, 1731–62'. SRO, GD 72/564/2–32, Hay of Park Mss., 'Stock accounts, 1718–30'.
[15] SRO, GD 220/6/1413–1579, Duke of Montrose Mss., 'Buchanan farm accounts, 1752–75'.

2 The link between tallow and candle price (tables 6.17–6.19)

The town council statute price series for tallow and candle (tables 6.17– 6.19), though valuable in their own right, are of particular interest here because there is reason to believe that they were set with regard to contemporary livestock prices, particularly those of sheep. It is a matter of some complexity, and must therefore be considered in detail.

Tallow and candle prices were unquestionably linked, the latter being dependent on the former. In fact, the relationship was equivalent to that between wheat and wheatbread; the town council would determine the price of tallow (which unlike wheat, they themselves set) and, adding to it the candlemakers' allowance, thereby establish the price at which candle should be sold. As with wheatbread, there was an annual assize of the price of candle. Thus in Edinburgh in February 1736, the town council first fixed the candlemakers' allowance at 12s. for each stone of common candle, 18s. for each stone of 'bald-wick' candle and 24s. for each stone of cotton-wick candle, then allowed the manufacturers to charge according to the current price of tallow and 'the King's duty'.[16] In order to discover the price of tallow, a jury of fifteen citizens was to be summoned by a town baillie within one month and required to 'fix and settle an assize for candle' to last until December. Thereafter this process was to be repeated annually, but in the future in November and not in February.[17]

This procedure, according to the council, followed from the requirements of an Act of Parliament of 1426.[18] A similar procedure appears to have been used in Banff where in 1549 it was stated that the 'lb. candle maid [shall] conform to the price of the tawcht [tallow], i.e. 10 candles to ilk pund',[19] and in Elgin where in 1550 it was enacted that 'it sall be lesum to any persoun to by tallow within the burgh for 8s. the stane to mak candill thairof for serving of the Quenis legis'.[20]

With the exception of the 1736 instance quoted above, however, the candlemakers' allowance is usually unknown, although it was clearly not uniform across the country. Thus in Dundee in 1712, when the price of candle was raised, the council explained that it was 'By reasoune of the scarcity of tallow, occasioned by the badness of the weather; and such as doth come in is for a great part carried out of the Burgh and disposed of at other places where they have greater allowance for candle.'[21]

This obscurity defeats any attempt accurately to predict tallow price from candle, but even so there was clearly a close relationship between the two, as table 6A demonstrates.[22]

[16] Tallow was bought by the tron stone whereas candle was sold by the troy stone. The former weighed some 10 per cent more than the latter, and this difference was allowed to the candlemakers for waste.

[17] NLS, Mss., EE3.40/13. 'Act of Edinburgh council in regulating the price of candle'.

[18] *APS*, vol. 2, p. 13, c3, 30 September 1426.

[19] William Crammond, *The annals of Banff*, vol. 1, New Spalding Club (Aberdeen, 1891), p. 24.

[20] William Crammond, *The records of Elgin, 1234–1800*, vol. 1, New Spalding Club (Aberdeen, 1903), p. 104.

[21] William Hay, *Charters, writs and public documents of the royal burgh of Dundee, 1292–1880* (Dundee, 1880), p. 160.

[22] The measure of relationship used [r] is the product-moment correlation coefficient. This provides a measure of linear relationship where − 1 indicates a perfect 'negative' relationship where *Y* decreases as *X* increases, and + 1 a perfect 'positive' relationship with both *X* and *Y* increasing together. A value of, or near, zero shows there to be no linear relationship.

Table 6A *Relationship of tallow and candle prices, 1547–1760*

Aberdeen	Candle = 0.98 times the price of 'Moltin' tallow	$n = 46$ (1590–1701) $r = 0.916$
	Candle = 1.16 times the price of 'sheep' tallow	$n = 67$ (1547–1701) $r = 0.973$
	Candle = 1.30 times the price of 'nolt' tallow	$n = 68$ (1547–1701) $r = 0.962$
Edinburgh	Candle = 1.26 times the price of tallow	$n = 49$ (1562–1693) $r = 0.967$
Glasgow	Candle = 1.14 times the price of tallow	$n = 103$ (1574–1717) $r = 0.944$
	'Common bleacht weekt' candle = 1.08 times the price of tallow	$n = 35$ (1718–1754) $r = 0.942$
	'Fine bleacht weekt' candle = 1.13 times the price of tallow	$n = 31$ (1721–1754) $r = 0.944$
	'Cotton weekt' candle = 1.21 times the price of tallow	$n = 34$ (1718–1754) $r = 0.942$
Perth	Candle = 1.28 times the price of tallow	$n = 51$ (1694–1760) $r = 0.657$
Stirling	Candle = 1.23 times the price of tallow	$n = 48$ (1522–1664) $r = 0.937$

Although it is not at all clear cut, these figures do suggest that, unless otherwise specified, the candle to which the statutes referred was of equivalent quality to what in eighteenth-century Glasgow was called 'cotton-wick candle' and that the tallow was sheep's tallow.

These candle and tallow prices, it must be remembered, were 'statute' prices and may thus not immediately reflect market prices. A good illustration of how councils may have used their statutes to try to keep prices low, at least in the short run, comes from the Edinburgh accounts in 1658. The council, on 27 October heard the deacon of the fleshers and a colleague declare that the 'lowest price they would afforde the tallow for' was 56s. the stone, while three candlemakers declared the lowest price of candle would be 66s.8d. the stone. Council then set the price of tallow at 54s. and candle at 64s.[23]

Establishing a link between tallow and livestock prices is more difficult and rests primarily on the fact that, where such prices were set, the statute prices for mutton and tallow were as closely related as were those for tallow and candle. Aberdeen was the only burgh which regularly set the price of livestock and is thus the only one for which meaningful comparisons with tallow prices are possible.

For an unknown reason, for a few years in the 1580s and 1590s the town council distinguished between fleshers' and butchers' mutton, but for the rest of the period between 1547 and 1701 the carcases were merely referred to as 'mutton'. The council only regularly began to set the price of beef carcases in 1656 and it always distinguished

[23] M. Wood, *Extracts from the records of the burgh of Edinburgh, 1655–1665* (Edinburgh, 1940), p. 122.

between ox beef and cow beef. These prices can be compared with those for sheep's and nolt's tallow respectively and the relationship tested. There was little, if any, relationship between the price of ox beef or cow beef and nolt tallow, but the relationship between mutton and sheep's tallow, especially before 1662, was nearly as close as that between sheep's tallow and candle.[24]

It may be presumed, therefore, that the price of sheep's tallow was determined directly from the contemporary price of mutton. This would make sense, for tallow was rendered down from the internal fat deposits of beef and mutton carcases. These deposits are still known as the 'tallow fat'. After 1662 there was, in Aberdeen, a marked divergence between mutton and tallow prices, possibly because the allowance given to the fleshers for making tallow increased: nevertheless after a few years it settled down again at an adjusted ratio.

Overall, it appears that the price of tallow can be used as a broad guide to the movements in the price of mutton; that is to say, fluctuations in the price of tallow are most likely to have been caused by fluctuations in the price of livestock. This is illustrated by the comment made in the Perth burgh accounts in 1713 which explained that the price of tallow and candle was 'so high on account of the great and frequent rains and [because] the cattle etc. not so well grown'.[25] It would be tempting, having observed the situation in Aberdeen prior to 1662, to extrapolate and presume that the price of a mutton carcase was approximately two-thirds the price of a stone of tallow: but it would be dangerous, as shown by the sudden shift after that date to a situation in which a stone of tallow was invariably costing more than twice the price of a carcase of sheep. It would perhaps be wisest to use tables 6.17–6.19 as a broad guide to short-term mutton price fluctuations rather than as a direct proxy for sheep prices. Also, of course, candle and tallow prices are of considerable interest in their own right as referring to essential industrial and domestic materials used in every business and household in the land.

3 Seasonal variation in meat prices

One of the problems which complicates any understanding of animal prices is, as already observed, the remarkable extent of variation throughout the year. Our examination of the household books of the Earl of Leven and Melville, 1690–1702, was designed to illuminate this, and also to see whether there was any observable effect on animal prices of the very high grain prices during 'King Williams Ill Years' in the second half of the 1690s.

Table 6.11 shows the result. Seasonal variation is seen at its most extreme in the case of the meat of young animals, veal and lamb, and for two reasons: firstly, the beasts themselves were comparatively uniform in size and absolutely so in age, so the complications that arise from selling very varied adult animals do not arise, and, secondly, the supply was by definition seasonal – in terms of both quality and quantity.

[24] A stone of sheep tallow cost 1.86 times a bowk of mutton: $n = 78, r = 0.854$ (1547–1702). For mutton observations 1547–1661, the relationship was that sheep tallow cost 1.51 times a bowk of mutton, $n = 26, r = 0.959$. But a stone of nolt tallow cost 0.25 times a carcase of ox-beef $n = 36$, $r = 0.262$; and 0.36 times a carcase of cow beef $n = 35$, $r = 0.265$ (1656–1701).   [25] SRO, B/59/17/3, Perth burgh records.

In the case of lambs, very high prices of £7–£8 a head (once over £12) were reached for the earliest ones in January or February, falling to £2–£3 in March and April and to around 30s. in June, July and August, when the supply ceased. Mutton carcases varied in a more random way, but were only irregularly purchased between September and January: the highest prices between March and May were often double those later in the summer. In the case of veal, the highest prices, roughly in the range of £7–£12, were normally between December and March, and were down by a third or a half, sometimes more, by late summer. The price of beef carcases was probably influenced more by size and age than by season, both the lowest and the highest quotations happening to occur in March and April, but normally little was bought between the end of September and early March. Salted beef was presumably the staple of the winter months.

At first sight there is very little sign of any positive impact on meat prices from the dearth of grain in the famine years (Fife fiars prices for oatmeal, for example, rose from £3 in 1692 to £7 in 1696 and to £7.13s.4d. in both 1698 and 1699 before dropping to £3.10s.0d. in 1701). If anything, there is a tendency for an inverse relationship, lamb prices inclining lower in the dear grain seasons and mutton being more available in the autumn than was usually the case. Plainly, at no point was the price of meat so low or the price of grain so high that consumers might be tempted to switch from one source of calories to another: they were not really substitution goods, though at least in the eighteenth and nineteenth centuries there were soup kitchens where small quantities of meat eked out with vegetables supplied the poor when oatmeal was too dear. On the other hand, the effect of grain dearth was likely to make livestock producers in upland areas liquidate some of their stock in order to buy in supplies of meal urgently and expensively: hence a downward pressure on prices in the spring when a higher proportion of lambs were sold, and a bigger supply in the autumn when the peasants decided they could not afford to hold on to all breeding ewes until the next season. If the buyer was wealthy, and a consumer of meat like the household of the Earl of Leven and Melville, the extra costs implied in a bad grain harvest might thus be partly offset by cheaper animals. On the other hand, if this process was too protracted the upland farmers would run breeding stocks so low that there would, in following years, be a shortage of animals and thus higher prices. Some of the cattle prices for the 1620s and 1690s examined in the following section appear to reflect such an impact of glut followed by scarcity.

4 The long-term trends of cattle prices

As we have demonstrated in the introduction, the problems of diverse and confusing data are considerable in the measurement of cattle prices: but long-term trends can nevertheless be discerned by careful examination of the data.

The scrappy sixteenth-century figures in tables 6.1, 6.2 and 6.4 refer to animals bought as carcases or received as rent and sold onwards, probably at the age of four years and upwards. The adult Scottish beef animal was not large. The best available estimate is that it would have contained at that age on average about 240 lbs. of edible meat and fat, or

310 lbs. deadweight carcase: this was appreciably smaller than English or Irish animals, and when the English customs officials valued Irish and Scottish beasts in the 1660s they estimated the average price of a Scottish beast at only 60 per cent of its Irish equivalent, presumably mainly on account of its size.[26]

In the sixteenth century, there was no indication of inflation in Scottish cattle prices until the mid 1530s, but there was then a doubling in price between that point and the early 1560s, when the price of a saleable beast stood at around £2 (a price reached in 1555 for the first time). In the second part of the century, inflation of cattle prices, as with other goods, was much more rapid, climbing to £5–£7 and more by the 1580s and £10–£12 by the end of the 1590s. It can be seen from the Exchequer quotations in table 6.4 that much of the impression depends on from where the crown was obtaining its animals. Bute beasts were valued at £1 in 1505, which at that time was entirely comparable with purchases from other sources: the price was increased modestly to 24s. in 1536, but remained at that level for over half a century. Presumably that was a long-term contract price and we have accordingly omitted these prices from table 6.4 after that date. Ross prices were much more variable and, presumably, realistic, being a shade lower than Bute prices at the start of the century, £1.10s. by 1539, £3.6s.8d. by the 1560s and £5.6s.8d. by 1589, when Bute animals were still being reckoned at 24s. Supplies from Perthshire came in first at £2 in 1555, reached £5 by 1587 and £10 by 1598. This final figure was slightly below that set by Privy Council in a general attempt to fix prices in the same year. It must be Ross and Perthshire which came closer to prices in the markets where most meat was bought and sold; even so their quotations were on the low side compared to the brief run of prices in table 6.1 for St Andrews, 1587–91, where carcases were being bought for around £7 instead of £5. By contrast, the valuations for stolen beasts laid out in table 6.6 are likely to have been on the high side, standing at the end of the century at up to double the prices suggested by the Exchequer data. Truth no doubt lay between the two extremes, but over the span of the price revolution, inflation of cattle prices was substantially less than that for grains.

The seventeenth century is best seen as a period in which cattle prices undulated, but ultimately followed an upward trend in the second half of the century. As with grain, the price revolution for cattle appeared largely to have run its course by the middle of the first decade. Dumfries probate quotations (table 6.5) settled down at a little over £10 for cows. The important Book of Rates valuation of 1612 (table 6.10) also put the price of beasts to be exported to England at £10, a trifle below the highest quotations of the 1590s, and the valuations on stolen cattle also appeared to be stationary or edging down. Data that Julian Goodare have made available to us from the unpublished Exchequer records, 1602–34, show that 'marts' were valued by the comptroller at £8 in 1603, falling as low as £6.13s.8d. in 1609, but then rising to £9 in 1613 and settling at £10 from 1616 to 1634. Another burst of data from St Andrews, 1617–21, suggest a mean of beef carcases rather over £11 (table 6.1). This stability was, however, rudely interrupted by the events of 1626, when a sudden increase in English demand, exacerbated, no doubt, by a

---

[26] A.J. Gibson, 'The size and weight of cattle and sheep in early modern Scotland', *Agricultural History Review*, vol. 36 (1988), pp. 162–71; D. Woodward, 'Anglo-Scottish trade and English commercial policy during the 1660s', *Scottish Historical Review*, vol. 56 (1977), p. 154.

shortage of stock in Scotland following sales and slaughter in the famine of 1622–4, produced from the Justices of the Peace the comprehensive statistics of Lowland cattle prices described in table 6.7. The general opinion of the magistrates (who appear to have been particularly worried about the impact on tillage from the effect on oxen prices) was that the price of most animals had risen by about a third from the level of former years; already in 1627 it was tending to fall again in most places. The price of £18 for Highland drove cows at Stirling is perhaps the most important to note for comparative purposes with the 1612 and later quotations.

The Exchequer figures, however, never waver during this crisis from what had by then perhaps become a customary £10 valuation. The Dumfries testamentary figures of table 6.5 increased in these years, but only slightly, and it is an interesting comment on the nature of probate valuation that they were still being put at a good third below what the local magistrates believed to be the true price of cows: perhaps we should not expect inventories of this type ever to reflect accurately a sudden rise in the market.

It seems unlikely that the inflated prices which the justices reported in 1626–7 remained the norm in the second quarter of the seventeenth century, which ended in serious disruption of the droving trade by war. It is true that Dumfriesshire inventory prices rose to new (if rather modest) heights between 1638 and 1642, but when English officials gathered particulars of Scottish crown rentals in 1650 they again put the price of 'beeves' sold from the estates at the traditional £10 (table 6.10). The situation, however, obviously improved after the Restoration, and in 1662 English customs officials again stated that the prime cost of animals imported from Scotland stood at £18. Perhaps thereafter there was another sag in prices: Aberdeen town council statute prices for beef carcases (table 6.9), at least, were down by a quarter in the late 1660s from the levels earlier in the decade, but recovered by the 1680s. The later 1690s, however, again seemed to be a period in which prices were driven up, eventually, by the shortage of beasts following years of high grain prices. The Aberdeen valuation of ox beef carcases doubled to £24 between 1697 and 1701, and English customs officials, attempting a renewed valuation of the prime cost of animals on the drove, put the price at £12 in 1697–8 (which probably reflects oversupply in a famine year) rising to £22.10s.0d. the following year (reflecting that slaughter). Prices paid to the Macleod lairds by the drovers in Skye are of course lower: they had to bear the costs of the journey to Falkirk or Crieff first. On the other hand, prices paid by the St Andrews colleges were generally higher than the Aberdeen statute price in the period 1671–75, and again in 1686–1700, though St Leonard's college is paying one third more for its beef in the 1690s than in the earlier 1670s.

The first half of the eighteenth century saw a continuation of these undulations, largely determined by conditions of supply in Scotland and demand in England – as exemplified in 1705 when the threat by the English government to prohibit the trade in Scottish cattle, unless negotiations were started for a union, allegedly brought a collapse in cattle prices and opportunities for speculation that were remembered for generations. It has to be said, however that the only series that we have covering these years, from St Andrews, show no such drama, only a mild dip in prices between 1703 and 1709.

Eighteenth-century data are more plentiful than figures for earlier periods, but also in some respects more confusing. This is partly because, apart from the St Andrews college accounts, they are drawn from estate records in different parts of Scotland, and there were substantial regional differences – what Malcolm Gray has called 'a mosaic of partly disconnected markets, with local peculiarities of breed, varying transport costs, and sometimes local non-competitive control'.[27] It is also because the animals themselves became more diverse in size and value as the process of agricultural improvement pursued its uneven way across the country. A comparison of Argyll and Wigtownshire data (tables 6.12 and 6.14) provides a good illustration. At Carskey in Kintyre there was no upward trend in the price of any class of beast between 1716 and 1740. At Park in Wigtownshire there was a leap in price of stots (bullocks) and oxen, even in the shorter time span of 1718–29. Argyll was not, at this stage, a significantly improving county, but Wigtownshire, along with Kirkcudbright and Dumfries, was involved in a new kind of cattle ranching that probably included bringing much heavier Irish cattle over to improve the breed: indeed, the peasant Levellers, who led an agrarian revolt against this new capitalist farming in 1724, were confident that the lairds were illegally selling imported Irish animals under the colour of Scottish.[28] But it must be the Carskey figures that were more representative of the majority of Scottish, and especially Highland, producers: the scrappier figures from Campbell of Knockbuy (also in Argyll) (table 6.13) and from more remote Harris and Skye,[29] are entirely in line with them.

There seems, in fact, to be no convincing evidence of a general rise in Scottish cattle prices between the late seventeenth century and some time after 1740. Despite the apparent price turbulence immediately before the treaty, the Union of 1707 itself made no discernible difference to the trend. Thus Clerk of Penicuik put the price of Scots cattle for export in 1733 at £20,[30] and though he commented that this was one third above what it had been twenty years earlier, his figure is in fact much the same as the pre-Union English customs valuation. From St Andrews there are almost annual quotations between 1700 and 1750 – the mean price paid for carcases in the autumn only once slips below £16 or rises above £24, and though some runs of years tend towards the lower end (e.g., 1706–8, 1735–8) and others to the upper (1712–20, 1739–43), there is no consistent trend at all.

On the other hand, there is much indication of a general, though uneven, upward movement in the third quarter of the eighteenth century. Gray, examining a mass of diverse information on Highland beasts, found most three-year olds selling for £12 or less in the 1740s, for around £18 in the 1750s and 1760s, reaching a new peak about £24 in the 1770s.[31] This level is lower than the general run of our quotations because he was referring to animals younger than most that went to slaughter or to the drove, and

[27] M. Gray, *The Highland economy, 1750–1850* (Edinburgh, 1957), p. 142.

[28] J. Leopold, 'The Galloway Levellers' revolt of 1724', in A. Charlesworth (ed.), *Rural social change and conflicts since 1500* (Hull, 1982), p. 30.

[29] C.L. Horricks, 'Economic and Social Change in the Isle of Harris, 1680–1754', University of Edinburgh Ph.D. thesis, 1974, pp. 291–2. The price of marts is put at £10, 1706–1720; £10.13s.4d., 1724; £14.0s.0d., 1744; and £20.0s.0d. in 1754.

[30] T.C. Smout (ed.), 'Sir John Clerk's "Observations on the present circumstances of Scotland"', *Miscellany X* (Scottish History Society, 1965), p. 195, footnote.   [31] Gray, *Highland economy*, p. 142.

possibly because he drew data largely from valuations of the estate of the deceased, which as we have seen often appear to understate market price. The trend, however, is similar to that in our tables. The Melville estate in Fife shows (table 6.15) prices clearly rising from the late 1730s, through the 1740s and early 1750s. In Knockbuy (table 6.13), the upward drift begins in the 1740s. For the third quarter of the century there are two good series. St Andrews beef prices (table 6.3) grew by one half between 1750–3 and 1760–3, hit a peak in 1766–7 that was about double the starting point, and settled back in the later 1770s at the level of the early 1760s. The accounts from Buchanan farm in Stirlingshire (table 6.16), show very clearly how complex and varied the picture was from year to year and from one type of beast to another. The movement in the price of cows had much less buoyancy than that of stots, for which, in respect to stock sold, the real leap came around 1770 from £40–£60 to a new level of £75–£100. Yet the more summarised evidence from Knockbuy in Argyll indicates a much smaller increase at this time, which may say something about the relative speed of improvement in the two estates.

John Ramsay of Ochtertyre took over the management of his Stirlingshire estate around 1760, and, writing around 1800, had very clear recollections of price movements.[32] He recalled a traditional price for 'the best Highland cows, when fat' of £16, which after 1747 suddenly moved up to £21–£24 due to the combined effects of Jacobite rebellion and of cattle disease in the south of England. By 1760, he said, the same kind of cattle were sold at £30–£33, with another leap in 1766–9 to a level of £40–£48, followed by a fall in 1770: 'though there were various ups and downs in the course of the next ten or twelve years, prices never fell so low as preceding 1766, nor rose as high as in that and the three following years'. Not all the details fit with our tables, but the general outline interestingly corroborates our statistics.

In 1775 Adam Smith in *The Wealth of Nations* expressed the view that the price of Highland cattle had tripled since the beginning of the century: 'of all the commercial advantages, however, that Scotland has derived from the union with England, this rise in the price of cattle is, perhaps, the greatest. It has not only raised the value of all highland estates, but it has, perhaps, been the principal cause of the improvement of the low country.'[33] One might venture the further observation that the increase in the price of cattle relative to that of grain was a most important feature of the entire period from 1660 to 1780: higher prices encouraged more cattle, more cattle allowed more dung, and more dung increased the productivity of grain-producing land. But whatever the justice of the general observation, he was broadly right about the scale of the price movement. While he may have exaggerated the increase for some cases, it would unquestionably be correct to say that generally cattle prices had more than doubled since the late 1730s, and that some prices for animals to be sold on to the drove were indeed at least three times the old level. There was to be further large inflation in the final two decades of the eighteenth century, but that does not concern us here.

---

[32] A. Allardyce (ed.), *Scotland and Scotsmen in the eighteenth century from the Mss of John Ramsay Esq. of Ochtertyre* (Edinburgh and London, 1888), vol. II, pp. 223, 249.

[33] A. Smith, *The wealth of nations* (Everyman edition, London, 1910), vol. I, pp. 135, 204.

5 The long-term trend of sheep, tallow and candle prices

The course of sheep prices in the sixteenth century can be discerned from tables 6.2 and 6.4, drawing mainly on St Andrews' evidence and on the Exchequer Rolls, and table 6.8, drawing on town council assessments. The trend is again difficult to pick out because of different ways of measuring prices and problems about animal age and size, but something emerges. A Ross-shire animal which had been valued in the exchequer at 2s. in 1522, had risen to 3s. by 1536 and 5s. by 1560. Five years later it was worth 6s.8d., and there it remained until revalued at 13s.4d. in the 1590s. This looks like a six- or seven-fold rise in price over the sixteenth century, or roughly a tripling since mid century. These animals must, however, have been either very young or very cheap at sale. The Aberdeen mutton carcase prices (themselves lower than the Edinburgh ones) show a wavering price between 1547 and 1560, then a three-fold rise to the end of the century when the price stood at £1.4s.0d. Such a price had already been reached at St Andrews by 1588, and even this was less than the £2 fixed for a mutton carcase in the Privy Council assessments of 1598, but the trends here, and also the trends revealed in the valuation of stolen beasts, are all in line. An average carcase weight of 30lbs. appears a reasonable estimate for the size of a grown Scottish sheep before the late eighteenth-century improvers introduced the Linton and the Cheviot.[34]

In the seventeenth century the two best direct series on sheep prices (both broken) are for St Andrews and for Aberdeen (tables 6.2 and 6.9), supplemented by Dumfries inventory material. In the first two decades there was apparently only a modest advance over late sixteenth-century levels, but prices in Aberdeen in 1640s and 1650s were a good 50 per cent above that plateau. If we take into account the opinions of the Justices of the Peace in 1626–7, sheep prices had reached or even exceeded those mid century heights at the start of the second quarter of the seventeenth century, when the average price of a wedder or a ewe with lamb in several counties was around £4 (table 6.7). This was (as expected) very much higher than the Dumfries probate valuations, a series which was not inflexible but which never between 1600 and 1660 valued a sheep as high as £2. The Exchequer figures extracted by Goodare valued a mutton carcase at only 4s. between 1602 and 1623, then at £1 from 1624 to 1634 – there must surely be special reasons behind what appear to be unrealistically low valuations. There were falls, however, in the second half of the century in the Aberdeenshire series, coming right down to £1.4s.0d. between 1666 and 1676, and hardly made up even during the partial recovery to 1701, though Leven and Melville prices (table 6.11) again seem to be at a higher level, 1690–1702, than those prevailing in Aberdeen. Evidence from St Andrews, 1670–1700, shows much the same level as at the start of the century.

Direct evidence of sheep prices in the eighteenth century is too tenuous to be of much value. The only series, from Buchanan in Stirlingshire between 1754 and 1773 (table 6.16), shows wedders selling from the farm at around £7.10s.0d, a price so high compared to seventeenth-century values as to raise questions about its representative nature. These wedders were considerably larger than most sold in Scotland in the third

[34] A.J. Gibson, 'Size and weight of cattle and sheep'.

quarter of the eighteenth century and probably belonged to an exceptional, improved breed. Farm accounts for Buchanan show that they weighed, on average, over 51 lbs. per carcase (two-thirds larger than the Scottish average). The same accounts valued the mutton consumed by the family at 3s. per pound, 1752–68, 3s.6d. per pound, 1770, 4s.6d. per pound in 1773–76 and 4s. per pound in 1779 and 1780. Casual observations of other, scattered quotations of sheep and mutton prices, for example from St Andrews, from Monymusk,[35] and Skye and Glenelg[36] do not bear out the impression that there was any sharp increase in their level, at least before the 1770s. Ramsay of Ochtertyre's observations are again interesting here, especially as he was speaking of the same general area where the Buchanan farm was situated: 'between 1760 and 1770, the carse tenants of their own accord gave over keeping sheep, from a conviction that more was lost by the nipping up the spring grass than was got by their dung and wool'. He quoted prices from £1.4s.0d. up to £3, the last for 'the best country ewes and wedders'. The grazing was then switched from sheep to cows.[37] In this case he was speaking not of the large improved sheep which, at the same time, were beginning to invade the southern Highlands and to increase in the Southern Uplands, but of the small unimproved animals kept on Lowland traditional farms as much to improve the ground by being folded on infield land as to provide meat or wool.

Significant indirect evidence on sheep price movements can also be deduced, as we saw in the introductory section, from data on tallow and candle prices, though the ratios between them do not everywhere remain unchanged. In fact, tallow and candle prices, originating from town council assessments, provide us with one of the longest series that we have for any goods, extending with few breaks from 1547 to 1760, and covering a variety of burghs (tables 6.17–6.19). Sixteenth-century inflation can at once be discerned, following, as would be expected, much the same pattern as for sheep and continuing until around 1605. Tallow and candle prices then levelled off in all towns for which evidence survives (Aberdeen was missing at this point), with little sign of shortages caused by the events examined by the justices in 1626 and 1627, though perhaps the town council assessments were designed to compel manufacturers to adjust to such a short-term increase in their raw material costs. At mid century, though, especially in years disturbed by war and plague, there were some very high prices. This was followed by a drop to a little above the previous level, with the lowest prices of the second half of the century being recorded in the late 1660s. Such a fall in tallow and candle prices did not, however, take place in Aberdeen, though a fall in sheep prices did, as we have seen: the ratio was altered at that point in Aberdeen, and probably tallow and candle prices in other towns from then on reflect the movement of sheep prices rather better. There was recovery from lowest prices, but no great increase to new levels, at the end of the century.

Eighteenth-century figures for tallow and candle prices come solely from Glasgow and Perth and do not extend beyond 1760. They show no particular upward movement;

---

[35] SRO, GD 345/990. Monymusk Mss., Aberdeenshire, livestock accounts. For instance, in 1712 sheep sold at £1.6s.8d.–£2; in 1738 at £1.13s.0d.–£2.6s.8d.; in 1762 at 13s.–£1.10s.0d.

[36] Horricks, thesis, pp. 291–2. Sheep from Skye and Glenelg were valued at £1.6s.8d. in 1735, 1744 and 1759.

[37] Allardyce, *Scotland and Scotsmen*, vol. II, pp. 250–1.

though there are some years of very low prices, especially in the mid 1730s, there was no sharply falling trend. In short, a citizen of Glasgow hardly had to pay more for his tallow in the 1720s than he had done in the 1620s, and, if the price was some 25 per cent higher than that by the 1750s, this too was about what he would have paid in the 1650s. Relative long-term stability was the keynote.

Sheep and their products did not, of course, play as large a part in Scottish commercial life in the seventeenth and eighteenth centuries as cattle. We have the word of several commentators, including Adam Smith, that the Union of 1707 led to a fall in the price of wool, and thus in the profitability of Border estates where the sheep-run had been the mainstay of income.[38] In the Highlands before around 1760 sheep were scarcely kept for the market at all: they were subsistence animals, like goats, and cattle alone were disposed of to pay the rent. On many Lowland farms, they had a similar role, alongside that of helping to manure the arable land. In these circumstances it is not surprising that data are thin, and price trends, where we can detect them, not very buoyant.

6 The price of butter and eggs (tables 6.20–6.21)

The only long-term series for the price of butter and eggs, goods that were associated in particular with sales made by the farmer's and cottar's wife, come from the accounts of the St Andrews colleges (tables 6.20 and 6.21). Comparing the earliest St Leonard's accounts of 1587–91 with those of the next earliest of 1617–21, it is interesting to see that butter prices rose slightly less than those of beef over the period (by 53 per cent as opposed to 62 per cent), to a level of 4s.5d. a pound. They touched 5s. and even 6s. in the 1690s, perhaps under the influence of dearth, but the average price in the first five years of the eighteenth century was still only 4s.8d. By the late 1730s it was always at least 5s., by the early 1750s at least 6s. and from 1764 to 1780 consistently 7s.6d. In the two centuries from the 1580s it thus about doubled in price, whereas beef carcases went up by about four or five times, which perhaps gives some indication of where the demand pressures were for animal products.

The price of eggs was about 1s.1d. a dozen in the late 1580s, and 62 per cent higher by 1617–21, but (except in the late 1690s) it did not generally reach 2s. until the 1720s or 3s. until the 1770s. Here, as elsewhere, there were some signs of inflation in Scotland in the third quarter of the eighteenth century of a kind that had not been seen since the late sixteenth century. They were not as yet very pronounced, but they were to continue past 1780 into the period of the *Statistical accounts* of 1791–6: at that point ministers frequently picked out the price of butter and eggs as among the commodities that had increased smartly in price in the course of the previous fifty years.

---

[38] Smout, 'Sir John Clerk's "Observations"', p. 205; Smith, *Wealth of nations*, vol. I, p. 216.

INTRODUCTION TO TABLES 6.1–6.21

These tables have no particular complexities, but should nevertheless be read in conjunction with the text for a full explanation of their meaning.

Sources

St Andrews University Library muniments: diet books of the colleges of St Leonard's, St Mary's, St Salvator's and United College.

Exchequer Rolls of Scotland, vols. xiv–xxiii (Edinburgh, 1893–1908).

W.K. Coutts, 'Social and economic history of the Commissariot of Dumfries from 1600–1665, as disclosed by the registers of testaments'; unpublished University of Edinburgh M.Litt. thesis, 1982.

Register of the Privy Council of Scotland (first series) vols. 6 and 7; (second series), vols. 1 and 2 (Edinburgh 1877–1908).

Aberdeen Town House manuscripts: Town Council Registers.

M. Wood (ed.), *Extracts from the records of the burgh of Edinburgh 1642–1665* (two vols., Edinburgh 1938–40).

SRO, GD 26/6/132/1–14, Leven and Melville Mss., 'House day books'.

GD 26/5/559, Leven and Melville Mss., 'Account book of Melville Estate, 1731–62'.

GD 72/564/2–32, Hay of Park Mss., 'Stock accounts, 1718–30'.

GD 220/6/1413–1579, Duke of Montrose Mss., 'Buchanan farm accounts 1752–75'.

F.F. Mackay (ed.), *Macneill of Carskey: his estate journal 1703–1743* (Edinburgh, 1955).

For additional details of town council records used for tables 6.17 and 6.18, see introduction to the tables in chapter 2.

Table 6.1 *Beef carcases: St Andrews University, 1587–1759*

Date	St Leonard's College L. s. d.	St Salvator's College L. s. d.	Date	St Leonard's College L. s. d.	St Salvator's College L. s. d.	St Mary's College L. s. d.
1587	6 14 0		1711	21 3 0		
1588	7 11 0		1712	22 1 0	23 5 0	
1589	7 4 0		1713	22 16 0	23 1 0	
1590	6 12 0		1714	21 7 0	21 5 0	
1591	7 13 0		1715	17 19 0		
			1716	20 12 0		
			1717	24 4 0		
1617	12 10 0					
1618	10 18 0					
1619	10 16 0		1720		22 1 0	
1620	11 16 0					
1621	11 18 0					
			1726			18 6 0
			1727			17 18 0
1671	15 2 0		1728			17 0 0
1672	18 19 0		1729			18 15 0
1673	15 16 0		1730	19 6 0		17 19 0
1674	12 4 0		1731	20 18 0		
1675	14 10 0		1732	22 6 0		
			1733		17 4 0	
			1734		18 14 0	
1686		15 17 0	1735		16 7 0	
1687		16 16 0	1736		16 19 0	
1688		18 2 0	1737		19 0 0	
1689		17 2 0	1738		17 17 0	
1690			1739		20 5 0	
1691		19 2 0	1740		19 4 0	
1692		19 0 0	1741	20 6 0		
1693	22 13 0	21 15 0	1742	23 5 0		
1694	25 2 0	19 7 0	1743			23 1 0
1695	18 18 0	18 11 0	1744			18 16 0
1696	17 8 0	19 9 0	1745			15 12 0
1697	16 3 0	17 1 0	1746			17 19 0
1698		20 12 0	1747			19 18 0
1699	20 6 0		1748			21 13 0
1700	19 12 0		1749			21 5 0
1701	21 8 0		1750			20 5 0
1702	20 8 0		1751			21 16 0
1703	22 16 0		1752			23 7 0
1704	18 13 0		1753			26 17 0
1705	18 8 0		1754			28 0 0
1706	17 7 0		1755			28 4 0
1707	17 18 0		1756			25 1 0
1708	16 8 0	13 1 0	1757			25 3 0
1709	19 12 0		1758			25 3 0
1710	19 0 0		1759			27 9 0

Table 6.2 *Mutton carcases: St Andrews University, 1587–1708*

Date	St Leonard's College L. s. d.			Date	St Leonard's College L. s. d.			St Salvator's College L. s. d.		
1587	1	0	0	1686				1	14	0
1588	1	4	0	1687						
1589	1	0	0	1688				1	15	0
1590	1	3	0	1689				1	14	0
1591	1	4	0	1690						
				1691				1	16	0
				1692						
1617	2	0	0	1693	1	17	3	1	16	0
1618	1	13	4	1694				1	16	0
1619	1	13	4	1695	1	18	0	1	16	0
1620	1	12	0	1696	1	14	0	1	16	0
1621	1	13	4	1697	1	12	0	1	16	0
				1698				1	16	0
				1699	1	15	0			
1671	1	12	0	1700	2	1	0			
1672	1	10	0							
1673	1	10	0							
1674	1	12	0	1708				1	12	0

Table 6.3 *Fresh beef and mutton (per stone): St Andrews University, 1750–1780*

Date	St Mary's College beef L. s. d.			Date	St Mary's College beef L. s. d.			United College beef L. s. d.			United College mutton L. s. d.		
1750	1	7	0	1766	2	19	0						
1751	1	11	0	1767	2	16	0						
1752	1	6	0	1768	2	9	0						
1753	1	13	0	1769	1	18	0	1	12	0	1	15	0
1754	1	19	0	1770	1	18	0						
1755	1	18	0	1771	2	0	0						
1756	1	17	0	1772	1	18	0	1	16	0	2	2	0
1757	1	14	0	1773	2	1	0						
1758	1	14	0	1774	2	4	0	2	4	0	2	9	0
1759	1	19	0	1775	2	3	0						
1760	2	0	0	1776	2	2	0						
1761	2	8	0	1777	2	1	0						
1762	2	3	0	1778	2	4	0	2	0	0	2	5	6
1763	2	8	0	1779	2	1	0	2	0	0	2	2	0
1764	2	12	0	1780	2	0	0						
1765	2	6	0										

Table 6.4 *Cattle and sheep: miscellaneous quotations, 1505–1599*

Date	Cattle	Sheep	Source
1505	20s. 0d.	--	*E.R.* (Bute)
1506	18s. 0d.	--	*E.R.* (Ross)
1507	20s. 0d.	--	*E.R.* (Bute)
1511	16s. 0d.	--	*E.R.* (Ross)
	18s. 0d.	--	*Arnot*[1]
1512	20s.–70s.	48d.–72d.	*Arnot*[2]
1513	20s. 0d.	34d.–48d.	*High Treasurer*
	20s. 0d.	--	*E.R.* (Bute)
1515	17s. 0d.	48d.	*High Treasurer*
1516	18s.–26s. 8d.	48d.	*Fife* [Valuation]
1518	--	108d.	*High Treasurer*
1521	13s. 4d.	--	*E.R.* (Bute)
1522	13s. 4d.	--	*E.R.* (Bute)
	--	24d.	*E.R.* (Ross)
1524	13s. 4d.	--	*E.R.* (Bute)
	20s. 0d.	24d.	*E.R.* (Ross)
1526	13s. 4d.	--	*E.R.* (Bute)
1527	20s. 0d.	--	*E.R.* (Bute)
1528	20s. 0d.	--	*E.R.* (Bute)
1529	20s. 0d.	--	*E.R.* (Bute)
1530	20s. 0d.	--	*E.R.* (Bute)
1531	20s. 0d.	--	*E.R.* (Bute)
1532	20s. 0d.	--	*E.R.* (Bute)
1533	20s. 0d.	--	*E.R.* (Bute)
	24s.–29s. 9d.	--	*High Treasurer*
1534	30s. 0d.	--	*E.R.* (Bute)
1535	20s. 0d.	--	*E.R.* (Bute)
1536	24s. 0d.	--	*E.R.* (Bute)
	24s. 0d.	36d.	*E.R.* (Ross)
1538	26s. 8d.	36d.	*E.R.* (Ross)
1539	30s. 0d.	36d.	*E.R.* (Ross)
1540	30s. 0d.	36d.	*E.R.* (Ross)
1549	32s. 2d.	120d.	*High Treasurer*
1555	40s. 0d.	--	*E.R.* (Perthshire)
1556	36s. 0d.	72d.	*Elgin* [Valuation]
1559	40s. 0d.	--	*E.R.* (Perthshire)
	160s. 0d.	--	*High Treasurer*
1560	40s. 0d.	--	*E.R.* (Perthshire)
	46s. 8d.	60d.	*E.R.* (Ross)
1561	--	72d.	*Benefices* (General)
1562	40s. 0d.	72d.	*Benefices* (Bewly & Kinloss)
	53s. 4d.	108d.	*Benefices* (Aberdeen)
	26s. 8d.	--	*Benefices* (Orkney)
1564	66s. 8d.	--	*E.R.* (Ross)
1565	66s. 8d.	80d.	*E.R.* (Ross)
1566	66s. 8d.	80d.	*E.R.* (Ross)
1568	66s. 8d.	80d.	*E.R.* (Ross)
1569	--	72d.	*Benefices* (Inverness)
1570	--	80d.	*Benefices* (Inverness)
1571	--	37½d.–120d.	*Elgin* [Valuation]
1573	--	80d.	*E.R.* (Ross)
1579	136s. 3d.	160d.	*Aberdeen Diet*
1580	--	80d.	*E.R.* (Ross)
1583	100s. 0d.	--	*E.R.* (Perthshire)

Table 6.4 *(cont.)*

Date	Cattle	Sheep	Source
1587	100s. 0d.	--	*E.R.* (Perthshire)
	--	80d.	*E.R.* (Ross)
1588	--	80d.	*E.R.* (Ross)
	223s. 0d.	288d.	*St Andrews Diet*[1]
1589	106s. 8d.	80d.	*E.R.* (Ross)
1590	--	160d.	*E.R.* (Ross)
1591	--	160d.	*E.R.* (Ross)
	133s. 4d.	--	*E.R.* (Perthshire)
1592	--	160d.	*E.R.* (Ross)
1593	133s. 4d.	--	*E.R.* (Perthshire)
1597	266s. 8d.	40d.	*St Andrews Diet*[2] [Estimate]
	200s. 0d.	--	*E.R.* (Perthshire)
1598	200s. 0d.	--	*E.R.* (Perthshire)
	240s. 0d.	480d.	*RPCS*
1599	--	160d.	*E.R.* (Ross)

Arnot	Hugo Arnot, *History of Edinburgh* (2nd edition, Edinburgh, 1816) 'A Table of the Prices of Provisions', quoting prices extracted from: 1) 'Compt of the King's Household Expense' made by the Bishop of Caithness, Comptroller. 2) James IV's Household Book.
E.R. (Bute) etc.	Prices recorded by treasurers of the Crown estates of Bute, Ross and 'Dishoir et Toyer' (Perthshire) published in the *Exchequer Rolls of Scotland.*
High Treasurer	Ship provisioning accounts in *Accounts of the Lord High Treasurer,* vol. IV (Edinburgh, 1902), vol. V (Edinburgh, 1903), and vol. VI (Edinburgh, 1905).
Fife	W.C. Dickinson, *The Sheriff Court Book of Fife, 1515–1522,* Scottish History Society, 3rd series, vol. 12 (Edinburgh, 1928).
Elgin	W. Crammond, *The Records of Elgin, 1234–80,* New Spalding Club, (2 vols., Aberdeen, 1903 and 1908).
Benefices (General) etc.	G. Donaldson, *Accounts of the Collectors of Thirds of Benefices, 1561–1572,* Scottish History Society, 3rd series, vol. 42 (Edinburgh, 1949). In 1561 prices were noted only by the Collector-General. Thereafter they were recorded by the Sub-Collectors for Bewley and Kinloss, Aberdeen, Orkney and Inverness.
Aberdeen Diet	Aberdeen University Diet Account of 1579 published in Cosmo Innes, *Fasti Aberdoneses,* Spalding Club (Aberdeen, 1854).
St Andrews Diet	St Andrews University Diet Accounts: 1) St Leonards College Diet Books, St Andrews University Library Mss., SL 530/3. 2) Crawfurd and Balcarres Mss., National Library of Scotland.
RPCS	*Register of the Privy Council of Scotland,* 1st series, vol. 5, p. 507: price assessment.

Table 6.5 *Cattle and sheep: Dumfries Commissariot probate inventories, 1600–1662*

Date	Cows L. s. d.			Sheep L. s. d.			Date	Cows L. s. d.			Sheep L. s. d.		
1600	8	10	0	1	7	6	1630	10	9	0	1	15	0
1601	8	4	6	1	5	6							
1602	10	0	0	1	10	0	1638	12	11	6	1	18	6
1603	10	8	0	1	9	6	1639	12	8	6	1	14	0
1604	10	3	6	1	14	0	1640	11	14	6	1	11	6
1605	10	8	0	1	14	6	1641	11	10	6	1	15	0
1606	10	12	6	1	15	0	1642	13	11	6	1	19	6
1607	10	15	6	1	18	0	1643	12	4	6	1	19	6
1608	10	15	0	1	17	0							
1609	11	15	0	1	19	0	1656	12	11	0	1	18	6
							1657	10	16	0	1	11	6
1624	10	16	0	1	17	0	1658	10	12	0	1	9	6
1625	10	16	0	1	19	0	1659	11	6	0	1	12	6
1626	11	14	6	1	18	0							
1627	11	9	0	1	18	6	1661	13	2	0	1	9	6
1628	11	14	6	1	18	0	1662	13	9	6	1	8	0
1629	10	10	0	1	17	0							

Table 6.6 *Cattle and sheep: Privy Council valuations of stolen beasts, 1565–1610*

Date of case	Date of raid	County	Price	Animal (cattle)	RPCS
1565	1565	Dumfriesshire	£6	kye	I.344
1573	1573	Stirlingshire	£2	stirks and cows	III.251
1580	--	Dumfriesshire	£10.13.4	nolt	III.254
1583	1583	Dumfriesshire	£7	kye and oxen	III.585
1597	1594	Argyll	£13.6.8	cow	V.381
1597	--	Dumfriesshire	£24	cows and oxen	V.400
1597	--	Dumfriesshire	£20	cows with calf	V.469
1598	1597	Morayshire	£20	cows with calf	V.498
1598	1597	Angus	£24	nolt and oxen	V.747
1599	1598	Midlothian	£33.6.8	oxen	V.522
1599	1598	Midlothian	£30	oxen	V.540
1599	1598	Dumfriesshire	£20	cows	VI.3
1600	1595	Perthshire	£16	kye	VI.93
1600	1595	Perthshire	£10.13.6	kye	VI.93
1600	--	Dumfriesshire	£16–£20	kye	VI.115
1600	1600	Dumfriesshire	£13.6.8	cows	VI.119
1600	1598	Dumfriesshire	£13.6.8–£20	oxen	VI.180
1601	1600	Perthshire	£13.6.8	nolt	VI.229
1601	1600	Perthshire	£25	oxen	VI.239
1602	--	Perthshire	£24	cows with calf	VI.363
1602	1601	Dumfriesshire	£12	oxen and cows	VI.483
1602	1595	Morayshire	£20	kye	VI.416
1602	1598	Perthshire	£20	kye and oxen	VI.441
1602	1597	Kirkcudbrightshire	£20	oxen	VI.471
1603	1601	Dumfriesshire	£20	kye and oxen	VI.516
1605	--	Ayrshire	£20	kye and oxen	VII.100
1605	1601	Borders	£24	cow with calf	VII.148
1606	--	Perthshire	£13.6.8	kye	VII.644
1607	1606	Perthshire	£16	drawing oxen	VII.330
1607	1606	Perthshire	£12	cow and calfs	VII.330

Table 6.6 *(cont.)*

Date of case	Date of raid	County	Price	Animal (sheep)	*RPCS*
1565	1565	Dumfriesshire	£1	sheep	I.344
1565	1565	Dumfriesshire	£0.8.0	lamb	I.344
1573	1573	Stirlingshire	£1	ewes and sheep	II.251
1583	1583	Dumfriesshire	£1.4.0	sheep	III.585
1597	--	Dumfriesshire	£4	ewes	V.400
1598	1597	Morayshire	£1.6.8	ewes	V.498
1599	1598	Dumfriesshire	£2.10.0	ewes	VI.3
1600	1598	Dumfriesshire	£2	sheep	VI.116
1601	1599	Dumfriesshire	£1.6.8	lamb	VI.210
1602	1596	Perthshire	£2.13.4	sheep	VI.414
1602	1600	Morayshire	£3.6.8	wedder	VI.416
1602	1600	Dumfriesshire	£2	sheep	VI.436
1602	1592	Perthshire	£1.10.0	sheep	VI.437
1602	1595	Perthshire	£2	sheep	VI.463
1605	--	Ayrshire	£4	sheep	VII.100
1610	--	--	£2.10.0	sheep	VIII.831
1610	--	--	£1	lamb	VIII.831

Table 6.7 *Cattle and sheep: JP's investigations, 1626–7*

	Oxen	Cows	Cows with calf	2 year olds	Yearlings
1626					
Berwickshire	£26.13.4–£30	£18	£24		
Roxburghshire	£36–£40	£24–£30			
Selkirkshire	£16–£24		£16–£18		
East Lothian	£32–£42		£20–£28		
West Lothian	£33.6.8–£50	£24–£30		£12–£13.6.8	£5.6.8–£8
Angus	£20–£33.6.8		£24		
Perthshire	£20–£33.6.8		£16–£24		
1627					
Berwickshire	£16–£26.13.4	£15–£18	£12–£18		
Roxburghshire	£24–£30	£18–£24			
Selkirkshire	£18–£24		£16–£18		
Dumfriesshire	£20–£22	£16–£18			
West Lothian	£26.13.4–£40			£8–£12	£5–£6.13.4
Stirlingshire	£20–£30	£18	£22	£10.13.4	
Perthshire	£20–£33.6.8		£16–£24		
Kincardineshire	£33.6.8	£26.13.4			

	Wedders	Ewes	Ewes with lamb	Hogs	Lambs
1626					
Berwickshire	£4	£3	£4.6.8	£2.13.4	£1.4.0
Roxburghshire	£4.13.4		£4.4.0	£3.6.8	
Selkirkshire	£3.10.0		£3.10.0	£2.13.4	
East Lothian	£4–£5		£4–£4.13.4	£2.18.0–£3.6.8	£1.6.8–£2
Angus	£3.6.8–£4.10.0			£2.5.0	£1.6.8
Perthshire	£4		£3.6.8		
1627					
Berwickshire	£3.6.8–£4	£3–£3.6.8	£3.6.8–£4	£2.10.0–£3	£1–£1.8.0
Roxburghshire	£4.13.8–£5		£3.13.4–£4		
Selkirkshire	£3.6.8–£4		£3–£3.6.8	£2.10.0	£1.0.0
Dumfriesshire	£3.6.8			£2.13.4	£1.4.0
Stirlingshire	£4		£3.13.4	£2	

Table 6.8 *Fresh beef and mutton: Aberdeen and Edinburgh council statutes, 1547–1598*

| Date | Aberdeen statutes | | | | Edinburgh statutes | |
| | Beef carcase | Mutton carcase | Mutton (fleshers') carcase | Mutton (butchers') carcase | Mutton (best) carcase | Mutton (second) carcase |
	L. s. d.	s. d.	s. d.	s. d.	s. d.	s. d.
1547		6 8				
1548						
1549		6 8				
1550		7 0			14 0	12 0
1551		7 0				
1552		6 8			10 0	8 0
1553	1 4 0	5 0				
1554	1 4 0	5 0				
1555		6 0				
1557					8 0	6 0
1558	1 4 0	5 0				
1559		6 0				
1560		8 0			8 0	6 0
1561		8 0				
1562		14 0				
1563		10 0				
1564		10 0			12 0	8 0
1565						
1566		8 0				
1567		12 0				
1570		10 0				
1571		10 0				
1572		10 0				
1573		10 0				
1574		12 0				
1575		10 0				
1576		14 0				
1577		14 0				
1578		10 0				
1579		13 4				
1580		13 0				
1581		13 4				
1582			15 0	12 0		
1583			15 0	12 0		
1584			15 0	10 0		
1585			15 0			
1586		20 0	16 0			
1587		16 0				
1588			20 0			
1589			20 0	18 0		
1590			18 0	16 0		
1591						
1592			20 0			
1593			24 0	20 0		
1594						
1595			20 0	20 0		
1596						
1597		24 0				
1598		24 0				

Table 6.9 *Fresh beef and mutton: Aberdeen council statutes, 1600–1701*

Date	Cow beef carcase L. s. d.			Ox beef carcase L. s. d.			Mutton carcase s. d.	
1600							30	0
1601								
1602							26	8
1603							33	4
1604							26	8
1605							33	4
1606							26	8
1607							26	8
1608								
1609							33	4
1610							33	4
1611							33	4
1644							48	0
1648							53	4
1649							46	0
1650							46	0
1651							46	0
1652							46	0
1653							46	0
1656	9	0	0	12	0	0	36	0
1657	9	0	0	12	0	0	36	0
1658	9	0	0	12	0	0	36	0
1659	8	0	0	10	13	4	32	0
1660	8	0	0	10	13	4	36	0
1661				10	13	4	34	0
1662	8	0	0	10	13	4	30	0
1663	8	0	0	10	13	4	30	0
1664	9	0	0	12	0	0	33	4
1665	8	0	0	10	13	4	30	0
1666	7	0	0	10	0	0	26	8
1667	6	0	0	9	0	0	24	0
1668	6	0	0	8	0	0	24	0
1669	6	0	0	8	0	0	24	0
1670	6	0	0	9	0	0	24	0
1671	6	0	0	9	0	0	24	0
1672	7	0	0	10	0	0	24	0
1673	7	0	0	10	0	0	24	0
1674	7	0	0	10	0	0	24	0
1675	7	0	0	10	0	0	24	0
1676	7	0	0	10	0	0	24	0
1677	8	0	0	11	0	0	26	8
1678	8	0	0	11	0	0	26	8
1679	8	0	0	12	0	0	29	0
1680	8	0	0	12	0	0	29	0
1681	7	6	8	10	13	4	26	8
1682	7	6	8	10	13	4	26	8
1683	7	6	8	10	13	4	26	8
1684	8	0	0	12	0	0	26	8
1685	8	0	0	12	0	0	26	8
1686	8	0	0	12	0	0	26	8
1687	8	0	0	12	0	0	26	8
1688	8	0	0	12	0	0	26	8
1689	8	0	0	12	0	0	26	8
1697	10	0	0	12	0	0	26	8
1701	14	0	0	24	0	0	40	0

Table 6.10 *Cattle and sheep: miscellaneous quotations, 1607–1707*

Date	Cattle	Sheep	Source
1607	£20.6.8	60s. 0d.	*Lennox*
1612	£10.0.0	40s. 0d.	Book of Rates, *RPCS*
1614	£13.6.8		*Urie* [Valuation]
1615	£12.0.0	20s. 0d.	*RPCS*, X.747
1620	£10.0.0	66s. 8d.	*Urie* [Valuation]
		30s.–50s.	*RPCS*, XII.181
1626	£10.0.0	60s. 0d.	*Urie* [Valuation]
1627	£10.0.0		*Urie* [Valuation]
1628		60s. 0d.	*Urie* [Valuation]
1629	£10.0.0		*Urie* [Valuation]
	£6.13.4	30s. 0d.	*Arnot*
1632	£10.0.0		*Urie* [Valuation]
1634	£10.0.0	60s. 0d.	*Urie* [Valuation]
1639	£10.0.0–£13.6.8		*Glasgow Diet*
1640	£6.13.4–£12.0.0		*Glasgow Diet*
1641	£9.0.0–£24.0.0		*Glasgow Diet*
1642		40s. 0d.	*Horricks* (Badenoch)
1650	£12.0.0	48s. 0d.	*Aberdeen Diet*[1]
	£14.13.4–£30.0.0	66s. 8d.–80s. 0d.	*Green Cloth*
	£10.0.0	40s. 0d.	*Thurloe Ms*
1651	£9.3.0	42s. 0d.	*Aberdeen Diet*[2]
1653	£15.10.0		*Arnot*
1662	£18.0.0		*Shaftesbury Ms*
1665	£18.10.0		*Stitchill*
	£16.0.0	40s. 0d.	*Horricks* (Urquhart)
1670	£17.0.0		*Stitchill*
1671	£8.0.0–£18.13.4	38s. 0d.–53s. 4d.	*St Andrews Diet*
1673		41s. 0d.	*Stitchill*
1674		66s. 8d.	*Stitchill*
1675		28s. 0d.	*Stitchill*
1682	£14.0.0–£18.0.0	30s. 0d.	*St Andrews Diet*
1683	£25.0.0–£40.0.0		*St Andrews Diet*
		66s. 0d.	*Stitchill*
1684		26s. 8d.	*Horricks* (Badenoch)
1690	£8.0.0–£24.0.0	40s. 0d.–46s. 6d.	*Jacobite Papers* [Valuation]
1696/7	£18.0.0		*PRO Customs*
1697/8	£12.0.0		*PRO Customs*
1698	£10.6.8		*Horricks* (Macleod)
1699	£21.0.0–£24.0.0		*PRO Customs*
1700	£18.0.0–£24.0.0		*PRO Customs*
	£13.6.8		*Horricks* (Macleod)

Table 6.10 *(cont.)*

Date	Cattle	Sheep	Source
1701	£18.0.0–£24.0.0	30s. 0d.	*PRO Customs* *Horricks* (Badenoch)
1702	£18.0.0–£24.0.0		*PRO Customs*
1703	£21.0.0		*PRO Customs*
1706	£10.0.0		*Horricks* (Macleod)
1707	£12.0.0		*Horricks* (Macleod)

Lennox	'Household Account of Ludovick Duke of Lennox, when Commissioner to the Parliament of Scotland, Anno 1607', *Miscellany of the Mailtland Club, vol. 1*, Maitland Club, vol. 25 (Edinburgh, 1834).
RPCS	*Register of the Privy Council of Scotland*, First Series.
Urie	D.G. Barron (ed.), *The Court Book of the Barony of Urie*, Scottish History Society, 1st Series, vol. 12 (Edinburgh, 1892).
Arnot	Hugo Arnot, *History of Edinburgh* (2nd edition, Edinburgh, 1816) 'A Table of the Prices of Provisions'. Prices are unattributed.
Glasgow Diet	'Schedule of Boarders in the College and accounts relative to them, 1633–40' (*Glasgow University Archives*, Mss. 26731), and 'Accounts the provisions, etc., for the Boarders at the Common Table, 1639–46' (*Glasgow University Archives*, Mss. 26733).
Horricks	C.L. Horricks, 'Economic and Social Change in the Isle of Harris, 1680–1754', University of Edinburgh Ph.D. Thesis, 1974. The name in brackets indicates the estate from which the quotation comes.
Thurloe Ms	*A Collection of the State Papers of John Thurloe, Esq.* (ed. Thos. Birch, London, 1742). 'The rental of the whole revenue of Scotland', p. 153.
Aberdeen Diet[1]	Aberdeen University Diet Accounts for 1650, published in Cosmo Innes, *Fasti Aberdoneses*, Spalding Club (Aberdeen, 1854).
Aberdeen Diet[2]	Aberdeen University Diet Accounts for 1651 in 'Liber Rationum Coll. Regal. Aberdonen., 1579–1653', Aberdeen University Library, Mss. K.2.
Green Cloth	'Minute Book of the Board of the Green Cloth, 8 July 1650 to 27 June 1651', *S.R.O.*, E.31/19.
Shaftsbury Ms	D. Woodward, 'Anglo-Scottish trade and English commercial policy during the 1660s', *Scottish History Review*, vol. 56 (1977), p. 164.
Stitchill	G.B. Gunn (ed.), *Records of the Baron Court of Stitchill, 1655–1807*, Scottish History Society, 1st series, vol. 50 (Edinburgh, 1905).
St Andrews Diet	St Leonard's College Diet Books, St Andrews University Library Mss., SL 530/3
Jacobite Papers	J. Allardyce, *Historical Papers relating to the Jacobite Period, 1699–1750*, vol. 1, New Spalding Club (Aberdeen, 1895).
PRO Customs	Import books of Scottish–English trade, Public Record Office, Customs 3.

Table 6.11 *Monthly meat prices: Leven and Melville accounts, March 1690 – April 1702*

Date		Beef	Veal	Mutton	Lamb
			all prices per carcase		
		L. s. d.	L. s. d.	L. s. d.	L. s. d.
March	1690	39 8 10	7 7 5	5 18 7	3 13 10
April	1690	40 2 3	6 16 8	6 5 5	3 3 8
May	1690	46 8 0	6 14 2	5 8 9	2 10 9
June	1690	32 2 0	5 19 10	3 14 5	1 15 9
July	1690	24 16 8	5 0 2	2 19 0	1 10 5
Dec.	1691		8 12 0	3 0 0	
Jan.	1692		7 11 4	3 4 1	3 4 0
Feb.	1692		6 2 3	3 16 0	5 4 0
March	1692		7 6 6	5 18 0	3 13 4
April	1692		5 16 9		2 19 6
May	1692		4 16 0	6 19 7	2 4 10
June	1692		5 5 3	6 7 1	1 16 9
July	1692		5 0 0	3 18 3	1 13 2
Aug.	1692		3 6 8		1 13 8
Dec.	1692		6 8 0	2 16 0	
Jan.	1693		7 14 8	2 16 0	
Feb.	1693		7 17 4		7 0 0
March	1693		6 5 7		3 18 5
April	1693		6 1 2	5 4 0	3 1 4
May	1693		5 3 4	4 3 4	2 8 8
June	1693		5 12 0	3 18 8	1 12 11
July	1693				1 9 8
Dec.	1694		10 9 7	3 2 0	
Jan.	1695		11 2 0	4 4 11	8 0 0
Feb.	1695		9 16 10	5 4 7	6 13 8
March	1695		6 17 5	6 4 0	4 3 0
April	1695		7 19 7	8 9 7	2 14 4
June	1695		7 2 10	7 13 9	2 12 8
July	1695		6 10 8	4 9 9	2 2 7
Aug.	1695	19 4 0			
Nov.	1695		3 6 8		
Dec.	1695		2 14 0	2 16 0	
Jan.	1696	14 17 4			
Feb.	1696	20 0 0		5 16 0	
March	1696	23 6 0	3 16 0		
April	1696	11 0 0	7 4 0		2 17 5
May	1696	16 0 0		4 8 0	2 2 3
July	1696			2 4 8	1 15 0
Aug.	1696	22 0 0		4 0 0	1 9 4
Sept.	1696	23 8 0	4 4 0		
Dec.	1696		7 16 0	3 2 0	

Table 6.11 *(cont.)*

Date		Beef			Veal			Mutton			Lamb		
							all prices per carcase						
		L. s. d.			L. s. d.			L. s. d.			L. s. d.		
Jan.	1697				8	12	2	3	15	6	6	0	0
Feb.	1697				7	10	2	4	5	6	12	13	4
March	1697				9	1	2				4	15	7
April	1697	15	0	0	5	0	0				2	1	0
May	1697	20	8	11	5	8	0				1	8	10
June	1697	16	0	0							1	7	8
July	1697	17	6	8	5	0	0	6	17	2	1	7	0
Aug.	1697							3	14	10	1	9	9
Sept.	1697							3	0	7			
Oct.	1697							2	15	6			
Nov.	1697							2	12	5			
Dec.	1697				7	7	2	2	14	4			
Jan.	1698				7	4	0						
March	1698	26	16	8	6	16	5	6	0	0	3	11	0
April	1698	26	18	4	4	16	0				1	17	4
May	1698	27	6	8	5	6	8				1	12	0
June	1698	26	13	4	4	10	0						
July	1698	22	0	0	3	10	0				1	6	0
Aug.	1698	13	16	0	1	6	8				1	12	6
Sept.	1698	14	0	0				2	8	0			
Nov.	1698	15	0	0				2	8	0			
Dec.	1698				8	0	0	3	2	0			
Jan.	1699				8	11	6	3	12	7			
Feb.	1699				11	1	9	5	4	0	4	4	0
March	1699				7	3	4	6	5	4	4	0	7
April	1699	26	6	8	6	3	4	7	17	9	3	0	10
May	1699	24	0	0	3	5	1	5	0	0			
June	1699	24	0	0	2	8	10	3	0	0			
July	1699				2	3	9				1	8	6
Aug.	1699				1	16	0						
Sept.	1699	14	0	0				2	12	0	1	12	0
Oct.	1699	16	0	0	6	13	0						
Nov.	1699	18	13	4	8	17	9						
Dec.	1699				6	6	8						
July	1700							5	7	2	1	13	4
Aug.	1700							3	3	8	1	13	2
Sept.	1700							2	17	9			
Oct.	1700	15	0	0									
Nov.	1700	16	0	0				3	0	0			
Dec.	1700	20	18	3	11	0	0	2	15	8			
Jan.	1701	23	11	1	9	18	4	3	2	6			
Feb.	1701				10	6	1	3	12	0	7	9	4
March	1701	11	6	6	10	2	6				6	2	1
April	1701	24	16	8	6	14	5				2	18	6
May	1701	27	17	6	5	1	0	5	6	0	2	15	0
June	1701	30	2	6	4	10	4	5	1	9	2	0	0
July	1701	32	0	0	4	13	4	4	0	0			
Aug.	1701	34	16	8	4	10	0						
Sept.	1701	30	10	0									
Oct.	1701	22	0	0									
Dec.	1701				9	4	7	3	17	7			
Jan.	1702				12	18	2	3	19	0			
Feb.	1702				6	1	7	2	16	0			
March	1702				7	5	0				2	12	8
April	1702							4	8	0	2	1	2

Table 6.12 *Cattle: Carskey, Argyll, 1716–1740*

Date	Adult beasts L. s. d.		Three-year olds L. s. d.	Two-year olds L. s. d.	One-year olds L. s. d.
4/1716				5 3 4	
5/1716			9 10 0	5 6 8	
11/1716	11 6 8	Cow		8 0 0	4 13 3
1/1717					4 0 0
11/1719	14 0 0	Cow			
1/1720	13 6 8	Tydie Cow [1]			
5/1721	13 6 8	Stots			
11/1721	16 0 0				
12/1721			10 0 0		
1/1722				6 13 4	5 6 8
3/1725			10 0 0		
5/1731	15 0 0	Nolt			
1/1734	9 0 0	Cow, Stirk			
5/1734	14 0 0	Nolt			
1/1735			10 0 0		
11/1735	10 13 4	Cow			
2/1736				6 13 4	
2/1737	9 0 0	Cow			3 6 8
11/1740	10 0 0	Cow			
12/1740	15 0 0	Tydie Cow [1]			

1 A 'Tydie Cow' was a cow in calf.

Table 6.13 *Cattle: Knockbuy, Argyll, 1729–1774*

Date	Average price of cows L. s. d.	Date	Average price of cows L. s. d.	Date	Average price of cows L. s. d.
1729	14 18 0	1741		1753	17 6 0
1730	15 18 0	1742	16 15 0	1754	
1731	16 15 7	1743	23 5 5	1755	19 10 0
1732	13 0 0	1744	16 16 8	1756	18 3 0
1733	13 5 4	1745	19 1 9	1757	19 16 0
1734	14 10 10	1746	18 7 8	1758	17 14 0
1735	12 15 0	1747	16 3 4	1759	18 6 0
1736	13 2 2	1748	17 4 4	1760	17 8 0
1737	12 6 8	1749		1761	17 2 0
1738	12 13 11	1750	24 0 0	1760–4 (ave.)	18 0 0
1739	13 10 4	1751	26 13 4	1765–9 (ave.)	24 0 0
1740	15 14 5	1752		1770–4 (ave.)	25 16 0

Table 6.14 *Cattle: Park estate, Wigtownshire, 1718–1729*

Date	Stots	Cows	Oxen
1718	£6.4.0–£18.0.0		
1719		£11.0.0	£14.13.4–£25.0.0
1720	£13.0.0–£19.0.0		
1721	£10.6.8–£24.0.0		£14.0.0–£24.0.0
1722	£11.0.0–£24.0.0		
1723		£11.10.0	£13.10.0–£20.0.0
1724	£13.6.8–£26.0.0		
1725	£12.0.0–£25.11.0	£9.13.6–£14.0.0	£16.0.0–£32.0.0
1726	£22.2.5–£26.13.4	£10.0.0–£20.6.0	£20.0.0–£33.6.8
1727			
1728	£24.0.0–£30.1.0		£19.0.0–£35.0.0
1729	£20.0.0–£30.0.0	£10.10.0–£16.3.0	

Table 6.15 *Cattle and sheep: Melville estate, Fife, 1731–1762*

Date	Cows	Highland cows	3-yr. old cows	2-yr. old cows	Year-lings	Calves
12/1731	£12.18.0–£18.0.0					
5/1732						
11/1732	£13.6.0					
11/1733	£24.0.0–£36.0.0	£15.5.4–£20.0.0		£17.2.10	£10.0.0	
5/1735	£26.6.0–£27.8.7	£18.0.0	£27.1.4			£4.0.0
11/1735	£30.0.0	£18.0.0	£30.0.0	£18.0.0	£16.13.4	£12.0.0
11/1736	£24.0.0–£30.0.0	£13.4.0	£24.0.0	£18.0.0	£12.0.0	£6.0.0
10/1737	£30.0.0	£18.0.0		£16.0.0	£12.0.0	£6.13.4
10/1738	£30.0.0–£40.0.0	£16.0.0				£8.11.5
10/1739	£30.0.0–£48.0.0	£18.0.0		£19.16.0	£18.0.0	£12.0.0
11/1742	£48.0.0–£60.0.0	£24.0.0		£24.0.0	£18.0.0	£12.0.0
11/1744	£48.0.0–£60.0.0	£19.1.6				
12/1746	£26.0.0–£50.0.0		£30.0.0	£24.0.0	£18.0.0	£9.0.0
11/1747	£30.0.0–£53.8.0		£28.0.0	£21.0.0	£18.12.0	£9.5.5
11/1748	£33.0.0–£50.0.0		£27.0.0	£9.9.6	£12.0.0	£9.0.0
7/1750	£36.0.0–£54.0.0			£24.0.0	£18.0.0	£9.0.0
10/1754	£60.0.0	£24.0.0	£39.0.0	£28.10.0	£22.13.4	£12.0.0

Date	Wedders s.	Ewes s.	Rams s.	Gimmers s.	Hogs s.	Lambs s.
12/1731	48–54	36	36	48	24	
11/1733	48	30–42			30	
5/1735	48	30	30	30	24	18
10/1754	100	48	74	72	48	36
10/1762	70–228	55				

Table 6.16 *Cattle and sheep: Buchanan farm, Stirlingshire, 1752–1775*

Date	Stock bought			Stock sold		
	Milk cows	Cows	Stots	Milk cows	Cows	Stots
	L. s. d.	L. s. d.	L. s. d.	L. s. d.	L. s. d.	L. s. d.
1752			23 15 0			51 0 0
1753	30 0 0		29 2 0	43 16 0		
1754	46 4 0		25 11 6	52 8 0		41 0 0
1755	33 7 6		33 5 8	25 1 4		42 19 7
1756			29 3 9	33 0 0		56 0 0
1757	52 9 2		35 0 0		49 6 5	
1758			30 5 10	48 0 0		48 0 0
1759	48 6 0		30 10 0	35 19 0		38 7 2
1760			23 5 0			48 0 0
1761	58 6 5		32 1 6	40 8 0		60 0 0
1762			34 5 4	63 0 0		39 0 0
1763	54 8 0	26 2 10	29 14 0	39 2 5		47 10 0
1764	58 8 0	27 16 6	30 6 0	48 0 0	39 0 0	54 0 0
1765	76 4 6	31 19 6	36 0 0	46 5 3	41 12 0	
1766	69 19 2	34 5 6			45 17 0	
1767		44 18 11		57 15 0	53 2 6	
1768			43 14 0	41 6 8		
1769		37 16 0				43 4 0
1770	57 3 0		81 3 6	47 9 2	45 2 2	12 0 0
1771		35 2 6			38 13 4	
1772	33 6 0	38 12 0	24 12 0	43 10 0	43 18 1	72 0 0
1773		37 4 0	42 0 0			
1774			49 17 3	94 10 0	58 7 8	75 12 0
1775			52 13 0			77 7 6

Date	Stock bought			Stock sold		
	Wedders	Ewes	Ewes (with lambs)	Wedders	Ewes	Ewes (with lambs)
	L. s. d.	L. s. d.	L. s. d.	L. s. d.	L. s. d.	L. s. d.
1752	4 16 0					
1753	4 4 0					
1754	4 10 0		5 8 0			
1755	4 4 0		7 13 0			
1756	4 16 0		7 4 0			
1757	4 14 0		7 0 0	4 10 0		
1758	4 16 0		7 4 0			
1759		5 9 0	7 2 0	4 14 0		
1760	6 8 0					
1761		5 8 0	7 4 0	4 16 0		
1762						
1763	5 6 0	4 10 0		7 4 0		
1764	5 2 0	3 17 0		7 10 0		4 16 0
1765	4 19 0	3 14 0		8 2 0		
1766	5 15 0	4 4 0		7 16 0	3 18 0	7 16 0
1767	6 14 0	4 19 0		8 18 0	5 8 0	9 0 0
1768	6 6 0			7 4 0	4 4 0	
1769	6 0 0	4 10 0		7 10 0		
1770	7 16 0			4 16 0	4 4 0	
1771	8 8 0	5 14 0				
1772					4 4 0	
1773				7 8 0		

Table 6.17 *Mutton, tallow and candle: Aberdeen council statutes, 1547–1701*

Date	Mutton carcase (each) s. d.		Sheep's tallow (per stone) s. d.		Candle (per stone) s. d.		Stones tallow per mutton carcase	Stones candle per stone tallow	Stones candle per mutton carcase
1547	6	8	10	0	13	4	0.667	0.750	0.500
1548									
1549	6	8	10	0			0.667		
1550	7	0							
1551	7	0	12	0			0.583		
1552	6	8	10	0	13	4	0.667	0.750	0.500
1553	5	0							
1554	5	0	10	0	13	4	0.500	0.750	0.375
1555	6	0	10	0	13	4	0.600	0.750	0.450
1558	5	0	10	0	13	4	0.500	0.750	0.375
1559	6	0							
1560	8	0	14	0			0.571		
1561	8	0	14	0			0.571		
1562	14	0							
1563	10	0	14	0			0.714		
1564	10	0	14	0			0.714		
1565			16	0					
1566	8	0							
1567	12	0	18	0			0.667		
1568			18	0					
1569			18	0					
1570	10	0	12	0			0.833		
1571	10	0	12	0			0.833		
1572	10	0	16	0			0.625		
1573	10	0	18	0			0.555		
1574	12	0	16	0			0.750		
1575	10	0	14	0	16	0	0.714	0.875	0.625
1576	14	0	14	0	16	0	1.000	0.875	0.875
1577	14	0	20	0	24	0	0.700	0.833	0.583
1578	10	0	18	0	20	0	0.555	0.900	0.500
1579	13	4	20	0			0.667		
1580	13	0	24	0			0.542		
1581	13	4	20	0			0.667		
1582			20	0	26	8		0.750	
1583			24	0	26	8		0.900	
1584			24	0	26	8		0.900	
1585			28	0	34	8		0.808	
1586	20	0	24	0			0.833		
1587	16	0	24	0			0.667		
1588									
1589			26	8					
1590			28	0	32	0		0.875	
1591			28	0	32	0		0.875	
1592			28	0	32	0		0.875	
1593			33	4	40	0		0.833	
1594									
1595			36	0					
1596									
1597	24	0	33	6	42	8	0.716	0.785	0.562
1598	24	0	33	4	42	8	0.720	0.781	0.562
1599									
1600	30	0							
1601									
1602	26	8	36	8	48	0	0.727	0.764	0.556
1603	33	4	36	8	48	0	0.909	0.764	0.694
1604	26	8	36	8	48	0	0.727	0.764	0.556

Table 6.17 *(cont.)*

Date	Mutton carcase (each) s. d.		Sheep's tallow (per stone) s. d.		Candle (per stone) s. d.		Stones tallow per mutton carcase	Stones candle per stone tallow	Stones candle per mutton carcase
1605	33	4	53	4	37	4	0.625	1.429	0.893
1606	26	8	50	0	53	4	0.533	0.937	0.500
1607	26	8	46	8	53	4	0.571	0.875	0.500
1608									
1609	33	4	46	8			0.714		
1610	33	4	46	8			0.714		
1611	33	4	53	4			0.625		
1640			60	0					
1641			60	0					
1642			60	0	72	0		0.833	
1643					72	0			
1644	48	0							
1648	53	4	66	8	80	0	0.800	0.833	0.667
1649	46	0	73	4	80	0	0.627	0.917	0.575
1650	46	0	73	4	80	0	0.627	0.917	0.575
1651	46	0	66	8	72	0	0.690	0.926	0.639
1652	46	0	66	8	72	0	0.690	0.926	0.639
1653	46	0	66	8	72	0	0.690	0.926	0.639
1654			66	8	72	0		0.926	
1655									0.500
1656	36	0			72	0			0.562
1657	36	0	55	0	64	0	0.655	0.859	0.450
1658	36	0	60	0	80	0	0.600	0.750	
1659	32	0	55	0			0.582		
1660	36	0	58	0	72	0	0.621	0.806	0.500
1661	34	0	66	8	72	0	0.510	0.926	0.472
1662	30	0	58	0	72	0	0.517	0.806	0.417
1663	30	0	58	0	72	0	0.517	0.806	0.417
1664	33	4	73	4	80	0	0.455	0.917	0.417
1665	30	0	58	0	72	0	0.517	0.806	0.417
1666	26	8	66	8	74	8	0.400	0.893	0.357
1667	24	0	58	0	72	0	0.414	0.806	0.333
1668	24	0	58	0	72	0	0.414	0.806	0.333
1669	24	0	58	0	64	0	0.414	0.906	0.375
1670	24	0	58	0	72	0	0.414	0.806	0.333
1671	24	0	58	0	72	0	0.414	0.806	0.333
1672	24	0	58	0	72	0	0.414	0.806	0.333
1673	24	0	58	0	72	0	0.414	0.806	0.333
1674	24	0	53	4	72	0	0.450	0.741	0.333
1675	24	0	63	4	72	0	0.379	0.880	0.333
1676	24	0	63	4	72	0	0.379	0.880	0.333
1677	26	8	60	0	72	0	0.444	0.833	0.370
1678	26	8	80	0	80	0	0.333	1.000	0.333
1679	29	0	66	8	72	0	0.435	0.926	0.403
1680	29	0	66	8	72	0	0.435	0.926	0.403
1681	26	8	66	8	72	0	0.400	0.926	0.370
1682	26	8	66	8	72	0	0.400	0.926	0.370
1683	26	8	66	8	72	0	0.400	0.926	0.370
1684	26	8	60	0	72	0	0.444	0.833	0.370
1685	26	8	60	0	72	0	0.444	0.833	0.370
1686	26	8	60	0	72	0	0.444	0.833	0.370
1687	26	8	60	0	72	0	0.444	0.833	0.370
1688	26	8	60	0	72	0	0.444	0.833	0.370
1689	26	8	60	0	72	0	0.444	0.833	0.370
1697	26	8	60	0	64	0	0.444	0.937	0.417
1701	40	0	66	8	80	0	0.600	0.833	0.500

Table 6.18 *Tallow and candle (per stone): various councils' statutes, 1508–1699*

Date	Edinburgh tallow	Edinburgh candle	Glasgow tallow	Glasgow candle	Kirkcud- bright candle	Stirling tallow	Stirling candle
	s. d	s. d.	s. d.	s. d.	s. d.	s. d.	s. d.
1508		4 0					
1522						4 0	6 0
1523						4 0	
1526							6 0
1529		8 0					
1551		12 0					
1552		12 0					
1553							
1554		12 0				9 0	
1555		12 0					14 8
1556							9 4
1557		10 8					
1560		13 4					
1561		13 4					
1562	13 0	17 4					
1566							16 0
1574			17 0	14 0			
1575			18 0	16 4			
1576			16 0	16 4			
1577		21 4	18 0	17 6			
1578		21 4		18 8			
1579				18 8			
1580	18 0	21 4	18 0	18 8			
1581			18 0	18 8			
1582			16 0	16 4			
1583	20 0	24 0		23 4			
1584	24 0						
1585				23 4			
1586							
1587		28 0					
1588							
1589		32 0	30 0	36 0			
1592	28 0						
1593							
1594				37 4			
1595							
1596		37 4			2 8		
1597					2 8		
1598							
1599		48 0	44 0	53 4		44 0	45 4

Table 6.18 *(cont.)*

Date	Edinburgh tallow	Edinburgh candle	Glasgow tallow	Glasgow candle	Kirkcud-bright candle	Stirling tallow	Stirling candle
	s. d.	s. d.	s. d.	s. d.	s. d.	s. d.	s. d.
1600		40 0	30 0	40 0	4 0	40 0	42 8
1601					4 0	33 4	40 0
1602	38 0	45 4				36 0	42 8
1603						33 4	40 0
1604		44 0				35 0	42 8
1605			38 0	53 4		40 0	48 0
1606			40 0				
1607		48 0	40 0	53 4		40 0	53 4
1608						40 0	53 4
1609		48 0	38 0	46 8		36 0	48 0
1610	40 0		40 0	53 4	5 4	40 0	53 4
1611				53 4	5 4	40 0	53 4
1612		53 4	42 0	52 0			
1613					5 4	40 0	48 0
1614	42 0	53 4			5 4	40 0	48 0
1615	42 0	53 4			4 0	40 0	53 4
1616	42 0	53 4			5 4	40 0	48 0
1617					5 4	46 8	53 4
1618	42 0	53 4			5 4	42 0	53 4
1619	40 0	51 2				40 0	53 4
1620		51 2			5 4	40 0	53 4
1621	42 0	53 4			5 4	40 0	53 4
1622	42 0	53 4			5 4	40 0	53 4
1623	40 0	51 2	36 0	45 4	5 4	36 0	48 0
1624	40 0	51 2	36 0	44 0	5 4	40 0	48 0
1625	43 4	53 4	40 0	18 0	5 4	40 0	48 0
1626	44 0	55 5	40 0	42 0	5 4	45 0	48 0
1627	44 0	56 10	40 0	48 0	5 4		
1628	44 0	55 5	40 0	48 0	5 4	46 8	56 0
1629	44 0	55 5	48 0	53 4	5 4	46 8	56 0
1630	40 0	55 5	46 8	53 4	5 4	40 0	53 4
1631	45 0	56 6	40 0	48 0		40 0	53 4
1632	45 0	56 6				46 8	58 8
1633	45 0	56 6	40 0	48 0		46 8	58 8
1634	45 0	56 6		53 4	5 4	48 0	56 0
1635			48 0	53 4	5 4		
1636			46 8	53 4		46 8	53 4
1637			40 0	48 0		45 0	53 4
1638			46 8	53 4	5 4	46 8	53 4
1639			46 0	53 4		43 4	53 4
1640			46 0	53 4		45 0	53 4
1641						54 0	64 0
1642			48 0	56 0	5 4	54 0	64 0
1643						46 8	53 4
1644				48 0	5 4	43 4	53 4
1645			43 4	50 0	6 8		
1646					6 8		
1647	53 4	68 3		80 0	8 0	80 0	88 0
1648			60 0	66 8	8 0		
1649	58 0	72 6	60 0	66 8	6 8	66 8	80 0

Table 6.18 *(cont.)*

Date	Edinburgh tallow	Edinburgh candle	Glasgow tallow	Glasgow candle	Kirkcud-bright candle	Stirling tallow	Stirling candle
	s. d.	s. d.	s. d.	s. d.	s. d.	s. d.	s. d.
1650			56 0	64 0	8 0		
1651			60 0	68 0	8 0		
1652	54 0	68 3	50 0	58 0	8 0		
1653	53 0	69 4	50 0	58 0	6 8	56 8	69 4
1654			50 0	58 0	8 0		
1655	52 0	66 1	56 8	66 8			
1656	52 0	64 0	46 8	53 4	6 8		
1657	48 0	61 10	40 0	48 0	6 8		
1658			46 8	55 0			
1659	56 0	70 4	46 0	54 0			
1660			48 0	56 0			
1661	52 0	66 1	50 0	58 0			
1662	54 0	68 3	50 0	58 0			
1663	54 0	68 3	50 0	58 0		43 0	69 4
1664	56 0	72 6	46 0	54 0		60 0	72 0
1665	53 4	68 3	48 0	56 0			
1666	40 0	56 10	40 0	48 0			
1667			48 0	54 0			
1668	46 0	49 0	40 0	48 0			
1669			40 0	48 0			
1670	53 4	56 10	40 0	48 0			
1671	56 0	59 8	41 8	48 0			
1672			41 4	48 0			
1673			41 4	48 0			
1674	53 4	67 6	46 8	53 4			
1675	50 0	68 3	48 0	56 0			
1676	54 0	68 3	48 0	53 4			
1677	56 0	68 3	50 0	58 0			
1678	56 0	68 3	50 0	56 8		Perth tallow	Perth candle
1679			50 0	58 0			
						s. d.	s. d.
1680	52 0	64 0	50 0	58 0			
1681			46 8	53 4			
1682			40 0	46 8			
1683			40 0	48 0			
1684	48 0	61 10	44 0	50 8			58 8
1685			46 0	52 0			
1686			48 0	54 8			
1687	48 0	59 8	46 8	53 4			
1688			46 8	53 4			
1689			48 0	56 0			53 4
1690			48 0	56 0			
1691			41 4	48 0			
1692			40 0	46 8			58 8
1693	48 0	61 10	48 0	56 0		50 0	58 8
1694			53 4	60 0		50 0	58 8
1695			60 0	68 0			
1696			57 0	64 0			
1697			48 0	54 8		50 0	58 8
1698			48 0	54 8			
1699			50 0	56 8			

Table 6.19 *Tallow and candle (per stone): various councils' statutes, 1700–1760*

Date	Glasgow tallow		Glasgow candle		Glasgow common 'bleacht' wick candle		Glasgow fine 'bleacht' wick candle		Glasgow cotton wick candle		Perth tallow		Perth candle	
	s.	d.	s.	d.	s.	d.	s.	d.	s.	d.	s.	d.	s.	d.
1700	53	4	60	0										
1701	64	0	72	0							65	9	76	0
1702	55	4	60	0							56	0	64	0
1703	50	0	56	8										
1704	42	0	48	8							41	0	48	0
1705	41	0	48	0										
1706	39	0	46	0							42	0	40	0
1707	40	0	46	8							46	0	60	0
1708	43	4	50	0							46	0	53	4
1709	45	0	48	0										
1710	51	0	54	0										
1711	53	0	56	0							50	0	74	8
1712	53	0	56	0										
1713	53	0	56	0							55	0	80	0
1714	51	0	54	0							45	4	53	4
1715	51	0	54	0							45	4	53	4
1716	49	0	52	0							45	4	53	4
1717	53	0	56	0							49	0	56	0
1718	51	0			54	0			60	0	54	0	58	8
1719	49	0			52	0					53	4	58	8
1720	49	0			52	0			58	0	49	0	53	4
1721	49	0			52	0	54	0	56	0	51	0	56	0
1722	41	0			44	0	46	0	48	0	51	0	56	0
1723	41	0			44	0	46	0	48	0	43	0	64	0
1724	46	0			50	0	54	0	54	0	41	0	48	0
1725	48	0			52	0	56	0	58	0	47	0	53	4
1726	50	0			54	0	58	0	60	0	49	0	72	0
1727	48	0			52	0	56	0	60	0	49	0	72	0
1728	56	0			59	0	62	0	65	0	53	0	76	0
1729	58	0			61	0	64	0	67	0	56	0	64	0
1730	58	0			62	0	64	0	66	0	56	0	64	0
1731	56	0			60	0	62	0	64	0	52	0	58	8
1732	56	0			60	0	62	0	64	0	52	0	58	8
1733	44	0			48	0	50	0	52	0	48	0	53	4
1734	38	0			42	0	44	0	46	0	43	0	53	4
1735	34	0			38	0	40	0	42	0	33	8	42	8
1736											36	0	32	0
1737	38	0			42	0	44	0	48	0	36	0	32	0
1738	48	0			52	0			58	0	39	0	48	0
1739	56	0			60	0	62	0	66	0	45	4	53	4
1740	58	0			62	0	64	0	70	0				
1741	62	0			66	0	68	0	74	0				
1742	64	0			68	0	70	0	76	0	60	0	69	4
1743	56	0			60	0	62	0	68	0	54	0	53	4
1744	58	0			62	0	64	0	70	0	46	8	72	0
1745	58	0			62	0	64	0	70	0				
1746	50	0			54	0	56	0	62	0	48	0	74	8
1747	56	0			60	0	62	0	68	0	48	0	74	8
1748	58	0			62	0	64	0	68	0	45	8	72	0
1749	58	0			62	0	64	0	74	0	48	0	74	8
1750	52	0			56	0	58	0	68	0	45	4	72	0
1751	48	0			52	0	54	0	64	0				
1752											48	0	74	8
1753	54	0			58	0	60	0	66	0				
1754	66	0			86	0	90	0	94	0	53	4	80	0
1755											61	0	88	0
1756														
1757											53	0	80	0
1758											45	0	72	0
1759											53	0	80	0
1760											53	0	80	0

Table 6.20 *Butter (mean price per pound): St Andrews University, 1587–1780*

Date	St Leonard's College s. d.		St Salvator's College s. d.		St Mary's College s. d.		Date	St Leonard's College s. d.		St Salvator's College s. d.		St Mary's College s. d.	
1587	3	4					1730					4	9
1588	2	8											
1589	2	6					1733			4	6		
1590	2	7					1734			4	6		
1591	3	4					1735			5	0		
							1736			5	0		
1617	4	5					1737			5	0		
1618	4	5					1738			5	0		
1619	4	5					1739			5	0		
1620	4	5					1740			6	0		
1621	4	6					1741	6	1				
							1742	5	6				
1672	3	6					1743					5	0
							1744					5	0
1686			3	7			1745					6	6
1687			3	7			1746					5	8
1688			3	7			1747					5	0
1689			4	9			1748					5	0
1690							1749					5	6
1691			4	0			1750					7	0
1692			4	6			1751					6	0
1693	5	0	5	0			1752					6	6
1694	5	0	5	0			1753					6	0
1695	5	8	5	6			1754					6	0
1696			4	8			1755					6	0
1697	4	10	4	3			1756					6	0
1698			5	4			1757					6	3
1699	6	8					1758					6	3
1700	6	0					1759					6	3
1701	5	0					1760					6	3
1702	6	0					1761					6	3
1703	5	0					1762					7	6
1704	3	9					1763					8	0
1705	3	9					1764					7	6
1706	4	3					1765					7	6
1707	5	5					1766					7	6
1708	5	7	5	0			1767					7	6
1709	6	2					1768					7	6
1710	5	6					1769			7	0	7	6
1711	5	0					1770					7	6
1712	4	6	4	6			1771					7	6
1713	5	0	5	0			1772			7	6	7	6
1714	5	0	5	0			1773					7	6
1715	4	0					1774			7	4	7	6
1716	5	0					1775					7	6
							1776					7	6
1720			5	0			1777					7	6
							1778			7	6	7	6
1726					4	10	1779			7	6	7	6
1727					4	10	1780					7	6
1728					4	0							
1729					5	9							

Table 6.21 *Eggs (mean price per dozen): St Andrews University, 1587–1780*

Date	St Leonard's College s. d.	St Salvator's College s. d.	St Mary's College s. d.	Date	St Salvator's College s. d.	St Mary's College s. d.
1587	1 0			1730		2 0
1588	1 0					
1589	1 2			1743		2 0
1590	1 2			1744		1 10
1591	1 1			1745		2 0
				1746		2 0
1617	1 5			1747		2 0
				1748		2 0
1621	1 8			1749		2 0
				1750		2 0
1671	1 8			1751		2 0
1672	1 8			1752		2 0
1673	1 7			1753		2 0
1674	1 9			1754		2 0
1675	2 0			1755		2 0
				1756		2 0
1686		1 11		1757		2 0
1687		1 9		1758		2 0
1688		1 11		1759		2 0
1689		2 0		1760		2 0
1690				1761		2 0
1691		1 8		1762		2 0
1692		1 8		1763		2 0
1693		1 8		1764		2 6
1694		1 8		1765		2 6
1695		1 8		1766		2 6
1696	1 8	2 0		1767		2 6
1697	1 7	2 0		1768		3 0
1698		1 10		1769	2 6	2 6
1699	2 0			1770		3 0
1700	2 0			1771		3 0
				1772	2 6	3 0
1712		1 8		1773		3 0
1713		1 6		1774	2 6	3 0
1714		1 8		1775		3 0
1715	1 6			1776		3 0
				1777		3 0
1720		2 0		1778	2 10	3 0
				1779	3 0	3 0
1726			1 10	1780		3 0
1727			2 0			
1728			2 0			
1729			2 0			

7 ✤ Food

What was the food of the Scottish population in the period between the end of the sixteenth century and the end of the eighteenth – what were the main ingredients, how satisfactory was it in terms of quantity and nutritional content, how did it change? Most explorations of Scottish economic and social history, though willing to mention famines, have steered well clear of any detailed examination of diet. In a study of prices and wages which has as one of its central purposes the exploration of the standard of living, and which concerns a society in which the wage itself was frequently paid partly or entirely in kind, food history must nevertheless be a central theme. Late eighteenth-century budgets suggest that among the labouring population at least two-thirds of family income was devoted to food, (see chapter 9 below). The proportion must have been the same, or greater, earlier. Food, therefore, was what the standard of living was largely about.

In this chapter we have deliberately eschewed discussing the problem of famine and dearth, partly because it has been considered elsewhere, but also because it was very much the exceptional and not the ordinary lot of the population. Even in the seventeenth century fewer than ten years can be identified as ones of widespread grain shortage, and even these were not universal across Scotland; in the eighteenth century the number is about five. We are here concerned about ordinary people in ordinary times.

No doubt earlier neglect of the history of diet in Scotland is partly due to methodological problems. Evidence before the middle of the nineteenth century falls into two main categories – the generalised accounts of contemporaries, and institutional records of food purchases and allowances. The former may be suspect on a number of grounds: many of the observers were travellers whose sojourn in Scotland was brief and whose intention was sometimes to denigrate or to sensationalise; others were Scots whose perspectives may have been equally distorted by an intention to inflate or to moralise; most of those whose declared intention was to present 'useful facts', in the *Statistical accounts* and *General reports of agriculture*, come from a slightly later period, in the 1790s, a decade after our end date, and given their general inclination to cry up the achievements of their own day and to devalue those of their predecessors, even their judgements might not have been as value free as they would like us to suppose.

Institutional accounts at first sight seem to offer safer ground and a beguiling opportunity for quantification: their interpretation, however, involves a very detailed knowledge of weights and measures in a situation where there is often much ambiguity and opportunity for error – and even when this appears to have been overcome there remains a major problem about their typicality. Those records that survive deal with sheltered situations, ranging from the royal court and landed households down to orphanages, but most Scots lived most of their lives in very different and more independent situations as cottars, small farmers, craftsmen or labourers. Nevertheless, a systematic and careful use of both types of evidence yields results.

By the late sixteenth century it can be readily established that, in the Lowlands, most labourers, farm servants and small tenants were already dependent on farinacious foods, principally upon oatmeal but also upon bearmeal and (in some places) peasemeal. It is likely that (as we have discussed elsewhere) in the late Middle Ages more meat, cheese, butter and milk had been consumed, and that in the Highlands an animal-based diet remained more prominent for some time to come.[1] Landowners, large tenants, merchants, lawyers and so forth, of course, continued to enjoy meat throughout the period and middling-sized tenants and skilled craftsmen clearly had a more varied diet than average. It was characteristic of early modern society in Scotland as elsewhere that ostentatious eating and drinking was a mark of social distinction.[2] We are concerned here primarily with the consumption patterns of those at the foot of the social pyramid, which was so wide and deep as to contain most Scots.

The situation at the turn of the century was clearly described by contemporaries. For example, in 1598 the English traveller Fynes Morrison, stated that the population ate 'little fresh meat' (though he did refer to salted beef) and added 'they vulgarly eate harth Cakes of Oates, but in Cities have also wheaten bread'.[3] This distinction between the burghs and the countryside was to persist for centuries, the business of the craft of baxters in the towns being often restricted to baking loaves of wheat, barley or rye bread, while oatcakes or 'oatbread' were in most places and at most times made privately at home by the housewife using an iron griddle (often of Culross manufacture) over an open fire. This fare had been vigorously defended by Scots since at least the days of John Major (1521): 'I say for my part I would rather eat the British oaten bread than bread of wheat or barley'; but oatbread (or oatcake) was usually found unpalatable by English travellers like Celia Fiennes and Samuel Johnson.[4] Scotland was 'the land of cakes' because the population ate oatcakes. The nutritional benefits, as we shall see, were substantial.

In 1605 Sir Thomas Craig, the Scottish jurist, considering the advantages that might come to England and Scotland by a mutual union, argued that the poverty of Scotland had been overstated:

Less fertile than England she may be, but she lacks none of the necessaries of life. Fewer of her people die of starvation... Nowhere else is fish so plentiful... We have meat of every kind... We eat barley bread as pure and white as that of England and France.

---

[1] A.J. Gibson and T.C. Smout, 'Scottish food and Scottish history, 1500–1800', in R.A. Houston and I. Whyte (eds.), *Scottish society, 1500–1800* (Cambridge, 1989), pp. 59–84.

[2] A.J. Gibson and T.C. Smout, 'Food and hierarchy in Scotland, 1550–1650', in L. Leneman (ed.), *Perspectives of Scottish social history – essays in honour of Rosalind Mitchison* (Aberdeen, 1989).

[3] P. Hume Brown (ed.), *Early travellers in Scotland* (Edinburgh, 1891), pp. 88–9.

[4] J.H. Macadam (ed.), *The baxter books of St Andrews* (Leith, 1903), pp. 54–7; John Major quoted in A. M. Mackenzie, *Scottish pageant* (Edinburgh, 1946), p. 55; C. Morris (ed.), *The illustrated journeys of Celia Fiennes c.1682–c.1712* (London, 1982), p. 173; S. Johnson, *A dictionary of the English language* (London, 1772), under 'oats'.

Such a diet referred only to the better-off in society, and he added:

Our servants are content with oatmeal, which makes them hardy and long-lived. The greater number of our farm hands eat bread made of peas and beans... should there be a bad harvest the Highlanders are able to supply us with cheese, which is often used, without any injury to health when the supply of cereals is short.

The Highlanders themselves, however, he described as a robust long-lived, active people, 'in spite of their entire dependence on cheese, flesh and milk', like the Scythians.[5]

This broad set of generalisations is borne out by much other evidence. The abundance of food available to the upper classes is confirmed not only by the great quantities of provisioning available at court and in the houses of the nobility, but also in the extremely generous allowances at the universities of St Andrews and Glasgow, including a vast amount of meat and fish: wheatbread, though, is more evident at this social level than the barley bread of Craig's observations. The reference to farm servants eating bread made from peas and beans was particularly valid for the south-east of Scotland, including the Lothians, where peasemeal remained an appreciated staple even in the mid nineteenth century.

Craig's remarks on the Highlanders echo earlier and later commentators, though they were overdrawn: several areas of the Highlands, especially such islands as Islay and Tiree in the Hebrides, were famed for their production of meal which was traded to less fertile parts. The Irish Franciscans writing to Rome between 1624 and 1636 from the mission field in the Hebrides and adjacent mainland shores round Moidart and Arisaig had many comments on the desperately meagre diet they were forced to endure. Wine and wheatbread (for Mass) was unobtainable except from Ireland or the Lowlands; beer was not seen for months at a time, and they drank only water or milk; on Colonsay they lived only on shellfish taken from the shore; in sum 'the people generally use milk foods and, in summer, they have scarcely any bread'.[6] Craig was obviously right to draw attention to a perceived distinction between Highland and Lowland diets in which the former still substantially depended on local animal produce (though seldom actually meat) and the latter on grain foods.

These observations were followed in 1615 by the comments of another English traveller, Richard James, who visited the Lowlands and travelled north as far as Orkney. He emphasised the meat dishes, broths and stews with which he was entertained by the gentlemen in whose houses he stayed, but he also described a 'pottage they make of oate meale flour boilde in water, which they eate with butter, milk or ale' as being 'eaten by the common people and school children at breakfast, and by Ladies allso'.[7] This is the first clear description of Scottish porridge that we have encountered, though it was probably nothing new. The inhabitants of Anstruther in Fife, for instance, had entertained the shipwrecked Spanish armada vessel's crew who were brought to their town in 1588 with

[5] C. Stanford Terry (ed.), *Sir Thomas Craig's 'De Unione Regnorum Britanniae Tractatus'* (Scottish History Society, 1st series, vol. 60, Edinburgh, 1909), pp. 416–17, 447.

[6] C. Giblin (ed.), *Irish Franciscan mission to Scotland; documents from Roman archives* (Dublin, 1964), pp. 35, 48, 52–3, 56, 171–2.

[7] E. MacGillivray (ed.), 'Richard James 1592–1638; description of Shetland, Orkney and the Highlands of Scotland', *Orkney miscellany*, vol. I (1953), pp. 53–4. Despite the title, the description of food is general to all of Scotland.

'keall, pottage and fische', which perhaps included the same thing.[8] Eating porridge with butter persists in Denmark to this day, but appears to have died out in Scotland at an early date. Eating it with ale rather than milk remained common, until the later eighteenth or nineteenth centuries.

There is no direct reference by James to humble people eating meat, and later seventeenth-century observers also simply fail to refer to the consumption of meat by the lower orders. At the same time the Privy Council ceased to concern itself with trying to ensure adequate meat supplies in time of famine, though this had been done throughout the sixteenth century. Martin Martin, writing the first insider's account of diet in his native Hebrides around 1700, observed that 'the generality eat but little Flesh, and only Persons of distinction eat it every day ... and they eat more Boil'd than Roasted'. The preference for boiled meat was also noted by James; roasting ovens appear to have been a less common feature of Scottish houses than of English until recent times, though seventeenth-century inventories often mention spits. Martin went on to describe a diet of butter, cheese, milk, potatoes, cabbage and oatmeal – 'the latter taken with some bread is the constant Food of several Thousands of both Sexes in this [Skye] and other Isles, during the Winter and Spring'. The passage is interesting both for its early references to potatoes and because of its emphasis on the continuing significance of other animal products – butter and cheese – even when meat itself was unavailable on the common table.[9] Another seventeenth-century Highland document, *Chronicles of the Frasers* was self-congratulatory about how the clan, living near Inverness, escaped a dearth affecting the Lowlands because the produce of its flocks and herds was unaffected.[10] These features, however, were not destined to last through the next century, except possibly in some very remote areas of the far north.

For most of the eighteenth century accounts for Highland and Lowland alike almost uniformly contrive to give an impression of a country where meat was eaten only in small quantities by the great majority of the population, except in the form of broth with barley and vegetables: 'flesh meat they seldom or never taste' was one brusque summary.[11] The marketing itself was inadequate. In 1729 James Mackintosh of Borlum stated that: 'For half the year, in many towns of Scotland there is no beef or mutton to be seen in the shambles and, if any, it is like carrion meat, yet dearer than ever I saw in England.'[12] His remarks are echoed in recollections at the end of the century. For example, William Fullarton in Ayrshire in 1793 observed that fifty years earlier no more than fifty cattle were slaughtered annually in the town of Ayr, though it contained 4,000–5,000 inhabitants. In winter, he went on to say, meat was only ever used as broth by the common people.[13] Others at that time speak of very little meat being eaten earlier by the lower classes apart from, for example, 'salted meat in winter' (at Inveresk, Midlothian)

---

[8] J. Melvill, *The diary of Mr James Melvill, 1556–1601* (Bannatyne Club, vol. 34, Edinburgh, 1829), p. 176. 'Kail' is Fife dialect for soup, which suggests that 'pottage' could easily have been porridge.

[9] M. Martin, *A description of the Western Isles of Scotland* (2nd edn, London, 1716), p. 201.

[10] W. Mackay (ed.), *Chronicles of the Frasers* (Scottish History Society, 1st series, vol. 47, Edinburgh, 1905), p. 345.

[11] D. Herbert (ed.), *The works of Tobias Smollett* (Edinburgh, 1887), p. 559.

[12] J. Mackintosh, *An essay on ways and means of enclosing* (Edinburgh, 1729), p. 131.

[13] W. Fullarton, *General view of the agriculture of the county of Ayr* (Edinburgh, 1793), pp. 11–12.

or 'the off-falls of their flocks, which died either by poverty or disease' (at Tongland in Kircudbright), or 'a little with their greens in winter' (at Falkirk in Stirlingshire). At Kilsyth also in Stirlingshire the minister in 1795 recalled that formerly 'the most respectable tradesman never used more than a leg of beef in a year'.[14]

In the Highlands, Thomas Pennant, who travelled extensively in the region in 1769 and 1772 only once, in many references to diet, noted the presence of meat: in winter, on Arran, 'some dried mutton or goat is added to their hard fare' of meal and potatoes.[15] William Marshall in his agricultural survey of the Central Highlands in 1794 was equally clear that Highlanders in his area of survey even then seldom tasted meat of any kind and Sir John Sinclair said the same about Cromarty: a family of small farmers would not consume 5 lbs. of flesh in a year.[16] Interestingly, some parishes in Banffshire reported in the 1790s that meat-eating had declined within living memory. At Fordyce 'they can seldom afford any flesh meat now, except at Christmas, but formerly could afford a little through the winter', at Grange 'formerly every householder ... killed a sheep now and then out of his little stock', and at Kirkmichael 'fifty years ago' cottagers kept sheep and sometimes ate meat, which they did no longer. In the latter two parishes the change was attributed to the rise of commercial farming which determined that local livestock had to be sold externally and 'the fold is kept sacred for the market.'[17] It was not the only comment to associate hardship with the switch from a subsistence to a commercial environment. Upper-class observers would not necessarily see everything – the snared rabbit or elderly hens that found their way into the cottar's pot, or the occasional poached deer or braxy mutton (carrion found dead on the hill) which cheered the common people's fare. But the general point they were making, that meat formed either an occasional treat or an insubstantial proportion of the daily food, is obviously true.

The extent to which eggs, butter, cheese and fish made up for the absence of meat is debatable. An Act of Parliament of 1641 sought to restrict the export of eggs so that the poor labouring man who eats only bread and drinks water could have the benefit of eggs with his meals: the way it is expressed suggested that eggs were not usual in his food, though no doubt present sometimes.[18] In Sir John Sinclair's Cromarty 160 years later, for tenants 'an egg is a luxury that is seldom or never indulged in, far less a fowl'.[19] In the Lowlands there is an impression of small quantities of cheese and butter regularly consumed by some to cheer an oatmeal diet, but also that not everyone could afford it. Ayrshire was a dairying area but one eighteenth-century commentator noted that the wives of small tenants, expert at making cheese and butter, sold it all at the market and could not afford to give it to their families.[20] Sir James Steuart similarly spoke of Lanarkshire labourers drinking only skimmed milk and selling all the butter made from their cow's cream for £2 sterling a year.[21]

[14] *OSA*, vol. 2 (*Lothians*), p. 317; vol. 5 (*Kirkcudbright*), p. 333; vol. 9 (*Stirling*), pp. 302, 500.
[15] T. Pennant, *A tour of Scotland and voyage to the Hebrides in 1772* (Edinburgh, 1776), part 1, p. 176.
[16] W. Marshall, *General view of the agriculture of the central Highlands* (London, 1794), p. 21; J. Sinclair, *General view of the agriculture of the northern counties of Scotland* (London, 1795), p. 82.
[17] *OSA*, vol. 16, pp. 155–6, 214, 307.   [18] *APS*, vol. 5, p. 420.   [19] Sinclair, *Northern counties*, p. 82.
[20] W.J. Dickson (ed.), 'Memories of Ayrshire about 1780 by the Reverend John Mitchell', *Miscellany of the Scottish History Society, vol. 6* (Scottish History Society, 3rd series, vol. 33, Edinburgh, 1930), p. 272.
[21] James Steuart, *Works* (London, 1805), vol. 5, p. 291–2.

In the Highlands, Duncan Forbes of Culloden could still speak in 1746 of the fare of the 'inhabitants of the mountains' in terms reminiscent of Martin Martin and the Irish Franciscans: 'The Grounds that are cultivated yield small quantities of mean Corns, not sufficient to feed the Inhabitants, who depend for their nourishment on milk, butter, cheese etc, the produce of their cattle.'[22] Pennant referred to Skye peasants eating their 'meal pudding' with milk, butter or treacle, Pococke to 'cured' meat in Sutherland diets in 1760, and Marshall, more generally, to Highlanders consuming milk 'and its products'.[23] In some very remote places where market forces had scarcely penetrated before the Napoleonic period, archaic food habits could persist. As late as 1812 John Henderson was to comment of Sutherland that the inhabitants of the coastal areas lived mainly 'upon fish, potatoes, milk and oat or barley-cakes': that is exactly as one would expect, but he continued:

Those in the interior or more Highland part feed upon mutton, butter cheese, milk and cream with oat or barley-meal cakes in the summer months ... in winter ... the poorer classes live upon potatoes and milk, and at times a little oat or barley cakes. In times of scarcity, in summer, they bleed their cattle, and after dividing it into square cakes, they boil it, and eat it with milk or whey instead of bread.[24]

The only new element there was potatoes, although the bleeding of cattle in times of dearth, practised in the seventeenth-century and earlier eighteenth-century Highlands, is unexpected in the nineteenth century: more generally, the mutton and dairy-produce diet also recalls the older accounts of Craig and Martin, rather than William Marshall's near contemporary account of the Central Highlands, which included milk but excluded meat.

Yet overall there is a strong impression that in the hills the eating of dairy produce was becoming more and more irregular. It is little mentioned in the *Statistical account*, where the emphasis is rather on meal and potatoes, with pessimistic observations such as the one in Bower, Caithness, to the effect that the people 'live on a very spare and scanty diet, and perhaps much less comfortably than before'. Certainly by the 1840s butter and cheese was sold rather than consumed: thus at Glenshiel 'butter and cheese, though favourite articles, they rarely indulge in'.[25] Once again the rise of a market for local produce seems to have led to a deterioration in the variety and content of diet.

The importance of fish depended very much on distance from the sea. Smollet in 1771 could call a pickled herring a 'delicacy' for the country people of Scotland and Sinclair in 1795 described 'a haddock occasionally' in summer as a 'wonderful regalement' in the northern Highlands; but along the coasts in Highland and Lowland alike herring, haddock, saithe and various shellfish were a common item – over reliance on fish and shellfish in times of dearth along the coasts was sometimes blamed for outbreaks of

[22] Quoted in A.J. Youngson, *After the '45* (Edinburgh, 1973), p. 23.
[23] Pennant, *Tour ... 1772*, part 1, p. 309; D.W. Kemp (ed.), *Bishop Pococke's tours in Scotland, 1747–1760* (Scottish History Society, 1st series, vol. 1, Edinburgh, 1886), p. 127; Marshall, *Central Highlands*, p. 21.
[24] J. Henderson, *General view of the agriculture of the county of Sutherland* (London, 1812).
[25] *OSA*, vol. 18 (*Caithness*), p. 6; I. Levitt and T.C. Smout, *The state of the Scottish working class in 1843* (Edinburgh, 1979), p. 26.

disease.[26] At St Andrews in the 1790s it was recalled that previously haddock had 'formed the chief article of animal food of the poorer sort, and were seen at every table'. At Inveresk, another coastal parish, salted herring had been, for the common people before ca. 1760, 'a great part of their *kitchen* . . . a word that signifies whatever gives relish to bread or *porridge*' – an observation that echoes Smollett's 'delicacy', though with the implication that here it was not that unusual.[27] Inland, there was the possibility of salmon and trout caught by all sorts of licit and illicit means, but little indication (despite traditional stories of apprentice indentures that prohibited the excessive provision of salmon) that it was more than an occasional treat.

The overwhelming impression from literary sources in the eighteenth century remains of a diet based on oatmeal in most places, increasingly, after about 1750, supplemented by potatoes where incomes were especially low or where the ground was less suitable for oats. Smollett gave a good account of the daily meals of 'the country people of North Britain', meaning the Scottish lowlanders: 'Their breakfast is a kind of hasty pudding of oatmeal, or peasemeal eaten with milk. They have commonly pottage to dinner composed of cale or cole, leeks, barley or big and butter and this is reinforced with bread and cheese made of skimmed milk. At night they sup on sowens flummery of oatmeal.'[28]

Robert Hope, writing in Sinclair's *General report of the agricultural state of Scotland* of 1814, which summarised the data from the 1790s investigations as well as describing the contemporary scene, stated that at breakfast a man would consume three imperial pints of porridge, containing about 15.5 oz. of oatmeal.[29] The daily intake of meal, though, could double that breakfast consumption. Sir James Steuart in 1770 described the weekly allowance for a labourer in Scotland as traditionally 16 lbs. Scottish troy weight, which works out at about 40 oz. avoirdupois.[30] The same figure was given in 1794 by observers in Lothian, Fife and Angus; James Donaldson being particularly explicit in writing of the unmarried farmhands in the Carse of Gowrie, where the workers got $6\frac{1}{2}$ bolls of meal a year:

They receive an English pint of sweet milk, or double that quantity of butter-milk, to breakfast, dinner and supper; so that oatmeal with milk, which they cook in different ways, is their constant food, three times a day, throughout the year, Sundays and holidays included, the quantity of meal allowed being thirty-six ounces to each man a day.[31]

Sinclair described in the north, for a man 'the usual rate of six bolls for one year's board', and for his wife, four bolls. Six bolls would produce about 37 oz. avoirdupois of meal for consumption a day. A household could indeed cut its intake from an estimated 27 bolls a

[26] Tobias Smollett, *Works* (ed. D. Herbert, Edinburgh, 1887), p. 559; Sinclair, *Northern counties*, p. 82; T. Ferguson, *The dawn of Scottish social welfare* (London, 1948), p. 24.

[27] *OSA*, vol. 2 (*Lothians*), p. 317.

[28] Smollett, *Works*, p. 559: 'big' was a form of barley.

[29] R. Hope, 'On rural economy', in Sir John Sinclair, *General report of the agricultural state, and political circumstances of Scotland* (Edinburgh, 1814), vol. 3, p. 256.

[30] James Steuart, *Inquiry into the principles of political economy* (Dublin, 1770), book 2, p. 403.

[31] J. Donaldson, *General view of the agriculture of the Carse of Gowrie* (London, 1794), p. 24. See also R. Beatson, *General view of the agriculture of Fife* (London, 1794), p. 16; G. Buchan-Hepburn, *General view of the agriculture and rural economy of East Lothian* (London, 1794), p. 91.

year to feed four adults and four children to 21 bolls, but food like this provided too little 'to give spirit or strength for labour'.[32]

The physical problem of consuming about 37 oz. of oatmeal in a day must have been substantial: not for nothing was breakfast traditionally taken standing up, for as a Scottish proverb has it 'a standing sack fills fullest'. To eat it all as porridge was certainly not practicable: one large bowl provides only $1\frac{1}{2}$ oz. of oatmeal. Nor could it all have been eaten as oatcake: it would be the equivalent of $3\frac{1}{2}$ packets of Walker's Highland oatcake at the present day. Some would be eaten as brose, where boiling water is poured over uncooked meal, and more than three times the quantity can then be put in the same space as in one bowl of porridge. Sowens (or flummery) was another dish: here the meal or oats were steeped in water, allowed to ferment slightly, and boiled up. Porridge itself could be allowed to go cold and solidify, and be eaten as slices: unsuspecting purchasers of old Scottish dressers have occasionally found in them a drawer solid with the uneaten porridge of a former age.

In the late eighteenth century a diet supplemented by potatoes was gaining ground among certain sectors of the population. Pennant noticed its increase in the Highlands, and William Marshall, writing of the Central Highlands in 1794, described potatoes as 'a principal food of the common people especially in winter' and 'the greatest blessing that modern times have bestowed on the country', having 'more than once saved it from the miseries of famine'. But he is clear that oatmeal is still 'the great support and strength of the Highlander', and Sinclair made the same point for the north – potatoes helped for some of the year, but between the end of April and the start of September meal-based foods 'constitute their food invariably and without a change'.[33] Potatoes were useful in husbanding the cash income of a parish. At Moulin in Perthshire they were reckoned to have the advantage of obviating the need to import meal: certainly the need to feed the Highland population on increasing quantities of meal as population rose and cattle were exported had been an increasingly prominent feature of Highland life since the late seventeenth century.[34]

In the Lowlands, dearths after the middle of the century also encouraged the development of potatoes as a second string to oatmeal: it had this effect in Stirlingshire after 1756–7, and potatoes were an important part of the Aberdeenshire food supply in the dearth of 1782–3.[35] In 1777 Hugo Arnot called potatoes the 'chief article of the poor' in Edinburgh[36] and many observations in the *Statistical account* indicate the extent to which their cultivation had spread. Thus at Abernyte in Perthshire, where oatmeal was still the 'staple provision among the labouring class, as in almost all Scotland', the minister noted two recent changes: pease and barleymeal were being replaced by wheat flour, and between August and April 'potatoes in a great measure are substituted for oatmeal'. At Bathgate, in West Lothian, potatoes constituted 'nearly two-thirds' of the food of a labouring man's family for nine months of the year. At Penport in Dumfriesshire the

---

[32] Sinclair, *Northern counties*, p. 82.
[33] Marshall, *Central Highlands*, p. 21; Sinclair, *Northern counties*, p. 82.
[34] *OSA*, vol. 12 (*Perths*), p. 755; Gibson and Smout, 'Scottish food and Scottish history', pp. 78–9, 81–2.
[35] T.C. Smout, *A history of the Scottish people, 1560–1830* (London, 1969), p. 270.
[36] H. Arnot, *The history of Edinburgh* (Edinburgh, 1779), p. 347.

main food of labourers was 'oatmeal and potatoes'. At Carnwarth in Lanarkshire potatoes made up 'a considerable part' of the food of the poor for 'more than six months in the year'. At Cupar in Fife potatoes had enabled the poor to enjoy 'a vast additional supply' of food.[37] At the close of the 1790s the Earl of Selkirk found in Galloway that 'in ordinary years' cottagers and their families, 'taken at an average of all years' ate daily 8 oz. of oatmeal, nearly 1 oz. of pot barley in their broth and from $1\frac{1}{2}$ to 2 lbs. of potatoes.[38] Clearly there was by then a partial substitution of a potato diet for an oatmeal diet, but except among the poorest Highlanders this was very incomplete: and the problems attached to keeping quantities of potatoes over the summer meant that at best they could only substitute for meal for part of the year.

Many reports from the 1790s and especially those from the *Statistical account* which were mainly published between 1791 and 1794, indicate a situation where gently rising incomes were providing a wider choice in everyday diet. Generally, however, these were reported only from favoured localities where agricultural improvement, proximity to a large town or the linen manufacture pushed up wage rates and earnings, and here present plenty was usually contrasted with past scarcity. At Inveresk and Dalmeny, on either side of Edinburgh, labourers had come to eat wheatbread and (at least in the latter) to drink tea, though they still had 'seldom any butcher meat'.[39] In lowland Perthshire the reporter for Longforgan could write of:

the lesser farmers and manufacturers ... have plenty of good wholesome food; many are supplied with butcher-meat at times; and both they and the labourers not only use oat-meal and potatoes, with the produce of their yards or gardens, but they frequently use wheaten bread, the consumption of which has increased much within these few years, and there are very few who have families, who do not use tea and its accompanyments.

This he also contrasted with the lot of farm servants who 'formerly lived with the family' and were given as their usual food 'broth made of kail and barley, or *grotts* (unhusked oats), without meat, and bannocks made of pease and bean meal'.[40]

At Crieff, in the same county, the scene of one of the famous 'trysts' where animals from the Highlands were sold to Lowland and English drovers, the minister wrote that 'ten times' more butcher's meat was sold locally than twenty years before; at Auchterarder nearby 'there is now four times the quantity of butcher-meat' used compared to a few years before. At Kilbrachan, one of the most prosperous Renfrewshire handloom-weaving villages the minister wrote that 'about 20 years ago tea and butcher's meat were very seldom tasted by any of the lower ranks. Now they are more or less used by people of every description.' The reporter for Cambuslang, outside Glasgow, said that in 1790 'a great deal of butcher's meat is consumed', and compared it with an earlier generation when only gentleman farmers killed their fat cattle. At Forfar, where between Hallow'-een and Christmas twenty-four beeves were killed in a week, previously 'a man who had bought a shilling's worth of beef or an ounce of tea would have concealed it from his

---

[37] *OSA*, vol. 11 (*Perths*), p. 25; vol. 2 (*Lothians*), p. 693; vol. 4 (*Dumfries*), p. 443; vol. 7 (*Lanarks*), p. 181; vol. 10 (*Fife*), p. 229. The minister of Cupar also called the potato 'the richest present which the new world ever made to Europe', vol. 10 (*Fife*), p. 226.

[38] J.M. Bumsted (ed.), *The collected writings of Lord Selkirk, 1799–1809* (Manitoba Record Society publications, vol. 7, 1984), pp. 90–1.   [39] *OSA*, vol. 2 (*Lothians*), pp. 317, 729.   [40] *OSA*, vol. 11 (*Perths*), p. 345.

neighbours like murder'. Similar reports of more meat-eating referred, for example, to farmers at Eccles (Berwickshire), Linton (Peeblesshire), Kilsyth (Stirlingshire), Twyne-holme and Kirk-Christ (Kirkcudbrightshire) and Fowlis Wester (Perthshire), to 'trades-men' in town at Kilsyth and in Kelso (Roxburghshire), and to 'labouring families' in Falkirk and Baldernock (Stirlingshire) and Strachur and Stralachan (Argyll). In a few places, like Dowally in Perthshire, Cupar in Fife, and Lochmaben in Dumfriesshire, this is related to new opportunities for the cottars to keep swine, itself no doubt facilitated by the cultivation of potatoes on the refuse of which they were fed. James Donaldson in 1794 considered that in the Carse of Gowrie in Perthshire 'pork and bacon constitute a greater proportion of the food of the poorer inhabitants here than in any other part of Scotland and there is scarcely a manufacturer, tradesman or labourer who does not feed one or two pigs every year, for the use of his family'.[41]

Nevertheless, it is evident that increased consumption of meat and other better quality or 'luxury' items was heavily circumscribed both by region and level of income. There is very little mention of improvement north of Angus, Perthshire and southern Argyll; indeed in parts of the north-east it was said that consumption of meat had fallen. Even in the south there were many parishes where diet for most people was still very narrow in its variety. Thus in as central a county as Fife it was reported from Kinglassie that 'the lower class use no animal food, but live on meal, potatoes, milk and small beer, with kail', from Largo that except at festivals 'they do not in general taste butcher-meat. Meagre broth, potatoes, cheese, butter in small quantities and a preparation of meal in different forms, make up their constant fare', and from Auchterderran that a family which spent £10.10s.7d. on grain foods and potatoes would spend nothing on meat, only 17s.4d. on milk and 12s.6d. on salt, cheese and butter.[42] In summary, there was no general return to meat-eating by most people within the eighteenth century or for a long time afterwards; tea-drinking did not become general until late in the nineteenth century; and wheat flour was not much consumed outside the towns and parts of the south-eastern countryside before the 1880s.[43]

What does a study of the surviving institutional diets from essentially 'sheltered' or 'special' situations add to these more general impressions of contemporaries? We have selected ten such diets for detailed analysis, falling within the time-span 1639 to 1790. Details are given in the appendix to this chapter. We disregarded certain others because the particulars provided, though interesting, were seriously incomplete, or because they were of a clearly upper-class character, analogous to the fare on the table of a landed gentleman rather than a reflection of common experience.[44]

The diets on which our analysis concentrates comprise two soldiers' diets (1639 and 1689), two orphanage diets (1649 and 1740), the latter indicating the level of the servants'

---

[41] *OSA*, vol. 12 (*Perths*), p. 291; vol. 11 (*Perths*), p. 50; vol. 7 (*Renfrew*), pp. 764, 793; vol. 13 (*Angus*), p. 256; vol. 3 (*Borders*), pp. 152, 807; vol. 9 (*Stirling*), pp. 500–1; vol. 5 (*Kirkcudbright*), p. 364; vol. 12 (*Perths*), p. 447; vol. 3 (*Borders*), p. 520; vol. 9 (*Stirling*), pp. 171, 302; vol. 8 (*Argyll*), p. 414; vol. 12 (*Perths*), p. 373; vol. 10 (*Fife*), p. 229; vol. 4 (*Dumfries*), p. 394. James Donaldson, *General view of the agriculture of the Carse of Gowrie in the County of Perth* (London, 1794), p. 30.   [42] *OSA*, vol. 10 (*Fife*), pp. 46–7, 499, 574.
[43] Levitt and Smout, *Scottish working class*, chapter 2.
[44] But we have examined some of these elsewhere: Gibson and Smout, 'Food and hierarchy', in Leneman (ed.), *Perspectives*.

nutrition as well as that of the orphans themselves, three diets of a pauper hospital (1740, 1780 and 1790), two diets of servants in landed households (1739 and 1743) and one of bursars at St Leonard's College in St Andrews in 1731, when it was a very much poorer place than it had been in the previous centuries and attracting bursars from fairly humble origins, though this diet is still much closer to the pattern of the upper orders of society than the others. Though the 1731 St Andrews' bursars' diet showed the highest percentage of calories obtained through eating meat of all these diets (19.2 per cent compared to a mean of 6.6 per cent), it was one third below the proportion in a diet planned 'for bursars and common servants' at St Andrews in 1597, when it had been 33.2 per cent (both these observations are biased upwards as they apply to 'meat days', and there were at the college normally three days in the week when only fish was provided, the nutritional value of which we cannot in these instances calculate).

Table 7.1 demonstrates very clearly the narrow range of foodstuffs shown by these institutional accounts as available to soldiers, servants, students and paupers in seventeenth- and eighteenth-century Scotland, as detailed inspection of tables 7.4–7.13 will confirm. 'Bread' almost always meant oatbread, 'meal' was oatmeal, 'meat' was generally either mutton or (less frequently) beef. Ale was the principal drink mentioned, and half-a-dozen other commodities cover everything. Overwhelmingly, these institutional diets were based on grain: on average, 82 per cent of the calories were grain derived, including the contribution of the ale brewed from barley, and 17 per cent animal-derived, of which merely 6.5 per cent was directly from meat. The qualitative impressions of travellers and contemporary Scottish observers are substantiated, especially when one considers that all the diets relate to sheltered positions where, if anything, diet is likely to have been above that of the most desperate in society. Soldiers have to march and to fight, servants to labour efficiently, and the health of bursars, orphans and elderly recipients of indoor poor relief must not be so undermined by their meagre fare that their charitable and municipal patrons are ashamed to meet them. A majority of the inmates of Glasgow Town Hospital would have been elderly women, who were the commonest recipients of indoor relief in pre-industrial Scotland.

Bearing that consideration in mind, the combined impressions of tables 7.1 and 7.2 (which provide a summary analysis of nutrient intake) are nevertheless of a decidedly well-fed group of people, with the exception of the Glasgow paupers in the difficult year of 1740. With respect to the intake of calories, no one else goes short except possibly the Edinburgh orphans, also in 1740: without knowing more about the age structure of the inmates even that is doubtful, and certainly the servants who looked after them were positively over-provided. The soldiers, too, were over-provided, though their diet was dull. Lady Grisell Baillie who ran the household at Mellerstane in 1743 might seem to be coming a little close to the margin with her employees, and she was indeed known to be a careful mistress unlikely to provide much over the odds. But many of her servants were adolescent girls with a calorie need well below the average level provided, and it is unlikely that anyone really went hungry round her table. We must, of course, emphasise again that these figures only apply to those in sheltered situations; outside, it is reasonable to suppose that, while the general structure of the diet would have been the same, variety would have been less and the quantities would not always have been so great. A servant who, as a teenager, came into Lady Grisell Baillie's household might well have found herself better provided for than ever she had been earlier as the child of a cottar, or ever was to be again as the wife of one.

When the nutritional components of the diet are considered, the scores are more than adequate for most requirements – for protein, iron, vitamin B_1, vitamin B_2 and niacin almost all the diets score well over the DHSS recommended daily intake, which are themselves above the *minimum* intake requirements for daily health. The secret lies very largely in the splendid nutritional qualities of oatmeal. Table 7.3 shows how the average daily quantity of oatmeal consumed, either directly or in the form of bread or biscuit, ran well below the 32 to 36 oz. mentioned by some of our commentators in other situations, presumably because these institutional diets were more varied by other foods. Nevertheless a mean of 20 oz. would provide 68 per cent of the calories, two-thirds of the calcium and all the iron, vitamin B_1 and niacin required by a very active adult male. If one adds to that something over two pints of ale also consumed, on average, according to the figures in table 7.3, the percentage of calories rises to 78 per cent, the proportion of calcium to about 87 per cent of the daily need, and of vitamin B_2 to nearly two-thirds. That was just on two staple ingredients. Numerous commentators spoke of the vigour of the Scottish people despite their plain fare. Thus Francis Douglas, writing in 1782 of the food of small farmers in the north-east, remarked that though flesh was rarely seen in their houses except at Christmas and Fasten Ev'n, they were strong and active, slept soundly, and lived long.[45] William Marshall spoke of the Highlanders' 'vegetable diet, with milk and its productions', based mainly on oatmeal, with bear and pease bannocks as supplementaries, along with potatoes: the strength of the diet was oatmeal, 'the most substantial of vegetable foods. In supporting severe bodily exercise, it is found to be much superior to wheat flour.'[46] Since there is no nutrional element in meat that is irreplaceable from other commodities, properly selected, we need not be surprised.

Nevertheless there appear to be three potential short-comings in this diet, quite apart from the fact that it might not be so generously enjoyed outside sheltered situations. One is a possible shortfall in calcium. The quantity provided might be significantly too little for growing children whose needs substantially exceed those of adults. Similarly for lactating mothers (who need 1,200 mg. a day) the normal provision in these diets of around 500 mg. of calcium would have been grossly inadequate unless the need was recognised and appropriate extra nourishment such as milk was provided. A second defect is the shortage of vitamin A, which would cause eye complaints (xerophthalmia) unless remedied by eating such foods as root vegetables (e.g., carrots) or certain animal offal. A third is the apparent absence in most of these diets of vitamin C, principally found in fresh vegetables: the consequence of this would be apparent in skin complaints, possibly even chronic scurvy. Did the seventeenth- and eighteenth-century Scottish diet really expose the population to these risks? Were there items which would have helped to

[45] F. Douglas, *A General description of the east coast of Scotland from Edinburgh to Cullen* (second edn, Aberdeen, 1826), pp. 138–9.   [46] W. Marshall, *Central Highlands*, p. 21.

reduce these risks but which did not appear in our institutional diets because they were essentially free goods, or for some other reason?

The biggest question concerns the availability and quality of milk in seventeenth- and most of eighteenth-century Scotland. One pint a day of unskimmed or 'sweet' milk would by itself have provided virtually all the calcium a growing child would need, and two pints would have sufficed for a lactating mother. Evidently, though, all that was often available was skimmed milk ('buttermilk') from which much of the vitamin A, most of the vitamin C, the fat and up to a third of the calorie value had been removed. Before the invention of the centrifuge in the nineteenth century, milk was allowed to separate under gravity, and when the cream was removed the liquid left would still contain more vitamins and fat than if it had been processed as skimmed today. In the *Statistical accounts* it was explicitly stated that buttermilk alone was available for instance at Dalmeny (West Lothian) and Longforgan (Perthshire), and it was surely implicit in areas where most of the milk was made into butter and cheese for the market, such as Ayrshire, Lanarkshire and Aberdeenshire.[47] In Aberdeenshire, James Anderson explained, the farm servants were given 'for drink whenever they like', the whey or buttermilk left over from making butter and cheese, and it was used instead of water in making 'pottage'.

Thus statements like 'every peasant possesses a milk cow' from Abernyte in Perthshire and Kemnay in Aberdeenshire do not necessarily imply that they enjoyed a regular supply of sweet milk, even allowing for the fact that in any case a cow would only give milk for about half the year.[48] A Highland cow 'was considered a good milker if she gave five pints a day' and rarely produced a calf 'oftener than every second year'.[49] Without milk, as the reporter from Ruthven (Angus) noted, the inhabitants could not enjoy porridge or sowens but 'were necessitated to have recourse to the wretched substitute of skrine, or unboiled flummery, prepared from the refuse of oatmeal soaked in water'.[50] Sir James Steuart writing of Lanarkshire in 1769 categorically stated that, although day labourers owned cows, 'no sweet milk is consumed in general' by their families.[51]

In the nineteenth century the use of milk was certainly widespread in the countryside. Robert Hutchison in his investigation into the diet of the Scottish rural labourer in 1869 found sweet milk in the diet of almost all of the families he surveyed: the same was true of 'milk' in the Poor Law investigation of 1843, though sometimes it was specified as buttermilk.[52] Robert Hope in the *General report* of 1814 shows that milk was equally common at the beginning of the nineteenth century – all the different types of labourers then had a quantity of milk with their food, though the amount varied from one district to another.[53]

[47] *OSA*, vol. 2 (*Lothians*), p. 729; vol. 11 (*Perths*), p. 345; James Anderson, *General view of the agriculture of Aberdeenshire* (London, 1794), p. 181. We are grateful to Dr R.Y. Thomson for pointing out the significance of skimmed milk to us.   [48] *OSA*, vol. 11 (*Perths*), p. 25; vol. 14 (*Aberdeen*), p. 534.

[49] I.F. Grant, 'The income of tenants on a Scotch open field farm in the eighteenth century', *Economic Journal*, vol. 34 (1924), pp. 83–9.   [50] *OSA*, vol. 13 (*Angus*), p. 610.   [51] Steuart, *Works*, vol. 5, p. 292.

[52] R. Hutchison, 'Report on the dietaries of Scotch agricultural labourers', *Transactions of the Highland and Agricultural Society of Scotland*, fourth series, vol. 2 (1869); Levitt and Smout, *Scottish working class*, pp. 25–6, 39, 48, 274.   [53] Hope, 'On rural economy', pp. 253–8.

The *Statistical account* and *General reports on agriculture* of the 1790s, often, as we have seen, refer to milk, though seldom without ambiguity as to its quality. Marshall, for example, stressed the general availability of 'milk' in the Central Highlands and Fullarton spoke of 'some milk' in the Ayrshire diet.[54] Occasionally it was plentiful: the bothy farm servants of Longforgan Perthshire were given three quarts of skimmed milk a day. Sometimes the entry implies its unimportance; a budget at Auchterderran in Fife for a working family only allowed 4d. a week for milk.[55]

Institutional diets, where they mention milk, generally do so in a way that implies its unimportance. Most strikingly, the orphans in Edinburgh in 1739 were allowed less than a third of a pint in a week, compared to over six pints of ale: admittedly they had a fair amount of cheese, but for growing children their intake of calcium appears to have been deficient by about one third. The children at the Merchant Maiden's Hospital, which was for orphans of a much higher class, were given milk for breakfast but ale for supper. The able-bodied pauper adults at 'St Pauls Work' in 1731 – essentially the Edinburgh workhouse – were given ale with their porridge but no milk at all; the sick poor tended in the Royal Infirmary at the same time got milk but no ale. In the Glasgow Town Hospital (essentially a pauper institution) the inmates got more ale than milk (much more in 1740), and most of the milk they had was skimmed. In Glasgow University in 1640, a quarter of a pint of milk a day was allowed compared to five times as much beer.[56]

All these, of course, are urban diets, and the critical difference may be between town and country. There is an implication in Lady Grisell Baillie's account book that at Mellerstane milk could, in the 1740s, on occasion, be substituted for ale, but that ale was normal; however Francis Douglas implied in 1782 that in the north-east milk was normal and ale the less usual substitute.[57]

Modern historians have themselves differed in their assessment of the place of milk in the eighteenth-century Scottish diet, Marjorie Plant and Maisie Steven, for example, stressing its abundance and accessibility,[58] and Henry Hamilton emphasising its scarcity. On the whole, the balance of evidence before the last part of the century may favour Hamilton, who, discussing the accounts of Monymusk between 1735 and 1750 noted that: 'Milk does not appear in the accounts, partly because it was produced locally and no market price had been placed on it, and partly because the amount consumed was very small. Dairy farming was as yet little practised, cows being valued for their powers of draught and for their meat.'[59] If this is the case, the spread of milk drinking in the Lowland countryside from around the middle of the eighteenth century could indeed be considered a significant improvement in diet over the seventeenth and earlier eighteenth

[54] Marshall, *Central Highlands*, p. 21; Fullarton, *Ayr*, pp. 11–12.
[55] *OSA*, vol. 11 (*Perths*), p. 345; vol. 10 (*Fife*), pp. 46–7.
[56] J. Richardson, 'Some notes on the early history of the Dean Orphan Hospital', *Book of the Old Edinburgh Club* (*BOEC*), vol. 27 (1949), pp. 162–3; E.S. Towill, 'The minutes of the Merchant Maiden Hospital', *BOEC*, vol. 29 (1956), pp. 34–5; M. Wood, 'St Paul's Work', *BOEC*, vol. 17 (1930), pp. 71–2; R. Thin, 'The old infirmary and earlier hospitals', *BOEC*, vol. 15 (1927), p. 158; *OSA*, vol. 7 (*Lanarks*), p. 316; Glasgow University archives, MS 26732–3.   [57] Douglas, *General description*, pp. 138–9.
[58] M. Plant, *The domestic life of Scotland in the eighteenth century* (Edinburgh, 1952), pp. 101–2; M. Steven, *The good Scots diet: what happened to it* (Aberdeen, 1985), pp. 37–45.
[59] H. Hamilton, *Life and labour on an Aberdeenshire estate, 1735–50* (Third Spalding Club, Aberdeen, 1945), pp. xiii–xiv.

centuries, even if much of it may, in the event, still have been skimmed milk (perhaps we should call it semi-skimmed) at the end of the century. One would expect its more widespread consumption to be reflected in the improved health of children and mothers through additional calcium, and thereby, among other things, to increase the average height of, at least, the rural population. There is no evidence of rickets in the eighteenth-century population, though in Britain this disease was always primarily caused not by low levels of calcium in the diet but by lack of vitamin D, which can be synthesised by the body if there is reasonable exposure to sunshine: rickets was characteristic of the late nineteenth-century slum dwellers in, for example, smoky cities such as Glasgow and Dundee.

The question of vitamin A and C deficiencies in our period is also important. Vitamin A occurs in sweet milk (though some would survive in semi-skimmed), in certain vegetables, and in animal offal. It has the additional quality of being able to be stored in the body over long periods, so that an occasional orgy of haggis or liver could provide most of what was needed with a little topping up from other sources. It is very likely that most Scots obtained enough that way even if it only appears occasionally in our surviving diets. At Gordon Castle, for instance, a little offal provided more than enough vitamin A, while at Mellerstane haggis or blood pudding was an alternative to cheese once a week. Probably most households, whether institutional or otherwise, made comparable use of such cheap and nutritious fare to vary their meals.

The only instance we have discovered that suggests poor health through vitamin A deficiency comes from the remote Argyll parish of Lismore, where Thomas Pennant found: 'The inhabitants in general are poor, and much troubled by sore eyes; and in Spring are afflicted with a costiveness that often proves fatal. At that season all their provisions are generally consumed; and they are forced to live on sheep's milk boiled, to which the distemper is attributed.'[60] The sore eyes may possibly have been xerophthalmia, an affliction caused by inadequate vitamin A in the diet; the costiveness, or constipation, was undoubtedly a consequence of a lack of roughage in the diet: presumably their supplies of meal did not stretch into the spring. Whatever the problems associated with such a diet, the inhabitants of Lismore clearly had little alternative. Their plight, however, was not typical of that of the majority of rural populations, even in the Highlands.

Whether the Scots suffered from vitamin C deficiency depends on how far they had access to fresh vegetables. Unfortunately, as with milk, it is very difficult to establish in detail their part in the Scottish diet. Of the accounts in the appendix only five mention the presence of vegetables: orphans at Hutchesone's Hospital in Glasgow in 1649 received one shilling's worth of kale per month; bursars at St Leonard's College, St Andrews, were provided with broth – presumably, though not necessarily, containing vegetables; orphans at the Dean Hospital, Edinburgh, in 1739–40 got both potatoes and kale in their broth; and the servants of Lady Grisell Baillie in 1743 received broth which, on some days at least, contained kale. In only two cases – the provision of potatoes to the orphans

---

[60] Pennant, *Tour . . . 1772*, part 2; there is bound with this in the 1776 edition a section called 'additions to the tour in Scotland, 1769', where this reference is found on p. 32.

in Edinburgh in 1740 and to the paupers in Glasgow in 1780 – is it possible to estimate the nutritional value of the vegetables provided.

Are we to presume from this that vegetables were not a common element in the Scottish diet? Or was the provision of vegetables excluded from the accounts only because they came from the institution or household's own gardens? St Leonard's College at St Andrews, for example, employed a gardener and though almost the only fruit or vegetables to enter the accounts were 'plumdames' (prunes to move the bowels) it is inconceivable that garden fare did not appear on the college table. It is, once again, to the comments of contemporary observers that we must turn.

Fynes Morrison declared in 1598 that the lower orders 'eate much red Colewort and Cabbage, but little freshe meate'.[61] James in 1615 spoke of the Scottish fondness for what we would now call Scotch broth with kale, as well as of dishes of cabbages and kale, some of them identifiable even today:

these they use minst and hole: the minst with butter and suggar they call champed long keale and the hole is layd in the platter with beefe; sometimes they stirre it into barley broth and that they call green Keale or Brusas another thing they have which they call stoue of the yonge blades of callords and beete leaves and other leaves of the garden which they boile with lams heads and entrails, all disht together with vinegar.[62]

Later travellers said much the same, Ray in the 1660s referring to 'much use of pottage made of cole-wort, which they call keal, sometimes broth of decorticated barley'.[63] In fact in the Lowlands of Scotland the cottager's kaleyard and the laird's garden – in the eighteenth century a point of pride to all improvers – were (or became) established features of the countryside. There is no reason at all to suppose that here, as long as most people had access either to a little holding or to the kitchen table of the better off, there would be any deprivation of vitamin C. References to the consumption of 'kale', or 'greens', occasionally of 'cabbage', occur over a wide area of Scotland in the *Statistical account* of the 1790s, ranging from Dalmeny (West Lothian), Tongland (Kirkcudbright-shire), Falkirk (Stirlingshire) and Kinglassie (Fife), up to Rayne and Udney in Aberdeenshire, Fordyce and St Fergus in Banff, Speymouth in Moray and Dingwall in Ross. Rayne, St Fergus and Speymouth also mention turnips.[64]

There is an interesting recipe given in the *Scots Magazine* for 1740 for 'hard time, when bread-corn was very dear and flesh-meat indifferent cheap', said to have been 'given to a poor weaver' by a 'soldier, who by his pay did thus feed his wife and three children fat and fair'. He took 2 lbs. of meat (salted or dried), and boiled it in 6 quarts of water with a quarter of a pound of carrots or parsnips, the same quantity of turnips or a few sliced potatoes, about 2 oz. of onions or leeks, and 'other greens according to discretion such as kail, cabbage, lettuce, sallary etc', the whole thickened with about a quart of oatmeal or some other grain such as knocked barley or pease. 'These well boiled together and seasoned with a little pepper or ginger, and salt, make an excellent well relished soup or

[61] Hume Brown (ed.), *Early travellers*, pp. 88–9.   [62] MacGillivray (ed.), 'Richard James', pp. 53–4.
[63] Hume Brown (ed.), *Early travellers*, p. 231.
[64] *OSA*, vol. 2 (*Lothians*), p. 729; vol. 5 (*Kirkcudbright*), p. 333; vol. 9 (*Stirling*), p. 302; vol. 10 (*Fife*), p. 499; vol. 15 (*Aberdeen*), pp. 480, 556; vol. 16 (*Banff, Moray, Nairn*), pp. 155, 415, 426, 675–6; vol. 17 (*Ross and Cromarty*), p. 366.

hodge-podge, which served the whole family a day, without bread or drink.' The total expense was said to be 7s.[65] Whether this was a genuine folk recipe or a genteel version of one (the pepper and ginger seem to lack authenticity), it probably indicates what went into broths of this sort, and especially the ingredients of famine-relief soups dispensed from charitable kitchens in the towns in the eighteenth century and later. It would certainly contain quantities of vitamin C.

On the other hand, the situation was much less obviously satisfactory in remote areas, and perhaps in many places before the general spread of potatoes as an ingredient in diet from the middle of the eighteenth century. Coleworts were included by Martin Martin in his list of the foodstuffs of Skye around 1700, and kaleyards are found in Highland rentals, as in seventeenth-century Breadalbane: but Highlanders had a reputation for 'the itch', as did the inhabitants of some remote communities in the southern hills, such as the lead miners of Wanlockhead in Dumfriesshire. Lead mining communities here and at Leadhills in Lanarkshire are known to have had a problem from scurvy. In the north a taste for vegetables other than potatoes was slow to develop, and as late as 1824 the traveller John Macculloch could say of the Highlanders that they never make a garden, and that 'you might as well seek for tropical fruits as for an onion, a leek, a turnip or a cabbage'.[66] To some extent, perhaps, the gap was met by wild foods. Martin Martin refers to the use of silverweed, several observers to nettles, and the *Statistical account* for Clunie in Perthshire lists watercress, sloes, hips and haws, wild raspberries, hazelnuts and crab apples.[67] Coastal parishes throughout Scotland could gather 'scurvy grass', a fleshy green plant growing in the sward or rocks behind the beach.

Nevertheless, it is from the northern half of Scotland that most late eighteenth-century reports come indicating the extent to which scurvy, the consequence of vitamin C deficiency, was a common disease. The *Statistical account* in the 1790s reveals something of its past and present extent. It had been rampant in St Fergus, Banff, until the introduction of greens and potatoes; it was reported in Arngask, Perthshire and in Blackford, also in Perthshire, where the minister recorded that 'Scurvy is the most predominant disease'. Just how predominant it could become, and how poorly understood its cause, is revealed by the comments of the minister of Forbes and Kearn, Aberdeenshire: 'of all diseases that prevail in this country, the scurvy is the most epidemical, and may justly be called the bane and scourge of human nature ... 9 out of 10 have it latent in the body'.[68]

Earlier in the century, even among the orphans of the burgess class at the Merchant Maiden Hospital in Edinburgh, scurvy had been endemic. The diet sheet shows a very generous fare but one fatally deficient in vegetables. For breakfast there was 'pottage and milk', for supper 'pottage and ale', or bread and ale. On Sunday there was an egg for dinner and meat for supper, on Monday and Friday, boiled meat and broth, on Tuesday and Thursday, roast meat, Wednesday, two eggs, Saturday, bread and butter. When

[65] *Scots Magazine*, vol. 2 (1740), appendix, p. 601.
[66] John Macculloch, *The Highlands and Western Isles of Scotland* (London 1824), vol. 2, p. 291.
[67] *OSA*, vol. 12 (*Perths*), pp. 230–1.
[68] *OSA*, vol. 16 (*Banff, Moray, Nairn*), p. 426; vol. 11 (*Perths*), p. 33; vol. 12 (*Perths*), p. 87; vol. 15 (*Aberdeen*), p. 139.

scurvy broke out the management blamed it on excessive pottage and substituted more bread and ale or bread and milk, having no inkling that a modicum of fresh greens would have cured the problem.[69]

Thus, whatever we might read of the presence of vegetables in the Scottish diet, it is clear that for a great many in the north or in other situations where there was no access to a kaleyard the amount consumed cannot have been sufficient to avoid vitamin C deficiency until the coming of the potato. As no more than 2 or 3 mg. of vitamin C is required daily to avoid scurvy, and as this would be supplied by less than an ounce of kale, this must mean that in such circumstances, to all intents and purposes, no greenstuffs were eaten.

Scottish diet for the commonality, then, in so far as it can be judged within the sheltered settings of institutions and upper-class households, appears to have been liberal in quantity and generally to have been of satisfactory or good nutritional content, with reservations about the quantity of calcium and especially of vitamin C available before the end of the eighteenth century.

How far such a relatively optimistic verdict might be true outside the sheltered situations is still an open question, and one that cannot be resolved by analysing expenditure patterns or diet sheets, since cottars, labourers and small tenants obviously kept no records. The evidence we have considered about standard allowances in the Lowlands, though, suggests that where these were paid the main difference between a sheltered and unsheltered situation is that a worker was more likely to live on oatmeal, with water or milk as a free good, and less likely to have ale, meat or cheese (except as part of a harvest diet). In effect, the increase in the average intake of oatmeal from about 20 oz. (in sheltered diets) to 30 oz. and more (in unsheltered ones) makes up for the deficit of other ingredients. The nutritional consequences of this would not have been at all disastrous: William Marshall was right when he said that oatmeal was 'probably the most substantial of vegetable foods', because 30 oz. would by itself provide all the calories needed to keep an active man hard at work, and meet DHSS recommended levels of protein, iron, vitamin B_1, and niacin. A small deficiency of calcium and vitamin B_2 would be made up even with a little milk: vitamin C would be completely absent unless some green vegetable such as kale was available, but that was also true in sheltered diets.

The remaining question, therefore, is the problem of diet when for one reason or another the standard allowance is not paid (because of unemployment, or because the person in question is a small tenant who has to raise his own food and it does not stretch so far), or where the allowance had to feed more than one person (as in a family where the wife and children are not earning). This we will explore in greater depth in the last chapter, but clearly such situations might be common at points in the life cycle. It is interesting that Sir John Sinclair thought that when a family lived on only about 75 or 80 per cent of the traditional allowances, they were lacking in 'spirit or strength for labour', and there must have been many such.[70] There was also the problem of dearths, and of populations like those of much of the Hebrides where grain growing was difficult and

[69] Towill, 'Merchant Maiden hospital', pp. 34–5.   [70] Sinclair, *Northern counties*, p. 82.

standard allowances simply did not apply. Though observers in the 1790s referred to recent improvements in diet for at least some of the population, few considered that labouring populations as a whole had anything but a struggle to make ends meet. The minister at Dalmeny in West Lothian, for instance, thought that the population was still less adequately nourished than the English lower classes.[71]

Nevertheless, even for the poor, the qualities of oatmeal as a staple of life ensured that the Scots as a nation were less likely to suffer from chronic malnutrition than many others in the early modern world. Indeed, as a diet full of roughage and other good nutritional qualities, some historians have considered the traditional Scottish fare, for all its narrow range and daunting volumes, as superior to that of the present day.[72] Some evidence that at least it was superior to that of most other parts of the United Kingdom at the start of the nineteenth century may be found in Floud, Wachter and Gregory's recent study of British height. Since stature is, to a degree, an indication of nutritional health in children and their mothers, it is interesting to see that Scottish males before 1850 appear to have been the highest of those in any of the British regions: 'Our average rural Scotsman turning 20 around 1837 is nine-tenths of an inch taller than our average Londoner. . . . If Sherlock Holmes had been forced to guess, at the start of his career, which of two suspects was a Scots husbandman and which a London hodcarrier, he would have had a two-to-one chance of guessing right on the basis of height alone.'[73] It is quite possible that earlier, this differential had been even more striking: Scottish-born recruits to the army in America who had been born in the period 1740–60 averaged almost an inch and a half taller in height than their English-born equivalents.[74] However, 'the significant Scottish advantage in height over the rest of the United Kingdom, so apparent in the eighteenth century, was eroded during the nineteenth century and had disappeared entirely in the twentieth':[75] that they are now almost the shortest (though still taller than their forefathers) must indicate a major change in relative nutritional standards. In money earnings the Scots were not by any means towards the top of the league in 1800: but in terms of the healthy quality of their food, they evidently were.

INTRODUCTION TO TABLES 7.1–7.13

Information on the diet of the Scottish people in the seventeenth and eighteenth centuries can be drawn from two types of contemporary evidence. On the one hand are the rather general, but nevertheless invaluable, descriptions handed down to us by Scottish commentators and foreign visitors alike. These we discuss at length in the text. In many instances they provide some broad indication of the quality and quantity of the principal foodstuffs which were consumed, but it is never possible to establish the full nutritional value of the diets described. For that we must turn to institutional accounts

---

[71] *OSA*, vol. 2 (*Lothians*), p. 729.   [72] E.g., Steven, *The good Scots diet*.
[73] R. Floud, K. Wachter and A. Gregory, *Height, health and history: nutritional status in the United Kingdom, 1750–1890* (Cambridge, 1990), p. 73.   [74] *Ibid.*, p. 193.   [75] *Ibid.*, p. 275.

which record in more precise detail the food which was provided to a known number of people. These accounts refer, of course, to conditions in sheltered situations and as such are unlikely fully to reflect the experience of the vast majority of Scots. Nevertheless, real light can be cast on diet if a detailed analysis of these accounts is taken in conjunction with more general observations.

The following tables, which summarise our analysis of ten such institutional accounts, present tentative estimates of overall nutritional value. We have used only the most detailed and straightforward accounts available, but in each case serious problems emerge in establishing the nutritional value of the particular foodstuffs referred to. These fall into three categories.

First, there is the ever-present question of the weights and measures used to describe the quantity of food that was being consumed. It is not always clear whether Scottish troy, tron, or English weight was being used. Nor can one rest completely comfortably with the assumption (which we nevertheless have made) that national standards were always employed to measure grain quantities. In view of this, tables 7.4–7.13, which present our most detailed calculations with respect to each of the diets we have chosen, commence with as full a description of the diet as is possible in the space available, as well as with a reference to the source from which each has been drawn. This is followed by our interpretation (still in terms of the system of measurement employed in the original account) of what that might have meant in terms of an individual's daily or weekly diet. In that interpretation we use square brackets to indicate where we have had to make some assumptions regarding the system of measurement (usually of weight) employed with respect to each of the items listed in the diet. On the basis of such assumptions, and in the light of the general observations regarding the weights and measures used in Scotland during the seventeenth and eighteenth centuries discussed in appendix I, we have calculated in terms of modern avoirdupois weight how much food was being provided. Any specific interpretative problems are then discussed in footnotes to the appropriate tables.

Second, there is the problem of items which were not given a specific weight or quantity, but were rather left in terms of a certain number of 'pieces of meat', herrings, eggs, chickens or the like. Here we have used a series of commonsense assumptions. Fortunately, even if some of these assumptions turn out to be rather wide of the truth, the dietary contribution made by those items tends to be slight in comparison to the oatmeal and ale, which stand at the very heart of all of these diets.

Finally, there is the difficulty of relating early modern foodstuffs to modern ones which have been subjected to nutritional analysis. This is no trivial matter, for although we have been able to use the detailed statistics on a vast range of foodstuffs in A.A. Paul and D.A.T. Southgate's *McCance and Widdowson's The composition of foods* (4th revised edn., HMSO, London, 1978), it must be emphasised that the grains, meats and other items analysed in the twentieth century are likely to have been somewhat different, in nutritional terms, to those available in early modern Scotland. For instance, we know that Scottish soldiers in 1639 were being provided with 30 fluid ounces of ale each day, but we can have little idea how comparable it would have been to the ales analysed by

Paul and Southgate. The nature of the ale provided in our various diets poses, in fact, a particularly intractable problem, as early modern descriptions range from those which suggest that it was a thick highly nutritious and potent brew to those which suggest that it was a thin watery concoction: and no doubt this variation reflected contemporary realities. As ale comprised a significant element in virtually all of the diets, this is an important question. The remarkable quantities which were being consumed have inclined us to suppose that it was not normally very strong.

Other assumptions must also be made. We use Paul and Southgate's nutritional analysis for oatmeal as given, though we must acknowledge that two centuries of crop selection might have altered, in ways we cannot begin to estimate, its nutritional value. Even different methods of milling will have had an effect. Similarly, our estimates of the nutritional value of various types of meat, although modified in the light of what is known regarding the fat content of pre-improvement cattle and sheep (discussed in A.J.S. Gibson, 'The size and weight of cattle and sheep in early modern Scotland', *Agricultural History Review*, vol. 36, 1988, pp. 162–71), must constitute at best a general estimate. Finally, many of the foodstuffs analysed in *The composition of foods* were cooked by methods unknown in early modern Scotland. To take a particularly extreme example, relying upon figures for 'Skate, fried in batter', is clearly unsatisfactory, given that the skate provided at Gordon Castle in 1739 would probably have been served up in some form of broth; but those are the only figures we have. It is fortunate that skate comprised only a minute proportion of the overall diet at Gordon Castle.

In the note below we have described the assumptions to convert the various descriptions of the foodstuffs in our accounts into specific quantities (in modern avoirdupois weight) of the modern foods analysed by Paul and Southgate, though we have not found space to justify all of them. Tables 7.1–7.13 must clearly be viewed with caution, for although we are satisfied that they provide a useful guide to the nutritional value of known diets, we claim no more of them than that.

Assumptions used in dietary calculations

In establishing the nutritional value of our diets we have followed the methods described in the general introduction to *The composition of foods*. Particular note should be made of the fact that figures for vitimin A and niacin (nicotinic acid) are of their total equivalents, calculated as described on pp. 12–13 of *The composition of foods*.

We have chosen not to include in the tables any analysis or discussion of the 'quality' of the protein provided by each diet even though the balance of amino acids to a large extent determines the proportion of the protein that will actually be available for metabolic functions. (For a full discussion, see *Protein requirements*, World Health Organisation technical reports series, no. 301, Geneva, 1965.) This becomes an important factor only with respect to very restricted diets, particularly those based on wheat, in which perhaps as little as 50 per cent of the protein present may actually be available. In fact, the oatmeal which is at the heart of all of our diets provides a remarkably good balance of amino acids. Thus even the most restricted diet, that of

Scottish soldiers in 1639, returns a protein score of 70.4 (the limiting amino acid being lysine). With some 70 per cent of protein thus being available, this is comparable to the level which would be expected from a good mixed diet. Direct comparisons with the DHSS recommendations concerning protein consumption, which assume a protein score of 70 or more, may thus be made.

For those many foodstuffs which are given precise weights, the only assumption we need to make is which modern food analysed in *The composition of foods* is to be used for the purpose of estimating the nutritional value of the diet. We have taken the following equivalences, in each case noting the entry number in *The composition of foods*:

Wheatbread	wholemeal bread (30).
Ale	draught mild (894).
Barley	pearl barley, boiled (2).
Oatmeal	oatmeal, raw (17).
Brandy	spirits, 90 per cent proof (919).
Cheese	cheese, cheddar type (152).
Butter	butter, salted (140).
Potatoes	old potatoes, boiled (640).
Milk	whole milk, fresh, summer (124).
Sweet milk	whole milk, fresh, summer (124).
Butter milk	skimmed milk, fresh (131).
Peasemeal	dried peas, raw (626).
Groats	oatmeal, raw (17).

There are also a number of items referred to in the accounts which require an estimate of the amount of edible matter provided as well as an assumption regarding their modern food equivalent. Thus:

Chickens	2 lbs. cooked meat per bird; chicken, roast, with meat and skin (322).
Capons	2 lbs. of cooked meat per bird; chicken, roast, with meat and skin (322).
Fowls	5 lbs. of cooked meat per bird; chicken, roast, with meat and skin (322).
Poultry	5 lbs. of cooked meat per bird; chicken, roast, with meat and skin (322).
Geese	10 lbs. of cooked meat per bird; goose, roast, meat only (331).
Turkeys	12 lbs. of cooked meat per bird; turkey, roast, with meat and skin (344).
Cod	8 lbs. cooked flesh per fish; cod, baked (440).
Haddock	8 oz. cooked flesh per fish; haddock, smoked (456).
Herring	4 oz. cooked flesh per fish; herring, grilled (485).
Skate	2 lbs. cooked flesh per fish; skate, fried in batter (514).
Eggs	2 oz. each; eggs, boiled (169).
Venison	4 lbs. cooked meat each piece; venison, haunch, roast (353).

Finally, there are those elements of the diet referred to in the accounts for which there are no obviously equivalent modern foods. It is thus necessary to make further assumptions in order to establish their approximate nutritional value.

Oatbread	80 per cent by weight as raw oatmeal (17).
Beef	a carcase is taken to provide 206 lbs. of lean meat and 38 lbs. of edible fat. This ratio is the basis of our estimate of the nutritional value of the meat consumed, using figures from *The composition of foods* for raw lean beef (237) and raw beef fat (240). A piece we take to comprise 8 lbs. of meat and fat in the same proportions as above.
Mutton	a carcase is taken to provide 20 lbs. of lean meat and 3.5 lbs. of edible fat. Using the same principle as for beef, we have thus estimated the nutritional value of mutton using raw lean lamb (266) and raw lamb fat (269). We take there to have been 8 pieces per carcase.
Offal	a piece we reckon to have weighed 7 lbs. once cooked. For the purpose of establishing its approximate nutritional value we have presumed it to have comprised equal quantities of fried lamb kidney (364), stewed ox kidney (367), fried calf liver (372), stewed ox liver (378), fried sweetbreads (385) and steamed sheep tongue (388).

Table 7.1 Selected Scottish diets: per cent of calories provided by different foods

	Bread & meal, etc.[1]	Potatoes	Ale	Meat	Fish	Cheese	Butter	Eggs	Milk
Scottish soldiers, 1639	93.7	-	6.3	-	-	-	-	-	-
Orphans, Glasgow, 1649	82.2	-	4.7	5.6	7.5	-	-	-	-
Scottish soldiers, circa 1689[2]	66.5	-	6.5	-	-	12.8	11.7	-	-
Bursars, St Andrews, 1731[3]	56.9	-	14.7	19.7	-	-	-	8.6	-
Servants, Gordon Castle, 1739	62.3	-	19.2	10.2	0.7	-	7.6	Tr.	-
Orphanage, Edinburgh, 1739–40	75.1	3.5	6.7	8.2	3.3	2.3	-	-	0.8
Paupers, Glasgow, 1740	79.0	-	4.7	5.0	2.5	3.2	2.8	0.3	2.4
Servants, Mellerstane, circa 1743	73.4	-	12.4	8.4	5.0	-	-	0.9	-
Paupers, Glasgow, 1780	75.5	1.7	4.1	4.0	1.2	4.1	4.2	1.2	4.0
Paupers, Glasgow, 1790	75.9	2.0	3.3	4.2	1.2	4.8	4.2	0.9	3.5
Mean	74.1	0.7	8.3	6.5	2.1	2.7	3.1	1.2	1.1

1 Always oatbread or oatmeal except in the soldiers' diet of 1639 when 28 per cent was wheatbread: small quantities (2.5 per cent or less of total Kcal) of pot barley are included in this heading for the two orphanage diets and the Mellerstane diet.

2 Brandy, amounting to 2.4 per cent of Kcal, is omitted from the columns.

3 Meat days only.

Tr. Trace in diet.

Table 7.2 *Selected Scottish diets: daily nutrient intakes*

	Energy kcal	Protein g.	Fat g.	Carbo-hydrate g.	Calcium mg.	Iron mg.	Vit. A µg.	Vit. B_1 mg.	Vit. B_2 mg.	Niacin mg.	Vit. C mg.
Scottish soldiers, 1639 (active adult males)	3,358	111	58	599	481	34	Tr.	16.5	1.1	52	0.0
Orphans, Glasgow, 1649 (children under 14)	3,001	116	80	457	439	28	56	3.2	1.2	41	Tr.
Scottish soldiers, circa 1689 (active adult males)	4,885	144	186	611	1,819	34	1,396	4.1	2.0	45	Tr.
Bursars, St Andrews, 1731 (boys, 14–16)	2,895	114	98	288	583	22	238	11.1	2.3	47	0.0
Servants, Gordon Castle, 1739 (active adults, both sexes)	3,226	105	90	358	649	26	797	13.0	1.7	42	0.9
Orphans, Edinburgh, 1739–40 (children under 14)	1,930	71	52	292	380	16	70	1.9	0.9	27	7.7
Orphanage servants, Edinburgh, 1739–40 (active adults, both sexes)	3,859	142	103	584	760	33	139	3.7	1.7	53	15.3
Paupers, Glasgow, 1740 (elderly adults)	1,649	61	47	247	450	14	143	1.7	0.9	20	2.1
Servants, Mellerstane, circa 1743 (active adults and adolescents)	2,648	101	70	369	424	23	54	2.4	1.4	39	Tr.
Paupers, Glasgow, 1780 (elderly adults)	2,300	86	67	345	764	19	286	2.3	1.4	27	8.0
Paupers, Glasgow, 1790 (elderly adults)	1,991	74	60	303	628	17	258	2.0	1.1	24	7.7
DHSS recommended daily intake of nutrients, 1979											
Very active adult men	3,350	84			500	10	750	1.3	1.6	18	30
Very active adult women	2,500	62			500	12	750	1.0	1.3	15	30
Boys aged 14	2,640	66			700	12	725	1.1	1.4	16	25
Girls aged 14	2,150	53			700	12	725	0.9	1.4	16	25
Women aged 56–74, sedentary	1,900	47			500	10	750	0.8	1.3	15	30

Table 7.3 *Selected Scottish diets: daily consumption of oatmeal and ale*

	Oatmeal [1] (oz. Av.)	Ale (Imperial pints)
Scottish soldiers, 1639	17.4	1.50
Orphans, Glasgow, 1649	19.9	1.00
Bursars, Aberdeen, 1650 [2]	18.6	0.75
Scottish soldiers, circa 1689	28.6	2.25
Bursars, St Andrews, 1731	14.5	3.00
Servants, Gordon Castle, 1739	22.1	4.37
Servants, Orphanage, Edinburgh, 1739–40	24.6	1.82
Paupers, Glasgow, 1740	10.5	0.55
Servants, Mellerstane, circa 1743	16.4	2.25
Paupers, Glasgow, 1780	13.8	0.66
Paupers, Glasgow, 1790	12.2	0.46
Mean (excluding paupers)	20.3	2.12
Mean (overall)	18.1	1.69

1   This column presents the amount of oatmeal consumed either directly or in the form of oatbread or oat biscuit. When we only have figures for the weight of bread or biscuit (as described in tables 7.4–7.13), we have converted these to oatmeal equivalents on the understanding that 80 per cent by weight of the bread or biscuit would have been oatmeal.

2   Although accounts describing the bursars' diet at Aberdeen University in 1640 are not detailed enough for us to estimate its full nutritional value, the amount of oatbread and ale which was provided is clearly stated. The 'Liber Rationum Collegi Aberdonensis, 1579–1653' (Aberdeen University Library, Mss. K.2) for May 1650 (reprinted in Cosmo Innes, *Fasti Aberdonensis,* Spalding Club, 1854, pp. 585–99) records that each bursar was allowed 2 loaves of oatbread and a quarter of a Scots pint of ale per day. As it was reported in 1652 that 240 loaves of bursar bread were to be baked from each boll of oatmeal, we may infer that each loaf would have contained 9.3 oz. avoirdupois.

Table 7.4 *Scottish soldiers: June 1639*

[G. M. Paul, 'Fragment of the diary of Sir Archibald Johnston, Lord Warriston, May 21 – June 25, 1639',
  Scottish History Society, vol. 26 (Edinburgh, 1896), p. 55.]

> to everie souldier two pound weight of aite bread in the day and
> twentie eight ounce of wheat bread ane pynt of aile in the day.

This diet was almost certainly meant to support two men; a soldier and his 'follower'. If so, both would have been
very active males, and each would have received, daily:

		Avoirdupois
Oatbread	1 lb. [tron]	21.76 oz.
Wheatbread	14 oz. [tron]	19.04 oz.
Ale	0.5 pints Scots	30.00 fl. oz.

This would have provided, for very active adult males, the following daily diet:

	Energy	Protein	Fat	Carbo-hydrate	Calcium	Iron	Vit.A	Vit.B$_1$	Vit.B$_2$	Niacin	Vit.C
	Kcal	g.	g.	g.	mg.	mg.	μg.	mg.	mg.	mg.	mg.
Oatbread	1,978.9	61.2	43.0	359.3	271.5	20.2	0.0	2.4	0.40	18.9	0.0
Wheatbread	1,166.0	47.6	14.7	225.6	124.1	13.5	0.0	14.1	0.38	30.3	0.0
Ale	213.0	1.8	Tr	13.8	85.2	Tr	Tr	Tr	0.30	2.7	0.0
Total	3,357.9	110.6	57.7	598.7	480.8	33.7	Tr	16.5	1.08	51.9	0.0

Table 7.5   *Orphans: Hutchesones hospital, Glasgow, 1649*

[J.D. Marwick, 'Orders set down by the committee for planting the poor in Hutchesones Hospital,
1 December 1649', *Extracts from the records of the burgh of Glasgow, 1630–1662* (Glasgow, 1881), pp. 178–9]

For the Young Ones

It is thought expedient that none bot ophantir be thair, gif they can be had, and necessar they eitt and bed within the hous.

Item, it is thought that the fyre in the hous quhair the schoole now is may suffice thame all, and that twa rowmes and twa beds in each of thame may suffice, and each of tham to have ane peck of meill weiklie.

Item, they must have one quha will mak thai meit and wash thair cloathes, quha must have food and rayment, and thairfor at leist must have 4s. per diem, and that scho be tain speciall notice of to be trustie.

Item, they must have once eache day ane herring to ilk ane of thame ewerie vther nicht. It is thought they wald have kaill, and so for this must have twa peckis of grottis in the monethe and a schilling in that tyme for the kaill and also a leg of beife in the monthe.

Item, it is thought meit that they be small drink browne to theme, about twelfe pennies the pynt, by some neichbour, quhairof they must have four pyntis eache day.

Elsewhere (William H. Hill, *History of Hospital and School in Glasgow founded by George and Thomas Hutcheson,* Glasgow, 1881, pp. 207, 250) it is stated that there were to be twelve children at the school. If so, the above account appears to imply that each child was to receive:

		Avoirdupois
Oatmeal	1 peck weekly	19.9 oz.
Herring	1 every other day	4.0 oz.
Groats	2 pecks a month shared between the 12 children	1.8 oz.
Beef	1 leg a month shared between the 12 children	2.9 oz.
Ale	4 pints Scots a day shared between the 12 children	20.0 fl. oz.

(In addition to which there was a shilling's worth of kaill per person per month.)

This would have provided for each child the following daily diet:

	Energy	Protein	Fat	Carbo-hydrate	Calcium	Iron	Vit.A	Vit.B$_1$	Vit.B$_2$	Niacin	Vit.C
	Kcal	g.	g.	g.	mg.	mg.	μg.	mg.	mg.	mg.	mg.
Oatmeal	2,261.7	70.0	49.1	410.6	310.2	23.1	0.0	2.8	0.60	21.5	0.0
Groats	204.6	6.3	4.4	37.1	28.1	2.1	0.0	0.3	0.05	1.9	0.0
Beef	167.0	15.2	11.8	0.0	6.1	1.6	Tr	0.1	0.17	6.9	0.0
Herring	225.7	23.1	14.8	0.0	37.4	1.1	55.6	Tr	0.20	8.8	Tr
Ale	142.0	1.2	Tr	9.2	56.8	Tr	Tr	Tr	0.20	1.8	0.0
Total	3,001.0	115.8	80.1	456.9	438.6	27.9	55.6	3.2	1.22	40.9	Tr

The addition of some kaill to the diet would certainly have contributed to the vitamin A and C intake. To what extent the obvious deficiency in these two vitamins would have been reduced would depend on the amount of kaill eaten, and this we do not know.

Table 7.6 *Scottish soldiers: circa 1689*

[SRO, GD 26/9/525, 'A calculation of the provisions necessary for 100 men for a month, circa 1689'.]

To each man 2 pecks of meal a week	Inde monthly at 30 days	50 bolls
To each man a pound biscuit a day	Inde	3,000 weight
To each man half pound cheese a day	Inde	93 stan 12 lb.
To each man a quarter pound butter	Inde	46 stan 14 lb.
To each 3 choppins ale a day	Inde	551 gallons 4 pints
To each a gill brandy		187 pints

It is almost certain that this was actually meant to provide for 100 soldiers and their followers, in total 200 men. It has been necessary to presume that the biscuit was oat biscuit and that it was nutritionally equivalent to oatbread. Thus each man would have received, daily:

		Avoirdupois
Oatmeal	18.29 oz. [Scottish troy]	19.90 oz.
Oat biscuit	8.0 oz. [tron]	10.88 oz.
Cheese	4.0 oz. [tron]	5.44 oz.
Butter	2.0 oz. [tron]	2.72 oz.
Ale	0.75 pints Scots	45.00 fl. oz.
Brandy	0.0625 pints Scots	1.88 fl. oz.

This would have provided, for very active adult males, the following daily diet:

	Energy	Protein	Fat	Carbo-hydrate	Calcium	Iron	Vit.A	Vit.B$_1$	Vit.B$_2$	Niacin	Vit.C
	Kcal	g.	g.	g.	mg.	mg.	μg.	mg.	mg.	mg.	mg.
Oatmeal	2,261.7	70.0	49.1	410.6	310.2	23.1	0.0	2.8	0.60	21.5	0.0
Oat biscuit	989.4	30.6	21.5	179.7	135.7	10.1	0.0	1.2	0.20	9.4	0.0
Cheese	626.1	40.1	51.7	Tr	1,233.8	0.6	636.2	0.1	0.76	9.6	0.0
Butter	570.6	0.3	63.2	Tr	11.6	0.1	759.5	Tr	Tr	0.1	Tr
Ale	319.5	2.7	Tr	20.7	127.8	Tr	Tr	Tr	0.45	4.1	0.0
Brandy	118.1	Tr	Tr	Tr	Tr	Tr	0.0	0.0	0.00	0.0	0.0
Total	4,885.4	143.7	185.5	611.0	1,819.1	33.9	1,395.7	4.1	2.01	44.7	Tr

Table 7.7   *Bursars: St Leonard's College, St Andrews, Fife, 1731*

['Ane account of the diet of the bursars of St Leonards College, 1731', St Andrews University Mss.]

Breakfast is one third of a scon and a mutchkin of ale.

Dinner is one half scon, mutchkin and a half of ale, and four bursars have ane ashet of broth and a portion of beef, mutton, veal or hens, and when they get fish they have them in ashets proportionately and in place of broth they have soppes.

Supper, each gets half a scon and one and a half mutchkins of ale and three eggs or the equivalent.

Sabbath, additional food is at supper broth and fresh meat and half scon of bread and one a half mutchkins of ale.

Elsewhere this account states that each 'scon' weighs 10 oz., and that the ordinary leg of mutton or veal comprised two portions and a hen one portion.

We cannot, unfortunately, provide a full nutritional account of this diet. We do not know how much fish was provided, how large a portion of beef was, or even how often the various alternatives were provided. However, some indication of the nutritional value of this diet can be obtained for those weekdays when a leg of mutton was provided. This we estimate to have comprised an eighth part of a carcase providing, as discussed in the introduction to these tables, 23.5 lbs. of flesh. On such days, therefore, assuming the scones to have been of oatbread (or at least its nutritional equivalent), each bursar would have received:

		Avoirdupois
Oatbread	13.33 oz. [tron] each	18.1 oz.
Ale	4 mutchkins	60.0 fl. oz.
Mutton	1/32 part of a carcase	11.8 oz.
Eggs	3	6.0 oz.

This would have provided, for boys of 14–16 years old, the following daily diet:

	Energy	Protein	Fat	Carbo-hydrate	Calcium	Iron	Vit.A	Vit.B$_1$	Vit.B$_2$	Niacin	Vit.C
	Kcal	g.	g.	g.	mg.	mg.	µg.	mg.	mg.	mg.	mg.
Oatbread	1,648.7	44.4	35.9	260.5	307.5	14.7	0.0	10.7	0.36	13.6	0.0
Ale	426.0	3.6	Tr	27.6	170.4	Tr	Tr	Tr	0.60	5.4	0.0
Mutton	570.5	44.7	43.6	0.0	16.8	3.5	Tr	0.3	0.59	21.7	0.0
Egg	250.0	20.9	18.5	Tr	88.4	3.4	238.1	0.1	0.78	6.2	0.0
Total	2,895.2	113.6	98.0	288.1	583.1	21.6	238.1	11.1	2.33	46.9	0.0

Table 7.8   *Servants: Gordon Castle, Banffshire, January – March 1739*

[SRO, GD 44/52/131/7–11, 'Gordon Castle household accounts, 1739–41' (printed in B. Horn, 'The domestic life of a Duke: Cosmo George, 3rd Duke of Gordon', unpublished Ph.D. thesis, Edinburgh, 1977, Tables 22 and 23).]

The household accounts show the provisions which were purchased in the months of January, February and March of 1739 (a total of 90 days). Although it is not stated explicitly how many servants were present during this period, in the Gordon castle account of 1743 (SRO, GD 44/52/133/3) it is revealed that each servant was to receive 1.5 loaves of bread and 1.5 pints of ale daily. If so, given that only servants were in residence at the time, the fact that 2,335 loaves and 2,226 pints were consumed implies that an average of 16 or 17 people were present.

Assuming that what was purchased was actually consumed, knowing from internal evidence that 192 loaves of bread were baked from each boll of oatmeal, and by adopting some common sense estimates of the size of the fowls, turkeys, geese and other items referred to in the accounts (as discussed in the introduction to these tables), it is possible to quantify the approximate nutritional value of the diet allowed to servants at Gordon Castle in early 1739.

Provisions purchased during the 90-day period for an average of 17 servants		Daily provision per person (Avoirdupois)
Oatbread	2,335 loaves	22.10 oz.
Ale	2,226 pints Scots	87.30 fl. oz.
Chickens	21 fowls	1.10 oz.
Beef	36 pieces	3.01 oz.
Butter	82 pounds [tron]	1.17 oz.
Haddocks	166.75	0.88 oz.
Turkeys	15	1.88 oz.
Geese	3	0.31 oz.
Offal	5 pieces	0.37 oz.
Venison	4 pieces	0.30 oz.
Eggs	18	0.02 oz.
Cod	2	0.10 oz.
Skate	1	0.02 oz.

This would have provided, for very active male and female adults and adolescents, the following daily diet:

	Energy	Protein	Fat	Carbo-hydrate	Calcium	Iron	Vit.A	Vit.B$_1$	Vit.B$_2$	Niacin	Vit.C
	Kcal	g.	g.	g.	mg.	mg.	μg.	mg.	mg.	mg.	mg.
Oatbread	2,009.8	54.1	43.8	317.6	374.8	17.9	0.0	13.0	0.44	16.6	0.0
Ale	619.8	5.2	Tr	40.2	247.9	Tr	Tr	Tr	0.87	7.9	0.0
Fowls	67.4	7.1	4.4	0.0	2.8	0.3	Tr	Tr	Tr	1.3	0.0
Beef	131.8	12.0	9.3	0.0	4.8	6.1	Tr	Tr	0.14	5.5	0.0
Butter	245.5	0.1	27.2	Tr	5.0	0.1	326.7	Tr	Tr	Tr	Tr
Haddock	18.2	4.2	0.2	0.0	4.4	0.2	Tr	Tr	Tr	1.8	0.0
Turkey	74.6	15.4	1.4	0.0	4.8	0.5	Tr	Tr	0.11	7.4	0.0
Goose	28.0	2.6	2.0	0.0	0.9	0.4	Tr	Tr	Tr	0.5	Tr
Offal	15.9	1.7	0.9	0.2	1.2	0.5	469.9	Tr	0.16	0.9	0.9
Venison	9.8	1.7	0.3	0.0	1.4	0.4	Tr	Tr	Tr	0.3	0.0
Eggs	0.8	0.1	0.1	Tr	0.3	Tr	0.8	Tr	Tr	Tr	0.0
Cod	3.7	0.9	Tr	0.0	0.7	Tr	Tr	Tr	Tr	0.2	0.0
Skate	1.1	0.1	0.1	Tr	0.3	Tr	Tr	Tr	Tr	Tr	Tr
Total	3,226.4	105.2	89.7	358.0	649.3	26.4	797.4	13.0	1.72	42.4	0.9

Table 7.9 *Orphans and servants: Dean Orphanage, Edinburgh, 1739–40*

[SRO, GD 1/140/16/(1), 'Scheme of maintenance of the Orphans Hospital from 1 November 1739 to
1 February, 1740'.]

This detailed 'scheme of maintenance' provides an account of the food to be provided for the 66 children and
7 servants at the orphanage at each meal during the course of a week. This weekly menu was to be repeated
throughout the quarter. Servants were allocated a double ration of the diet allowed for the orphans. All items in the
diet were given precise measures except the 'flesh and broth' which was provided three days a week, the 'fleshless
kaill' which was provided on a further three days, and the butter provided to make the bread more palatable. There
is, however, a gloss stating that six salted cows, 10 sheep, and 14 stone of salted butter were consumed in the
quarter. Making a series of assumptions (discussed in the introduction to these tables) it is possible to estimate the
approximate nutritional value of the diet allowed to servants at the Dean Orphanage:

	Provided weekly for each servant	Daily provision per person (Avoirdupois)
Oatmeal	6.5 lbs. Scottish troy	16.16 oz.
Oatbread	68 oz. [tron]	10.57 oz.
Barley	1.2 lbs. [tron]	2.98 oz.
Potatoes	0.1 pecks	5.97 oz.
Ale	4.25 pints Scots	36.43 fl. oz.
Milk	0.2 pints Scots	1.71 fl. oz.
Cheese	4 oz. [tron]	0.78 oz.
Herrings	2	2.29 oz.
Beef	6/520ths of a carcase	6.44 oz.
Mutton	1/52nd of a carcase	1.03 oz.

This would have provided, for active male and female adults and adolescents, the following daily diet:

	Energy	Protein	Fat	Carbo-hydrate	Calcium	Iron	Vit.A	Vit.B$_1$	Vit.B$_2$	Niacin	Vit.C
	Kcal	g.	g.	g.	mg.	mg.	μg.	mg.	mg.	mg.	mg.
Oatmeal	1,837.1	56.9	39.9	333.5	251.9	18.7	0.0	2.3	0.48	17.5	0.0
Oatbread	961.3	29.7	20.9	174.5	131.9	9.8	0.0	1.2	0.19	9.1	0.0
Barley	101.4	2.3	1.4	23.3	2.5	0.2	0.0	Tr	Tr	1.4	0.0
Potatoes	135.4	2.4	0.2	33.4	6.7	0.5	Tr	0.1	0.06	1.9	11.9
Ale	258.6	2.2	Tr	16.8	103.5	Tr	Tr	Tr	0.36	3.3	0.0
Milk	31.5	1.6	1.8	2.3	58.2	Tr	18.7	Tr	0.09	0.4	3.4
Cheese	87.5	5.6	7.2	Tr	172.4	0.1	88.9	Tr	0.11	1.3	0.0
Herring	129.2	13.2	8.5	0.0	21.4	0.6	31.8	Tr	0.10	5.1	0.0
Beef	267.1	24.3	18.8	0.0	9.8	2.6	Tr	0.1	0.28	11.1	0.0
Mutton	50.0	3.9	3.8	0.0	1.5	0.3	Tr	Tr	0.05	1.9	0.0
Total	3,859.1	142.1	102.5	583.8	759.8	32.8	139.4	3.7	1.72	53.0	15.3

Whilst the orphans, who were allocated half the diet provided for the servants, would have received daily:

	Energy	Protein	Fat	Carbo-hydrate	Calcium	Iron	Vit.A	Vit.B$_1$	Vit.B$_2$	Niacin	Vit.C
	Kcal	g.	g.	g.	mg.	mg.	μg.	mg.	mg.	mg.	mg.
Total	1,929.6	71.1	51.3	291.9	379.9	16.4	69.7	1.9	0.86	26.5	7.7

Table 7.10 *Paupers: Glasgow town hospital, 1740*

['Table, shewing the expence of the Town's Hospital, and the consumption of certain articles in it, at different periods', *OSA*, vol. 7, p. 316]

The minister's table describes the provisions supplied to the hospital and the numbers present in 1740, 1780 and 1790. In 1740 there were 259 paupers present and the average cost of supporting each was £3.4.5 Sterling (£38.12.0 Scots) per annum. In addition to the items listed below, a further £46 Scots was spent on 'petty provisions'. As this amounts to only 3s.7d. per person for the year, the nutritional value of any such additional purchases would have been minimal.

	Provisions for the 259 paupers for the year	Weekly per person (Avoirdupois)
Oatmeal	444 bolls	73.5 oz.
Peasemeal	6 bolls	1.0 oz.
Pease	8 bolls	2.8 oz.
Barley	27 cwts. (Eng. wt.)	3.6 oz.
Groats	18 bolls	3.0 oz.
Ale	2,166 gallons Scots	77.2 fl. oz.
Mutton[1]	442 stones tron	11.8 oz.
Herrings	£9 worth [8,640][2]	5.1 oz.
Butter	57 stones tron	1.5 oz.
Cheese	120 stones tron	3.2 oz.
Eggs	497 dozen (5,964)	0.9 oz.
Sweet Milk	1,019 pints Scots	4.5 fl. oz.
Butter Milk	4,493 pints Scots	20.0 fl. oz.

This would have provided, for elderly male and female paupers, the following weekly diet:

	Energy Kcal	Protein g.	Fat g.	Carbo-hydrate g.	Calcium mg.	Iron mg.	Vit.A µg.	Vit.B$_1$ mg.	Vit.B$_2$ mg.	Niacin mg.	Vit.C mg.
Oatmeal	8,349.9	258.6	181.4	1,516.0	1,145.1	85.2	0.0	10.3	2.20	79.3	0.0
Peasemeal	81.0	6.1	0.4	14.2	17.3	1.3	11.8	0.2	0.09	1.8	Tr
Pease	226.8	17.1	1.1	39.8	48.4	3.6	33.0	0.6	0.25	5.0	Tr
Barley	122.2	2.8	1.7	28.1	3.1	0.2	0.0	Tr	Tr	1.7	0.0
Groats	341.1	10.5	7.5	61.8	46.8	3.6	0.0	0.3	0.09	3.3	0.0
Ale	548.1	4.6	Tr	35.5	219.2	Tr	Tr	Tr	0.77	7.0	0.0
Mutton	579.5	44.7	44.6	0.0	16.8	3.5	Tr	0.3	0.60	21.7	0.0
Herring	286.7	29.4	18.8	0.0	47.6	1.4	70.6	Tr	0.26	11.3	0.0
Butter	319.7	0.2	35.4	Tr	6.5	0.1	425.6	Tr	Tr	0.1	0.0
Cheese	369.2	23.6	30.5	Tr	727.5	0.4	375.1	Tr	0.45	5.7	0.0
Eggs	36.9	3.1	2.7	Tr	13.1	0.5	35.2	Tr	0.12	0.9	0.0
Sweet Milk	83.7	4.3	4.9	6.0	154.4	0.1	49.8	Tr	0.23	1.1	9.1
Butter Milk	198.6	19.8	0.6	29.0	703.6	0.4	Tr	0.2	1.00	0.4	5.6
Total	11,543.4	424.8	329.6	1,730.4	3,149.4	100.3	1,001.1	11.9	6.06	139.3	14.7

Which equates to a daily per capita intake of:

	Energy Kcal	Protein g.	Fat g.	Carbo-hydrate g.	Calcium mg.	Iron mg.	Vit.A µg.	Vit.B$_1$ mg.	Vit.B$_2$ mg.	Niacin mg.	Vit.C mg.
Total	1,649.1	60.7	47.1	247.2	449.9	14.3	143.0	1.7	0.87	19.9	2.1

1   The table actually refers to 'butcher meat'. This was probably largely mutton.

2   There is no real way of knowing how many herrings £9 would have bought, but in 1739–40 the Dean Orphanage in Edinburgh was paying 3d. per dozen and this seems a reasonable working figure for contemporary Glasgow.

Table 7.11   *Lady Grisell Baillie's servants: Mellerstane, Berwickshire, circa 1743*

[R. Scott-Moncrieff, 'The household book of Lady Grisell Baillie, 1692–1733', *Scottish History Society*, 2nd series, vol. 1, 1911, pp. 277–8]

Each servant was to receive 3 mutchkins of ale a day, Scottish measure.

One stone of meal (or brown flour) was to provide 17 servants with bread for one day.

One pound of barley or grots was to provide 17 servants with broth for one day and when the broth contained meat, each servant was to have half a pound of beef.

Sunday	Bread and ale, boiled beef and broth
Monday	Bread and ale, boiled beef and broth, one herring each
Tuesday	Bread and ale, broth and beef
Wednesday	Bread and ale, broth and two eggs each
Thursday	Bread and ale, broth and beef
Friday	Bread and ale, broth and herring (one each)
Saturday	Bread and ale, broth without meat; cheese, or a puden or blood pudens, or what is most convenient.

This proposed diet implies that each servant was to recieve daily:

Avoirdupois

Oatmeal	15.06 oz. [Scottish troy]	16.38 oz.	(In addition to
Ale	0.75 pints Scots	45.00 fl. oz.	which there was
Barley	0.94 oz. [tron]	1.28 oz.	an unknown, but
Beef	4.57 oz. [tron]	6.22 oz.	valuable, amount
Egg	2 weekly	0.57 oz.	of cheese, blood
Herring	1 weekly	2.28 oz.	pudding and haggis.)

This would have provided, for very active male and female adults and adolescents, the following daily diet:

	Energy	Protein	Fat	Carbo-hydrate	Calcium	Iron	Vit.A	Vit.B$_1$	Vit.B$_2$	Niacin	Vit.C
	Kcal	g.	g.	g.	mg.	mg.	µg.	mg.	mg.	mg.	mg.
Oatmeal	1,862.1	57.6	40.5	338.1	255.4	19.0	0.0	2.3	0.49	17.7	0.0
Ale	319.5	2.7	Tr	20.7	127.8	Tr	Tr	Tr	0.45	4.1	0.0
Barley	43.5	1.0	0.6	10.0	1.1	0.1	0.0	Tr	Tr	0.6	0.0
Beef	270.8	24.8	19.0	0.0	10.0	2.6	Tr	0.1	0.29	11.3	0.0
Egg	23.8	2.0	1.8	Tr	8.4	0.3	22.6	Tr	0.07	0.6	0.0
Herring	128.6	13.2	8.4	0.0	21.3	0.6	31.7	Tr	0.11	5.0	Tr
Total	2,648.3	101.3	70.3	368.8	424.0	22.6	54.3	2.4	1.41	39.3	Tr

The addition of some cheese, blood pudding and haggis would have greatly enhanced this diet. It would probably have resulted in an adequate intake of vitamin A, though still leaving a deficiency in vitamin C.

Table 7.12   *Paupers: Glasgow town hospital, 1780*

['Table, shewing the expence of the Town's Hospital, and the consumption of certain articles in it, at different periods', *OSA*, vol. 7, p. 316]

The minister's table describes the provisions supplied to the hospital and the numbers present in 1740, 1780 and 1790. In 1780 there were 254 paupers present and the average cost of supporting each was £4.8.2 Sterling (£52.18.0 Scots) per annum. In addition to the items listed below, a further £81 Scots was spent on 'petty provisions'. As this amounts to only 6s.5d. per person for the year, the nutritional value of any such additional purchases would have been minimal.

	Provisions for the 254 paupers for the year	Weekly per person (Avoirdupois)
Oatmeal	573 bolls	96.7 oz.
Barley	75 cwts. (Eng. wt.)	10.2 oz.
Pease	24 bolls	8.7 oz.
Groats	7 bolls	1.2 oz.
Potatoes	15 bolls (of 622 lbs. Eng. wt. each)	12.0 oz.
Ale	2,560 gallons Scots	93.0 fl. oz.
Mutton[1]	478 stones Tron	13.0 oz.
Herrings	£14.0.0 worth [5,760][2]	3.5 oz.
Butter	118 stones Tron	3.2 oz.
Cheese	210 stones Tron	5.7 oz.
Eggs	2,467 dozen (29,604)	4.5 oz.
Sweet Milk	2,100 pints Scots	9.5 fl. oz.
Butter Milk	10,214 pints Scots	46.4 fl. oz.

This would have provided, for elderly male and female paupers, the following weekly diet:

	Energy Kcal	Protein g.	Fat g.	Carbo-hydrate g.	Calcium mg.	Iron mg.	Vit.A μg.	Vit.B$_1$ mg.	Vit.B$_2$ mg.	Niacin mg.	Vit.C mg.
Oatmeal	10,988.0	340.2	238.7	1,995.0	1,506.9	112.1	0.0	13.4	2.90	104.4	0.0
Barley	346.2	7.8	4.9	79.6	8.7	0.6	0.0	Tr	Tr	4.9	0.0
Pease	704.9	53.2	3.2	123.2	150.3	11.6	102.7	1.5	0.74	16.0	Tr
Groats	136.4	4.2	3.0	24.7	18.7	1.4	0.0	0.1	0.04	1.3	0.0
Potatoes	272.8	4.8	0.4	67.2	13.6	1.1	Tr	0.2	0.12	3.7	24.1
Ale	660.6	5.6	Tr	42.8	264.2	Tr	Tr	Tr	0.93	8.4	0.0
Mutton	639.0	49.3	49.2	0.0	18.6	3.9	Tr	0.3	0.66	23.9	0.0
Herrings	195.8	20.1	12.8	0.0	32.5	1.0	48.2	Tr	0.17	7.7	Tr
Butter	674.7	0.4	74.8	Tr	13.7	0.2	898.1	Tr	Tr	0.1	Tr
Cheese	658.8	42.2	54.4	Tr	1,298.2	0.6	669.4	0.1	0.80	10.1	0.0
Eggs	186.8	15.6	13.9	Tr	66.1	2.6	177.9	0.1	0.58	5.1	0.0
Sweet Milk	175.8	9.0	10.3	12.7	324.5	0.1	104.6	0.1	0.48	2.3	19.1
Butter Milk	460.3	45.9	1.4	67.3	1,630.9	0.9	Tr	0.5	2.32	0.9	13.0
Total	16,100.1	598.3	467.0	2,412.5	5,346.9	136.1	2,000.9	16.3	9.74	188.8	56.2

Which equates to a daily per capita intake of:

	Energy Kcal	Protein g.	Fat g.	Carbo-hydrate g.	Calcium mg.	Iron mg.	Vit.A μg.	Vit.B$_1$ mg.	Vit.B$_2$ mg.	Niacin mg.	Vit.C mg.
Total	2,300.0	85.5	66.7	344.6	763.8	19.4	285.8	2.3	1.39	27.0	8.0

1   The table actually refers to 'butcher meat'. This was probably largely mutton.

2   There is no real way of knowing how many herrings £14 would have bought, but Hugo Arnot (*The history of Edinburgh*, 2nd edn., Edinburgh, 1816, pp. 268–9) gives a price range of 4d.–9d. per dozen in 1777. We have taken a working figure of 7d. per dozen for near contemporary Glasgow.

Table 7.13   *Paupers: Glasgow town hospital, 1790*

['Table, shewing the expence of the Town's Hospital, and the consumption of certain articles in it, at different periods', *OSA*, vol. 7, p. 316]

The minister's table describes the provisions supplied to the hospital and the numbers present in 1740, 1780 and 1790. In 1790 there were 330 paupers present and the average cost of supporting each was £4.9.9 Sterling (£53.17.0 Scots) per annum. In addition to the items listed below, a further £89 Scots was spent on 'petty provisions'. As this amounts to only 5s.5d. per person for the year, the nutritional value of any such additional purchases would have been minimal.

	Provisions for the 330 paupers for the year	Weekly per person (Avoirdupois)
Oatmeal	659 bolls	85.6 oz.
Barley	109 cwts. (Eng. wt.)	11.4 oz.
Pease	23 bolls	6.4 oz.
Groats	8 bolls	1.0 oz.
Potatoes	20 bolls (of 662 lbs. Eng. wt. each)	12.3 oz.
Ale	2,304 gallons Scots	64.4 fl. oz.
Mutton[1]	569 stones Tron	11.9 oz.
Herrings	£16.0.0 worth [6,583][2]	3.1 oz.
Butter	133 stones Tron	2.8 oz.
Cheese	276 stones Tron	5.8 oz.
Eggs	2,138 dozen (25,656)	3.0 oz.
Sweet Milk	2,920 pints Scots	10.2 fl. oz.
Butter Milk	8,766 pints Scots	30.7 fl. oz.

This would have provided, for elderly male and female paupers, the following weekly diet:

	Energy Kcal	Protein g.	Fat g.	Carbo-hydrate g.	Calcium mg.	Iron mg.	Vit.A µg.	Vit.B$_1$ mg.	Vit.B$_2$ mg.	Niacin mg.	Vit.C mg.
Oatmeal	9,555.6	301.2	211.3	1,766.0	1,333.9	99.3	0.0	12.0	2.57	92.4	0.0
Barley	387.2	8.8	5.5	89.0	9.7	0.7	0.0	Tr	Tr	5.5	0.0
Pease	518.5	39.2	2.4	90.6	2.7	8.5	75.5	1.1	0.54	11.8	Tr
Groats	113.7	3.5	2.5	20.6	15.6	1.2	0.0	0.1	0.03	1.1	0.0
Potatoes	280.0	4.9	0.4	69.0	13.9	1.1	Tr	0.2	0.12	3.8	24.7
Ale	457.6	3.9	Tr	29.6	183.0	Tr	Tr	Tr	0.64	5.8	0.0
Mutton	585.5	45.2	45.0	0.0	17.0	3.5	Tr	0.3	0.60	21.9	0.0
Herrings	173.2	17.7	11.4	0.0	28.7	0.9	42.6	Tr	0.15	6.8	Tr
Butter	585.4	0.3	64.9	Tr	11.9	0.1	779.1	Tr	Tr	0.1	Tr
Cheese	666.5	42.7	55.0	Tr	1,313.2	0.6	677.1	0.1	0.81	10.2	0.0
Eggs	124.6	10.4	9.2	Tr	44.1	1.7	118.7	0.1	0.39	3.1	0.0
Sweet Milk	188.2	9.6	11.0	13.6	347.3	0.1	111.9	0.1	0.51	2.5	20.4
Butter Milk	304.1	30.3	0.9	44.4	1,077.4	0.6	Tr	0.3	1.53	0.6	8.6
Total	13,940.1	517.7	419.5	2,122.8	4,398.4	118.3	1,804.9	14.3	7.89	165.6	53.7

Which equates to a daily per capita intake of:

	Energy Kcal	Protein g.	Fat g.	Carbo-hydrate g.	Calcium mg.	Iron mg.	Vit.A µg.	Vit.B$_1$ mg.	Vit.B$_2$ mg.	Niacin mg.	Vit.C mg.
Total	1,991.4	74.0	59.9	303.3	628.3	16.9	257.8	2.0	1.13	23.7	7.7

1   The table actually refers to 'butcher meat'. This was probably largely mutton.

2   There is no real way of knowing how many herrings £16 would have bought, but Hugo Arnot (*The history of Edinburgh*, 2nd edn., Edinburgh, 1816, pp. 268–9) gives a price range of 4d.–9d. per dozen in 1777. We have taken a working figure of 7d. per dozen for near contemporary Glasgow.

8 ✦ Wages in money and kind

1 Introduction to the sources

Wages were highly complex in early modern society, in Scotland as elsewhere. They might be paid entirely in money or entirely in kind, or in a mixture of both. They might be paid differently to the same person for different kinds of work (money with food at harvest, money alone for other day labour). They might be paid at a higher rate in summer than in winter. They would certainly be paid higher to some categories of worker than to others. The jobs might be described by age and sex as well as by skill and task ('herd lass', 'journeyman wright'), but what was understood by certain critical terms ('master mason', 'agricultural servant') might vary nevertheless from one period to another or from one locality to another. Any attempt at the objective measurement of change through time is clearly going to be fraught with difficulties.

In our investigation we have used four kinds of evidence; *wages from accounts* extracted from the account books and papers of employers (tables 8.1–8.7); *assessed wages*, statements of maximum wage rates set down by town councils and justices of the peace (tables 8.8–8.10); *estimated wages* as reported retrospectively by the ministers and others in the *Statistical account* of the 1790s (tables 8.11–8.16), and *poll-tax wages* (tables 8.17–8.18) as declared to the authorities who levied a percentage tax on wages in the 1690s. Each of these has its own advantages and pitfalls, so it is best to begin with some description of the sources.

1.1 Wages from accounts (tables 8.1–8.7)

When we consider money wages we are, ideally, trying to discover 'the going rate for the job', that is, the accepted wage to pay someone of good average ability for their allotted task, neither exceptionally skilled and quick nor handicapped and slow. A cohort of workers was likely to contain people at both extremes, but with most receiving the going rate: when faced with a mass of data from accounts, it is usually better therefore to seek for the mode than for the mean or the median.

Since we are above all seeking a long-term perspective, we have in the main sought details of wage payments in series of accounts that will at least run over several decades, where the jobs can be readily identified and where most or all of the payment was in money. As other historians of wages have found,[1] this generally means, for urban workers, concentrating on the building trades: master masons, their journeymen and their unskilled day labourers called 'barrowmen', master wrights and their journeymen. The *Accounts of the Masters of the Works*, working for the crown in various parts of Scotland have been published for the sixteenth and much of the seventeenth centuries.[2] Their diligent editors have saved us much work in extracting wage rates. To these we have added runs of data relating to urban construction projects, especially from the Edinburgh Town Treasurer's accounts and the Dean of Guild's tradesmens' accounts and from the Town Treasurer's accounts and the Shorework accounts at Aberdeen:[3] and we have used building accounts from Newbattle Abbey and Glasgow and St Andrews Universities.[4] For rural labour, primarily day labourers, we have used the records of estates where the landlord employed workers directly. Particularly useful have been the Yester records in East Lothian, running back to 1672, and for the eighteenth century, those from Buchanan in Stirlingshire, Panmure in Angus, Drylaw in Midlothian and Gordon Castle in Aberdeenshire.[5]

There is a sense in which these details of actual wages paid over to the recipients and formally entered in the accounts of the employer come closest to recording the truth as we want to know it. Nevertheless, the evidence is seldom free of difficulties, which we can illustrate from one typical example, the accounts of St Leonard's College, St Andrews. The college was a building of only modest size on which masons and wrights were engaged intermittently in the late seventeenth and early eighteenth centuries to effect repairs and some reconstruction. Sometimes the work was paid by the piece, or in a form that does not permit analysis: 'for wrights' work, £55.0.0'. Often, though, it was paid on a daily basis, and in a way that implies that food and drink was not supplied by the college to workmen on the job as part of their normal wage, though occasionally, especially at the completion of work, drink might be allowed as an extra, as in April 1702: 'given to the masons by the master's order two gallons of ale and at the finishing thereof one; given to the wrights when putting up the house two gallons of ale'. Thus we are usually able to collect a number of apparently straightforward statements about money wages in most years when building at the college was most active.

Can we, however, be absolutely sure that the worker in question received the whole of the wage paid over by the college? Individual master masons and wrights sent in their

---

[1] H. Phelps Brown and S.V. Hopkins, 'Seven centuries of building wages', *Economica*, vol. 22 (1955); 'Seven centuries of the prices of consumables, compared with builders' wage-rates', *Economica*, vol. 23 (1956); both reprinted in H. Phleps Brown and S.V. Hopkins, *A perspective of wages and prices* (London, 1981).

[2] H.M. Paton, *Accounts of the Master of Works, I, 1529–1615* (Edinburgh, 1957); J. Imrie and J.G. Dunbar, *Accounts of the Master of Works, II, 1616–1649* (Edinburgh, 1982).

[3] Edinburgh Town council accounts (1553–1780), comprising the town treasurer's accounts, the Dean of Guild tradesmen's accounts and the Parliament House building accounts, all held in the City Chambers, Edinburgh; Aberdeen town council accounts (1594–1706), comprising the kirk and bridge work accounts and the shore work accounts, both held in the Town House, Aberdeen; L.B. Taylor, *Aberdeen shore work accounts, 1596–1670* (Aberdeen, 1972).

[4] SRO, GD 40, Newbattle estate accounts; Glasgow University archives, building accounts; St Andrews University archives, building accounts of St Leonard's college.

[5] SRO, GD 45, Dalhousie muniments, Panmure estate accounts; SRO, GD 28, Yester estate accounts; SRO, GD 220, Montrose papers, Buchanan estate accounts; SRO, GD 268, Spencer Loch of Drylaw muniments, Drylaw estate accounts; SRO, GD 44, Richmond and Gordon muniments, Gordon Castle estate accounts.

accounts for themselves and their men to be paid by the college and often received their money one, two or three years in arrears. There was never any allowance made in them either for interest or for profit and it could have been that the master took a cut and handed on lower wages to his workers, as, for example, was the case in eighteenth-century Copenhagen.[6] Or perhaps, since in St Andrews and most other places, except perhaps later eighteenth-century Edinburgh, we are dealing with very small-scale craft businesses where the master worked side-by-side with his men, it was all paid over in the amounts indicated on the document. We simply do not know.

Again, how are we to account for such variation in wages as those in the St Leonard's accounts before 1717, wrights occasionally being paid 12s. though usually 10s., masons 10s. though usually 13s.4d, barrowmen 4s. though usually 5s.? It does not appear always to be a matter of seasonal variation, but it could sometimes be: winter wages, with the shorter day, were often paid about one-sixth less than summer wages. But we might equally be dealing in some years with a requirement for unusually skilled, or conversely unskilled men; or it could be that the pressures of demand and supply on the labour force did indeed vary from year to year in a way that occasionally sent the 'going rate' up and down.

Certainly our tabulations inevitably sacrifice much interesting detail that is embodied in accounts of this sort. Thus at St Leonard's in 1693 John Gilbert, mason, charged 13s.4d. a day for his own services, 5s. for a barrowman's and 10s. for his own son's – obviously assisting his father in his trade; in 1706 the college disbursed 12s. a day on a wright, 8s. on his 'servant' and 5s. a day on a 'plasterer's assistant'; in 1719 Alexander Boutson charged 13s.4d. a day for himself on wright's work, plus two men and an apprentice 'at sawin', one man being paid 10s., the other 4s. and the apprentice nothing.

The problems of estate account books are simpler to the extent that the wages entered are certainly those which were received by the worker, and for day labourers this is usually very straightforward and easy to tabulate. The position can, however, become very complicated with agricultural and domestic servants paid by the year and paid to a varying extent in money and kind. An interesting example is provided on the estates of the Earl of Leven and Melville in Fife,[7] where the employer in the period 1766 to 1784 calculated that he paid each of three agricultural servants £36 a year, plus two pecks of oatmeal a week: however, deductions were made for the holdings they rented, at £15 a year (they were in effect cottars); for their houses, from £4 to £8; and in two cases for 'alley', food received at his table. The upshot was that in money terms one received a 'fie' of £10.12s.0d., one £13.4s.0d. and one £17.0s.0d., though the estate reckoned that overall they were treated alike. When one considers also the value of the oatmeal provided, about £54 a year at current Fife fiar's prices in this period, the money element in the total wage of these three individuals was 13 per cent, 15 per cent and 19 per cent respectively. For this and other reasons we have not attempted to tabulate the wages of similar categories of workers from estate accounts.

It is also worth considering how completely intractable to summation are the details of

---

[6] Edit Rasmussen, *Mester og svend: studier over kobenhavnske tomrer – og murersvendes lonproblemes og sociale forhold, 1756–1800* (Arhus, 1985). [7] SRO, GD 26/6, Leven and Melville estate accounts.

wage bargains that survive in account books from much less monetised parts of Scotland. Macneill of Carskey's book from Kintyre[8] is full of entries of this character:

Novr 1720 Then agreed with Donald McIlheanie and Mall:

McGibbon for making ane fensible Ditch betwixt the foot of

Achnaha and Garvalt, for which I gave ym ane Kow to slaughter

and they are to finish sd Ditch.

I payt Malcome McGibbon in pairt payt of his Summer Ditching,

half ane Crown money at Lambas Last	£1.10.0.
Item ane Daill board yt he got for his Sons Coffine	£0.18.0.
Item two shill Scots Lent money	£0.02.0.

Feby 6d. 1721 Cleard.

The employer thus paid McGibbon for the shared digging of a ditch with part of a cow, a coffin board, a fragment of a loan and a sterling coin. With bargains so unstandardised, wages become direct personal transactions, unique events incapable of having a trend. We should never lose sight of the fact that this must have been the case in many parts of Scotland for most of our period.

1.2 Assessed wages (tables 8.8–8.10)

Scotland had no general Statute of Artificers such as governed wage regulation in sixteenth-century England, but she did have wage assessments. They came in two forms – those carried out by town councils in the sixteenth and seventeenth centuries under legislation empowering them to fix the prices of craftmen's work, going back to at least 1426,[9] and those made by county justices of the peace in the seventeenth and eighteenth centuries. Of the first, only the series from Aberdeen is important:[10] the magistrates here, possibly because their isolation from other large burghs provided more realistic opportunities to fix the labour market than occurred in the south, can be found ordering the wages of masons, wrights and their labourers from at least as early as the 1560s to the end of the seventeenth century (table 8.8). They also concerned themselves from time to time with the wages of slaters, women servants, tapsters and nurses, and, at least at the end of the seventeenth century they fixed the remuneration of shoemakers, pewterers, smiths and coopers by regulating the price of their end product – just as in Edinburgh and elsewhere the earnings of baxters and brewers were fixed (see chapter 2 above). Sometimes the rules in Aberdeen demonstrate a job hierarchy: the master mason is distinguished from the 'underlayer' and both from the 'barrowman'; the master slater is distinguished from the 'trowel' and both from the 'carrier' who is paid the same unskilled wage as the mason's barrowman. The prices they decreed for labour were of course maxima: no one should venture to employ a craftsman or barrowman at more than the assessed wage on pain of punishment. What relation Aberdeen assessed wages had to the real going rate in the city is not totally clear, but where they can be compared

---

[8] F.F. Mackay (ed.), *Macneill of Carskey: his estate journal 1703–1743* (Edinburgh, 1955), p. 61.

[9] *APS*, vol. I, p. 13.

[10] Annual wages statutes (1565–1701) set by the town council of Aberdeen and recorded in the minutes of the town council held in the Town House, Aberdeen.

to paid wages, as they can from time to time for day labourers employed on harbour works and municipal buildings in the seventeenth century, they seem comfortingly realistic.

Other burghs also intermittently levied wage assessments, which occasionally provide interesting detail. Thus at Dundee in 1659 six master masons, complaining that strangers and 'insufficient' men were taking their work from them, were allowed to combine to protect their position in return for submitting to strict regulations. For a day of twelve hours (6a.m.–6p. m.), with half an hour off to rest in the morning and an hour at noon, they were, from March to September, to receive 16s.8d. if no drink was supplied by the employer: with drink, the rate fell to 13s.4d. It was unusual to be so explicit about this detail, but the difference of 3s.4d. was material. Variation about what was tacitly understood as extras could account for some of the apparent differences from place to place or time to time, without this always being clear from the sources.[11]

The wage assessments made by the justices fixing country wages do not in general lend themselves to complete tabulation because their survival is too scrappy and their operation in any case only intermittent (tables 8.9–8.10). Nevertheless they are of great interest in their descriptions of rural jobs and methods of wage payments, and their definitions of employment according to age and sex. They are particularly useful for understanding the very complicated position of farm servants paid by the year or half year.

The justices of the peace were established under legislation of James VI, in imitation of English statute, and as early as 1611 firmly included among their duties the fixing of 'the ordinair hyre and wadgeis of laubouraris, workemen and servandis'.[12] Two assessments have survived from 1611, from the Fife justices sitting at Cupar and from Perth.[13] The Fife document (which also regulated the activities of tanners and shoemakers, fixed the price of hides and shoes, and concerned itself with the terms of servants' contracts and the vagabondage law), laid out the terms for five categories of wage labour. Firstly, no more than £6 Scots for the half year was to be paid as 'fie and bountie' to a labouring workman, that is to say a farm servant, defined here as 'ane holder of the pleuch, thresher of the bairne, staker of cornis, theiker of houssis with thak and davit, ganger with laide horse and doer of sic labor'. Secondly, no more than six merks (i.e., £4) for the half year, was to be given to 'callers of plewis, hirds and uthers of that degree' – that is to say, inferior or immature agricultural servants. Thirdly, no more than £3 for the half year was to be given to a woman servant and £1.10s to a 'lasse'. Fourthly, no more than four merks (i.e., £2.13s.4d.) for the half year, plus four ells of grey cloth, was to be paid to a horse keeper. Lastly, day labourers, except at harvest, were to be paid 2s. a day with food and 5s. without food.

Wages in the Perth document were identical in every respect, except that engagements were for the year, the horse keeper was defined as the 'horse boy', and assessments were

---

[11] Annette Smith, *The three united trades of Dundee: masons, wrights and slaters* (Abertay Historical Society Publication no. 26, Dundee, 1987), p. 46.

[12] *Register of the Privy Council of Scotland*, 1st series, vol. IX (1899), p. 222.

[13] St Andrews University Library archives: Anstruther Wester papers; 'Justice of the Peace wage assessment, Perth, 1611', transcribed and published in S. Cowan, *The ancient capital of Scotland*, vol. 2 (London, 1904), pp. 106–7.

given for cooks, baxters, brewsters and 'gentleman's servants' at £12 a year (half that, for the cook's assistant or 'foreman').

These assessments contrast in many significant ways with that made, following a new attempt to provide JPs with effective powers under Cromwell, by the justices of Midlothian in 1656 (there were also assessments made for Peeblesshire and Ayrshire in the same year).[14] Midlothian was part of a region comprehending the other Lothians and much of the eastern Borders where the organisation of farm work was fundamentally different from elsewhere in Scotland. The unit of labour was the 'hind' and his family; the hind was a skilled workman able to 'plow, to sow, to stack, to drive carts, etc.' He was expected to bring with him to work 'an able fellow-servant', whom he lodged and fed himself (he might of course be his own son). Between them they undertook 'the labour of a whole plough'. The 'half-hind' was similar, but had no obligation to bring a servant. Their wives completed the working unit: they were 'to shear dayly in harvest' and assist their husbands 'in winning their master's hay and peats, setting of his lime-kills, gathering, filling, carting and spreading their master's muck, and all other sort of fuilzie . . . all manner of work, at barns and byres, to bear and carry the stacks from the barn-yards to the barns for threshing', carry fodder to the animals, 'muck, cleange and dight the byres and stables, and help winnow and dight the cornes'. As payment the hind (or the family) received a cottage and a kailyard, an allowance of ground to sow grain, grazing for two or three cows, 15 bolls of oats and $1\frac{1}{2}$ bolls of peas. There was no money 'fie' at all. Other skilled rural workers, the 'half-hind', the shepherd and the 'tasker' who did the bulk of the threshing were paid in the same way, the half-hind getting one half of the hind's allowances. The only people, apart from craftsmen, in this assessment who received cash were certain living-in servants of both sexes who received a 'fie' in addition to their keep and day labourers who were paid 6s. a day without food or 3s. a day with.

The Midlothian assessment also contained unusually elaborate regulations for the wages of rural craftsmen – masons (including the unskilled cowans who generally built dry-stone dykes), wrights, thatchers, slaters, taylors, shoemakers and malt men, both day rates and piece rates. Weavers were left out on the grounds that their price lists were too complicated, but exhorted not to charge more than they had in the past. The day rate with food was invariably twice that of the day rate without food, a merk for a mason being reduced to half a merk, eight shillings for a cowan being reduced to four shillings, six shillings for a barrowman being reduced to three shillings, and so on. This implies, of course, much more plentiful or more tasty food for the mason. The assessment also noted that craftsmen's and labourers' wages were to be reduced by one sixth between 1 October and 1 March 'because of the Winter Season, and shortnesse of the Day; Except such as Work by Candle-light'. Finally, it attempted to limit entertainment costs: 'The makers of penny-bridals are not to exceed ten shillings Scots, for a man, and eight shillings Scots, for a woman, whether at dinner or supper.' It was much more elaborate and comprehensive than most assessments that have come down to us.

Our third and last example is characteristic of a group of eighteenth-century

---

[14] C.H. Firth (ed.), *Scotland and the Protectorate* (Scottish History Society, 1899) 1st series, vol. 31, pp. 405–11.

assessments. It was made by the justices of Lanarkshire in 1708.[15] Like Fife, the Western Lowlands were an area where almost all farm servants received at least some cash. The exception was the thresher, who was paid entirely in kind; his wage was one twenty-fifth part of what he threshed, plus (for his work and that of his wife outside the harvest season) a cottage and kailyard, a boll of meal in summer, pasture for a cow and food for himself and wife during the harvest. Otherwise, an ordinary agricultural servant able to do 'all manner of work relating to husbandry, viz. to plow, sow, stack, drive carts and lay on loads' was to have £24 a year for fee and bounty 'and no more'. A 'manservant of younger years', a 'halfling', living in, was to have £16 fee and bounty, 'boyes or lads' similarly placed half that; a woman servant 'strong and sufficient ... for barns, byres, shearing, brewing, baking, washing and other necessary work' had £14, and a lass £8. Harvest workers were separately assessed on day rates, being given food and drink and, for a 'sufficient man shearer' 6s. a day, a 'sufficient woman shearer' 5s., and younger workers proportionately. Outside harvest, day labourers (as in Midlothian) were to be paid 6s. without food, 3s. with food. This assessment also fixed the daily wages of craftsmen, masons, wrights, barrowmen, thatchers and tailors, again in every case halved if food was provided. Arrangements for winter wages were the same as in Midlothian.

In considering the use that might be made of justices' assessments, it is necessary to remember that they arose from a perceived need to combat excessive or increasing labour costs, what an Act of Parliament of 1621 called 'the fraude and malice off servantis who ... refuis to be hyired without gryit and extraordinarie waiges'.[16] They were the maximum rates supposed to be tolerated, and from time to time justices did indeed punish those who paid or received higher wages, at least until around 1760. After this, few assessments are to be found, though the courts in Scotland continued to have a role in arbitrating wage claims until the nineteenth century.

The Commonwealth period in Roxburghshire provides an example when prosecutions were particularly frequent, significantly when wages in various parts of Scotland seemed to be reaching a peak and employers no doubt felt under pressure.[17] In 1656 six masters and eight servants were charged with paying and receiving more than the law allowed. One such was John Riddell, younger, who confessed that he gave to Thomas Riddell 'his brother, ane servant' a fie of £7 Scots, a boll of bear, a pair of shoes and a pair of hose. Thomas admitted only to receiving ten 'shillings' (probably in sterling money, or £6 Scots), plus the boll of bear, and the magistrates concluded that he had, altogether, been paid £4 over what the acts allowed. The more effective the acts, the more one would expect to find in periods of pressure for wage rises that the employer conceded more in fringe benefits or non-monetised extras that were less easy for JPs to trace or to complain about.

On the other hand, where the money element of paid wages can be checked against assessments they generally appear to be in line. The 5s.–6s. a day for day labour found in

[15] C.A. Malcolm (ed.), *The minutes of the Justices of the Peace for Lanarkshire 1707–23* (Scottish History Society, 1931), 3rd series, vol. 17, pp. 16–21.   [16] *Acts of the Parliaments of Scotland*, vol. IV, p. 623.
[17] National Library of Scotland: MS 5439, Roxburgh JP records.

the assessments seems fairly general in accounts in Scotland in the seventeenth century, especially outside large burghs. The craftsmens' wages laid down by the Lanarkshire justices in 1708 are almost identical to those paid for the same jobs in St Andrews in that period. The Kelsalls, in their examination of 'a wide range of daily wages for work of many different kinds' mentioned in the account books of Border households in the late seventeenth and early eighteenth centuries, found 'not many cases where *less* was paid' than the rates given in the Midlothian and Lanarkshire assessments cited, and only a few where more was paid (though thatchers sometimes received 13s.4d in place of the 8s. allowed in 1656 and the 10s. allowed in 1708). There was, they considered, 'a broad correspondence between actual daily wages paid and the maxima laid down by the justices'.[18] This, of course, does not rule out the possibility that more benefits in kind were sometimes given than the magistrates bargained for.

Certainly, the fact that assessed wages are not identical with the totality of paid wages creates problems when, for example, we try to compare Fife and Perthshire in 1611 with Lanarkshire in 1708. On the face of it, the fee for ordinary agricultural service paid by the year has doubled from £12 to £24, the more remarkable when one considers that the wage of the day labourer has only risen from 5s. a day all year, in 1611, to 6s. in summer and 5s. in winter, in 1708. It could be that the justices in 1611 had tried to set the fee unrealistically low. Or it could be that the money element in this wage did indeed double, but that some other part of the wage paid in kind (for example, meal or house rent), unstated and unregulated, diminished in proportion. The justices' assessment in Peebles in 1664[19] envisaged an able farm servant with all-round skills as being paid for the half year £8 in money with a pair of shoes and six quarts of 'grog', or an extra £2 'for grog and shoon' if he preferred that option. For a woman servant 'of the first sort', able to milk, make cheese, work in the barn and byre, spin, card and do all sorts of household work, the choice for the summer half year was between 'fourty shillings in money a ston of wooll and a pare of single sohl shoone', or 'six pounds seven shillings in money': it trebled her money wage if she took the last option.

An example derived from an actual contract, rather than from a justice's assessment, comes from Culross in 1656, where a woman servant hired for the winter half year, Martinmas to Whitsunday, accepted £5 in Scots money as 'fie', a groat sterling, or 4s. Scots, as 'arles' – earnest money – and as 'bounteth' or payment in kind, three ells of 'hardine' worth 24s., an ell of linen worth 12s., a pair of shoes worth 24s. and 'ane old wylie coat' (petticoat) worth 30s. The wage was calculated to be worth £9.14s.0d., of which about 46 per cent was in kind. And this takes no account of the free food she can be expected to have received in the employer's kitchen in the performance of her duties. She broke the contract and was consequently fined by the town magistrates.[20]

In Renfrewshire in the late seventeenth century and early eighteenth century, Sheriff Court records (apparently relating to cases where workers sued employers for non-payment of wages) similarly show great variation in the percentage value of the total

[18] H. and K. Kelsall, *Scottish lifestyles 200 years ago* (Edinburgh, 1986), p. 164.
[19] SRO, JP 3/2/3, 'Justice of the Peace wage assessment, Peebles, 1664'.
[20] D. Beveridge, *Culross and Tulliallan* (Edinburgh, 1885), vol. I, pp. 294–5.

wage paid in kind. Thus in 1686 one manservant was paid a harvest fee of £8 plus, as 'bontage', an ell of plaiding and a pair of shoes worth 11s.; another was paid a half year fee of £6 plus 'bontages' of a pair of shoes at 24s., an ell of linen at 10s. and a shirt at 15s. In this case the total earnings of the two men were almost identical, but the money wage substantially larger in the first instance. For Renfrewshire women the proportion paid in kind also clearly varied. For example in 1687 a woman servant was paid £6 fee for a half year, plus 'bontages' worth £3.16s.0d. in shoes, aprons and hose; in 1709 a woman was paid the same money fee, received 'bontages' of shoes, apron and hose worth only £2.2s.0d.; in 1724 two women received the £6 fee, one with 'bontages' of £2.0s.0d., the other with 'bontages' of £1.11s.0d. The money element was the same as thirty-seven years earlier, but the element in kind had clearly fallen.[21]

For farm servants paid by the year or half year it is almost always difficult to guess what is happening to their total wage if the data relates only to the money portion, and one strongly suspects that much of the flexibility in the real wage bargain occurred over elements in kind that could not easily be regulated.

1.3 Estimated wages (tables 8.11–8.16)

In addition to accounted and assessed wages, there were also retrospectively estimated wages. From time to time, especially in the eighteenth century, commentators on the Scottish scene made judgements as to what the prevailing rate of wages was at the time, or had been in the past. These may be interesting, and sometimes surprisingly accurate like Adam Smith's observation in 1775 that in the previous century the normal rate of day labour in Scotland had been 6s. in summer and 5s. in winter, much the same as it still was in the Highlands, while the normal Lowland rate had risen to 8s., with 10s.–12s. paid in industrial districts and the south-east.[22] They are, however, not generally numerous or systematic enough to be of much value to us.

The exception, however is the important and plentiful data collected by the ministers and other reporters to the *Statistical account of Scotland* of the 1790s; they were generally replies, at least in rural parishes, to Sir John Sinclair's question about the rates of wages current in their parishes at the time, and in a significant number of cases they then valuably compared these modern wages with those of the immediate past.[23] These quotations have been a mine of information for historians since the time they were first noted and summarised by A.L. Bowley as part of a much larger study.[24] Bowley's

21 William Hector (ed.), *Selections from the judicial records of Renfrewshire* (Paisley, 1876), pp. 334–5.
22 Adam Smith, *The wealth of nations* (Everyman edn, 1910), vol. I, p. 68.
23 Our citations from the *Statistical account of Scotland*, edited by Sir John Sinclair between 1791 and 1799, refer to the useful modern edition, rearranged by counties, under the general editors D.J. Withrington and I.R. Grant (Wakefield, 1973–83).
24 A.L. Bowley, 'The statistics of wages in the United Kingdom during the last hundred years, part II, agricultural wages, Scotland', *Journal of the Royal Statistical Society*, vol. 62 (1899), pp. 140–50; A.L. Bowley, 'The statistics of wages in the United Kingdom during the last hundred years, part VII, wages in the building trades (cont) 'Scotland and Ireland', *JRSS*, vol. 63 (1900), pp. 485–98. For recent restatements of Bowley's citations, see E.H. Hunt, 'Industrialization and regional inequality: wages in Britain, 1760–1914', *Journal of Economic History*, vol. 46 (1986), pp. 935–96, esp. p. 937, and J.H. Treble, 'The standard of living of the working class', in T.M. Devine and R. Mitchison (eds.), *People and society in Scotland*, vol. I, *1760–1830* (1988), pp. 188–226.

methods of summary seem to have been alarmingly cavalier, though historians have often used his figures uncritically. For example, in his treatment of pre-1790 building craftsmen's wages he gives eight citations, including those for Aberdeen, Ayr, Cupar, Forfar, Haddington and Perth, though the *Statistical accounts* contain no such information in their returns for these burghs (sometimes they do for rural parishes in the same county). The return for Monimail in Fife cites the rate for the 'master mason' but not for the journeyman mason, which would have seemed more appropriate. That for Dunfermline turns out to be based on a statement that '30 years ago' wages were 'half' what they are now, in 1794, which is probably an admissible guess by the reporter. It is impossible to be certain, from the information given, how Bowley arrived at his summaries for early agricultural wages. Among modern scholars, Valerie Morgan's work has been quite independent of Bowley's, and she has written most valuably on the *Statistical account*, analysing statements relating to agricultural wages in 500 parishes in the 1790s and to more than 100 retrospective estimates.[25]

We are not concerned here to provide a detailed consideration of the reports of wages current in the 1790s, a task already undertaken by Morgan and others, and one that falls in any case just beyond our terminal point around 1780. Nevertheless we have included as table 8.16 Robert Hope's almost contemporary analysis of this material in Sir John Sinclair's, *General report of the agricultural state and political circumstances of Scotland* (Edinburgh, 1814), to provide a perspective against which to see earlier change. We are, though, concerned with the retrospective estimates from Sinclair's *Statistical account*, which stretch in some cases back into the first half of the eighteenth century, and we have therefore constructed a number of tables with more than 300 observations from all over Scotland, mainly for the period 1740–80, on male and female farm servants fees, harvest wages, and day labourers and craftsmen's wage rates. They form a substantial body of potentially useful data.

How reliable are such retrospective estimates? Most historians following Bowley have taken them at their face value and reproduced them without comment. Morgan, however, concluded that what was reported to the *Statistical account* about current wages 'indicated a large measure of comparability between the ministers' findings and those of other contemporary observers', and noted that ministers themselves were often experienced employers, both of domestic service and, through glebe land, of agricultural labour.[26] Yet there must be real doubts about the ability of the ministers to quote wage rates accurately for up to half a century past: only occasionally did they cite old accounts or 'some authentic documents' as their authority, and simple recollection of figures running back several decades seems a slender foundation for certainty. To this must be added the fact that they had some interest in making the rate of wages seem to be rising rapidly, both because their efforts to increase their own stipends and those of the parish schoolmasters which would be strengthened by evidence of a general wage increase for those of humble status, and because the eighteenth-century improver liked to take the

[25] V. Morgan, 'Agricultural wage rates in late eighteenth-century Scotland', *Economic History Review*, 2nd series, vol. 24 (1971), pp. 181–201.   [26] *Ibid.*, p. 183.

optimistic line that things had recently got much better than they ever were in the benighted past.

Nevertheless, comparisons between the broad profile given by the *Statistical account* retrospective quotations and that of other sources are fairly encouraging, and the ministers at least present a broadly coherent but regionally varied pattern. If taken, like most other historical sources, with care and scepticism, they can be used with the rest.

1.4 Poll tax wages (tables 8.17–8.18)

Finally, there is information to be gleaned about wages from the poll tax returns of the late seventeenth century. There were four poll taxes ordered by the Scottish Parliaments in the 1690s, the first in 1693, one in 1695 and two more in 1698. Those of 1698 are of no interest to us since they do not contain wage data, but the two earlier acts required servants to be taxed according to the value of their annual 'fee and bounteth'. In 1693, the tax equalled one-twentieth of that fee and bounteth, in 1695, one-fortieth in addition to a general poll of 6s.[27] With servants' wages being explicitly stated, or implicit in the tax that was paid, the poll tax returns appear a most beguiling source, particularly for the study of the geographical variation of servants' wages at a single point in time.

Though the effective coverage of the country was patchy, and the survival of records patchier still, in aggregate the number of lists of taxpayers and their obligations is considerable. Comprehensive records appear to survive for Aberdeenshire, Renfrewshire, West Lothian and Edinburgh, whilst most of the parishes in Orkney are listed, along with some in Berwickshire, Selkirkshire, Peeblesshire, Lanarkshire, Fife, Banffshire, Argyll and Ross.[28]

Unfortunately, the path to their interpretation is strewn with pitfalls. First, doubts have been raised regarding the comprehensiveness of the returns. R.E. Tyson has estimated, for instance, that the poll books for Aberdeenshire should have contained about 81,650 pollable persons whereas in fact they contain only 51,656 persons (or 63.3 per cent of the expected total).[29] Second, the poll tax wage returns deal solely with the 'fee and bounteth' that was due to servants; i.e., the money element of the wage plus the value of such extras as shoes or clothes that were specified in hiring agreements. Whilst it seems unlikely that the fee and bounteth are systematically understated (there were severe penalties for evasion and, perhaps more significantly, it was the employer who reported the fee and bounteth upon which their servants paid taxes), this would exclude any payments in food, rent, land allowance and so forth which, as we have seen, would often greatly exceed the value of the fee and bounteth. The tax also took no account of the value of gratuities, which for domestic servants of the landed classes could be considerable. The Kelsalls found that in this period 'in Polwarth House and other places

[27] *APS*, vol. IX, pp. 266, 381–4; Vol. X, pp. 152, 179.
[28] See the discussion in M.W. Flinn (ed.), *Scottish population history from the seventeenth century to the 1930s* (Cambridge, 1977), pp. 55–7 and the detailed list of surviving Poll Tax records held in SRO, E.70.
[29] R.E. Tyson, 'The population of Aberdeenshire, 1695–1755: a new approach', *Northern Scotland*, vol. 6 (1985), pp. 113–31.

where visitors frequently came to stay, the effect of sharing out the drink money they left must often have doubled the money wages received for their employment'.[30]

The real difficulties behind the interpretation of the poll tax returns arise, however, when we use them to examine the way in which servants' wages varied geographically. Such a goal is effectively one of comparison and if this is to be achieved, then we must ensure that we compare like with like. Unfortunately, it is clear that the term 'servant' could be used to describe almost anyone in employment who was neither a day labourer nor a craftsman. Encompassing all from a herd-boy to a gentleman's gentleman, this effectively ranged from those earning as little as £2 Scots per annum at one end of the spectrum to about £100 per annum at the other. Clearly, a straightforward comparison between the means of servants' wages in two localities need not tell us very much about relative wage levels; it may instead reveal no more than the relative numbers of servants of different classes in the two localities.

Much of the variation in the classes of employees comprehended by the term 'servant' can be removed by excluding from our survey all who worked in the houses of large landowners, craftsmen or merchants, and concentrating on those who worked for tenant farmers and small heritors, whom we have devined as those holding land valued at less than £500 Scots. This effectively removes all the more prestigious servants and brings us much closer to targeting the same population in different areas, namely agricultural servants hired by the year. Even this strategy has problems. First, as some farm servants, especially in Renfrewshire, were only hired for the half year or for the harvest, their declared wages in the tax returns were proportionately, and misleadingly, low. This is a quirk which we suspect is not always made explicit and which cannot always be allowed for. Second, as even the relatively restricted category of 'agricultural servant' contains many degrees of experience and skill, individuals within it were provided with a similar diversity of reward. The difficulty here is that the care which the assessors took to distinguish between agricultural servants of different sorts varied considerably from one area to another. Thus in some areas herds, hyremen and hyrewomen, boys and girls were all listed separately from servants, whilst in other areas, all these occupations were comprehended under a generic use of the term 'servant'. It is the variable inclusion of juvenile labour which is of particular concern. We have excluded them when they can be identified, for it is the spatial variation of wages paid to able-bodied adult farm servants in which we are primarily interested, but we cannot be sure that the results do not, at least in part, reflect spatial variations in the way in which the poll tax returns describe the servant community.

Nevertheless, with evidence on the 'fees and bounteth' of 3,334 male and 2,380 female servants of small tenants and heritors spread over eighty-five parishes in Aberdeenshire, and 307 and 566 such male and female servants in sixteen parishes in Renfrewshire, the poll tax data provide a unique insight into the spatial distribution of high and low wage areas in these two counties (see section 3 below).[31] The poll tax data can, moreover, be

---

[30] Kelsall, *Scottish lifestyles*, p. 156.

[31] J. Stuart (ed.), *List of pollable persons within the shire of Aberdeen, 1696* (Spalding Club, Aberdeen, two vols., 1844); David Semple's articles on the pollable persons of Renfrewshire reprinted from the *Glasgow Herald*, various dates, 1864, brought together in a bound volume in SRO, T.335.

used in other ways. They provide, for instance, a particularly valuable perspective on female employment and renumeration, as other sources on this subject are comparatively rare (see section 2.5 below).

2 Trends in wages

2.1 Skilled building workers (tables 8.1–8.5, 8.8–8.9, 8.15–8.16)

The wages we are considering here are those paid entirely in money to men described as 'masons' and 'wrights', as 'master masons' and 'master wrights' and as 'servant masons' and 'servant wrights'. There are considerable terminological problems. A 'master' is clearly an employer as well as a working craftsman and we have already noted that in submitting his accounts he may possibly include an element of mark-up for his own wages and those of his employees to cover overheads and profit. This seems to be evident in Aberdeen in the seventeenth century, where master masons and wrights were being paid, according to both the town council and shorework accounts (tables 8.2 and 8.3) significantly more than town council assessment stipulated as their personal wage (table 8.8). A 'servant' is equally clearly an employee, perhaps a qualified journeyman or perhaps an unqualified assistant who had not served an apprenticeship, a 'cowan'. The term 'mason' or 'wright' used by itself is particularly ambiguous, not least because of differences in skill even among qualified men. The Master of Works accounts for Holyrood in 1559 include 'masons' working on the chapel paid at 4s. a day and other 'masons' repairing the park dyke at 2s.6d. or 3s. a day.[32] In country areas at least one can take the term to indicate a self-employed, fully qualified craftsman able to do all simple jobs, though even so some rural assessments also give separate rates for 'cowans' who were characteristically employed on dyking.

In large burghs, especially in Edinburgh, we may take it that master masons gradually assumed more entrepreneurial functions, deploying numbers of journeymen and welcoming into their ranks country masons who found it more profitable to become employees than to work on their own.[33] In Edinburgh in 1764 and again in 1778 there were strikes by building trades journeymen, both masons and wrights, against their masters: the first was triggered by an attempt by the journeymen masons to alter a traditional wage of 13s.4d. a day in summer and 10s. in winter, which they claimed had been set 120 years earlier, when the cost of living had been, they said, with no historical evidence, only a quarter of what it was at the present time.[34]

We have constructed figure 8.1 in order to demonstrate trends in the wage payments to masons and wrights. Because of the ambiguities, we have expressed the quotations as a range, the top end usually alluding to 'masters' and the bottom to 'servants' where they are distinguished in the sixteenth and seventeenth centuries, though highs and lows in the

---

[32] H.M. Paton, *Accounts of the Masters of Works, 1529–1615* (Edinburgh, 1957).

[33] For this development in the eighteenth century, see W.H. Fraser, *Conflict and class: Scottish workers, 1700–1838* (Edinburgh, 1988), chapter 2.

[34] Fraser, *Conflict and class*, p. 50; H. Hamilton, *An economic history of Scotland in the eighteenth century* (Oxford, 1963), pp. 348–9.

eighteenth century may be produced by town and country variation. We have, however, excluded the wages paid to 'master' masons and wrights in the Aberdeen town council and shore work accounts as they appear to include an element above and beyond payment for their own labour. The diagrams are principally compiled from information for Edinburgh and for the 'servant' masons and wrights in Aberdeen. It is a misfortune that while we have information from both burghs simultaneously for some years in the sixteenth century, for the seventeenth century the data are almost entirely drawn from Edinburgh alone in the first half, and from Aberdeen almost, but not quite, alone in the second. For the eighteenth century we are dependent on Edinburgh (though no town council payments are available before 1736), supplemented by reports from St Andrews and from some rural localities, including data from the *Statistical account*. It is encouraging that during the sixteenth century rates in Edinburgh and Aberdeen kept roughly in line, but it would have been helpful to be able to check whether this was also true subsequently, especially as the Edinburgh rates are from paid accounts that do not specifically distinguish master from servant masons, whilst the Aberdeen ones are from assessments and paid accounts that do make such a distinction. In the largest burghs, building workers are perhaps more likely to have been paid at roughly equivalent levels, but at least in the eighteenth century there was not just one rate across the country. The information from the St Andrews accounts, and from occasional rural assessments and the *Statistical account* show lower wages in smaller, more rural and more isolated places.

In comparing the masons with the wrights, it is not possible to see any consistent differences in rates of pay in the early period. They are treated as identical in the Aberdeen assessments of the sixteenth century (table 8.8) and are usually paid about the same in Edinburgh then and in the first half of the seventeenth century (table 8.1). In Aberdeen after 1665 master wrights came to be assessed higher than master masons, while servant wrights were assessed lower than servant masons, though these distinctions do not always appear in the paid accounts. Later, in rural evidence (table 8.4) and accounts from St Andrews and Edinburgh (tables 8.2 and 8.5), masons are often paid more than wrights, sometimes the same, but very seldom less. All the wages cited here are of course given in Scots money throughout, and are assumed to be at summer day wage rates without food, unless explicitly stated otherwise.

In both trades, however, the broad outlines of the trends are clear enough. Edinburgh rates in the 1530s hovered around 2s.6d. and were about 3s. or 4s. in both Edinburgh and Aberdeen in the 1560s. From this they nearly doubled by the 1580s and then doubled again, to 12s., by 1620. In Edinburgh they stabilised at the traditional 'merk Scots', or 13s.4d. by the 1630s, though this rate was not achieved by the servant masons in Aberdeen for another thirty years. In the Aberdeen assessments, rates rose as high as 17s.9d. for master craftsmen around the time of the Restoration, though they slipped back after 1665 to stabilise at 13s.4d. for master masons, 16s.8d. for master wrights. That this peak was not just a quirk of the Aberdeen assessors is shown by a short but significant series from Haddington, where masons were paid 18s. in 1661, falling to 16s. in 1663 and 12s. by 1677. Here and elsewhere the 1650s and 1660s appear as a high water mark in money wages, not to be surpassed for the next century.

In the eighteenth century, mason's wages held remarkably steady at 16s.8d. in the Edinburgh town council building accounts from when they are first reported in 1736 until 1760, though the journeymen later recollected the rate at this time and earlier as 13s.4d.: the difference is probably due to mark-up accounting procedures, but it might be due to different grades of mason being described. Short series from Drylaw, St Andrews and Newbattle mostly indicate payments at the lower end of this range, with some as high as 18s. for unspecified work at Drylaw. After 1760 masons' wages everywhere began to rise, in Edinburgh reaching 19s. by 1780 and 26s. by 1787.[35] The evidence from the *Statistical account* of rural craftsmen's wages shows a range from 12s. to 24s. in the 1790s in the different counties, but most are from around 16s. to 18s. by then: the lowest wages are in the north, the highest in the Central Belt. Comparison with retrospective quotations here again suggests that there had been little movement until after 1760, with rural masons in the middle of the eighteenth century earning 10s.–12s., and wrights 8s.–10s. (quotations at half these rates are presumably with food allowed).

It appears likely, therefore, that craftsmen in eighteenth-century Edinburgh, though better paid than in the country, probably increased their wages less than their country cousins – unless, of course, the ministers tended to overstate the rural improvement. Masons in the capital enjoyed an increase of, at most, about 50 per cent between the 1760s and the 1790s, rural masons and wrights apparently one of between 50 and 100 per cent. Such increases at this point kept pace with or slightly outstripped the price of meal.

In the long perspective from around 1530 there were three phases in the development of wages. First there was a period of money wage increases lagging behind the general inflation that ended just after the middle of the seventeenth century. How far this ultimately left the building craftsman worse off in terms of what food his wage could buy is a question discussed further in the next chapter, but between 1530 and 1600 there was a drop of about 45 per cent in the quantity of wheatbread he could buy for his money, and the fall was at its most precipitous in the 1580s and 1590s, with some appreciable bounce back in the early seventeenth century. As we shall see, the deterioration was rather worse for craftsmen than for labourers, and taking the period of the price revolution as a whole was less grave if measured in oatmeal than if measured in wheatbread. The second phase, from the mid seventeenth to the mid eighteenth century comprised a long period of near stagnation in which wages tended to tip downwards from their mid seventeenth-century peak. Finally, there was another positive upward tendency after 1760, which in this case moved rather faster than the increase in living costs.

There are interesting contrasts here with the experience of the south of England outlined by Phelps Brown and Hopkins.[36] Firstly, in the first half of the seventeenth century, craftsmen's wages rose at roughly the same rate – by about 60 per cent in Scotland, 50 per cent in England. By the 1640s Scottish daily wages at about one merk (13s.4d.) in central Lowland Scotland, compared to southern English wages at 16s.–18s. Scots – a fairly narrow margin of about a third in England's favour. For a short time in the 1650s and 1660s it was possible to find building craftsmen in some parts of Scotland

---

[35] Fraser, *Conflict and class*, p. 36, suggests only 20s.–24s. by 1787.
[36] H. Phelps Brown and S.V. Hopkins, *Perspective of wages*, chapter 1.

paid as much as their English equivalents. After mid century, however, wages went on rising in England while they stagnated or fell in Scotland: by the 1730s an English craftsman earning 24s. had almost a 50 per cent margin over his Scottish counterpart, even allowing for a generous interpretation of the Edinburgh mason's wage: it rose to an 80 per cent margin compared to the traditional merk Edinburgh working masons still considered they were paid, and was at least double Scottish country wages. Even after 1760, when there was renewed growth of Scottish craftsmen's wages, a differential of this order seems to have been maintained. Dr Hunt's investigations suggests that in the 1765–95 period wrights in Aberdeen and Edinburgh never reached more than 40–5 per cent of the wages of wrights in London (Aberdeen was lower), and hardly two-thirds of their wages in Manchester or Exeter.[37] No wonder the finest road a Scotsman ever saw led to England.

A second point of contrast relates to the ratio between skilled and unskilled work in the building trades in the two countries. In Scotland from the middle of the sixteenth century a 'mason' in Edinburgh consistently earned about twice the wage of his labourer, or 'barrowman', though there is reason to think that in the 1530s the gap had been more like three times. In the seventeenth century very much the same ratio of two to one continued – e.g., in the royal Master of Works accounts, a merk for the mason, half a merk for the barrowman. In country areas a mason might earn a little more than twice the unskilled wage. This did not vary in the eighteenth century until the 1760s, when day labourers' wages, except in the extreme north of Scotland, began to gain on those of craftsmen, reducing the difference to about 60 per cent by 1780. In England, on the other hand, craftsmen throughout the period were paid only half as much again as their labourers, Phelps Brown and Hopkins picking out this 50 per cent ratio as a peculiarly stable feature in their statistics over several centuries. Economists consider the extent of the skilled–unskilled differential to be a useful measure of relative economic growth in different countries, the wider the difference the more retarded the economy: in this case it would measure Scotland as very substantially behind England until the 1760s, then suddenly accelerating to narrow the gap.

There is also an interesting comparison to be made in this respect with Ireland, which we have discussed at greater length elsewhere.[38] Briefly, while the wages of craftsmen in Ireland at least in the eighteenth century were often not out of line with those in England and therefore higher than Scottish craft wages, the wages of labourers came to be very much lower. This appears, from scrappy data, consistently to give differentials of skilled to unskilled wages of more than two to one, and often of three to one, in seventeenth-century Ireland, while in Irish country areas in the 1770s rather fuller data measure the skilled to unskilled ratio at roughly three to one or four to one, though more like two to one in Dublin. Using this yardstick, therefore, of the three British kingdoms, England is always comfortably the more advanced, Scotland occupies the middle position and

[37] E.H. Hunt, 'Industrialization and regional inequality', p. 937.
[38] L.M. Cullen, T.C. Smout and A. Gibson, 'Wages and comparative development in Ireland and Scotland, 1565–1780', in R. Mitchison and P. Roebuck (eds.), *Economy and society in Scotland and Ireland, 1500–1939* (Edinburgh, 1988), pp. 105–16.

Ireland comes last, though the difference between Scotland and Ireland only became striking in the third quarter of the eighteenth century.

2.2 Day labourers (tables 8.6–8.10, 8.13–8.14, 8.16)

What contemporaries called 'day labour' was unskilled work performed by strong adult males hired on a day-to-day basis as required. In towns such people might be the masons' 'barrowmen', who brought and mixed building materials for the craftsmen, or they might be carters, scavengers, coalheavers, assistants and odd-job men of many kinds where muscle was required. New Mills cloth manufactory at Haddington around 1700 paid native Scottish shearmen and dyers at the ordinary rate of day labour.[39] In the country there were similarly many tasks for which an employer would hire day labour – ditching, dyking, roof-mending, assisting other workers round the fields and yards. When in the mid eighteenth century Lady Balgarvie in Fife wanted a muck-heap moved she hired four labourers, paid them 5s. a day each and gave them some ale.[40] At harvest time labour was also hired by the day, but at a much higher rate and with food almost invariably provided: we discuss harvest wages at the end of this subsection.

Exactly who performed day labour is not always clear. Poll tax returns occasionally pick out such occupations as coalheavers and even 'labourers' or 'lawbourers', but, in Fife at least, the latter also appeared to have possessed small-holdings in the burghs. When Acts of Parliament referred to 'poor labouris of the ground' they meant small tenants, who themselves employed the labour of 'servants'.[41] In the countryside those who provided day labour were frequently, probably usually, cottars. Thus at Polwarth in Berwickshire in the 1690s the Kelsalls were able to trace eleven men whom Lady Grisell Baillie paid by the day for tasks such as quarrying, mending dykes, thatching and helping with shearing and stacking: they were all entered in the poll tax as cottars, paying an annual rent of around £4 for their holding. Their wives sometimes sold poultry, eggs and butter to the big house, and in July 'virtually all of them' sold their wool for between £1.4s. and £1.15s. each. Indeed, as we see in the following chapter, so meagre were the returns of day labour that it was unlikely that a family could subsist on them without a holding on the land from which to grow some of their own food and sell a little of the surplus. It is clear that the concept 'landless labourer' can hardly be applied in the Scottish countryside before the agricultural revolution of the late eighteenth and early nineteenth centuries.

Wage records themselves can give a rather misleading impression that day labour was paid entirely in money, though not invariably so: we have, for example, seen how both in the Fife wage assessment of 1611 and the Lanarkshire assessment of a century later, 3s. a day was deducted from the going rate if food was provided, which amounted to half or more of the total wage. However, careful inspection of actual wage payments, where

[39] W.R. Scott (ed.), *The records of a Scottish cloth manufactory at New Mills, Haddingtonshire, 1681–1703* (Scottish History Society, 1st series, vol. 46, Edinburgh, 1905), p. xxiii.

[40] St Andrews University Library archives: Lady Balgarvie's account book.

[41] *APS*, vol. IV, p. 623.

evidence of them survives, suggests that in the countryside coins may have been handed over relatively infrequently. Most day wages, though certainly reckoned in money, would have been at least partly paid in an equivalent value of oatmeal, or in terms of miscellany of goods including, for example, fuel or cow dung, or in calculated allowances set against rent. The rates cited in our tables, therefore, reflect not so much coins or notes handed over, as an accounting mechanism for an entitlement that would often be paid in some other medium. They are no less valid for that.

Something over the going rate might be paid for exceptionally heavy work; for example if the barrowmen at a building site were employed for a short intensive burst moving stones, they might be paid 8s. instead of 6s. There is a striking example of this in the Aberdeen shore work account of 1668 when eight workmen were paid double rates (13s.4d. instead of 6s.8d.) for 'bringing ane hillfull of stones from the shore to the bulwark anent the over cran they going at four in the morning and cam not hom till nyn hours at night'. Often, however, this particular group of labourers was paid less than the going rate, perhaps at only 4s. a day when their work on the harbour was limited by the coming and going of the tide, or at 5s. or 6s. a day if they were merely filling sand.[42] In all our tables we have ignored such payments if they seem obvious and exceptional, and we have always tried to quote a standard day rate. Nevertheless it is possible that some of the upward or downward variation in some years might be due to such factors entering undetected. Generally, also, there were differing rates for summer and winter work, the latter being one-sixth lower to allow for a shorter working day. Unless stated to the contrary, our tables refer to summer rates throughout, but again it is possible that certain low rates are due to winter rates creeping in unrecognised.

We have constructed figure 8.2 to show the range of day labourers wages accounted in money terms from quotations in town and countryside. Rural wage quotations do not go back far beyond the middle of the seventeenth century, but where they can be compared thereafter they are almost always below the rate in the large burghs. No doubt this was, in part at least, a real distinction, but we must note again that much of the burgh data are from building accounts where the possibility of a mark-up to allow for the master mason's or wright's profits cannot usually be excluded.[43]

The trend in towns is not unlike that of the skilled building workers. The normal wage in the 1530s seems to have been edging up from 10d. a day, but was 1s.6d. to 2s. by the 1560s except perhaps for work that demanded extraordinary exertion. By the end of the century it had reached 5s., and by the next decade 6s., though higher in the Master of Works accounts (except Dumbarton), lower in Edinburgh's town council building records. By mid century it was usually either 6s.8d. or 8s., momentarily 9s. in Glasgow, occasionally even higher in the Aberdeen shore work accounts in the second half of the century, but this may be due to unusual tasks on hand. In the eighteenth century, at least in Edinburgh, the usual rate was around 7s. until mid century, when it began to rise more steeply than the rate for skilled building workers, achieving 12s. by the early 1770s and

---

[42]   L.B. Taylor (ed.), *Aberdeen shore work accounts, 1596–1670* (Aberdeen, 1972), p. 580.

[43]   We at least know that in 1807 in Dundee the mason's incorporation 'not only fixed the prices but laid down what the master's profit should be – 6d. per day on a journeyman's labour, 4d. on a labourers'. A. Smith, *The three united trades of Dundee*, p. 23.

14s. by the late 1780s.[44] Nevertheless it shows the same approximate profile – a century of inflation which plainly did not keep up with the long-term trend in food prices though some of the losses were recouped before 1630, followed by a century of stagnation tending to decline, followed by a period of renewed growth.

Rural day wages seem to have followed an identical trend where they can be traced after 1660, though they were distinctly lower. Until the 1750s or 1760s they followed more firmly the traditional 6s. a day in summer (5s. in winter) in the south of Scotland, a shilling or two lower north of the Tay. An interesting exception, significantly from the 1660s, comes from Panmure in Angus, where labourers received 8s. daily in summer, 6s. in winter. The estimated wages in the *Statistical account* appear to give a more varied impression than wages drawn from account books; this may be partly from faulty recollection, and partly because some of the very low quotations omitted to state that an equal value of food was also provided. After 1760 day labourers' wages in most areas increased with rapidity until by the early 1790s they were about 14s. a day in summer (12s. in winter) in the central belt, 12s. a day in summer (10s. in winter) in the north-east and western borders and 7s. a day in summer (still 5s. in winter) in Ross and Cromarty. There was thus throughout most of Scotland a considerably greater gain for unskilled day labour than for skilled building workers in the thirty years after 1760 – generally, it was at least a doubling in money terms and therefore clearly outpaced inflation of food prices.

Making the comparison with unskilled building workers studied by Phelps Brown and Hopkins and by Bowden in England, both trends and levels of pay again look rather different in the two regions.[45] The English equivalents of the 'barrowman' and the agricultural day labourer were earning 8s.–10s. in Scots money for a day's work in the first forty years of the seventeenth century, almost within reach of a Scottish worker, whose highest wages came within that range, though most would be about a third lower. After 1650, however, workman's wages in the south of England climbed out of sight while in Scotland they levelled off or even fell a little. Agricultural day wages in Essex and Sussex by the first half of the eighteenth century were 12s.–18s. in Scots money, builders' wages in Oxford 14s., in London upward of 20s., compared to the 8s. or so even in Edinburgh, 6s. in the countryside. Nothing could illustrate more sharply the basic success of the English economy, or the basic failure of the Scottish economy, than this sharp divergence in remuneration for the unskilled, though in Yorkshire and Lancashire at least before 1750 day labourers rates at 8s. were much closer to Scottish levels. Then, however, the tide turned once more: unskilled building workers' wages in the south of England in the 1790s were running at 19s.–22s. compared to 12s.–14s. over most of Scotland, a much narrower ratio where the Scots were again only a little over a third lower. It surely goes some way to explain the confidence with which the commentators in the *Statistical account* regarded the increasing prosperity of at least the southern half of Scotland, though we should also note that inflation had by the final decade of the eighteenth century rubbed some of the gilt off the gingerbread.

[44] Fraser, *Conflict and class*, p. 36, also gives 14s. by 1790.
[45] Phelps Brown and Hopkins, *Perspective of wages*, pp. 1–12; P.J. Bowden, 'Statistical appendix' in J. Thirsk (ed.), *The agrarian history of England and Wales*, vol. IV (Cambridge, 1967), p. 684, vol. V, pt. 2 (1985), p. 877.

Finally, it is worth making a comment on harvest earnings, which would be available to virtually all rural, and no doubt many urban, day labourers for several weeks in the late summer and autumn. They were always paid with free food over and above the wage accounted in money, which was an important consideration, and the latter wage itself was equal to or higher than the usual summer wage rate. Thus in Lanarkshire in 1708 it was 6s. with food, at Yester in East Lothian in 1761 it was 9s. with food, and according to the *Statistical account* by the 1790s it was, over most of Scotland, between 12s. and 18s. with food, with a mode at 14s. In real terms probably another 3s. or 4s. could be added to these 'money' wages to account for the value of the food. At Yester in the early eighteenth century 12s. a day was paid for the similar hard labour of mowing or cutting hay, in this case without food.

Sometimes the contract was for the whole harvest rather than by the day: thus the Peebles justices in 1656 envisaged harvest workers either as being paid 4s. a day with food (women 3s.4d.) or as hiring themselves 'for the harvest . . . till all the cornes be put in barne and barnyeard'. In the latter case a 'sufficient and best man' able to stack and bind was to get £7.6s.8d., with food and drink while both a halfling who could only shear and a 'sufficient woman shearer' were paid £6.0s.0d., also with food and drink. Renfrewshire Sheriff Court records, 1686–1728, note 'fees for service in hairst' for males from £6.12s.0d. to £9.13s.0d., sometimes with additional payment in kind (plaiding, shoes, meal, groats, even 'two cwt. coals at pit'). For women the range was from £3.0s.0d. to £8.0s.0d., without 'bontages' though presumably still with food. Cash sums of this sort were often equivalent to, or even in excess of, the standard half year hiring fees in the same area.[46]

The *Statistical account* also put the value of most harvest earnings for males in the range of £6–£7 before about 1760, doubling by the 1770s and ranging above £20 in some places by the 1790s. This was a rate of increase greater than that of ordinary wages, which was to be expected if at the end of the period an increasing proportion of the workforce on the farms were becoming full-time landless labourers, rather than the traditional underemployed cottars whose labour could more readily be drawn upon at harvest time. Such periods of high earnings helped to offset the lower winter rates as well as the broken time that occurred when bad weather or sheer lack of employment drove the day labourer out of work.

2.3 Regularity of work for labourers and craftsmen

What proportion of the year a labourer or skilled craftsman could expect to find work was, of course, of the utmost importance. Labourers, masons and all manner of other building and agricultural workers paid by the day tended to be employed only when the need arose. Often they appear in the accounts for only a few days here and there, but even when fortunate enough to be employed for longer periods they remained exposed to the vagaries of the weather and the seasonal demands of agriculture or the building trade. Their problem was that, by and large, if there was no work to be done on a particular day

[46] SRO, JP 3/2/1, 'Justice of the Peace wage assessment, Peebles, 1656'; Hector (ed.), *Records of Renfrewshire*, pp. 334–5.

or half day, then they would earn no money. Indeed, in some cases it appears that employment was in fact by the hour, the amount paid being reduced if the usual twelve-hour day had, for whatever reason, to be shortened.

For cottars employed periodically by the estate on which they lived this was perhaps not too critical; they had land which needed their attention and, in any case, any waged labour they obtained was probably a valuable extra rather than the central mainstay of their livelihood. For those more dependent upon waged labour, however, the balance between days worked and days lost could mean the difference between relative comfort and abject poverty.

In this respect long-term trends in the number of days worked per year is an important, if in the end rather conjectural, factor to consider when examining the thorny question of changing living standards. This is a problem to which we return in chapter 9. For the moment, however, it is necessary to place in context our discussion of wage rates by identifying, at least in broad terms, what a daily rate of pay was likely to have meant in terms of an overall annual income. We are not here concerned with the problem of family incomes (this too will be considered in the next chapter), merely with evidence on the number of days worked per year by those labourers and skilled workmen whose daily rates of pay we have attempted to chart for the period 1550–1780.

There is first the evidence provided by a small number of estate and building accounts from which it is possible to determine the number of days individual labourers worked over the course of a year or series of years. Whilst these are invaluable, for they reveal the experience of individuals and thus come as close to the reality of employment as it is possible to get, they are nevertheless limited in two respects. First, they cast light on the employment of no more than a tiny, and possibly biased, proportion of all those labourers who were employed by the day. Second, the accounts upon which we depend were compiled from the point of view of the employer rather than the employed, and it is thus impossible to know for sure whether or not individuals found alternative sources of waged employment when they were absent from the accounts.

Such accounts nevertheless provide a useful starting point, and none more so than those prepared for the Duke of Montrose with respect to employment on his Stirlingshire estate of Buchanan between 1723 and 1783. As discussed in detail elsewhere,[47] a significant shift in employment patterns took place around mid century. In the first half of the eighteenth century most day labour was provided by individuals, almost certainly cottars, working for comparatively short periods each year. But as the century wore on, an increasing proportion of the work undertaken by day labourers at Buchanan was directed towards a relatively small group of men, each of whom tended to work for an ever greater proportion of the year. Thus, as table 8A indicates, during the period 1723–40 only a very small proportion of labourers were able to find work for even 220 days each year. After 1752, on the other hand, the vast majority of those employed worked for at least that length of time. By 1772–83, of those neither hired nor fired in the course of the year, the average number of days worked was no less than 276 per annum. Indeed, it was not unusual to find labourers working for more than 300 days a year, with the

---

[47] A. Gibson, 'Proletarianization? The transition to full-time labour on a Scottish estate, 1723–1787', *Continuity and Change*, vol. IV (1990), pp. 357–389.

Table 8A *Availability of employment for day labour: days worked per year*[48]

| Place and period | Number of labourers working given days per year (aggregate of annual totals) | | | | | Individual maximum days worked |
	1–19	20–119	120–219	220–79	280+	
Buchanan, 1723–40	72	255	114	4	0	274½
Buchanan, 1752–64	5	37	36	88	132	292
Buchanan, 1772–83	0	0	9	19	97	308½
Yester, 1672–5	0	8	19	17	9	310
Yester, 1687–96	5	15	10	32	3	283
Yester, 1744–5	0	0	1	9	4	295½
Aberdour, 1742–4	20	27	7	5	7	301½
Panmure, 1768	0	1	6	6	0	274
Glasgow, 1637	0*	4	6	0	0	182½
Glasgow, 1655	19	11	6	0	0	219
Glasgow, 1718	3	7	4	0	0	203½

Note:
* There were, in addition, some 82 days worked by an unstated number of men. The implication is that this was short-term employment for men not elsewhere mentioned in the accounts.

maximum being the 308½ days worked by Walter Mitchell in 1772. Given that the Sabbath was a rest day, and there was thus a maximum of 313 working days, this represents a remarkably high proportion of the year.

The emergence at Buchanan of a group of labourers who were able to find such a high level of employment was in part dependent upon the massive demand for year-round labour which was needed to fuel the Duke of Montrose's improvements. In this the situation at Buchanan would not have been unique, but even at the height of the agricultural revolution it must have been unusual. Few estates could have afforded the level of investment required for such a rapid transformation of the landscape as was being wrought at Buchanan. Certainly the evidence from other accounts would suggest that elsewhere it would have been rare for a labourer to have found work for more than 280 days in a year, and that even 220 days would have been fortunate. As summarised by table 8A, of the remaining records only the 1687–96 and 1744–5 accounts for Yester show more than half the workforce to have been employed for as many as 220 days in the year.[49]

[48] These statistics were extracted from the following sources: Buchanan 1723–40, SRO, GD 220/6/812–29; 1752–64, SRO, GD 220/6/1415–48; and 1772–83, SRO, GD 220/6/1547–74. Yester 1672–5, SRO, GD 28/2081 and GD 28/2095/1–3; 1687–96, NLS, MS 14638; and 1744–5, NLS, MS 14667/67–90. Aberdour 1742–4, SRO, GD 150/2394/1–2. Panmure 1768, SRO, GD 45/8/2274. Glasgow 1637, Glasgow University Archives, MS 26748; 1655, Glasgow University Archives, MS 26627; 1718, SRO, GD 220/6/1326.

[49] This is not to say that there is not clear evidence of individuals working for almost the entire year in other accounts. Often the documentary record is too meagre to allow for the analysis of the employment pattern of the workforce as a whole, yet still alludes to individuals such as John Hunter who, over the four years from 1756 to 1759 found, respectively, 264, 300, 288½ and 282 days work per year at Yester (NLS, MS 14667, pp. 160–192).

This table should, of course, be read with some caution, for in some cases wages were undoubtedly being earned in other ways. Leaving aside the earning potential of a small plot of land for those who had it, probably the most important source of extra income was the harvest. In addition, piece work, or even the supply of simple manufactured items such as nails or baskets, was occasionally used to enhance the overall income of an individual. The Yester accounts are particularly revealing in this context, for separate receipts were kept to account for all payments made to each individual, be they for day labour, piece work or for the harvest. For most individuals the contribution was slight, a matter of a few pounds Scots here or there, but for some, particularly in the period 1687–96, these other sources of income could prove very much more significant. To take but one example, in 1687 it was recorded that Thomas Burn worked some 152½ days for the estate at 6s.8d. per day. In addition to this, however, he was paid £21.8s.0d. for mowing in the meadow and a further £18.16s.0d. for erecting 47 roods of turf dyke at 8s. per rood. Over the course of the year he was therefore able to earn a total of £91.0s.8d., of which only £50.16s.8d. came through traditional day labour.[50]

It seems likely that Yester was only unusual in the manner and detail with which its records were kept. Perhaps it was rare for a man to appear for more than 220 days in the accounts, but that same man may have been picking up piece work, either on the estate or elsewhere, building dykes, winning stones, carting lime or sand, or simply working at the harvest. At Yester it is possible to gauge the contribution of these sources of income; elsewhere their value remains unknown. What, then, to make of the experience of George Mitchell at Aberdour between 1742 and 1744? He was fortunate enough to obtain 304¼ days work in 1743, the greatest number of days worked by any individual in any one year during this period, but in 1742 and 1744 he was only able to find work for 131 and 260 days respectively.[51] On the face of it this seems to epitomise the insecurity of the day labourer's annual income, but perhaps in these other years he merely directed his labour in other directions.

This possibility was no doubt particularly significant in the urban environment where alternative sources of employment were presumably much more readily available than in the relatively closed world of large estates such as Buchanan or Yester. The employment profile for Glasgow must be seen in this context. None of the labourers who appear in the Glasgow College accounts were able, in either 1655 or 1718, to obtain even 220 days employment with the College. This may to some extent reflect the strongly seasonal character of the building calendar, but it seems very likely that labourers who disappear from the College's accounts were, for at least some of the time, simply working elsewhere in the city.

Nevertheless, the overall impression to be gained from table 8A, that few labourers could have relied on being employed for even two-thirds of the year, cannot be dismissed lightly. In this respect a comparison between the rewards of day labour and farm service is revealing. The work undertaken by each category of labour was often similar (and at Yester there were individuals who were employed interchangeably from one year to the next), but the annually hired farm servant was generally also required to undertake more

[50] NLS, MS 14638.   [51] SRO, GD 150/2394/1–2.

skilled activities such as ploughing and sowing. Indeed, in many cases day labour appears to have been treated as little more than a top-up to the work provided by farm servants. Bearing this in mind, it seems strange that, wherever the comparison can be made, a day labourer would have been able, had he been employed for the whole year, to earn significantly more than the more highly regarded farm servant. To take but one example, between 1724 and 1742, a day labourer who could work for 313 days a year at Gordon Castle in Aberdeenshire[52] could, at the standard summer rate of 5s. a day (for 40 weeks) and winter rate of 4s. per day (for 12 weeks), earn about £74, yet an unskilled farm servant could only have earned £21 in cash plus his traditional 6½ bolls of oatmeal. In an average year the latter was worth, according to the Aberdeenshire fiars, about £29.15s.0d. The farm servant was, at least for the time being, in secure employment, and he had the considerable advantage of knowing he was to receive those 6½ bolls of oatmeal however expensive the staple foodstuff became, but the difference between his and the day labourer's potential income is nevertheless remarkable. The only reasonable conclusion is that a day labourer would very seldom have worked the entire year, perhaps even that he could hardly be sure of the 203 days work per year (or about four days per week) that would have brought him level, at summer rates, with the farm servant's total income of money plus the whole of his oatmeal in kind.

Such a conclusion seems intuitively likely with respect to others employed by the day, namely craftsmen such as masons and wrights. The evidence, as summarised in table 8B is sparse, and there is no comparable group paid by the year against whom comparisons can be made, but these men would have been at least as exposed to the vagaries of the weather and the seasonal nature of their trades as their unskilled contemporaries. At the level of the individual, insecurity of employment must have been a fact of life for all but the very lucky. But even at the aggregate level there seems little doubt that, as hinted at by table 8B, conditions varied markedly from year to year and even from one area to the next. At Buchanan, for instance, between 1752 and 1764 there were some twenty cases of individual masons being employed for more than 220 days a year. But these were all in the three years 1752–4 and outside of this relatively short period of hectic demand the greatest number of days worked in a year by a single individual was the 179 days worked by Robert Burrell in 1761.[53]

Occasionally, of course, relatively long-term contracts were entered into, such as that between the Earl of Panmure and John Milne, Master Mason, for the employment of fourteen masons and two apprentice masons from the 4 April until the middle of October 1666.[54] But even then bad weather was an ever present threat to earnings, and unemployment was only an indiscretion away:

If any of the aforesaid workmen shall neglect to attend their worke either wholl day or half day, their wages are to be detained from them accordinglie or such as shall be found given to drink and so neglect their dutie shall be put from the work and others put in their places.

Clearly it is rash to generalise about annual earnings on the basis of the limited evidence which is available. But we must, for one point is clear, neither labourers nor craftsmen

52 SRO, GD 44/52/64/3–5 and GD 44/51/379.   53 SRO, GD 220/6/1423/18.   54 SRO, GD 45/27/128.

Table 8B *Availability of employment for craftsmen: days worked per year*

	Number of masons working given days per year (aggregate of annual totals)					Individual maximum days
Place and period	1–19	20–119	120–219	220–79	280+	worked
Masons:						
Buchanan, 1752–64	17	27	23	7	13	301½
Buchanan, 1772–83	2	6	3	5	6	308
Glasgow, 1637	0	4	12	0	0	156
Glasgow, 1655	3	8	12	0	0	172
Wrights:						
Buchanan, 1752–64	3	9	7	9	18	305½
Buchanan, 1772–83	2	1	8	4	18	306

could generally rely on waged labour throughout the year and our understanding of the value of their daily rates of pay must be amended accordingly. The figure is perhaps uncomfortably conjectural, but if we assume that such men were able, on average, to work for the equivalent of only four days per week (or 57 per cent of the year) at summer rates of pay it seems unlikely that we shall be far from the mark. This is the figure we shall adopt in the next chapter as we begin to consider what wages in cash and kind would have meant in real terms.

2.4 Male farm servants paid by the year (tables 8.9, 8.11)

There are few problems in Scottish wage history more intractable than that of calculating the wage trends of male agricultural workers paid annually, or in some cases twice a year. Such men were widely called 'farm servants', but they are also simply called 'workmen'. In the south-east of Scotland, the Lothians and the eastern Border counties, where the farm servant was generally married and lived in a cottage, he was termed the 'hind' or 'half-hind', as described in the Midlothian wage assessment of 1656. In other parts of Scotland he might be what the Linlithgow assessment of 1673, as well as the Lanarkshire assessment of 1708 and others, called a 'domestic serving man' or 'inn servant', that is, not one who performed domestic service or lived in a hostelry, but one who lived domestically in the employer's household, and was unmarried. Just as there was a clear preference in the south-east for married men, so there was evidently a preference in the west and north for unmarried ones. Other areas, like Fife and Angus, evidently had mixed preferences.[55]

Married or unmarried, the job of the farm servant generally contained the same crucial elements – the best or 'sufficient' man had to be able to plough, to sow, to thresh,

[55] I. Levitt and C. Smout, *The state of the Scottish working-class in 1843* (Edinburgh, 1979), pp. 70–5, 83, 91, show the spatial distribution of these preferences in the 1840s: there is no reason to think they were different in earlier centuries.

to stack, to cart and, where appropriate, to be able to cut peat or turf. Some assessments differentiated the wage according to the arduous nature and skill of the task. Gathering seaweed ('ware') from the shore to spread as fertiliser on the fields was particularly demanding work and a Banffshire assessment in 1760 distinguished 'the best man servant, who drags the ware, and is capable to big [build] and sow', from second and third grades who merely loaded the 'ware horse' and could not build or sow, though they could thresh and reap. Their annual fee varied from £27 for the best servant to £20 for the third man: but for inland parishes where work with seaweed was not required the three grades varied in their fees from £23 to £13.6s.8d. – so there was more than 100 per cent difference between the top and bottom of the Banffshire range.[56] Many assessments allowed for such ranges of skills, characteristically distinguishing 'an able servant' from a 'servant of second rank', who could perform most but not all of the core tasks, and 'a boy or lad for keeping of cattell'. The middle rank was sometimes called a 'half lang man' or a 'halfling' ('between a man and a boy'),[57] which seems to imply some progression with age: but just as often he is simply described as a 'second man'. Often, across Scotland, he was also expected to be able to thatch, but at the end of the eighteenth century that task was increasingly performed by a specialised thatcher. The farm servant was thus a jack-of-all-trades, but those that knew most and worked hardest were best rewarded.

Almost always the farm servant's wage had two or three main elements: food and 'fee' (a cash payment) if he was unmarried, food, fee and entitlement to house and land if he was married. In some cases, as with the Lothian hinds in 1656, the married hind and half-hind had no money fee at all, but was relatively generously paid in grain, which he could turn into food for his family or market, at his own option. Very often there was another minor element of payment in kind, the 'bounteth' or 'bontage', paid as a few ells of cloth or a pair or two of shoes, sometimes as an extra allowance of drink. The historian's problem is of course in attempting to measure the value of all these things.

At first sight it appears that the easiest element to study must be the fee. It is, after all, the element cited in paid wages from estate account books, in the asessments, the poll tax records and the opinions of the contributors to the *Statistical account*. It is also of some intrinsic interest in its own right, since, as Valerie Morgan observes, the amount of cash an agricultural worker had to spend determined what he could buy in the market or lay up as savings, and this in turn throws light on the spread of a market economy within the Scottish regions.[58] There are, however, as we shall see, certain anomalies, in that in some parts of Scotland most in touch with the market the tradition of payment in kind survived longest.

It is not difficult to see, at least in crude outline for the south of Scotland, the course of change in the payment of money fees to farm servants paid by the year. The Fife and Perth assessments of 1611, although isolated quotations, both give a fee of £12 for a 'sufficient man'. The Ayrshire assessment of 1656 raises it to £24, and the Peebles assessment of 1664 puts it at £16 to £20 depending on how much of the bounteth is taken

---

[56] A. Fenton, *The shape of the past 2: essays in Scottish ethnology* (Edinburgh, 1986), p. 56.
[57] *OSA*, vol. XIII (Angus), p. 612.   [58] Morgan, 'Agricultural wage rates', p. 182.

in kind; the Linlithgow figure of 1673 is £20.13s.4d. and the Lanarkshire one of 1708 is again £24, roughly substantiated by the Renfrewshire poll tax of about the same period. The retrospective estimates of the *Statistical account* and surviving assessments from Wigtownshire and Dumfries suggest that a figure of around £24–£30 was still general until the 1750s, after which they began to move rapidly upwards until they reached a Scottish average of about £80 in the early 1790s according to Morgan, about £100 according to Hope.[59] Thus we can propose a doubling of money wages between 1611 and 1656, followed by a plateau of a century during which little happened; then we can more securely estimate an increase in money wages of upwards of 300 per cent in the three decades after 1760. Morgan has also shown how money wages in the latter period did not rise evenly across the southern half of Scotland, the increase being more pronounced in the west central belt and to a lesser extent in the linen districts of Angus and its environs.

Away from the southern half of Scotland, it is impossible to say anything about trends for male farm workers hired by the year before the middle of the eighteenth century, but from the *Statistical account* estimates it is clear that there was a much lower level of fee even before 1760 in the Highlands and in north-east Scotland than elsewhere: only four out of twenty-four citations are over £20, whereas to the south thirty-four out of forty-three are above that sum, and sixteen (including all those in south-east Scotland) are of £30 or more. That the north was already an area of low money wages, before the major economic developments of the second part of the eighteenth century widened the gap still further, has perhaps been insufficiently appreciated.[60] This difference persisted or became more accentuated by the 1790s, but a significant increase in the fee was common to all regions by that date.

What does an increase, over the years 1760–90, in the fee for farm servants of three-fold or four-fold mean? It seems remarkable, compared to a modest rise of at most half in building craftsmen's wages, and of a doubling in the wages of day labourers. It is, however, the sort of comparison we must not make without further consideration, for in the case of craftsmen and day labourers we were measuring their entire wage, for farm servants only one element among several. Only if we are able to calculate what the other elements are worth can we approach any estimate of the actual rate of increase in farm servants' wages.

This process is unusually difficult, since we may be dealing with situations in which some of the rents and prices of goods that were part of the wage moved in ways that are difficult to detect and also with the possibility, that in some places, as more was paid in money so the amount paid in kind may have diminished. This could have been true of the minor element, the bounteths of clothing, shoes and drink that in many places topped up the cash fee: the *Statistical account* occasionally noted their abolition by the 1790s.[61] It is less likely to have been true of the basic food allowances. We know that in 1843 the quantities of grain and other allowances in kind that a Lothian hind received were very similar to what he had received in 1656. Furthermore in 1843 over much of Scotland the

[59] Morgan, 'Agricultural wage rates', p. 191.   [60] Morgan, 'Agricultural wage rates', pp. 189–91.
[61] E.g. *OSA*, vol. 12 (Perths), p. 644.

farm servant received six and a half bolls of oatmeal a year, or two pecks a week. This was exactly the amount given in Fife and Aberdeenshire, for example, in the middle of the eighteenth century and in Angus in the seventeenth century. It looks as though the money element in the wage and not the amount given in food allowances, was what varied in the eighteenth century itself.

Bearing this in mind, at least one calculation can be made that might illuminate our problem. In Fife around 1760 oatmeal cost around £6 a boll: six and a half bolls a year would be valued at £39. An unmarried servant living with his employer and earning £24 fee would thus have a total income of £63. In the early 1790s meal cost around £9.10s.0d. a boll, the six and a half bolls then being valued at £62. The fee, according to Hope, was then £88, making a total income of £150, from which a little should be deducted if bounteths had been abolished. The increase between the two dates was thus slightly more than a doubling, which was better than, but comparable to, the improvement for a day labourer, and, of course, the main element in the overall cost of food was, by definition, protected from the increase in the cost of living. The percentage of the entire wage which in this case was paid in money was rather under 40 per cent in 1760, rising to almost 60 per cent in 1790. However one looks at it, these do look to be improving times for farm workers.

It would be a mistake, however, simply to equate a high or increasing percentage of the wage being paid in cash with progress out of subsistence farming and into production for the market. Nowhere in Scotland enjoyed more technically advanced or market-oriented farming than the south-east, especially East Lothian and the eastern Borders; but it was here, above all, that the system of hinding held sway, with most payments in kind to the married ploughman and his family. As late as 1843, in this region, where the value of the total wage to married agricultural workers was then demonstrably the highest in Scotland, the percentage paid in money was by far the lowest: it varied only from 5 per cent to 20 per cent.[62] We cannot make exactly the same calculation here for the eighteenth century, but it would be surprising if the overall picture was very different.

One other point is worth reiterating from section 2.3 above, in comparing the position of rural day labourers with farm servants. The former, had they been able to work all weekdays, winter and summer, would have earned more than farm servants: in the case just cited, a Fife day labourer earning a daily average 6s.6d. in 1760 and 13s. in 1790 (this does not allow for harvest earnings) would have had an income of £102 and £203 respectively, compared to £63 and £150 for the farm servant. Since there is no evidence that his labour was more highly regarded, but rather that it was normally considered as a top-up to that of the more highly skilled farm servant, the day labourers' total annual income must surely have been lower than that of the farm servants. The detailed examination of the regularity of work at Buchanan shows that in the period 1723–40 an average of twenty-five men employed worked only seventy-nine days a year. However, following the basic reorganisation of labour that accompanied the improvers' movement at Buchanan, this had changed by 1772–83 to an average of thirteen men who

---

[62] Levitt and Smout, *State of the Scottish working class*, p. 73.

worked 276 days a year.[63] Men working at this latter intensity may indeed have come to be as well off as the traditional farm servants, but (as discussed above) they probably remained the exception even into the nineteenth century. It was the farm servant who remained the sturdy backbone of Scottish rural labour force throughout the agricultural revolution and beyond.

2.5 Women (tables 8.12–8.13, 8.16)

The role of women in the labour force of Scotland before the Industrial Revolution has until recently been little noticed by historians,[64] but a glance at the poll tax returns for the 1690s indicates at once how important they were. In Aberdeenshire the percentage of 'servants' (including here farm servants, herds and similar designations as well as unspecified household servants) who were female ranged from 24 per cent in Towie up to about 75 per cent in Aberdeen. In the more purely rural parishes the percentage of women servants usually ranged from 30 per cent to 50 per cent, and the mean in households of tenants and small heritors was 42 per cent. In Renfrewshire female servants were even more numerous, ranging from 44 per cent in Eaglesham to 86 per cent in Paisley town and 92 per cent in the burgh of Greenock. Here the normal range was for 50–70 per cent of the servants to be women; overall the mean for the county was 61 per cent. In both counties about a fifth of the entire pollable population was entered under the designation 'servant'. We are dealing here with a very significant sector of the working population.

It is also clear that the wages received by women were, on average, substantially lower than those received by men. In the 1690s in Aberdeenshire the mean money payment per year for 'servants' of all descriptions employed by small heritors and tenants was £10.1s.0d. for men and £6.7s.5d. for women, the latter thus receiving about two thirds of the former. However, these figures are no more than means, encompassing wide ranging types of workers subsumed under the poll tax designation of 'servant'. Even in the agricultural sector this might include everyone from very young servants of either sex earning £2 or £4 a year to fully mature and capable men and women: at Greenlaw in Berwickshire the top 10 per cent of male servants earned £26–£32 a year, while the highest rate for women was £16, though that rate was earned by 20 per cent of females.[65] As illustrated by figure 8.3, the range for women revealed by the poll tax seems generally to have been much narrower and more strongly skewed than for men, but with relatively more women paid towards the top end.

Perhaps a more exact approach to examining the relative wages of men and women is through wage rates for comparable jobs, though the data here are meagre before 1750. The Fife assessment of 1611 envisaged the highest fee for a mature woman servant as half that for a man (and that of a 'lasse' as half that of a woman). A hundred years later the

---

[63] A.J. Gibson, 'Proletarianization?', pp. 357–90.
[64] But see R.A. Houston, 'Women in the economy and society of Scotland, 1500–1800', in R.A. Houston and I.D. Whyte (eds.), *Scottish society, 1500–1800* (Cambridge, 1988), pp. 118–47.
[65] Kelsall, *Scottish lifestyles*, p. 155.

Lanarkshire assessment of 1708 put the highest money payment for a 'strong and sufficient woman' at £14, which was 58 per cent that of the top male rate in husbandry. A 'lass or young maide' was to have £8, the same as 'boyes or lads', which confirms an impression from the poll tax that the gender difference was unimportant for children at the bottom end of the earning ladder in age and experience.

The retrospective wage quotations in the *Statistical account* give a wide and rather confusing variety of statements, but a female farm servant's annual fee in the south of Scotland was seldom more than one half of a man's; in the north-east it was a slightly higher proportion of a male's wage, but a smaller absolute sum. Highland women seem to have been particularly ill paid, perhaps because of a lack of commercial linen spinning which elsewhere in Scotland had begun to compete with field and dairy work. Between 1750 and 1790 the fee in the south probably at least doubled to around £36 a year; it also doubled in the north, but did not range so high. Valerie Morgan believes the women gained less than the men after mid century: 'both overall change and regional contrast are less marked'.[66] By the 1790s the money fee was about 40 or 50 per cent of the male equivalent, and they would be entitled to only half as much food.

Harvest work was another area where the labour of men and women can be compared. The Lanarkshire assessment of 1708 proposed to pay the shearers, per day, with food, at the rate of 6s. for a man, 5s. for a woman, 4s. for a male 'halflin', 3s. for 'younger maids'. The *Statistical account* quotes a number of cases where harvest fees were paid for cutting the complete harvest: before 1760, the mean for men was £6.13s.4d., for women £5.0s.0d. Women were long accepted as being particularly tough and useful in the harvest field, and these narrow differentials between the sexes recognise the fact.

Ordinary day labour, on the other hand, reverted to more typical ratios, as in the industrial work at New Mills, Haddington, in the 1680s. Women here got 3s.8d. a day (without food), for cleaning and picking wool, the same rate as that awarded for spinning (and also given to boys, for tasks such as scribbling and mixing wool): male weavers got 8s., more than twice as much.[67] A century later, in the 1790s, women employed by the day on field labour were earning 4s. or 5s. over most of Scotland, roughly a third of the male labourer's summer wage. Characteristically these would be involved in weeding or lifting turnip and potato crops, new tasks in this period.

Overall, there was no tendency for the wage rates of women to improve relative to those of men during our period. In the 1840s it was a safe rule of thumb to suggest that the going rate for a woman's work was about half that for man's work, in so far as it was ever possible to compare the two. The same figure had occurred to the Fife magistrates in 1611, and, except with respect to harvest work, a ratio of two to one or three to one was fairly general in the intervening years. Women probably reached their highest level of earnings sooner than men, so that (as the Renfrewshire poll tax data in particular suggest) more earned the maximum and the actual wage bill paid out to the two sexes may not have been quite so unequal as wage rates alone suggest. On the other hand, this situation arose because women were not given the opportunity to develop paid skills

[66] Morgan, 'Agricultural wage rates', p. 195.
[67] W.R. Scott (ed.), *Records of a Scottish cloth manufactory*, p. xxiii.

which they could then use to earn higher rewards as young or maturing adults: the dead end came sooner.

Finally, it would be useful to be able to say something about women's wage rates in domestic industry, especially in textile spinning. There is no doubt that earnings opportunities here were extremely important, as we shall see, but detailed reliable information on rates is very difficult to obtain before the end of the eighteenth century. Durie tells us that in Kintyre in 1744 a good spinner might have earned 7s.–8s. a week – 'but it is perhaps safest to say merely that earnings varied widely'. In 1755 a spinner might have taken away, after the cost of flax had been deducted, 16s. a week at Brechin in Angus, but only 12s. at Banff 'and even less at Huntly' in Aberdeenshire. Perthshire rates in 1755 were at 15s. to 16s.6d. a week, but two years earlier had ranged from 21s. to 30s. a week – much depended on demand for yarn and on the price of flax.[68] Adam Smith, probably as well informed on this as on other details of prices and wages, observed in 1775 that in most parts of Scotland 'she is a good spinner who can earn twentypence a week' – i.e., 20s. in Scottish money.[69] The *Statistical account* contains many quotations for female textile labour, as discussed later, for the 1790s: many of them suggest that a woman spinning could earn about a third of a male day labourer's wage. Yet the fact that such employment opportunities were there at all was, as we shall see in chapter 9, of the first importance in relation to family income opportunities in the eighteenth century.

3 The geographical variation of wages

Our understanding of how wage rates evolved over the sixteenth, seventeenth and eighteenth centuries relies upon a handful of series derived, until the final part of the seventeenth century, almost entirely from the principal burghs. Whilst we have no doubts that these provide a realistic guide to the movement of wages over time, it is worth emphasising that the geographical variation of wages was always a fact of life in the early modern period.

Such variation was to be found at all scales. In the mid seventeenth century, for instance, masons in Edinburgh could earn about two-thirds of the wage received by their counterparts in London, though by the middle of the eighteenth century (before the upturn in prosperity) this proportion had dropped to about 50 per cent. At the earlier of these two dates a similar differential applied between the wages of day labourers in the two capitals, those in Edinburgh earning about two-thirds of those in London. Before the mid eighteenth century, however, day labourers in Edinburgh had lost much ground, obtaining for a day's work little more than a third of that received in the English capital.

Wage differentials of similar magnitude were also to be found from one part of Scotland to another. The evidence (table 8.7) is most complete for the period 1747–9, when labourers' wages ranged from as little as 4s. per day at Monymusk (in central Aberdeenshire), through 5s. per day at Gordon Castle (Morayshire) and 6s. per day at Aberdour (Fife), Buchanan (Stirlingshire), Dalmahoy (Midlothian) and Yester (East

---

[68] A.J. Durie, *The Scottish linen industry in the eighteenth century* (Edinburgh, 1979), pp. 43, 76–7.
[69] A. Smith, *The wealth of nations* (Everyman edn, 1910), vol. I, p. 106.

Lothian), to as much as 7s. per day in Drylaw (Midlothian) and Edinburgh. A similar patttern of high wages in the central lowlands falling away further from the Forth–Clyde axis can be seen in the case of craftsmen. Thus the 10s. per day wage that masons were being paid at Gordon Castle in 1737 (table 8.4) contrasts markedly with the 16s.8d. being received in Edinburgh at the same time (table 8.1).

Such isolated comparisons notwithstanding, there is relatively little evidence upon which to assess the development of regional differentials in wage rates over the course of the seventeenth and eighteenth centuries. At no earlier point can we mirror Robert Hope's excellent snap shot of one moment, which he produced on the basis of ministers' comments in the *Statistical account* of the 1790s (table 8.16). This is unfortunate, for wage differentials constituted an important element of the Scottish economy and serve as a crude measure of the relative demand for labour and thus of economic development. They would, moreover, doubtless have acted as a spur to the migration of labour from areas of low demand and poor remuneration to the growing towns of the central lowlands.

There is, however, one area in which we can usefully add to the picture. Just as there were considerable differences between wages in different parts of Scotland, so too did wage levels vary within individual counties. The poll tax returns of the late seventeenth century provide an unrivalled opportunity to examine the scale and character of this (tables 8.17–8.18).

The interpretative pitfalls of these records have already been discussed, but by isolating the 'fee and bounteth' upon which the servants of tenants and small heritors were taxed we may feel fairly secure that we have identified as best we can the wage paid to 'agricultural servants' employed by the year or half year, excluding, of course, any additional payments made by way of food, rent, land allowance and so forth. This has been undertaken for both Aberdeenshire and Renfrewshire and although in both counties this procedure substantially cuts the number of servants whose wages we can examine, with 3,334 male and 2,380 female servants of tenants and small heritors spread over eighty-five parishes in Aberdeenshire,[70] and 307 and 566 such male and female servants spread over sixteen parishes in Renfrewshire,[71] this still constitutes a substantial sample upon which to base an analysis of the geographical variation of wage levels.

The situation in Renfrewshire (figure 8.4) can be described quite simply, on account of the small number of parishes in the county for which evidence is available. As described in table 8.17 and illustrated by figure 8.5, the means of both male and female servants' wages show a pronounced upward trend towards the more fertile parishes along the River Clyde, the Black Cart Water and the White Cart Water. Male servants in Cathcart, for instance, were earning on average about twice the wages of their counterparts in the three most westerly parishes of Inverkip, Greenock Landward and Kilmacolm. The mean for female servants, meanwhile, was nearly 50 per cent more in the east than in the west of the county.

[70] There are no servants in households of small heritors or tenants in the parishes of Old Aberdeen and the Burgh of Aberdeen.
[71] There are no data available for the parish of the Burgh of Renfrew, and there are no servants of small heritors or tenants in the parish of the towns of Greenock.

In Aberdeenshire, average wages for both male and female agricultural servants also varied significantly from one part of the county to the next (table 8.18). Average wage rates were, however, generally much lower; male and female wages being, on average, about 60 and 50 per cent of those received by their counterparts in Renfrewshire. Moreover, whilst the scale of wage variation for male servants was of a similar magnitude to that found in Renfrewshire, the differential was much more pronounced with respect to female servants. Male wages were at their highest in central Aberdeenshire where servants could earn, on average, £13.12s.0d. Scots per annum.[72] They were at their lowest in the three most south-westerly parishes of Crathie and Braemar, Glenmuick, Tullich and Glengairn, and Aboyne and Glentanar where wages were, on average, only £7.5s.3d. Scots. Female wages, meanwhile, were at their highest in the immediate vicinity of Aberdeen where servants could earn, on average, £9.11s.10d. Scots per annum,[73] and at their lowest in those parishes around the upper reaches of the River Don where wages were, on average, only £3.18s.0d. Scots.[74] Within Aberdeenshire, therefore, average male wages varied by about 90 per cent, but female wages by nearly 250 per cent.

Illustrating the geographical variation of wage rates in Aberdeenshire is somewhat more complex than in Renfrewshire for here there were a total of eighty-five parishes. An aggregative procedure has thus been adopted to highlight the general trends in wage rates across the county. This procedure is based on the idea of running means, except that it is two-dimensional so as to deal with a pattern of interlocking spatial units. Thus the 'running mean' wage rate for each parish is taken as the mean of that parish's wage (weighted according to the number of servants of small tenants and heritors) alongside the weighted means of its immediate neighbours. This 'running mean' is then ascribed to that parish's centroid. Repeating this for each of the eighty-five parishes, it is then possible to overlay 'contours' of equal wage rates and thereby to create what might be termed an 'iso-wage' map. Although this technique is limited insofar as the total number of parishes included in each of the samples from which the 'running-means' are calculated varies from one parish to the next, and because it involves the translation of areal data into point data, it nevertheless effectively aggregates the data without emphasising discontinuities.

With regard to male servants, as can be seen in figure 8.6, there was a pronounced band of high average wage rates running north-west from Aberdeen along the valleys of the rivers Don and Urie and across into the Dovern valley. A broadly similar pattern emerges with respect to female wages, save in this case the burgh of Aberdeen apparently had a very much greater, although perhaps more localised, influence on average wage rates. Thus whilst female wages in the immediage vicinity of Aberdeen were, on average, £9.11s.10d. Scots per annum,[75] just ten miles or so to the west, in the parishes of Drumoak, Echt and Midmar, wages were, on average, only £5.18s.5d. Scots per annum.

---

[72] The average wage in the parishes of Premnay, Leslie and Keig.
[73] The average wage in the parishes of Belhelvie, Dyce and Newhills.
[74] The average wage in Glenbuchat, Logie-Coldstone, Tarland and Strathdon.
[75] This average wage is considerably higher than might be expected according to figure 8.6. This is because the 'running means' used tend to smooth-out extreme values.

In general terms, the further one travels from the burgh of Aberdeen the lower were the wages paid to female agricultural servants until, in the far west and south-west, average wages fall below £4.0s.0d. per annum.

It would appear, therefore, that notwithstanding the relatively short distances involved, in both Renfrewshire and Aberdeenshire there were very significant differences between the wages which could be obtained in different areas. In Renfrewshire, for instance, little over twenty miles separated the parish of Innerkip in the far west from that of Cathcart in the east, yet over that distance male wages rose by no less than 100 per cent.

It is difficult to be certain just what these differences in average wage rates mean. It seems unlikely, for instance, that the overall value of agricultural labour would have shown the same degree of variation as is implied by the 'fee and bounteth' recorded in the Poll Tax books. We know from other sources that the value of this element of the wage would very often have been outweighed by the value of payments made in food, or by way of rent or land allowances. If the value of these additional payments remained broadly stable from one part of the country to another, then the remarkable wage differentials shown in figures 8.5 and 8.6 would have been reduced quite significantly.

The problem is that we have no evidence whatsoever on the contemporary value of these additional payments. It is even possible, for instance, that variations in the 'fee and bounteth' (which was primarily the cash element of the wage) was actually compensated for by variations in the other element. In other words, it is possible that our maps measure, not trends in the value of agricultural labour, but rather the penetration of a cash-based economy in late seventeenth-century Renfrewshire and Aberdeenshire. We cannot dismiss this possibility entirely, though the pattern of average male servants' wage rates in Aberdeenshire does tend to weigh against it. In this part of Scotland the burghs of Aberdeen and Old Aberdeen would surely have been the focus of any cash-based economy, yet the average value of the 'fee and bounteth' was at a maximum in central Aberdeenshire. With regard to female wage rates in Aberdeenshire and to both male and female wage rates in Renfrewshire the evidence is inconclusive, but it nevertheless seems probable that figures 8.5 and 8.6 provide a genuine insight into the spatial variation of the value of agricultural labour, albeit one in which the differentials are exaggerated.

There is another sense in which the wage differentials may be misleading. It is undoubtedly the case that in different parts of the two counties a different mix of servants, and particularly of male servants, would have been required to service the different types of agriculture pursued. The obvious distinction is between the mixed arable and pastoral parishes of the lowlands and the predominately pastoral parishes of the uplands. In the former there would have been a relatively high proportion of, to follow the terminology used by the justices of the peace, 'sufficient' men who were 'eable to performe all manner of work relating to husbandry, viz. to plow, sow, stack, drive carts and lay on loads'. Their presence, with their particular skills being rewarded by relatively high wages, would have pushed up average wage rates in the mixed farming regions compared with the more strictly pastoral districts.

This certainly appears to have been the case in Renfrewshire which, according to Francis H. Groome,[76] can be divided into two quite distinct regions. The correspondence between parish boundaries and the topography of the county is not exact (figure 8.4), but Groome's 'bleak hilly moorland' region broadly coincides with the seven parishes of Kilmacolm, Lochwinnoch, Eaglesham, Mearns, Neilston, Inverkip and Greenock Landward, where average male wages were only £13.11s.5d. per annum. This contrasts with the average male wage of £18.4s.6d. in the nine parishes of Eastwood, Kilbrachan, Houston and Killane, Erskine, Cathcart, Renfrew, Inchinnane and the two Paisleys which together constitute Groome's 'gently rising district' and 'flat laich lands'. Assuming that the nature of agriculture broadly reflected this basic topography, wage rates were significantly higher in the mixed farming parishes than in the more purely pastoral parishes of the 'bleak hilly moorland'.[77]

The situation with respect to male wages in Aberdeenshire was similar. Here the pastoral parishes of the uplands can be distinguished from the mixed farming parishes which comprised the majority of the county on the basis of the ratio of acres to valued rent (figure 8.7).[78] A significant difference exists between wages paid in those parishes with more than 10 acres of land per pound Scots of valued rent (on average, £7.15s.6d. Scots per annum) and those paid elsewhere in the county (on average, £11.13s.8d. per annum).

The employment profile of the agricultural workforce in different areas was obviously important, but local conditions of supply and demand, both of labour in general and of agricultural servants in particular, must also have played a part in determining the geography of average male wage rates in both Renfrewshire and Aberdeenshire. Whilst this is difficult to demonstrate in Renfrewshire because the urban centres of the lower Clyde were located just where the more skilled workforce of the mixed arable and pastoral farming lowlands would have been inflating average wage rates anyway, in Aberdeenshire the impact of local conditions of supply and demand can be more readily isolated. Thus whilst the tongue of highly valued arable land shown on figure 8.6 is mirrored by a zone of high wages which extends up the Don and Urie valleys, elsewhere the relationship is less clear cut. The area of high-value arable land also, for instance, extended up the east coast as far north as Fraserburgh, but male wages decline significantly with increasing distance from the burgh of Aberdeen.

An important factor behind this pattern may have been the rewards which could have been had through weaving, principally of plaiding, a coarse cloth made from combed wool. In remote country districts the industry was organised through the *kaufsystem*, whereby workers supplied their own raw materials and sold their products at local markets and fairs. The limited rewards available under such a system would have placed

---

[76] F. H. Groome, *Ordnance gazetteer of Scotland: a survey of Scottish topography, statistical, biographical and historical* (6 vols., Edinburgh, 1885).

[77] This is a statistically significant difference with a confidence limit of 99 per cent.

[78] Tyson has divided the county into three districts on the basis of the valued rent of parishes in 1674: R.E. Tyson, 'The rise and fall of manufacturing industry in rural Aberdeenshire', in J.S. Smith and D. Stevenson (eds.), *Fermfolk and fisherfolk; rural life in Northern Scotland in the eighteenth and nineteenth centuries* (Aberdeen, 1989), pp. 63–82, p. 75. By definition these regions reflect the agricultural worth of the land and thus, at least to a degree, the relative proportion of arable as opposed to pastoral farmland in each parish.

little upward pressure on male agricultural servants' wages, particularly at a time when the industry was experiencing a long and severe crisis.[79] Closer to Aberdeen, however, the industry was organised under the *verlagssystem* or putting-out system. Under this system the price which could be obtained for plaiding decreased the further the merchants had to travel to deliver the raw materials and collect the finished products. Given that the industry was monopolised by merchants from Aberdeen, both the income which could be generated through weaving and the upward pressure on agricultural wages would have decreased the further one went from that burgh.

This factor no doubt also played a part in determining the geography of female agricultural servants' average wage rates in Aberdeenshire. The underlying pattern of agriculture would certainly have been less significant than with male servants; even in mixed arable and pastoral areas women tended to be engaged in activities, often domestic, which did not permit the development of particularly well-rewarded skills. Nevertheless, although the bulk of the labour force involved in the production of plaiding was made up of the women and children who spun the wool before it was woven by the men, and although the production of stockings (the other major cottage industry in Aberdeenshire at this time) was almost entirely carried out by women,[80] the very sharp and relatively localised peak in female wage rates in the parishes adjacent to Aberdeen suggests that other forces were at work.

According to the Poll Books there were some 800 female servants in the burghs of Aberdeen and Old Aberdeen (and this unquestionably understates the real number). This amounts to nearly 18 per cent of all female servants recorded in Aberdeenshire as a whole and, as a large proportion of these servants were presumably drawn from outside the two burghs, this exceptionally high demand for female labour must have pushed up female wage rates in the area surrounding the two burghs. This may have been further compounded by the presence of unusually skilled female agricultural servants employed in the production of butter and cheese for the urban market.

Whatever the precise explanation, and this must include factors which influenced the actual value of labour as well as those which influenced the relative proportion of skilled and thus better paid agricultural servants within the labour force as a whole, it is clear that average wage rates varied significantly over quite short distances in both Aberdeenshire and Renfrewshire. It seems clear, moreover, that what was true of these two counties would have been true throughout the country as a whole.

If we have been able merely to scratch the surface of the geography of wages in the 1690s, we can do little more concerning the development of that geography in the following century. The changes that took place at a national level have already been alluded to, but there are clues from the *Statistical account* that significant changes in wage differentials also took place at local level. Some forty-two ministers reported in the *Statistical account* on the wages paid to female agricultural servants in Aberdeenshire, their estimates varying from £24 to £42 Scots per annum. Wages had increased

[79] By 1700, cloth that had sold for 11s.6d. per ell in 1674 could be bought for as little as 6s. or 7s: R.E. Tyson, 'Proto-industrialization in Aberdeenshire; woollen cloth and knitted stockings', unpublished paper presented to the 'Proto-industrialization in the North' conference held at St Andrews, 23 April 1988, p. 2.

[80] R.E. Tyson, 'The rise and fall of manufacturing, p. 70.

throughout the county, but at a vastly greater rate in those parishes which had shown the lowest average wages in 1695. Thus in the parishes of Glenbuchat, Logie-Coldstone, Tarland and Strathdon, where female agricultural servants had been paid, on average, only £3.18s.0d. Scots per annum in 1695, the going rate in the 1790s was about £27 Scots, an increase of no less than 690 per cent over the course of a century. On the other hand, in those parishes in the immediate vicinity of Aberdeen where female servants had, on average, received £9.11s.10d. in 1695, the going rate in the late eighteenth century was also in the region of £27 Scots per annum, representing an increase of only 280 per cent. Moreover, not only had female wage differentials within Aberdeenshire been significantly reduced by the 1790s, the reports of the ministers show no convincing pattern of wage variation across the county.

Similarly, although male agricultural servants' wages in Aberdeenshire were still subject to a similar magnitude of variation in the 1790s as had been the case in 1695, once again the clear geographical trends which had been obvious at the end of the seventeenth century had largely disappeared. It is quite possible, therefore, that those differences which do emerge in the *Statistical account* with respect to both male and female wage rates were a consequence of the lack of accuracy, and perhaps even bias, of the individual ministers reporting on the wages paid in their parishes. In Renfrewshire, meanwhile, wage differentials had also decreased markedly by the end of the eighteenth century; average male wages by then ranged from about £96 to £132 per annum (a 38 per cent difference compared to the 100 per cent recorded in 1695); whilst average female wages ranged from about £36 to £48 per annum (a 33 per cent as opposed 50 per cent difference).

All this evidence refers, of course, only to the money element of the wage. Possibly these developments may reflect little more than a changing balance in different parts of the country between payments made in cash as opposed to kind, in effect, the penetration of an incrasingly cash-based economy into the more remote parts of the countryside. To what extent these changes nevertheless reflect underlying developments in the geography of the actual value of labour, and what the reasons for these changes may have been, lies beyond the scope of this survey.

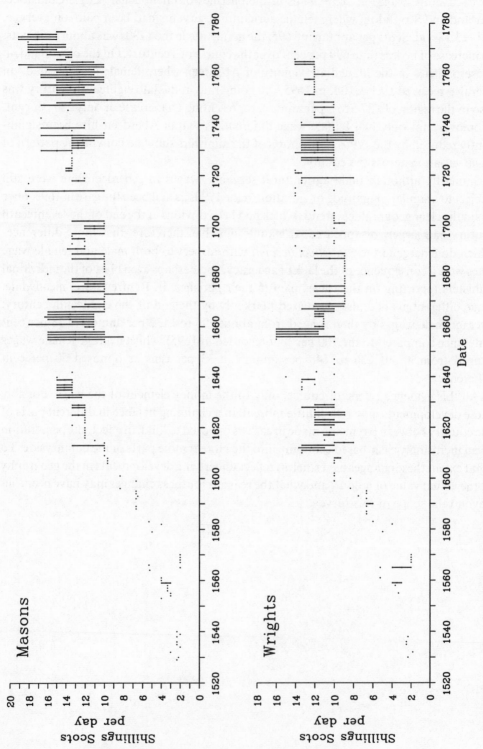

8.1 Craftsmen's daily wages: Scotland, 1529–1780

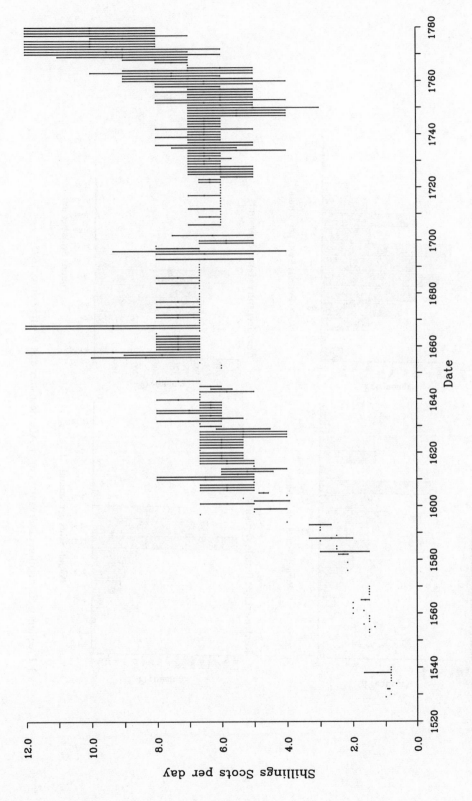

8.2 Labourers' daily wages: Scotland, 1529–1780

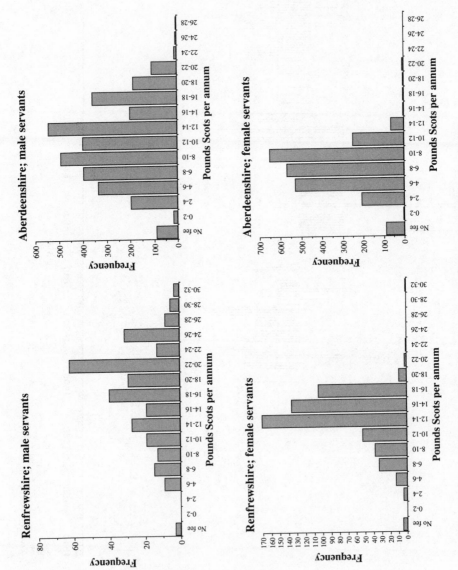

8.3 Frequency distribution of servants' wages: Aberdeenshire and Renfrewshire, 1695

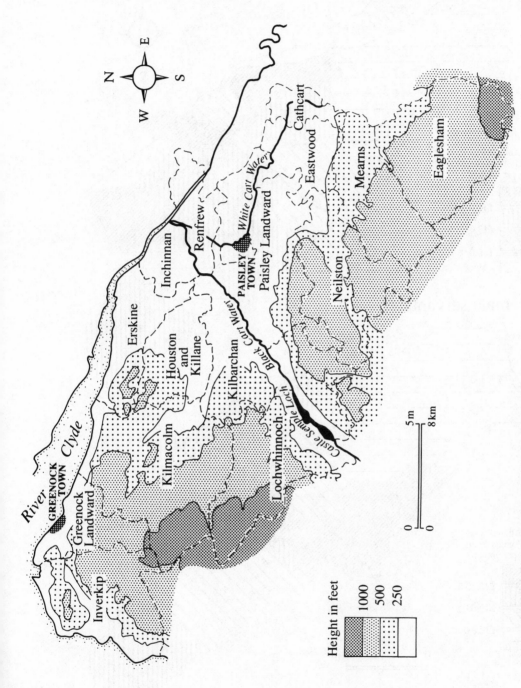

Height in feet

1000
500
250

8.4 Renfrewshire: topography and parochial division

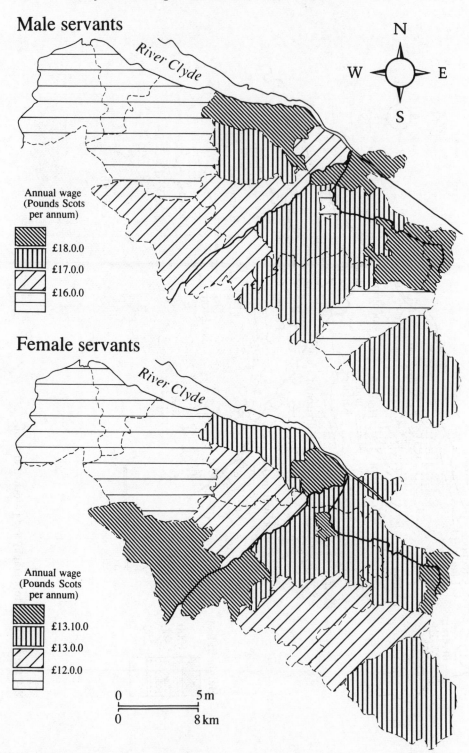

8.5 Male and female servants' annual fees: Renfrewshire, 1695

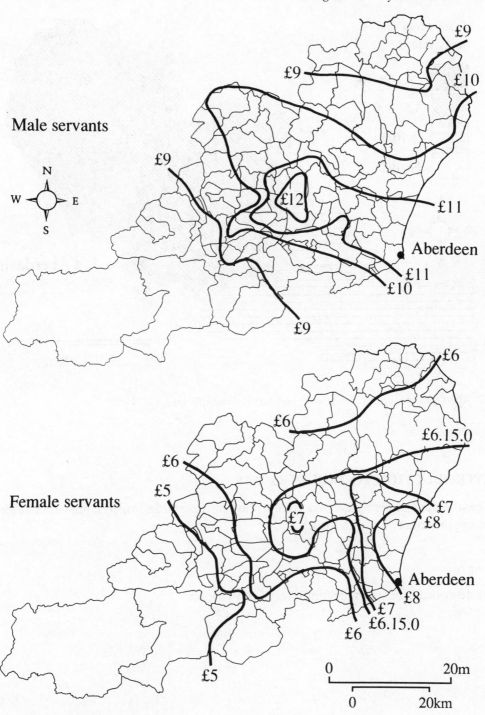

8.6 Servants' wages: Aberdeenshire, 1695

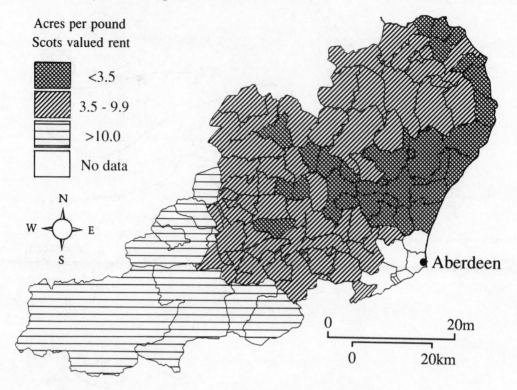

8.7 Aberdeenshire regions: acres per pound Scots of rateable value (1674)

INTRODUCTION TO TABLES 8.1–8.18

The whole of chapter 8 serves as a commentary on these tables, which should not be used except in conjunction with the text.

Sources

As described in detail in the footnotes of this chapter.

Table 8.1 *Edinburgh building craftsmens' daily wages, 1529–1790*

	Masons		Wrights	
Date	Town council accounts s. d.	Master of Works' accounts s. d.	Town council accounts s. d.	Master of Works' accounts s. d.
1529		2 4		* 2 2
1530		2 2		2 4
1532		3 0		1 10
1535		2 4		2 6
1536		2 4		2 6
1538				2 4
1553	4 0			
1554	3 0			
1555	3 0		3 4	
1556	3 4		* 4 4	
1557	3 4			
1558	3 4		3 8	
1559	4 0	3 0	4 0	3 0
1560	4 0			
1561	4 0		5 3	
1564	5 3		5 3	
1565			4 0	
1566	5 4		* 5 0	
1579		5 0		5 0
1582	* 6 8		* 5 0	
1583	5 4		6 0	
1584	* 5 0		* 5 0	
1585	* 7 6		* 5 0	
1586	* 6 10			
1587	* 8 4		6 8	
1588	6 8			
1589	6 8			
1590			6 8	
1591	* 3 0			
1592	6 8			
1593	6 6		7 6	
1596	8 4		8 4	
1598			*10 10	
1599			* 6 8	10 0
1600			8 4	
1601	8 4		* 8 4	
1604			* 6 8	
1606	* 9 8			
1607	9 8			
1608	9 8		9 3	
1609	10 0			
1611	10 0		10 0	10 0
1612	10 0		11 0	
1613	10 0	13 4	10 0	
1614	10 0	10 0	10 0	8 0
1615	11 0		11 0	

* denotes sparse data.

Table 8.1 *(cont.)*

Date	Masons		Wrights	
	Town council accounts	Master of Works' accounts	Town council accounts	Master of Works' accounts
	s. d.	s. d.	s. d.	s. d.
1616	12 0	12 0	12 0	12 0
1617	12 0	12 0	11 1	10 0
1618	12 0	12 0	12 0	8 11
1619	12 0			
1620	12 0		10 4	
1621	13 4		12 0	
1622	12 0	12 0	12 0	8 11
1623	12 0		12 0	
1624	12 0		12 0	
1625	12 0	13 4	12 0	8 11
1626	12 0	12 0	12 0	8 11
1627	12 0		12 0	
1628	12 0	13 4	12 0	13 4
1629	12 0	13 4	12 0	10 0
1632	13 4			
1633	13 4	*14 0		*12 0
1634	13 4			
1635	13 4		13 4	
1636	13 4		13 4	
1637	13 4		12 0	
1638	13 4		13 4	
1639	13 4	13 4	12 0	13 4
1640			*10 0	
1642	13 4		11 10	

Date	Town council accounts		Date	Town council accounts	
	Masons s. d.	Wrights s. d.		Masons s. d.	Wrights s. d.
1736	16 8	*14 0	1772	19 0	
1739	16 8		1774	19 0	
			1775	19 0	
1743	16 8		1776	*19 0	18 0
			1777	*18 0	
1748	16 8		1778	*19 0	
			1779	*19 0	
1752	16 8		1780	19 0	*19 0
			1781	20 0	
1756	16 8		1782	20 0	
			1783	20 0	
1759	16 8		1784	21 0	
1760	16 8		1785	24 0	
1763	18 0		1787	26 0	
1764	19 0				
			1789	26 0	
1771	*19 0		1790	26 0	

* denotes sparse data.

Table 8.2 *Provincial masons' daily wages, 1594–1736*

Date	Aberdeen master masons		Aberdeen servant masons		Glasgow masons	Haddington masons
	Town council accounts s. d.	Shore work accounts s. d.	Town council accounts s. d.	Shore work accounts s. d.	College accounts s. d.	Town treasurers' accounts s. d.
1594	13 4		6 8			
1595	13 4		6 8			
1599	13 4		6 8			
1603	13 4					
1604	13 4					
1605	13 4					
1606	13 4					
1611	13 4					
1612	13 4					
1613	13 4					
1617	13 4					
1621	13 4					
1623	14 0					
1624	13 4					
1625	13 4					
1626	13 4					
1627	13 4					
1628	13 4					
1632					15 0	
1633			10 0			
1634	13 4		13 4			
1635	16 4	16 8			15 0	
1636					15 0	
1637					15 0	
1639					15 0	
1640					15 0	
1642	13 4					
1643		15 7				
1647	13 4					
1654	20 0		10 0			
1655	20 0		10 0		16 0	
1656	23 4	20 0	8 0		16 0	
1657		20 0			16 0	
1658		20 0			16 0	
1659	20 0		11 1			
1660	20 0	20 0	12 0			
1661				13 4		18 0
1662				13 4		
1663				13 4		16 0
1664				16 4		16 0
1665	20 0			16 0		16 0
1666						16 0
1667		20 0				
1668				13 4		
1669				12 0		

Table 8.2 *(cont.)*

Date	Aberdeen master masons		Aberdeen servant masons		Glasgow masons	Haddington masons	St Andrews masons
	Town council accounts	Shore work accounts	Town council accounts	Shore work accounts	College accounts	Town treasurers' accounts	St Leonard's college accounts
	s. d.	s. d.	s. d.	s. d.	s. d.	s. d.	s. d.
1670		26 8					
1671	18 0					16 0	
1672	18 0						
1673	13 4	18 0	6 8				
1674				13 4			
1676				13 4			
1677						12 0	
1678	20 0			13 4			
1679				13 4			
1681				16 0			
1687				13 4			
1689				13 4			
1690				13 4			
1691	20 0		14 0	13 4			
1693				13 4			13 4
1695	20 0						13 4
1696							13 4
1697							13 4
1698	20 0						
1699		20 0					10 0
1700		20 0					10 0
1701		20 0					
1702					13 4		10 0
1706		18 0					
1714							13 4
1718					13 4		
1719							12 0
1722					13 4		
1723					13 4		
1727					13 4		
1729					13 4		
1730					13 4		
1732					12 0		
1733					12 0		
1734					13 4		
1735					13 4		
1736					13 4		

Table 8.3 *Provincial wrights' daily wages, 1586–1741*

Date	Aberdeen master wrights		Aberdeen servant wrights		Glasgow wrights
	Town council accounts	Shore work accounts	Town council accounts	Shore work accounts	College accounts
	s. d.	s. d.	s. d.	s. d.	s. d.
1586			6 8		
1589			6 8		
1590	10 0		6 0		
1592			6 8		
1594	10 0		6 8		
1595	10 0		6 8		
1601	13 4		10 0		
1602	13 4		10 0		
1606	13 4		10 0		
1607	13 4		10 0		
1608	13 4		10 0		
1610	16 8		13 4		
1611	16 8	15 0	13 4		
1612	16 8	15 0	13 4		
1613	16 8		13 4		
1615	13 4				
1617	13 4				
1618	13 4		10 0		
1621	13 4		10 0		
1623	13 4		10 0		
1624	13 4				
1625	13 4		10 0		
1626	13 4		10 0		
1628	13 4		10 0		
1629		20 0			
1631	13 4		10 0		
1632	13 4				
1634	13 4		10 0		
1635	13 4				
1639		13 4			
1640					15 0
1641	13 4	13 4	10 0		
1642		13 4			
1643	13 4				
1644	13 4	12 0			
1645			10 0		
1647	13 4		10 0		
1655					16 0
1656					16 0
1657					16 0
1658					16 0
1659	20 0		12 0		16 0
1660			12 0		

Table 8.3 *(cont.)*

Date	Aberdeen master wrights		Aberdeen servant wrights		Glasgow wrights	St Andrews wrights
	Town council accounts	Shore work accounts	Town council accounts	Shore work accounts	College accounts	St Leonard's college accounts
	s. d.	s. d.	s. d.	s. d.	s. d.	s. d.
1661	20 0					
1664	20 0		12 0			
1665		20 0	12 0	12 0		
1666	20 0	20 0		12 0		
1667			12 0	13 4		
1668	20 0	20 0	12 0			
1669	20 0		12 0			
1672		20 0		12 0		
1674	20 0		12 0			
1676	20 0		13 4			
1677		18 0				
1685		20 0				
1687				13 4		
1689		20 0		13 4		
1690				13 4		
1693						10 0
1694						10 0
1696	20 0					
1697						12 0
1699		20 0				10 0
1700						10 0
1701						10 0
1702						10 0
1703						10 0
1704						10 0
1705						10 0
1706						12 0
1714						10 0
1717						13 4
1718					13 4	
1719						13 4
1721					13 4	
1723					13 4	13 4
1726					13 4	
1727					13 4	
1729					13 4	
1730					13 4	
1731					13 4	
1732					13 4	
1733					13 4	
1734					13 4	
1735					13 4	
1736					13 4	
1740					13 4	
1741					13 4	

Table 8.4 *Estate masons' daily wages, 1691–1777*

Date	Gordon Castle s. d.	Monymusk s. d.	Panmure s. d.	Buchanan s. d.	Dalmahoy s. d.	Drylaw s. d.	Newbattle s. d.	Wedderburn s. d.
1691			12 0					
1692			12 0					
1694			12 0					
1695			12 0					
1699			12 0					
1700			12 0					
1709						18 0		
1712						18 0		
1714			10 0			18 0		
1717						18 0		
1718			12 0					
1721			12 0					
1722							14 0	
1723				13 4			14 0	
1724				13 4				
1725				13 4				
1726				13 4				
1727				13 4				
1729				13 4			13 4	
1730				13 4		16 8	13 4	
1731			12 0	13 4			13 4	
1732				13 4			13 4	
1733				13 4				
1734	12 0			13 4				
1735	10 0			13 4				
1736	10 0			13 4				
1737	10 0	*14 0						
1738				13 4				
1739				12 0		16 8		
1741	10 0							
1748					12 0			
1749		15 0			12 0			
1752		15 0						
1753	11 0	15 0						
1754	11 0	15 0						
1755	12 0	15 0						
1756	11 0	15 0						
1757	10 0	15 0						
1758	10 0	15 0						15 0
1759	10 0							15 0
1760	11 0							15 0
1761	10 0							15 0
1762	11 0							16 0
1763	10 0							
1764	10 0			15 0				
1765	11 0			13 4				
1766		14 0		15 0				
1767		14 0		13 4				
1768		16 0		13 4				
1769		16 0		13 4		18 0		
1770				15 0		18 0		16 0
1771				14 0		18 0		16 0
1772				14 0		18 0		16 0
1773								16 0
1774				15 0				15 0
1775				15 0				15 0
1776			15 0					15 0
1777			15 0					

Table 8.5 *Estate wrights' daily wages, 1692–1778*

Date	Gordon Castle	Monymusk	Panmure	Buchanan	Dalmahoy	Drylaw	Newbattle	Wedderburn
	s. d.	s. d.	s. d.	s. d.	s. d.	s. d.	s. d.	s. d.
1692						14 0		
1696							12 0	
1697						14 0	12 0	
1700			10 0					
1712						14 0		
1713						14 0		
1715						14 0		
1719		8 0				13 4		
1721							14 0	
1722							14 0	
1724				10 0				
1725				10 0				
1726				10 0				
1727		10 0		10 0				
1728				10 0				
1729				10 0			14 0	
1730				10 0				
1731				10 0				
1732				10 0			12 0	
1733				10 0				
1734				10 0				
1735	8 0			10 0				
1736	8 0			10 0				
1737	8 0			10 0				
1738				10 0				
1739	10 0			10 0				
1740				10 0				
1742				10 0				
1743		10 0				12 0		
1744						12 0		
1745						12 0		
1746						12 0		
1747						12 0		
1748					10 0			
1749					10 0	12 0		
1752						12 0		13 0
1753		12 0				12 0		
1754	12 0							
1755	12 0							
1756	12 0							
1757	12 0							
1758	12 0							13 0
1759	12 0							
1760	12 0	10 0						
1761	12 0							
1762	12 0							
1763	12 0							
1764	12 0					14 0		
1765	12 0					14 0		
1766						14 0		
1767				12 0				
1769						14 0		
1775				12 0				
1778						18 0		

Table 8.6 *Building labourers' daily wages, 1529–1706*

Date	Aberdeen town council accounts s. d.	Aberdeen shore work accounts s. d.	Edinburgh town council accounts s. d.	Edinburgh Master of Works accounts s. d.	Falkland Master of Works accounts s. d.	Linlithgow Master of Works accounts s. d.
1529				1 0		
1530				0 10		
1532				1 0	1 0	
1534						0 8
1535				0 10		
1536				0 10		
1537					0 10	
1538				1 8	0 10	
1539					0 10	
1540				0 10	0 10	
1553			1 6			
1554			1 6			
1555			1 4			
1556			1 8			
1557			1 6			
1558			1 6			
1559			1 6	1 6		
1560			2 0			
1561			1 8			
1562			2 0			
1564			2 0			
1565			1 9			
1576				2 2		
1579				2 2		
1582			2 6			
1583	1 6		3 0			
1584			2 6			
1585			2 6			
1587			3 0			
1588			3 4			
1589			2 6			
1590			* 6 0			
1591			3 0			
1592			3 0			
1593			3 4			
1594	* 2 6		4 0			
1595	* 3 4					
1596		6 8	4 0			
1597		6 8				
1598			5 0			
1599			4 0	5 0		

* denotes sparse data.

Table 8.6 *(cont.)*

Date	Aberdeen town council accounts	Aberdeen shore work accounts	Edinburgh town council accounts	Edinburgh Master of Works' accounts	Glasgow college building accounts	Linlithgow [1] Master of Works' accounts	Linlithgow town treasurers' accounts
	s. d.	s. d.	s. d.	s. d.	s. d.	s. d.	s. d.
1601	6 8		5 0				
1602	5 0		3 11				
1603	5 4						
1604			4 0				
1605	5 0		4 5				
1606	6 8		5 0				
1607	5 0	6 8	5 0				
1608	5 0	6 8	6 0				
1609	5 0						
1610	8 0		5 0				
1611	8 0		5 0				
1612	6 0		5 0				
1613	6 0		4 5	6 0			
1614	4 0		5 0	6 0			
1615			5 0				
1616			5 0	6 8		6 8	
1617			5 0	6 8		6 8	
1618		6 8	5 0	6 8		6 8	
1619		6 0	5 4	6 8		6 8	
1620			5 4	6 8		6 8	
1621	6 8			6 8		6 8	
1622			5 4	6 8		6 8	
1623	6 0		5 4	6 8		6 8	
1624	6 0		5 4	6 8		6 8	
1625	6 0	4 0	5 4	6 8		6 8	
1626	6 0	4 0	5 0	6 8		6 8	
1627	6 0	4 0	5 4	6 8		6 8	
1628	5 0	5 0	5 4	6 8		6 8	
1629		6 8	6 0	6 8		6 8	
1630		6 0		6 8		6 8	
1631		6 8		6 8		6 8	
1632			6 0	6 8	8 0	6 8	6 0
1633	5 4		6 0	6 8		6 8	
1634	6 8	6 0	6 0	6 8		6 8	
1635	6 8	6 8	6 0	6 8	8 0	6 8	
1636		5 0	6 0	6 8	8 0	6 8	
1637			6 0	6 8		6 8	6 0
1638		6 8	6 0	6 8		6 8	
1639		6 8	6 0	6 8	6 0	6 8	
1640		6 8			8 0	6 8	
1641		6 8					
1642	6 8	6 8	6 8				
1643	5 0	6 8					6 0
1644		6 8					6 0
1645	6 8	6 8					6 0
1646							6 0
1647	6 8						8 0
1652							6 0
1653							6 0

1 Falkland and Stirling Master of Works accounts are identical to Linlithgow in wages and years.

Table 8.6 *(cont.)*

Date	Aberdeen town council accounts		Aberdeen shore work accounts		Edinburgh town council accounts		Haddington town treasurers' accounts		Glasgow college building accounts		St Andrews St Leonard's college accounts	
	s.	d.	s.	d.	s.	d.	s.	d.	s.	d.	s.	d.
1656	10	0	6	8	8	0			9	0		
1657			6	8	8	0			9	0		
1658	12	0	6	8					9	0		
1659	8	0	6	8								
1660	6	8	6	8								
1661			6	8			8	0				
1662			6	8								
1663			6	8			8	0				
1664	8	0	6	8			8	0				
1666	6	8	6	8								
1667	12	0	6	8								
1668	12	0	6	8								
1669			6	8								
1670			6	8			6	8				
1671			6	8			8	0				
1672	8	0	8	0								
1673			6	8								
1675			8	0								
1676			6	8								
1677			6	8			8	0				
1678	6	8	6	8								
1680			6	8								
1681			6	8								
1683			6	8								
1684			8	0								
1685			6	8								
1686			9	0								
1687			6	8								
1688			6	8								
1689			6	8								
1690	6	8	13	4[1]								
1691	6	8	6	8								
1693	8	0	6	8							5	0
1694			13	4[1]								
1695	8	0	6	8							5	0
1696	8	0	9	4							4	0
1697	8	0									4	0
1698	8	0										
1699			6	8							5	0[2]
1700			6	8							5	0
1701			6	8								
1702									7	6	5	0[2]
1706			6	8					7	0		

1 For exceptional work.

2 Although 'wrights' men' received 8s. Scots per day.

Table 8.7 Building and estate labourers' daily wages, 1707–1799

Date	Gordon Castle estate accounts	Monymusk estate accounts	Panmure estate accounts	St Andrews St Leonard's college accounts	Aberdour estate accounts	Buchanan estate accounts	Glasgow college accounts	Dalmahoy estate accounts	Drylaw estate accounts	Edinburgh town council accounts	Newbattle estate accounts	Yester estate accounts	Wedderburn estate accounts
	s. d.	s. d.	s. d.	s. d.	s. d.	s. d.	s. d.	s. d.	s. d.	s. d.	s. d.	s. d.	s. d.
1707												6 0	
1708												6 0	
1709							6 8					6 0	
1710												6 0	
1711												6 0	
1712									7 0			6 0	
1713												6 0	
1714									6 0			6 0	
1715												6 0	
1716												6 0	
1717									7 0			6 0	
1718							*7 6					6 0	
1719				6 0								6 0	
1720												6 0	
1721												6 0	
1722				6 7		6 0	6 8					6 0	
1723				6 0		6 0	6 8					6 0	
1724	5 0					6 0	7 0					6 0	
1725	5 0					6 0	7 0					6 0	
1726	5 0					6 0	7 0					6 0	
1727	5 0					6 0	7 0		7 0			6 0	
1728						6 0	7 0		7 0			6 0	
1729						6 0	7 0		7 0			6 0	
1730						6 0	7 0		7 0			6 0	
1731						6 0	7 0		7 0		6 0	6 0	
1732		6 0				6 0	7 0		7 0		6 0	6 0	
1733						6 0	7 0		7 0			6 0	
1734						6 0	7 0		7 0			6 0	
1735	5 0					6 0	7 0		7 0			6 0	
1736	5 0					6 0	7 0		7 0	8 0		6 0	
1737	5 0	6 0				6 0	7 0		7 0			6 0	
1738						6 0			7 0			6 0	
1739						6 0			7 0	8 0		6 0	

* denotes sparse data.

Table 8.7 (cont.)

Date	Gordon Castle estate accounts		Monymusk estate accounts		Panmure estate accounts		St Andrews St Leonard's college accounts		Aberdour estate accounts		Buchanan estate accounts		Glasgow college accounts		Dalmahoy estate accounts		Drylaw estate accounts		Edinburgh town council accounts		Newbattle estate accounts		Yester estate accounts		Wedderburn estate accounts	
	s.	d.	s.	d.	s.	d.	s.	d.	s.	d.	s.	d.	s.	d.	s.	d.	s.	d.	s.	d.	s.	d.	s.	d.	s.	d.
1740	6	0									6	0					7	0	7	0			6	0		
1741	6	0									6	0					7	0	7	0			6	0		
1742	5	0									6	0					7	0	7	0			6	0		
1743									6	0	6	0					7	0	7	0			6	0		
1744	6	0							6	0	6	0			6	0	7	0	7	0			6	0		
1745									6	0	6	0			6	0	7	0	7	0			6	0		
1746									6	0	6	0					7	0	7	0			6	0		
1747	5	0	4	0					6	0	6	0			6	0	7	0	7	0			6	0		
1748	5	0	4	0					6	0	6	0			6	0	7	0	7	0			6	0		
1749	5	0	4	0					6	0	6	0			6	0	7	0	7	0			6	0		
1750	5	0	4	0					6	0	6	0					7	0	7	0			6	0		
1751	5	0							6	0	6	0					7	0	7	0			6	0		
1752	5	0									6	0					7	0					6	0		
1753	5	0									6	0					7	0					6	0		
1754	5	0									6	0					7	0					6	0		
1755	5	0	6	0							6	0					7	0					6	0		
1756	5	0	5	0							6	0					7	0					6	0		
1757	6	0	5	0							6	0					7	0	7	0			6	0	8	0
1758	6	0									6	0					7	0					6	0	8	0
1759	6	0	5	0							6	0					7	0					6	0		
1760	6	0	5	0							6	0					7	0	7	0			6	0	9	0
1761	6	0	5	0							6	0					7	0	9	0			6	0	9	0
1762	6	0									7	0					7	0					6	0		
1763	6	0	5	0							7	0					7	0					6	0		
1764	6	0	5	0							7	0					7	0	10	0			6	0		
1765	6	0	5	0							7	0					7	0	9	0			6	0		
1766											7	0														
1767			8	0	7	0					7	0					11	0								
1768			9	0	7	0					7	0														
1769	8	0	9	0	7	0					7	0														

Table 8.7 (cont.)

Date	Gordon Castle estate accounts		Monymusk estate accounts		Panmure estate accounts		St Andrews St Leonard's college accounts		Aberdour estate accounts		Buchanan estate accounts		Glasgow college accounts		Dalmahoy estate accounts		Drylaw estate accounts		Edinburgh town council accounts		Newbattle estate accounts		Yester estate accounts		Wedderburn estate accounts	
	s.	d.	s.	d.	s.	d.	s.	d.	s.	d.	s.	d.	s.	d.	s.	d.	s.	d.	s.	d.	s.	d.	s.	d.	s.	d.
1770	8	0			7	0					7	0					12	0							10	0
1771					7	0					8	0					12	0	10	0					10	0
1772					8	0					8	0					12	0	12	0					10	0
1773					8	0					8	0							12	0					10	0
1774	9	0			8	0					8	0							12	0						
1775	10	0			8	0					8	0							10	0						
1776	8	0			8	0					8	0							12	0					10	0
1777	7	0			8	0					8	0							12	0						
1778					8	0					8	0							12	0						
1779					8	0					8	0							12	0						
1780					8	0					8	0							12	0						
1781					8	0					8	0							12	0						
1782					8	0					8	0							12	0						
1783					8	0					8	0							12	0						
1784					8	0					10	0							13	0						
1785					8	0					10	0							14	0						
1786					8	0					10	0							14	0						
1787					8	0					10	0							14	0						
1788																			14	0						
1789					10	0													16	0						
1790					10	0													16	0						
1791					10	0													16	0						
1792					10	0													18	0						
1793					10	0																				
1794																										
1795																										
1796					18	0																				
1797					18	0																				
1798					18	0																				
1799																			20	0						

Table 8.8 *Aberdeen wage assessments: day rates, 1565–1593 and 1654–1701*

Date	Day labourers' rate		Master masons' rate		Servant masons' rate		Master wrights' rate		Servant wrights' rate	
	s.	d.	s.	d.	s.	d.	s.	d.	s.	d.
1565	1	6	3	0	2	0	3	0	2	0
1567	1	6	3	0	2	0	3	0	2	0
1568	1	6	3	0	2	0	3	0	2	0
1569	1	6	3	0	2	0	3	0	2	0
1570	1	6	3	0	2	0	3	0	2	0
1582	2	0	5	0	4	0	5	0	4	0
1588	2	0	5	0			5	0		
1593	2	8	6	8			6	8		
1654	6	8	15	6	10	0	13	4	10	0
1656	6	8	15	6	10	0	13	4	10	0
1657	6	8	15	6	10	0	15	6	11	8
1658	6	8	15	6	10	0	15	6	11	8
1659	8	0	17	9	11	1	17	9	11	1
1660	8	0	17	9	11	1	17	9	11	1
1661	8	0	17	9	11	1	17	9	11	1
1662	8	0	17	9	11	1	17	9	11	1
1663	8	0	17	9	11	1	17	9	11	1
1664	8	0	17	9	11	1	17	9	11	1
1665	8	0	17	9	11	1	17	9	11	1
1666	6	8	16	8	10	0	17	9	10	0
1667	6	8	11	1	10	0	17	9	10	0
1668	6	8	11	1	10	0	16	8	8	11
1669	6	8	13	4	10	0	16	8	8	11
1670	6	8	13	4	10	0	16	8	8	11
1671	6	8	13	4	10	0	16	8	8	11
1672	6	8	13	4	10	0	16	8	8	11
1673	6	8	13	4	10	0	16	8	8	11
1674	6	8	13	4	10	0	16	8	8	11
1675	6	8	13	4	10	0	16	8	8	11
1676	6	8	13	4	10	0	16	8	8	11
1677	6	8	13	4	10	0	16	8	8	11
1678	6	8	13	4	10	0	16	8	8	11
1679	6	8	13	4	10	0	16	8	8	11
1680	6	8	13	4	10	0	16	8	8	11
1681			13	4			15	7	6	8
1682	6	8	13	4	10	0	16	8	8	11
1683	6	8	13	4	10	0	16	8	8	11
1684	6	8	13	4	10	0	16	8	8	11
1685	6	8	13	4	10	0	16	8	8	11
1686	6	8	13	4	10	0	16	8	8	11
1687	6	8	13	4	10	0	16	8	8	11
1688	6	8	13	4	10	0	16	8	8	11
1689	6	8	13	4	10	0	16	8	8	11
1697	6	8	13	4	10	0	16	8	8	11
1701	6	8	13	4	10	0	16	8	8	11

Table 8.9 *County JP's wage assessments: annual fees and day wages, 1611–1751*

Occupation	Annual fee (with board)	Daily wage (without food)	Payments in kind
Fife, 1611			
Farm Servant	£12.0.0		
Thresher, Stacker	£12.0.0		
Horse Driver	£12.0.0		
Plough Caller	£8.0.0		
Herd	£8.0.0		
Woman Servant	£6.0.0		
Lass	£3.0.0		
Horse Keeper	£5.6.8		4 ells grey cloth
Labourer		5s.	(or 2s. plus food)
Perth, 1611			
Farm Servant	£12.0.0		
Thresher	£12.0.0		
Horse Driver	£12.0.0		
Cook, Baxter, Brewer	£12.0.0		
Gentleman's Servant	£12.0.0		
Cook's Foreman	£6.0.0		
Woman Servant	£6.0.0		
Horse Boy	£5.6.8		
Labourer		5s.	(or 2s. plus food)
Midlothian, 1656			
Whole Hind (with wife and one servant)	No cash or board except harvest food		Cot, kailyard, 15 bolls oats, 6 firlot pease, ground to sow 6 firlots of oats and 1 firlot bear, plus 2–3 soums of grass. Food only in harvest.
Half Hind (with wife but no servant)	No cash or board except harvest food		As above, but half the allowances plus an extra 2 firlots oats.
Herd (with one servant)	No cash or board		Cot, kailyard, 8 bolls of oats, 1 boll pease, an acre of land, plus 2–3 soums of grass.
Thresher	No cash or board		1/25th of grain threshed
Thresher (on Mains Farm, with wife)	No cash or board except harvest food		1/25th of grain, cot, kailyard, 1 boll pease, 1 soum of grass.
Farm Servant (inservant)	£26.13.4		
Halfling	£13.6.8		
Boy	£6.13.4		
Able Woman	£13.6.8		
Lass	£6.13.4		
Labourer		6s.	(or 3s. plus food)
Mason		13s. 4d.	(or 6s. 8d. plus food)
Wright		12s.	(or 6s. plus food)
Cowan		8s.	(or 4s. plus food)
Barrowman		6s.	(or 3s. plus food)
Thatcher		8s.	(or 4s. plus food)
Tailor			4s. plus food
Peebles, 1664			
Farm Servant	£20.0.0		(or £16 plus two pairs shoes and 12 qts. grog worth £4)
Second Farm Servant	£14.13.4		(or £10.13.4 plus above)
Boy Herd	£5.6.8		2 ells grey cloth, 2 pairs shoes
Best Woman Servant	£12.14.0		(or £4.0.0 plus 2 stones wool and 2 pairs shoes)
Lass	£6.7.0		(or half above)

Table 8.9 *(cont.)*

Occupation	Annual fee (with board)	Daily wage (without food)	Payments in kind
Linlithgow, 1673			
Best Farm Servant	£26.13.4		
Second Farm Servant	£20.0.0		
Halfling	£13.6.8		
Able Farm Woman	£16.0.0		
Second Farm Woman	£12.0.0		
Domestic Woman	£8.0.0		
Banff, 1702			
Best Farm Servant	£17.6.8		2 bolls bear
Best Tailor (with apprentice			4s. plus food
Second Tailor (without apprentice)			2s. plus food
Wright			5s. plus food
Cooper			6s. 8d. plus food
Lanark, 1708			
Farm Servant (inservant)	£24.0.0		
Halfling	£16.0.0		
Boy	£8.0.0		
Able Farm Woman	£14.0.0		
Lass	£8.0.0		
Thresher			1/25th of grain threshed.
Thresher (on Mains Farm, with wife)	No cash or board except harvest food		1/25th of grain, cot, kailyard, 1 boll meal, 1 soum grass, and food in harvest.
Mason		13s. 4d.	(or 6s. 8d. plus food)
Wright		12s.	(or 6s. plus food)
Thatcher		10s.	(or 6s. plus food)
Tailor			3s. 4d. plus food
Aberdeen, 1743			
Best Farm Servant	£20.0.0		£2.8.0 for shoes
Second Farm Servant	£16.0.0		£1.4.0 for shoes
Third Farm Servant or Plough Caller	£12.0.0		
Best Farm Woman	£10.13.4		
Second Woman	£9.6.8		
Wigtown, 1749			
Farm Servant	£27.0.0		
Woman Servant	£13.10.0		
Aberdeen, 1750			
Best Farm Servant	£20.0.0		£2.8.0 for shoes
Second Farm Servant	£18.0.0		£1.4.0 for shoes
Boy	£6.0.0		
Best Farm Woman	£12.0.0		

Table 8.9 *(cont.)*

Occupation	Annual fee (with board)	Daily wage (without food)	Payments in kind
<u>Dumfries, 1751</u>			
Farm Servant	£27.0.0		two pairs of shoes or £3.0.0
Barn Man	£22.0.0		two pairs of shoes
Lad	£11.0.0		one pair of shoes
Able Woman	£15.0.0		two pairs of shoes or £3.0.0
Lass	£8.0.0		two pairs of shoes or £2.0.0

Table 8.10 *County JP's wage assessments: harvest wages, 1656–1743*

Occupation	Fee for whole harvest	Day rate [1]
<u>Peebles, 1656</u>		
Best Man	£7.6.8	
Halfling	£6.0.0	
Woman Shearer	£6.0.0	
Lass	£4.13.4	
Man		4s.
Woman		3s. 4d.
<u>Banff, 1702</u>		
Best Man	£5.0.0	
Best Woman	£3.6.8	
<u>Banff, 1703</u>		
Best Man	£5.13.4	
Best Woman	£3.13.4	
<u>Lanark, 1708</u>		
Best Man		6s.
Halfling		4s.
Best Woman		5s.
Lass		3s.
<u>Aberdeen, 1743</u>		
Best Man	£6.13.4	
Second Man	£5.6.8	
Best Woman	£4.13.4	

1 In every case, food and drink was provided in addition to cash.

Table 8.11 *Male farm servants: annual fees, c.1714–1789, from the* OSA

South-east Scotland

Parish	County	Date	Fee
Castleton	Roxburgh	1740	£36–£42
Duddingston	Lothian	1746	£36.0.0 [1]
Carriden	Lothian	[1750]	£36.0.0
Innerwick	Lothian	[1750]	£30.0.0
Yester	Lothian	[1750]	£30.0.0
Greenlaw	Berwick	[1754]	£36–£48
Cramond	Lothian	1760	£96.12.0
Whittingehame	Lothian	1760	£28.16.0–£36 [2]
Edinburgh	Lothian	1763	£78.0.0
Eccles	Berwick	[1772]	£48–£60
Bo'ness	Lothian	[1774]	£72.0.0 [3]
Cramond	Lothian	1775	£109.4.0
Castleton	Roxburgh	1778	£36–£72

1 'plus 2 pecks of meal a week as kitchen'
2 'plus food in the house not calculated'
3 'does not include the value of his victual'

South-west Scotland

Parish	County	Date	Fee
Torthorwald	Dumfries	1730	£27.12.0
Dailly	Ayr	[1730]	£12.0.0
Torthorwald	Dumfries	1739	£27.12.0
Kilwinning	Ayr	1742	£21–£24
Torthorwald	Dumfries	1744	£36.0.0 [1]
Cambuslang	Lanark	1750	£36–£48 [2]
Kelton	Kirkcudbright	[1750]	£24.0.0
Penpont	Dumfries	[1750]	£24.0.0
Auchinleck	Ayr	1752	£48.0.0
Walston	Lanark	[1753]	£36.0.0
Sanquhar	Dumfries	1760	£30–£36
Kirkmichael	Dumfries	[1760]	£36–£48
Parton	Kirkcudbright	1761	£30.0.0
Closeburn	Dumfries	[1772]	£48.0.0
Douglas	Lanark	[1773]	£30.0.0
Libberton	Lanark	[1786]	£66.0.0
Libberton	Lanark	[1786]	£48.0.0
Sorn	Ayr	1789	£84–£96

1 'plus 2 pairs of shoes'
2 'plus food'

Note: Dates in square brackets have been estimated on the basis of vague comments such as 'some twenty years ago a farm servants could earn ....'.

Table 8.11 *(cont.)*

Central eastern Scotland

Parish	County	Date	£Fee
Campsie	Stirling	1714	£18–£24
Forfar	Forfar	[1730]	£18–£24
Portmoak	Kinross	[1730]	£21.0.0
Caputh	Perth	1735	£8.0.0 [1]
Caputh	Perth	1739	£24.0.0 [2]
Clunie	Perth	1740	£18.0.0
Tillicoultry	Clackmannan	1740	£36.0.0
Oathlaw	Forfar	[1740–60]	£24.0.0 [3]
Ruthven	Forfar	[1742–57]	£24.0.0
Ruthven	Forfar	[1742–57]	£7.0.0
Ruthven	Forfar	[1742–57]	£3.0.0
Moulin	Perth	1743	£19.16.0
Campsie	Stirling	1744	£36–£48
Moulin	Perth	1750	£23.8.0
Monimail	Fife	1750	£24–£30 [4]
Farnell	Forfar	[1750]	£24.0.0
Glenisla	Forfar	[1750]	£16.0.0 [5]
Lethnot	Forfar	[1750]	£20.0.0
Lundie & Fowlis	Forfar	[1750]	£24.0.0 [2]
Stracathro	Forfar	1751	£20.0.0
Kippen	Stirling	[1753]	£24.0.0 [2]
Monifieth	Forfar	[1753]	£25.4.0
Auchterderran	Fife	1755	£28.0.0
Kincardine	Perth	[1755]	£30.0.0
Monikie	Forfar	[1755]	£30.0.0
Monikie	Forfar	[1755]	£24.0.0 [6]
Campsie	Stirling	1759	£60–£72
Leslie	Fife	1759	£30–£36
Mains	Forfar	1760	£36.0.0
Callender	Perth	[1760]	£36.0.0
Kinfauns	Perth	[1760]	£48–£60
Kippen	Stirling	[1763]	£60–£72 [2]
St Andrews	Fife	[1763]	£36.0.0
Kincardine	Perth	[1765]	£60.0.0
Anstruther Wester	Fife	1768	£48–£60
Kinnoull	Perth	1770	£50.8.0–£63
Airth	Stirling	[1770]	£60–£72
Callender	Perth	[1770]	£48.0.0
Fowlis Wester	Perth	[1770]	£54–£60 [7]
Fowlis Wester	Perth	[1770]	£30–£36 [8]
Kincardine	Perth	[1770]	£24.0.0
Redgorton	Perth	[1770]	£48–£60
Creiff	Perth	1772	£40.0.0 [9]
Lochlee	Forfar	1772	£30–£36 [10]
Drymen	Stirling	[1772]	£48.0.0
Alyth	Perth	1773	£63–£75.12.0
Weem	Perth	1778	£36.0.0 [5]
Longforgan	Perth	1781	£78.0.0
Bendochy	Perth	1785	£60.0.0
Cargill	Perth	1785	£60.0.0
Kilconquhar	Fife	1785	£48–£60

1 'plus bounty of clothing worth £6.18.0'
2 'plus bounty'
3 'plus board'
4 'plus 2 pecks of meal weekly'
5 'with maintenance'
6 'carter'

7 'best man'
8 'inferior man'
9 'plus 6½ bolls meal at £8.0.0 the boll and 8s. weekly for milk; worth, in all, £72.16.0'
10 'plus pasture for a score of sheep'

Table 8.11 *(cont.)*

North-east Scotland

Parish	County	Date	£Fee
Keith	Banff	1740	£16–£20
Mary-Kirk	Kincardine	1740	£18.0.0 [1]
Alford	Aberdeen	[1740]	£16–£20
Dyke & Moy	Moray	[1743]	£20.0.0
Bourtie	Aberdeen	1744	£9.12.0–£18
Turriff	Aberdeen	1744	£16.0.0
Banff	Banff	1748	£16.0.0 [2]
Fyvie	Aberdeen	1749	£18.0.0
Forres	Moray	1750	£18.8.0
Grange	Banff	1750	£20.0.0
Grange	Banff	1750	£16.0.0
Mary-Kirk	Kincardine	1750	£36.0.0 [1]
Cluny	Aberdeen	[1750]	£20.0.0 [3]
Cushnie	Aberdeen	[1750]	£18.0.0
Monquhitter	Aberdeen	[1750]	£20.0.0
Tyrie	Aberdeen	[1750]	£24–£27.12.0
Fordyce	Banff	[1755]	£20–£48
Kinellar	Aberdeen	1758	£22.0.0
Ordiquhill	Banff	[1760]	£30.0.0
Tullynessie	Aberdeen	[1760]	£16–£20
Crathie & Braemar	Aberdeen	[1763]	£21–£24
Peterhead	Aberdeen	[1764]	£30.0.0
Leslie	Aberdeen	[1770]	£36.0.0
Meldrum	Aberdeen	[1770]	£48–£60
Mary-Kirk	Kincardine	1771	£48–£54 [1]
Turriff	Aberdeen	1774	£54.0.0

1 'besides keep'
2 'plus a pair of shoes'
3 'plus victuals'

Highlands and Islands

Parish	County	Date	£Fee
Avoch	Ross & Cromarty	1734	£20.0.0
Kilmartin	Argyll	[1745]	£15.16.0–£18
Petty	Inverness	[1750]	£16.0.0 [1]
Tain	Inverness	[1750]	£18.0.0
Bower	Caithness	[1750]	£12.0.0 [2]
Moy & Dalarossie	Argyll	[1755]	£12–£14.8.0 [3]
Eddrachillis	Sutherland	[1760]	£4.13.4–£5.6.8
Kilmoden	Argyll	1770	£36.0.0
Watten	Caithness	[1775]	£21.12.0–£24
Kilfinichen & Kilvickeon	Western Isles	1780	£25.4.0–£30.12.0 [4]

1 'plus 6 bolls victual, two parts barleymeal to one part oatmeal'
2 'plus 5½ bolls victual'
3 'men either get food with family, or 6 bolls victual per annum'
4 'plus four pairs of brogues'

Table 8.12 *Female farm servants: annual fees, c.1700–1789, from the* OSA

South-east Scotland

Parish	County	Date	Fee
Castleton	Roxburgh	1740	£12.18.0
Duddingston	Lothian	1746	£18.0.0
Carriden	Lothian	[1750]	£12–£13.4.0
Innerwick	Lothian	[1750]	£15.0.0
Yester	Lothian	[1750]	£18.0.0 [1]
Greenlaw	Berwick	[1754]	£24–£30
Cramond	Lothian	1760	£21.12.0
Whittingehame	Lothian	1760	£12.0.0 [2]
Edinburgh	Lothian	1763	£36–£48
Eccles	Berwick	[1772]	£24.0.0
Bo'ness	Lothian	[1774]	£18.0.0
Cramond	Lothian	1775	£27.12.0

1 'all articles included'
2 'plus £6.0.0 perks'

South-west Scotland

Parish	County	Date	Fee
Dually	Ayr	[1730]	£8.0.0 [1]
Kilwinning	Ayr	1742	£15.12.0–£18
Torthorwald	Dumfries	1744	£12.0.0
Cambuslang	Lanark	1750	£24–£30
Kelton	Kirkcudbright	[1750]	£9.0.0
Penpont	Dumfries	[1750]	£8.0.0
Auchinleck	Ayr	1752	£20.0.0
Walston	Lanark	[1753]	£24.0.0
Sanquhar	Dumfries	1760	£21–£30
Kirkmichael	Dumfries	[1760]	£21–£27
Parton	Kirkcudbright	1761	£18.0.0
Closeburn	Dumfries	[1772]	£24.0.0
Douglas	Lanark	[1773]	£30.0.0
Libberton	Lanark	[1786]	£30.0.0
Sorn	Ayr	1789	£36–£42

1 'plus an apron and a pair of shoes'

Table 8.12 *(cont.)*

Central eastern Scotland

Parish	County	Date	Fee
Campsie	Stirling	1714	£12.0.0
Forfar	Forfar	[1730]	£2.0.0 [1]
Portmoak	Kinross	[1730]	£9.0.0
Caputh	Perth	1735	£2.0.0 [2]
Clunie	Perth	1740	£7.4.0
Oathlaw	Forfar	[1740–60]	£18.0.0
Ruthven	Forfar	[1742–57]	£8.0.0
Moulin	Perth	1743	£9.12.0
Campsie	Stirling	1744	£30–£24
Monimail	Fife	1750	£24–£30
Fernell	Forfar	[1750]	£12.0.0
Lethnot	Forfar	[1750]	£9.0.0 [2]
Lundie & Fowlis	Forfar	[1750]	£12.0.0 [2]
Strickathro	Forfar	1751	£12.0.0
Kippen	Stirling	[1753]	£9–£10 [2]
Monifieth	Forfar	[1753]	£15.12.0
Auchterderran	Fife	1755	£18.0.0
Moulin	Perth	1755	£11.6.0
Monikie	Forfar	[1755]	£15–£18
Campsie	Stirling	1759	£30–£36
Leslie	Fife	1759	£24–£30
Mains	Forfar	1760	£18.0.0
Callender	Perth	[1760]	£14.8.0
Kippen	Stirling	[1763]	£21–£27
Anstruther Wester	Fife	1768	£19.4.0–£24
Airth	Stirling	[1770]	£24–£30
Callender	Perth	[1770]	£21.0.0
Fowlis Wester	Perth	[1770]	£12–£15
Redgorton	Perth	[1770]	£24–£30
Creiff	Perth	1772	£25.4.0 [3]
Alyth	Perth	1773	£24.0.0
Dunkeld	Perth	1776	£18.0.0
Weem	Perth	1776	£18.0.0
Cargill	Fife	1785	£24.0.0
Kilconquhar	Fife	1785	£24–£30
Kirriemuir	Forfar	1786	£24–£36

1 'plus harvest wage'
2 'plus bounties'
3 'plus board of 4 bolls 14 pecks meal and 6s. weekly' (worth £54.12.0)

Table 8.12 *(cont.)*

North-east Scotland

Parish	County	Date	Fee
Keith	Banff	1740	£7.4.0–£13.4.0
Alford	Aberdeen	[1740]	£10.13.0
Dyke & Moy	Moray	[1743]	£9.4.0 [1]
Turriff	Aberdeen	1744	£10.16.0
Banff	Banff	1748	£8.0.0
Fyvie	Aberdeen	1749	£14.8.0
Forres	Moray	1750	£10–£12
Grange	Banff	1750	£9.12.0
Mary-Kirk	Kincardine	1750	£14.8.0 [2]
Cluny	Aberdeen	[1750]	£12.0.0
Monquitter	Aberdeen	[1750]	£12.0.0
Tyrie	Aberdeen	[1750]	£12–£18
Fordyce	Banff	[1755]	£9.12.0–£12
Mary-Kirk	Kincardine	[1760]	£12.0.0 [2]
Crathie & Braemar	Aberdeen	[1763]	£12–£18
Peterhead	Aberdeen	[1764]	£14.8.0–£18
Mary-Kirk	Kincardine	1771	£24–£30 [2]
Turriff	Aberdeen	1774	£18.0.0

1 'plus brogues or an apron worth 12s.'
2 'plus keep'

Highlands and Islands

Parish	County	Date	Fee
Sandwick & Stromness	Orkney	1700	£3.0.0
Avoch	Ross & Cromarty	1734	£7.19.0
Moy & Dalarossie	Inverness	[1740]	£7.4.0–£8.8.0
Kilmartin	Argyll	[1745]	£8.0.0
Bower	Caithness	[1755]	£6.0.0 [1]
Eddrachillis	Sutherland	[1760]	£4.0.0
Watten	Caithness	[1775]	£9.12.0 [2]

1 'plus 2 bolls 3 firlots victual'
2 'plus 1 boll 2 firlots victual'

Table 8.13 *Harvest fees, c.1730–1780, from the* OSA

Men

Parish	County	Date	Fee
Forfar	Forfar	[1730]	£6.6.0
Caputh	Perth	1735	£6.0.0
Ruthven	Forfar	[1742–57]	£6.13.4
Turriff	Aberdeen	1744	£6.16.0
Forres	Moray	1750	£6.0.0
Grange	Banff	1750	£7.4.0
Penpont	Dumfries	[1750]	£5.0.0
Kippen	Stirling	[1753]	£8–£10
Monifieth	Forfar	[1753]	£7.0.0
Lesley	Aberdeen	[1770]	£12.0.0
Turriff	Aberdeen	1774	£17.8.0
Longforgan	Perth	1780	£12.0.0

Women

Parish	County	Date	Fee
Forfar	Forfar	[1730]	£4.16.0–£6
Caputh	Perth	1735	£5.0.0
Ruthven	Forfar	[1742–57]	£4.19.8
Turriff	Aberdeen	1744	£5.5.0
Grange	Banff	1750	£3.12.0
Penpont	Dumfries	[1750]	£3.0.0
Kippen	Stirling	[1753]	£6–£8
Monifieth	Forfar	[1753]	£6.0.0
Turriff	Aberdeen	1774	£10.10.0

Table 8.14 *Labourers: day wages, c.1730–1789, from the* OSA

South-east Scotland

Parish	County	Date	Wage
Castleton	Roxburgh	1740	6s.
Duddingston	Lothian	1746	7s.
Innerwick	Lothian	[1750]	5s.
Yester	Lothian	[1750]	6s.
Carriden	Lothian	[1750]	7s.
Greenlaw	Berwick	[1754]	6s.
Cramond	Lothian	1760	7s.
Whittingehame	Lothian	1760	4–6s.
Bo'ness	Lothian	[1774]	12s.
Cramond	Lothian	1775	10s.

South-west Scotland

Parish	County	Date	Wage
Dually	Ayr	[1730]	2s.+food
Kilwinning	Ayr	1742	8s.
Cambuslang	Lanark	1750	6–7s.
Penpont	Dumfries	[1750]	6s.
Auchinleck	Ayr	1752	8s.
Walston	Lanark	[1753]	8s.
Rothesay	Bute	[1770]	6–8s.
Closeburn	Dumfries	[1772]	6s.
Douglas	Lanark	[1773]	10–12s.
Sorn	Ayr	1789	12s.

Highlands and Islands

Parish	County	Date	Wage
Avoch	Ross & Cromarty	1734	4s.
Petty	Inverness	[1750]	7s.
Moy & Dalrossie	Inverness	[1755]	7s.

Table 8.14 *(cont.)*

Central eastern Scotland

Parish	County	Date	Wage
Portmoak	Kinross	[1730]	3s.+food
Tillicoultry	Clackmannan	[1742]	5–6s.
Oathlaw	Forfar	[1740–60]	2s.6d.
Ruthven	Forfar	[1742–57]	3s.
Monimail	Fife	17550	5s.
Lethnot	Forfar	[1750]	2s.+food
Strickathow	Forfar	1751	2s.+food
Monifieth	Forfar	1753	6s.
Kippen	Stirling	[1753]	4s.
Leslie	Fife	1759	8s.
Kincardine	Perth	[pre-1760]	5s.
Mains	Forfar	1760	6s.
St Andrews	Fife	[1763]	6s.
Anstruther Wester	Fife	1764	7s.
Redgorton	Perth	[1770]	8s.
Lochlee	Forfar	1772	4s.+food
Creiff	Perth	1772	9s.
Drymen	Stirling	[1772]	8–10s.
Kincardine	Perth	1775	8s.
Longforgan	Perth	1777	8–9s.
Auchterderran	Fife	1778	8s.
Kippen	Stirling	[1783]	6s.
Kilconquhar	Fife	1785	7–10s.

North-east Scotland

Parish	County	Date	Wage
Grange	Banff	1750	3s.
Cluny	Aberdeen	[1750]	4s.+food
Tyrie	Aberdeen	[1750]	6s.
Fordyce	Banff	[1755]	5–6s.
Peterhead	Aberdeen	[1764]	8s.
Lesley	Aberdeen	[1770]	4s.+food

Table 8.15 *Building craftsmen: day wages, 1734–1786, from the* OSA

Masons

Parish	County	Date	Wage
Avoch	Ross & Cromarty	1734	11s.
Tillicoultry	Clackmannan	[1740]	12s.
Duddingston	Lothian	1746	13s.9d.
Cambuslang	Lanark	1750	8–10s.
Forres	Moray	1750	13s.4d.
Grange	Banff	1750	6s.
Monimail	Fife	1750	7–8s.
Auchinleck	Ayr	1752	12s.
Mains	Forfar	1760	10s.
Cramond	Lothian	1760	13s.6d.
Whittingehame	Lothian	1760	13s.4d.
Kippen	Stirling	[1763]	6s. [1]
St Andrews	Fife	[1763]	12s.
Peterhead	Aberdeen	[1764]	12s.
Cramond	Lothian	1775	16s.
Longforgan	Perth	1777	14s.
Kirriemuir	Forfar	1786	15–18s.
Sorn	Ayr	1786	20s.

1 'plus victuals'

Wrights

Parish	County	Date	Wage
Avoch	Ross & Cromarty	1734	8s.
Duddingston	Lothian	1746	10s.
Cambuslang	Lanark	1750	7–9s.
Grange	Banff	1750	4s.
Monimail	Fife	1750	7–8s.
Mains	Forfar	1760	6s.
Whittingehame	Lothian	1760	12s.
Kippen	Stirling	[1763]	6s. [1]
Peterhead	Aberdeen	[1764]	12s.
Longforgan	Perth	1777	12s.

1 'plus victuals'

Table 8.16 *Rural wages, 1790–1794, according to Robert Hope, from General Account*

	1794 Unmarried man's wages, with board (annual) L.s.d.	1790 Labourer's wages			1790 Women's wage (day) s.	1790 Carpenter's wage (day) s.	1790 Mason's wage (day) s.	1790 Thatcher's wage (day) s.
		Winter (day) s.	Summer (day) s.	Harvest (day) s.				
West Lothian	£88.04.0	12	14	12	5	-	-	-
Midlothian	£88.04.0	12	14	12	5	16	16	15
East Lothian	£96.00.0	12	14	12	5	24	24	24
Berwickshire	£96.00.0	12	14	18	5	18	20	18
Roxburghshire	£96.00.0	12	14	18	5	16	20	16
Selkirkshire	£84.00.0	12	14	18	5	16	15	20
Peeblesshire	£96.00.0	10	12	12	4	16	15	20
Dumfriesshire	£96.00.0	10	12	12	4	16	18	18
Galloway		10	12	14	-	-	-	-
Ayrshire	£120.00.0	12	16	18	9	18	24	18
Lanarkshire	£120.00.0	12	14	14	-	16	18	14
Renfrewshire	£120.00.0	12	14	14	-	-	-	-
Dunbartonshire	£108.00.0	12	14	14	-	-	-	-
Stirlingshire	£108.00.0	12	14	14	-	-	-	-
Clackmannanshire	£88.04.0	10	14	14	5	-	-	-
Kinrosshire	£88.04.0	10	14	13	5	16	16	14
Fifeshire	£84.00.0	10	14	14	5	16	16	14
Perthshire	£96.00.0	10	14	14	5	14	14	12
Forfarshire	£96.00.0	10	14	14	5	18	18	14
Kincardineshire	£96.00.0	12	16	15	5	18	18	18
Aberdeenshire	£72.00.0	9	12	10	4	12	14	18
Banffshire	£72.00.0	9	12	10	4	-	-	-
Morayshire	£72.00.0	9	12	10	4	-	-	-
Nairnshire	£72.00.0	9	12	10	4	12	14	18
Inverness-shire	£96.00.0	8	12	12	4	-	-	-
Argyleshire	£96.00.0	8	12	12	4	16	19	13
Ross and Cromarty	£60.00.0	5	7	6	3	12	15	12
Caithness	£16.16.0	6	11	8	-	-	-	-

Table 8.17 *Agricultural servants' annual fees: Renfrewshire, 1695*

Parish	Total polled population	Male Servants			Female Servants		
		All servants	Target sample[1]	Average wage	All servants	Target sample[1]	Average wage
Cathcart	290	33	16	£22.00.00	49	18	£14.04.10
Eaglesham	659	83	20	£17.07.08	65	27	£13.05.08
Eastwood	456	52	21	£19.12.06	70	26	£13.08.02
Erskine	554	75	23	£18.01.04	113	48	£13.01.09
Greenock Landward	559	22	6	£ 7.18.11	27	5	£ 9.16.00
Houston and Kilellan	538	75	19	£17.07.07	80	28	£12.04.06
Inchinnan	361	56	13	£16.06.07	83	18	£14.17.07
Inverkip	1071	21	5	£11.17.04	48	6	£12.00.00
Kilbarchan	977	72	21	£16.02.01	123	72	£12.13.03
Kilmacolm	901	49	15	£11.04.05	103	50	£ 9.18.01
Lochwinnoch	971	81	27	£16.10.03	105	75	£13.18.10
Mearns	532	24	21	£12.19.08	44	36	£12.08.05
Neilston	932	98	28	£17.01.11	123	55	£12.09.04
Paisley Landward	1399	132	56	£17.17.07	218	85	£13.00.05
Paisley Town	1129	18	4	£13.10.00	111	3	£16.00.00
Renfrew	225	36	12	£18.18.06	64	14	£13.00.03
Total/Average[2]	11,554	927	307	£16.16.05	1,426	566	£12.16.00

1. This represents the number of adult servants employed by small tenant farmers and heritors (defined as those with land valued at less than 500 pounds Scots) in each parish. The average wage has been calculated on the basis of this sample which, as discussed in the text, is likely to have been of a broadly uniform cohort of 'servants in husbandry'.
2. There is no information available for the burgh of Renfrew, and the Poll Books record no servants of small tenants or heritors in Greenock Town.

Table 8.18 *Agricultural servants' annual fees: Aberdeenshire, 1695*

Parish	Total polled population	Male Servants			Female Servants		
		All servants	Target sample [1]	Average wage	All servants	Target sample [1]	Average wage
Aberdour	615	75	23	£ 8.01.03	48	19	£ 5.09.04
Aboyne & Glentanner	595	66	50	£ 6.06.05	34	23	£ 3.17.04
Alford	482	76	55	£10.18.10	40	33	£ 6.10.08
Auchindoir	346	35	21	£ 7.16.02	40	29	£ 4.08.03
Auchterless	776	108	41	£ 9.12.03	52	29	£ 5.14.07
Banchory Devenick	225	17	17	£12.04.08	32	18	£ 7.19.03
Belhelvie	730	86	58	£12.19.09	70	56	£ 9.14.06
Birse	575	76	70	£ 8.10.10	45	38	£ 5.07.04
Bourtie	268	26	20	£ 6.06.06	17	13	£ 6.16.11
Cabrach	159	16	8	£ 9.14.02	11	11	£ 6.10.04
Cairney	713	105	60	£ 9.19.01	69	39	£ 6.02.07
Chapel of Garioch	673	81	21	£11.19.08	52	31	£ 7.07.06
Clatt	331	31	27	£ 9.09.00	39	35	£ 6.12.06
Cluny	340	34	31	£12.06.11	26	24	£ 5.12.08
Coull	449	64	51	£10.00.07	27	21	£ 6.07.05
Crathie and Braemar	1466	64	45	£ 7.05.06	38	26	£ 4.19.06
Crimond	453	51	17	£11.07.10	39	20	£ 5.10.06
Cruden	1234	181	67	£10.03.00	100	57	£ 5.17.08
Culsalmond	446	55	35	£12.14.09	44	32	£ 8.11.08
Cushnie	231	28	19	£ 7.12.03	18	13	£ 5.04.01
Daviot	374	38	14	£12.17.04	22	12	£ 8.01.01
Deer	1314	174	45	£ 8.08.06	103	54	£ 6.09.08
Drumblade	697	99	61	£10.15.09	78	49	£ 6.04.02
Drumoak	307	54	46	£ 7.03.10	20	15	£ 6.09.09
Dyce	231	46	41	£10.15.01	21	18	£ 9.10.00
Echt	769	55	48	£ 8.11.00	59	47	£ 5.04.08
Ellon	1095	157	126	£ 9.12.11	89	58	£ 7.07.09
Fintray	443	53	46	£11.15.06	38	32	£ 7.01.11
Forbes and Kearn	254	55	39	£ 9.02.09	25	20	£ 6.12.00
Forgue	1092	120	88	£10.00.06	83	65	£ 5.17.08
Foveran	845	106	46	£12.03.03	72	37	£ 8.02.10
Fraserburgh	813	62	24	£ 7.03.07	66	21	£ 5.10.09
Fyvie	1405	212	60	£10.19.10	92	48	£ 6.01.03
Gartly	377	41	22	£ 8.11.06	25	20	£ 5.05.08
Glass	431	62	34	£ 8.16.08	43	34	£ 6.05.01
Glenbuchat	179	10	8	£ 6.02.06	7	6	£ 3.06.08
Glenmuick, Tullich and Glengairn	936	90	73	£ 7.17.11	56	45	£ 5.00.11
Huntly	876	123	45	£11.10.03	105	47	£ 6.03.10
Insch	534	61	47	£10.07.04	52	39	£ 6.11.00
Inverurie	382	48	20	£11.09.02	31	14	£ 5.15.11
Keig	324	23	19	£12.15.00	17	14	£ 7.07.07
Keithhall and Kinkell	599	105	56	£11.07.05	54	25	£ 7.17.11
Kemnay	303	33	20	£12.01.08	15	11	£ 6.07.03
Kennethmont	443	39	26	£10.09.09	38	29	£ 6.00.11
Kildrummy	230	32	21	£10.14.03	19	11	£ 6.03.08
Kincadine O'Neil	873	88	75	£10.05.08	67	48	£ 6.04.02
King Edward	818	91	48	£ 7.17.11	64	51	£ 5.08.06
Kinnellar	207	24	22	£ 7.18.02	16	12	£ 4.13.04
Kintore	402	40	30	£11.06.02	31	22	£ 4.01.10

Table 8.18 *(cont.)*

Parish	Total polled population	Male Servants			Female Servants		
		All servants	Target sample[1]	Average wage	All servants	Target sample[1]	Average wage
Leochel	259	39	21	£12.08.07	16	13	£ 7.01.10
Leslie	320	50	26	£14.12.02	43	30	£ 7.05.11
Logie-Buchan	455	83	71	£ 9.06.02	37	25	£ 8.04.10
Logie-Coldstone	520	40	34	£ 8.11.05	30	25	£ 4.00.00
Longside	777	115	16	£12.04.03	68	9	£ 7.01.04
Lonmay	729	92	41	£ 8.13.07	50	31	£ 6.15.07
Lumphanan	328	34	19	£12.01.05	19	9	£ 5.15.07
Meldrum	629	34	26	£10.11.09	31	19	£ 6.13.00
Methlick	744	76	37	£11.06.10	68	31	£ 7.17.00
Midmar	371	48	41	£ 8.13.06	34	25	£ 6.17.07
Monquitter	518	63	30	£ 7.13.10	39	27	£ 4.13.04
Monymusk	738	120	57	£13.03.11	61	26	£ 7.04.07
New Deer	1265	88	68	£ 7.19.01	83	61	£ 5.18.10
Newhills	210	26	20	£12.13.04	21	15	£ 9.04.00
New Machar	528	52	25	£13.09.07	49	27	£ 7.03.11
Old Machar	883	105	73	£10.13.03	90	48	£ 7.06.11
Oyne	323	22	17	£10.08.08	15	11	£ 7.09.08
Peterculter	324	27	23	£ 9.16.10	25	18	£ 6.01.06
Peterhead	870	68	48	£10.12.08	75	23	£ 6.10.03
Pitsligo	501	56	30	£ 9.18.07	42	19	£ 4.18.09
Premney	317	27	19	£13.01.05	20	15	£ 6.10.08
Rathen	710	75	13	£ 8.07.04	33	16	£ 4.17.10
Rayne	538	65	33	£12.01.01	33	21	£ 8.03.10
Rhynie and Essie	458	52	32	£ 9.11.06	34	19	£ 6.05.03
Skene	622	84	44	£10.03.11	43	35	£ 5.15.03
Slains	542	55	36	£ 8.18.02	39	28	£ 6.03.11
Strathdon	535	46	32	£ 8.11.03	20	17	£ 3.11.04
Strichen	402	52	11	£ 9.12.01	25	22	£ 5.04.03
Tarland	435	58	56	£ 7.13.07	26	25	£ 4.03.02
Tarves	1059	115	94	£10.18.00	77	53	£ 7.12.02
Tough	332	34	28	£10.17.10	24	19	£ 7.01.07
Towie	282	32	24	£10.09.05	10	10	£ 5.16.00
Tullynessie	258	37	11	£13.06.05	25	10	£ 5.15.08
Turriff	1009	145	71	£ 8.19.05	78	62	£ 5.02.11
Tyrie	288	27	12	£ 9.01.08	30	21	£ 6.05.03
Udny	828	139	109	£11.03.01	68	44	£ 7.16.06
Total/Average[2]	48,567	5,697	3,334	£10.01.00	3,730	2,380	£ 6.07.05

1. This represents the number of adult servants employed by small tenant farmers and heritors (defined as those with land valued at less than 500 pounds Scots) in each parish. The average wage has been calculated on the basis of this sample which, as discussed in the text, is likely to have been of a broadly uniform cohort of 'servants in husbandry'.

2. There were no servants of small farmers or heritors listed in the Poll Books for the burghs of Aberdeen or Old Aberdeen, although there were, in all, 244 male and 673 female servants (out of a total polled population of 2,194) in Aberdeen, and 28 male and 127 female servants (out of a polled population of 824) in Old Aberdeen.

9 ✦ Real wages

The problems of investigating the standard of living in Scotland at any point before the mid twentieth century are enormous, as they must be for any country before government begins to collect modern statistical data on income, prices and employment. These problems are of two kinds: conceptual, concerning the nature and meaning of a 'standard of living', and practical, concerning the accumulation of appropriate evidence.

The first kind we shall for the moment side step, defining for our purposes the standard of living as what contributes to real income, whether in money or in kind: that is to say, we assume the standard to be rising if wages rise faster than prices and if employment opportunities for an individual or family remain the same or, better, improve. This admittedly dodges very real problems of having to weight benefits and costs, if higher incomes are accompanied (as no doubt they often were) by more laborious toil or a deteriorating environment for life at home and work.

The second problem is the evidential one. What sort of data are relevant to the exploration of the standard of living? They may be both qualitative and quantitative, but those on which Scottish historians have chiefly relied for their judgements before 1800 have hitherto mainly been qualitative – i.e., the broad opinions of contemporaries concerning what was happening in the world about them. Where they are available they are not to be underrated, though they may be unfashionable: contemporary observers had, after all, the inestimable advantage of being alive at a time when we were not. Nevertheless, their disadvantages are also undeniable – they survive only patchily, tend by their nature to be impressionistic and imprecise, and have their own types of biases. Travellers' tales and topographical accounts, for instance, in striving to be interesting, too often tend towards the sensational, and, in the case of English travellers, also tend to denigrate, a fashion that stretches at least from Sir Anthony Weldon in 1617 to Dr Johnson in 1772. Even descriptions from Scottish improvers and their friends in the eighteenth century tend to exaggerate the advances of their own day and play down the achievements and standards of their predecessors. Travellers' accounts have, indeed, only very limited uses, and those mainly to confirm what is sufficiently obvious from the general course of economic history, that Scotland was visibly poorer than England throughout the centuries with which we are concerned. Continental travellers, however, for example from France or Sweden, never found any difference in the general condition of the common people in Scotland and their own countries worth remark.

By far and away the largest and most useful account of contemporary opinions, however, were those collected by Sir John Sinclair from all the parishes in Scotland in the *Statistical account* of the 1790s. They cannot of course be accepted uncritically. They were mainly, but not exclusively, the views of the clergy, and the ministers were overwhelmingly in favour of agricultural improvement (though by no means uniformly uncritical of its social repercussions). Like others, they were inclined to puff the present and despise the past. Nevertheless, there is a consistency and pattern in their reports which itself should encourage the historian to consider them seriously.

The first impression that comes across universally from the *Statistical account* is that there was very little recollection of altered living standards until very recent times. Occasionally there were reports of variation in the prosperity of communities beyond the immediate period of living memory – for example Anstruther in Fife was reported as having decayed immediately following the Union of Parliaments, in this case almost certainly incorrectly, as severe decay predated the Union and to judge from local building activity some mild improvement probably followed.[1] But there was nothing to suggest that the ministers reporting to the *Statistical account* knew of any long-term trend either up or down in living standards, either for individual social groups or on a wide geographical scale.

Secondly, though there were many striking reports of significant improvement since the middle of the eighteenth century, these tended to be grouped in specific geographic areas. This itself lends confidence, as there is no reason to think that the distribution of excessively optimistic ministers would be other than random. There were, for instance, few positive reports from the Western Isles, though there were some from Orkney, where, for instance, in Kirkwall the 'lower classes of people live much better in point of food, clothing and houses'; in Shetland there were several reports of a spreading taste for tea, whisky and imported clothes, though not clearly accompanied by rising incomes.[2] There were not many positive reports from the length and breadth of the mainland Highlands. In, Ross and Cromarty, Sutherland and Caithness, for example, such reports of the spread of 'luxury' as there were similarly referred to an increase in dram drinking (due mainly to the malt tax affecting the relative cost of beer and whisky) or – in more prosperous coastal parishes like Dornoch – to the replacement of homespun woollens by textiles, often linen, imported from southern Scotland and England (again perhaps as much a function of shifting relative prices as of rising income). When remarks are made (as at Dingwall) about luxuries which 'when once known, soon come into general use', the context makes it clear that they refer only to the households of urban merchants and their allies, and of neighbouring gentlemen whose 'style of living, and their expences, are widely different from those of their ancestors'.[3] They are balanced by occasional observations about deterioration, as at Bower in Caithness where the minister believed the common people ate less well precisely in order to be able to purchase more 'fineries' of dress.[4] Even in the broad north-eastern Lowland plain beyond Aberdeen there were

[1] Sir John Sinclair (ed.), *The statistical account of Scotland 1791–1799*, EP edition, general editor D.J. Withrington (Wakefield, 1973–1983) (henceforth abbreviated to *OSA*), vol. 10 (*Fife*), pp. 38–9.
[2] *OSA*, vol. 19 (*Orkney*) pp. 15–16, 124, 271 (*Shetland*) pp. 375, 381, 398, 560.
[3] *OSA*, vol. 17 (*Ross and Cromarty*) pp. 365–9; vol. 18 (*Caithness*) pp. 22, 81, 231 (*Sutherland*) pp. 342, 370.
[4] *OSA*, vol. 18 (*Caithness*) p. 6.

few convincing reports of a rising standard of living, though many of rising wages accompanied by rising prices. Improvements here were again mainly observed in dress, with dram drinking and occasionally tea drinking (as at Peterhead and Montquitter), but there is also much talk of poverty and sometimes of poorer diet (as at Fordyce and Grange).[5]

Further south, there was much stronger evidence of a rising standard of living after about 1750, though again it varied from place to place. Dumfries and Galloway did not provide much more unequivocal evidence than the north-east: where things were better it was sometimes associated with country potatoes and pig keeping rather than with rising cash incomes, except in parishes associated with the new textiles, like Tongland.[6] Even in the south of Scotland, the ministers of those rural communities that were relatively detached from a thriving market because of poor communications seldom complained or boasted of the spread of luxury. When any such progress was reported, it was often mentioned (as at Kelso) that it was the larger farmers and the more considerable tradesmen who enjoyed most of its benefits – for example in the consumption of meat or white bread.[7] If in such parishes the common people – smaller tenants, labourers, weavers – were also often said to be appreciably better off than their fathers and grandfathers, commentators also noted that rising prices had in recent decades eaten into rising wages and, as in the north, that the most obvious signs of new affluence were often in dress and whisky drinking.

There were, however, two characteristic types of locality south of the line from Dumbarton to Stonehaven where the common people seemed to be quite clearly better off by the 1790s. One was in rural areas which were close enough to urban labour markets for the people to feel the strong upward tug on wage rates and regularity of employment, and also for them to be involved in selling a surplus of grain or animals either to the towns or over the Border to England. Thus advantageously situated were the day labourers of Anstruther Wester in Fife: 'when they are frugal and industrious, they live very comfortably, and their children are well fed and educated. Thrice the quantity of butcher meat and wheatbread are used now, that were 20 years ago in this parish.'[8] Their brothers, the 'labourers and mechanicks' of Mid-Calder in Midlothian ate more meat, began to drink tea and had abandoned, also within the last twenty years, woollen bonnets, homespun stockings and clothes of local cloth, for hats, English cloth, fustian breeches, cotton stockings and 'slight neat shoes', and their womenfolk had gone over to silk bonnets, cotton gowns, white petticoats, muslin neckerchiefs 'and sometimes there is an addition of a shawl'.[9]

The other type of favoured locality were centres of manufacture, in town and country alike. Thus at Coupar Angus in southern Perthshire, a parish with 101 weavers, the minister in 1795 compared the state of the populace with '40 years ago'. Then, he said 'the broad blue bonnet' and a coat of 'home manufacture' was the universal male dress,

[5] *OSA*, vol. 15 (*N. and E. Aberdeen*) pp. 325, 451; vol. 16 (*Banff*) pp. 155, 212–13.
[6] *OSA*, vol. 4 (*Dumfriesshire*) p. 394; vol. 5 (*Kirkcudbright*), p. 257, 326, 331–3.
[7] *OSA*, vol. 3 (*Roxburghshire*), p. 520.   [8] *OSA*, vol. 10 (*Fife*) p. 32.
[9] *OSA*, vol. 2 (*Lothians*) pp. 96–7.

and 'the tartan plaid, applied closely over a head-dress of linen' was that of women. Now, however:

few servant lads are to be seen at church without their coats of English cloth, hats on their heads, and watches in their pockets. At the period just referred to, a watch, an eight-day clock, or a tea kettle, were scarcely to be met with. At present, there are few houses without one or other of these articles; perhaps one half of the families in the parish are possessed of all of them.[10]

Over the Tay, at Ceres in Fife, a parish with many weavers and with coal and lime works, as well as 'a great number of freeholdings', wheatbread had largely replaced barley and peasemeal, the quantity of butcher meat eaten had doubled in thirty years, tea was used by three-quarters of the families, half the houses had been rebuilt and many new ones erected, women had abandoned the plaid for the cloak and bonnet and men had replaced the bonnet by the hat. 'The servant men are generally clothed with English cloth, and many of them have watches in their pockets.'[11]

Similarly, in the west of Scotland, the reporter from the weaving parish of Cambuslang in Lanarkshire could contrast the period around 1750 with the present age: previously only people of wealth and quality had used wheatbread, sugar or tea, and killed fat cattle; now wheat bread was used by all, sugar and tea occasionally by many and fat cattle killed 'by all farmers, tradesmen, and manufacturers',[12] and in another weaving parish, Houston and Killallan in Renfrewshire, the people were even better dressed than in Coupar Angus:

scarlet is now worn by the lowest and poorest people. The women generally wear black silk cloaks, bonnets of various shapes, and high crowned hats, and riding habits; and the congregation on Sunday appears like an assembly of well dressed and fashionable ladies.[13]

Interesting additional evidence about Lanarkshire comes from a pamphlet by Sir James Steuart in 1769, discussing rising incomes among the labouring classes in the county and pointing out its benefits in better nutrition and more buoyant demand for agricultural goods. He was more sympathetic than many of the ministers towards the small new fineries of dress almost everyone detected among the girls, and used an anthropological argument about this form of consumption. The girls, who were spinners in their own homes, wore 'little superfluities of dress, which they hold out, I suppose, as a fund at their disposal, for the maintenance of children, in case any young fellow should wish to take them for a wife. Were it not for the use of ribbands, and such little ornaments now in fashion, a country lad could form no judgement of the industry and frugality of the young women of the parish.'[14]

Quotations from the *Statistical account* could be multiplied many times, and help to build up a picture of central Scotland, from Angus to Dumbarton and from Ayrshire back to Berwickshire, where rising living standards appear to have been evident in many communities after the middle of the century. It is encouraging to the historian to see the

---

[10] *OSA*, vol. 11 (*S. and E. Perthshire*) p. 97.   [11] *OSA*, vol. 10 (*Fife*) pp. 150–1.
[12] *OSA*, vol. 7 (*Lanarkshire*) p. 93.   [13] *OSA*, vol. 7 (*Renfrew*) p. 730.
[14] Published pseudonomously as Robert Frame, *Considerations on the interest of the County of Lanark* (Glasgow, 1769), p. 16.

evidence fit into a geographical and economic pattern like this, since its consistency confirms the value of the individual fragments and repels the charge, sometimes made, that the ministers were everywhere overly facile in reporting the world about them.

This valuable body of evidence thus places central Scotland among a rather small number of areas in Europe where the living standards of the common people were improving in the second half of the eighteenth century. Stagnation or deterioration of real wages was reported not only in the Scottish Highlands, but in most of Ireland, southern England, the Low Countries and Scandinavia. Improvement, however, was also reported in the north of England, where it was also associated with the earliest stages of industrialisation.[15]

The modern economic and social historian, however, does not wish to rest a case solely on contemporary qualitative opinions from one point in time, but demands in addition materials that can be quantified and which contain enough observations to constitute a time series, ideally one stretching over a century or more. The classic study in English history is of course the Henry Phelps Brown–Shiela Hopkins work of 1955–6 where the wage rates of building craftsmen and labourers were measured against the cost of a basket of consumables to provide an index of the standard of living over seven centuries.[16] This approach had several forebears in England, back to Arthur Young's attempt in 1812 to measure carpenters' and masons' wages from the fourteenth century to the eighteenth century in terms of the quantity of corn and other foodstuffs that the wage could buy, and William Playfair's similar attempt in 1822 to measure the wage of 'good mechanics' from 1565 to 1819 against the price of wheat.[17]

Such approaches are readily criticised. It is difficult to fill a basket of consumables with items that remain equally in demand over seven centuries: Phelps Brown for the period before 1800 relied solely on the needs of two priests and a servant at Bridport in Dorset in the 1450s, and the reports of Davies and Eden on the consumption of the English poor in the 1790s. It is difficult to distinguish, in the building accounts of the sixteenth and seventeenth century, small contractors charging various overheads from craftsmen receiving no more than a wage. It is hard to take account of perquisites, or wages paid partly in kind which may add very considerably to the value of the money wage.[18] The attempt to obtain long series either of prices or wages may force the researcher unwittingly to untypical sources, relating to institutions which perhaps bought cheaply on long-term contracts or alternatively paid over the odds if they had no flexibility to shop around for bargains. Similarly, labour working on colleges or palaces may have enjoyed a degree of security not typical of the wider market place, but may possibly have been paid at a lower daily wage rate as a result. Institutional sources in short, may not

[15] L.M. Cullen, T.C. Smout and A. Gibson, 'Wages and comparative development in Ireland and Scotland, 1565–1780', in R. Mitchison and P. Roebuck (eds.), *Economy and society in Scotland and Ireland, 1500–1939* (Edinburgh, 1988), pp. 105–16; G. Karlsson (ed.), *Levestandarden i Norden, 1750–1914* (Reykjavik, 1987); E.W. Gilboy, *Wages in eighteenth century England* (Cambridge, Mass. 1934); E.W. Hunt, 'Industrialization and regional inequality: wages in Britain, 1760–1914', *Journal of Economic History*, vol. 46 (1986), pp. 935–66.

[16] The papers are conveniently collected in H. Phelps Brown and S.V. Hopkins, *A perspective of wages and prices* (London, 1981), pp. 1–98.   [17] Phelps Brown and Hopkins, *A perspective*, pp. 99–105.

[18] M. Sonenscher, 'Work and wages in Paris in the eighteenth century', in M. Berg, P. Hudson and M. Sonenscher (eds.), *Manufacture in town and country before the factory* (London, 1983).

completely reflect the volatility of the unsheltered world. There is a danger, again, of forgetting that wages have not always been as important a source of income and sustenance to the common people as access to land: the waged labour that was the norm in the nineteenth century certainly was not so in the sixteenth, but a simple index invites us to assume that its variations tells us as much about the general standard of living in one period as another. By a similar misperception there is a risk of allowing wage rates to stand as a valid proxy for earnings, though the main source of variability in the standard of living in an early period could well be in the number of days a year in which waged work could be found, and in the differing opportunities of family members to contribute to the household income. The objections to using Phelps Brown and Hopkins or similar works as a straightforward index to the standard of living in the long run are legion.[19]

Yet, as scholars have discovered, it is a great deal easier to criticise this approach than to replace it with any better perspective on long-term trends in the standard of living. It has the considerable merits of convenience and clarity. The historian can very reason-ably ask what *does* it mean when an index of wages suddenly begins to move ahead or fall behind an index of prices, because it would be a very rash scholar who assumed it meant nothing at all. If, for example, the wage rates rise faster than food prices for a decade or more, it is difficult to imagine that this is not sound evidence that labour as a whole is becoming better off, always providing that the wage rates in question are typical of those paid in a range of occupations – such an assumption seems especially reasonable for unskilled work with a good deal of interchangeability possible between, say, a building site and a farm. Similar assumptions of improvement or decline can be made by sudden short-term lurches in either direction caused by seasons of plenty and dearth, and the fact that the magnitude of these lurches is generally far more obvious than the trends, tells us the important fact that early modern people experienced much greater variability in their standard of living in the short term than in the medium or long term, in contrast to the experience of western Europeans in the last hundred years. Again, if real wage rates move up in one country or region but not in another, it is a reasonable hypothesis that the populace is experiencing differing fortunes in different places. It is not quite so clear, however, that the standard of living cannot improve even if the adult male real wage index appears to be stagnant over several decades, since it is possible that if employment opportunities for women and children are growing, or if the man gets more waged work in the year, families could afford more. In short, while it is not reasonable to assume that every detectable shift in the index would have the same significance to the mass of the population then as it would have today, an index well constructed and cautiously used can be an invaluable tool for the historian, if it is not used naively or in isolation from other evidence.

In our study we have experimented cautiously in the Phelps Brown–Hopkins tradition. One approach has been to estimate the daily wages divided by the price of oatmeal or of wheatbread, to demonstrate what quantity of meal or bread a wage could buy. Oatmeal

---

[19] D. Woodward, 'Wage rates and living standards in pre-industrial England', *Past and Present*, no. 91 (1981), pp. 28–45.

was the staff of life of the Scots in the seventeenth and eighteenth centuries, the most important item in the budget of a labouring family, perhaps accounting for half or more of total household expenditure. This calculation provides the simplest and most vivid indication of varying prosperity that we could devise. Wheatbread was eaten more in towns than in the country, and even there probably not by the poorest. We have included estimates of how much wheatbread could be bought by the labourers and masons of Edinburgh, partly to facilitate international comparisons with wheat-eating societies elsewhere but mainly because the price records for wheatbread are better than those for oatmeal in the sixteenth and early seventeenth centuries. The price of the two grains are of course related: in individual years there might be shifts in the ratio, but as a rough measure of trends in the cost of subsistence, bread price is a good second to meal price.

Let us consider the estimates of the purchasing power of labour in terms of the quantity of wheatbread or of oatmeal that could be bought with a day's wage (figures 9.1–9.2). Before the eighteenth century we are dealing with meagre data, and that mainly relating to Edinburgh masons and building labourers: even here it is necessary, before 1636, to use Fife oatmeal fiars as a proxy for the local (Midlothian) prices, as the latter are unknown. The main effect of this substitution is to render uncertain individual figures rather than to discredit the trends, as in the later seventeenth century when both are available there is at least a broad similarity between meal prices in Fife and Midlothian.

The first impression to emerge from scrutiny of the graphs for all periods is one of extreme variability of experience from one year to another, a short-term instability between seasons brought about by the inflexibility of wages and the volatile character of the grain market. To take an example, the Edinburgh mason in 1554 could have bought 20 lbs. of wheatbread with his day's wage, three years later only 10 lbs. (all these bread and meal weights are in Scottish troy, for which see appendix I). It was not at all unusual to experience fluctuations of 50 to 100 per cent or even more within two or three seasons even as late as the eighteenth century – as at Buchanan between 1741 and 1744 (from 3.5 to 9.2 lbs. of oatmeal for his day's wage), between 1757 and 1760 (from 4.0 to 7.0 lbs.) or between 1780 and 1783 (from 7.4 to 3.9 lbs.). For contemporaries who had to survive, and budget for their subsistence, this must obviously have been the most important feature of price behaviour.

Secondly, there is evidence of longer-term alterations. There is skimpy but conclusive witness that in the sixteenth century the European-wide decline in food purchasing power for wage earners did not exclude Scotland. The oatmeal series puts 1560 as the best year on record for Edinburgh labourers in 250 years (14.5 lbs. a day could be bought for the day's wage), and 1587 as the worst (1.9 lbs.) – but it is full of gaps, not least for the 1590s. More persuasive are the wheatbread graphs, showing falls of about 30 per cent in the purchasing power of labourers, measuring the period from 1530 to 1540 against the period 1590 to 1600; most of this fall came after 1570. For Edinburgh masons the trend is the same but, the absolute decline appears steeper, more like a fall of 45 per cent. The period from 1596 to 1607 contains several years even worse than any in the 1580s. A half century followed which, on the whole, marked a distinct improvement on the nadir of the late 1590s without fully restoring the situation to what it had been in the middle of the sixteenth century.

These are steeper falls than those now accepted for the trend of workers' real wages in sixteenth-century England, where the Phelps Brown and Hopkins estimate of a fall in the real wages of skilled and semi-skilled workers in southern England of 57 per cent over the Tudor period has recently been revised to 29 per cent by Rappaport in his study of London, and, with relatively minor changes in consumption patterns, to as little as 17 per cent.[20] But one is not exactly comparing like with like. The English data are based on a 'basket of consumables' with many observations of many commodities, ours only on wheatbread and oatmeal. The data for wheatbread are stronger than for meal, but both have relatively few observations. Furthermore, if the comparison is not between the 1530s and 1590s, but the periods 1550–65 and 1625–40 (both of which yield a significant number of observations), the Edinburgh masons lost 32 per cent of their purchasing power measured in wheatbread but only 25 per cent measured in oatmeal, and the Edinburgh labourers lost 25 per cent of their purchasing power measured in wheatbread but 17 per cent measured in oatmeal. These are appreciable but by no means catastrophic falls.

In any case, at least after the final quarter of the sixteenth century, which was clearly a particularly bad period throughout Europe, contemporaries would surely have found the extreme swings more notable than the trend. The labourers' low oatmeal purchasing power of 1624, 1629, 1631, 1636 and 1637, for example, contrasted with those about twice as high in 1633 and 1637. If our data were better we would be better able to identify more runs of good and bad runs of years, especially after 1640, but it simply does not hold up enough to do that. One needs no graph to discover the particular difficulties of the later 1690s, of course.

In the eighteenth century, for Edinburgh labourers, there is clearly a striking improvement in terms of their oatmeal purchasing power after about 1750, after an ambiguous experience in the two previous decades. For Edinburgh masons, interestingly, there is no sign of improvement before 1780 – a phenomenon that probably accounts for the increasing restiveness of skilled labour in the capital in the decades between 1760 and the end of the century.

The data sets for rural estates covering the century after 1680 (figure 9.2) provide an important warning against relying on Edinburgh or any other single series as a base for generalisations about the Scottish experience as a whole. Some estate variations may be due to sudden bursts of house building or estate improvements that die away again after a few years, but right up to the 1790s the overwhelming impression is of stability of trend. It is really not evident, even in Yester and Buchanan where the influence of the improvers and the urban market should have been clear at a relatively early stage, that things were better in the 1780s than the 1680s.

Considering that the average daily intake of a Scottish workman might be around 30 oz. avoirdupois of oatmeal a day, the discovery that a labourer's day wage could often buy five or six lbs., and sometimes considerably more, appears at first sight to provide

[20] S. Rappaport, *Worlds within worlds; structures of life in sixteenth-century London* (Cambridge, 1989), esp. p. 160.

rather an optimistic perspective on his standard of living. This is deceptive. First, probably only about half to two-thirds of household income would be available to be spent on meal: the proportion would vary with the poverty of the worker, two-thirds applying to the poorest. Second, the calculation is one of food prices divided by a daily wage rate, but while food was needed daily, waged employment could at best be provided six days out of seven, and even on weekdays it is a generous assumption for most of our period, averaging summer and winter, that work would be found even for an urban labourer for as many as two days out of three: if so, wages would only be paid for 57 per cent of the days in the year – this is discussed at length in chapter 8, section 2.3 above. Indeed, for most rural labourers before the agricultural revolution in Scotland, there would probably be only very intermittent waged labour available. Finally, a man might have to support dependants – a wife, children, perhaps aged parents – from his wage. The remaining graphs attempt to explore these problems so as to approach the real standard of living more closely.

Our second type of calculation involves modelling the cost of subsistence in certain defined situations. Figures 9.3–9.5 show tentative calculations from Edinburgh, Glasgow and Buchanan based as far as possible on local price and wage data. The weekly cost of living is calculated in three situations – first, a single man living in a household, for example that of his parents, paying for food and clothing but not paying rent; next, a young couple just married and living in their own rented cottage but unencumbered with children; last, a couple similarly housed but with four children under ten.

In estimating the cost of living, the largest single component is obviously the cost of food, as the first priority is to maintain physical efficiency, ideally by securing at least 3,350 calories for the man, 2,500 for the woman and proportionally smaller amounts for the four young children. Our calculations assume that all the food was bought (i.e., that the money wages were equivalent to the entire wage) and that it consisted only of the most basic kind of food discussed in chapter 7, based on 30 oz. avoirdupois of oatmeal for adult males, 20 oz. for adult females, and between 11.5 oz. and 15.5 oz. for the children: we assume that the family drank water or milk obtained free of charge. Meal prices are not available for all the localities or for all the years for which there are wage data, or where a wage can reasonably be interpolated from existing data; where they are missing they can sometimes be calculated closely enough from oat prices. We assume, next, from evidence in the *Statistical account*, that clothing costs are equal to one-third of the cost of respective food needs. Budgets in the *Statistical account* give reasonably consistent figures for annual clothing expenses for unskilled labourers – £21 Scots at Poatmoak in Kinross, £13.10s.0d. at Auchterarder and £19.6s.0d. at Moulin in Perthshire; £18 at Graitney in Dumfriesshire.[21] The Moulin entry details exactly what was involved – a coat and waistcoat (the latter lined and backed from the wife's old clothes), breeches and hose, two pairs of shoes and two shirts: also a great coat, a bonnet and a handkerchief every second year. It sounds like the basic minimum for working outdoors in the Scottish climate, and it is hard to believe labourers made do with less in earlier centuries. Estimates of the annual cost of women's clothing vary from £8.5s.0d. at

---

[21] *OSA*, vol. 4 (*Dumfriesshire*) p. 187; vol. 11 (*S. and E. Perthshire*) pp. 45, 674; vol. 12 (*N. and W. Perthshire*) p. 758.

Auchterarder to £19.1s.0d. at Moulin where, however, it was assumed that the wife brought sufficient body blothes into the marriage as will 'reduce the yearly expense of her own and her children's clothing one third'. We have estimated a woman's clothing at two-thirds the cost of a man's clothing over the period. The Moulin record explains what is involved – a gown and petticoats, two shirts, hose, a pair of shoes, a neck handkerchief and an apron, plus a bodice every second year. Clothing costs for four small children we reckoned to be equivalent to the father's total clothing bill, which has some support from the budgets for Graitney, Auchterarder and Moulin if one assumes frugality.

How do we turn these figures for the 1790s into a fair base for reckoning a component for clothing in our standard of living calculations? At both Moulin and Poatmoak the sum spent on basic clothes represented an addition equivalent to one third of what a man was spending on himself on food. We may perhaps assume that the same ratio applied in the past, but in order to avoid the appearance of an unjustifiable leap in clothing costs whenever there is a dearth, it is safer to express clothing expenses as equivalent to 33 per cent of a running mean of food costs over an eleven-year period.

The element of fuel and rent was likely in reality to be a particularly variable cost, the first depending partly on the proximity to a peat bank, furze common or coal heugh, the latter on whether a town or country labourer was involved. Some workers would have had both fuel and rent 'free' or, more accurately, in the case of fuel, for the labour of cutting it, in the case of rent, under some such arrangement as for the Lothian and Border 'hind' whereby the wife or 'bondager' worked a specified number of days in harvest in return for occupation of the cottage. Our assumption, however, is that the man had to pay both fuel and rent from his wage. In the *Statistical account* at both Graitney and Moulin fuel costs were £12 Scots a year, at Auchterarder £15; rent was £9 at Moulin and £12 at Graitney; whilst the implication at Portmoak was that the two elements together cost about £24. We have assumed an average of £12 each, and calculated them each throughout as about as expensive as the woman's clothes.

What we have listed does not quite exhaust the list of a family's needs. At Moulin 'soap and blue for washing' was costed at £2.14s.0d. Scots and 'oil for light' at £1.4s.0d.; at Auchterarder lamp oil was estimated at £2.2s.0d., candle at £1.9s.0d., expenses during in-lying, sickness, etc., at £9, and needles, pins and thread 10s.; whilst at Graitney 'soap, candles, and salt, etc.' came to £9, with 'school wages for two of the children' at £7.4s.0d. At Moulin it was also mentioned that even poor families 'by some means or other . . . give their children such education as the nearest school affords', but no cost was put on it. We have disregarded education costs as not in the strictest sense a 'necessity', and allowed £6 (or half the cost of the woman's clothes) for these other miscellaneous expenses for the full household with four children.

The method that we have followed allows for about 67 per cent of the labouring family expenditure in the full household to be devoted to food. Is this plausible? The family of four at Moulin spent 70 per cent on food, and Murray has calculated 'something in the region of 70 per cent' as typical for handloom weaver's families in Scotland, 1810–1830. Such was also typical of family expenditures in England and Denmark in the eighteenth and nineteenth centuries.[22] A little over two-thirds thus seems a safe enough proportion to work with.

Our graphs, as calculated, therefore have certain undeniable and unavoidable weaknesses. Firstly, for non-food elements, they rest on budgeting from the early 1790s, and not from any earlier decades. Secondly, non-food costs (clothing, rent, fuel in particular) are assumed to have borne the same ratio to average food costs throughout the period as they bore in the early 1790s. This seems reasonable, as the two centuries before the 1790s were not a time of dramatically changing technology which might have altered relative prices: it is true that clothing may have become somewhat cheaper in the eighteenth century but we have other testimony that the populace spent more on it than before, so perhaps these two alterations can be regarded as cancelling each other out. It is nevertheless important to recognise that the graphs are only rough and ready guides to the experience of the past.

Taking them, for the moment, at their face value, what lessons can be learned from this exercise? Firstly, in those circumstances where we have envisaged the labourer as a single man, paying for his meal, ale and other food, but living in another's household rent free, his wage almost invariably left a margin after the demands of meeting simple physical efficiency had been met. The margin varied from period to period and place to place. Given the nature of the data and the calculations one should perhaps not make too much of the differences, but our graphs show how the rural labourers of Stirlingshire in the eighteenth century were the most pinched of all. The higher real wages in towns of which contemporaries such as Adam Smith spoke were certainly a reality. At least the urban labourer would have experienced his bachelor years as by and large economically easy ones (in contrast to what was to come), providing, of course, he could rely on employment for two-thirds of the year. In reality he was likely to need to save something in the full employment weeks of summer to tide him over the winter when jobs were harder to come by. It can be seen, nevertheless, that even a single labourer in constant employment might be pressed in certain years of high grain prices, and would have then been unlikely to have been able to meet the requirements of full physical efficiency – he would have gone hungry, his work would have suffered, but he would not have starved.

Our second scenario imagines a recently married couple in which the man alone contributes to the income. The skilled craftsmen in these circumstances can normally manage readily enough, just as the unskilled managed when he was unmarried, though there are plainly years (most obviously in the 1690s) when the shoe pinches. The unskilled labourer, however, is left by marriage in difficulty, even if our graphs possibly overdraw his plight. In our model, he could scarcely by dint of his own wage alone hope to keep the household going at levels of full physical efficiency. What might be possible, most of the time, was a bare scraping subsistence. Moreover, when one adds, in the third scenario, the prospect of the couple attempting to maintain four children under ten, the

²² N. Murray, *The Scottish hand loom weavers 1790–1850: a social history* (Edinburgh, 1978), p. 99; Phelps Brown's figures (around 80 per cent) do not allow for rent: *A perspective*, p. 14; P. Thestrup, 'The standard of living in Denmark since c.1750', in *Levestandarden i Norden*, p. 35.

situation appears to become an impossibility. It appears somewhat beyond the reach even of a skilled worker (though note that if he had full employment rather than work for two thirds of the year it would be within his grasp), while for the labourer the expense appears superficially to be quite beyond his means. For instance, the wage of the Stirlingshire labourer in the 1750s looks to be only about a third of the sum needed to support a family of this size at levels of physical efficiency. Even making allowances for unduly harsh assumptions, it is hard to see how it could have been more than half.

It is improbable that all elements of a household's expenditure needed to be carried through periods of particular hardship. Rent arrears and all manner of other debts are commonplace in estate records of the seventeenth and eighteenth centuries, and no doubt just as ubiquitous among the labouring classes in the towns. For a time a family could pull their belts in and go hungry without actually perishing. Figure 9.6 attempts to trace the fortunes of a 'model' Edinburgh labourer with his wife and four children, attempting to purchase oatmeal over two and a half centuries, with no other costs attributed to their budget. It shows how a decent diet could have been maintained for most of the time, but that there were significant periods when even the barest minimum was beyond reach, all non-essential costs already having been stripped away. Hard physical work could hardly have been possible under these circumstances. That such families could survive at all seems remarkable. Yet the Scottish population married and reproduced successfully, and some labouring families (perhaps not many, we have no accurate means of telling) were able to raise a family of four children under ten to maturity. How can it be explained?

It can only be explained if we understand that our models are no more than illuminating devices, throwing light on reality but not corresponding to it. They show that, normally, a wife could not herself possibly afford to be unemployed, even if pregnancy and childcare confined her to the home, to the needle, the knitting needle and the spinning wheel or rock. They show how imperative it would be to the family economy to have contributions from the children at as early an age as possible. They show the importance of exceptional earning opportunities, like harvest wages which were always larger in money terms and better provided with food entitlements than the day rates graphed. They show how a family must have depended on income from other things than waged labour – indeed, at these rates of pay a married agricultural labourer would have been unthinkable without land on which he and his wife could raise produce both for immediate consumption and for sale. Even a craftsman might need a holding if he was to raise a family with much comfort, especially in the less well-paid rural areas. They show of what significance extras and perquisites would have been, varying from the allowances of free milk that a rural labourer might expect, to the opportunity to take away 'waste' materials available to burgh craftsmen; this is the sort of thing that Michael Sonenscher and others have emphasised.[23] They indicate the importance of eighteenth-century opportunities for substitution, milk for ale, and especially potatoes for oatmeal, at the bottom end of the earnings scale. They indicate how unlikely it was that a subsistence based on generous provision of oatmeal and ale, found at the employer's

[23] M. Sonenscher, 'Work and wages in Paris', pp. 161–2.

table for unmarried servants and reckoned as optimal for maintaining physical efficiency, could have been sustained in the labourer's household itself: calorie input is likely to have dropped on marriage. Finally, and perhaps most interestingly of all, they throw into sharp relief in a preindustrial society the same kind of poverty cycle that Rowntree discovered in York at the opening of the twentieth century: an adolescence and early adulthood of relative ease, poverty accompanying the establishment of a new household, turning to real hardship when the children arrived, some easing of the situation as they found employment, and an old age or widowhood of deep poverty if one survived so long. It should be emphasised that in most areas of Scotland, outside the south-east where a different system prevailed, most farm servants were young and unmarried and lived in with the farmer; they received free food and a small money wage, generally worth only about 40 per cent of the value of their total wage in money and kind. This of course insulated them from fluctuations in food prices until they got married. Then they generally became cottars, providing day labour for the farmer and receiving a wage calculated almost solely in money. They might indeed purchase meal with this money directly from the farmer, or fall into debt with him in dear years for meal credited to them, but they were fully exposed to fluctuations in food prices. In these circumstances the poverty cycle, especially the difference between the married and unmarried state, was likely to be accentuated.

The puzzle is how they managed. One commentator who understood rural life very well was Sir James Steuart, whose *Considerations on the interest of the county of Lanark* (1769) included the earliest detailed attempt we have seen to outline a labourer's budget.[24] He began by the observation that in recent years the lot of agricultural labourers had greatly improved: 'had you asked them formerly how they lived, they would have told you, "By the Providence of God". The answer was good and proper. Their industry was then so miscellaneous; the employment they found was so precarious and uncertain that they could not give it a name.' Lanarkshire, of course, was at the heart of the region where the standard of living had begun noticeably to rise from the middle of eighteenth century and significantly Steuart's calculations assumed that by this date the day labourers' employment was no longer precarious and uncertain but steady through the year. 'Let us suppose', he says, 'the lowest wages of a day Labourer to amount, through the year, to about Nine Pound Sterling [£108 Scots], or Three Shillings and Sixpence per week [£2.2s.0d. Scots a week, or 7s. Scots a day]: and let us allow this for the maintenance alone of his family.' By maintenance he means food; the labourer, though, needs also to provide for fire, clothes and house rent. Firing was, says Stewart, 'a mere triffle, from the abundance of fewel in most places of the Country'. He would, however, also need 'one half rood of ground', dug and manured, for producing greens and potatoes, 'which two articles occasion a great saving on the oatmeal in the autumn and winter'. The rent of the cottage and small holding would be 13s.4d. [£8 Scots] plus that of a summer's grazing for a cow on the adjacent farms, £1 to £1.10s. [£12–£18 Scots]: the produce of the cow, amounting to about a cwt of butter a year, would fetch £2 [£24 Scots] and more than pay the rent charges (he pointed out that the family would only drink

[24] Steuart, *Considerations*, pp. 2–3.

skimmed milk). All his original figures were of course in sterling. Anything left, along with the produce of the wife's spinning, would provide for clothing and other needs. . . . 'in this way can our day-labourers live, when oatmeal is at One Shilling per peck, which for three years past it has been'. But when they get old, either charity or their children must support them.

The evidence in the *Statistical account* of the following generation also shows how readily the outline of the theoretical picture depicted in our graphs can be filled with telling detail. Like ourselves and like Steuart, the reporters were often puzzled to understand how labouring families managed, especially where paid day labour was less regularly available. The minister at Mortlach in Banff, for example, said that 'as to the labouring man at sixpence [6s. Scots] a day with his victuals, when married and with a few young children, it is rather surprising how he makes out at all, considering that he cannot get work all the year round, unless the winter season be uncommonly mild'.[25] It was 'inconceivable' to see how the labourer with a large family survived, observed his colleague at Dingwall in Ross and Cromarty, 'but habits of frugal management, taught by poverty to the indigent, are found to effect what the affluent do not imagine and cannot easily believe'.[26]

If there was one point to which the commentators drew particular attention, it was that if a labourer was to marry and raise a family, the household economy demanded an input from all its members, not just the man, united by a common moral commitment to frugality. The woman's role was pivotal. A typical brief comment was that by the minister of Cleish, in Kinross-shire: 'the wages of labourers are sufficient, if they and their wives are industrious, and enjoy an ordinary measure of health, to enable them to bring up a family'.[27] More explicit and helpful was this observation from Montquitter in Aberdeenshire:

The maintenance of a tradesman's or a day-labourer's family does not entirely depend on what he himself gains; for if his wife and children are industrious, they share the merit of furnishing subsistence. When a day-labourer or tradesman rents a croft, his wife commonly pays landlord and merchant by the produce of her cows and by manufacture; and leaves it for the husband, by the sale of cattle and by his work, to furnish bread. During infancy and childhood of their family, parents of these classes are generally poor, but gradually rise to easy circumstances, as their children become capable of relieving the hand, and assisting in the industry of the mother.[28]

Even clearer and more elaborate was the report from Udney, also in Aberdeenshire:

It is not easy precisely to ascertain the expence of a common labourer when married. He has a boll's sowing or two from the tenant; it is plowed to him; his cow kept in summer with the farmer's cattle; and the straw of his corn from his croft maintains the cow during winter. He has liberty to cast turf for himself, and sometimes a few peats. He works to the farmer in harvest, attends the plough during winter and spring, at which time he either receives his victuals at the farmer's house, or has allowed to him 2 pecks of oat-meal a-week. What time he has to spare in summer, from Whitsunday to harvest, he works for day's wages to different persons. His wife and children weave stockings . . . until the boys are fit for herding cattle. What is thus earned, if he and his wife are industrious, and his family keeps in health, maintains them in a sober way.[29]

[25] *OSA*, vol. 16 (*Banff*) pp. 340–1.   [26] *OSA*, vol. 17 (*Ross and Cromarty*) p. 366.
[27] *OSA*, vol. 11 (*S. and E. Perthshire*) p. 641.   [28] *OSA*, vol. 15 (*N. and E. Aberdeenshire*) pp. 325–6.
[29] *OSA*, vol. 15 (*N. and E. Aberdeenshire*) pp. 555–6.

The essentially heterogeneous nature of income in a pre-industrial labouring household could not be better expressed than by these Aberdeenshire examples. Subsistence was obtained not only (perhaps not mainly) by buying food and fuel, but by growing and digging it: the budget was balanced not only by wage payments but by sales of cattle, dairy produce and textiles. The situation is similar to Steuart's Lanarkshire example of 1769, but income was still more heterogeneous. We begin to have a clearer idea how the yawning chasms on our graphs were bridged.

It is also made very clear in all parts of Scotland that children were expected to contribute to their keep from an early age. Steuart implied elsewhere, in a passage that seems to refer to the Highlands, that such child labour was often provided without a cash wage at all, and emphasised the difference when a textile industry was introduced and 'the cottars begin to spin' so that children who 'tended herds of cattle for a poor maintenance will turn themselves to a more profitable occupation'.[30] At Humbie in East Lothian the *Statistical account* explained that the wages of a farm servant:

with the earnings of his wife, enable him to rear a family of 4 or 5 children; but during this period, the whole family are very poorly fed indeed. The first relief he meets with is from the oldest of his children, who go as early as possible to service, and give him whatever they can spare for bringing up their younger brothers and sisters ... when their filial exertions are no longer necessary, the young people turn their attention to dress.[31]

At Johnston in Dumfriesshire it was observed that from the age of seven or eight children could be employed tending cattle, for which they were given board and lodging as well as a wage – and the fact that another household took over the responsibility of feeding was surely at least as important as the few pence they obtained as a cash wage.[32] At Kinnettles in Angus eight was the age at which a child could help the mother to earn and ten was the age for a boy or girl to go into service, 'and the burden of that child is taken away ... when a few of the children get above 10 years, they increase the living of the family very considerably'.[33] At Lethnot in the same county children became useful at eight or nine, receiving keep in exchange for herding as in Dumfriesshire.[34] So the top line in our graph of a couple with four unsupported children under ten years old represents a situation that was rare or at least lasted only briefly.

It may also be remarked that if the labour of children was highly valued in the household, so was their education, to the point of providing at least for minimal school attendance. Steuart reported seeing children in Lochaber at the age of fourteen ('numbers of idle, poor, useless hands') doing nothing except herding and going to school, as if no other occupation was possible. He did not approve at all. The ministers of the *Statistical account* were more sympathetic.[35] At Bathgate in West Lothian the minister said that many labouring parents bringing up three, four or five children 'paid for teaching their sons to read, write and sometimes arithmetic, and their daughters to read, often to sew and write'.[36] At Dalmeny in the same county 'scarce any fail to put

[30] Sir James Steuart, *Inquiry into the principles of political economy* (Dublin, 1770), vol. I, pp. 103–5.
[31] *OSA*, vol. 2 (*Lothians*), p. 509.   [32] *OSA*, vol. 4 (*Dumfriesshire*) p. 253–4.
[33] *OSA*, vol. 13 (*Angus*) p. 333.   [34] *OSA*, vol. 13 (*Angus*) p. 384.
[35] Steuart, *Political economy*, vol. I, p. 106.   [36] *OSA*, vol. 2 (*Lothians*) p. 694.

their children to school to learn English, writing and arithmetic'.[37] At Strachur and Stralachlan in Argyll labouring families with four or five children 'give them a suitable education'.[38] At St Quivox in Ayrshire the children of day labourers 'almost without exception ... are taught to read and write', though in another industrial parish, Old Monkland in Lanarkshire, 'the boys and girls get wages for tambouring, sewing muslin etc. at so early a period there is great danger of their education being neglected'.[39] At Moulin in Perthshire, as in other places, the minister marvelled that poor parents were able to afford their children's schooling, but noticed that they almost always did.[40] Fees at the parish school for reading and writing in the second half of the eighteenth century were very generally 30s. Scots a quarter (12s. for reading alone). With a family of even three of school age it would surely be unthinkable for all of them to attend all the year, but if the girls learned reading and not writing (which was very common), and both sexes attended only in winter and spring (to leave summer and autumn free for herding and similar work), school attendance over a year or two might be practical. There is no reason to think that the Scottish standard of living was so low that most people could not afford basic literacy, but equally no reason to think that economic circumstances allowed it to be more than very basic indeed.

It is important to pay careful attention to those occasions when observers in the *Statistical account* and elsewhere report an improvement in the standard of living. An increase in the rate of wages is often referred to, especially as a disadvantage to the employer. As the minister of Deskford in Banff put it, in a nice parody of the political slogan, 'the wages of servants "have increased, are increasing and, in the opinion of the farmer, ought to be diminished"'.[41] On the other hand, it was often pointed out in the 1790s that the improvement had been heavily eroded, though not cancelled out, by inflation, as at St Vigeans in Angus, where, since 1754 'wages are more than double, and prices generally as three to two'.[42]

Improvements in the standard of living were almost invariably seen as having complex causes, in which rises in wage rates were only one. Thus at Cupar in Fife, the improvement in the condition of the labourer was seen to be due to his own wages having risen more than the cost of provisions, to the introduction of the potato which enabled him to enjoy 'a vast additional supply' of food and also to rear pigs and poultry, and to the fact that unlike his father, 'he can depend on being employed during the course of the whole year'.[43] Such points were often made in other parishes, particularly about the importance of potatoes as a substitute for more expensive meal, and the greater regularity of employment through the year, which (like the rise in wage rates itself) was often seen as a consequence of spreading industry and improving agriculture. Sometimes the point is effectively made through comparison with non-improving areas. Thus at Craignish in Argyll, though a labourer was paid 12s. Scots a day (about the Lowland rate at that point in the 1790s) his work was not constant as 'there are no works of any

[37] *OSA*, vol. 2 (*Lothians*) p. 729.   [38] *OSA*, vol. 8 (*Argyll*) p. 414.
[39] *OSA*, vol. 6 (*Ayrshire*) p. 523; vol. 7 (*Lanarkshire*) p. 526.
[40] *OSA*, vol. 12 (*N. and W. Perthshire*) p. 759.   [41] *OSA*, vol. 16 (*Banff*) p. 142.
[42] *OSA*, vol. 13 (*Angus*) p. 628.   [43] *OSA*, vol. 10 (*Fife*) p. 229.

importance of extent carrying on'. Consequently his income did not exceed £108 or £120 Scots a year (a good third below, say, earnings in Fife) and out of this 'he must pay a smart rent for the miserable hut' his family lived in, and render twelve days unpaid work to his superior. Furthermore, his children, until they were fit for herding, were 'a dead weight' upon him, and his wife 'can contribute little to the common stock: for she must, in some places, spin so much to the landlady without food or payment; and she must draw money from the poor husband's pocket to purchase half a dozen of hens and eggs, to be given also to the landlady as a present, or rather as a further token of vassalage'.[44]

Studies made on the Buchanan estate in Stirlingshire (more fully reported else-where)[45] show in detail from the records of an eighteenth-century estate how one employer made a complete break around mid century from a system employing a large number of labourers on day rates for a few days in the year, to one employing a small number of labourers for around 300 days in the year. In the former situation, of course, the labourers would undoubtedly have had to live predominately from their own holdings, and they were well described as cottars; in the latter, they would scarcely have had the time to cultivate their holdings by their own labour (though their families might) – they were much more like what we think of as farm labourers. Arguably a rise in the rate for day labour might therefore have been necessary just to maintain them at the same level of subsistence, to compensate for the time they would otherwise have spent raising their own food.

It is probable, indeed, that the most substantial increases in the standard of living in late eighteenth-century Scotland came about less through the expansion of wage rates and employment opportunities for males than for their expansion for women and children. This was true even in non-textile areas. Take, for example, the agricultural workers of Lothian and the eastern Borders where the distinctive 'hinding' system prevailed. The male hind was hired by the year (he was no casual day labourer), and was a married man with a cot holding. He was paid by an annual allowance in kind in the seventeenth century and in many places on into the nineteenth century. It is a startling fact that his allowances scarcely varied between the assessment of 1656 and the reports of 1843, so the only scope for improvement in his situation would be that afforded by the substitution of potato ground for oatground, and the ability to take advantage, as the farmer did, of rising prices for the grain he was given in excess of what he and his family needed to eat.[46] On the other hand, where his wife (the 'bondager') and his son had been expected to give their labour for nothing in 1656, by 1843 they were both receiving substantial money wages – it was their contribution to the household income that had so notably grown. In the 1790s in this region there were several reports of how employment for women had recently multiplied – thus at Cramond a woman could then earn 6s. Scots a day 'working in the fields' for six months of the year, the new root crops having multiplied jobs for turnip hoeing, weeding and picking, and 3s. Scots a day at spinning,

[44] *OSA*, vol. 8 (*Argyll*) pp. 79–80.

[45] A. Gibson, 'Proletarianization? The transition to full-time labour on a Scottish estate, 1722–1727', *Continuity and Change*, vol. 5 (1990), pp. 357–89.

[46] I. Levitt and C. Smout, 'Farm workers' incomes in 1843', in T.M. Devine (ed.), *Farm servants and labour in Lowland Scotland, 1770–1914* (Edinburgh, 1984) p. 160.

for the other six months.[47] This would have yielded a cash income of £70 Scots a year. At Heriot, much more upland and isolated, women could earn £15 or £18 for their winter work, and twice that rate for summer work because the farmer needed more hands to milk the ewes, cut the crops and hoe the turnips: that suggests an income in the range of £48 a year.[48] These may be compared to estimated values of the man's work of £151–£156 at Gladsmuir, £168 at Humbie, both in the same area.[49] If the women's £48–£70 look like gender exploitation from one angle, they look from another like an increase in total family income of 30 to 45 per cent.

In the areas of 'protoindustrialisation' where the textile industries in the countryside were most important, the contribution of rising female wage rates and increasing employment opportunities to improvements in family income was possibly even greater. The extreme cases were parishes such as Dumbarton, where a girl flowering muslin in the 1790s was said to be able to earn as much as 12s. Scots a day 'and upwards', and Kirrimuir, where flax spinners wages ranged as high as 15s. a day – sums equal to or exceeding those of male agricultural workers in many parts even of the Lowlands.[50] More typical were rates close to or a little higher than those quoted for female agricultural work in Midlothian – for instance 6s. a day for spinning wool at Galashiels in the Borders, 6s.–8s. a day for flax spinning at Auchtertool in Fife (but the same scale was quoted even for eight- and nine-year old girls at Old Monkland in Lanarkshire), 5s.–7s. at Carnbee in Fife, 7s.–8s.6d. at Abernyte in Perthshire, 4s. at Kilcalmonnell and Kilberry in Argyll.[51] Poverty, indeed, was partly accounted for by the low rate of wool spinners wages in Stirling – only 3s. a day;[52] but that kind of rate was commoner in the north, where protoindustrialisation meant knitting stockings: – at Keithhall and Kirkell in Aberdeenshire, 3s.–3s.6d. a day, at Rothiemay in Banffshire, 3s.6d. to 4s. 'A poor pittance, indeed!', exclaimed the minister of the last parish, 'and till manufactures be established here (a thing more to be desired than expected), there is little reason to hope that female labour will find a better, at least an adequate reward.'[53] Nevertheless, in the last case, the male labourer would only earn without victuals 9s. a day, so the proportionate female contribution to household income from such employment was still as substantial as in the south. The situation was also seen to be a poor one from the point of view of the family budget in parishes like Dingwall in Ross and Cromarty where 'there is no room for children to exert industry as there are no manufactures'.[54]

Such quotations relate to situations where the woman or girl was able to work the whole time at spinning, flowering or knitting, but it is clear from many quotations that protoindustrial labour was also expected and forthcoming from mothers bringing up large families, even if they could not earn so much – characteristically they then earned 3s. or 3s.6d a day while looking after three or four children. At Lethnot in Angus, a very prosperous parish with much industrial activity, the minister believed that 'a woman's

[47] *OSA*, vol. 2 (*Lothians*) p. 169.   [48] *OSA*, vol. 2 (*Lothians*) p. 273.
[49] *OSA*, vol. 2 (*Lothians*) pp. 492, 509.   [50] *OSA*, vol. 9 (*Dunbartonshire*) p. 44; vol. 13 (*Angus*) p. 361.
[51] *OSA*, vol. 3 (*Eastern Borders*) p. 25; vol. 7 (*Lanarkshire*) p. 531; vol. 8 (*Argyll*) p. 193; vol. 10 (*Fife*) pp. 69, 108; vol. 12 (*S. and E. Perthshire*) p. 24.   [52] *OSA*, vol. 9 (*Stirlingshire*) p. 625.
[53] *OSA*, vol. 15 (*N. and E. Aberdeenshire*) p. 231; Vol 16 (*Banffshire*) p. 403.
[54] *OSA*, vol. 17 (*Ross and Cromarty*) p. 26.

work in this country turns to more account than it appears to do in England'; a married woman busy with her family could earn 18s. a week, a girl could earn the same by the time she was fourteen or fifteen, and a woman working full time could earn £1.16s.0d. a week.[55] In Steuart's view, many women 'subsist with great ease by spinning', and in 1769 he quoted earnings of 20s. to 24s. a week in Lanarkshire – 'with this they are clothed and nourished'.[56] Adam Smith, as so often, flatly contradicted him by pointing out that any woman who tried to earn a living by spinning alone would earn 'but a scanty subsistance'.[57] Smith, however, rather missed the point. Additions of this order to the household income could make the difference between doing all right and doing well (as in Lethnot), or between not coping and getting by. The minister of Cushnie in Aberdeenshire summed up the latter case:

I cannot positively ascertain the expence of a labourer, when married; but it is well known that such have great difficulty in rearing their families, as it is only for a few months in summer that they can get employment; and were it not for that the women make something by knitting stockings, and that the female children are employed in that way as soon as capable, it would be absolutely impossible for them, without assistance, to make a shift to live.[58]

It could well be that in the areas of specialised textile production in the central belt children were less readily sent into farm or domestic service in another household, but kept at home to contribute to family income until they left on early marriage to set up their own households. This is very much what Steuart describes. Sufficient work has not yet been done in Scotland to confirm the validity of this, but it is not hard to see what a difference textiles could make. Two daughters in their late teens in the 1790s, living at home and working constantly at a wage of 12s. a day could each earn £180 Scots a year, and thus easily bring the household income to three times the sum that the adult male alone was able to earn. Women with young children had lower productivity due to the distractions of child care, but these children were themselves soon another pair of hands, increasingly expert, and were being continuously trained by their mothers for a burst of high earning power in their middle and later teens. The most prosperous families and the biggest gains in real income seem likely to have been in those counties where employment opportunity was growing fastest for subordinate family members.

Conversely, of course, this prosperity would not have been felt in the same way where women and children could not be set to work in novel ways. This was obviously true of the Highlands and remote rural areas less in touch with industrial outlets, but would also have been true in families of certain kinds of urban skilled workers. The Edinburgh mason, for example, does not seem to have enjoyed particularly buoyant wages himself in the third quarter of the eighteenth century, and he would have had little chance to gain from wider employment of his family. His contemporary discontent was entirely understandable.[59]

In conclusion, we should reiterate the point that any study of the standard of living is

---

[55] *OSA*, vol. 13 (*Angus*) pp. 384–5.   [56] Steuart, *Considerations* p. 16.

[57] Adam Smith, *Wealth of nations* (Everyman edn, 1957), vol. 1, p. 106.

[58] *OSA*, vol. 14 (*S. and W. Aberdeenshire*) p. 481.

[59] W.H. Fraser, *Conflict and class: Scottish workers 1700–1838* (Edinburgh, 1988), pp. 50, 53.

beset with very substantial technical difficulties for the historian, that the study of wages makes up only part of it, and the study of male wages a smaller part still. Income was earned in several ways, and by all the household, so the only fully legitimate way into the problem is through the examination of a total household economy. Such a strategy is difficult enough for the middling and upper ranks: for the commonality it is perhaps impossible to pursue with acceptable rigour. Nevertheless, it would be difficult to argue that in the period from the late sixteenth to the late eighteenth centuries in Scotland that there was any clear upward change in the general fortunes of the population except, in some favoured areas, in the closing few decades of the period. Until then by far the most obvious causes in variation of welfare were the surges and slumps in oatmeal prices, not movements of income. And when, at last, the level of real income did hesitantly begin to advance, it looks as though improving opportunities owed as much to women's labour as to men's. There is much more work to be done on the interface of women's history and economic history.

INTRODUCTION TO FIGURES 9.1–9.6

To obtain the long-term series which chart the purchasing power of labour and the expenditure of sample households it has been necessary to make a number of assumptions, to interpolate some figures and to use the occasional surrogate price series. The nature of the Scottish data makes this unavoidable, though we have been conscious throughout that any computed series would lose all validity should we stray too far from direct comparisons between the actual wages and prices obtained at particular places at specific times. This section describes in full the steps we took in creating figures 9.1–9.6.

With regard to figures 9.1 and 9.2, which chart the purchasing power of labour, our goal was to draw as many comparisons as possible between wage rates and food prices in Edinburgh and the four rural estates of Buchanan, Yester, Gordon Castle and Panmure. When we use wheatbread prices, which were usually set in November of one year to apply until the same time the following year, we have taken them to apply to the year following their promulgation. When we use oatmeal prices, which derive from fiars struck at the beginning of one year with respect to the preceding year's crop, we have taken them to apply to the year in which they were actually struck. As both oatmeal and wheatbread were commonly highly volatile over the very short term, we have avoided any interpolation of food prices. Wages were more stable, and these we have interpolated if the same wage rates were reported at the beginning and end of a period of not more than five years of missing data.

The conversion of wheatbread prices, given in the sources in terms of ounces per penny Scots (or multiple thereof), to pence per pound Scots is straightforward, except in the case of eighteenth-century Edinburgh where we have allowed for the fact that the bread was being baked under the authority of the newly imposed British statutes. We have used the 'Scottish standard' series listed in table 2.1 and calculated as described in the footnotes to that table.

Our conversion of oatmeal prices, given in the fiars per boll Scots, to pence Scots per pound has assumed the boll to have weighed 128 lbs. Scottish troy, as defined by legislation of 1696. We have also added 10 per cent to prices to allow for the fact, as discussed in chapter 3, that the fiars were struck on the basis of wholesale transactions whilst the grain obtained by those whose purchasing power we wish to measure would have been bought at retail prices.

Unfortunately, it has not always been possible to find local price series against which to compare known wage rates and thus a number of surrogate series have had to be employed. Oatmeal prices in Edinburgh go no further back than the 1635 crop – prior to that date we have used the Fife fiars. These two series, when we can compare them, are similar in terms of both their absolute levels and the direction of their year-on-year movements. With respect to the four rural estates, only at Buchanan can wage rates be compared directly to the appropriate county fiars price series. There are no oatmeal fiars available for Haddington (East Lothian) and thus Yester wages have been set against Edinburgh (Midlothian) fiars. Similarly, both the Forfar and Banff fiars are in some way defective and we have thus used the Perthshire and Aberdeenshire fiars for comparison with wages paid at Panmure and Gordon Castle respectively.

Turning to figures 9.3–9.5, here we have tried to estimate household expenditure in three situations in each of Edinburgh, Glasgow and Buchanan. These situations were of a single man living in a household paying only for his food and clothes, a young couple paying for their food and clothes as well as for rent and fuel for their cottage and, finally, that same couple with four children below the age of ten whom they fed and clothed. The manner in which we have estimated the budgets of each of these households is discussed in the text, here it is only necessary to observe that each budget would have been based on highly variable food costs and much more stable clothing, rent, fuel and miscellaneous costs.

The former we have calculated, whenever possible, on the basis of local oatmeal fiars prices (reckoning the boll to have weighed 128 lbs. Scottish troy and allowing for a 10 per cent retail mark-up). In Edinburgh, when these are not available, we have used the Fife fiars, and in both Edinburgh and Glasgow, when there are no appropriate oatmeal prices, we have turned to wheatbread prices to provide a surrogate series. These have been used allowing for the fact that, when comparisons can be made prior to 1700, the price by weight of oatmeal was, on average, 88 and 84 per cent of the price of wheatbread in Edinburgh and Glasgow respectively. Those remaining years not covered by these sources have been ascribed an estimated oatmeal price by means of linear interpolation. Having established a long-term oatmeal price series we have assumed, as discussed in the text, that a single man would have required 30 oz., a couple 50 oz. and a couple plus four children 103.4 oz. avoirdupois of oatmeal daily.

Non-food costs cannot be derived directly, the information simply does not exist. Nevertheless, a number of eighteenth-century descriptions of household budgets do allow us to estimate the level of those costs relative to food costs. The evidence, and our use of it, is discussed in the text, but from the point of view of calculating non-food costs we have assumed that a single man would have spent the equivalent of one-third of his total food bill on clothing, that a couple would have spent three times as much on clothing, rent, fuel and miscellaneous items, and that a couple with four children would have spent, for all their needs, four and a third times as much. These non-food costs would not, of course, have fluctuated year-on-year in the manner of food costs and thus we have used an eleven-year running mean of a single man's food costs as the basis for our calculations.

Finally, figure 9.6 attempts to illustrate the margin available between an optimal diet, taken as that recommended by the DHSS in 1979 (see table 7.2), and one just able to keep body and soul together. Exactly what is needed to sustain life is, of course, impossible to define precisely. Many factors are involved of which adequate energy intake is but one critical requirement. The minimum diet presumed here (following S. Davidson and R. Passmore, *Human nutrition and dietetics*, 1967) would, however, almost certainly have prevented life-threatening malnutrition, though little active work could have been undertaken. The cost of these two diets (and there is no allowance here for clothes, rent or fuel) has been calculated in the same manner as described above for figures 9.3–9.5.

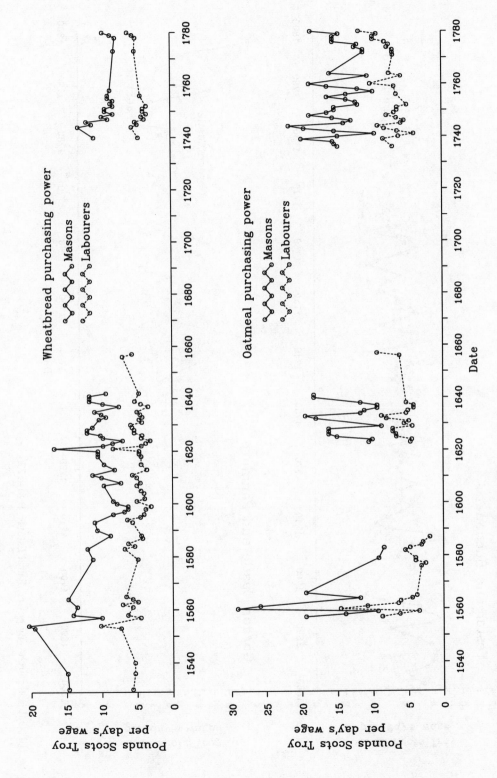

9.1 Purchasing power of labour: Edinburgh, 1530–1780

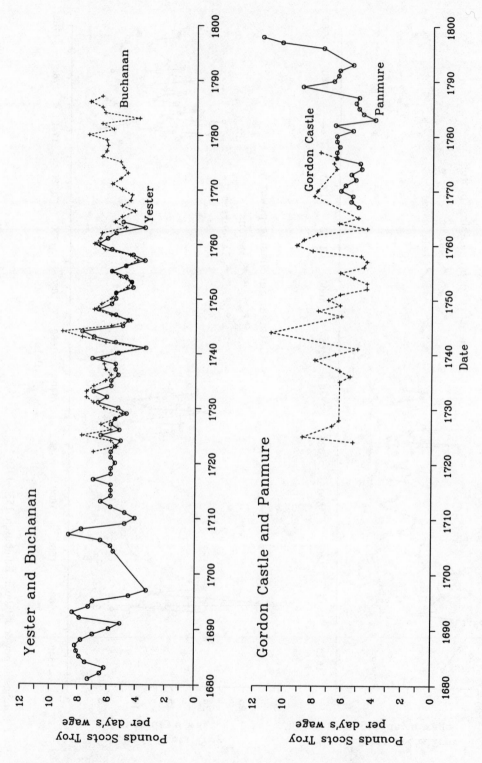

9.2 Oatmeal purchasing power: Rural Estates, 1681–1790

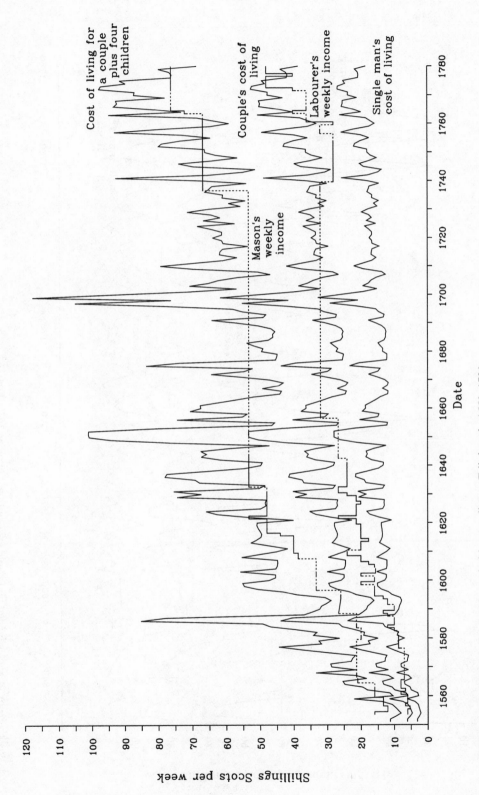

9.3 Weekly incomes and estimated household expenditure: Edinburgh, 1550–1780

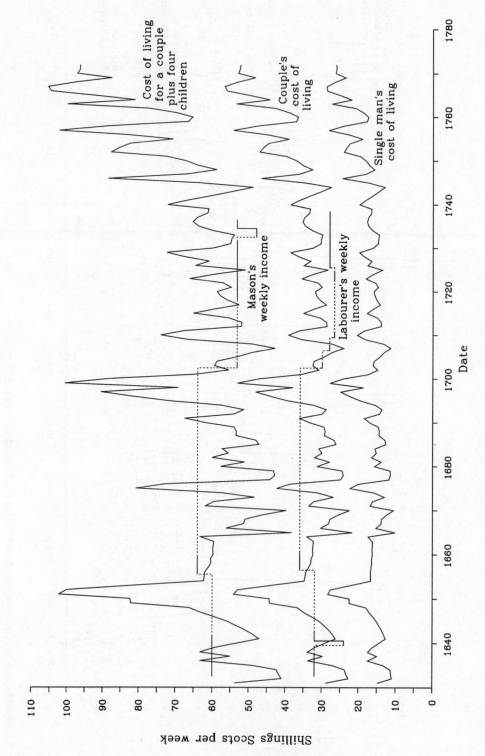

9.4 Weekly incomes and estimated household expenditure: Glasgow, 1630–1780

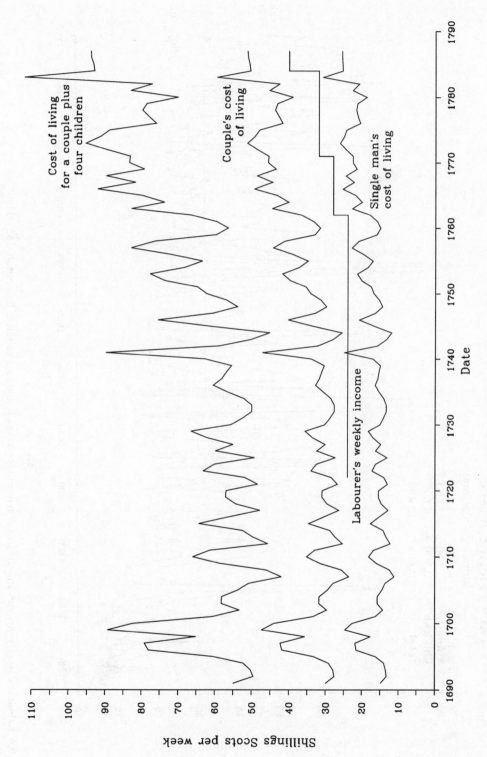

9.5 Weekly incomes and estimated household expenditure: Buchanan, 1691–1787

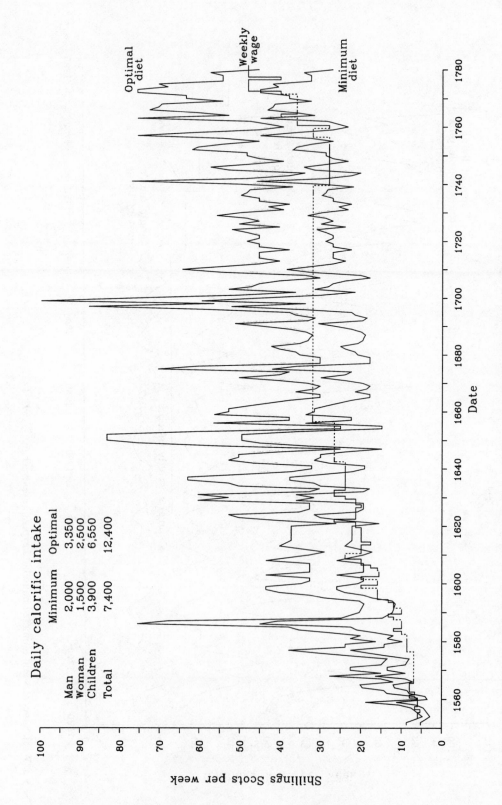

9.6 Labourers' weekly incomes and the cost of oatmeal for a couple and four children: Edinburgh, 1553–1790

APPENDIX I Scottish weights and measures, 1580–1780

Although the early modern period was marked by increasing legislative concern with the standardisation of weights and measures, this was a process which made only gradual headway prior to the nineteenth century. With a plethora of local weights and measures standing alongside the still evolving national standards, identifying which particular system of weight or measurement was in use in various contexts has posed one of the most intractable evidential problems we have had to face. Zupko's paper on weights and measures in Scotland makes clear how complex the situation could be.[1] In Forfarshire, to take one example, butcher meat was sold by Scottish troy weight, but butter and cheese according to a tron pound which varied in size across the county from 22 oz. avoirdupois in Dundee, Arbroath and Cupar to 27 oz. avoirdupois in Kirriemuir. In spite of Zupko's work and the invaluable evidence to be found in John Swinton's late eighteenth-century plea for standardisation,[2] a full understanding of the regional use of customary systems remains elusive.

Interpreting the price series in the foregoing tables is, to some extent confused rather than clarified by the process of standardisation that was underway. Thus whilst many of the longer price series, in particular the fiars, were probably initially set down in terms of local customary measures, in time the national standards came to be adopted. A good example of this process is provided by the manner in which the various county oatmeal fiars responded to the 1696 legislation requiring that oatmeal should be sold according to a boll defined by weight rather than by measure.[3] The Fife fiars court responded almost immediately and for the crop of the following year was reporting prices by both 'weight' and 'measure'. In Perth and Lanark it was not until the crops of 1703 and 1723 respectively that the fiars explicitly shift to the boll by weight. Whilst in Aberdeen only with the 1741 crop did the fiars begin to value white meal according to the boll by weight (albeit of 9 stone Scottish troy), and not until the 1771 crop that they finally began to use the boll by weight for mercat meal (of 8 stone Scottish troy, as had been required by the legislation). When we know of them, these developments have been noted in the tables, but by and large the records remain silent regarding such issues and our understanding of their impact on long-term price series must remain largely conjectural.

[1] R.E. Zupko, 'The weights and measures of Scotland before the Union', *Scottish Historical Review*, vol. 56 (1977), pp. 119–45.
[2] J. Swinton, *A proposal for uniformity of weights and measures in Scotland* (Edinburgh, 1779; 2nd edn, 1789).
[3] *APS*, vol. 10, p. 34, c6, 25 September 1696.

The use of customary measures, overlain by this gradual imposition of centrally defined national standards, thus renders problematic the comparison of prices over both time and space. We have nevertheless resisted the temptation to standardise the price series according to some set of nominal measures. Such would be unduly speculative, for it would require a far more precise knowledge of the weights and measures in use at various times and in various places than is currently available. We have, therefore, always reported prices exactly as we found them. This is not, however, to deny the importance of an understanding of the weights and measures used with respect to the various commodities for which we have price statistics. It is the purpose of this appendix to describe briefly what is known, acknowledging that this is a very partial picture soon to be significantly enhanced by work in progress.[4]

1 The measurement of weight

Early modern Scotland possessed two indigenous systems of weight for goods other than gold and silver,[5] the troy and the tron. The latter was the more widely used, at least by the eighteenth century, but it was the former that came to the attention of the Scottish parliaments as they sought to define and impose a standard system of weights on the kingdom. The relative neglect of historical metrology in Scotland has meant that the origins and early evolution of both systems remain unclear. At the time of David I the Scottish system of weights seems to have shared a common penny-weight, shilling and ounce with the English tower system, but whereas the English pound weighed 12 ounces of 450 English troy grains, the Scottish pound contained 15 ounces.[6] By implication this Scottish mint pound weighed 6,750 English troy grains (437.39 grams).[7] What happened thereafter is difficult to follow; there had apparently been 20 pennies to the ounce in David's system, but in 1306 × 1329 and then in 1393 this ratio was redefined, first as 21 pennies and then as 32 pennies to the ounce.[8] Whether this implies some redefinition of the weight of the pound and the ounce, or merely of the penny (and shilling) as the systems of coinage and weight began to diverge is uncertain. The picture is then further complicated by the statute of 1426 which mentions, for the first time, a 'trois' pound weight of 16 ounces.[9] Only following legislation in 1618[10] and the redefinition of the troy pound on the basis, it is believed,[11] of the Amsterdam pound, does it become possible to assess the actual weight of the Scottish troy pound.

Inscriptions on the stone-weight lodged in Lanark and the pound-weight at Edin-

---

[4] R.D. Connor and A.D.C. Simpson are shortly to publish the results of their recent work in this field; *The weights and measures of Scotland* (forthcoming, HMSO with the National Museums of Scotland).

[5] According to Zupko the troy pound used in Scotland to weight gold and silver was of 5,760 troy grains, or 12 ounces of 480 troy grains each ('Weights and measures', p. 134). Weighing 373.24 grams, this was in fact the English troy weight outlawed in that country in 1587 save for 'the weighing of bread, gold, silver and electuaries and for no other thing' ('The proclamation for weights, 16 December 1587', in E. Nicholson, *Men and measures* (London, 1912), p. 102).

[6] *APS*, vol. 1, p. 673; A.D.C. Simpson, 'Grain packing in early standard capacity measures: Evidence from the Scottish dry capacity standards', *Annals of Science*, vol. 49 (1992), pp. 337–50.

[7] The following equivalences have been taken for the purpose of converting between the Scottish and English measures and the metric system of the present day; 1 kilogram = 2.20462 pounds avoirdupois (or 15,432.3 English troy grains).   [8] Swinton, *Proposal*, 2nd edn, p. 132; *APS*, vol. 1, pp. 569–70, 24 October 1393.

[9] *APS*, vol. 2, p. 12, c22, 11 March 1426.   [10] *APS*, vol. 4, p. 587.   [11] E. Nicholson, *Measures*, p. 263.

burgh, both of which were raised on the authority of the 1618 act, state that the pound weighed 7,620 English troy grains.[12] A calculation in the *Scots Magazine* in 1743, meanwhile, determined the troy pound to be 7,594 English troy grains,[13] whilst John Swinton and John Sinclair reckoned it to weigh 7,616 and 7,621.8 English troy grains in 1779 and 1814 respectively.[14] These discrepancies have little practical consequence, and for the sake of argument we have chosen to follow Swinton. Its weight prior to 1618 must remain somewhat conjectural, though its appears likely that it was not so very different. Burrell argues that it was slightly larger at 7,680 English troy grains,[15] whilst circumstantial evidence that it could not have changed significantly since at least 1555 is provided by the fact that, according to the assize of wheatbread, 140 pounds of bread were to be baked from each boll of wheat from the middle of the sixteenth century through to the Union in 1707.[16]

The Scottish tron system of weight, meanwhile, was perhaps not so much a system as the generic name given to the customary measures used in the various markets of the kingdom.[17] The Scottish parliaments may have had some success establishing a standard troy weight, but their parallel attempts to outlaw the use of the infuriatingly variable tron pound were to no avail, as Swinton's remarkable table of the weights still in use towards the end of the eighteenth century attests. Moreover, not only did the tron weight vary from one market to the next, it may also have changed over time. Swinton claimed that in his day the Edinburgh tron pound weighed 20 oz. Scottish troy, but just over a century and a half earlier Alexander Hunter had stated that it weighed $19\frac{1}{2}$ oz.,[18] although this may just reflect some imprecision of measurement. These are, of course, ratios drawing a comparison between the troy and tron systems; there were apparently 16 oz. to the pound in both, so the tron ounce would also have varied in size from one market to the next.

The third system of weight which was to find acceptance in Scotland, although only gradually and largely during the course of the eighteenth century, was the English avoirdupois weight. This comprised a stone of 14 lbs., each of which again weighed 16 oz.. This had effectively been the only commercial system of weight in England since the sixteenth century, and as early as 1582 had been defined as 7,000 English troy grains (453.59 grams).[19] The avoirdupois ounce, therefore, weighed $437\frac{1}{2}$ English troy grains compared to the nominal Scottish troy ounce of 480 English troy grains or, as it had been determined by Swinton, of 476 English troy grains.

[12] E. Nicholson, *Measures*, p. 148; R.W. Cochran-Patrick, *Mediaeval Scotland* (Glasgow 1892), p. 161.
[13] *The Scots Magazine*, 1743, vol. 5, p. 613.
[14] Swinton (*Proposal*, 2nd edn, p. 38) has clearly used in all his comparative work the measurements and calculations made by James Gray in 1754, 'The weights and measures of Scotland compared with those of England', *Edinburgh physical and literary essays*, vol. 1 (1754), pp. 200–2; Sir John Sinclair, *General report of the agricultural state, and political circumstances of Scotland* (Edinburgh), 1818, p. 349.
[15] Lawrence Burrell, 'The standards of Scotland', unpublished paper presented to the Institute of Weights and Measures, Scottish Branch, Montrose, 14 October 1960.
[16] For further discussion of the wheatbread assize see chapter 2.
[17] The term 'tron' in fact refers to the public weighing machine that would have been located in all markets. The Trongate in Glasgow and Tron Kirk in Edinburgh were, no doubt, named after their respective trons.
[18] Alexander Hunter, *A treatise of weights, mets and measures of Scotland* (Edinburgh, 1624; reprinted Amsterdam, 1974), p. 2.
[19] E. Nicholson, *Measures*, pp. 99–102; A.E. Berriman, *Historical metrology* (London, 1953), pp. 147–51.

Table App. A *A comparison of weights in use in early modern Scotland*

A The national 'standards'

	Weight in English troy grains			Weight in grams		
	Stone	Pound	Ounce	Stone	Pound	Ounce
Scottish troy[1]	121,856	7,616	476	7,896.06	493.50	30.84
Scottish tron[2]	152,320	9,520	595	9,870.08	616.88	38.55
Avoirdupois	98,000	7,000	437.5	6,350.23	453.59	28.35

B Local usage[3]

	Commodity	System	Unit	Grams equivalent	Tables
Aberdeen[4]	tallow	troy	stone	7,896.06	6.17
	–or–	tron	stone	12,700.47	6.17
Edinburgh	tallow	tron	stone	9,870.08	6.18
Glasgow	tallow	tron	stone	9,870.08	6.18–19
Perth	tallow	tron	stone	9,978.94	6.18–19
Stirling	tallow	tron	stone	9,900.92	6.18–19
St Andrews	flesh	troy	stone	7,896.06	6.3
	butter	tron	pound	616.88	6.20

Notes:

[1] The troy ounce and pound is taken as reckoned by Swinton in the late eighteenth century.

[2] Swinton takes 20 oz. Scottish troy as the 'nominal' weight of the Scottish tron pound. Where we have had to assume the weight of the tron pound, as in the diet calculations in chapter 7, this is the value we have used.

[3] Neither Swinton nor others provide explicit evidence on the system of weight used with respect to candles or oatbread. It seems likely, however, that they were sold in each place according to the same tron weight as was being used for tallow. Wheatbread was most probably everywhere sold according to Scottish troy weight.

[4] Swinton states that tallow was sold retail according to the troy system, but William Kennedy claims that it was sold by a tron pound weighing 28 oz. avoirdupois (*Annals of Aberdeen*, 2 vols., London, 1818, vol. 2, p. 293).

Whilst it is impossible to determine with certainty which system of weight was being used with respect to each of the various commodities for which we have prices per ounce, pound or stone, table App. A above attempts to provide some broad guidelines. It is largely derived from Swinton's late eighteenth-century observations and should thus be seen as a snap-shot of usage at the very end of the period covered by our price statistics. It is, for instance, quite possible that the local tron weights had evolved over the period covered by our price statistics, though about such matters we can say nothing.

2 The measurement of liquid capacity

The early history of the gallon and the pint is as difficult to discern as that of the stone, pound and ounce. The earliest known Scottish gallon was defined in the middle of the

Table App. B *The evolution of the pint in Scotland*

	Definition by weight[1] (English Troy grains of water)	Capacity[2] cubic inches	litres
David I, ca. 1150	13,500	53.57	.88
James I, 1426	19,680	78.10	1.28
James VI, 1618	26,400	104.76	1.72
Swinton's 'standard' of 1779		103.404	1.69
English pint	8,750	34.72	0.57

Notes:

[1] This takes the ounce of David I to be 450 English troy grains, and that of the Scottish troy system used in 1426 and 1618 to be 480 English troy grains. The English pint was defined as one eighth of a 10 lbs. avoirdupois gallon, i.e. 0.125 x 10 x 7,000 = 8,750 English troy grains.

[2] These figures assume a cubic inch of water to weigh 252 English troy grains and a litre equal to 61.0236 cubic inches.

twelfth century as 12 lbs. of water.[20] Given that this probably refers to the Scottish mint pound (of 15 oz. each of 450 English troy grains) and that at this time the gallon was apparently divided into 6 pints,[21] the implication is that the pint weighed 28.125 Scottish troy oz. of 480 grains. If so, significant enlargement had clearly taken place, or was brought about, by the act of 1426 in which it was explicitly stated that the pint weighed 41 oz. Scottish troy.[22] By that date the system of division which was to survive through into the eighteenth century and beyond had become established, namely:

4 gills = 1 mutchkin

2 mutchkins = 1 choppin

2 choppins = 1 pint

8 pints = 1 gallon

Significantly predating any of the prices we report in tables 2.8 and 2.9 for either ale or wine, in the present context neither the enlargement of the pint nor the change from six to eight pints per gallon is of concern. Not so a further enlargement which appears to have taken place by the time of the important legislation of 1618. This defined the pint as 55 oz. Scottish troy of the clear running water of Leith although, as surviving physical standards make clear, this must actually have represented the legal confirmation of a measure already established by the middle of the sixteenth century.[23] Until further research determines the precise nature and timing of this putative second enlargement it

[20] *APS*, vol. 1, p. 673.   [21] A.D.C. Simpson, 'Grain packing', p. 340.

[22] *APS*, vol. 2, p. 12, c22, 11 March 1426.

[23] With a cubic inch of water weighing 252 English troy grains, the pint of 55 ounces Scottish troy (each of 480 English troy grains) would have had a volume of 104.76 cubic inches (1.72 litres). The Jedburgh Jug of 1563, the Edinburgh chopin of 1555, the St Andrews pint of 1574, and the undated but probably sixteenth-century Dundee and Stirling pint measures all had volumes which put the mid sixteenth-century pint at between 103 and 109.5 cubic inches. The larger measures may have incorporated a brewer's allowance of one-sixteenth.

Table App. C *The regional variation of the pint according to Swinton*[1]

	Cubic inches	Litres	Relative to Scottish standard
Aberdeen[2]	108.89	1.784	1.0531
Banff	105.284	1.725	1.0182
Dunbarton	100.50	1.647	0.9719
Dunfermline (Fife)	[103.404]	[1.694]	[1.0000]
Edinburgh	[103.404]	[1.694]	[1.0000]
Elgin	105.438	1.728	1.0197
Glasgow (Lanark)	[103.404]	[1.694]	[1.0000]
Haddington	[103.404]	[1.694]	[1.0000]
Kirkcudbright	122.00	1.999	1.1798
Perth	104.344	1.710	1.0091
Roxburgh	109.86675	1.800	1.0625
Stirling (Scottish standard)	103.404	1.694	1.0000

Notes:

[1] Where Swinton makes no specific mention of the size of the pint measure it may be presumed that he found it to be, as indicated in square brackets, the Scottish standard. All comparisons are with respect to his reckoning that this standard was of 103.404 cubic inches.

[2] William Kennedy (*Annals of Aberdeen*, London, 1818, vol. 2, p. 295.) states that the Aberdeen pint weighs 26,600 English troy grains, which would make it 105.56 cubic inches, or 1.0209 the Scottish standard.

is impossible to know how it might affect the interpretation of the earliest runs of ale prices given in table 2.8.

In addition to this rather late and quite substantial enlargement, the pint poses a number of problems due to its regional variation. It may have been defined by Parliament in terms of a certain weight of water, but its actual size was determined by various physical standards which, according to Swinton's late eighteenth-century observations, varied significantly from one locality to the next. Table App. C above extracts from his more extensive account just those local measures to which ale prices in table 2.8 presumably refer.

Once again, representing the situation towards the end of the eighteenth century, a detailed understanding of the evolution of these local pint measures would need to be established before due allowance could be made for their possible variation from county to county and burgh to burgh in earlier times. In any case, with regard to ale prices, differences in quality were at least as likely to have influenced relative price levels as any differences in the size of the pint measure itself.

Where it has been necessary to assume the size of the pint, as in the diet calculations in chapter 7, we have followed the popular eighteenth-century reckoning which held the Scottish pint to be equivalent to three English pints. With 55 ounces Scottish troy weighing 59.84 or 60.34 ounces avoirdupois (depending on whether one takes the Scottish troy ounce to weigh 476 or 480 English troy grains) this was certainly a reasonable estimate of its legal size and was no doubt adequate for all practical purposes.

Table App. D *The firlot and boll as defined by the Scottish parliaments of 1426 and 1618*[24]

	Scottish cubic inches	Litres
1426 Assize		
firlot	1,200	19.98
trading boll (4 firlots + allowance)	5,600	93.26
1618 Assize		
wheat firlot	2,110	35.14
barley firlot	3,030	50.46

3 The measurement of dry capacity

Until the legislation of 1696 required oatmeal to be sold by weight, all grain in Scotland was sold according to a system of dry capacity measures which, usually, was sub-divided as follows:

  4 lippies = 1 peck
   4 pecks = 1 firlot
    4 firlots = 1 boll

There were, however, two separate sets of measures, the larger 'heaped' measures used for barley, oats and malt and the 'straiket', or level, measures used for wheat, pease, beans and rye.

The early history of this system has yet to be satisfactorily explored and explained, although this is currently being addressed by R.D. Connor and A.D.C. Simpson.[25] Nevertheless it already appears that the hitherto confusing dual definition of the firlot and boll, in terms of both the number of pints they contained and their physical dimensions, has at last been reconciled. As a result it now appears likely that the firlot and boll measures may have been enlarged within the period for which we have data.[26] As with the evolution of the pound and ounce, however, the long-term stability of the wheatbread assize gives some reason to suspect that any significant enlargement must have taken place prior to 1555. Once again, until the precise nature and timing of this process of enlargement has been established the earliest runs of grain prices given in tables 2.2–2.7, 2.10 and 3.1 must be treated with great caution.

These were, although legal definitions, purely nominal capacities laid down by parliament. The actual size of the firlot and boll was effectively determined by local

---

[24] The Scottish inch was reckoned to be 1.0054 English inches (Swinton, *Proposal*, 2nd edn, p. 134). This inch was legally superseded by the English inch in 1685 *APS*, (vol. 8, p. 494, c59, 16 June 1685) though it remained in common use throughout the eighteenth century. A cubic Scottish inch, in which terms the physical definition of the firlot and boll would have been established, was thus 1.01629 English cubic inches. The litre equivalents in this table have been calculated making allowance for this conversion.

[25] R.D. Conner and A.D.C. Simpson, *The weights and measures of Scotland* (forthcoming, HMSO with the National Museums of Scotland).

[26] A.D.C. Simpson, 'Grain packing', table 1, p. 347.

physical standards which may or may not have attempted to replicate the Linlithgow measures, as the national standards became known. Thus in his account of the regional diversity of weights and measures in late eighteenth-century Scotland, Swinton shows that, although in many places the Linlithgow standards were ostensibly adhered to, the actual physical standards often differed significantly from them. In some instances such variation may have been due to carelessness on the part of those who built the local measures, but it is clear that systematic adjustments were being made.

In the legislation of 1618 the wheat and barley firlots were defined in terms of both their physical dimensions and the number of pints they contained. Unfortunately, if one takes the pint to be of water then these two definitions are incompatible; the size of the firlot established as a certain number of fills of a pint being significantly larger than that determined by the measurements laid down by the act. Once the prototype standards in Linlithgow were lost confusion was inevitable as the authorities tried to decide which of the act's two definitions should be followed. Surviving physical standards with Linlithgow markings show that at least in some instances it was the number of fills of a pint of water that was used to determine the size of the wheat and barley firlots. Yet this was, as Simpson has convincingly demonstrated,[27] an erroneous interpretation of the 1618 act. This legislation had intended that the firlot be established on the basis of a certain number of pint measures containing grain rather than water; 21.25 fills of grain into the wheat firlot, 31 fills into the barley firlot. Due to the manner in which grain packs as it is poured, such a definition is brought almost perfectly into line with the definition by measurement.

Thus not only did the legislation change, but so did the manner in which that legislation was interpreted, apparently well into the eighteenth century. In a sense, however, this is all rather academic, for if the enormous diversity of local grain measures to be found in the late eighteenth century is any guide, parliamentary legislation defining the size of the wheat and barley firlots was always likely to have had only a marginal impact on actual usage. It may be that future research will establish a precise understanding of the evolution of the national standards, but it seems improbable that many, if any, of our price series would have been based upon them.

The size of the boll and firlot measures being used in various localities remains, of course, the crucial question, though for the early period at least it will probably never be answered satisfactorily. What seems likely, however, is that the various grain measures in use towards the end of the eighteenth century, which is when we first begin to find reliable evidence concerning their size, will provide a more reliable guide to those earlier measures than any study of the national legislation, even if many of the local measures were in some sense or another derived from the national standards. It is thus to the work of Swinton and Bald and their detailed descriptions of the county grain measures still being used in the late eighteenth century that we must turn.[28]

Both authors attempt to provide a detailed account of, as Bald puts it, 'the conformity which the wheat [and barley] measures of the several counties of Scotland have with each other'. Both describe, to no less than three decimal places, the size of the local measures

[27] *Ibid.*   [28] Swinton, *Proposal*; A. Bald, *The farmer and corn dealer's assistant* (Edinburgh, 1780).

Table App. E *Regional measures of dry capacity; the wheat and barley bolls*[1]

		Wheat boll[2] (The 'level' measure)		Oats or Barley boll[3] (The 'heaped' measure)	
		Cubic inches	Relative to Linlithgow measure	Cubic inches	Relative to Linlithgow measure
Linlithgow[4] (Scottish standard)		8,789.0	1.0000	12,822.0	1.0000
Aberdeen[5]		10,754.0	1.2236	14,062.9	1.0968
Ayr[6]	(1)	8,601.7	0.9787	17,203.4	1.3417
	(2)	9,830.4	1.1185	14,487.0	1.1299
	(3)	10,178.8	1.1581	16,286.1	1.2702
Banff		9,265.0	1.0542	13,476.4	1.0510
Berwick[7]	(1)	12,901.5	1.4680	12,901.9	1.0062
	(2)	13,847.8	1.5756	13,847.8	1.0800
	(3)	11,374.4	1.2942	17,061.7	1.3307
Bute		11,512.3	1.3099	17,268.5	1.3468
Clackmannan[8]		9,513.2	1.0824	13,752.7	1.0726
Dumfries[9]		26,557.4	3.0217	34,406.3	2.6834
Dunbarton		10,251.0	1.1663	13,668.0	1.0660
Edinburgh		8,944.4	1.0177	13,028.9	1.0161
Elgin		9,384.0	1.0677	13,496.1[10]	1.0526
Fife		9,099.6	1.0353	13,235.7	1.0323
Forfar[11]	(1)	9,099.5	1.0353	13,235.7	1.0323
	(2)	9,099.5	1.0353	13,442.5	1.0484
	(3)			13,442.5	1.0484
	(4)	9,383.9	1.0677	12,925.5	1.0081
	(5)	8,892.7	1.0118	13,028.9	1.0161
	(6)	8,892.7	1.0118	13,442.5	1.0484
Glasgow[12]		9,256.8	1.0532	13,357.6	1.0418
Haddington		9,047.9	1.0294	13,209.9	1.0302
Inverness		10,059.9	1.1446	14,076.9[13]	1.0979
Kincardine		9,926.8	1.1294	13,649.3	1.0645
Kinross		9,022.0	1.0265	13,209.9	1.0302
Kirkcudbright		14,274.0	1.6241	23,653.4	1.8447
Lanark[14]	(1)	9,256.8	1.0532	13,357.6	1.0418
	(2)	8,789.0	1.0000	13,235.7	1.0323
Nairn		10,720.9	1.2198	14,294.5[15]	1.1148
Perth[16]	(1)	9,096.6	1.0350	12,941.3	1.0093
	(2)	9,051.8	1.0299	13,356.0	1.0416
Renfrew		8,789.0[17]	1.0000	13,623.5	1.0625
Roxburgh[18]		11,374.4	1.2942	13,649.3	1.0645
Stirling[19]		9,513.2	1.0824	13,752.7	1.0726
Wigtown		17,206.4	1.9577	25,805.0	2.0126
Winchester bushel (all grains):		2150.4 cubic inches			

Notes:
[1] Where more than one set of figures is provided, it is the first entry which was most probably used for official purposes such as the fiars.

[2] Usually known as the wheat boll, the level boll was, unless stated to the contrary, used to measure wheat, pease, beans, rye and, prior to 1696, oatmeal. After that date, in theory at least, oatmeal was to be sold by a boll of 8 stones Scottish troy (often taken as 140 lbs. avoirdupois).

[3] Variously known as the oats or barley boll, this 'heaped' measure was, unless stated to the contrary, used for oats, barley and malt.

[4] The nominal size of the Linlithgow firlot has been taken from Swinton, although its precise size does vary slightly between authors.

[5] William Kennedy states the wheat and barley firlots to have been 1.24221 and 1.1135 times their respective national standards (*Annals of Aberdeen*, London, 1818, vol. 2, pp. 296–8). He further notes that malt and oatmeal was sold by a boll measure equal to the Winchester quarter, thus of 17,203.36 cubic inches or 1.3417 times the Linlithgow boll.

[6] Swinton notes that within the county two sets of measures 'now laid aside' had been used; these were for (1) Kyle and Carrick, and (2) Cunninghame. The burgh of Ayr lies within the former. The Winchester bushel (3) was by his time commonly used, taking 4 bushels to the wheat boll and 8 to the barley boll.

[7] Swinton states that the same boll measure was used for all grains. In Berwick itself (1) this boll was taken as 6 Winchester bushels. In Duns and its neighbourhood (2) it was apparently 8 per cent better than the Linlithgow standard, whilst in Lauder (3) the 5-firlot boll of Roxburgh was used.

[8] Swinton notes that the Linlithgow firlot had been much used for wheat since 1754, but that the customary measures (reported here) were still used for all other grains.

[9] Swinton draws attention to a number of surviving customary measures, the most common (1) being raised from the Nithsdale or Dumfries peck. The Winchester bushel was, however, most in use by his time (presumably, as elsewhere, with 4 to the wheat and 8 to the barley boll). None of Swinton's customary measures can have been those used by Bald who calculated that the Dumfries wheat and barley measures were 3.0219 and 2.6834 times their respective Linlithgow standards.

[10] This heaped measure was used for barley and malt. Oats were usually sold according to a 5-firlot boll (16,870.16 cubic inches, or 1.3157 times the Linlithgow boll), although the boll could vary from 5 to 8 firlots. The idea here being of 'a boll of oats being what will produce a boll of meal, so that in some places where the grain is good, 18 or 19 pecks will make a boll'. The inferior black oats were sold according to an 8-firlot boll (26,870.16 cubic inches, or 2.0956 the Linlithgow boll).

[11] Swinton notes different measures for (1) Forfar, (2) Montrose, (3) Kirriemuir, (4) Arbroath, (5) Dundee and (6) Brechin. A note in the Forfar fiars for 1764 (SRO, GD 45/ 12/86) notes that black oats were sold according to a 'double boll'.

[12] Swinton states that in Glasgow the measures in use were those for the Lower Ward of Lanarkshire. The level firlot (as given in the table) was used for wheat and rye, whilst pease and beans were sold according to a boll of 13,084.8 cubic inches (or 1.4888 times the Linlithgow standard).

[13] The boll for oats, although often of 5 firlots (thus being 17,596.125 cubic inches, or 1.3723 times the Linlithgow boll), would vary according to the principle that a boll oats was to provide a boll oatmeal.

[14] Swinton divides Lanarkshire into (1) Lanark and the Upper Ward and (2) Glasgow and the Lower Ward. A note in the Lanark fiars (SRO, SC 38/19/1) notes that from 1730 malt was sold according to the Linlithgow firlot, and from 1731 bear and pease likewise. As the figures Swinton provides are relatively close to the Linlithgow measure and were thus probably derived from it, this implies that prior to 1730 there were in use customary measures now lost.

[15] Oats were sold according to a 5-firlot boll of 17,868.16 (or 1.3936 times the Linlithgow measure). Black oats were sold by the 'pease firlot', that is the level firlot, reckoning 9 such firlots to the boll (which would thus have been 24,121.98 cubic inches, or 1.8813 times the Linlithgow measure).

[16] Swinton reports that a new set of Linlithgow firlots were obtained in 1774.They were carefully tried in March 1788 and found to contain the figures given in (2). The previous measures for the wheat and barley firlots (1) Swinton describes as respectively 3.5 and 0.93 per cent larger than their Linlithgow standards, although only the barley firlot was by then still extant.

[17] Beans, pease and vetches were sold by a boll of 9616.57 cubic inches (or 1.09416 times the Linlithgow measure).

[18] A 5-firlot boll (given here) was used for all grains, though in the Kelso market Swinton notes that the measure used of late was the Berwickshire boll of (12,902.47 cubic inches) which was held equal to 6 Winchester bushels.

[19] The Linlithgow firlot, Swinton states, had been much used since 1754, though the local customary measures for grain (given here) remained in use.

as a percentage of the Linlithgow standard, whilst Swinton also gives the actual capacity of the measures in terms of cubic inches, again to three decimal places. Whether they themselves provide completely reliable witnesses is, of course, another matter. The fact that they agree one with the other is no guide, as Bald almost certainly used Swinton's tables, which had been published in the previous year, to compile his 'ready reckoner'. But the very fact that Bald was providing a practical tool for the corn dealers who needed to be able to compare the prices they were quoted from all parts of Scotland is encouraging. If the tables Bald, or for that matter Swinton, provided were inaccurate then their labours would have been worthless and their books would not have sold. That we can trust them as a guide to regional measures and their usage at the time they were written thus seems highly likely, though how reliable they are as a guide to local measures and their usage prior to the latter part of the eighteenth century must remain doubtful. As we have already seen, the national standards were hardly immune from either re-interpretation or mis-interpretation, and the same processes must have been working on the presumably much less closely managed local standards.

The figures supplied in Table App. E above should, therefore, be used with caution. Describing the size of the various local measures likely to have been used towards the end of our period, they may or may not cast light on those used in earlier periods. Comprehending only those counties from which price statistics have been drawn, all figures relate to the size of the boll – the unit to which all but one of our grain prices refer. The exception is the Edinburgh meal prices given in tables 4.5–4.7 which refer to the peck, which is a sixteenth part of the local boll.

APPENDIX II Accessing the data

The tables within this book present but a part (albeit a significant part) of the material we have collected during the course of an ESRC-funded research project on Scottish wages and prices. This larger body of data which, in addition to further wage and price material, includes a number of long-term demographic and meterological series for Edinburgh, is held on computer and is being deposited with the ESRC Data Archive at University of Essex. Hardcopy printout is also being deposited with the Scottish Record Office in Edinburgh and in St Andrews University Library. In addition, the full database has been retained for developmental purposes at Exeter University, and may be retrieved, in whole or in part, using remote file transfer via the Joint Academic Network (JANET). Any academic interested in obtaining the data in such a way should in the first instance contact the authors via electronic mail at the following address: ajgibson@uk.ac.exeter

Bibliography

I MANUSCRIPT SOURCES

Scottish Record Office, Edinburgh
B 30, Haddington burgh records
B 48, Linlithgow burgh records
B 59, Perth burgh records

E 5/5, Exchequer fiars, 1708–86

GD 1/651, Craw, Hewitt; miscellaneous documents
GD 6, Biel papers
GD 10, Broughton and Callie muniments
GD 16, Airlie muniments
GD 22, Cunninghame Graham muniments
GD 25, Aisla muniments
GD 26, Leven and Melville muniments
GD 28, Hay of Yester papers
GD 30, Shairp of Houston papers
GD 40, Newbattle (Lothian) papers
GD 44, Richmond and Gordon muniments
GD 45, Dalhousie muniments
GD 49, Barclay Allardice muniments
GD 72, Hay of Park papers
GD 75, Dundas of Dundas muniments
GD 103, Papers of the Society of Antiquaries
GD 109, Bargany papers
GD 110, Hamilton-Dalrymple of North Berwick muniments
GD 150, Morton muniments
GD 170, Campbell of Barcaldine papers
GD 180, Cathcart of Genoch and Knockdolian muniments
GD 220, Montrose papers
GD 224, Buccleuch muniments
GD 267, Home-Robertson papers
GD 268, Spencer Loch of Drylaw muniments
GD 345, Grant of Monymusk muniments
GD 399, Papers of the Incorporation of Carters, Leith

JP 3/2, Justice of the Peace, wage assessments, Peebles
JP 12/2, Justice of the Peace, wage assessments, Dumfries

JP 15/2, Justice of the Peace, wage assessments, West Lothian
JP 17/2, Justice of the Peace, wage assessments, Wigtown
JP 26/2, Justice of the Peace, wage assessments, Aberdeen

PE 1/1/100, Index to Perth council minutes

SC 6, Sheriff Court records, Ayr
SC 38, Sheriff Court records, Lanark
SC 49, Sheriff Court records, Perth
SC 67, Sheriff Court records, Stirling

T 335, Pollable persons of Renfrewshire, 1695
T 644, Kirkcudbright town council minutes, 1576–1658

National Library of Scotland, Edinburgh

MS EE.3.40/13. Act of Edinburgh Town Council of regulating the price of a candle
Roxburgh JP records, MS 5439
Yester mss., MS 14590–14745
Crawfurd and Balcarres mss.
The Caledonian Mercury
The Scots Magazine

Town House, Aberdeen

Aberdeen town council accounts (1594–1706), comprising the kirk and bridge work accounts and
    the shore work accounts.
Aberdeen town council register, vols. 17–58, 1541–1701, comprising the proceedings of the
    council, and the baillie, guild and head courts.

City Chambers, Edinburgh

Edinburgh town council accounts (1553–1780), comprising the town treasurer's accounts, the
    Dean of Guild tradesmens' accounts and the Parliament House building accounts.

Glasgow University Archives

Building accounts and vouchers, 1630–1767, MS 26625–41615
Accounts of the provisions for the common table, 1639–46, MS 26733
Schedule of boarders in the College and accounts, 1633–40, MS 26731,26748
Accounts of the ordinary revenue of the College, 1664–1776, MS.26652,26670

Perth Museum and Art Gallery

James Scott, 'Prices of victual at Perth, 1525–1685', Acc. No. 270

St Andrews University Library

Building accounts of St Leonard's college
Anstruther Wester papers Poll Tax records for St Andrews and Anstruther-Wester

Lady Balgarvie's account book
Pittenweem sea box book, 1633–1755
Diet books of the colleges of St Leonard's, St Mary's, St Salvator's, and United College.
Untitled St Andrews University diet account, 1597.

In private possession
Unpublished diary of John Mackinnon
Unpublished memoir, 'Records of the families of Maxwell and Chalmers ... by Alexander
  Maxwell and his son George'

II PRINTED SOURCES

Acts of the Parliaments of Scotland, 1124–1707 (12 vols., Edinburgh, 1814–75).

Adams, I.H., 'Economic process and the Scottish land surveyor', *Imago Mundi*, vol. 27 (1975), pp.
  13–18.

Allardyce, A. (ed.), *Scotland and Scotsmen in the eighteenth century from the Mss of John Ramsay
  Esq. of Ochtertyre* (2 vols., Edinburgh and London, 1888).

Anderson, J., *General view of the agriculture of Aberdeenshire* (London, 1794).

Anon., 'Household account of Ludovick, Duke of Lennox, when Commissioner to the Parliament of Scotland, 1607', *Miscellany of the Maitland Club*, vol. 2 (Maitland Club, 25,
  Edinburgh, 1834), pp. 160–91.

Armet, C.H. (ed.), *Kirkcudbright town council records, 1576–1658* (2 vols., Edinburgh, 1939 and
  1958).

Arnot, H., *The history of Edinburgh* (Edinburgh, 1779).

Bald, A., *The farmer and corn dealer's assistant* (Edinburgh, 1780).

Ballard, A., 'The theory of the Scottish burgh', *Scottish Historical Review*, vol. 12 (1916), pp. 16–
  27.

Barclay, G., 'Account of the parish of Haddington', *Archaeologia Scotica: or Transactions of the
  Society of Antiquaries of Scotland*, vol. I (Edinburgh, 1792), pp. 40–121.

Barrow, G.W.S., *Kingship and unity: Scotland, 1000–1306* (London, 1981).

Baulaut, M. and Meuvret, J., *Prix des cereales extraits de la Mercuriale de Paris*, vol. 1, 1520–1620
  (Paris, 1960).

Beatson, R., *General view of the agriculture of Fife* (London, 1794).

Berriman, A.E., *Historical metrology* (London, 1953).

Beveridge, D., *Culross and Tulliallan* (2 vols., Edinburgh, 1885).

Beveridge, E. (ed.), *Burgh records of Dunfermline, 1488–1589* (Edinburgh, 1917).

Beveridge, W., *et al.*, *Prices and wages in England from the twelfth to the nineteenth century* (New
  York, 1939).

Bieganska, A., 'A note on the Scots in Poland, 1550–1800', in Smout, T.C. (ed.), *Scotland and
  Europe, 1200–1850* (Edinburgh, 1986), pp. 157–66.

Bowden, P.J., 'Agricultural prices, farm profits and rents', and 'Statistical appendix', in J. Thirsk
  (ed.), *The agrarian history of England and Wales*, vol. IV, *1500–1640* (Cambridge, 1967), pp.
  593–695, 814–65.

  'Agricultural prices, wages, farm profits and rents', and 'Statistical appendix III; Statistics' in
  Thirsk J.,(ed.), *The agrarian history of England and Wales*, vol. V(2), *1640–1750* (Cambridge,
  1985), pp. 1–118, 827–902.

Bowley, A.L., 'The statistics of wages in the United Kingdom during the last hundred years; part
  II, agricultural wages, Scotland', *Journal of the Royal Statistical Society*, vol. 62 (1899), pp.
  140–50.

  'The statistics of wages in the United Kingdom during the last hundred years, part VII, wages in the building trades (cont), Scotland and Ireland', *Journal of the Royal Statistical Society*, vol. 63 (1900), pp. 485–98.

Wages and income in the United Kingdom since 1860 (London, 1937).

Brown, H.P. and Hopkins, S.V., 'Seven centuries of building wages', *Economica*, vol. 22 (1955), pp. 195–206.

'Seven centuries of the prices of consumables, compared with builders' wage-rates', *Economica*, vol. 23 (1956), pp. 296–314.

A perspective of wages and prices (London, 1981).

Brown, J.J., 'The social, political and economic influences of the Edinburgh merchant elite' (unpublished University of Edinburgh Ph.D. thesis, 1986).

Brown, K.M., 'The price of friendship', in Mason, R.A. (ed.), *Scotland and England 1286–1815* (Edinburgh, 1987).

'Aristocratic finances and the origins of the Scottish revolution', *English Historical Review*, vol. 104 (1989), pp. 46–87.

Brown, P. Hume (ed.), *Early travellers in Scotland* (Edinburgh, 1891).

Buchan-Hepburn, G., *General view of the agriculture and rural economy of East Lothian* (Edinburgh, 1794).

Bumsted, J.M. (ed.), *The collected writings of Lord Selkirk, 1799–1809* (Manitoba Record Society publications, vol. 7, Winnipeg, 1984).

Burrell, L., 'The standards of Scotland' (unpublished paper presented to the Institute of Weights and Measures Administration, Scottish branch, at the Guild Hall, Montrose, 14 October 1960).

Cage, R.A., 'The standard of living debate: Glasgow, 1800–1850', *Journal of Economic History*, vol. 43 (1983), pp. 175–82.

Campbell, R.H., *The rise and fall of Scottish industry, 1707–1939* (Edinburgh, 1980).

Challis, C.E., 'Debasement: the Scottish experience in the fifteenth and sixteenth centuries', in Metcalf, D.M. (ed.), *Coinage in medieval Scotland 1100–1600* (British Archaeological Reports, British series, vol. 45, Oxford, 1977), pp. 171–96.

Chambers, W. (ed.), *Charters and documents relating to the burgh of Peebles, 1165–1710* (Scottish Burgh Record Society, Edinburgh, 1872).

Clyde, J.A., *Hope's Major Practicks, 1608–1633* (2 vols., Stair Society, vols. 3 and 4, Edinburgh, 1937 and 1938).

Cobbet, W., *Cottage economy* (1823; 1926 edn, London).

Cochran, L.E., *Scottish trade with Ireland in the eighteenth century* (Edinburgh, 1985).

Cochran-Patrick, R.W., *Records of the coinage of Scotland from the earliest period to the Union* (Edinburgh, 1876).

Mediaeval Scotland (Glasgow, 1892).

Colville, J. (ed.), *The house book of accompts, Ochtertyre, 1739–9* (Scottish History Society, 1st series, vol. 55, Edinburgh, 1907).

Connor, R.D. and Simpson, A.D.C., *The weights and measures of Scotland* (forthcoming, HMSO with the National Museums of Scotland).

Court of Sessions, *Acts of Sederunt of the Lords of Council and Session* (Edinburgh, 1811).

Acts of Sederunt of the Lords of Council and Session, from the 15th of January 1553, to the 11th of July, 1790 (Edinburgh, 1790).

Coutts, W.K., 'Social and economic history of the Commissariot of Dumfries from 1600 to 1665, as disclosed by the registers of testaments' (unpublished University of Edinburgh M.Litt thesis, 1982).

Cowan, S., *The ancient capital of Scotland* (2 vols., London, 1904).

Crammond, W., *The records of Elgin, 1234–1800* (New Spalding Club, 2 vols., Aberdeen, 1903 and 1908).

Crammond, W. (ed.), *The annals of Banff* (New Spalding Club, 2 vols., Aberdeen, 1891 and 1893).

Cregeen, E.R., 'The tacksmen and their successors: a study of tenurial reorganisation in Mull, Morvern and Tiree in the early 18th century', *Scottish Studies*, vol. 13 (1969), pp. 93–144.

Cullen, L.M., Smout, T.C. and Gibson, A., 'Wages and comparative development in Ireland and Scotland, 1565–1780', in Mitchison, R. and Roebuck, P. (eds.), *Economy and society in Scotland and Ireland, 1500–1939* (Edinburgh, 1988), pp. 105–16.

Davidson, H.M., *Report on the subject of the fiars of East Lothian* (Edinburgh, 1850).

Davidson, S. and Passmore, R., *Human nutrition and dietetics* (Edinburgh, 1967).

DesBrisay, G., 'Authority and discipline in Aberdeen, 1650–1700' (unpublished University of Aberdeen Ph.D. thesis, 1989).

Dickinson, W.C., *Scotland from the earliest times to 1603* (Edinburgh, 1961).

Dickinson, W.C. (ed.), *The court book of the barony of Carnwath, 1523–1542* (Scottish History Society, 3rd series, vol. 29, Edinburgh, 1937).

Dickson, W.J. (ed.), 'Memories of Ayrshire about 1780 by the Reverend John Mitchell', *Miscellany of the Scottish History Society, 6th volume* (Scottish History Society, 3rd series, vol. 33, Edinburgh, 1930).

Dodds, J. (ed.), *Diary and account book of William Cunningham of Craigends, 1673–1680* (Scottish History Society, 1st series, vol. 2, Edinburgh, 1887).

Dodgshon, R.A., *Land and society in early Scotland* (Oxford, 1981).

Donaldson, G., *Scotland: James V–James VIII* (Edinburgh, 1965).

Donaldson, J., *General view of the agriculture of the Carse of Gowrie in the County of Perth* (London, 1794).

Douglas, F., *A General description of the east coast of Scotland from Edinburgh to Cullen* (1782; 2nd edn, Aberdeen, 1826).

Dumbarton Burgh Council, *Records of the burgh of Dumbarton, 1627–1746* (Dumbarton, 1860).

Dunbar, J.G., 'The building of Yester House, 1670–1878', *Transactions of the East Lothian Antiquarian and Field Naturalists Society*, vol. 13 (1972), pp. 20–42.

Duncan, A.A.M., *Scotland, the making of the kingdom* (Edinburgh, 1975).

Durie, A.J., *The Scottish linen industry in the eighteenth century* (Edinburgh, 1979).

Elliot, N., *The position of the fiars prices* (Edinburgh, 1879).

Everitt, A., 'Farm Labourers', in Thirsk, J. (ed.), *The agrarian history of England and Wales*, vol. IV, *1500–1640* (Cambridge, 1967), pp. 396–465.

The Exchequer Rolls of Scotland (Rotuli Scaccarii Regum Scotorum), 1264–1600 (23 vols., Edinburgh, 1878–1908).

Feavearyear, A.E., *The pound sterling; a history of English money* (2nd edn, Oxford, 1963).

Fenton, A., *The shape of the past 2: essays in Scottish ethnology* (Edinburgh, 1986).

Fenton, A., and Smout, T.C., 'Scottish farming before the improvers: an exploration', *Agricultural History Review*, vol. 13 (1965), pp. 73–93.

Ferguson, T., *The dawn of Scottish social welfare* (London, 1948).

Firth, C.H. (ed.), *Scotland and the Protectorate* (Scottish History Society, 1st series, vol. 31, Edinburgh, 1899).

Flinn, M.W., 'Agricultural productivity and economic growth in England, 1700–1760: a comment', *Journal of Economic History*, vol. 26 (1966), pp. 93–8.

Flinn, M.W. (ed.), *Scottish population history from the seventeenth century to the 1930s* (Cambridge, 1977).

Floud, R., Wachter, K. and Gregory, A., *Height, health and history: nutritional status in the United Kingdom, 1750–1890* (Cambridge, 1990).

Folco, J.A. di, 'Aspects of seventeenth century social life in central and north Fife' (unpublished M.Phil. thesis, St Andrews, 1975).

Fraser, W.H., *Conflict and class: Scottish workers, 1700–1838* (Edinburgh, 1988).

Fullarton, W., *General view of the agriculture of the county of Ayr* (Edinburgh, 1793).

Giblin, C. (ed.), *Irish Franciscan mission to Scotland; documents from Roman archives* (Dublin,

1964).

Gibson, A.J.S., 'The size and weight of cattle and sheep in early modern Scotland', *Agricultural History Review*, vol. 36 (1988), pp. 162–71.

'Proletarianization? The transition to full-time labour on a Scottish estate, 1723–1787', *Continuity and Change*, vol. V (1990), pp. 357–89.

Gibson, A.J.S. and Smout, T.C., 'Food and hierarchy in Scotland, 1550–1650', in Leneman, L. (ed.), *Perspectives of Scottish social history – essays in honour of Rosalind Mitchison* (Aberdeen, 1989), pp. 33–52.

'Scottish food and Scottish history, 1500–1800', in Houston, R.A. and Whyte, I. (eds.), *Scottish society, 1500–1800* (Cambridge, 1989), pp. 59–84.

Gilbert, J.M., 'The usual money of Scotland and exchange rates against foreign coin', in Metcalf, D.M. (ed.), *Coinage in medieval Scotland, 1100–1600* (British Archaeological Reports, British series, vol. 45, Oxford, 1977), pp. 131–53.

Gilboy, E.W., *Wages in eighteenth century England* (Cambridge, Mass., 1934).

Gillespie, R., *Colonial Ulster: the settlement of east Ulster, 1600–1641* (Cork, 1985).

Gourvish, T.R., 'The cost of living in Glasgow in the early nineteenth century', *Economic History Review*, 2nd series, vol. 25 (1972), pp. 65–80.

Grant, A., *Independence and nationhood: Scotland, 1306–1469* (London, 1984).

Grant, I.F., 'The income of tenants on a Scotch open field farm in the eighteenth century', *Economic Journal*, vol. 34 (1924), pp. 83–9.

The social and economic development of Scotland before 1603 (Edinburgh, 1930).

Gray, J., 'The weights and measures of Scotland compared with those of England', *Edinburgh physical and literary essays*, vol. 1 (1754), pp. 200–2.

Gray, M., *The Highland economy, 1750–1850* (Edinburgh, 1957).

Groome, F. H., *Ordnance gazetteer of Scotland* (6 vols., Edinburgh, 1882–5).

Guy, I., 'The Scottish export trade, 1460–1599, from the Exchequer Rolls' (unpublished University of St Andrews M.Phil thesis, 1984).

Hallen, A.W.C. (ed.), *Account book of Sir John Foulis of Ravelston, 1671–1707* (Scottish History Society, 1st series, vol. 16, Edinburgh, 1894).

Hamilton, H., *Life and labour on an Aberdeenshire estate, 1735–50* (Third Spalding Club, Aberdeen, 1945).

An economic history of Scotland in the eighteenth century (Oxford, 1963).

Hannay, R. K. (ed.), *Acts of the Lords of Council in Public Affairs, 1501–1554; selections from the Acta Dominorum Concilii* (Edinburgh, 1932).

Hay, W., *Charters, writs and public documents of the royal burgh of Dundee, 1292–1880* (Scottish Burgh Record Society, Dundee, 1880).

Hector, W. (ed.), *Selections from the judicial records of Renfrewshire* (Paisley, 1876).

Henderson, J., *General view of the agriculture of the county of Sutherland* (London, 1812).

Hill, W.H., *History of the hospital and school in Glasgow founded by George and Thomas Hutcheson* (Glasgow, 1881).

Holderness, B.A., 'Prices, productivity and output', Thirsk, J. (ed.), *The agrarian history of England and Wales*, vol. VI, *1750–1850* (Cambridge, 1967), pp. 84–189.

Home, H. (Lord Kames), *The decisions of the Court of Session from its first institution to the present time* (4 vols., Edinburgh, 1791–7).

Hope, R., 'On rural economy', in Sir John Sinclair, *General report of the agricultural state, and political circumstances of Scotland* (Edinburgh, 1814), vol. 3, pp. 225–88.

Horn, B.L.H., 'Domestic life of a duke. Cosmo George, 3rd Duke of Gordon' (unpublished University of Edinburgh Ph.D. thesis, 2 vols., 1977).

Horricks, C.L., 'Economic and Social Change in the Isle of Harris, 1680–1754' (unpublished University of Edinburgh Ph.D. thesis, 1974).

Houston, R.A., 'Women in the economy and society of Scotland, 1500–1800', in Houston, R.A.

and Whyte, I.D. (eds.), *Scottish society, 1500–1800* (Cambridge, 1988), pp. 118–47.

Hunt, E.H., *Regional wage variations in Britain, 1850–1914* (Oxford, 1973).

'Industrialization and regional inequality: wages in Britain, 1760–1914', *Journal of Economic History*, vol. 46 (1986), pp. 935–96.

Hunter, A., *A treatise of weights, mets and measures of Scotland* (Edinburgh, 1624; reprinted Amsterdam, 1974).

Hunter, D., *Report of the committee on fiars prices to the General Assembly of the Church of Scotland* (Edinburgh, 1895).

Hutchison, R., 'Report on the dietaries of Scotch agricultural labourers', *Transactions of the Highland and Agricultural Society of Scotland*, 4th series, vol. 2 (1869), pp. 1–29.

Imrie, J. and Dunbar, J.G., *Accounts of the Master of Works*, vol. II *1616–1649* (Edinburgh, 1982).

Innes, C. (ed.), *Fasti Aberdonenses* (Spalding Club, Aberdeen, 1859).

Extracts from the council register of the burgh of Aberdeen, vol. II, *1570–1625* (Spalding Club, Aberdeen, 1898).

Innes, C. and Renwick, R., *Ancient laws and customs of the burghs of Scotland* (2 vols., Scottish Burgh Record Society, Edinburgh, 1868 and 1910).

Irving, J. (ed.), *Dumbarton burgh records, 1627–1746* (Dumbarton, 1860).

John, A.H., 'The course of agricultural change, 1660–1760', in Presnell, L.S. (ed.), *Studies in the industrial revolution* (London, 1960), pp. 125–55.

'Statistical appendix', in Thirsk, J. (ed.), *The agrarian history of England and Wales*, vol. VI, *1750–1850* (Cambridge, 1989), pp. 972–1155.

Johnson, S., *A dictionary of the English language* (London, 1772).

Jutikkala, E., 'The great Finnish famine in 1696–7', *Scandinavian Economic History Review*, vol. 3 (1955), pp. 48–63.

Karlsson, G. (ed.), *Levestandarden i Norden, 1750–1914* (Reykjavik, 1987).

Kelsall, H. and K., *Scottish lifestyles 200 years ago* (Edinburgh, 1986).

Kemp, D.W. (ed.), *Bishop Pococke's tours in Scotland, 1747–1760* (Scottish History Society, 1st series, vol. 1, Edinburgh, 1886).

Kennedy, W., *Annals of Aberdeen* (2 vols., London, 1818).

Kerr, R., *General view of the agriculture of the county of Berwick* (London, 1813).

Kirk, J. (ed.), *The Books of Assumption: the Scottish ecclesiastical rentals at the Reformation* (British Academy Records of Social and Economic History, forthcoming).

Lamb, H.H., *Climate, history and the modern world* (London, 1982).

Law, R., *Memorialls: or, The memorable things that fell out within this island of Brittain from 1638 to 1684* (Edinburgh, 1818).

Leopold, J., 'The Galloway Levellers' revolt of 1724', in Charlesworth, A. (ed.), *Rural social change and conflicts since 1500* (Hull, 1982), pp. 18–41.

Levitt, I. and Smout, T.C., *The state of the Scottish working class in 1843* (Edinburgh, 1979).

'Farm workers' incomes in 1843', in Devine, T.M. (ed.), *Farm servants and labour in Lowland Scotland, 1770–1914* (Edinburgh, 1984), pp. 156–87.

Littlejohn, D., 'Aberdeenshire fiars', *Miscellany of the New Spalding Club, vol. 2* (New Spalding Club, Aberdeen, 1906), pp. 2–43.

Lynch, M., *Scotland, 1470–1623* (London, 1981).

Lynch, M. (ed.), *The early modern town in Scotland* (London, 1987).

Lynch, M., Spearman, M. and Stell, G. (eds.), *The Scottish medieval town* (Edinburgh, 1988).

Lythe, S.G.E., *The economy of Scotland in its European setting, 1550–1625* (Edinburgh, 1960).

'The Tayside meal mobs, 1772–3', *Scottish Historical Review*, vol. 46 (1967), pp. 26–36.

Lythe, S.G.E. and Butt, J., *An economic history of Scotland, 1100–1939* (Glasgow, 1975).

Macadam, J.H. (ed.), *The baxter books of St Andrews* (Leith, 1903).

Macculloch, J., *The Highlands and Western Isles of Scotland* (London, 1824).

MacGillivray, E. (ed.), 'Richard James 1592–1638; description of Shetland, Orkney and the Highlands of Scotland', *Orkney miscellany*, vol. I (1953), pp. 48–56.

Mackay, F.F. (ed.), *Macneill of Carskey: his estate journal, 1703–1743* (Edinburgh, 1955).

Mackay, W. (ed.), *Chronicles of the Frasers* (Scottish History Society, 1st series, vol. 47, Edinburgh, 1905).

Mackenzie, A.M., *Scottish pageant* (Edinburgh, 1946).

Mackenzie, W.M., *The Scottish burghs* (Edinburgh, 1949).

Mackintosh, J., *An essay on ways and means of enclosing* (Edinburgh, 1729).

Madden, C., 'The Scottish Exchequer: the finances of the Scottish crown in the later Middle Ages' (unpublished University of Glasgow Ph.D. thesis, 1975).

Makey, W., *The church of the covenant, 1637–1651* (Edinburgh, 1979).

Malcolm, C.A. (ed.), *The minutes of the Justices of the Peace for Lanarkshire, 1707–1723* (Scottish History Society, 3rd series, vol. 17, Edinburgh, 1931).

Marshall, W., *General view of the agriculture of the central Highlands* (London, 1794).

Martin, M., *A description of the Western Isles of Scotland* (1703; 2nd edn, London, 1716).

Marwick, J.D., *Edinburgh guilds and crafts* (Scottish Burgh Records Society, Edinburgh, 1909).

Marwick, J.D. (ed.), *Records of the Convention of the Royal Burghs of Scotland, 1295–1714* (Scottish Burgh Record Society, 2 vols., Edinburgh, 1870).

Marwick, J.D. and Hunter, T. (eds.), *Extracts from the records of the convention of the Royal Burghs of Scotland, 1615–1779* (Scottish Burgh Record Society, 5 vols., Edinburgh, 1878–1918).

Marwick, J.D. and Renwick, R. (eds.), *Extracts from the records of the burgh of Glasgow, 1573–1759* (Scottish Burgh Records Society, vols. 11–12, 16, 19, 22 and 29, Glasgow, 1876–1911).

Marwick, J.D., Wood, M., Hannay, R.K. and Armet, H. (eds.), *Extracts from the records of the burgh of Edinburgh, 1403–1718* (13 vols., Edinburgh, 1869–1967).

Melvill, J., *The diary of Mr. James Melvill, 1556–1601* (Bannatyne Club, 34, Edinburgh, 1829).

Metcalf, D.M. (ed.), *Coinage in medieval Scotland, 1100–1600* (British Archaeological Reports, British series, vol. 45, Oxford, 1977).

Metcalf, W.M. (ed.), *Charters and documents relating to the burgh of Paisley, 1163–1665* (Scottish Burgh Record Society, Paisley, 1902).

Mingay, G.E., 'The agricultural depression, 1730–1750', *Economic History Review*, 2nd series, vol. 8 (1955–6), pp. 323–38.

English landed society in the eighteenth century (London, 1963).

Miscellany of the Maitland Club, vol. I, Maitland Club, vol. 25 (Edinburgh, 1834).

Mitchison, R., 'The movements of Scottish corn prices in the seventeenth and eighteenth centuries', *Economic History Review*, 2nd series, vol. 18 (1965), pp. 278–91.

A history of Scotland (London, 1970).

Molland, R. and Evans, G., 'Scottish farm wages from 1870 to 1900', *Journal of the Royal Statistical Society*, series A (general), vol. 113 (1950), pp. 220–7.

Moore, J.S., 'Prices and wages in Scotland, 1450–1860' (unpublished SSRC report, HR 400/1, 1970).

Morgan, V., 'Agricultural wage rates in late eighteenth-century Scotland', *Economic History Review*, 2nd series, vol. 24 (1971), pp. 181–201.

Morris, C. (ed.), *The illustrated journeys of Celia Fiennes, c.1682–c.1712* (London, 1982).

Mossman, R.C., 'On the price of wheat at Haddington from 1627–1897', *The Accountants' Magazine*, vol. 4 (1900), pp. 94–110.

Murray, N., *The Scottish hand loom weavers, 1790–1850: a social history* (Edinburgh, 1978).

Nicholson, E., *Men and measures* (London, 1912).

Nicholson, R., *Scotland: the later middle ages* (Edinburgh, 1974).

'Scottish monetary problems in the fourteenth and fifteenth centuries', in Metcalf, D.M. (ed.),

Coinage in medieval Scotland, 1100–1600 (British Archaeological Reports, British series, vol. 45, Oxford, 1977), pp. 103–114.

Pagan, T., *Convention of the Royal Burghs* (Glasgow, 1926).

Parry, M.L., 'Secular climatic change and marginal agriculture', *Transactions of the Institute of British Geographers*, no. 64 (1975), pp. 1–13.

Paterson, G., *An historical account of the fiars in Scotland* (Edinburgh, 1852).

Paton, H.M., *Accounts of the Masters of Works, 1529–1615* (Edinburgh, 1957).

Paul, A.A. and Southgate, D.A.T., *McCance and Widdowson's The composition of foods* (4th revised edn, HMSO, London, 1978).

Paul, G.M., 'Fragment of the diary of Sir Archibald Johnston, Lord Warriston, May 21–June 25, 1639', Scottish History Society (1st series, vol. 26, Edinburgh, 1896), pp. 1–98.

Pennant, T., *A tour of Scotland and voyage to the Hebrides in 1772* (Edinburgh, 1776).

Perceval-Maxwell, M., *The Scottish migration to Ulster in the reign of James I* (London, 1973).

Plant, M., *The domestic life of Scotland in the eighteenth century* (Edinburgh, 1952).

Post, J.D., *Food Shortage, climatic variability and epidemic disease in preindustrial Europe: the mortality peak in the early 1740s* (Ithaca, 1985).

Price, S.F., 'Riveters' earnings in Clyde shipbuilding, 1889–1913', *Scottish Economic and Social History*, vol. I (1981), pp. 42–65.

Pryde, G.S. (ed.), *Ayr burgh accounts, 1534–1624* (Scottish History Society, 3rd series, vol. 28, Edinburgh, 1937).

Rappaport, S., *Worlds within worlds: structures of life in sixteenth-century London* (Cambridge, 1989).

Rasmussen, E., *Mester og svend: studier over kobenhavnske tomrer – og murersvendes lonproblemes og sociale forhold, 1756–1800* (Arhus, 1985).

Register of the Privy Council of Scotland (1st series, *1545–1625*, 14 vols., Edinburgh, 1877–98; 2nd series, *1625–60*, 3 vols., 1898–1908; 3rd series, *1661–1691*, 16 vols., 1908–70).

Renwick, R. (ed.), *Extracts from the records of the royal burgh of Stirling, 1519–1666* (Scottish Burgh Record Society, Glasgow, 1887).

Extracts from the records of the royal burgh of Stirling, 1667–1752 (Scottish Burgh Record Society, Glasgow, 1889).

Extracts from the records of the royal burgh of Peebles, 1652–1714 (Scottish Burgh Record Society, Glasgow, 1910).

Report of the General Assembly's committee on the fiars; presented to the Assembly in 1831, Parliamentary papers, 1834, vol. 49 (259), pp. 49–61.

Richardson, J., 'Some notes on the early history of the Dean Orphan Hospital', *Book of the Old Edinburgh Club*, vol. 27 (1949), pp. 155–68.

Rick, E.E. and Wilson, C. H. (eds.), *The Cambridge economic history of Europe*, vol. IV, *The economy of expanding Europe in the sixteenth and seventeenth centuries* (Cambridge, 1967).

Robertson, J.D., *A handbook to the coinage of Scotland* (London, 1878).

Rodger, R.G., 'The invisible hand: market forces, housing and the urban form in Victorian cities', in Fraser, D. and Sutcliffe, A. (eds.), *The pursuit of urban history* (London, 1980), pp. 190–211.

Rogers, J.E.T., *A history of agriculture and prices in England, 1259–1793* (6 vols., Oxford, 1866–1902).

Salaman, R.N., *The history and social influence of the potato* (Cambridge, 1949).

Sanderson, M.H.B., *Scottish rural society in the sixteenth century* (Edinburgh, 1982).

Scott, W.R. (ed.), *The records of a Scottish cloth manufactory at New Mills, Haddingtonshire, 1681–1703* (Scottish History Society, 1st series, vol. 46, Edinburgh, 1905).

Scott, W.W., 'Sterling and the usual money of Scotland, 1370–1415', *Scottish Economic and Social History*, vol. 5 (1985), pp. 4–22.

Scott-Moncrieff, R. (ed.), *The household book of Lady Grisell Baillie, 1692–1733* (Scottish History Society, 2nd series, vol. 1, Edinburgh, 1911).

Scottish Office and the Board of Agriculture and Fisheries, Committee on Fiars Prices in Scotland, *Fiars Prices in Scotland* (London, 1911)

Sen, A., *Poverty and famines: an essay on entitlement and deprivation* (Oxford, 1981).

Shearer, A. (ed.), *Extracts from the burgh records of Dunfermline in the sixteenth and seventeenth centuries* (Dunfermline, 1951).

Simpson, A.D.C., 'Grain packing in early standard capacity measures: Evidence from the Scottish dry capacity standards', *Annals of Science*, vol. 49 (1992), pp. 337–50.

Sinclair, J., *General view of the agriculture of the northern counties of Scotland* (London, 1795).

General report of the agricultural state, and political circumstances of Scotland (Edinburgh, 1818).

Smith, A., *An inquiry into the nature and causes of the wealth of nations* (1776; Everyman edn, 2 vols., London, 1957).

The three united trades of Dundee: masons, wrights and slaters (Abertay Historical Society Publication, 26, Dundee, 1987).

Smith, A.M., 'A Scottish aristocrat's diet, 1671', *Scottish History Review*, vol. 61 (1982), pp. 146–65.

Smollet, T., *Works* (ed. D. Herbert, Edinburgh, 1887).

Smout, T.C., *Scottish trade on the eve of Union, 1660–1707* (Edinburgh, 1963).

A history of the Scottish people, 1560–1830 (London, 1969).

'Famine and famine relief in Scotland', in Cullen, L.M. and Smout, T.C. (eds.), *Comparative aspects of Scottish and Irish economic and social history* (Edinburgh, 1976), pp. 21–31.

'Improvements before the improvers', *Times Literary Supplement*, 1982, p. 389.

'Where had the Scottish economy got to in the third quarter of the eighteenth century?', in Hont, I. and Ignatieff, M., *Wealth and virtue: the shaping of political economy in the Scottish Enlightenment* (Cambridge, 1983), pp. 45–72.

Smout, T.C. (ed.), 'Sir John Clerk's "Observations on the present circumstances of Scotland"', *Miscellany of the Scottish History Society, vol. 10* (Scottish History Society, 4th series, vol. 2, Edinburgh, 1965), pp. 175–212.

Sonenscher, M., 'Work and wages in Paris in the eighteenth century', in Berg, M., Hudson, P. and Sonenscher, M. (eds.), *Manufacture in town and country before the factory* (London, 1983), pp. 1–32.

Statistical accounts of Scotland, 1791–1799, edited by Sir John Sinclair, new edition by I.R. Grant and D.J. Withrington, vols. 1–20 (Wakefield, 1972–83).

Steuart, J., (as Robert Frame) *Considerations on the interest of the county of Lanark* (Glasgow, 1769).

Inquiry into the principles of political economy (2 vols., Dublin, 1770).

The works, political, metaphysical, and chronological, of the late Sir James Steuart of Coltness (6 vols., London, 1805).

Steven, M., *The good Scots diet: what happened to it?* (Aberdeen, 1985).

Stewart, I.H., *The Scottish coinage* (1955; revised edn, London, 1967).

Stuart, J. (ed.), *Extracts from the council register of the burgh of Aberdeen, vol. I, 1398–1570* (Spalding Club, Aberdeen, 1844).

List of pollable persons within the shire of Aberdeen, 1696 (2 vols., Spalding Club, Aberdeen, 1844).

Extracts from the council register of the burgh of Aberdeen, 1625–1747 (2 vols., Scottish Burgh Record Society, Aberdeen, 1871–72).

Swinton, J., *A proposal for uniformity of weights and measures in Scotland* (1779; 2nd edn, Edinburgh, 1789).

Taylor, L.B. (ed.), *Aberdeen shore work accounts, 1596–1670* (Aberdeen, 1972).

Terry, C.S. (ed.), *Sir Thomas Craig's 'De Unione Regnorum Britanniae Tractatus'* (Scottish History Society, 1st series, vol. 60, Edinburgh, 1909).

Thestrup, P., *The standard of living in Copenhagen, 1730–1800; some methods of measurement* (Copenhagen University Institute for Economic History publication number 5, Copenhagen, 1971)

'The standard of living in Denmark since c.1750', in Karlsson, G. (ed.), *Levestandarden i Norden, 1750–1914* (Reykjavik, 1987), pp. 25–45.

Thin, R., 'The old infirmary and earlier hospitals', *Book of the Old Edinburgh Club*, vol. 15 (1927), pp. 135–63.

Thirsk, J. (ed.), *The agrarian history of England and Wales*, vol. IV, *1500–1640* (Cambridge, 1967). *The agrarian history of England and Wales*, vol. VI, *1750–1850* (Cambridge, 1967).

Towill, E.S., 'The minutes of the Merchant Maiden Hospital', *Book of the Old Edinburgh Club*, vol. 29 (1956), pp. 1–92.

Treble, J.H., 'The standard of living of the working class', in Devine, T.M. and Mitchison, R. (eds.), *People and society in Scotland*, vol. 1, *1760–1830* (1988), pp. 188–226.

Trotter, J., *General view of the agriculture of the county of West Lothian* (London, 1811).

Tyson, R.E., 'The population of Aberdeenshire, 1695–1755: a new approach', *Northern Scotland*, vol. 6 (1985), pp. 113–32.

'Famine in Aberdeenshire, 1695–1699: anatomy of a crisis', in Stevenson, D. (ed.), *From lairds to louns: country and burgh life in Aberdeen, 1600–1800* (Aberdeen, 1986), pp. 32–51.

'Proto-industrialization in Aberdeenshire: woollen cloth and knitted stockings', unpublished paper presented to the 'Proto-industrialization in the North' conference held at St Andrews, 23 April, 1988.

'The rise and fall of manufacturing industry in rural Aberdeenshire', in Smith, J.S. and Stevenson, D. (eds.), *Fermfolk and fisherfolk; rural life in Northern Scotland in the eighteenth and nineteenth centuries* (Aberdeen, 1989), pp. 63–82.

'Contrasting régimes: population growth in Ireland and Scotland during the eighteenth century', in Houston, R.A. *et al.* (eds.), *Conflict and identity in the social and economic history of Ireland and Scotland* (Edinburgh, forthcoming).

Warden, A., *Burgh laws of Dundee* (London, 1872).

Whyte, I., *Agriculture and society in seventeenth-century Scotland* (Edinburgh, 1979).

Wood, M., 'St Paul's Work', *Book of the Old Edinburgh Club*, vol. 17 (1930), pp. 49–75.

Woodward, D., 'Anglo-Scottish trade and English commercial policy during the 1660s', *Scottish Historical Review*, vol. 56 (1977), pp. 153–74.

'Wage rates and living standards in pre-industrial England', *Past and Present*, no. 91 (1981), pp. 28–45.

Wormald, J., *Court, kirk and community; Scotland, 1470–1623* (London, 1981).

Wrigley, E.A. and Schofield, R.S., *The population history of England, 1541–1871* (Cambridge, 1981).

Youngson, A.J., *After the '45* (Edinburgh, 1973).

Zupko, R.E., 'The weights and measures of Scotland before the Union', *Scottish Historical Review*, vol. 56 (1977), pp. 119–45.

Persons index

Place index

Subject index